See what students love about LearningCurve.

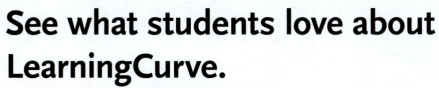 learningcurveworks.com

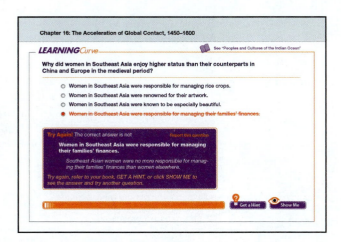

Students using LaunchPad receive access to LearningCurve for *Understanding World Societies.*

Each chapter-based LearningCurve activity gives students **multiple chances to understand key concepts**, return to the narrative textbook if they need to reread, and answer questions correctly.

Over 90% of students report satisfaction with LearningCurve's **fun and accessible game-like interface.**

Assigning LearningCurve in place of reading quizzes is easy for instructors, and the **reporting features help instructors track overall class trends** and spot topics that are giving students trouble so that they can adjust lectures and class activities.

To learn more about LearningCurve, visit learningcurveworks.com.

LearningCurve: Everyone's got a learning curve — what's yours?

THE CONTEMPORARY WORLD

0 | 1,500 | 3,000 miles
0 | 1,500 | 3,000 kilometers

ARCTIC OCEAN

RUSSIAN FEDERATION

NORWAY
SWEDEN
FINLAND
ESTONIA
LATVIA
LITHUANIA
DEN.
GERMANY
POLAND
LUX.
BELARUS
CZ.
SLK.
UKRAINE
AUS.
HUNG.
MOLDOVA
SLN.
ROMANIA
ITALY
B.H.
BULGARIA
MO.
KO.
MAC.
SE.
ALB.
GREECE
TUNISIA
MALTA
CYPRUS
ISRAEL
GEORGIA
ARMENIA
AZERBAIJAN
TURKEY
SYRIA
LEBANON
IRAQ
West Bank
Gaza Strip
JORDAN
KUWAIT
QATAR
UNITED ARAB
EMIRATES
IRAN
BAHRAIN
SAUDI ARABIA
OMAN
YEMEN

KAZAKHSTAN
UZBEKISTAN
KYRGYZSTAN
TURKMENISTAN
TAJIKISTAN
AFGHANISTAN
PAKISTAN

MONGOLIA

CHINA

N. KOREA
S. KOREA
JAPAN

PACIFIC OCEAN

NEPAL
BHUTAN
BANGLADESH
INDIA
MYANMAR
(BURMA)
LAOS
VIETNAM
THAILAND
CAMBODIA

Taiwan

Mariana Is.
(U.S.)

Guam
(U.S.)

MARSHALL
IS.

ALGERIA
LIBYA
EGYPT
NIGER
CHAD
SUDAN
ERITREA
DJIBOUTI
NIGERIA
BENIN
TOGO
CAMEROON
EQ.
GUINEA
GABON
CONGO
CENTRAL
AFRICAN REP.
SOUTH
SUDAN
ETHIOPIA
SOMALIA
SÃO
TOMÉ
& PRÍNCIPE
RWANDA
UGANDA
KENYA
DEM. REP. OF
THE CONGO
BURUNDI
TANZANIA

MALDIVES

SRI
LANKA

PHILIPPINES

BRUNEI

PALAU

FEDERATED STATES
OF MICRONESIA

NAURU

KIRIBATI

MALAYSIA

SINGAPORE

INDONESIA

PAPUA
NEW
GUINEA

SOLOMON
IS.

TUVALU

ANGOLA
ZAMBIA
MALAWI
NAMIBIA
ZIMBABWE
BOTSWANA
MADAGASCAR
COMOROS
SEYCHELLES

INDIAN OCEAN

MAURITIUS

TIMOR
LESTE

VANUATU

FIJI

MOZAMBIQUE
SOUTH
AFRICA
SWAZILAND
LESOTHO

AUSTRALIA

New Caledonia
(Fr.)

NEW
ZEALAND

Tasmania
(Aust.)

ANTARCTICA

ABBREVIATIONS	
ALB.	ALBANIA
AUS.	AUSTRIA
BEL.	BELGIUM
B.H.	BOSNIA AND HERZEGOVINA
CR.	CROATIA
CZ.	CZECH REPUBLIC
DEN.	DENMARK
HUNG.	HUNGARY
KO.	KOSOVO
LUX.	LUXEMBOURG
MAC.	MACEDONIA
MO.	MONTENEGRO
NETH.	NETHERLANDS
SE.	SERBIA
SLK.	SLOVAKIA
SLN.	SLOVENIA
SWITZ.	SWITZERLAND

160°W 140°W 120°W 100°W 80°W 60°W 40°W 20°W

Arctic Circle

NORTH AMERICA

R O C K Y   M T S.

APPALACHIAN MTS.

Mississippi

ATLANTIC OCEAN

Tropic of Cancer

Gulf of Mexico

PACIFIC OCEAN

Caribbean Sea

Equator

Amazon R.

SOUTH AMERICA

A N D E S   M T S.

Tropic of Capricorn

N
W   E
S

ATLANTIC OCEAN

0   1,000   2,000   3,000 miles
0 1,000 2,000 3,000 kilometers

Antarctic Circle

EUROPE

ALPS

ASIA

AFRICA

SAHARA

ARABIAN DESERT

URAL MTS.

Volga R.

Ob R.

GOBI

Yellow R. (Huang He)

HIMALAYA MTS.

Ganges R.

Yangzi R.

Mediterranean Sea

Nile R.

Congo R.

Zambezi R.

KALAHARI DESERT

Arabian Sea

Bay of Bengal

South China Sea

PACIFIC OCEAN

INDIAN OCEAN

AUSTRALIA

Arctic Circle

80°N

60°N

40°N

Tropic of Cancer

20°N

Equator 0°

20°S

Tropic of Capricorn

40°S

60°S

Antarctic Circle

80°S

20°E 40°E 60°E 80°E 100°E 120°E 140°E 160°E

Vegetation zones

- Tundra
- Northern forest
- Temperate forest
- Temperate grassland
- Desert and dry shrub
- Mediterranean shrub
- Mountain grassland
- Tropical grassland and savanna
- Tropical forest
- Permanent ice cover

Understanding
World Societies

A HISTORY SECOND EDITION

VOLUME 2 **Since 1450**

John P. McKay
University of Illinois at Urbana-Champaign

Bennett D. Hill
Late of Georgetown University

John Buckler
Late of University of Illinois at Urbana-Champaign

Patricia Buckley Ebrey
University of Washington

Roger B. Beck
Eastern Illinois University

Clare Haru Crowston
University of Illinois at Urbana-Champaign

Merry E. Wiesner-Hanks
University of Wisconsin–Milwaukee

Jerry Dávila
University of Illinois at Urbana-Champaign

Bedford / St. Martin's
Boston • New York

For Bedford/St. Martin's

Vice President, Editorial, Macmillan Higher Education Humanities: Edwin Hill
Publisher for History: Michael Rosenberg
Director of Development for History: Jane Knetzger
Associate Editor for History: Robin Soule
Production Editor: Annette Pagliaro Sweeney
Senior Production Supervisor: Dennis Conroy
Executive Marketing Manager: Sandra McGuire
Project Manager: Katrina Ostler, Jouve
Editorial Assistant: Arrin Kaplan
Cartography: Mapping Specialists, Ltd.
Photo Researcher: Bruce Carson
Director of Rights and Permissions: Hilary Newman
Senior Art Director: Anna Palchik
Cover Design: William Boardman
Cover Art: Alfredo Ramos Martinez
La Pintora de Uruapan (The Painter of Uruapan), circa 1930
tempera on board
47.5 × 38.75 inches; 120.65 × 98.43 centimeters
© The Alfredo Ramos Martinez Research Project, reproduced by permission.
Composition: Jouve
Printing and Binding: RR Donnelley and Sons

9 8 7 6 5 4
f e d c b a

For information, write: Bedford/St. Martin's, 75 Arlington Street, Boston, MA 02116
(617-399-4000)

ISBN 978-1-4576-9992-4 (Combined Edition)
ISBN 978-1-319-00837-6 (Volume 1)
ISBN 978-1-319-00838-3 (Volume 2)

Understanding
World Societies

A HISTORY

VOLUME 2

How to use this book to figure out what's really important

The **chapter title** tells you the subject of the chapter and identifies the time span that will be covered.

The **opening question** and **chapter introduction** identify the most important themes, events, and people that will be explored in the chapter.

16
THE ACCELERATION OF GLOBAL CONTACT
1450–1600

> **What new global connections were forged in the fifteenth and sixteenth centuries?** Chapter 16 examines the causes, course, and effects of European expansion in the fifteenth and sixteenth centuries. Before 1500 Europeans were relatively marginal players in a centuries-old trading system that linked Africa, Asia, and Europe. By 1550 the European search for better access to Asian trade goods had led to a new overseas empire in the Indian Ocean and the accidental discovery of the Western Hemisphere. With this discovery South and North America were drawn into an international network of trade centers and political empires, which Europeans came to dominate. The era of globalization had begun, creating new political systems and forms of economic exchange as well as cultural assimilation, conversion, and resistance.

 **LearningCurve**
After reading the chapter, use LearningCurve to retain what you've read.

Memorizing facts and dates for a history class won't get you very far. That's because history isn't just about "facts." This textbook is designed to help you focus on what's truly significant in the history of world societies and to give you practice thinking like a historian.

Nezahualpilli At the time of the arrival of Europeans, Nezahualpilli was ruler of the city-state of Texcoco, the second most important city in the Aztec Empire after Tenochtitlan. (Nezahualpilli, portrait from *Codex Ixtlilxochitl*, 1582, pigment on European paper/Bibliothèque Nationale, Paris, France/De Agostini Picture Library/akg-images)

> What was the Afroeurasian trade world like prior to the era of European exploration?

> Why and how did Europeans undertake ambitious voyages of expansion?

> What was the impact of Iberian conquest and settlement on the peoples and ecologies of the Americas?

> How was the era of global contact shaped by new commodities, commercial empires, and forced migrations?

> How did new encounters shape cultural attitudes and beliefs in Europe and the New World?

The **chapter-opening questions** are also the questions that open the new sections of the chapter and will be addressed in turn on the following pages. You should think about answers to them as you read.

Each section has tools that help you focus on what's important.

The **question in red** asks about the specific topic being discussed in this section. Pause to answer each one after you read the section.

> ### How was the era of global contact shaped by new commodities, commercial empires, and forced migrations?

A New World Sugar Refinery in Brazil

Sugar was the most important and most profitable plantation crop in the New World. This image shows the processing and refinement of sugar on a Brazilian plantation. Sugarcane was grown, harvested, and processed by African slaves who labored under brutal and ruthless conditions to generate enormous profits for plantation owners. (The Bridgeman Art Library/Getty Images)

THE CENTURIES-OLD AFROEURASIAN trade world was forever changed by the European voyages of discovery and their aftermath. For the first time, a truly global economy emerged in the sixteenth and seventeenth centuries, and it forged new links among far-flung peoples, cultures, and societies.

The Columbian Exchange

Key terms in the margins give you background on important people, ideas, and events. Use these for reference while you read, but also think about which terms are emphasized and why they matter.

Columbian exchange
▶ The exchange of animals, plants, and diseases between the Old and the New Worlds.

The travel of people and goods between the Old and New Worlds led to an exchange of animals, plants, and diseases, a complex process known as the Columbian exchange. As we have seen, the introduction of new diseases to the Americas had devastating consequences. But other results of the exchange brought benefits not only to the Europeans but also to native peoples.

Everywhere they settled, the Spanish and Portuguese brought and raised wheat. Grapes and olives brought over from Spain did well in parts of Peru and Chile. Perhaps the most significant introduction to the diet of Native Americans

| CHAPTER LOCATOR | What was the Afroeurasian trade world like prior to the era of European exploration? | Why and how did Europeans undertake ambitious voyages of expansion? |

to pay tributes in cash, rather than in labor. To respond to a shortage of indigenous workers, royal officials established a new government-run system of forced labor, called *repartimiento* in New Spain and *mita* in Peru. Administrators assigned a certain percentage of the inhabitants of native communities to labor for a set period each year in public works, mining, agriculture, and other tasks.

Spanish systems for exploiting the labor of indigenous peoples were both a cause of and a response to the disastrous decline in the numbers of such peoples that began soon after the arrival of Europeans. Some indigenous people died as a direct result of the violence of conquest and the disruption of agriculture and trade caused by warfare. The most important cause of death, however, was infectious disease. Having little or no resistance to diseases brought from the Old World, the inhabitants of the New World fell victim to smallpox, typhus, influenza, and other illnesses.

The pattern of devastating disease and population loss established in the Spanish colonies was repeated everywhere Europeans settled. Overall, population declined by as much as 90 percent or more but with important regional variations. In general, densely populated urban centers were worse hit than rural areas and tropical, low-lying regions suffered more than cooler, higher-altitude ones.

Colonial administrators responded to native population decline by forcibly combining dwindling indigenous communities into new settlements and imposing the rigors of the encomienda and the repartimiento. By the end of the sixteenth century the search for fresh sources of labor had given birth to the new tragedy of the Atlantic slave trade (see page 598).

Patterns of Settlement

The century after the discovery of silver in 1545 marked the high point of Iberian immigration to the Americas. Although the first migrants were men, soon whole families began to cross the Atlantic, and the European population began to increase through natural reproduction. By 1600 American-born Europeans, called *Creoles*, outnumbered immigrants.

Iberian settlement was predominantly urban in nature. Spaniards settled into the cities and towns of the former Aztec and Inca Empires as the native population dwindled through death and flight. They also established new cities in which settlers were quick to establish urban institutions familiar to them from home: city squares, churches, schools, and universities.

Despite the growing number of Europeans and the rapid decline of the native population, Europeans remained a small minority of the total inhabitants of the Americas. Iberians formed sexual relationships with native women leading to a substantial population of mixed Iberian and Indian descent known as *mestizos* (meh-STEE-zohz). The large-scale arrival of enslaved Africans, starting in Brazil in the mid-sixteenth century, added new ethnic and racial dimensions to the population (see pages 598–603).

QUICK REVIEW <

What factors help explain the conquest of the mighty Inca and Aztec Empires by the Spanish?

What was the impact of Iberian conquest and settlement on the peoples of the Americas?	How was the era of global contact shaped by new commodities and forced migrations?	How did new encounters shape cultural attitudes and beliefs in Europe and the New World?	LearningCurve Check what you know.

473

The quick review helps you check your recall of the section before you resume reading.

The chapter locator at the bottom of the page puts this section in the context of the chapter as a whole so you can see how this section relates to what's coming next.

The Chapter Study Guide provides a process that will build your understanding and your historical skills.

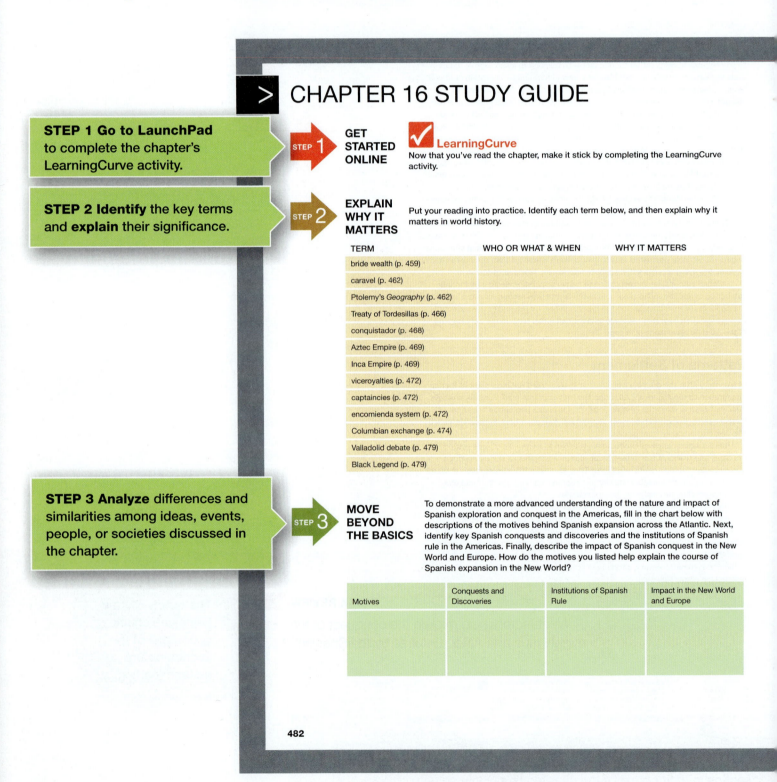

STEP 1 Go to LaunchPad to complete the chapter's LearningCurve activity.

STEP 2 Identify the key terms and **explain** their significance.

STEP 3 Analyze differences and similarities among ideas, events, people, or societies discussed in the chapter.

> CHAPTER 16 STUDY GUIDE

STEP 1 GET STARTED ONLINE

✓ **LearningCurve**
Now that you've read the chapter, make it stick by completing the LearningCurve activity.

STEP 2 EXPLAIN WHY IT MATTERS

Put your reading into practice. Identify each term below, and then explain why it matters in world history.

TERM	WHO OR WHAT & WHEN	WHY IT MATTERS
bride wealth (p. 459)		
caravel (p. 462)		
Ptolemy's *Geography* (p. 462)		
Treaty of Tordesillas (p. 466)		
conquistador (p. 468)		
Aztec Empire (p. 469)		
Inca Empire (p. 469)		
viceroyalties (p. 472)		
captaincies (p. 472)		
encomienda system (p. 472)		
Columbian exchange (p. 474)		
Valladolid debate (p. 479)		
Black Legend (p. 479)		

STEP 3 MOVE BEYOND THE BASICS

To demonstrate a more advanced understanding of the nature and impact of Spanish exploration and conquest in the Americas, fill in the chart below with descriptions of the motives behind Spanish expansion across the Atlantic. Next, identify key Spanish conquests and discoveries and the institutions of Spanish rule in the Americas. Finally, describe the impact of Spanish conquest in the New World and Europe. How do the motives you listed help explain the course of Spanish expansion in the New World?

Motives	Conquests and Discoveries	Institutions of Spanish Rule	Impact in the New World and Europe

STEP 4 **PUT IT ALL TOGETHER** Now, take a step back and try to explain the big picture. Remember to use specific examples from the chapter in your answers.

STEP 4 Answer the big-picture questions using specific examples or evidence from the chapter.

THE AFROEURASIAN TRADE WORLD BEFORE COLUMBUS

▶ Which states were at the center of global trade prior to 1492? Why?

▶ Why were Europeans at a trading disadvantage prior to 1492? How did geography limit European participation in world trade? What role did Europe's economy and material culture play in this context?

DISCOVERY AND CONQUEST

▶ In your opinion, what was the most important motive behind European expansion? What evidence can you provide to support your position?

▶ What was the Columbian exchange? How did it transform both Europe and the Americas?

CHANGING VALUES AND BELIEFS

▶ How did European expansion give rise to new ideas about race?

▶ How did expansion complicate European's understanding of themselves and their place in the world?

LOOKING BACK, LOOKING AHEAD

▶ If Europe was at the periphery of the global trading system prior to 1492, where was it situated by the middle of the sixteenth century? What had changed? What had not?

▶ What connections can you make between our own experience of globalization in the twenty-first century and the experience of globalization in the sixteenth century? In what ways are the experiences similar? In what ways do they differ?

> IN YOUR OWN WORDS Imagine that you must give an oral report to the class answering the following question: **What new global connections were forged in the fifteenth and sixteenth centuries?** What would be the most important points and why?

ACTIVE RECITATION Explain how you would answer the chapter-opening question in your own words to make sure you have a firm grasp of the most important themes and events of the chapter.

PREFACE: Why This Book This Way

U*nderstanding World Societies* grew out of many conversations we have had among ourselves and with other instructors about the teaching and learning of history. We knew that instructors wanted a world history text that introduced students to the broad sweep of history but that also re-created the lives of ordinary men and women in appealing human terms. We knew that instructors wanted a text that presented cutting-edge scholarship in new fields of historical inquiry. We also knew that many instructors wanted a text that would help students focus as they read, keep their interest in the material, and encourage them to learn historical thinking skills. It is our hope that *Understanding World Societies* addresses all of these concerns.

The second edition of *Understanding World Societies* continues to provide the social and cultural focus, comprehensive regional organization, and global perspective that have long been hallmarks of the book. All three of these qualities have been greatly enhanced by the addition of a new member to the author team, Jerry Dávila from the University of Illinois, who brings expertise in Latin America and the twentieth century. A renowned scholar of Brazil whose work focuses on race and social policy, Jerry offers a fresh perspective to our coverage of Latin America and to the final chapters in the book, which he has completely reconceptualized. Not only do we thus continue to benefit from a collaborative team of regional experts with deep experience in the world history classroom, but we are also pleased to introduce a suite of digital tools designed to save you time and help students gain confidence and learn historical thinking skills.

New Tools for the Digital Age

Because we know that your classroom needs are changing rapidly, we are excited to announce that *Understanding World Societies* is available with **LaunchPad**. Free when packaged with the book, or heavily discounted as a stand-alone product, LaunchPad's course space and interactive e-book is ready to use as is or can be edited and customized with your own material and assigned right away. Developed with extensive feedback from history instructors and students, LaunchPad includes the complete narrative e-book, as well as abundant primary documents, maps, images, assignments, and activities. The aims of key learning outcomes are addressed via formative and summative assessment, short-answer and essay questions, multiple-choice quizzing, and **LearningCurve**, an adaptive learning tool designed to get students to read before they come to class. Available with training and support, LaunchPad can help you take your teaching into a new era. To learn more about the benefits of LearningCurve and LaunchPad, see the "Versions and Supplements" section on page xxvii and see below on how specific skills-based features of *Understanding World Societies* benefit from the ability to assign and track student work in LaunchPad.

Understanding World Societies: Bringing the Past to Life for Students

In this age of global connections, with its influence on the global economy, global migration patterns, popular culture, and global warming, among other things, the study of world history is more vital and urgent than ever before. An understanding of the broad sweep of the human past helps us comprehend today's dramatic changes and enduring continuities. People now migrate enormous distances and establish new lives far from their places of birth, yet migration has been a constant in history since the first humans walked out of Africa. Satellite and cell phones now link nearly every inch of the planet, yet the expansion of communication networks is a process that is thousands of years old. Children who speak different languages at home now sit side by side in schools and learn from one another, yet intercultural encounters have long been a source of innovation, transformation, and at times, unfortunately, conflict.

This book is designed for twenty-first-century students who will spend their lives on this small interconnected planet and for whom an understanding of only local or national history will no longer be sufficient. We believe that the study of world history in a broad and comparative context is an exciting, important, and highly practical pursuit. It is our conviction, based on considerable experience in introducing large numbers of students to world history, that a book reflecting current trends in scholarship can excite readers and inspire an enduring interest in the long human experience.

Our strategy has been twofold. First, we have made social and cultural history the core elements of our narrative. We seek to re-create the lives of ordinary people in appealing human terms and also to highlight the interplay between men's and women's lived experiences and the ways they reflect on these to create meaning. Thus, in addition to foundational works of philosophy and literature, we include popular songs and stories. We present objects along with texts as important sources for studying history, and this has allowed us to incorporate the growing emphasis on material culture in the work of many historians. At the same time, we have been mindful of the need to give great economic, political, and intellectual developments the attention they deserve. We want to give individual students and instructors an integrated perspective so that they can pursue—on their own or in the classroom—the themes and questions that they find particularly exciting and significant.

Second, we have made every effort to strike an effective global and regional balance. The whole world interacts today, and to understand the interactions and what they mean for today's citizens, we must study the whole world's history. Thus we have adopted a comprehensive regional organization with a global perspective that is clear and manageable for students. For example, Chapter 7 introduces students in depth to East Asia, and at the same time the chapter highlights the cultural connections that occurred via the Silk Road and the spread of Buddhism. We study all geographical areas, conscious of the separate histories of many parts of the world, particularly in the earliest millennia of human development. We also stress the links among cultures, political units, and economic systems, for these connections have made the world what it is today. We make comparisons and connections across time as well as space, for understanding the unfolding of the human story in time is the central task of history.

An Inquiry-Based Model Designed for Understanding

By employing innovative pedagogy, we believe that *Understanding World Societies* helps students not only understand the book's major developments but also begin to grasp the question-driven methodology that is at the heart of the historian's craft. Each chapter opens with a **new chapter-opening question** that drives students toward the overarching themes of the chapter, followed by a **brief chapter introduction** that identifies the most important events and people to be discussed. **Section-opening headings** expressed as questions and **section-ending quick review questions** further model the kinds of questions historians ask and help students engage in inquiry-based reading and understanding.

Chapter Study Guides Designed for Active Learning

At the core of the unique pedagogical features of *Understanding World Societies* are the revised **Chapter Study Guides** that provide a carefully structured four-step process to help students build deep understanding of the chapter material. In **Step 1**, students go to LaunchPad to complete the LearningCurve activity to ensure that they have a grasp of the basic content and concepts of the chapter. In **Step 2**, students not only identify the chapter's key terms but also explain why each matters. In **Step 3**, they begin to apply their understanding of the chapter material through activities that ask them to consider comparison, change over time, or cause and effect. In **Step 4**, analytical and synthetic questions require students to engage in higher-order historical thinking. And, finally, in an active recitation exercise, students **answer the chapter-opening question** to fully realize their understanding of the chapter. In LaunchPad, instructors can assign the **NEW Guided Reading Exercise** for each chapter, which prompts students to read actively to collect information that answers a broad analytic question central to the chapter as a whole.

Primary Sources for Teaching Critical Thinking and Analysis

Understanding World Societies offers an extensive program of primary source assignments to help students master a number of key learning outcomes, among them **critical thinking**, **historical thinking**, **analytical thinking**, **argumentation**, and learning about the **diversity of world cultures**. When assigned in LaunchPad, all primary source features are accompanied by multiple-choice quizzes that help you ensure that students come to class prepared.

New assignable **Online Document Projects** in LaunchPad offer students more practice in interpreting primary sources. Each project, based on the Individuals in Society feature described below, prompts students to explore a key question through analysis of multiple sources. Chapter 22, for example, asks students to analyze documents on the complexities of the Haitian Revolution and the conditions that made Toussaint L'Ouverture's story possible. Auto-graded multiple-choice questions based on the documents help students analyze the sources.

Finally, we have revised our **primary source documents collection**, *Sources for World Societies*, to add more visual sources and to closely align the readings with the chapter topics and themes of the second edition. The documents are now available in a fully assignable and assessable electronic format within each LaunchPad unit, and the accompanying multiple-choice questions measure comprehension and hold students accountable for their reading.

Student Engagement with Biography

In our years of teaching world history, we have often noted that students come alive when they encounter stories about real people in the past. To give students a chance to see the past through ordinary people's lives, each chapter includes one of the popular **Individuals in Society** biographical essays, each of which offers a brief study of an individual or a group, informing students about the societies in which the individuals lived. This feature grew out of our long-standing focus on people's lives and the varieties of historical experience, and we believe that readers will empathize with these human beings who themselves were seeking to define their own identities. The spotlighting of individuals, both famous and obscure, perpetuates the book's continued attention to cultural and intellectual developments, highlights human agency, and reflects changing interests within the historical profession as well as the development of "micro-history." As mentioned previously, the majority of these features are tied to **NEW Online Document Projects**, available in LaunchPad, that allow students to explore further the historical conditions in which these individuals lived. **NEW** features include essays on Sudatta, a lay follower of the Buddha; Cosimo and Lorenzo de' Medici; Malintzin; and Sieng, a Mnong refugee living in the United States.

Geographical and Visual Literacy

We recognize students' difficulties with geography and visual analysis, and the new edition retains our **Mapping the Past map activities** and **Picturing the Past visual activities**. Included in each chapter, these activities ask students to analyze the map or visual and make connections to the larger processes discussed in the narrative, giving them valuable practice in reading and interpreting maps and images. In LaunchPad, they are assignable, and students can submit their work. Throughout the textbook and online in LaunchPad, more than **92 full-size maps** illustrate major developments in the chapter. In addition, **74 spot maps** are embedded in the narrative to show specific areas under discussion.

Chronological Reasoning

To help students make comparisons, understand change over time, and see relationships among contemporaneous events, each chapter begins with a **chapter chronology** that reviews major developments discussed in the chapter. This chronology, available from every page in LaunchPad, allows students to compare developments over the centuries.

Better-Prepared Students

To help students fully understand their reading and come to class prepared, instructors who adopt LaunchPad for *Understanding World Societies* can assign the **LearningCurve** formative assessment activities. This online learning tool is popular with students because it helps them rehearse content at their own pace in a nonthreatening, game-like environment. LearningCurve is also popular with instructors because the reporting features allow them to track overall class trends and spot topics that are giving students trouble so they can adjust their lectures and class activities. When LearningCurve is assigned, students come to class better prepared, and instructors can better evaluate and adjust their classes.

To further encourage students to read and fully assimilate the text as well as measure how well they do this, instructors can assign the **new multiple-choice summative quizzes** in LaunchPad, where they are automatically graded. These secure tests not only encourage students to study the book, they can be assigned at specific intervals as high-stakes testing and thus provide another means for analyzing class performance.

Organizational and Textual Changes

To meet the demands of the evolving course, we have made several major changes in the organization of chapters to reflect the way the course is taught today. The most dramatic changes are the reordering of Chapter 17: "The Islamic World Powers, 1300–1800" (formerly Chapter 20) and a complete overhaul of the final section of the book, covering the postwar era. This new placement for our coverage of Islam reflects a growing interest among instructors and students in the Islamic world and highlights early Islamic cultural contributions.

To address the concerns of instructors who teach from the second volume of the text, we have added a new section on the Reformation to Chapter 18 so that students whose courses begin with Chapters 15 or 16 will now receive that coverage in Volume 2. The new section includes the Protestant and Catholic Reformations, as well as religious violence and witch-hunts.

In its examination of the age of revolution in the Atlantic world, Chapter 22 now incorporates revolutions in Latin America. In order to provide a more global perspective on European politics, culture, and economics in the early modern period, Chapter 23 on the Industrial Revolution considers industrialization more broadly as a global phenomenon with a new section titled "The Global Picture." Together, the enhanced global perspectives of these chapters help connect the different regions of the globe and, in particular, help explain the crucial period when Europe began to dominate the rest of the globe.

The final section of the text covering the post-1945 period has also been completely reworked. In addition to updating all of the postwar chapters through 2014, Jerry Dávila substantially rewrote and streamlined the last four chapters into three to create a more tightly focused and accessible section that now divides the period chronologically as follows: *Chapter 31: Decolonization, Revolution, and the Cold War, 1945–1968*; *Chapter 32: Liberalization, 1968–2000s*; *Chapter 33: The Contemporary World in Historical Perspective*. The last three chapters are now organized around two dominant themes of the postwar world: liberation movements that challenged power structures such as colonialism and racial supremacism and the spread of liberalization that characterized the end of the Cold War in particular, marking the rise of free markets and liberal political systems. The final chapter examines the significance of social movements in shaping a contemporary world that continues to struggle with historic conflicts and inequalities.

In terms of specific textual changes, we have worked hard to keep the book up to date and to strengthen our comprehensive, comparative, and connective approach. Moreover, we revised every chapter with the goal of readability and accessibility. Highlights of the new edition include:

- Chapter 1 includes new information on the recent archaeological find at Göbekli Tepe in present-day Turkey that suggests that cultural factors may have played a role in the development of agriculture.
- Chapter 2 has new coverage on Egyptian society and a discussion of gender distinctions in Sumerian society.
- In Chapter 6, the section on the founding of Rome has been completely rewritten.
- Chapter 8 contains a new section on Christian missionaries and conversion, and it explains the process of the Christianization of barbarian Europe.
- Chapter 11 now centers on the ways in which systems of religious belief shaped ancient societies of the Americas and provided tools that people used to understand and adapt their world. It also looks at the role of sources produced after the European encounter in shaping our understanding of the histories of indigenous American empires.
- An expanded discussion of witchcraft in Chapter 15 now discusses practices of indigenous peoples in the New World.
- Chapter 18 has expanded coverage of Russian imperial expansion as well as a new section called "Peoples Beyond Borders" that includes piracy and gives students a feeling for the ways in which imperial borders were often more real on the map than in real life.
- In Chapter 19, a new section called "The Early Enlightenment" clarifies the mixture of religious, political, and scientific thought that characterized the early period of the Enlightenment.
- Chapter 22 emphasizes the indigenous origins of the Haitian revolution by highlighting the African backgrounds of slaves and the considerable military experience many of them had, which helps explain how they could defeat the French and British.
- Chapter 23 has been heavily revised to reflect new scholarship on industrialization and to provide a broader, more comparative perspective.
- A new section in Chapter 24 on social and economic conflict connects the industrialization of continental Europe with the political coverage of the revolutions of 1848.
- Chapter 27 now focuses on the Americas within the framework of liberalism and examines connections between the experiences with settlement, state formation, and economic integration in the United States and Latin America.
- Chapter 29 contains more detail on the reforms of emir Amanullah Khan in the section on the modernization of Afghanistan.
- As noted previously, the final three chapters of the book have been entirely rewritten by new author Jerry Dávila.

In sum, we have tried to bring new research and interpretation into our global history, believing it essential to keep our book stimulating, accurate, and current for students and instructors.

Acknowledgments

It is a pleasure to thank the many instructors who critiqued the parent textbook, *A History of World Societies*, Tenth Edition. Their feedback helped inform the shape this book has taken.

Stewart Anderson, *Brigham Young University*

Brian Arendt, *Lindenwood University*

Stephen Auerbach, *Georgia College*

Michael Bardot, *Lincoln University*

Natalie Bayer, *Drake University*

Michael Bazemore, *William Peace University*

Brian Becker, *Delta State University*

Rosemary Bell, *Skyline College*

Chris Benedetto, *Granite State College*

Wesley L. Bishop, *Pitt Community College*

Robert Blackey, *California State University–San Bernardino*

Edward Bond, *Alabama A&M University*

Nathan Brooks, *New Mexico State University*

Jurgen Buchenau, *The University of North Carolina at Charlotte*

Paul Buckingham, *Morrisville State College*

Steven B. Bunker, *University of Alabama*

Kate Burlingham, *California State University, Fullerton*

David Bush, *The College of the Siskiyous*

Laura M. Calkins, *Texas Tech University*

Robert Caputi, *Erie Community College–North Campus*

Lucia Carter, *Mars Hill College*

Lesley Chapel, *Saginaw Valley State University*

Nevin Crouse, *Chesapeake College*

Everett Dague, *Benedictine College*

Peter de Rosa, *Bridgewater State University*

Jeffrey Demsky, *San Bernardino Valley College*

Nicholas Di Liberto, *Newberry College*

Randall Dills, *University of Louisville*

Shawn Dry, *Oakland Community College*

Roxanne Easley, *Central Washington University*

John Fielding, *Mount Wachusett Community College*

Barbara Fuller, *Indian River State College*

Dolores Grapsas, *New River Community College*

Emily Fisher Gray, *Norwich University*

Gayle Greene-Aguirre, *Mississippi Gulf Coast Community College*

Neil Greenwood, *Cleveland State Community College*

Christian Griggs, *Dalton State College*

W. Scott Haine, *Cañada College*

Irwin Halfond, *McKendree University*

Alicia Harding, *Southern Maine Community College*

Jillian Hartley, *Arkansas Northeastern College*

Robert Haug, *University of Cincinnati*

John Hunt, *Utah Valley University*

Fatima Imam, *Lake Forest College*
Rashi Jackman, *De Anza College*
Jackie Jay, *Eastern Kentucky University*
Timothy Jenks, *East Carolina University*
Andrew Kellett, *Harford Community College*
Christine Kern, *Edinboro University*
Christopher Killmer, *St. Johns River State College*
Mark Klobas, *Scottsdale Community College*
Chris Laney, *Berkshire Community College*
Erick D. Langer, *Georgetown University*
Mary Jean Lavery, *Delaware County Community College*
Mark Lentz, *University of Louisiana, Lafayette*
Darin Lenz, *Fresno Pacific University*
Yi Li, *Tacoma Community College*
Jonas Liliequist, *Umeå University*
Ron Lowe, *University of Tennessee at Chattanooga*
Mary Lyons-Carmona, *University of Nebraska at Omaha*
Elizabeth S. Manley, *Xavier University of Louisiana*
Brandon D. Marsh, *Bridgewater College*
Sean F. McEnroe, *Southern Oregon University*
John McLeod, *University of Louisville*
Brendan McManus, *Bemidji State University*
Christina Mehrtens, *University of Massachusetts-Dartmouth*
Charlotte Miller, *Middle Georgia State College*
Robert Montgomery, *Baldwin Wallace University*
Curtis Morgan, *Lord Fairfax Community College*
Richard Moss, *Harrisburg Area Community College*
Larry Myers, *Butler Community College*
Erik Lars Myrup, *University of Kentucky*
April Najjaj, *Mount Olive College*
Katie Nelson, *Weber State University*
Lily Rhodes Novicki, *Virginia Western Community College*
Monica Orozco, *Westmont College*
Neal Palmer, *Christian Brothers University*
Jenifer Parks, *Rocky Mountain College*
Melinda Pash, *Fayetteville Technical Community College*
Tao Peng, *Minnesota State University–Mankato*
Patricia Perry, *St. Edward's University*
William Plants, *University of Rio Grande/Rio Grande Community College*
Joshua Pollock, *Modesto Junior College*
Fabrizio Prado, *College of William & Mary*
Daniel Prosterman, *Salem College*
Tracie Provost, *Middle Georgia College*
Melissa Redd, *Pulaski Technical College*
Charles Reed, *Elizabeth City State University*
Leah Renold, *Texas State University*
Kim Richardson, *Front Range Community College*
David Ruffley, *Colorado Mountain College*
Martina Saltalamacchia, *University of Nebraska at Omaha*

Karl Schmidt, *South Dakota State University*
Kimberly Schutte, *SUNY–The College at Brockport*
Eva Seraphin, *Irvine Valley College*
Courtney Shah, *Lower Columbia College*
Jeffrey Shumway, *Brigham Young University*
David Simonelli, *Youngstown State University*
James Smith, *Southwest Baptist University*
Kara D. Smith, *Georgia Perimeter College*
Ilicia Sprey, *Saint Joseph's College*
Rachel Standish, *San Joaquin Delta College*
Kate Staples, *West Virginia University*
Brian Strayer, *Andrews University*
Sonia Chandarana Tandon, *Forsyth Technical Community College*
James Todesca, *Armstrong Atlantic State University*
Elisaveta Todorova, *University of Cincinnati*
Dianne Walker, *Baton Rouge Community College*
Kenneth Wilburn, *East Carolina University*
Carol Woodfin, *Hardin-Simmons University*
Laura Zeeman, *Red Rocks Community College*

It is also a pleasure to thank the many editors who have assisted us over the years, first at Houghton Mifflin and now at Bedford/St. Martin's. At Bedford/St. Martin's, these include associate editor Robin Soule; senior development editors Sara Wise and Laura Arcari; editorial assistant Arrin Kaplan; former executive editor Traci Mueller Crowell; director of development Jane Knetzger; former publisher for history Mary Dougherty; map editor Charlotte Miller; photo researcher Bruce Carson; text permissions editor Eve Lehmann; and production editor Annette Pagliaro Sweeney, with the assistance of Erica Zhang and the guidance of Sue Brown, director of editing, design, and media production, and managing editor Michael Granger. We would also like to thank former vice president for editorial humanities Denise Wydra and former president Joan E. Feinberg.

VERSIONS AND SUPPLEMENTS

Adopters of *Understanding World Societies* and their students have access to abundant print and digital resources and tools, including documents, assessment and presentation materials, the acclaimed Bedford Series in History and Culture volumes, and much more. And for the first time, the full-featured LaunchPad course space provides access to the narrative with all assignment and assessment opportunities at the ready. See below for more information, visit the book's catalog site at **bedfordstmartins.com/mckayworldunderstanding/catalog**, or contact your local Bedford/St. Martin's sales representative.

Get the Right Version for Your Class

To accommodate different course lengths and course budgets, *Understanding World Societies* is available in several different formats, including 3-hole-punched loose-leaf Budget Books versions and low-priced PDF e-books, such as the *Bedford e-Book to Go* from our Web site and other PDF e-books from other commercial sources. And for the best value of all, package a new print book with LaunchPad at no additional charge to get the best each format offers—a print version for easy portability and reading with a LaunchPad interactive e-book and course space with loads of additional assignment and assessment options.

- **Combined Volume** (Chapters 1–33): available in paperback, loose-leaf, and e-book formats and in LaunchPad
- **Volume 1, To 1600** (Chapters 1–16): available in paperback, loose-leaf, and e-book formats and in LaunchPad
- **Volume 2, Since 1450** (Chapters 16–33): available in paperback, loose-leaf, and e-book formats and in LaunchPad

As noted below, any of these volumes can be packaged with additional titles for a discount. To get ISBNs for discount packages, see the online catalog at **bedfordstmartins.com/mckayworldunderstanding/catalog** or contact your Bedford/St. Martin's representative.

NEW Assign LaunchPad — A Content-Rich and Assessment-Ready Interactive e-book and Course Space

Available for discount purchase on its own or for packaging with new books at no additional charge, LaunchPad is a breakthrough solution for today's courses. Intuitive and easy-to-use for students and instructors alike, LaunchPad is ready to use as is, but it can be edited, customized with your own material, and assigned in seconds. *LaunchPad for Understanding World Societies* includes Bedford/St.

Martin's high-quality content all in one place, including the full interactive e-book and the *Sources of World Societies* documents collection plus LearningCurve formative quizzing, guided reading activities designed to help students read actively for key concepts, additional primary sources, images, videos, chapter summative quizzes, and more.

Through a wealth of formative and summative assessments, including short-answer questions, essay questions, multiple-choice quizzing, and the adaptive learning program of LearningCurve (see the full description below), students gain confidence and get into their reading *before* class. Map and visual activities engage students with visual analysis and critical thinking as they work through each unit, while special boxed features become more meaningful through automatically graded multiple-choice exercises and short-answer questions that prompt students to analyze their reading.

LaunchPad easily integrates with course management systems, and with fast ways to build assignments, rearrange chapters, and add new pages, sections, or links, it lets teachers build the courses they want to teach and hold students accountable. For more information, visit **launchpadworks.com** or contact us at **history@bedfordstmartins.com** to arrange a demo.

✅ NEW Assign LearningCurve So Your Students Come to Class Prepared

Students using LaunchPad receive access to LearningCurve for *Understanding World Societies.* Assigning LearningCurve in place of reading quizzes is easy for instructors, and the reporting features help instructors track overall class trends and spot topics that are giving students trouble so they can adjust their lectures and class activities. This online learning tool is popular with students because it was designed to help them rehearse content at their own pace, in a nonthreatening, game-like environment. The feedback for wrong answers provides instructional coaching and sends students back to the book for review. Students answer as many questions as necessary to reach a target score, with repeated chances to revisit material they haven't mastered. When LearningCurve is assigned, students come to class better prepared.

Take Advantage of Instructor Resources

Bedford/St. Martin's has developed a rich array of teaching resources for this book and for this course. They range from lecture and presentation materials and assessment tools to course management options. Most can be found in LaunchPad or can be downloaded or ordered at **bedfordstmartins.com/mckayworldunderstanding /catalog**.

▶ **Instructor's Resource Manual.** The instructor's manual offers both experienced and first-time instructors tools for preparing lectures and running discussions. It includes chapter content learning objectives, teaching strategies, and a guide to chapter-specific supplements available for the text, plus suggestions on how to get the most out of LearningCurve and a survival guide for first-time teaching assistants.

- ▶ **Guide to Changing Editions.** Designed to facilitate an instructor's transition from the previous edition of *Understanding World Societies* to the second edition, this guide presents an overview of major changes as well as of changes in each chapter.

- ▶ **Computerized Test Bank.** The test bank includes a mix of fresh, carefully crafted multiple-choice, short-answer, and essay questions for each chapter. All questions appear in Microsoft Word format and in easy-to-use test bank software that allows instructors to add, edit, re-sequence, and print questions and answers. Instructors can also export questions into a variety of formats, including Blackboard, Desire2Learn, and Moodle.

- ▶ *The Bedford Lecture Kit:* **PowerPoint Maps and Images.** Look good and save time with *The Bedford Lecture Kit*. These presentation materials are downloadable individually from the Instructor Resources tab at **bedfordstmartins .com/mckayworldunderstanding/catalog**. They include all maps, figures, and images from the textbook in JPEG and PowerPoint formats.

Package and Save Your Students Money

For information on free packages and discounts up to 50%, visit **bedfordstmartins .com/mckayworldunderstanding/catalog** or contact your local Bedford/St. Martin's sales representative. The products that follow all qualify for discount packaging.

- ▶ **The Bedford Series in History and Culture.** More than 100 titles in this highly praised series combine first-rate scholarship, historical narrative, and important primary documents for undergraduate courses. Each book is brief, inexpensive, and focused on a specific topic or period. For a complete list of titles, visit **bedfordstmartins.com/history/series**.

- ▶ *Rand McNally Atlas of World History.* This collection of almost 70 full-color maps illustrates the eras and civilizations in world history from the emergence of human societies to the present.

- ▶ *The Bedford Glossary for World History.* This handy supplement for the survey course gives students historically contextualized definitions for hundreds of terms—from *abolitionism* to *Zoroastrianism*—that they will encounter in lectures, reading, and exams.

- ▶ *World History Matters: A Student Guide to World History Online.* Based on the popular "World History Matters" Web site produced by the Center for History and New Media, this unique resource, edited by Kristin Lehner (The Johns Hopkins University), Kelly Schrum (George Mason University), and T. Mills Kelly (George Mason University), combines reviews of 150 of the most useful and reliable world history Web sites, with an introduction that guides students in locating, evaluating, and correctly citing online sources.

- ▶ **Trade Books.** Titles published by sister companies Hill and Wang; Farrar, Straus and Giroux; Henry Holt and Company; St. Martin's Press; Picador; and Palgrave Macmillan are available at a 50% discount when packaged with Bedford/St. Martin's textbooks. For more information, visit **bedfordstmartins.com /tradeup**.

▶ *A Pocket Guide to Writing in History.* This portable and affordable reference tool by Mary Lynn Rampolla provides reading, writing, and research advice useful to students in all history courses. Concise yet comprehensive advice on approaching typical history assignments, developing critical reading skills, writing effective history papers, conducting research, using and documenting sources, and avoiding plagiarism—enhanced with practical tips and examples throughout—has made this slim reference a best-seller.

▶ *A Student's Guide to History.* This complete guide to success in any history course provides the practical help students need to be successful. In addition to introducing students to the nature of the discipline, author Jules Benjamin teaches a wide range of skills, from preparing for exams to approaching common writing assignments, and explains the research and documentation process with plentiful examples.

BRIEF CONTENTS

LearningCurve
bedfordstmartins.com
/mckayunderstanding

16 | The Acceleration of Global Contact, 1450–1600 *454*

17 | The Islamic World Powers, 1300–1800 *484*

18 | European Power and Expansion, 1500–1750 *512*

19 | New Worldviews and Ways of Life, 1540–1790 *548*

20 | Africa and the World, 1400–1800 *582*

21 | Continuity and Change in East Asia, 1400–1800 *610*

22 | Revolutions in the Atlantic World, 1775–1825 *642*

23 | The Revolution in Energy and Industry, 1760–1850 *680*

24 | Ideologies of Change in Europe, 1815–1914 *710*

25 | Africa, the Ottoman Empire, and the New Imperialism, 1800–1914 *748*

26 | Asia and the Pacific in the Era of Imperialism, 1800–1914 *780*

27 | The Americas in the Age of Liberalism, 1810–1910 *812*

28 | World War and Revolution, 1914–1929 *844*

29 | Nationalism in Asia, 1914–1939 *882*

30 | The Great Depression and World War II, 1929–1945 *914*

31 | Decolonization, Revolution, and the Cold War, 1945–1968 *952*

32 | Liberalization, 1968–2000s *990*

33 | The Contemporary World in Historical Perspective *1028*

Endnotes *E-1*
Index *I-1*

CONTENTS

How to Use This Book *x*

Preface *xvii*

Versions and Supplements *xxvii*

Maps, Figures, and Tables *xliii*

Special Features *xlv*

16

THE ACCELERATION OF GLOBAL CONTACT

1450–1600 *454*

> What was the Afroeurasian trade world like prior to the era of European exploration? 456

The Trade World of the Indian Ocean 456 Peoples and Cultures of the Indian Ocean 458 Trade with Africa and the Middle East 459 Genoese and Venetian Middlemen 460

> Why and how did Europeans undertake ambitious voyages of expansion? 461

Causes of European Expansion 461 Technology and the Rise of Exploration 462 The Portuguese in Africa and Asia 463 Spain's Voyages to the Americas 464 Spain "Discovers" the Pacific 466 Early Exploration by Northern European Powers 467

> What was the impact of Iberian conquest and settlement on the peoples and ecologies of the Americas? 468

Spanish Conquest of the Aztec and Inca Empires 468 Portuguese Brazil 471 Colonial Administration 471 Indigenous Population Loss and Economic Exploitation 472 Patterns of Settlement 473

> How was the era of global contact shaped by new commodities, commercial empires, and forced migrations? 474

The Columbian Exchange 474 Sugar and Early Transatlantic Slavery 475 The Birth of the Global Economy 476

> How did new encounters shape cultural attitudes and beliefs in Europe and the New World? 478

Religious Conversion 479 European Debates About Indigenous Peoples 479 New Ideas About Race 479

CHAPTER SUMMARY 480

CONNECTIONS 481

☑ **LearningCurve**

CHAPTER 16 STUDY GUIDE 482

> **PICTURING THE PAST** Mixed Races 478

> **MAPPING THE PAST** Overseas Exploration and Conquest in the Fifteenth and Sixteenth Centuries 465

> **INDIVIDUALS IN SOCIETY** Doña Marina/Malintzin 470

 **ONLINE DOCUMENT PROJECT** 481

17

THE ISLAMIC WORLD POWERS

1300–1800   *484*

> How were the three Islamic empires established, and what sorts of governments did they set up? 486
   The Ottoman Turkish Empire's Expansion 487   The Ottoman Empire's Use of Slaves 490   The Safavid Empire in Persia 490   The Mughal Empire in India 493

> What cultural advances occurred under the rule of the Ottoman, Safavid, and Mughal Empires? 494
   The Arts 494   City and Palace Building 495   Gardens 496 Intellectual Advances and Religious Trends 497 Coffeehouses and Their Social Impact 498

> How did Christians, Jews, Hindus, and other non-Muslims fare under these Islamic states? 499

> How were the Islamic empires affected by the gradual shift toward trade routes that bypassed their lands? 501
   European Rivalry for Trade in the Indian Ocean 502 Merchant Networks in the Islamic Empires 502 From the British East India Company to the British Empire in India 505

> What common factors led to the decline of central power in the Islamic empires in the seventeenth and eighteenth centuries? 506

CHAPTER SUMMARY 508

CONNECTIONS 509

☑ **LearningCurve**

CHAPTER 17 STUDY GUIDE 510

> **PICTURING THE PAST** Coffee Drinking 498

> **MAPPING THE PAST** The Ottoman Empire at Its Height, 1566 488

> **INDIVIDUALS IN SOCIETY** Hürrem 491

 **ONLINE DOCUMENT PROJECT** 509

18

EUROPEAN POWER AND EXPANSION

1500–1750   *512*

> How did the Protestant and Catholic Reformations change power structures in Europe and shape European colonial expansion? 514
   The Protestant Reformation 514   The Catholic Reformation 516   Religious Violence 518

> How did seventeenth-century European states overcome social and economic crisis to build strong states? 519
   The Social Order and Peasant Life 519   Famine and Economic Crisis 520   The Thirty Years' War 520 European Achievements in State-Building 521

> How did absolutism evolve in the seventeenth century in Spain, France, and Austria? 523
   Spain 523   The Foundations of French Absolutism 524 Louis XIV and Absolutism 525   Expansion Within Europe 525   The Economic Policy of Mercantilism 527 The Austrian Habsburgs 527   The Absolutist Palace 528

> Why and how did the constitutional state triumph in England and the Dutch Republic? 529
   Religious Divides and Civil War 529   The Puritan Protectorate 530   Constitutional Monarchy 531 The Dutch Republic 531

> How did European nations compete for global trade and empire in the Americas and Asia? 534
   The Dutch Trading Empire 535   Colonial Empires of England and France 535   Mercantilism and Colonial Wars 537   People Beyond Borders 538

> How did Russian rulers build a distinctive absolutist monarchy and expand into a vast and powerful empire? 539
   Mongol Rule in Russia and the Rise of Moscow 539 Building the Russian Empire 540   Peter the Great and Russia's Turn to the West 541

CHAPTER SUMMARY 544

CONNECTIONS 544

☑ **LearningCurve**

CHAPTER 18 STUDY GUIDE 546

> **PICTURING THE PAST** *The Young Scholar and His Wife* 532

> **MAPPING THE PAST** Europe After the Peace of Utrecht, 1715 526

> **INDIVIDUALS IN SOCIETY** Glückel of Hameln 533

 **ONLINE DOCUMENT PROJECT** 545

19

NEW WORLDVIEWS AND WAYS OF LIFE

1540–1790 *548*

> What revolutionary discoveries were made in the sixteenth and seventeenth centuries, and why did they occur in Europe? 550

Why Europe? 550   Scientific Thought to 1550 552
Astronomy and Physics 553   Newton's Synthesis 553
Natural History and Empire 554   Magic and Alchemy 555

> What intellectual and social changes occurred as a result of the Scientific Revolution? 556

The Methods of Science 556   Medicine, the Body, and Chemistry 558   Science and Religion 559   Science and Society 559

> What new ideas about society and human relations emerged in the Enlightenment, and what new practices and institutions enabled these ideas to take hold? 561

The Early Enlightenment 561   The Influence of the Philosophes 563   Cultural Contacts and Race 565
The International Enlightenment 566   Enlightened Absolutism and Its Limits 568

> How did economic and social change and the rise of Atlantic trade interact with Enlightenment ideas? 572

Economic and Demographic Change 572   The Atlantic Economy 573   Urban Life and the Public Sphere 575
Culture and Community in the Atlantic World 576
The Atlantic Enlightenment 577

CHAPTER SUMMARY 578

CONNECTIONS 578

✓ **LearningCurve**

CHAPTER 19 STUDY GUIDE 580

> **PICTURING THE PAST** Enlightenment Culture 567

> **MAPPING THE PAST** The Partition of Poland, 1772–1795 570

> **INDIVIDUALS IN SOCIETY** Moses Mendelssohn and the Jewish Enlightenment 571

 **ONLINE DOCUMENT PROJECT** 579

20

AFRICA AND THE WORLD

1400–1800 *582*

> What different types of economic, social, and political structures were found in the kingdoms and states along the west coast and in the Sudan? 584

The West Coast: Senegambia and Benin 584   The Sudan: Songhai, Kanem-Bornu, and Hausaland 587   The Lives of the People of West Africa 588   Trade and Industry 590

> How did the arrival of Europeans and other foreign cultures affect the East African coast, and how did Ethiopia and the Swahili city-states respond to these incursions? 592

Muslim and European Incursions in Ethiopia, ca. 1500–1630 593   The Swahili City-States and the Arrival of the Portuguese, ca. 1500–1600 594

> What role did slavery play in African societies before the transatlantic slave trade began, and what was the effect of European involvement? 596

The Institution of Slavery in Africa 596   The Transatlantic Slave Trade 598   Impact on African Societies 603

CHAPTER SUMMARY 606

CONNECTIONS 606

✓ **LearningCurve**

CHAPTER 20 STUDY GUIDE 608

> **PICTURING THE PAST** Chinese Porcelain Plates 592

> **MAPPING THE PAST** West African Societies, ca. 1500–1800 586

> **INDIVIDUALS IN SOCIETY** Olaudah Equiano 600

 **ONLINE DOCUMENT PROJECT** 607

21

CONTINUITY AND CHANGE IN EAST ASIA

1400–1800 *610*

> What sort of state and society developed in China after the Mongols were ousted? 612

The Rise of Zhu Yuanzhang and the Founding of the Ming Dynasty 612   Problems with the Imperial Institution 615   The Mongols and the Great Wall 615   The Examination Life 616   Everyday Life in Ming China 618   Ming Decline 619

> Did the return of alien rule with the Manchus have any positive consequences for China? 620

The Rise of the Manchus 620   Competent and Long-Lived Emperors 622   Imperial Expansion 623

> How did Japan change during this period of political instability? 624

Muromachi Culture 624   Civil War 625   The Victors: Nobunaga and Hideyoshi 625

> What was life like in Japan during the Tokugawa peace? 627

Tokugawa Government 627   Commercialization and the Growth of Towns 629   The Life of the People in the Edo Period 629

> How did the sea link the countries of East Asia, and what happened when Europeans entered this maritime sphere? 633

Zheng He's Voyages 633   Piracy and Japan's Overseas Adventures 634   Europeans Enter the Scene 635   Christian Missionaries 636   Learning from the West 637   The Shifting International Environment in the Eighteenth Century 637

CHAPTER SUMMARY 638

CONNECTIONS 639

 **LearningCurve**

CHAPTER 21 STUDY GUIDE 640

> **PICTURING THE PAST** Interior View of a Theater 630

> **MAPPING THE PAST** The Qing Empire, ca. 1800 621

> **INDIVIDUALS IN SOCIETY** Tan Yunxian, Woman Doctor 617

LaunchPad ONLINE DOCUMENT PROJECT 639

22

REVOLUTIONS IN THE ATLANTIC WORLD

1775–1825 *642*

> What were the factors behind the age of revolution in the Atlantic world? 644

Social Change 644   Demands for Liberty and Equality 646   The Seven Years' War 647

> Why and how did American colonists forge a new, independent nation? 649

The Origins of the Revolution 649   Independence from Britain 650   Framing the Constitution 651   Limitations of Liberty and Equality 652

> How did the events of 1789 result in a constitutional monarchy in France, and what were the consequences? 653

Breakdown of the Old Order 653   The National Assembly 654   Constitutional Monarchy 655   The National Convention 655   The Directory 659

> How did Napoleon Bonaparte assume control of France and much of Europe, and what factors led to his downfall? 660

Napoleon's Rule of France 660   Napoleon's Expansion in Europe 661   The Grand Empire and Its End 662

> How did slave revolt on colonial Saint-Domingue lead to the creation of the independent nation of Haiti in 1804? 665

Revolutionary Aspirations in Saint-Domingue 665   The Outbreak of Revolt 667   The War of Haitian Independence 668

> Why and how did the Spanish and Portuguese colonies of North and South America shake off European domination and develop into national states? 671

The Origins of the Revolutions Against Colonial Powers 671   Resistance, Rebellion, and Independence 673   The Aftermath of Revolution in the Atlantic World 675

CHAPTER SUMMARY 676

CONNECTIONS 677

 **LearningCurve**

CHAPTER 22 STUDY GUIDE 678

> **PICTURING THE PAST** Contrasting Visions of the Sans-Culottes 657

> **MAPPING THE PAST** Napoleonic Europe in 1812 663

> **INDIVIDUALS IN SOCIETY** Toussaint L'Ouverture 669

LaunchPad ONLINE DOCUMENT PROJECT 677

23

THE REVOLUTION IN ENERGY AND INDUSTRY

1760–1850   *680*

> Why did the Industrial Revolution begin in Britain, and how did it develop between 1780 and 1850? 682

Why Britain? 682   Technological Innovations and Early Factories 684   The Steam Engine Breakthrough 685   Steam-Powered Transportation 688   Industry and Population 689

> How did countries in Europe and around the world respond to the challenge of industrialization after 1815? 691

National and International Variations 691   Industrialization in Continental Europe 693   Agents of Industrialization 693   The Global Picture 695

> How did work evolve during the Industrial Revolution, and how did daily life change for working people? 697

Work in Early Factories 697   Working Families and Children 698   The Sexual Division of Labor 699   Living Standards for the Working Class 700

> How did the changes brought about by the Industrial Revolution lead to new social classes, and how did people respond to the new structure? 702

The New Class of Factory Owners 703   Responses to Industrialization 703   The Early Labor Movement in Britain 704   The Impact of Slavery 706

CHAPTER SUMMARY 706

CONNECTIONS 707

 **LearningCurve**

CHAPTER 23 STUDY GUIDE 708

> **PICTURING THE PAST** Ford Maddox Brown, *Work* 704

> **MAPPING THE PAST** Continental Industrialization, ca. 1850 694

> **INDIVIDUALS IN SOCIETY** Josiah Wedgwood 687

LaunchPad ONLINE DOCUMENT PROJECT 707

24

IDEOLOGIES OF CHANGE IN EUROPE

1815–1914   *710*

> How did the allies fashion a peace settlement in 1815, and what radical ideas emerged between 1815 and 1848? 712

The Political and Social Situation After 1815 712   Conservatism After 1815 713   Liberalism and the Middle Class 715   The Growing Appeal of Nationalism 715   The Birth of Socialism 716

> Why did revolutions triumph briefly throughout most of Europe in 1848, and why did they fail? 718

Social and Economic Conflict 718   Liberal Reform in Great Britain 719   Revolutions in France 720   The Revolutions of 1848 in Central Europe 722

> How did strong leaders and nation building transform Italy, Germany, and Russia? 724

Cavour, Garibaldi, and the Unification of Italy 724   Bismarck and German Unification 726   The Modernization of Russia 729

> What was the impact of urban growth on cities, social classes, families, and ideas? 731

Urban Development 731   Social Inequality and Class 733   The Changing Family 734   Science for the Masses 736   Cultural Shifts 737

> How did nationalism and socialism shape European politics in the decades before the Great War? 739

Trends in Suffrage 739   The German Empire 740   Republican France 740   Great Britain and the Austro-Hungarian Empire 741   Jewish Emancipation and Modern Anti-Semitism 742   The Socialist Movement 743

CHAPTER SUMMARY 744

CONNECTIONS 745

 **LearningCurve**

CHAPTER 24 STUDY GUIDE 746

> **PICTURING THE PAST** The Triumph of Democratic Republics 721

> **MAPPING THE PAST** Europe in 1815 714

> **INDIVIDUALS IN SOCIETY** Giuseppe Garibaldi 727

LaunchPad ONLINE DOCUMENT PROJECT 745

25

AFRICA, THE OTTOMAN EMPIRE, AND THE NEW IMPERIALISM

1800–1914   *748*

> What were the most significant changes in Africa during the nineteenth century, and why did they occur? 750

Trade and Social Change 750   Islamic Revival and Expansion in Africa 753   The Scramble for Africa, 1880–1914 754   Southern Africa in the Nineteenth Century 756   Colonialism's Impact After 1900 758

> What were the causes and consequences of European empire building after 1880? 760

Causes of the New Imperialism 761   A "Civilizing Mission" 762   Critics of Imperialism 762   African and Asian Resistance 763

> How did the Ottoman Empire and Egypt try to modernize themselves, and what were the most important results? 765

Decline and Reform in the Ottoman Empire 765   Egypt: From Reform to British Occupation 767

> What were the global consequences of European industrialization between 1800 and 1914? 771

The Rise of Global Inequality 771   The World Market 772

> What fueled migration, and what was the general pattern of this unprecedented movement of people? 774

CHAPTER SUMMARY 776

CONNECTIONS 777

 **LearningCurve**

CHAPTER 25 STUDY GUIDE 778

> **PICTURING THE PAST** Pears' Soap Advertisement 752

> **MAPPING THE PAST** The Partition of Africa 755

> **INDIVIDUALS IN SOCIETY** Muhammad Ali 769

LaunchPad **ONLINE DOCUMENT PROJECT** 777

26

ASIA AND THE PACIFIC IN THE ERA OF IMPERIALISM

1800–1914   *780*

> In what ways did India change as a consequence of British rule? 782

The Evolution of British Rule 782   The Socioeconomic Effects of British Rule 783   The British and the Indian Educated Elite 784

> Why were most but not all Southeast Asian societies reduced to colonies? 787

The Dutch East Indies 787   Mainland Southeast Asia 788   The Philippines 789

> Was China's decline in the nineteenth century due more to internal problems or to Western imperialism? 791

The Opium War 791   Internal Problems 792   The Self-Strengthening Movement 793   Republican Revolution 794

> How was Japan able to quickly master the challenges posed by the West? 795

The "Opening" of Japan 795   The Meiji Restoration 796   Industrialization 798   Japan as an Imperial Power 799

> What were the causes and consequences of the vast movement of people in the Pacific region? 800

Settler Colonies in the Pacific: Australia and New Zealand 800   Asian Emigration 802

> What explains the similarities and differences in the experiences of Asian countries in this era? 806

CHAPTER SUMMARY 808

CONNECTIONS 809

 **LearningCurve**

CHAPTER 26 STUDY GUIDE 810

> **PICTURING THE PAST** Japan's First Skyscraper 798

> **MAPPING THE PAST** Asia in 1914 786

> **INDIVIDUALS IN SOCIETY** José Rizal 790

LaunchPad **ONLINE DOCUMENT PROJECT** 809

27
THE AMERICAS IN THE AGE OF LIBERALISM

1810–1910   *812*

> How and why did the process of nation-state consolidation vary across the Americas?   814

Liberalism and Caudillos in Spanish America   814   Mexico and the United States   816   Liberal Reform in Mexico   818   Brazil: A New World Monarchy   819

> Why did slavery last longer in the United States, Brazil, and Cuba than in the other republics of Spanish America? How did patterns of resistance shape slavery and abolition?   821

Slave Societies in the Americas   821   Independence and Abolition   823   Abolition in Cuba and Brazil   825

> As Latin America became more integrated into the world economy, how did patterns of economic growth shape social relations and political culture?   826

The Porfiriato and Liberal Stability in Mexico   826   Liberal Consolidation in South America   827   Latin America Re-enters the World Economy   828

> What factors shaped immigration patterns to the Americas? How did immigrants shape — and how were they shaped by — their new settings?   831

Immigration to Latin America   832   Immigration to the United States   833   Immigration to Canada   835

> In what ways did U.S. policies in the Caribbean and Central America resemble European imperialism? How did U.S. foreign policy depart from European imperialism?   837

U.S. Intervention in Latin America   837   The Spanish-American War   838   The Panama Canal   839

CHAPTER SUMMARY   840

CONNECTIONS   841

☑ **LearningCurve**

CHAPTER 27 STUDY GUIDE   842

> **PICTURING THE PAST** Slaves Sold South from Richmond, 1853   822

> **MAPPING THE PAST** Abolition in the Americas   824

> **INDIVIDUALS IN SOCIETY** Henry Meiggs, Promoter and Speculator   830

LaunchPad **ONLINE DOCUMENT PROJECT**   841

28
WORLD WAR AND REVOLUTION

1914–1929   *844*

> What were the long-term and immediate causes of World War I, and how did the conflict become a global war?   846

Origins and Causes of the Great War   846   The Outbreak of War   849   Stalemate and Slaughter   850   The War Becomes Global   852

> How did total war affect the home fronts of the major combatants?   854

Mobilizing for Total War   854   The Social Impact of War   855   Growing Political Tensions   857

> What factors led to the Russian Revolution, and what was its outcome?   858

The Fall of Imperial Russia   858   The Provisional Government   859   Lenin and the Bolshevik Revolution   860   Dictatorship and Civil War   862

> What were the global consequences of the First World War?   864

The End of the War   864   The Paris Peace Treaties   864   American Rejection of the Versailles Treaty   867

> How did leaders deal with the political dimensions of uncertainty and try to re-establish peace and prosperity in the interwar years?   868

Germany and the Western Powers   868   Hope in Foreign Affairs   870   Hope in Democratic Government   870

> In what ways were the anxieties of the postwar world expressed or heightened by revolutionary ideas in modern thought, art, and science and in new forms of communication?   872

Uncertainty in Philosophy and Religion   872   The New Physics   873   Freudian Psychology   874   Twentieth-Century Literature   874   Modern Architecture, Art, and Music   874   Movies and Radio   876

CHAPTER SUMMARY   878

CONNECTIONS   879

☑ **LearningCurve**

CHAPTER 28 STUDY GUIDE   880

> **PICTURING THE PAST** "Never Forget!"   854

> **MAPPING THE PAST** Territorial Changes in Europe After World War I   866

> **INDIVIDUALS IN SOCIETY** Vera Brittain   856

LaunchPad **ONLINE DOCUMENT PROJECT**   879

29
NATIONALISM IN ASIA

1914–1939 *882*

> Why did modern nationalism develop in Asia between the First and Second World Wars, and what was its appeal? 884

Asian Reaction to the War in Europe 884   The Mandates System 885   Nationalism's Appeal 886

> How did the Ottoman Empire's collapse in World War I shape nationalist movements in the Middle East? 888

The Arab Revolt 890   The Turkish Revolution 891   Modernization Efforts in Persia and Afghanistan 893   Gradual Independence in the Arab States 894   Arab-Jewish Tensions in Palestine 894

> What role did Gandhi and his campaign of militant nonviolence play in leading India to independence from the British? 896

British Promises and Repression 896   The Roots of Militant Nonviolence 898   Gandhi's Resistance Campaign in India 898

> How did nationalism shape political developments in East and Southeast Asia? 900

The Rise of Nationalist China 901   China's Intellectual Revolution 902   From Liberalism to Ultranationalism in Japan 902   Japan Against China 905   Striving for Independence in Southeast Asia 908

CHAPTER SUMMARY 910

CONNECTIONS 910

✔ **LearningCurve**

CHAPTER 29 STUDY GUIDE 912

> **PICTURING THE PAST** The Fate of a Chinese Patriot 900

> **MAPPING THE PAST** The Partition of the Ottoman Empire, 1914–1923 889

> **INDIVIDUALS IN SOCIETY** Ning Lao, a Chinese Working Woman 904

**ONLINE DOCUMENT PROJECT** 911

30
THE GREAT DEPRESSION AND WORLD WAR II

1929–1945 *914*

> What caused the Great Depression, and what were its consequences? 916

The Economic Crisis 916   Mass Unemployment 918   The New Deal in the United States 918   The European Response to the Depression 919   Worldwide Effects 920

> What was the nature of the new totalitarian dictatorships, and how did they differ from conservative authoritarian states and from each other? 922

Conservative Authoritarianism 922   Radical Totalitarian Dictatorships 923

> How did Stalin and the Communist Party build a totalitarian order in the Soviet Union? 925

From Lenin to Stalin 926   The Five-Year Plans 926   Life and Culture in Soviet Society 927   Stalinist Terror and the Great Purges 928

> How did Italian fascism develop? 930

The Seizure of Power 930   The Regime in Action 931

> Why were Hitler and his Nazi regime initially so popular, and how did their actions lead to World War II? 933

The Roots of Nazism 933   Hitler's Road to Power 934   The Nazi State and Society 935   Hitler's Popularity 936   Aggression and Appeasement, 1933–1939 936

> How did Germany and Japan build empires in Europe and Asia, and how did the Allies defeat them? 939

Hitler's Empire in Europe, 1939–1942 939   The Holocaust 942   Japan's Asian Empire 942   The Grand Alliance 943   The War in Europe, 1942–1945 945   The War in the Pacific, 1942–1945 946

CHAPTER SUMMARY 948

CONNECTIONS 949

✔ **LearningCurve**

CHAPTER 30 STUDY GUIDE 950

> **PICTURING THE PAST** British Conservative Party Poster, 1931 920

> **MAPPING THE PAST** World War II in the Pacific 947

> **INDIVIDUALS IN SOCIETY** Primo Levi 944

**ONLINE DOCUMENT PROJECT** 949

31

DECOLONIZATION, REVOLUTION, AND THE COLD WAR

1945–1968 *952*

> How did the Cold War and decolonization shape the postwar world? 954

The Cold War and the Division of Europe 954   The United Nations 957   The Politics of Liberation 957   Dependency and Development Theories 958   Interpreting the Postcolonial Experience 960

> How did religion and the legacies of colonialism affect the formation of new nations in South Asia and the Middle East after World War II? 961

Independence in India, Pakistan, and Bangladesh 962   Arab Socialism in the Middle East 963   The Arab-Israeli Conflict 964

> How did the Cold War shape reconstruction, revolution, and decolonization in East and Southeast Asia? 966

The Communist Victory in China 967   Conflict in Korea 968   Japan's American Reconstruction 968   The Vietnam War 969

> What factors influenced decolonization in Africa after World War II? 971

The Growth of African Nationalism 971   Ghana Shows the Way 973   French-Speaking Regions 974

> Why did populism emerge as such a powerful political force in Latin America? 976

Economic Nationalism in Mexico 976   Populism in Argentina and Brazil 978   Communist Revolution in Cuba 980

> Why did the world face growing social unrest in the 1960s? 981

The Soviet Union Struggles to Move Beyond Stalin 981   Western Europe's Postwar Challenge 982   America's Economic Boom and Civil Rights Revolution 984   The World in 1968 984

CHAPTER SUMMARY 986

CONNECTIONS 986

✔ **LearningCurve**

CHAPTER 31 STUDY GUIDE 988

> **PICTURING THE PAST** Communist China Poster Art 966

> **MAPPING THE PAST** Decolonization in Africa, 1947 to the Present 972

> **INDIVIDUALS IN SOCIETY** Eva Perón 979

🅛 LaunchPad **ONLINE DOCUMENT PROJECT** 987

32

LIBERALIZATION

1968–2000s *990*

> What were the short-term and long-term consequences of the OPEC oil embargo? 992

The OPEC Oil Embargo 992   Mexico Under the PRI 994   Nigeria, Africa's Giant 995

> How did war and revolution reshape the Middle East? 997

The Palestinian-Israeli Conflict 997   Egypt: Arab World Leader 998   Revolution and War in Iran and Iraq 999

> What effect did the Cold War and debt crisis have on Latin America? 1002

Civil Wars in Central America 1002   Boom and Bust in Chile 1003   The Dirty War in Argentina 1004   Development and Dictatorship in Brazil 1005

> How did white-minority rule end in southern Africa? 1007

Portuguese Decolonization and Rhodesia 1007   South Africa Under Apartheid 1008   Political Change in Africa Since 1990 1009

> How have East and South Asian nations pursued economic development, and how have political regimes shaped those efforts? 1011

China's Economic Resurgence 1011   "Japan, Inc." and the "Asian Tigers" 1013   Development Versus Democracy in India and Pakistan 1014

> How did decolonization and the end of the Cold War change Europe? 1016

The Limits of Reform in the Soviet Union and Eastern Europe 1017   Recasting Russia Without Communism 1019   Integration and Reform in Europe 1022

CHAPTER SUMMARY 1024

CONNECTIONS 1025

✔ **LearningCurve**

CHAPTER 32 STUDY GUIDE 1026

> **PICTURING THE PAST** Tiananmen Square, 1989 1012

> **MAPPING THE PAST** Abrahamic Religions in the Middle East and Surrounding Regions 1000

> **INDIVIDUALS IN SOCIETY** Václav Havel 1018

🅛 LaunchPad **ONLINE DOCUMENT PROJECT** 1025

33

THE CONTEMPORARY WORLD IN HISTORICAL PERSPECTIVE

1028

> Does the contemporary world reflect the "end of history"? 1030

Complexity and Violence in a Multipolar World 1031
An Expanding Atomic Age 1032   Al-Qaeda and Afghanistan 1033

> How have migration and the circulation of capital and technology continued to shape the world? 1036

Migration 1036   Urbanization 1037   Multinational Corporations 1041

> What challenges did social reformers address at the turn of the twenty-first century? 1043

Environmentalism 1044   Lesbian, Gay, and Transgender Rights 1045   Women's Right to Equality 1045   Children: The Right to Childhood 1046

> How have science and technology kept pace with population change? 1048

Intensified Agriculture and the Green Revolution 1048
Slowing Population Growth 1049   The Medical Revolution 1050   A Digital Revolution 1051

CHAPTER SUMMARY 1053

CONNECTIONS 1053

 **LearningCurve**

CHAPTER 33 STUDY GUIDE 1054

> PICTURING THE PAST Protest Against Genetically Modified Foods 1048

> MAPPING THE PAST The Global Distribution of Wealth, ca. 2010 1040

> INDIVIDUALS IN SOCIETY Sieng, a Mnong Refugee in an American High School 1038

LaunchPad ONLINE DOCUMENT PROJECT 1053

MAPS, FIGURES, AND TABLES

CHAPTER 16

MAP 16.1 The Fifteenth-Century Afroeurasian Trading World *458*

MAP 16.2 Overseas Exploration and Conquest in the Fifteenth and Sixteenth Centuries *465*

SPOT MAP Columbus's First Voyage in the New World, 1492–1493 *466*

SPOT MAP Invasion of Tenochtitlán, 1519–1521 *469*

SPOT MAP The Conquest of Peru, 1532–1533 *469*

SPOT MAP The Transatlantic Slave Trade *476*

MAP 16.3 Seaborne Trading Empires in the Sixteenth and Seventeenth Centuries *477*

CHAPTER 17

SPOT MAP Empire of Timur, ca. 1405 *487*

MAP 17.1 The Ottoman Empire at Its Height, 1566 *488*

MAP 17.2 The Safavid Empire, 1587–1629 *492*

SPOT MAP The Mughal Empire, 1526–1857 *493*

MAP 17.3 India, 1707–1805 *503*

MAP 17.4 The Muslim World, ca. 1700 *507*

CHAPTER 18

MAP 18.1 Religious Divisions, ca. 1555 *517*

MAP 18.2 Europe After the Thirty Years' War *522*

MAP 18.3 Europe After the Peace of Ultrecht, 1715 *526*

SPOT MAP Austrian Expansion, to 1699 *527*

SPOT MAP The English Civil War, 1642–1649 *530*

MAP 18.4 Seventeenth-Century Dutch Commerce *536*

SPOT MAP European Claims in North America, 1714 *537*

MAP 18.5 The Expansion of Russia, 1462–1689 *543*

CHAPTER 19

SPOT MAP The Pale of Settlement, 1791 *569*

MAP 19.1 The Partition of Poland, 1772–1795 *571*

MAP 19.2 The Atlantic Economy, 1701 *574*

FIGURE 19.1 Exports of English Manufactured Goods, 1700–1774 *575*

CHAPTER 20

MAP 20.1 West African Societies, ca. 1500–1800 *586*

SPOT MAP West African Trade Routes *590*

MAP 20.2 East Africa in the Sixteenth Century *593*

SPOT MAP Cape Colony, ca. 1750 *597*

SPOT MAP The Slave Coast of West Africa *598*

FIGURE 20.1 Estimated Slave Imports by Destination, 1501–1866 *599*

FIGURE 20.2 The Transatlantic Slave Trade, 1501–1866 *605*

CHAPTER 21

SPOT MAP Ming China, ca. 1600 *613*

MAP 21.1 The Qing Empire, ca. 1800 *621*

SPOT MAP Hideyoshi's Campaigns in Japan and Korea, 1592–1598 *626*

MAP 21.2 Tokugawa Japan, 1603–1867 *628*

MAP 21.3 East Asia, ca. 1600 *635*

CHAPTER 22

MAP 22.1 European Claims in North America and India Before and After the Seven Years' War, 1755–1763 *648*

SPOT MAP Loyalist Strength in the Colonies, ca. 1774–1776 *651*

SPOT MAP Areas of French Insurrection, 1793 *656*

SPOT MAP German Confederation of the Rhine, 1806 *662*

MAP 22.2 Napoleonic Europe in 1812 *663*

MAP 22.3 The War of Haitian Independence, 1791–1804 *667*

MAP 22.4 Latin America in ca. 1780 and 1830 *674*

CHAPTER 23

SPOT MAP Cottage Industry and Transportation in Great Britain in the 1700s *684*

MAP 23.1 The Industrial Revolution in Great Britain, ca. 1850 *688*

TABLE 23.1 Per Capita Levels of Industrialization, 1750–1913 *692*

MAP 23.2 Continental Industrialization, ca. 1850 *694*

CHAPTER 24

MAP 24.1 Europe in 1815 *714*

MAP 24.2 The Unification of Italy, 1859–1870 *725*

MAP 24.3 The Unification of Germany, 1866–1871 *728*

SPOT MAP The Crimean War, 1853–1856 *729*

SPOT MAP The Russian Revolution of 1905 *730*

CHAPTER 25

MAP 25.1 The Partition of Africa *755*
SPOT MAP The Struggle for South Africa, 1878 *758*
SPOT MAP Ottoman Decline in the Balkans, 1818–1830 *767*
SPOT MAP The Suez Canal, 1869 *768*
FIGURE 25.1 The Growth of Average Income per Person Worldwide, 1750–1914 *772*

CHAPTER 26

SPOT MAP The Great Revolt/Great Mutiny, 1857 *783*
MAP 26.1 Asia in 1914 *786*
SPOT MAP Chinese Rebellions, 1851–1911 *793*
SPOT MAP Japanese Expansion, 1875–1914 *799*
MAP 26.2 Australia *801*
MAP 26.3 Emigration Out of Asia, 1820–1914 *803*

CHAPTER 27

MAP 27.1 Displacement of Indigenous Peoples, 1780s–1910s *817*
MAP 27.2 Abolition in the Americas *824*
MAP 27.3 The Dominion of Canada, 1871 *835*

CHAPTER 28

MAP 28.1 European Alliances at the Outbreak of World War I, 1914 *848*
MAP 28.2 The Balkans, 1878–1914 *849*
SPOT MAP The Schlieffen Plan *850*
MAP 28.3 The First World War in Europe *851*
SPOT MAP The Russian Civil War, 1917–1922 *862*
MAP 28.4 Territorial Changes in Europe After World War I *866*
SPOT MAP French Occupation of the Ruhr, 1923–1925 *869*

CHAPTER 29

MAP 29.1 The Partition of the Ottoman Empire, 1914–1923 *889*
SPOT MAP Afghanistan Under Amanullah Khan *893*
SPOT MAP India, ca. 1930 *899*
MAP 29.2 The Chinese Communist Movement and the War with Japan, 1927–1938 *907*
SPOT MAP The Spanish-American War in the Philippines, 1898 *909*

CHAPTER 30

SPOT MAP Italy's Ethiopian Campaign, 1935–1936 *936*
MAP 30.1 The Growth of Nazi Germany, 1933–1939 *937*
SPOT MAP Vichy France, 1940 *940*
MAP 30.2 World War II in Europe and Africa, 1939–1945 *941*
SPOT MAP The Holocaust, 1941–1945 *942*
MAP 30.3 World War II in the Pacific *947*

CHAPTER 31

MAP 31.1 Cold War Europe in the 1950s *956*
MAP 31.2 The Partition of British India, 1947 *962*
MAP 31.3 The Middle East After 1947 *965*
MAP 31.4 Decolonization in Asia *967*
SPOT MAP The Korean War *968*
SPOT MAP The Vietnam War *970*
MAP 31.5 Decolonization in Africa, 1947 to the Present *972*
SPOT MAP Cuba *980*

CHAPTER 32

MAP 32.1 Abrahamic Religions in the Middle East and Surrounding Regions *1000*
SPOT MAP Asian "Economic Tigers" *1011*
MAP 32.2 The Breakup of Yugoslavia *1020*
MAP 32.3 Russia and the Successor States *1021*
MAP 32.4 The European Union, 2014 *1023*

CHAPTER 33

SPOT MAP Iraq, ca. 2010 *1035*
TABLE 33.1 Urban Population as a Percentage of Total Population in the World and in Eight Major Areas, 1925–2025 *1039*
MAP 33.1 The Global Distribution of Wealth, ca. 2010 *1040*
MAP 33.2 People Living with HIV/AIDS Worldwide, ca. 2010 *1051*

SPECIAL FEATURES

CHAPTER 16
PICTURING THE PAST Mixed Races *478*
INDIVIDUALS IN SOCIETY Doña Marina/Malintzin *470*

CHAPTER 17
PICTURING THE PAST Coffee Drinking *498*
INDIVIDUALS IN SOCIETY Hürrem *491*

CHAPTER 18
PICTURING THE PAST *The Young Scholar and His Wife* *532*
INDIVIDUALS IN SOCIETY Glückel of Hameln *533*

CHAPTER 19
PICTURING THE PAST Enlightenment Culture *567*
INDIVIDUALS IN SOCIETY Moses Mendelssohn and the Jewish Enlightenment *570*

CHAPTER 20
PICTURING THE PAST Chinese Porcelain Plates *592*
INDIVIDUALS IN SOCIETY Olaudah Equiano *600*

CHAPTER 21
PICTURING THE PAST Interior View of a Theater *630*
INDIVIDUALS IN SOCIETY Tan Yunxian, Woman Doctor *617*

CHAPTER 22
PICTURING THE PAST Contrasting Visions of the Sans-Culottes *657*
INDIVIDUALS IN SOCIETY Toussaint L'Ouverture *669*

CHAPTER 23
PICTURING THE PAST Ford Maddox Brown, *Work* *704*
INDIVIDUALS IN SOCIETY Josiah Wedgwood *687*

CHAPTER 24
PICTURING THE PAST The Triumph of Democratic Republics *721*
INDIVIDUALS IN SOCIETY Giuseppe Garibaldi *727*

CHAPTER 25
PICTURING THE PAST Pears' Soap Advertisement *752*
INDIVIDUALS IN SOCIETY Muhammad Ali *769*

CHAPTER 26
PICTURING THE PAST Japan's First Skyscraper *798*
INDIVIDUALS IN SOCIETY José Rizal *790*

CHAPTER 27
PICTURING THE PAST Slaves Sold South from Richmond, 1853 *822*
INDIVIDUALS IN SOCIETY Henry Meiggs, Promoter and Speculator *830*

CHAPTER 28
PICTURING THE PAST "Never Forget!" *854*
INDIVIDUALS IN SOCIETY Vera Brittain *856*

CHAPTER 29
PICTURING THE PAST The Fate of a Chinese Patriot *900*
INDIVIDUALS IN SOCIETY Ning Lao, a Chinese Working Woman *904*

CHAPTER 30
PICTURING THE PAST British Conservative Party Poster, 1931 *920*
INDIVIDUALS IN SOCIETY Primo Levi *944*

CHAPTER 31
PICTURING THE PAST Communist China Poster Art *966*
INDIVIDUALS IN SOCIETY Eva Perón *979*

CHAPTER 32
PICTURING THE PAST Tiananmen Square, 1989 *1012*
INDIVIDUALS IN SOCIETY Václav Havel *1018*

CHAPTER 33
PICTURING THE PAST Protest Against Genetically Modified Foods *1048*
INDIVIDUALS IN SOCIETY Sieng, a Mnong Refugee in an American High School *1038*

Understanding
World Societies

A HISTORY

VOLUME 2

16

THE ACCELERATION OF GLOBAL CONTACT

1450–1600

> **What new global connections were forged in the fifteenth and sixteenth centuries?** Chapter 16 examines the causes, course, and effects of European expansion in the fifteenth and sixteenth centuries. Before 1500 Europeans were relatively marginal players in a centuries-old trading system that linked Africa, Asia, and Europe. By 1550 the European search for better access to Asian trade goods had led to a new overseas empire in the Indian Ocean and the accidental discovery of the Western Hemisphere. With this discovery South and North America were drawn into an international network of trade centers and political empires, which Europeans came to dominate. The era of globalization had begun, creating new political systems and forms of economic exchange as well as cultural assimilation, conversion, and resistance.

LearningCurve
After reading the chapter, use LearningCurve to retain what you've read.

Nezahualpilli At the time of the arrival of Europeans, Nezahualpilli was ruler of the city-state of Texcoco, the second most important city in the Aztec Empire after Tenochtitlan. (Nezahualpilli, portrait from *Codex Ixtlilxochitl*, 1582, pigment on European paper/Bibliothèque Nationale, Paris, France/De Agostini Picture Library/akg-images)

> What was the Afroeurasian trade world like prior to the era of European exploration?

> Why and how did Europeans undertake ambitious voyages of expansion?

> What was the impact of Iberian conquest and settlement on the peoples and ecologies of the Americas?

> How was the era of global contact shaped by new commodities, commercial empires, and forced migrations?

> How did new encounters shape cultural attitudes and beliefs in Europe and the New World?

What was the Afroeurasian trade world like prior to the era of European exploration?

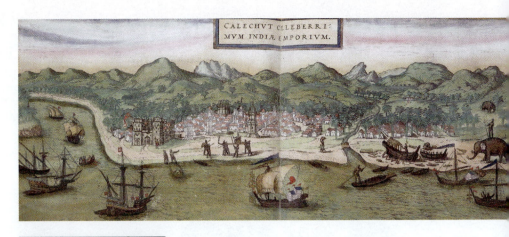

The Port of Calicut in India

The port of Calicut, located on the west coast of India, was a center of the Indian Ocean spice trade during the Middle Ages. Vasco da Gama arrived in Calicut in 1498 and obtained permission to trade there, leading to hostilities between the Portuguese and the Arab traders who had previously dominated the port. (Private Collection/The Stapleton Collection/The Bridgeman Art Library)

THE AFROEURASIAN TRADE WORLD linked the products and people of Europe, Asia, and Africa in the fifteenth century. The West was not the dominant player in this trading system. Nevertheless, wealthy Europeans were eager consumers of luxury goods from the East, which they received through Italian middlemen.

The Trade World of the Indian Ocean

The Indian Ocean was the center of the Afroeurasian trade world, serving as a crossroads for commercial and cultural exchanges between China, India, the Middle East, Africa, and Europe (Map 16.1). From the seventh through the fourteenth centuries, the volume of this trade steadily increased, declining only during the years of the Black Death.

Merchants congregated in a series of multicultural, cosmopolitan port cities strung around the Indian Ocean. Most of these cities had some form of autonomous self-government, and mutual self-interest had largely limited violence and attempts to monopolize trade. The most developed area of this commercial web was made up of the ports surrounding the South China Sea. In the fifteenth century the port of Malacca became a great commercial entrepôt (AHN-truh-poh), a trading post to which goods were shipped for storage while awaiting redistribution to other places.

CHAPTER LOCATOR | **What was the Afroeurasian trade world like prior to the era of European exploration?** | Why and how did Europeans undertake ambitious voyages of expansion?

CHAPTER 16
456 THE ACCELERATION OF GLOBAL CONTACT

1271–1295 Marco Polo travels to China	**1519–1522** Magellan's expedition circumnavigates the world
1443 Portuguese establish first African trading post at Arguin	**1521** Cortés conquers Aztec Empire
1492 Columbus lands on San Salvador	**1533** Pizarro conquers Inca Empire
1494 Treaty of Tordesillas ratified	**1571** Spanish establish port of Manila in the Philippines
1518 Atlantic slave trade begins	**1602** Dutch East India Company founded

The Mongol emperors opened the doors of China to the West, encouraging Europeans like the Venetian trader and explorer Marco Polo to do business there. Marco Polo's tales of his travels from 1271 to 1295 fueled Western fantasies about the Orient.

After the Mongols fell to the Ming Dynasty in 1368, China entered a period of agricultural and commercial expansion, population growth, and urbanization (see pages 612–619). Historians agree that China had the most advanced economy in the world until at least the beginning of the eighteenth century.

China also took the lead in exploration, sending Admiral Zheng He's fleet as far west as Egypt. Each of his seven expeditions from 1405 to 1433 involved hundreds of ships and tens of thousands of men (see page 633). The purpose of the voyages was primarily diplomatic, to enhance China's prestige and seek tribute-paying alliances. The high expense of the voyages in a period of renewed Mongol encroachment led to the abandonment of the maritime expeditions after the deaths of Zheng He and the emperor.

China's decision to forego large-scale exploration was a decisive turning point in world history, one that left an opening for European states to expand their role in Asian trade. Nonetheless, Zheng He's voyages left a legacy of increased Chinese trading in the South China Sea and Indian Ocean.

Another center of Indian Ocean trade was India, the crucial link between the Persian Gulf and the Southeast Asian and East Asian trade networks. The subcontinent had ancient links with its neighbors to the northwest. Trade among ports bordering the Indian Ocean was revived in the Middle Ages by Arab merchants who circumnavigated India on their way to trade in the South China Sea.

The inhabitants of India's Coromandel coast traditionally looked to Southeast Asia, where they had ancient trading and cultural ties. Hinduism and Buddhism arrived in Southeast Asia from India during the Middle Ages, and a brisk trade between Southeast Asian and Coromandel port cities persisted from that time until the arrival of the Portuguese in the sixteenth century. India itself was an important contributor of goods to the world trading system. Most of the world's pepper was grown in India, and Indian cotton and silk textiles were also highly prized.

What was the impact of Iberian conquest and settlement on the peoples of the Americas? | How was the era of global contact shaped by new commodities and forced migrations? | How did new encounters shape cultural attitudes and beliefs in Europe and the New World? | ✓ **LearningCurve** Check what you know.

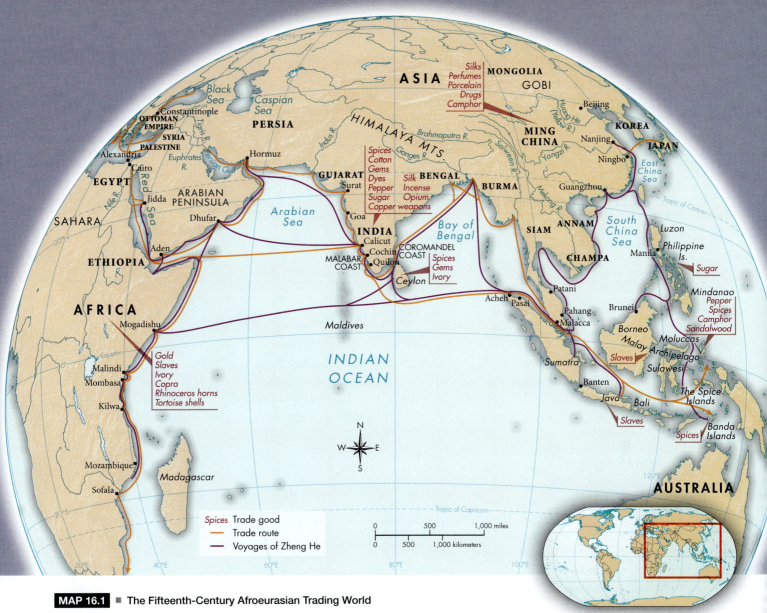

MAP 16.1 ■ The Fifteenth-Century Afroeurasian Trading World

After a period of decline following the Black Death and the Mongol invasions, trade revived in the fifteenth century. Muslim merchants dominated trade, linking ports in East Africa and the Red Sea with those in India and the Malay Archipelago. The Chinese admiral Zheng He followed the most important Indian Ocean trade routes on his voyages (1405–1433), hoping to impose Ming dominance of trade and tribute.

Peoples and Cultures of the Indian Ocean

Indian Ocean trade connected peoples from the Malay Peninsula (the southern extremity of the Asian continent), India, China, and East Africa, among whom there was an enormous variety of languages, cultures, and religions. In spite of this diversity, certain sociocultural similarities linked these peoples, especially in Southeast Asia.

In comparison to India, China, or even Europe after the Black Death, Southeast Asia was sparsely populated. People were concentrated in port cities and in areas of intense rice cultivation. Another difference between Southeast Asia and

CHAPTER LOCATOR

What was the Afroeurasian trade world like prior to the era of European exploration?

Why and how did Europeans undertake ambitious voyages of expansion?

India, China, and Europe was the higher status of women—their primary role in planting and harvesting rice gave them authority and economic power. At marriage, which typically occurred around age twenty, the groom paid the bride (or sometimes her family) a sum of money called **bride wealth**, which remained under her control. This practice was in sharp contrast to the Chinese, Indian, and European dowry, which came under the husband's control. Property was administered jointly, in contrast to the Chinese principle and Indian practice that wives had no say in the disposal of family property. All children, regardless of gender, inherited equally.

Respect for women carried over to the commercial sphere. Women participated in business as partners and independent entrepreneurs. When Portuguese and Dutch men settled in the region and married local women, their wives continued to play important roles in trade and commerce.

In contrast to most parts of the world other than Africa, Southeast Asian peoples had an accepting attitude toward premarital sexual activity and placed no premium on virginity at marriage. Divorce carried no social stigma and was easily attainable if a pair proved incompatible. Either the woman or the man could initiate a divorce.

bride wealth

▶ In early modern Southeast Asia, a sum of money the groom paid the bride or her family at the time of marriage. This practice contrasted with the dowry in China, India, and Europe, which the husband controlled.

> **Common Features of Southeast Asian Societies:**

- Austronesian languages
- Diet based on rice, fish, palms, and palm wine
- Rice, harvested by women, as the staple of the diet
- Fishing as the chief male occupation

Trade with Africa and the Middle East

On the east coast of Africa, Swahili-speaking city-states engaged in the Indian Ocean trade, exchanging ivory, rhinoceros horn, tortoise shells, copra (dried coconut), and slaves for textiles, spices, cowrie shells, porcelain, and other goods. The most important cities were Mogadishu, Mombasa, and Kilwa, which had converted to Islam by the eleventh century.

West Africa also played an important role in world trade. In the fifteenth century most of the gold that reached Europe came from the Sudan region in West Africa. Transported across the Sahara by Arab and African traders on camels, the gold was sold in the ports of North Africa. Other trading routes led to the Egyptian cities of Alexandria and Cairo.

Inland nations that sat astride the north-south caravan routes grew wealthy from this trade. In the mid-thirteenth century the kingdom of Mali emerged as an important player on the overland trade route. In later centuries, however, the diversion of gold away from the trans-Sahara routes would weaken the inland states of Africa politically and economically.

Gold was one important object of trade; slaves were another. Long before the arrival of Europeans. Arab and

Mansa Musa

This detail from the Catalan Atlas of 1375, a world map created for the Catalan king, depicts a king of Mali, Mansa Musa, who was legendary for his wealth in gold. European desires for direct access to the trade in sub-Saharan gold helped inspire Portuguese exploration of the west coast of Africa in the fifteenth century. (Detail from the *Catalan Atlas*, 1375 [vellum], by Abraham Cresques (1325–1387)/Bibliothèque Nationale, Paris, France/The Bridgeman Art Library)

| What was the impact of Iberian conquest and settlement on the peoples of the Americas? | How was the era of global contact shaped by new commodities and forced migrations? | How did new encounters shape cultural attitudes and beliefs in Europe and the New World? | ✓ LearningCurve Check what you know. |

African merchants took West African slaves to the Mediterranean to be sold in European, Egyptian, and Middle Eastern markets and also brought eastern Europeans to West Africa as slaves. In addition, Indian and Arab merchants traded slaves in the coastal regions of East Africa.

The Middle East served as an intermediary for trade between Europe, Africa, and Asia and was also an important supplier of goods for foreign exchange. Two great rival empires, the Persian Safavids and the Turkish Ottomans, dominated the region, competing for control over western trade routes to the East. By the mid-sixteenth century the Ottomans had established control over eastern Mediterranean sea routes to trading centers in Syria, Palestine, Egypt, and the rest of North Africa.

Genoese and Venetian Middlemen

Europe constituted a minor outpost in the world trading system, for European craftsmen produced few products to rival those of Asia. However, Europeans desired luxury goods from the East, and in the late Middle Ages such trade was controlled by the Italian city-states of Venice and Genoa. Venice had opened the gateway to Asian trade in 1304, when it established formal relations with the sultan of Mamluk Egypt and started operations in Cairo. Because Eastern demand for European goods was low, Venetians funded their purchases through shipping and trade in firearms and slaves.

Venice's ancient trading rival was Genoa. By 1270, Genoa dominated the northern route to Asia through the Black Sea. From then until the fourteenth century, the Genoese expanded their trade routes as far as Persia and the Far East.

In the fifteenth century, with Venice claiming victory in the spice trade, the Genoese shifted focus from trade to finance and from the Black Sea to the western Mediterranean. When Spanish and Portuguese voyages began to explore the western Atlantic (see page 461), Genoese merchants, navigators, and financiers provided their skills and capital to the Iberian monarchs.

A major element of Italian trade was slavery. Merchants purchased slaves in the Balkans of southeastern Europe. After the loss of the Black Sea trade routes—and thus the source of slaves—to the Ottomans, the Genoese sought new supplies of slaves in the West, eventually seizing or buying and selling the Guanches (indigenous peoples from the Canary Islands), Muslim prisoners and Jewish refugees from Spain, and, by the early 1500s, both black and Berber Africans. With the growth of Spanish colonies in the New World, Genoese and Venetian merchants became important players in the Atlantic slave trade.

> **QUICK REVIEW**

What role did the peoples of Southeast Asia play in the Afroeurasian trade world? What role did Europeans play?

CHAPTER LOCATOR | What was the Afroeurasian trade world like prior to the era of European exploration? | **Why and how did Europeans undertake ambitious voyages of expansion?**

460 CHAPTER 16 THE ACCELERATION OF GLOBAL CONTACT

Why and how did Europeans undertake ambitious voyages of expansion?

Pepper Harvest

To break the monotony of their bland diet, Europeans had a passion for pepper, which — along with cinnamon, cloves, nutmeg, and ginger — was the main object of the Asian trade. We can appreciate the fifteenth-century expression "as dear as pepper": one kilo of pepper cost 2 grams of silver at the place of production in the East Indies and from 1 to 10 grams of silver in Alexandria, Egypt; 14 to 18 grams in Venice; and 20 to 30 grams at the markets of northern Europe. Here natives fill vats, and the dealer tastes a peppercorn for pungency. (Bibliothèque Nationale, Paris, France/Archives Charmet/The Bridgeman Art Library)

AS EUROPE RECOVERED after the Black Death, new European players entered the scene with novel technology, eager to spread Christianity and to undo Italian and Ottoman domination of trade with the East. A century after the plague, Iberian explorers began the overseas voyages that helped create the modern world, with immense consequences for their own continent and the rest of the planet.

Causes of European Expansion

European expansion had multiple causes. The first was economic. By the middle of the fifteenth century Europe was experiencing a revival of population and economic activity after the lows of the Black Death. This revival created renewed demand for luxuries, especially spices, from the East. The fall of Constantinople and the subsequent Ottoman control of trade routes created obstacles to fulfilling these demands. European merchants and rulers eager for the profits of trade thus needed to find new sources of precious metal to exchange with the Ottomans or trade routes that bypassed the Ottomans.

| What was the impact of Iberian conquest and settlement on the peoples of the Americas? | How was the era of global contact shaped by new commodities and forced migrations? | How did new encounters shape cultural attitudes and beliefs in Europe and the New World? | ✓ LearningCurve Check what you know. |

Religious fervor and the crusading spirit were another important catalyst for expansion. Just seven months separated Isabella and Ferdinand's conquest of the emirate of Granada, the last remaining Muslim state on the Iberian Peninsula, and Columbus's departure across the Atlantic. Overseas exploration thus transferred the militaristic religious fervor of the reconquista (reconquest) to new non-Christian territories. As they conquered indigenous empires, Iberians brought the attitudes and administrative practices developed during the reconquista to the Americas.

A third motivation was the dynamic spirit of the Renaissance. Like other men of the Renaissance era, explorers sought to win glory for their exploits and demonstrated a genuine interest in learning more about unknown waters. The detailed journals kept by European voyagers attest to their fascination with the new peoples and places they visited.

The people who stayed at home had a powerful impact on the voyages of discovery. Merchants provided the capital for many early voyages and had a strong say in their course. To gain authorization and financial support for their expeditions, they sought official sponsorship from the Crown. Competition among European monarchs for the prestige and profit of overseas exploration thus constituted another crucial factor in encouraging the steady stream of expeditions that began in the late fifteenth century.

The small number of Europeans who could read provided a rapt audience for tales of fantastic places and unknown peoples. Cosmography, natural history, and geography aroused enormous interest among educated people in the fifteenth and sixteenth centuries. One of the most popular books of the time was the fourteenth-century text *The Travels of Sir John Mandeville*, which purported to be a firsthand account of the author's travels in the Middle East, India, and China.

Technology and the Rise of Exploration

Technological developments in shipbuilding, navigation, and weaponry enabled European expansion. Since ancient times, most seagoing vessels had been narrow, open boats called galleys, propelled by slaves or convicts manning the oars. The need for sturdier craft, as well as population losses caused by the Black Death, forced the development of a new style of ship that would not require much manpower. Over the course of the fifteenth century the Portuguese developed the **caravel**, a small, light, three-mast sailing ship with triangular lateen sails. The caravel was much more maneuverable than the galley. When fitted with cannon, it could dominate larger vessels.

This period also saw great strides in cartography and navigational aids. Around 1410 Arab scholars reintroduced Europeans to **Ptolemy's *Geography***. Written in the second century, the work synthesized the geographical knowledge of the classical world. It represented a major improvement over medieval cartography, but it also contained significant errors. Unaware of the Americas, Ptolemy showed the world as much smaller than it is, so that Asia appeared not very far to the west of Europe.

The magnetic compass made it possible for sailors to determine their direction and position at sea. The astrolabe, an instrument invented by the ancient Greeks and perfected by Muslim navigators, was used to determine the altitude

caravel
▶ A small, maneuverable, three-mast sailing ship developed by the Portuguese in the fifteenth century that gave the Portuguese a distinct advantage in exploration and trade.

Ptolemy's *Geography*
▶ A second-century-c.e. work that synthesized the classical knowledge of geography and introduced the concepts of longitude and latitude. Reintroduced to Europeans in 1410 by Arab scholars, its ideas allowed cartographers to create more accurate maps.

CHAPTER LOCATOR | What was the Afroeurasian trade world like prior to the era of European exploration? | **Why and how did Europeans undertake ambitious voyages of expansion?**

CHAPTER 16
462 THE ACCELERATION OF GLOBAL CONTACT

The Portuguese Fleet Embarked for the Indies

This image shows a Portuguese trading fleet in the late fifteenth century bound for the riches of the Indies. Between 1500 and 1635 over nine hundred ships sailed from Portugal to ports on the Indian Ocean in annual fleets composed of five to ten ships. Portuguese sailors used astrolabes, such as the one pictured here, to accurately plot their position. (fleet: British Museum/HarperCollins Publishers/The Art Archive at Art Resource, NY; astrolabe: © The Trustees of the British Museum/Art Resource, NY)

of the sun and other celestial bodies. It permitted mariners to plot their latitude, that is, their precise position north or south of the equator.

Like the astrolabe, much of the new technology that Europeans used on their voyages was borrowed from the East. Gunpowder, the compass, and the stern-post rudder were Chinese inventions. Advances in cartography also drew on the rich tradition of Judeo-Arabic mathematical and astronomical learning in Iberia. In exploring new territories, European sailors thus called on techniques and knowledge developed over centuries in China, the Muslim world, and trading centers along the Indian Ocean.

The Portuguese in Africa and Asia

For centuries Portugal was a small and poor nation on the margins of European life. Yet Portugal had a long history of seafaring and navigation. Blocked from access to western Europe by Spain, the Portuguese turned to the Atlantic. Nature favored the Portuguese: winds blowing along their coast offered passage to Africa, its Atlantic islands, and, ultimately, Brazil.

In the early phases of Portuguese exploration, Prince Henry (1394–1460), a dynamic younger son of the king, played a leading role. A nineteenth-century

What was the impact of Iberian conquest and settlement on the peoples of the Americas? | How was the era of global contact shaped by new commodities and forced migrations? | How did new encounters shape cultural attitudes and beliefs in Europe and the New World? | ✓ LearningCurve Check what you know.

463

scholar dubbed Henry "the Navigator" because of his support for the study of geography and navigation and for the annual expeditions he sponsored down the western coast of Africa.

Portugal's conquest of Ceuta, an Arab city in northern Morocco, in 1415 marked the beginning of European overseas expansion. In the 1420s, under Henry's direction, the Portuguese began to settle the Atlantic islands of Madeira (ca. 1420) and the Azores (1427). In 1443 they founded their first African commercial settlement at Arguin in North Africa. By the time of Henry's death in 1460, his support for exploration had resulted in thriving sugar plantations on the Atlantic islands, the first arrival of enslaved Africans in Portugal (see page 475), and new access to African gold.

The Portuguese next established fortified trading posts, called factories, on the gold-rich Guinea coast and penetrated into the African continent all the way to Timbuktu (Map 16.2). By 1500 Portugal controlled the flow of African gold to Europe. In contrast to the Spanish conquest of the Americas (see page 468), the Portuguese did not establish large settlements in West Africa or seek to control the political or cultural lives of those with whom they traded. Instead they sought to profit by inserting themselves into pre-existing trading systems.

In 1487 Bartholomew Diaz (ca. 1451–1500) rounded the Cape of Good Hope at the southern tip of Africa (Map 16.2), but storms and a threatened mutiny forced him to turn back. A decade later Vasco da Gama (ca. 1469–1524) succeeded in rounding the Cape while commanding a fleet in search of a sea route to India. With the help of an Indian guide, da Gama reached the port of Calicut in India. He returned to Lisbon with spices and samples of Indian cloth, having proved the possibility of lucrative trade with the East via the Cape route. Thereafter, a Portuguese convoy set out for passage around the Cape every March.

Lisbon became the entrance port for Asian goods into Europe, but this was not accomplished without a fight. Muslim-controlled port city-states had long controlled the rich trade of the Indian Ocean, and they did not surrender it willingly. From 1500 to 1515 the Portuguese used a combination of bombardment and diplomatic treaties to establish trading factories at Goa, Malacca, Calicut, and Hormuz, thereby laying the foundation for a Portuguese trading empire in the sixteenth and seventeenth centuries. The acquisition of port cities and their trade routes brought riches to Portugal, but, as in Africa, the Portuguese had limited impact on the lives and religious faith of peoples beyond Portuguese coastal holdings.

Inspired by the Portuguese, Spain had also begun the quest for empire. Theirs was to be a second, entirely different mode of colonization leading to large-scale settlement and the forced assimilation of huge indigenous populations.

Spain's Voyages to the Americas

Christopher Columbus, a native of Genoa, was an experienced seaman and navigator. He had worked as a mapmaker in Lisbon and had spent time on Madeira. He was familiar with such fifteenth-century Portuguese navigational aids as *portolans*—written descriptions of the courses along which ships sailed—and the use of the compass as a nautical instrument.

Columbus was also a deeply religious man. He had witnessed the Spanish conquest of Granada and shared fully in the religious fervor surrounding that event. Like the Spanish rulers and most Europeans of his age, Columbus under-

What was the Afroeurasian trade world like prior to the era of European exploration?

Why and how did Europeans undertake ambitious voyages of expansion?

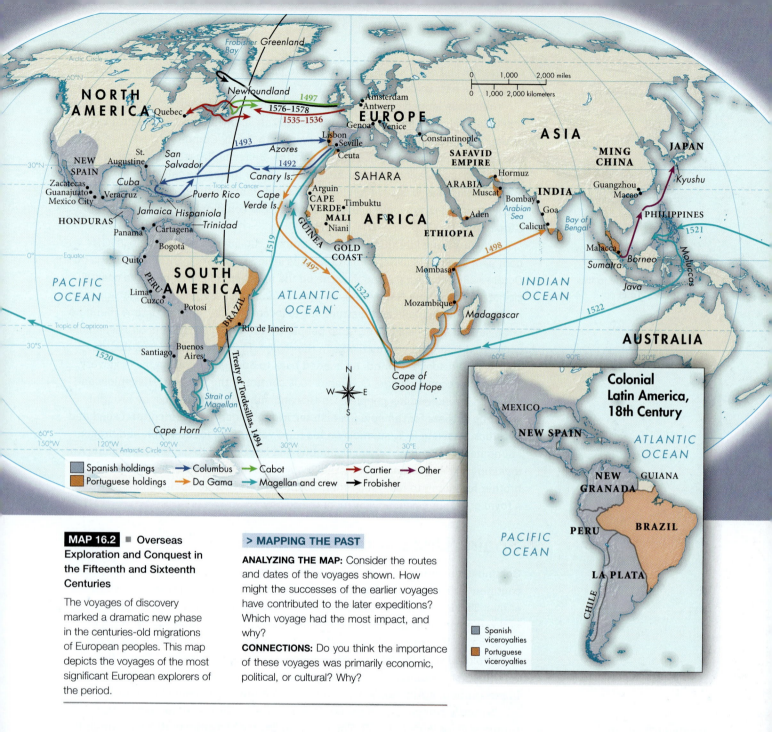

MAP 16.2 ■ Overseas Exploration and Conquest in the Fifteenth and Sixteenth Centuries

The voyages of discovery marked a dramatic new phase in the centuries-old migrations of European peoples. This map depicts the voyages of the most significant European explorers of the period.

> **MAPPING THE PAST**

ANALYZING THE MAP: Consider the routes and dates of the voyages shown. How might the successes of the earlier voyages have contributed to the later expeditions? Which voyage had the most impact, and why?

CONNECTIONS: Do you think the importance of these voyages was primarily economic, political, or cultural? Why?

stood Christianity as a missionary religion that should be carried to all places of the earth.

Rejected for funding by the Portuguese in 1483 and by Ferdinand and Isabella in 1486, Columbus finally won the support of the Spanish monarchy in 1492. Buoyed by the success of the reconquista and eager to earn profits from trade, the Spanish crown agreed to make him viceroy over any territory he might discover and to give him one-tenth of the material rewards of the journey.

Columbus and his small fleet left Spain on August 3, 1492. Columbus dreamed of reaching the court of the Mongol emperor, the Great Khan, not realizing that the Ming Dynasty had overthrown the Mongols in 1368. Based on Ptolemy's

| What was the impact of Iberian conquest and settlement on the peoples of the Americas? | How was the era of global contact shaped by new commodities and forced migrations? | How did new encounters shape cultural attitudes and beliefs in Europe and the New World? | ✓ LearningCurve Check what you know. |

Columbus's First Voyage to the New World, 1492–1493

Geography and other texts, he expected to pass the islands of Japan and then land on the east coast of China.

Columbus landed on an island in the Bahamas on October 12, which he christened San Salvador and claimed on behalf of the Spanish crown. In a letter he wrote to Ferdinand and Isabella on his return to Spain, Columbus described the natives as handsome, peaceful, and primitive. Believing he was somewhere off the east coast of Japan, in what he considered the Indies, he called them "Indians," a name that was later applied to all inhabitants of the Americas. Columbus concluded that they would make good slaves and could quickly be converted to Christianity.

Scholars have identified the inhabitants of the islands as the Taino (TIGH-noh) people. From San Salvador, Columbus sailed southwest, landing on Cuba on October 28. Deciding that he must be on the mainland of China near the coastal city of Quinsay (now Hangzhou), he sent a small embassy inland with letters from Ferdinand and Isabella and instructions to locate the city. Although they found no large settlement, the sight of Taino people wearing gold ornaments on Hispaniola suggested that gold was available in the region. In January, confident that its source would soon be found, he headed back to Spain to report on his discovery.

On his second voyage, Columbus took control of the island of Hispaniola and enslaved its indigenous peoples. On this and subsequent voyages, he brought with him settlers for the new Spanish territories, along with agricultural seed and livestock. Arriving in Hispaniola on his third voyage, he found revolt had broken out against his brother, whom Columbus had left behind to govern the colony. An investigatory expedition sent by the Spanish crown arrested Columbus and his brother for failing to maintain order. Columbus returned to Spain in disgrace and a royal governor assumed control of the colony.

Spain "Discovers" the Pacific

Columbus never realized the scope of his achievement: that he had found a vast continent unknown to Europeans, except for a fleeting Viking presence centuries earlier. The Florentine navigator Amerigo Vespucci (veh-SPOO-chee) (1454–1512) realized what Columbus had not. Writing about his discoveries on the coast of modern-day Venezuela, Vespucci stated: "Those new regions which we found and explored with the fleet . . . we may rightly call a New World." This letter was the first document to describe America as a continent separate from Asia. In recognition of Amerigo's bold claim, the continent was named for him.

To settle competing claims to the Atlantic discoveries, Spain and Portugal turned to Pope Alexander VI. The resulting **Treaty of Tordesillas** (tawr-duh-SEE-yuhs) in 1494 gave Spain everything to the west of an imaginary line drawn down the Atlantic and Portugal everything to the east.

The search for profits determined the direction of Spanish exploration and expansion in South America. Because its profits from Hispaniola and other Caribbean islands were insignificant compared to Portugal's enormous riches from the Asian spice trade, Spain renewed the search for a western passage to Asia. In 1519 Charles V of Spain commissioned Ferdinand Magellan (1480–1521) to find a direct sea route to Asia. Magellan sailed southwest across the Atlantic to Brazil, and after a long search along the coast he located the strait off the southern tip of South America that now bears his name (see Map 16.2). After passing through

Treaty of Tordesillas
▶ The 1494 agreement giving Spain everything west of an imaginary line drawn down the Atlantic and giving Portugal everything to the east.

CHAPTER LOCATOR | What was the Afroeurasian trade world like prior to the era of European exploration? | **Why and how did Europeans undertake ambitious voyages of expansion?**

the strait, his fleet sailed north up the west coast of South America and then headed west into the Pacific.

Terrible storms, disease, starvation, and violence haunted the expedition. Magellan himself was killed in a skirmish in the Malay Archipelago, and only one of the five ships that began the expedition made it back to Spain. This ship returned home in 1522 with only eighteen men aboard, having traveled from the east by way of the Indian Ocean, the Cape of Good Hope, and the Atlantic. The voyage—the first to circumnavigate the globe—had taken close to three years.

Despite the losses, this voyage revolutionized Europeans' understanding of the world by demonstrating the vastness of the Pacific. Magellan's expedition also forced Spain's rulers to rethink their plans for overseas commerce and territorial expansion. The westward passage to the Indies was too long and dangerous for commercial purposes. Thus Spain soon abandoned the attempt to oust Portugal from the Eastern spice trade and concentrated on exploiting its New World territories.

Early Exploration by Northern European Powers

Spain's northern European rivals also set sail across the Atlantic during the early days of exploration, searching for a northwest passage to the Indies. In 1497 John Cabot (ca. 1450–1499), a Genoese merchant living in London, landed on Newfoundland. The next year he returned and explored the New England coast. These forays proved futile, and at that time the English established no permanent colonies in the territories they explored.

News of the riches of Mexico and Peru later inspired the English to renew their efforts. Between 1576 and 1578 Martin Frobisher (ca. 1535–1594) made three voyages in and around the Canadian bay that now bears his name. Frobisher brought a quantity of ore back to England with him in hopes that it contained precious metals, but it proved to be worthless.

Early French exploration of the Atlantic was equally frustrating. Between 1534 and 1541 Frenchman Jacques Cartier (1491–1557) made several voyages and explored the St. Lawrence region of Canada, searching for a passage to the wealth of Asia. When this hope proved vain, the French turned to a new source of profit within Canada itself: trade in beavers and other furs. As had the Portuguese in Asia, French traders bartered with local peoples whom they largely treated as autonomous and equal partners. French fishermen also competed with the Spanish and English for the schools of cod they found in the Atlantic waters around Newfoundland.

QUICK REVIEW

How did the Portuguese lay the foundation for European overseas expansion?

What was the impact of Iberian conquest and settlement on the peoples of the Americas?

How was the era of global contact shaped by new commodities and forced migrations?

How did new encounters shape cultural attitudes and beliefs in Europe and the New World?

☑ LearningCurve
Check what you know.

What was the impact of Iberian conquest and settlement on the peoples and ecologies of the Americas?

Juan Vespucci's World Map, 1526

As chief pilot to the Spanish crown, Juan Vespucci oversaw constant revisions to royal maps necessitated by ongoing voyages of discovery and exploration. This map shows the progress of Spanish knowledge of the New World some thirty years after Columbus.

BEFORE COLUMBUS'S ARRIVAL, the Americas were inhabited by thousands of groups of indigenous peoples with distinct languages and cultures. These groups ranged from hunter-gatherer tribes organized into tribal confederations to settled agriculturalists to large-scale empires connecting bustling cities and towns. The best estimate is that the peoples of the Americas numbered between 35 and 50 million in 1492. Their lives were radically altered by the arrival of Europeans.

Spanish Conquest of the Aztec and Inca Empires

In the first two decades after Columbus's arrival in the New World, the Spanish colonized Hispaniola, Cuba, Puerto Rico, and other Caribbean islands. Based on rumors of a wealthy mainland civilization, the Spanish governor in Cuba sponsored expeditions to the Yucatán coast of the Gulf of Mexico, including one in 1519 under the command of the **conquistador** (kahn-KEES-tuh-dawr) Hernán Cortés (1485–1547). Alarmed by Cortés's ambition, the governor decided to withdraw his support, but Cortés quickly set sail before being removed from command. Cortés and his party landed on the Mexican coast on April 21, 1519. His

conquistador

▶ Spanish for "conqueror"; a Spanish soldier-explorer, such as Hernán Cortés or Francisco Pizarro, who sought to conquer the New World for the Spanish crown.

CHAPTER LOCATOR | What was the Afroeurasian trade world like prior to the era of European exploration? | Why and how did Europeans undertake ambitious voyages of expansion?

camp soon received visits by delegations of Aztec leaders bearing gifts and news of their great emperor.

The Mexica Empire, also known as the **Aztec Empire**, comprised the Mexica people and the peoples they had conquered. At the time of the Spanish arrival, the empire was ruled by Moctezuma II (r. 1502–1520), from his capital at Tenochtitlan (tay-nawch-teet-LAHN), now Mexico City. The Aztecs were a sophisticated civilization with an advanced understanding of mathematics, astronomy, and engineering. As in European nations at the time, a hereditary nobility dominated the army, the priesthood, and the state bureaucracy and reaped the gains from the agricultural labor of the common people.

Within weeks of his arrival, Cortés acquired translators who provided vital information on the empire and its weaknesses. (See "Individuals in Society: Doña Marina / Malintzin," page 470.) Through his interpreters, Cortés learned of strong local resentment against the Aztec Empire. Realizing that he could exploit dissensions within the empire to his own advantage, Cortés forged an alliance with Tlaxcala (tlah-SKAH-lah), a subject kingdom of the Aztecs. In October a combined Spanish-Tlaxcalan force occupied the Aztec city of Cholula, second largest in the empire, and massacred thousands of inhabitants. Strengthened by this victory, Cortés formed alliances with other native kingdoms. In November 1519, with a few hundred Spanish men and some six thousand indigenous warriors, he marched on Tenochtitlan.

Moctezuma's response to the arrival of the Spanish was weak and hesitant. Unlike other native leaders, he refrained from attacking the Spaniards but instead welcomed Cortés and his men into Tenochtitlan. Moctezuma was apparently deeply impressed by Spanish victories and believed the Spanish were invincible. When Cortés took Moctezuma hostage, the emperor's influence crumbled. During the ensuing attacks and counterattacks, Moctezuma was killed. The Spaniards and their allies escaped from the city suffering heavy losses. Cortés quickly began gathering forces and making new alliances against the Aztecs. In May 1521 he led a second assault on Tenochtitlan, leading an army of approximately one thousand Spanish and seventy-five thousand native warriors.[1]

The Spanish victory in late summer 1521 was hard-won and was greatly aided by the effects of smallpox, which had devastated the besieged population of the city. After establishing a new capital in the ruins of Tenochtitlan, Cortés and other conquistadors began the systematic conquest of Mexico.

More remarkable than the defeat of the Aztec Empire was the fall of the remote **Inca Empire** in Peru. Living in a settlement perched more than 9,800 feet above sea level, the Incas were isolated from the Mesoamerican civilization of the Aztecs. The Incas' strength lay largely in their bureaucratic efficiency. They divided their empire into four major regions, each region into provinces, and each province into districts. Officials at each level used the extensive network of roads to transmit information and orders. The Incas used a complex system of colored and knotted cords, called khipus, for administrative bookkeeping.

By the time of the Spanish invasion, however, the Inca Empire had been weakened by a civil war over succession and an epidemic of disease, possibly smallpox, spread through trade with groups in contact with Europeans. The Spanish conquistador Francisco Pizarro (ca. 1475–1541) landed on the northern coast of Peru on May 13, 1532, the very day the Inca leader Atahualpa (ah-tuh-WAHL-puh) won control of the empire. As Pizarro advanced across the Andes toward Cuzco, the capital of the Inca Empire, Atahualpa was also heading there for his coronation.

Aztec Empire

▶ Also known as the Mexica Empire, a large and complex Native American civilization in modern Mexico and Central America that possessed advanced mathematical, astronomical, and engineering technology.

Invasion of Tenochtitlán, 1519–1521

The Conquest of Peru, 1532–1533

Inca Empire

▶ The vast and sophisticated Peruvian empire centered at the capital city of Cuzco that was at its peak in the fifteenth century.

What was the impact of Iberian conquest and settlement on the peoples of the Americas?

How was the era of global contact shaped by new commodities and forced migrations?

How did new encounters shape cultural attitudes and beliefs in Europe and the New World?

✔ LearningCurve
Check what you know.

I n April 1519 Hernán Cortés and his followers received a number of gifts from the Tabasco people after he defeated them, including a group of twenty female captives. Among them was a young woman the Spanish baptized as Marina, which became Malin in the Nahuatl (NAH-wha-tuhl) language spoken in the Aztec Empire. Her high status and importance were recognized with the honorific title of *doña* in Spanish and the suffix *-tzin* in Nahuatl. Bernal Díaz del Castillo, who accompanied Cortés and wrote the most important contemporary history of the Aztec Empire and its conquest, claimed that Doña Marina (or Malintzin) was the daughter of a leader of a Nahuatl-speaking tribe. According to his account, the family sold Marina to Maya slave traders as a child to protect the inheritance rights of her stepbrother.

Marina possessed unique skills that immediately caught the attention of Cortés. Fluent both in Nahuatl and Yucatec Maya (spoken by a Spanish priest accompanying Cortés), she offered a way for him to communicate with the peoples he encountered. She quickly learned Spanish as well and came to play a vital role as an interpreter and diplomatic guide. Indigenous pictures and writings created after the conquest depict Malintzin as a constant presence beside Cortés as he negotiated with and fought and killed Amerindians. The earliest known images show her interpreting for Cortés as he meets with the Tlaxcalan lord Xicotencatl, forging the alliance that would prove vital to Spanish victory against the Aztecs. Malintzin also appears prominently in the images of the *Florentine Codex*, an illustrated history of the Aztec Empire and its conquest created near the end of the sixteenth century by indigenous artists working under the direction of Friar Bernardino de Sahagún. All the images depict her as a well-dressed woman standing at the center of interactions between the Spanish and Amerindians.

Malintzin bore Cortés a son, Don Martín Cortés, in 1522 and accompanied him on expeditions to Honduras between 1524 and 1526. It is impossible to know the true nature of their personal relationship. Cortés was married to a Spanish woman in Cuba at the time, and Malintzin was a slave, in no position to refuse any demands he made of her. Cortés recognized their child and provided financial support for his upbringing. Malintzin later married one of Cortés's Spanish followers, Juan Jaramillo, with whom she had a daughter. It is unknown when and how she died.

Bernal Díaz gave Malintzin high praise. In his history, written decades after the fact, he described her as beautiful and intelligent, revered by native tribesmen, and devotedly loyal to the Spanish. He stated repeatedly that it would have been impossible for them to succeed without her help. Cortés mentioned Malintzin only twice in his letters to Spanish king Charles V. He acknowledged her usefulness as his interpreter but described her only as "an Indian woman of this land," giving no hint of their personal relationship. No writings from Malintzin herself exist.

Doña Marina translating for Hernán Cortés.

Malintzin is commonly known in Mexico and Latin America as La Malinche, a Spanish rendering of her Nahuatl name. She remains a compelling and controversial figure. Popular opinion has often condemned La Malinche as a traitor to her people, whose betrayal enabled the Spanish conquest and centuries of subjugation of indigenous peoples. Other voices have defended her as an enslaved woman who had no choice but to serve her masters. As the mother of a *mestizo* (mixed-race) child, she has also been seen as a founder of the mixed-race population that dominates modern Mexico. She will always be a reminder of the complex interactions between indigenous peoples and Spanish conquistadors that led to the conquest and the new culture born from it.

QUESTIONS FOR ANALYSIS

1. Why was the role of interpreter so important in Cortés's conquest of the Aztec Empire? Why did Malintzin become such a central figure in interactions between Cortés and the Amerindians?
2. What options were open to Malintzin in following her path? If she intentionally chose to aid the Spanish, what motivations might she have had?

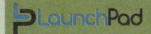

ONLINE DOCUMENT PROJECT

How did Spanish and Amerindian artists depict Malintzin? Examine Spanish and Amerindian representations of Malintzin's role in the conquest, and then complete a quiz and writing assignment based on the evidence and details from this chapter. *See inside the front cover to learn more.*

Like Moctezuma in Mexico, Atahualpa sent envoys to greet the Spanish. Motivated by curiosity about the Spanish, he intended to meet with them to learn more about them and their intentions. Instead the Spaniards ambushed and captured him, extorted an enormous ransom in gold, and then executed him in 1533. The Spanish then marched on to Cuzco, profiting, as with the Aztecs, from internal conflicts and forming alliances with local peoples. When Cuzco fell in 1533, the Spanish plundered immense riches in gold and silver.

A combination of factors made it possible for tiny Spanish forces to bring down the mighty empires of the Americas: the boldness and audacity of conquistadors like Cortés and Pizarro; the military superiority endowed by Spanish firepower and horses; the fervent belief in a righteous Christian God imparted by the reconquista; division within the Aztec and Inca Empires that produced native allies for the Spanish; and, of course, the devastating impact of contagious diseases among the indigenous population. Ironically, the well-organized, urban-based Aztec and Inca Empires were more vulnerable to wholesale takeover than more decentralized and fragmented groups like the Maya, whose independence was not wholly crushed until the end of the seventeenth century.

Portuguese Brazil

Unlike Mesoamerica or the Andes, the territory of Brazil contained no urban empires but instead had roughly 2.5 million nomadic and settled people divided into small tribes and many different language groups. In 1500 the Portuguese crown named Pedro Álvares Cabral commander of a fleet headed for the spice trade of the Indies. En route, the fleet sailed far to the west, accidentally landing on the coast of Brazil, which Cabral claimed for Portugal under the terms of the Treaty of Tordesillas.

In the 1520s Portuguese settlers brought sugarcane production to Brazil. They initially used enslaved indigenous laborers on sugar plantations, but the rapid decline in the indigenous population soon led to the use of forcibly transported Africans. In Brazil the Portuguese thus created a new form of colonization in the Americas: large plantations worked by enslaved people. This model of slave-worked sugar plantations would spread throughout the Caribbean in the seventeenth century.

Colonial Administration

By the end of the sixteenth century the Spanish and Portuguese had successfully overcome most indigenous groups and expanded their territory throughout modern-day Mexico, the southwestern United States, and Central and South America. In Mesoamerica and the Andes, the Spanish had taken over the cities and tribute systems of the Aztecs and the Incas, basing their control on the prior existence of well-established polities with organized tribute systems.

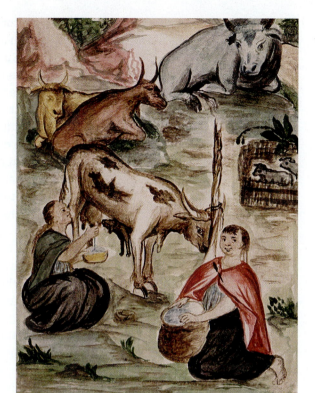

Inca Women Milking Cows

This illustration of Inca women milking cows is from a collection of illustrations by a Spanish bishop that offers a valuable view of life in Peru in the 1780s. (From *Codex Trujillo*, Bishop Baltasar Jaime Martínez Compañón, Palacio Real, Madrid, Spain/Photo: Albers Foundation/Art Resource, NY)

What was the impact of Iberian conquest and settlement on the peoples of the Americas?

How was the era of global contact shaped by new commodities and forced migrations?

How did new encounters shape cultural attitudes and beliefs in Europe and the New World?

✓ LearningCurve
Check what you know.

471

viceroyalties

▶ The name for the four administrative units of Spanish possessions in the Americas: New Spain, Peru, New Granada, and La Plata.

While early conquest and settlement were conducted largely by private initiatives, the Spanish and Portuguese governments soon assumed more direct control. In 1503 the Spanish granted the port of Seville a monopoly over all traffic to the New World and established the House of Trade, or *Casa de Contratación*, to oversee economic matters. In 1523 Spain created the Royal and Supreme Council of the Indies, with authority over all colonial affairs subject to approval by the king. Spanish territories themselves were divided initially into two **viceroyalties**, or administrative divisions: New Spain, created in 1535; and Peru, created in 1542. In the eighteenth century, two new viceroyalties, New Granada and La Plata, were created (see Map 16.2).

Within each territory, the viceroy, or imperial governor, exercised broad military and civil authority. The viceroy presided over the *audiencia* (ow-dee-EHN-see-ah), a board of judges that served as his advisory council and the highest judicial body. As in Spain, settlement in the Americas was centered on cities and towns. In each city, the municipal council, or *cabildo*, exercised local authority.

In Portugal, the India House in Lisbon functioned much like the Spanish House of Trade, and royal representatives oversaw its possessions in West Africa and Asia, as did governors in Spanish America. To secure the vast expanse of Brazil, however, the Portuguese implemented a distinctive system of rule, called **captaincies**, in the 1530s. These were hereditary grants of land given to nobles and loyal officials who bore the costs of settling and administering their territories. Over time, the Crown secured greater power over the captaincies, appointing royal governors to act as administrators.

captaincies

▶ A system established by the Portuguese in Brazil in the 1530s, whereby hereditary grants of land were given to nobles and loyal officials who bore the costs of settling and administering their territories

Throughout the Americas, the Catholic Church played an integral role in Iberian rule. The papacy allowed Portuguese and Spanish officials greater control over the church than was the case at home, allowing them to appoint clerics and collect tithes. This control helped colonial powers use the church as an instrument to indoctrinate indigenous people (see page 479).

Indigenous Population Loss and Economic Exploitation

From the time of Christopher Columbus in Hispaniola, the conquerors of the New World made use of the **encomienda system** to profit from the peoples and territories they encountered. This system was a legacy of the methods used to reward military leaders in the time of the reconquista. First in the Caribbean and then on the mainland, conquistadors granted their followers the right to employ groups of Native Americans as laborers and to demand tribute payments from them in exchange for providing food, shelter, and instruction in the Christian faith.

encomienda system

▶ A system whereby the Spanish crown granted the conquerors the right to forcibly employ groups of Indians; it was a disguised form of slavery.

A 1512 Spanish law authorizing the use of the encomienda called for indigenous people to be treated fairly, but in practice the system lead to terrible abuses. Spanish missionaries publicized these abuses, leading to debates in Spain about the nature and proper treatment of indigenous people (see page 479). King Charles V responded to such complaints in 1542 with the New Laws, which set limits on the authority of encomienda holders.

The New Laws provoked a revolt among elites in Peru and were little enforced throughout Spanish territories. Nonetheless, the Crown gradually gained control over encomiendas in central areas of the empire and required indigenous people

CHAPTER LOCATOR

What was the Afroeurasian trade world like prior to the era of European exploration?

Why and how did Europeans undertake ambitious voyages of expansion?

472   CHAPTER 16   THE ACCELERATION OF GLOBAL CONTACT

to pay tributes in cash, rather than in labor. To respond to a shortage of indigenous workers, royal officials established a new government-run system of forced labor, called *repartimiento* in New Spain and *mita* in Peru. Administrators assigned a certain percentage of the inhabitants of native communities to labor for a set period each year in public works, mining, agriculture, and other tasks.

Spanish systems for exploiting the labor of indigenous peoples were both a cause of and a response to the disastrous decline in the numbers of such peoples that began soon after the arrival of Europeans. Some indigenous people died as a direct result of the violence of conquest and the disruption of agriculture and trade caused by warfare. The most important cause of death, however, was infectious disease. Having little or no resistance to diseases brought from the Old World, the inhabitants of the New World fell victim to smallpox, typhus, influenza, and other illnesses.

The pattern of devastating disease and population loss established in the Spanish colonies was repeated everywhere Europeans settled. Overall, population declined by as much as 90 percent or more but with important regional variations. In general, densely populated urban centers were worse hit than rural areas and tropical, low-lying regions suffered more than cooler, higher-altitude ones.

Colonial administrators responded to native population decline by forcibly combining dwindling indigenous communities into new settlements and imposing the rigors of the encomienda and the repartimiento. By the end of the sixteenth century the search for fresh sources of labor had given birth to the new tragedy of the Atlantic slave trade (see page 598).

Patterns of Settlement

The century after the discovery of silver in 1545 marked the high point of Iberian immigration to the Americas. Although the first migrants were men, soon whole families began to cross the Atlantic, and the European population began to increase through natural reproduction. By 1600 American-born Europeans, called *Creoles*, outnumbered immigrants.

Iberian settlement was predominantly urban in nature. Spaniards settled into the cities and towns of the former Aztec and Inca Empires as the native population dwindled through death and flight. They also established new cities in which settlers were quick to establish urban institutions familiar to them from home: city squares, churches, schools, and universities.

Despite the growing number of Europeans and the rapid decline of the native population, Europeans remained a small minority of the total inhabitants of the Americas. Iberians formed sexual relationships with native women leading to a substantial population of mixed Iberian and Indian descent known as *mestizos* (meh-STEE-zohz). The large-scale arrival of enslaved Africans, starting in Brazil in the mid-sixteenth century, added new ethnic and racial dimensions to the population (see pages 598–603).

QUICK REVIEW <

What factors help explain the conquest of the mighty Inca and Aztec Empires by the Spanish?

What was the impact of Iberian conquest and settlement on the peoples of the Americas?

How was the era of global contact shaped by new commodities and forced migrations?

How did new encounters shape cultural attitudes and beliefs in Europe and the New World?

☑ LearningCurve
Check what you know.

How was the era of global contact shaped by new commodities, commercial empires, and forced migrations?

A New World Sugar Refinery in Brazil

Sugar was the most important and most profitable plantation crop in the New World. This image shows the processing and refinement of sugar on a Brazilian plantation. Sugarcane was grown, harvested, and processed by African slaves who labored under brutal and ruthless conditions to generate enormous profits for plantation owners. (Bibliothèque Nationale, Paris, France/Giraudon/The Bridgeman Art Library)

THE CENTURIES-OLD AFROEURASIAN trade world was forever changed by the European voyages of discovery and their aftermath. For the first time, a truly global economy emerged in the sixteenth and seventeenth centuries, and it forged new links among far-flung peoples, cultures, and societies.

The Columbian Exchange

The travel of people and goods between the Old and New Worlds led to an exchange of animals, plants, and diseases, a complex process known as the **Columbian exchange**. As we have seen, the introduction of new diseases to the Americas had devastating consequences. But other results of the exchange brought benefits not only to the Europeans but also to native peoples.

Everywhere they settled, the Spanish and Portuguese brought and raised wheat. Grapes and olives brought over from Spain did well in parts of Peru and Chile. Perhaps the most significant introduction to the diet of Native Americans

Columbian exchange

▶ The exchange of animals, plants, and diseases between the Old and the New Worlds.

CHAPTER LOCATOR | What was the Afroeurasian trade world like prior to the era of European exploration? | Why and how did Europeans undertake ambitious voyages of expansion?

came via the meat and milk of the livestock that the early conquistadors brought with them, including cattle, sheep, and goats. The horse enabled both the Spanish conquerors and native populations to travel faster and farther and to transport heavy loads more easily.

In turn, Europeans returned home with many food crops that became central elements of their diet. Crops originating in the Americas included tomatoes, squash, pumpkins, peppers, and many varieties of beans, as well as tobacco. One of the most important of such crops was maize (corn). By the late seventeenth century, maize had become a staple in Spain, Portugal, southern France, and Italy, and in the eighteenth century it became one of the chief foods of southeastern Europe and southern China. Even more valuable was the nutritious white potato, which slowly spread from west to east, contributing everywhere to a rise in population.

While the exchange of foods was a great benefit to cultures across the world, the introduction of European pathogens to the New World had a disastrous impact on the native population. The wave of catastrophic epidemic disease that swept the Western Hemisphere after 1492 can be seen as an extension of the swath of devastation wreaked by the Black Death in the 1300s, first on Asia and then on Europe. The world after Columbus was thus unified by disease as well as by trade and colonization.

Sugar and Early Transatlantic Slavery

Two crucial and interrelated elements of the Columbian exchange were the transatlantic trade in sugar and slaves. Throughout the Middle Ages, slavery was deeply entrenched in the Mediterranean, but it was not based on race. How, then, did black African slavery enter the European picture and take root in South and then North America? In 1453 the Ottoman capture of Constantinople halted the flow of European slaves from the eastern Mediterranean. Additionally, the successes of the Christian reconquest of the Iberian Peninsula drastically diminished the supply of Muslim captives. Cut off from its traditional sources of slaves, Mediterranean Europe turned to sub-Saharan Africa, which had a long history of slave trading.

As Portuguese explorers began their voyages along the western coast of Africa, one of the first commodities they sought was slaves. While the first slaves were simply seized by small raiding parties, Portuguese merchants soon found that it was easier and more profitable to trade with African leaders, who were accustomed to dealing in enslaved people captured through warfare with neighboring powers. From 1490 to 1530 Portuguese traders brought between three hundred and two thousand enslaved Africans to Lisbon each year.

In this stage of European expansion, the history of slavery became intertwined with the history of sugar. Population increases and greater prosperity in the fifteenth century led to increasing demand for sugar. The establishment of sugar plantations on the Canary and Madeira Islands in the fifteenth century testifies to this demand.

Sugar was a particularly difficult crop to produce for profit, requiring constant, back-breaking labor. The invention of roller mills to crush the cane more efficiently meant that yields could be significantly augmented, but only if a sufficient labor force was found to supply the mills. Europeans solved the labor problem by forcing first native islanders and then transported Africans to perform the backbreaking work.

| What was the impact of Iberian conquest and settlement on the peoples of the Americas? | **How was the era of global contact shaped by new commodities and forced migrations?** | How did new encounters shape cultural attitudes and beliefs in Europe and the New World? | ✓ LearningCurve Check what you know. |

475

The Transatlantic Slave Trade

The transatlantic slave trade that would ultimately result in the forced transport of over 12 million individuals began in 1518, when Spanish king Charles V authorized traders to bring enslaved Africans to New World colonies. The Portuguese brought the first slaves to Brazil around 1550. After its founding in 1621, the Dutch West India Company transported thousands of Africans to Brazil and the Caribbean, mostly to work on sugar plantations. In the late seventeenth century, with the chartering of the Royal African Company, the English began to bring slaves to Barbados and other English colonies in the Caribbean and mainland North America.

Before 1700, when slavers decided it was better business to improve conditions, some 20 percent of slaves died on the voyage from Africa to the Americas.[2] The most common cause of death was dysentery induced by poor-quality food and water, lack of sanitation, and intense crowding. On sugar plantations, death rates among enslaved people from illness and exhaustion were extremely high. Driven by rising demands for plantation crops, the tragic transatlantic slave trade reached its height in the eighteenth century.

The Birth of the Global Economy

With Europeans' discovery of the Americas and their exploration of the Pacific, the entire world was linked for the first time in history by seaborne trade. The opening of that trade brought into being three successive commercial empires: the Portuguese, the Spanish, and the Dutch.

In the sixteenth century the Portuguese controlled the sea route to India (Map 16.3). From their bases at Goa on the Arabian Sea and at Malacca on the Malay Peninsula, ships carried goods to the Portuguese settlement at Macao. From Macao Portuguese ships loaded with Chinese silks and porcelains sailed to Japan and the Philippines, where Chinese goods were exchanged for Spanish silver from New Spain. Throughout Asia the Portuguese traded in slaves. They also exported horses from Mesopotamia and copper from Arabia to India; from India they exported hawks and peacocks for the Chinese and Japanese markets. Back to Portugal they brought Asian spices that had been purchased with textiles produced in India and with gold and ivory from East Africa. They also shipped back sugar from their colony in Brazil, produced by African slaves whom they had transported across the Atlantic.

Becoming an imperial power a few decades later than the Portuguese, the Spanish were determined to claim their place in world trade. This was greatly facilitated by the discovery of immense riches in silver in the Americas. Silver poured into Europe through the Spanish port of Seville, contributing to steep inflation across Europe. Demand for silver also created a need for slaves to work in the mines.

The Spanish Empire in the New World was basically land based, but across the Pacific the Spaniards built a seaborne empire centered at Manila in the Philippines. The city of Manila served as the transpacific bridge between Spanish America and China. In Manila Spanish traders used silver from American mines to purchase Chinese silk for European markets.

In the seventeenth century the Dutch challenged the Spanish and Portuguese Empires. The Dutch East India Company was founded in 1602 with the stated

CHAPTER LOCATOR | What was the Afroeurasian trade world like prior to the era of European exploration? | Why and how did Europeans undertake ambitious voyages of expansion?

CHAPTER 16
476 THE ACCELERATION OF GLOBAL CONTACT

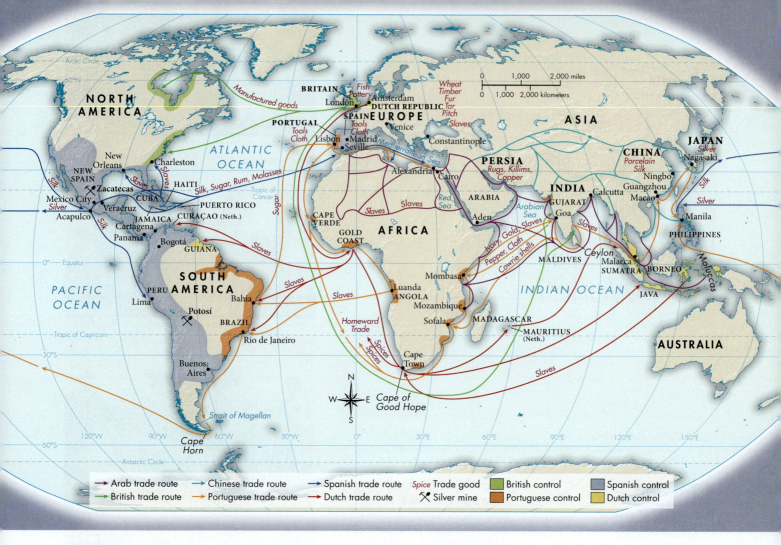

MAP 16.3 ■ Seaborne Trading Empires in the Sixteenth and Seventeenth Centuries

By the mid-seventeenth century trade linked all parts of the world except for Australia. Notice that trade in slaves was not confined to the Atlantic but involved almost all parts of the world.

intention of capturing the spice trade from the Portuguese. Drawing on their commercial wealth and long experience in European trade, by the end of the century the Dutch emerged as the most powerful worldwide seaborne trading power (see Chapter 19).

QUICK REVIEW <

How did European demand for sugar stimulate the expansion of the transatlantic slave trade?

| What was the impact of Iberian conquest and settlement on the peoples of the Americas? | **How was the era of global contact shaped by new commodities and forced migrations?** | How did new encounters shape cultural attitudes and beliefs in Europe and the New World? | ✓ LearningCurve
Check what you know. |

How did new encounters shape cultural attitudes and beliefs in Europe and the New World?

Español con India. Mestizo.

Mestizo con Española. Castizo.

Mulato con Española, Morisco.

Morisco con Española. Chino.

Lobo con China. Gibaro.

Gibaro con Mulata. Albarazado

Sanbaigo con Loba. Calpamulato.

Calpamulato con Canbuja. Tenteen el Aire.

Mixed Races

The unprecedented mixing of peoples in the Spanish New World colonies inspired great fascination. An elaborate terminology emerged to describe the many possible combinations of indigenous, African, and European blood, which were known collectively as *castas*. This painting belongs to a popular genre of the eighteenth century depicting couples composed of individuals of different ethnic origin and the children produced of their unions. (Schalkwijk/Art Resource, NY)

> PICTURING THE PAST

ANALYZING THE IMAGE: What do these images suggest about the racial composition of the population of Spanish America and the interaction of people with different racial and ethnic backgrounds? Who do you think the audience might have been, and why would viewers be fascinated by such images?
CONNECTIONS: What elements of this chapter might suggest that these are romanticized or idealized depictions of relations among different racial and ethnic groups?

THE AGE OF OVERSEAS EXPANSION heightened Europeans' contacts with the rest of the world. These contacts gave birth to new ideas about the inherent superiority or inferiority of different races. Religion became another means of cultural contact, as European missionaries aimed to spread Christianity in both the New World and East Asia. The East-West contacts also led to exchanges of influential cultural and scientific ideas.

CHAPTER LOCATOR

What was the Afroeurasian trade world like prior to the era of European exploration?

Why and how did Europeans undertake ambitious voyages of expansion?

Religious Conversion

Converting indigenous people to Christianity was one of the most important justifications for European expansion. The first missionaries to the New World accompanied Columbus on his second voyage, and more than 2,500 Franciscans, Dominicans, Jesuits and other friars crossed the Atlantic in the following century. Later French explorers were also accompanied by missionaries.

Catholic friars were among the first Europeans to seek an understanding of native cultures and languages as part of their effort to render Christianity comprehensible to indigenous people. They were also the most vociferous opponents of abuses committed by Spanish settlers.

Religion had been a central element of pre-Columbian societies, and many, if not all, indigenous people were receptive to the new religion that accompanied the victorious Iberians. In addition to spreading Christianity, missionaries taught indigenous peoples European methods of agriculture and instilled obedience to colonial masters. Despite the success of initial conversion efforts, authorities could not prevent the melding together of Catholic teachings with elements of pagan beliefs and practices.

European Debates About Indigenous Peoples

Iberian exploitation of the native population of the Americas began from the moment of Columbus's arrival in 1492. Denunciations of this abuse by Catholic missionaries, however, quickly followed, inspiring vociferous debates in both Europe and the colonies about the nature of indigenous peoples and how they should be treated. Bartolomé de Las Casas (1474–1566), a Dominican friar and former encomienda holder, was one of the earliest and most outspoken critics of the brutal treatment inflicted on indigenous peoples.

Mounting criticism in Spain led King Charles V to assemble a group of churchmen and lawyers to debate the issue in 1550 in the city of Valladolid. One side of the **Valladolid debate**, led by Juan Ginés de Sepúlveda, argued that conquest and forcible conversion were both necessary and justified to save indigenous people from the horrors of human sacrifice, cannibalism, and idolatry. To counter these arguments, Las Casas and his supporters depicted indigenous people as rational and innocent children, who deserved protection and tutelage from more advanced civilizations.

Elsewhere in Europe, audiences also debated these questions. Eagerly reading denunciations of Spanish abuses by critics like Las Casas, they derived the **Black Legend** of Spanish colonialism, the notion that the Spanish were uniquely brutal and cruel in their conquest and settlement of the Americas. This legend helped other European powers overlook their own record of colonial violence and exploitation.

New Ideas About Race

At the beginning of the transatlantic slave trade, most Europeans grouped Africans into the despised categories of pagan heathens or Muslim infidels. As Europeans turned to Africa for new sources of slaves, they drew on beliefs about Africans' primitiveness and barbarity to defend slavery.

Valladolid debate

▶ A debate organized by Spanish king Charles V in 1550 in the city of Valladolid that pitted defenders of Spanish conquest and forcible conversion against critics of these practices.

Black Legend

▶ The notion that the Spanish were uniquely brutal and cruel in their conquest and settlement of the Americas, an idea propagated by rival European powers.

What was the impact of Iberian conquest and settlement on the peoples of the Americas?

How was the era of global contact shaped by new commodities and forced migrations?

How did new encounters shape cultural attitudes and beliefs in Europe and the New World?

✓ LearningCurve
Check what you know.

Over time, the institution of slavery fostered a new level of racial inequality. Africans gradually became seen as utterly distinct from and wholly inferior to Europeans. In a transition from rather vague assumptions about Africans' non-Christian religious beliefs and general lack of civilization, Europeans developed increasingly rigid ideas of racial superiority and inferiority to safeguard the growing profits gained from plantation slavery. Black skin became equated with slavery itself as Europeans at home and in the colonies convinced themselves that blacks were destined by God to serve them as slaves in perpetuity. Support for this belief went back to the Greek philosopher Aristotle's argument that some people are naturally destined for slavery and to biblical associations between darkness and sin.

After 1700 the emergence of new methods of observing and describing nature led to the use of science to define race. Although previously the term referred to a nation or an ethnic group, henceforth "race" would be used to describe supposedly biologically distinct groups of people whose physical differences produced differences in culture, character, and intelligence. Biblical justifications for inequality thereby gave way to allegedly scientific ones (see page 736).

> ## QUICK REVIEW

How did European ideas about race change over the course of the early modern period?

CHAPTER SUMMARY

Prior to Columbus's voyages, well-developed trade routes linked the peoples and products of Africa, Asia, and Europe. Overall, Europe played a minor role in the Afroeurasian trade world. As the economy and population recovered from the Black Death, Europeans began to seek more direct and profitable access to the Afroeurasian trade world. Technological developments such as the invention of the caravel and the magnetic compass enabled explorers to undertake ever more ambitious voyages.

In the aftermath of their conquest of the Aztec and Inca Empires, the Spanish established new forms of governance to dominate native peoples and exploit their labor. The arrival of Europeans brought enormous population losses to native communities, primarily through the spread of infectious diseases. Disease was one element of the Columbian exchange, a complex transfer of germs, plants, and animals between the Old and New Worlds. These exchanges contributed to the creation of the first truly global economy. Tragically, a major component of global trade was the transatlantic slave trade, in which Europeans transported Africans to labor in the sugar plantations and silver mines of the New World. European nations vied for supremacy in global trade, with early Portuguese success in India and Asia being challenged first by the Spanish and then by the Dutch.

CHAPTER LOCATOR | What was the Afroeurasian trade world like prior to the era of European exploration? | Why and how did Europeans undertake ambitious voyages of expansion?

CHAPTER 16
480   THE ACCELERATION OF GLOBAL CONTACT

Increased contact with the outside world led Europeans to develop new ideas about cultural and racial differences. Debates occurred in Spain and its colonies over the nature of the indigenous peoples of the Americas and how they should be treated. Europeans had long held negative attitudes about Africans; as the slave trade grew, they began to express more rigid notions of racial inequality and to claim that Africans were inherently suited for slavery. Religion became another means of cultural contact, as European missionaries aimed to spread Christianity in the New World.

 **CONNECTIONS** Just three years separated Martin Luther's attack on the Catholic Church in 1517 and Ferdinand Magellan's discovery of the Pacific Ocean in 1520. Within a few short years western Europeans' religious unity and notions of terrestrial geography were shattered. In the ensuing decades Europeans struggled to come to terms with religious differences among Protestants and Catholics at home and with the multitudes of new peoples and places they encountered abroad.

Even as the voyages of discovery contributed to the fragmentation of European culture, they also played a role in state centralization and consolidation in the longer term. Henceforth, competition to gain overseas colonies became an integral part of European politics. While Spain's enormous profits from conquest ultimately led to a weakening of its power, over time the Netherlands, England, and France used profits from colonial trade to help build modernized, centralized states.

Two crucial consequences emerged from this era of expansion. The first was the creation of enduring contacts among five of the seven continents of the globe—Europe, Asia, Africa, North America, and South America. From the sixteenth century onward, the peoples of the world were increasingly entwined in divergent forms of economic, social, and cultural exchange. The second was the growth of European power. Europeans controlled the Americas and gradually assumed control over existing trade networks in Asia and Africa. Although China remained the world's most powerful economy until at least 1800, the era of European dominance was born.

ONLINE DOCUMENT PROJECT

Interpreting Conquest

How did Spanish and Amerindian artists depict Malintzin?

Examine Spanish and Amerindian representations of Malintzin's role in the conquest, and then complete a quiz and writing assignment based on the evidence and details from this chapter. *See inside the front cover to learn more.*

What was the impact of Iberian conquest and settlement on the peoples of the Americas?

How was the era of global contact shaped by new commodities and forced migrations?

How did new encounters shape cultural attitudes and beliefs in Europe and the New World?

✔ LearningCurve
Check what you know.

CHAPTER 16 STUDY GUIDE

STEP 1   GET STARTED ONLINE

 **LearningCurve**

Now that you've read the chapter, make it stick by completing the LearningCurve activity.

STEP 2   EXPLAIN WHY IT MATTERS

Put your reading into practice. Identify each term below, and then explain why it matters in world history.

TERM	WHO OR WHAT & WHEN	WHY IT MATTERS
bride wealth (p. 459)		
caravel (p. 462)		
Ptolemy's *Geography* (p. 462)		
Treaty of Tordesillas (p. 466)		
conquistador (p. 468)		
Aztec Empire (p. 469)		
Inca Empire (p. 469)		
viceroyalties (p. 472)		
captaincies (p. 472)		
encomienda system (p. 472)		
Columbian exchange (p. 474)		
Valladolid debate (p. 479)		
Black Legend (p. 479)		

STEP 3   MOVE BEYOND THE BASICS

To demonstrate a more advanced understanding of the nature and impact of Spanish exploration and conquest in the Americas, fill in the chart below with descriptions of the motives behind Spanish expansion across the Atlantic. Next, identify key Spanish conquests and discoveries and the institutions of Spanish rule in the Americas. Finally, describe the impact of Spanish conquest in the New World and Europe. How do the motives you listed help explain the course of Spanish expansion in the New World?

Motives	Conquests and Discoveries	Institutions of Spanish Rule	Impact in the New World and Europe

PUT IT ALL TOGETHER

Now, take a step back and try to explain the big picture. Remember to use specific examples from the chapter in your answers.

THE AFROEURASIAN TRADE WORLD BEFORE COLUMBUS

▶ Which states were at the center of global trade prior to 1492? Why?

▶ Why were Europeans at a trading disadvantage prior to 1492? How did geography limit European participation in world trade? What role did Europe's economy and material culture play in this context?

DISCOVERY AND CONQUEST

▶ In your opinion, what was the most important motive behind European expansion? What evidence can you provide to support your position?

▶ What was the Columbian exchange? How did it transform both Europe and the Americas?

CHANGING VALUES AND BELIEFS

▶ How did European expansion give rise to new ideas about race?

▶ How did expansion complicate European's understanding of themselves and their place in the world?

LOOKING BACK, LOOKING AHEAD

▶ If Europe was at the periphery of the global trading system prior to 1492, where was it situated by the middle of the sixteenth century? What had changed? What had not?

▶ What connections can you make between our own experience of globalization in the twenty-first century and the experience of globalization in the sixteenth century? In what ways are the experiences similar? In what ways do they differ?

> ## IN YOUR OWN WORDS

Imagine that you must give an oral report to the class answering the following question: **What new global connections were forged in the fifteenth and sixteenth centuries?** What would be the most important points and why?

17

THE ISLAMIC WORLD POWERS

1300–1800

> **What were the strengths and weaknesses of the three great Islamic empires?** Chapter 17 examines developments in Islamic empires during the early modern period. The Ottoman Empire was one of the largest, best-organized, and most enduring political entities in world history. In Persia (now Iran) the Safavid Dynasty created a Shi'a state and presided over a brilliant culture. In India the Mughal leader Babur and his successors gained control of much of the Indian subcontinent. Although often at war with each other, these three states shared important characteristics and challenges and were strongly linked culturally. Before the end of this period, Europeans were also active in trade in these empires, especially in India.

LearningCurve

After reading the chapter, use LearningCurve to retain what you've read.

Persian Princess The ruling houses of the Islamic empires were great patrons of art and architecture. This depiction of a princess in a garden is from an early-seventeenth-century palace built by Shah Abbas of the Safavid Dynasty in Persia. (Safavid Dynasty [fresco]. Chehel Sotun, or *The 40 Columns*, Isfahan, Iran/Giraudon/The Bridgeman Art Library)

> How were the three Islamic empires established, and what sorts of governments did they set up?

> What cultural advances occurred under the rule of the Ottoman, Safavid, and Mughal Empires?

> How did Christians, Jews, Hindus, and other non-Muslims fare under these Islamic states?

> How were the Islamic empires affected by the gradual shift toward trade routes that bypassed their lands?

> What common factors led to the decline of central power in the Islamic empires in the seventeenth and eighteenth centuries?

How were the three Islamic empires established, and what sorts of governments did they set up?

Sultan Mehmet II

Mehmet was called "the Conqueror" because at age twenty-one he captured Constantinople and ended the Byzantine Empire, but he is also known for his patronage of the arts and appreciation of beauty. (Topkapi Palace Museum, Istanbul, Turkey/ Giraudon/The Bridgeman Art Library)

BEFORE THE MONGOLS ARRIVED in Central Asia and Persia, another nomadic people from the region of modern Mongolia, the Turks, had moved west, gaining control over key territories from Anatolia to Delhi in north India. As Mongol strength in Persia and Central Asia deteriorated in the late thirteenth to mid-fourteenth centuries, the Turks resumed their expansion.

In the late fourteenth century the Turkish leader Timur (1336–1405), also called Tamerlane, built a Central Asian empire from his base in Samarkand that reached into India and through Persia to the Black Sea. After his death, his sons and grandson fought each other for succession. By 1450 his empire was in rapid decline, and power devolved to the local level. Meanwhile, Sufi orders (groups of Islamic mystics) thrived, and Islam became the most important force integrating the region. It was from the many small Turkish chiefs that the founders of the three main empires emerged.

CHAPTER LOCATOR | **How were the three Islamic empires established, what governments did they set up?** | What cultural advances occurred under the rule of the Ottoman, Safavid, and Mughal Empires?

486 CHAPTER 17
THE ISLAMIC WORLD POWERS

1299–1326 Reign of Osman, founder of the Ottoman Dynasty	**1521** Piri Reis produces *Book of the Sea*, a navigational map book
1299–1922 Ottoman Empire	**1526–1857** Mughal Empire
1336–1405 Life of Timur	**1556–1605** Reign of Akbar in Mughal Empire
ca. mid-1400s Coffeehouses become centers of Islamic male social life	**1570** Ottomans take control of Cyprus
1453 Ottoman conquest of Constantinople	**1571** First major Ottoman defeat by Christians, at Lepanto
1501–1524 Reign of Safavid Shah Isma'il	**1587–1629** Reign of Shah Abbas; height of Safavid power; carpet weaving becomes major Persian industry
1501–1722 Safavid Empire	**1631–1648** Construction of Taj Mahal under Shah Jahan in India
1520–1558 Hürrem wields influence in the Ottoman Empire as Suleiman's concubine and then wife	**1658–1707** Reign of Aurangzeb; Mughal power begins to decline
1520–1566 Reign of Ottoman sultan Suleiman I; period of artistic flowering in Ottoman Empire	**1763** Treaty of Paris recognizes British control over much of India

The Ottoman Turkish Empire's Expansion

The **Ottomans** took their name from Osman (r. 1299–1326), the chief of a band of seminomadic Turks that had migrated into western **Anatolia** while the Mongols still held Persia. The Ottomans gradually expanded at the expense of other small Turkish states and the Byzantine Empire (Map 17.1). Although temporarily slowed by defeat at the hands of Timur in 1402, the Ottomans quickly reasserted themselves after Timur's death in 1405.

Osman's campaigns were intended to subdue, not to destroy. The Ottomans built their empire by absorbing the Muslims of Anatolia and by becoming the protector of the Orthodox Church and of the millions of Greek Christians in Anatolia and the Balkans. A series of victories between 1326 and 1352 made the Ottomans the masters of the Balkans. After these victories, the Ottomans made slaves of many captives and trained them as soldiers. These troops were outfitted with guns and artillery and trained to use them effectively.

In 1453, during the reign of Sultan Mehmet II (r. 1451–1481), the Ottomans conquered Constantinople, capital of the Byzantine Empire. Once Constantinople was theirs, the Ottoman

Ottomans

▶ Ruling house of the Turkish empire that lasted from 1299 to 1922.

Anatolia

▶ The region of modern Turkey.

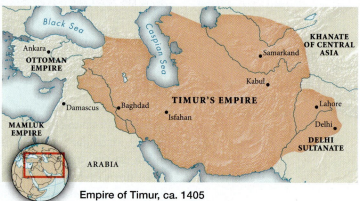

Empire of Timur, ca. 1405

How did Christians, Jews, Hindus, and other non-Muslims fare under these Islamic states?	How were the Islamic empires affected by trade routes that bypassed their lands?	What common factors led to the decline of central power in the Islamic empires?	✓ LearningCurve Check what you know.

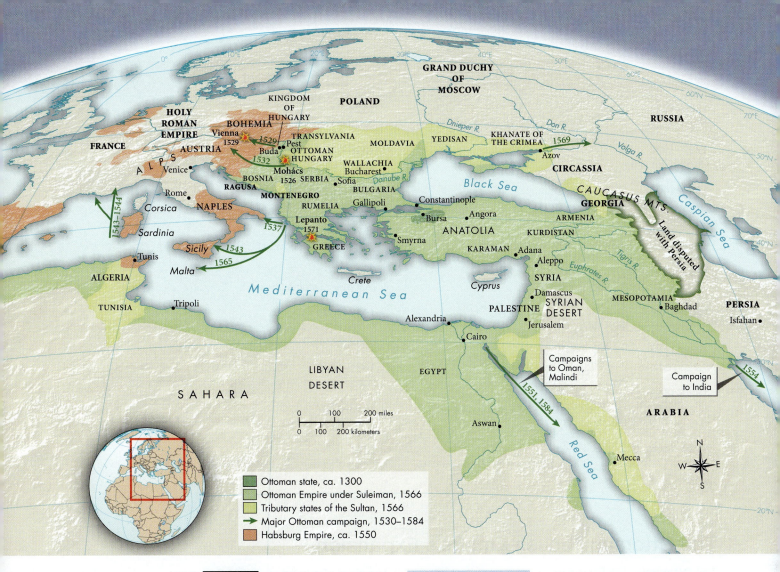

Ottoman state, ca. 1300
Ottoman Empire under Suleiman, 1566
Tributary states of the Sultan, 1566
→ Major Ottoman campaign, 1530–1584
Habsburg Empire, ca. 1550

MAP 17.1 ■ The Ottoman Empire at Its Height, 1566

The Ottomans, like their great rivals the Habsburgs, rose to rule a vast dynastic empire encompassing many different peoples and ethnic groups. The army and the bureaucracy served to unite the disparate territories into a single state.

> MAPPING THE PAST

ANALYZING THE MAP: Trace the coastlines of the Ottoman Empire. What were the major port cities of the empire? Which regions were encompassed within the empire at its height?

CONNECTIONS: If the Ottoman Empire is compared to Europe of the same period (see Map 18.2, page 522), which had more of its territory near the sea? How did proximity to the Mediterranean shape the politics of Ottoman-European relations in this period?

sultan

▶ An Arabic word originally used by the Seljuk Turks to mean authority or dominion; it was used by the Ottomans to connote political and military supremacy.

sultans considered themselves successors to both the Byzantine and Seljuk Turk emperors, and they quickly absorbed the rest of the Byzantine Empire. In the sixteenth century they continued to expand through the Middle East and into North Africa.

To begin the transformation of Constantinople (renamed Istanbul) into an imperial Ottoman capital, Mehmet ordered wealthy residents to participate in building mosques, markets, fountains, baths, and other public facilities. To make up for the loss of population through war, Mehmet transplanted inhabitants of other territories to the city, granting them tax remissions and possession of empty houses. He wanted them to start businesses, make Istanbul prosperous, and transform it into a microcosm of the empire.

CHAPTER LOCATOR | **How were the three Islamic empires established, what governments did they set up?** | What cultural advances occurred under the rule of the Ottoman, Safavid, and Mughal Empires?

Gunpowder, which was invented by the Chinese and adapted to artillery use by the Europeans, played an influential role in the expansion of the Ottoman state. In the first half of the sixteenth century, thanks to the use of this technology, the Ottomans gained control of shipping in the eastern Mediterranean and eliminated the Portuguese from the Red Sea. In 1514, under the superb military leadership of Selim (r. 1512–1520), the Ottomans turned the Safavids back from Anatolia. In addition, the Ottomans added Syria and Palestine (1516) and Egypt (1517). Before long the Ottomans had extended their rule across North Africa to Tunisia and Algeria. For the next four centuries a majority of Arabs lived under Ottoman rule.

Suleiman (r. 1520–1566) extended Ottoman dominion to its widest geographical extent (see Map 17.1). Suleiman's army crushed the Hungarians at Mohács in 1526. Three years later the Turks unsuccessfully besieged the Habsburg capital of Vienna. From the late fourteenth to the early seventeenth centuries, the Ottoman Empire was a key player in European politics. In 1525 Francis I of France and Suleiman struck an alliance; both believed that only their collaboration could prevent Habsburg domination of Europe. The Habsburg emperor Charles V retaliated by seeking an alliance with Safavid Persia. Suleiman renewed the French agreement with Francis's son, Henry II (r. 1547–1559), and this accord became the cornerstone of Ottoman policy in western Europe. Suleiman also allied with the German Protestant princes, forcing the Catholic Habsburgs to grant concessions to the Protestants. Ottoman pressure thus contributed to the official recognition of Lutheran Protestants at the Peace of Augsburg in 1555 and the consolidation of the national monarchy in France.

Though usually victorious on land, the Ottomans did not enjoy complete dominion on the seas. Competition with the Habsburgs and pirates for control of the Mediterranean led the Ottomans to conquer Cyprus in 1570 and settle thousands of Turks from Anatolia there. In response, Pope Pius V organized a Holy League against the Turks, which won a victory in 1571 at Lepanto off the west coast of Greece. Still, the Turks remained supreme on land and quickly rebuilt their entire fleet.

To the east, war with Safavid Persia occupied the sultans' attention throughout the sixteenth century. Several issues lay at the root of the long and exhausting conflict: religious antagonism between the Sunni Ottomans and the Shi'a Persians, competition to expand at each other's expense in Mesopotamia, desire to control trade routes, and European alliances. (For more on the Shi'a faith, see page 490.) Finally, in 1638 the Ottomans captured Baghdad, and the treaty of Kasr-I-Shirim established a permanent border between the two powers.

The Ottoman political system reached its classic form under Suleiman I. All authority flowed from the sultan to his public servants: provincial governors, police officers, military generals, heads of treasuries, and **viziers**. Suleiman ordered Lütfi Paşa (d. 1562), a poet and juridical scholar of slave origin, to draw up a new general code of laws that prescribed penalties for routine criminal acts. It also sought to reform bureaucratic and financial corruption. The legal code also introduced the idea of balanced government budgets. The head of the religious establishment was given the task of reconciling sultanic law with Islamic law. Suleiman's legal acts influenced many legal codes, including that of the United States.

The Ottomans ruled their more distant lands, such as those in North Africa, relatively lightly. Governors of distant provinces collected taxes and maintained trade routes, but their control did not penetrate deeply into the countryside.

viziers
▶ Chief assistants to caliphs.

| How did Christians, Jews, Hindus, and other non-Muslims fare under these Islamic states? | How were the Islamic empires affected by trade routes that bypassed their lands? | What common factors led to the decline of central power in the Islamic empires? | ✓ LearningCurve Check what you know. |

The Ottoman Empire's Use of Slaves

devshirme
▶ A process whereby the sultan's agents swept the provinces for Christian youths to be trained as soldiers or civil servants.

The power of the Ottoman central government was sustained through the training of slaves. Slaves were purchased from Spain, North Africa, and Venice; captured in battle; or drafted through the system known as **devshirme**, by which the sultan's agents compelled Christian families in the Balkans to sell their boys. The slave boys were converted to Islam and trained for the imperial civil service and the standing army. The brightest 10 percent entered the palace school, where they learned to read and write Arabic, Ottoman Turkish, and Persian in preparation for administrative jobs. Other boys were sent to Turkish farms, where they acquired physical toughness in preparation for military service. Known as **janissaries** (Turkish for "recruits"), they formed the elite army corps. They played a central role in Ottoman military affairs in the sixteenth century, adapting easily to the use of firearms. The devshirme system enabled the Ottomans to apply merit-based recruitment to military and administrative offices at little cost and provided a means of assimilating Christians living in Ottoman lands.

janissaries
▶ Turkish for "recruits"; they formed the elite army corps.

The Ottoman ruling class consisted partly of descendants of Turkish families that had formerly ruled parts of Anatolia and partly of people of varied ethnic origins who rose through the bureaucratic and military ranks, many beginning as the sultan's slaves. In return for their services to the sultan, they held landed estates for the duration of their lives. Because all property belonged to the sultan and reverted to him on the holder's death, Turkish nobles, unlike their European counterparts, did not have a local base independent of the ruler. The absence of a hereditary nobility and private ownership of agricultural land differentiates the Ottoman system from European feudalism.

concubine
▶ A woman who is a recognized spouse but of lower status than a wife.

Another distinctive characteristic of the Ottomans was the sultan's failure to marry. From about 1500 on, the sultans did not contract legal marriages but perpetuated the ruling house through concubinage. A slave **concubine** could not expect to exert power the way a local or foreign noblewoman could. (For a notable exception, see "Individuals in Society: Hürrem," page 491.) If one of the sultan's concubines delivered a boy, she raised him until the age of ten or eleven. Then the child was given a province to govern under his mother's supervision. Because succession to the throne was open to all the sultan's sons, fratricide often resulted upon his death, and the losers were blinded or executed.

Slave concubinage paralleled the Ottoman development of slave soldiers and slave viziers. All held positions entirely at the sultan's pleasure, owed loyalty solely to him, and thus were more reliable than a hereditary nobility. Great social prestige, as well as the opportunity to acquire power and wealth, was attached to being a slave of the imperial household.

The Safavid Empire in Persia

shah
▶ Persian word for "king."

Safavid
▶ The dynasty that encompassed all of Persia and other regions; its state religion was Shi'ism.

Qizilbash
▶ Nomadic Sufi tribesmen who were loyal to and supportive of the early Safavid state.

With the decline of Timur's empire after 1450, Persia was controlled by Turkish lords, with no single one dominant until 1501, when fourteen-year-old Isma'il (1487–1524) led a Turkish army to capture Tabriz and declared himself **shah** (king).

The strength of the early **Safavid** state rested on three crucial features. First, it had the loyalty and military support of nomadic Turkish Sufis known as **Qizilbash** (KIH-zihl-bahsh). The shah secured the loyalty of the Qizilbash by granting them

CHAPTER LOCATOR | **How were the three Islamic empires established, what governments did they set up?** | What cultural advances occurred under the rule of the Ottoman, Safavid, and Mughal Empires?

490   CHAPTER 17
THE ISLAMIC WORLD POWERS

Hürrem

Hürrem (1505?–1558) was born in the western Ukraine (then part of Poland), the daughter of a Ruthenian priest, and was given the Polish name Aleksandra Lisowska. When Tartars raided, they captured and enslaved her. In 1520 she was given as a gift to Suleiman on the occasion of his accession to the throne. The Venetian ambassador (probably relying on secondhand or thirdhand information) described her as "young, graceful, petite, but not beautiful." She was given the Turkish name Hürrem, meaning "joyful."

Hürrem apparently brought joy to Suleiman. Their first child was born in 1521. By 1525 they had four sons and a daughter; sources note that by that year Suleiman visited no other woman. But he waited eight or nine years before breaking Ottoman dynastic tradition by making Hürrem his legal wife, the first slave concubine so honored. For the rest of her life, Hürrem played a highly influential role in the political, diplomatic, and philanthropic life of the Ottoman state. First, great power flowed from her position as mother of the prince, the future sultan Selim II (r. 1566–1574). Then, as the intimate and most trusted adviser of the sultan, she was Suleiman's closest confidant. During his frequent trips to the far-flung corners of his multiethnic empire, Hürrem wrote him long letters filled with her love and longing for him and her prayers for his safety in battle. She also shared political information about affairs in Istanbul, the activities of the grand vizier, and the attitudes of the janissaries. At a time when some people believed that the sultan's absence from the capital endangered his hold on the throne, Hürrem acted as his eyes and ears for potential threats.

Hürrem was the sultan's contact with her native Poland, which sent more embassies to Istanbul than any other power. Through her correspondence with King Sigismund I, peace between Poland and the Ottomans was maintained. When Sigismund II succeeded his father in 1548, Hürrem sent congratulations on his accession, along with two pairs of pajamas (originally a Hindu garment but commonly worn in southwestern Asia) and six handkerchiefs. Also, she sent the shah of Persia gold-embroidered sheets and shirts that she had sewn herself, seeking to display the wealth of the sultanate and to keep peace between the Ottomans and the Safavids.

Hürrem depicted by a contemporary European artist. (© Mary Evans Picture Library/The Image Works)

The enormous stipend that Suleiman gave Hürrem permitted her to participate in his vast building program. In Jerusalem (in the Ottoman province of Palestine) she founded a hospice for fifty-five pilgrims that included a soup kitchen that fed four hundred pilgrims a day. In Istanbul Suleiman built and Hürrem endowed the Haseki (meaning "royal favorite concubine") mosque complex and a public bath for women near the Women's Market.

Perhaps Hürrem tried to fulfill two functions hitherto distinct in Ottoman political theory: those of the sultan's favorite and of mother of the prince. She also performed the conflicting roles of slave concubine and imperial wife. Many Turks resented Hürrem's interference at court. They believed she was behind the execution of Suleiman's popular son Mustafa on a charge of treason to make way for her own son to succeed as sultan.

Source: Leslie P. Peirce, *The Imperial Harem: Women and Sovereignty in the Ottoman Empire* (New York: Oxford University Press, 1993).

QUESTIONS FOR ANALYSIS

1. How does Hürrem compare to powerful women in other places, such as Empress Wu in China, Isabella of Castile, Catherine de' Medici of France, Elizabeth I of England, or any other you know about?
2. What was Hürrem's "nationality"? What role did it play in her life?

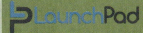

ONLINE DOCUMENT PROJECT

How did Europeans view the Ottoman Empire? Examine a Habsburg ambassador's impressions of the Ottoman Empire, and then complete a quiz and writing assignment based on the evidence and details from this chapter. *See inside front cover to learn more.*

vast grazing lands. In return, the Qizilbash supplied him with troops. Second, the Safavid state utilized the skills of urban bureaucrats and made them an essential part of the civil machinery of government.

The third source of Safavid strength was the Shi'a faith, which became the compulsory religion of the empire. The Shi'a believed that leadership among Muslims rightfully belonged to the Prophet Muhammad's descendants. Because Isma'il claimed descent from a line of twelve infallible imams (leaders) beginning with Ali (Muhammad's cousin and son-in-law), he was officially regarded as their representative on earth. Isma'il recruited Shi'a scholars to instruct and guide his people, and he persecuted and exiled Sunni **ulama**.

Safavid power reached its height under Shah Abbas (r. 1587–1629), who moved the capital from Qazvin to Isfahan. His military achievements, support for trade and commerce, and endowment of the arts earned him the epithet "the Great." In the military realm he adopted the Ottoman practice of building an army of slaves, who could serve as a counterweight to the Qizilbash, who had come to be considered a threat. He also increased the use of gunpowder weapons and made alliances with European powers against the Ottomans and Portuguese. In his campaigns against the Ottomans, Shah Abbas captured Baghdad, Mosul, and Diarbakr in Mesopotamia (Map 17.2). After Shah Abbas, Safavid power was sapped by civil war between tribal factions vying for control of the court.

ulama

▶ Religious scholars whom Sunnis trust to interpret the Qur'an and the Sunna, the deeds and sayings of Muhammad.

MAP 17.2 ■ The Safavid Empire, 1587–1629

In the late sixteenth century the power of the Safavid kingdom of Persia rested on its strong military force, its Shi'a Muslim faith, and its extraordinarily rich trade in rugs and pottery. Many of the cities on the map, such as Tabriz, Qum, and Shiraz, were great rug-weaving centers.

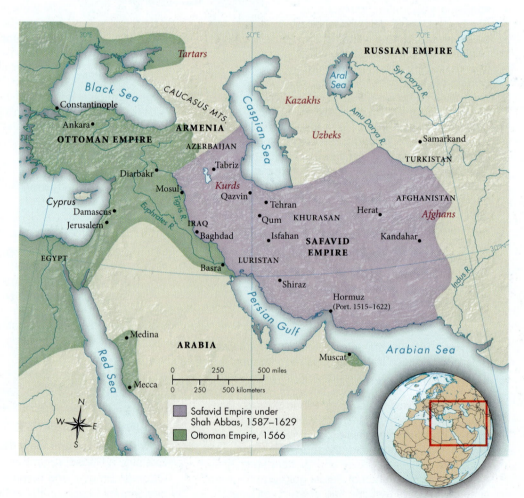

CHAPTER LOCATOR | How were the three Islamic empires established, what governments did they set up? | What cultural advances occurred under the rule of the Ottoman, Safavid, and Mughal Empires?

492 CHAPTER 17 THE ISLAMIC WORLD POWERS

The Mughal Empire in India

Of the three great Islamic empires of the early modern world, the **Mughal** Empire of India was the largest, wealthiest, and most populous. In the sixteenth century only the Ming Dynasty in China could compare.

In 1504 Babur (r. 1483–1530), a Turkish ruler forced out of a small territory in Central Asia, captured Kabul and established a kingdom in Afghanistan. Babur moved southward in search of resources to restore his fortunes. In 1526, with a force that was small but was equipped with firearms, Babur defeated the sultan of Delhi at Panipat. Babur's capture of the cities of Agra and Delhi, key fortresses of the north, paved the way for further conquests in northern India. Although many of his soldiers wished to return north with their spoils, Babur decided to stay in India.

During the reign of Babur's son Humayun (r. 1530–1540 and 1555–1556), the Mughals lost most of their territories in Afghanistan. Humayun went into temporary exile in Persia, where he developed a deep appreciation for Persian art and literature. The reign of Humayun's son Akbar (r. 1556–1605) may well have been the greatest in the history of India. Under his dynamic leadership, the Mughal state took definitive form and encompassed most of the subcontinent north of the Godavari River. No kingdom or coalition of kingdoms could long resist Akbar's armies. The once-independent states of northern India were forced into a centralized political system under the sole authority of the Mughal emperor.

To govern this vast region, Akbar developed an administrative bureaucracy centered on four co-equal ministers: finance and revenue; the army and intelligence; the judiciary and religious patronage; and the imperial household, whose jurisdiction included roads, bridges, and infrastructure throughout the empire. Under Akbar's Hindu finance minister, Raja Todar Mal, a uniform system of taxes was put in place. In the provinces imperial governors were appointed by and responsible solely to the emperor. Whereas the Ottoman sultans and Safavid shahs made extensive use of slaves for military and administrative positions, Akbar used the services of royal princes, nobles, and warrior-aristocrats. Initially these men were Muslims from Central Asia, but to reduce their influence, Akbar vigorously recruited Persians and Hindus. No single ethnic or religious faction could challenge the emperor.

Akbar's descendants extended the Mughal Empire further. His son Jahangir (r. 1605–1628) consolidated Mughal rule in Bengal. Jahangir's son Shah Jahan (r. 1628–1658) launched fresh territorial expansion. Faced with dangerous revolts by the Muslims in Ahmadnagar and the resistance of the newly arrived Portuguese in Bengal, Shah Jahan not only crushed this opposition but also strengthened his northwestern frontier. Shah Jahan's son Aurangzeb (r. 1658–1707), unwilling to wait for his father to die, deposed him and confined him for years in a small cell. A puritanically devout and strictly orthodox Muslim, as well as a skillful general and a clever diplomat, Aurangzeb ruled more of India than did any previous Mughal emperor, having extended the realm deeper into south India. His reign, however, also marked the beginning of the empire's decline. His non-Muslim subjects were not pleased with his religious zealotry, and his military campaigns were costly. In the south resistance to Mughal rule led to major uprisings. (For more on Aurangzeb's rule, see page 499.)

Mughal

▶ A term meaning "Mongol," used to refer to the Muslim empire of India, although its founders were primarily Turks, Afghans, and Persians.

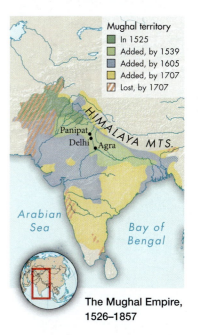

Mughal territory
- In 1525
- Added, by 1539
- Added, by 1605
- Added, by 1707
- Lost, by 1707

The Mughal Empire, 1526–1857

QUICK REVIEW

What role did slaves play in the government of each of the major Islamic empires?

How did Christians, Jews, Hindus, and other non-Muslims fare under these Islamic states?

How were the Islamic empires affected by trade routes that bypassed their lands?

What common factors led to the decline of central power in the Islamic empires?

✓ **LearningCurve**
Check what you know.

What cultural advances occurred under the rule of the Ottoman, Safavid, and Mughal Empires?

Music in a Garden

This illustration of a courtly romance depicts several women in a garden intently listening to a musician, with cups of a beverage in their hands.
(The Granger Collection, NYC — All rights reserved.)

ALL THREE ISLAMIC EMPIRES presided over an extraordinary artistic and intellectual flowering. At the same time, new religious practices (and conflicts) emerged. Artistic and intellectual advances spread from culture to culture, probably because of the common Persian influence on the Turks since the tenth century. This exchange was also aided by common languages.

The Arts

One of the arts all three empires shared was carpet making. Carpet designs and weaving techniques demonstrate both cultural integration and local distinctiveness. Turkic migrants carried their weaving traditions with them as they moved but also readily adopted new motifs, especially from Persia. In Safavid Persia, Shah Abbas was determined to improve his country's export trade and built the small cottage business of carpet weaving into a national industry. Women and children were often employed as weavers, especially of the most expensive rugs, because their smaller hands could tie tinier knots.

Another art that spread from Persia to both Ottoman and Mughal lands was miniature painting, especially for book illustration. This tradition had been

How were the three Islamic empires established, what governments did they set up?

What cultural advances occurred under the rule of the Ottoman, Safavid, and Mughal Empires?

enriched by the many Chinese artists brought to Persia during the Mongol period. There was also an interplay between carpets and miniature painting, with many motifs appearing in both book illustrations and carpets.

In Mughal India, as throughout the Muslim world, books were regarded as precious objects. Time, talent, and expensive materials went into their production, and they were highly coveted because they reflected wealth, learning, and power. Akbar reportedly possessed twenty-four thousand books when he died.

City and Palace Building

In all three empires strong rulers built capital cities and imperial palaces as visible expressions of dynastic majesty. Suleiman "the Magnificent" used his fabulous wealth to adorn Istanbul with palaces, mosques, schools, and libraries, and the city reached about a million in population. The building of hospitals, roads, and bridges and the reconstruction of the water systems of the great pilgrimage sites at Mecca and Jerusalem benefited his subjects. Safavid Persia and Mughal India produced rulers with similar ambitions.

The greatest builder under the Ottomans was Mimar Sinan (1491–1588), a Greek-born devshirme recruit who rose to become imperial architect under Suleiman. His masterpieces, the Shehzade and Suleimaniye Mosques in Istanbul, which rivaled the Byzantine church of Hagia Sophia, were designed to maximize the space under the dome. His buildings expressed the discipline, power, and devotion to Islam that characterized the Ottoman Empire under Suleiman.

Shah Abbas made his capital, Isfahan, the jewel of the Safavid Empire. He had his architects place a polo ground in the center and surrounded it with palaces, mosques, and bazaars. A city of perhaps 750,000 people, Isfahan also contained 162 mosques, 48 schools, 273 public baths, and the vast imperial palace. Private houses had their own garden courts, and public gardens, pools, and parks adorned the wide streets.

Akbar in India was also a great builder. The birth of a long-awaited son, Jahangir, inspired Akbar to build a new city, Fatehpur Sikri, to symbolize the regime's Islamic foundations. He personally supervised the construction of the city, which combined the Muslim tradition of domes, arches, and spacious courts

How did Christians, Jews, Hindus, and other non-Muslims fare under these Islamic states?

How were the Islamic empires affected by trade routes that bypassed their lands?

What common factors led to the decline of central power in the Islamic empires?

✓ **LearningCurve** Check what you know.

Isfahan Tiles

The embellishment of Isfahan under Shah Abbas I created an unprecedented need for tiles, as had the rebuilding of imperial Istanbul after 1453, the vast building program of Suleiman the Magnificent, and a huge European demand. Persian potters learned their skills from the Chinese. By the late sixteenth century Italian and Austrian potters had imitated the Persian and Ottoman tile makers. (Eileen Tweedy/Victoria & Albert Museum, London, UK/The Art Archive at Art Resource, NY)

with the Hindu tradition of flat stone beams, ornate decoration, and solidity. Unfortunately, because of its bad water supply, the city was soon abandoned.

Of Akbar's successors, Shah Jahan had the most sophisticated interest in architecture. Because his capital at Agra was cramped, in 1639 he decided to found a new capital city at Delhi. In the design and layout of the buildings, Persian ideas predominated. The walled palace-fortress alone extended over 125 acres. It included private chambers for the emperor; mansions for the wives, widows, and concubines of the imperial household; huge audience rooms for the conduct of public business; baths; and vast gardens filled with flowers, trees, and thirty silver fountains spraying water. In 1650, the palace-fortress housed fifty-seven thousand people. It also boasted a covered public bazaar.

Shah Jahan's most enduring monument is the Taj Mahal. Between 1631 and 1648 twenty thousand workers toiled over the construction of this memorial in Agra to Shah Jahan's favorite wife, who died giving birth to their fifteenth child. One of the most beautiful structures in the world, the Taj Mahal is both an expression of love and a superb architectural blending of Islamic and Indian culture.

Gardens

Many of the architectural masterpieces of this age had splendid gardens attached to them. Gardens represent a distinctive and highly developed feature of Persian culture. Identified with paradise in Arab tradition, gardens served not only as centers of prayer and meditation but also as places of leisure and revelry. After the incorporation of Persia into the caliphate in the seventh century, formal gardening spread west and east through the Islamic world.

Because it evoked paradise, the garden played a large role in Muslim literature. Some scholars hold that to understand Arabic poetry, one must study Arab

CHAPTER LOCATOR | How were the three Islamic empires established, what governments did they set up?

What cultural advances occurred under the rule of the Ottoman, Safavid, and Mughal Empires?

CHAPTER 17
496 THE ISLAMIC WORLD POWERS

gardening. The secular literature of Muslim Spain, rife with references such as "a garland of verses," influenced the lyric poetry of southern France, the troubadours, and the courtly love tradition.

Intellectual Advances and Religious Trends

Between 1400 and 1800 the culture of the Islamic empires developed in many directions. Particularly notable were new movements within Islam as well as advances in mathematics, geography, astronomy, and medicine. Building on the knowledge of earlier Islamic writers and stimulated by Ottoman naval power, the geographer and cartographer Piri Reis's *Book of the Sea* (1521) contained 129 chapters, each with a map incorporating all Islamic (and Western) knowledge of the seas and navigation. In the field of astronomy, Takiyuddin Mehmet (1521–1585) built an observatory at Istanbul. He also produced *Instruments of the Observatory*, which catalogued astronomical instruments and described an astronomical clock that fixed the location of heavenly bodies with greater precision than ever before.

There were also advances in medicine. Under Suleiman the imperial palace itself became a center of medical science, and the large number of hospitals established in Istanbul and throughout the empire testifies to his support for medical research and his concern for the sick. Recurrent outbreaks of the plague posed a challenge for physicians in Muslim lands. Muhammad had once said not to go to a country where an epidemic existed but also not to leave a place because an epidemic broke out. As a consequence, when European cities began enforcing quarantines to control the spread of the plague, early Muslim rulers dismissed such efforts. By the sixteenth century, however, a better understanding of contagion led to a redefinition of the proper response to a plague epidemic.

In the realm of religion, the rulers of all three empires drew legitimacy from their support for Islam. The Sunni-Shi'a split between the Ottomans and Safavids led to efforts to define and enforce religious orthodoxy on both sides. For the Safavids this entailed suppressing Sufi movements and Sunnis, even marginalizing—sometimes massacring—the original Qizilbash warriors, who had come to be seen as politically disruptive. Sectarian conflicts within Islam were not as pronounced in Mughal lands, perhaps because Muslims were greatly outnumbered by non-Muslims, mostly Hindus.

Sufi fraternities thrived throughout the Muslim world in this era, even when the states tried to limit them. In India Sufi orders also influenced non-Muslims. The mystical Bhakti movement among Hindus involved dances, poems, and songs reminiscent of Sufi practice. The development of the new religion of the Sikhs (seeks) was also influenced by Sufis. The Sikhs traced themselves back to a teacher in the sixteenth century who argued that God did not distinguish between Muslims and Hindus but saw everyone as his children.

Despite all the signs of cultural vitality in the three Islamic empires, none of them adopted the printing press or went through the sorts of cultural expansion associated with it in China and Europe. Until 1729 the Ottoman authorities prohibited printing books in Turkish or Arabic. Printing was not banned in Mughal India, but neither did the technology spread. The copying of manuscripts was a well-established practice, and those who made their living this way sometimes organized to keep competition at bay. It also needs to be noted that by the end of this period, scientific knowledge was not keeping up with advances made in Europe (see page 550).

| How did Christians, Jews, Hindus, and other non-Muslims fare under these Islamic states? | How were the Islamic empires affected by trade routes that bypassed their lands? | What common factors led to the decline of central power in the Islamic empires? | ✓ LearningCurve Check what you know. |

Coffee Drinking

This sixteenth-century miniature depicts men drinking coffee at a banquet. (© The Trustees of the Chester Beatty Library, Dublin, Ireland/The Bridgeman Art Library)

> PICTURING THE PAST

ANALYZING THE IMAGE: What activities are people engaged in? How does the artist convey differences in the ages of those drinking coffee?

CONNECTIONS: What made coffee a popular drink for people socializing?

Coffeehouses and Their Social Impact

In the mid-fifteenth century a new social convention spread throughout the Islamic world—drinking coffee. Arab writers trace the origins of coffee drinking to Yemen Sufis, who sought a trancelike concentration on God to the exclusion of everything else and found that coffee helped them stay awake. Merchants carried the Yemenite practice to Mecca in about 1490. From Mecca, where pilgrims were introduced to it, coffee drinking spread to Egypt and Syria. In 1555 two Syrians opened a coffeehouse in Istanbul.

Coffeehouses provided a place for conversation and male sociability; there a man could entertain his friends cheaply and more informally than at home. But coffeehouses encountered religious and governmental opposition, as some authorities saw them as a threat to public morality. On the other hand, the coffee trade was a major source of profit that local notables sought to control.

Although debate over the morality of coffeehouses continued through the sixteenth century, their eventual acceptance represented a revolution in Islamic life: socializing was no longer confined to the home. In the seventeenth century coffee and coffeehouses spread to Europe.

> **> Principle Arguments Against Coffeehouses:**

- Because of its composition, coffee is intoxicating, making it analogous to wine, prohibited to Muslims
- Coffee drinking was an innovation and therefore a violation of Islamic law
- Coffeehouses encouraged political discussions, facilitating sedition
- Coffeehouses attracted unemployed soldiers and other low types, encouraging immoral behavior, such as gambling, using drugs, and soliciting prostitutes
- Music at coffeehouses encouraged debauchery

> **QUICK REVIEW**

What factors facilitated cultural exchange between the Islamic empires?

CHAPTER LOCATOR | How were the three Islamic empires established, what governments did they set up? | What cultural advances occurred under the rule of the Ottoman, Safavid, and Mughal Empires?

Emperor Akbar in the City of Fatehpur Sikri

In 1569 Akbar founded the city of Fatehpur Sikri (the City of Victory) to honor the Muslim holy man Sheik Salim Chishti, who had foretold the birth of Akbar's son and heir Jahangir. Akbar is shown here seated on the cushion in the center overseeing the construction of the city. The image is contained in the Akbarnama, a book of illustrations Akbar commissioned to officially chronicle his reign. (Victoria & Albert Museum, London, UK/The Bridgeman Art Library)

How did Christians, Jews, Hindus, and other non-Muslims fare under these Islamic states?

DRAWING ON QUR'ANIC TEACHINGS, Muslims had long practiced a religious tolerance unknown in Christian Europe. Muslim rulers for the most part guaranteed the lives and property of Christians and Jews on their promise of obedience and the payment of a poll tax. In the case of the Ottomans, this tolerance was extended not only to the Christians and Jews who had been living under Muslim rule for centuries but also to the Serbs, Bosnians, Croats, and other Orthodox Christians in the newly conquered Balkans. In 1454 Rabbi Isaac Sarfati sent a letter to the Jews in the Rhineland, Swabia, Moravia, and Hungary, urging them to move to Turkey because of the good conditions for Jews there. A massive migration to Ottoman lands followed. When Ferdinand and Isabella of Spain expelled the Jews in 1492 and later, many immigrated to the Ottoman Empire.

| How did Christians, Jews, Hindus, and other non-Muslims fare under these Islamic states? | How were the Islamic empires affected by trade routes that bypassed their lands? | What common factors led to the decline of central power in the Islamic empires? | ✓ LearningCurve Check what you know. |

The Safavid authorities made efforts to convert Armenian Christians in the Caucasus, and many seem to have embraced Islam, some more voluntarily than others. Nevertheless, the Armenian Christian Church retained its vitality, and under the Safavids Armenian Christians were prominent merchants in long-distance trade (see page 502).

Babur and his successors acquired even more non-Muslim subjects with their conquests in India, which included not only Hindus but also substantial numbers of Jains, Zoroastrians, Christians, and Sikhs. Over time, the number of Indians who converted to Islam increased, but the Mughal rulers did not force conversion.

Akbar went the furthest in promoting Muslim-Hindu accommodation. He celebrated important Hindu festivals, and he wore his uncut hair in a turban as a concession to Indian practice. Also, Akbar twice married Hindu princesses, one of whom became the mother of his heir, Jahangir, and he appointed the Spanish Jesuit Antonio Monserrate (1536–1600) as tutor to his second son, Prince Murad. Eventually, Hindus totaled 30 percent of the imperial bureaucracy. In 1579 Akbar abolished the **jizya**, the poll tax on non-Muslims that guaranteed their protection. These actions infuriated the ulama, and serious conflict erupted between its members and the emperor. Ultimately, Akbar issued an imperial decree declaring that the Mughal emperor had supreme authority, even above the ulama, in all religious matters, to the dismay of the Muslim religious establishment.

Some of Akbar's successors, above all Aurangzeb, sided more with the ulama. Aurangzeb appointed censors of public morals in important cities to enforce Islamic laws. He forbade sati—the self-immolation of widows on their husbands' funeral pyres—and the castration of boys to be sold as eunuchs. He also abolished all taxes not authorized by Islamic law. To compensate for the loss of revenue, in 1679 Aurangzeb reimposed the tax on non-Muslims. Aurangzeb's reversal of Akbar's religious tolerance and cultural cosmopolitanism extended further. He ordered the destruction of some Hindu temples and tried to curb Sikhism. Aurangzeb's attempts to enforce rigid Islamic norms proved highly unpopular and aroused resistance that weakened Mughal rule.

jizya
▶ A poll tax on non-Muslims.

> **QUICK REVIEW**

Which of Akbar's policies were reversed by Aurangzeb? Why?

CHAPTER LOCATOR | How were the three Islamic empires established, what governments did they set up? | What cultural advances occurred under the rule of the Ottoman, Safavid, and Mughal Empires?

CHAPTER 17
500 THE ISLAMIC WORLD POWERS

English Dress Made of Indian Printed Cotton Cloth

Early British traders in India were impressed with the quality of the textiles made there and began ordering designs that would be popular with the English. This dress, created around 1770–1780 in England, is made of printed cotton (chintz) from the southeastern part of India. Chintz became so popular in England that it was eventually banned because it was threatening local textile industries. (Victoria & Albert Museum, London, UK/Art Resource, NY)

I

IT HAS WIDELY BEEN THOUGHT that a decline in the wealth and international importance of the Muslim empires could be directly attributed to the long-term shift in trading patterns that resulted from European overseas expansion. The argument is that new sea routes enabled Europeans to acquire goods from the East without using Muslim intermediaries, so that the creation of European colonial powers beginning in the sixteenth century led directly and indirectly to the eclipse of the Ottomans, Safavids, and Mughals. Recent scholars have challenged these ideas as too simplistic. First, it was not until the eighteenth century that political decline became evident in the three Islamic empires. Second, Turkish, Persian, and Indian merchants remained very active as long-distance traders into the eighteenth century and opened up many new routes themselves. It is true that in the Islamic empires New World crops fueled population increases less rapidly than in western Europe and East Asia. But economic growth does not always correlate with population increases.

How did Christians, Jews, Hindus, and other non-Muslims fare under these Islamic states?

How were the Islamic empires affected by trade routes that bypassed their lands?

What common factors led to the decline of central power in the Islamic empires?

☑️ **LearningCurve**
Check what you know.

Over the centuries covered in this chapter, the Islamic empires became not only more tied to European powers but also more connected to each other. Europeans gained deeper knowledge of Islamic lands, but so did residents of these lands, who more frequently traveled to other Islamic countries and wrote about their travels.

European Rivalry for Trade in the Indian Ocean

Shortly before Babur's invasion of India, the Portuguese had opened the subcontinent to Portuguese trade. In 1510 they established the port of Goa on the west coast of India as their headquarters and through an aggressive policy took control of Muslim shipping in the Indian Ocean and Arabian Sea, charging high fees to let ships through. As a result, they controlled the spice trade over the Indian Ocean for almost a century.

In 1602 the Dutch formed the Dutch East India Company with the stated goal of wresting the enormously lucrative spice trade from the Portuguese. In 1685 they supplanted the Portuguese in Ceylon (Sri Lanka). The scent of fabulous profits also attracted the English. With a charter signed by Queen Elizabeth, eighty London merchants organized the British East India Company. In 1619 Emperor Jahangir granted a British mission important commercial concessions. Soon, by offering gifts, medical services, and bribes to Indian rulers, the British East India Company was able to set up twenty-eight coastal forts/trading posts. By 1700 the company had founded the cities that became Madras and Calcutta (today called Chennai and Kolkata) and had taken over Bombay (today Mumbai), which had been a Portuguese possession (Map 17.3).

The British called their trading posts **factory-forts**. The term designated the walled compound containing company residences, offices, and warehouses. The company president exercised political authority over all residents.

Factory-forts existed to make profits from Asian-European trade, which was robust due to the popularity of Indian and Chinese wares in Europe in the late seventeenth and early eighteenth centuries. To pay for these goods, the British East India Company sold silver, copper, zinc, lead, and fabrics to the Indians. Profits grew even larger after 1700, when the company began to trade with China.

factory-forts

▶ A term first used by the British for their trading post at Surat that was later applied to all European walled settlements in India.

Merchant Networks in the Islamic Empires

The shifting trade patterns associated with European colonial expansion brought no direct benefit to the Ottomans and the Safavids, whose merchants could now be bypassed by Europeans seeking goods from India, Southeast Asia, or China. Yet merchants from these Islamic empires often proved adaptable, finding ways to benefit from the new trade networks.

In the case of India, the appearance of European traders led to a rapid increase in overall trade, helping Indian merchants and the Indian economy. Block-printed cotton cloth, produced by artisans working at home, was India's chief export. Through an Islamic business device involving advancing payment to artisans, banker-brokers supplied the material for production and money for

CHAPTER LOCATOR | How were the three Islamic empires established, what governments did they set up? | What cultural advances occurred under the rule of the Ottoman, Safavid, and Mughal Empires?

502 CHAPTER 17 THE ISLAMIC WORLD POWERS

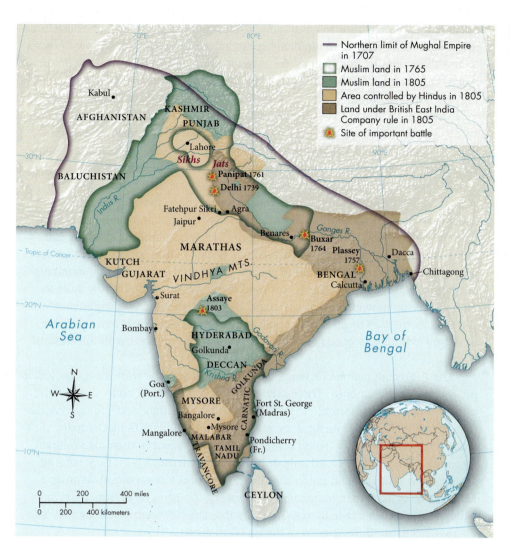

MAP 17.3 ■ India, 1707–1805

In the eighteenth century Mughal power gradually yielded to the Hindu Marathas and to the British East India Company.

Map legend:
- Northern limit of Mughal Empire in 1707
- Muslim land in 1765
- Muslim land in 1805
- Area controlled by Hindus in 1805
- Land under British East India Company rule in 1805
- Site of important battle

the artisans to live on while they worked; the cloth brokers specified the quality, quantity, and design of the finished products. This procedure resembles the later English "domestic" or "putting-out" system (see page 684), for the very good reason that the English took the idea from the Indians.

Within India the demand for cotton cloth, as well as for food crops, was so great that Akbar had to launch a wide-scale road-building campaign. From the Indian region of Gujarat, Indian merchant bankers shipped their cloth worldwide. Some scholars have compared India's international trade in the sixteenth century with that of Italian firms, such as the Medici. Indian trade actually extended over a far wider area, however. Indian merchants were often devout Hindus, Muslims, Buddhists, or Jains, evidence that undermines the argument of some Western writers, notably Karl Marx (see page 716), that religion retarded Asia's economic development.

Throughout Muslim lands both Jews and Christians were active in commerce. A particularly interesting case involves the Armenian Christians in the Safavid Empire in the sixteenth to eighteenth centuries. When the Portuguese first

| How did Christians, Jews, Hindus, and other non-Muslims fare under these Islamic states? | **How were the Islamic empires affected by trade routes that bypassed their lands?** | What common factors led to the decline of central power in the Islamic empires? | ✓ **LearningCurve** Check what you know. |

appeared on the western coast of India in 1498 and began to settle in south India, they found many Armenian merchant communities already there. A few decades later Akbar invited Armenians to settle in his new capital, Agra. In 1603 Shah Abbas captured much of Armenia, taking it from the Ottomans. Because defending this newly acquired border area was difficult, he forced the Armenians to move more deeply into Persia. Among them was the merchant community of Julfa, which was moved to a new suburb of Isfahan, which was renamed New Julfa. Shah Abbas made use of the Armenian merchants as royal merchants and financiers, but their economic mainstay continued to be long-distance trade.

The trading networks of Armenian merchants stretched from Venice and Amsterdam in western Europe, Moscow in Russia, and Ottoman-controlled Aleppo and Smyrna to all the major trading cities of India and even regions farther east, including Guangzhou in southern China and Manila in the Philippines. Many Armenian communities in these cities became quite substantial. Kinship connections were regularly used to cement commercial relations, and members of the community living in these scattered cities would return to New Julfa to marry, creating new kinship connections. Business, though, was conducted through contracts. The merchant about to take a journey would borrow a sum of money to purchase goods and would contract to pay it back with interest on his return.

The Armenian merchants would sail on whatever ships were available, including Dutch and Italian ones. The merchants could often speak half a dozen languages and were comfortable in both Islamic and Christian lands. In India Armenian merchants reached an agreement with the British East India Company that recognized their rights to live in company cities and observe their own religion. By the 1660s they had settled in Manila, and a few decades later they entered what is now Malaysia and Indonesia. By the end of the seventeenth century a small group of Armenian merchants had crossed the Himalayas from India and established themselves in Lhasa, Tibet. By the mid-eighteenth century they had also settled in the Dutch colony of Batavia (Indonesia).

Armenian Brass Bowl

The inscription on this bowl dates it to 1616 and places it in New Julfa, the Armenian quarter of Isfahan. It would have been used by an Armenian Christian priest to wash his hands. (© Ana Melikian 2007)

CHAPTER LOCATOR | How were the three Islamic empires established, what governments did they set up? | What cultural advances occurred under the rule of the Ottoman, Safavid, and Mughal Empires?

504 CHAPTER 17 THE ISLAMIC WORLD POWERS

From the British East India Company to the British Empire in India

Britain's presence in India began with the British East India Company and its desire to profit from trade. Managers of the company in London discouraged all unnecessary expenses and financial risks and thus opposed missionary activities or interference in local Indian politics. Nevertheless, the company responded to political instability in India in the early eighteenth century by extending political control. The company's factories evolved into defensive installations manned by small garrisons of native troops—known as **sepoys**—trained in Western military weapons and tactics.

From 1740 to 1763 Britain and France were engaged in a tremendous global struggle, and India, like North America in the Seven Years' War, became a battlefield and a prize. The French won land battles, but English sea power proved decisive by preventing the landing of French reinforcements. The Treaty of Paris of 1763 recognized British control of much of India, marking the beginning of the British Empire in India.

How was Britain to govern so large a territory? Eventually, the East India Company was pushed out of its governing role because the English Parliament distrusted the company, believing it was corrupt. The Regulating Act of 1773 created the office of governor general to exercise political authority over the territory controlled by the company. The India Act of 1784 required that the governor general be chosen from outside the company, and it made company directors subject to parliamentary supervision.

Implementation of these reforms fell to three successive governors: Warren Hastings (r. 1774–1785), Lord Charles Cornwallis (r. 1786–1794), and the marquess Richard Wellesley (r. 1797–1805). Hastings sought allies among Indian princes, laid the foundations for the first Indian civil service, abolished tolls to facilitate internal trade, placed the salt and opium trades under government control, and planned a codification of Muslim and Hindu laws. Cornwallis introduced the British style of property relations in which the rents of tenant farmers supported the landlords. Wellesley was victorious over local rulers who resisted British rule, vastly extending British influence in India. Like most nineteenth-century British governors of India, Wellesley believed that British rule strongly benefited the Indians.

sepoys
► The native Indian troops who were trained as infantrymen.

QUICK REVIEW <

How did European powers try to gain control of Indian Ocean trade?

| How did Christians, Jews, Hindus, and other non-Muslims fare under these Islamic states? | **How were the Islamic empires affected by trade routes that bypassed their lands?** | What common factors led to the decline of central power in the Islamic empires? | ☑ LearningCurve Check what you know. |

What common factors led to the decline of central power in the Islamic empires in the seventeenth and eighteenth centuries?

BY THE END OF THE EIGHTEENTH CENTURY all three of the major Islamic empires were on the defensive and losing territory (Map 17.4). They faced some common problems—succession difficulties, financial strain, and loss of military superiority—but their circumstances differed in significant ways as well.

The first to fall was the Safavid Empire. Persia did not have the revenue base to maintain a large standing army. Decline in the strength of the army encouraged increased foreign aggression. In 1722 the Afghans invaded from the east, seized Isfahan, and were able to repulse an Ottoman invasion from the west. In Isfahan thousands of officials and members of the shah's family were executed. In the following century no leader emerged capable of reuniting all of Persia. In this political vacuum, Shi'a religious institutions grew stronger.

The Ottoman Empire also suffered from poor leadership. Early Ottoman practice had guaranteed that the sultans would be forceful men. The sultan's sons gained administrative experience as governors of provinces and military experience on the battlefield as part of their education. After the sultan died, any son who wanted to succeed had to contest his brothers to claim the throne, after which the new sultan would have his defeated brothers executed. Although bloody, this system led to the succession of capable, determined men. After Suleiman's reign, however, the tradition was abandoned. To prevent threats of usurpation, sons of the sultan were brought up in the harem and confined there as adults, denied roles in government. The result was a series of rulers who were minor children or incompetent adults, leaving power in the hands of high officials and the mothers of the heirs. Political factions formed around viziers, military leaders, and palace women. In the contest for political favor, the devshirme was abandoned, and political and military ranks were filled by Muslims.

The Ottoman Empire's military strength also declined. The defeat of the Turkish fleet by the Spanish off the coast of Greece at Lepanto in 1571 marked the loss of Ottoman dominance in the Mediterranean. By the terms of a peace treaty with Austria signed at Karlowitz (1699), the Ottomans lost Hungary and Transylvania,

CHAPTER LOCATOR | How were the three Islamic empires established, what governments did they set up? | What cultural advances occurred under the rule of the Ottoman, Safavid, and Mughal Empires?

506 CHAPTER 17 THE ISLAMIC WORLD POWERS

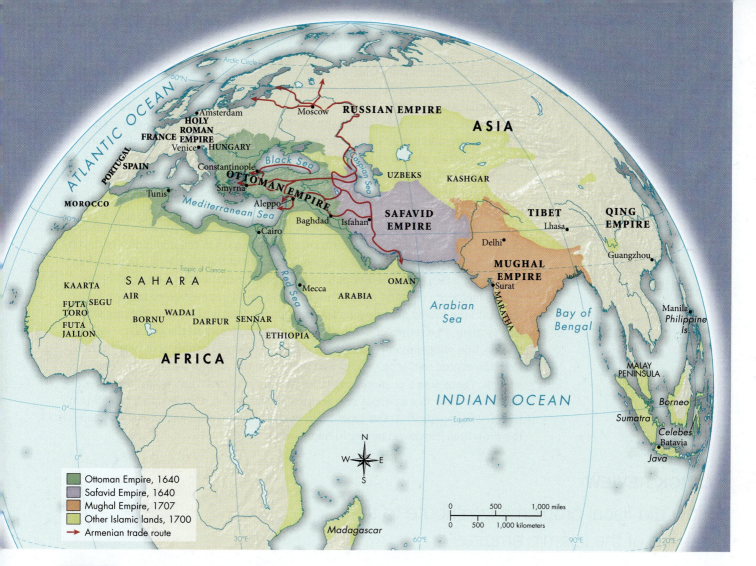

MAP 17.4 ■ The Muslim World, ca. 1700

The three great Islamic empires were adjacent to each other and of similar physical size. Many of their other neighbors were Muslim as well.

along with the tax revenues they had provided. Also, the Ottoman armies were depending more on mercenaries, and they did not keep up with the innovations in drill, command, and control that were then transforming European armies. From the late seventeenth century Ottoman armies began losing wars and territory along both northern and eastern borders. In 1774 the empire lost the lands on the northern bank of the Black Sea to Russia. In North Africa the local governors came to act more independently, sometimes starting hereditary dynasties.

Military challenges proved daunting in Mughal India as well. After defeating his father and brothers, Aurangzeb made it his goal to conquer the south. The stiffest opposition came from the Marathas, a militant Hindu group centered in the western Deccan. From 1681 until his death in 1707, Aurangzeb took many forts and won several battles, but total destruction of the Maratha guerrilla bands eluded him.

Aurangzeb's death led to thirteen years of succession struggles, shattering the empire. His eighteenth-century successors were less successful than the

How did Christians, Jews, Hindus, and other non-Muslims fare under these Islamic states?

How were the Islamic empires affected by trade routes that bypassed their lands?

What common factors led to the decline of central power in the Islamic empires?

LearningCurve
Check what you know.

Ottomans in making the dynasty the focus of loyalty. Mughal provincial governors began to rule independently, giving only minimal allegiance to the throne at Delhi. Meanwhile, the Marathas pressed steadily northward. Threats also came from the west. In 1739 the Persian adventurer Nadir Shah invaded India, defeated the Mughal army, and looted Delhi. Constant skirmishes between the Afghans and the Marathas for control of the Punjab and northern India ended in 1761 at Panipat, where the Marathas were crushed by the Afghans. At that point, India no longer had a state strong enough to impose order on the subcontinent or check the penetration of the Europeans.

In all three empires fiscal difficulties contributed to strain on the state. A long period of peace in the late sixteenth century and again in the mid-eighteenth century, as well as a decline in the frequency of visits of the plague, led to a doubling of the population. Increased population, coupled with the "little ice age" of the mid-seventeenth century, meant that the land could not sustain so many people, nor could the towns provide jobs for the thousands of agricultural workers who fled to them. The return of demobilized soldiers aggravated the problem. Inflation, famine, and widespread revolts resulted. The economic center of gravity shifted from the capital to the provinces, and politically the empire began to decentralize as well. There was a positive side to increasing provincial autonomy, however, because it drew more people into political participation, thus laying a foundation for later nationalism. At the time, however, central government officials perceived the growth in provincial power in negative terms.

> QUICK REVIEW

How did fiscal problems contribute to the decline of the Islamic empires?

CHAPTER SUMMARY

After the decline of the Mongols in Central Asia and Persia, many small Turkic-ruled states emerged in the region from Anatolia through Afghanistan. Three of them went on to establish large empires: the Ottomans in Anatolia, the Safavids in Persia, and the Mughals in India. The Ottoman Empire's political system reached its classic form under Suleiman I. All authority flowed from the sultan to his public servants. In Persia, the strength of the Safavid state rested in part on the skills of urban bureaucrats, who were vital to the civil machinery of government. Babur, from his base in Afghanistan, founded the Mughal Empire in India. His grandson Akbar extended Mughal rule far into India. All three empires quickly adapted to new gunpowder technologies.

Each of the three Islamic empires presided over an extraordinary artistic and intellectual flowering in everything from carpet making and book illustration to architecture and gardening, from geography and astronomy to medicine. Each of these empires drew legitimacy from their support for Islam. There were, however, key differences: the Ottomans and Mughals supported the Sunni tradition, the Safavids the Shi'a tradition.

CHAPTER LOCATOR | How were the three Islamic empires established, what governments did they set up? | What cultural advances occurred under the rule of the Ottoman, Safavid, and Mughal Empires?

508 CHAPTER 17 THE ISLAMIC WORLD POWERS

The three Islamic empires all had a substantial number of non-Muslim subjects. The Ottomans ruled over the Balkans, where most of the people were Christian, and Muslims in India were greatly outnumbered by Hindus.

European exploration opened new trade routes and enabled Europeans to trade directly with India and China, bypassing Muslim intermediaries in the Middle East. Within India British merchants increased their political control in politically unstable areas, leading before the end of the eighteenth century to a vast colonial empire in India.

By the end of the eighteenth century all three of the major Islamic empires were losing territory. The first to fall was the Safavid Empire. From the late seventeenth century Ottoman armies began losing wars along the northern and eastern borders, resulting in substantial loss of territory. Military challenges proved daunting in Mughal India as well. In all three empires, as central power declined, local notables and military strongmen seized power.

 **CONNECTIONS** From 1300 to 1800, Islamic civilization thrived under three dynastic houses: the Ottomans, the Safavids, and the Mughals. All three empires had a period of expansion when territory was enlarged, followed by a high point politically and culturally, and later a period of contraction, when territories broke away. At the cultural level, the borders of these three states were porous, and people, ideas, art motifs, languages, and trade flowed back and forth.

In East Asia the fifteenth through eighteenth century also saw the creation of strong, prosperous, and expanding states, though in the case of China (under the Qing Dynasty) and Japan (under the Tokugawa Shogunate) the eighteenth century was a cultural high point, not a period of decline. The Qing emperors were Manchus, from the region northeast of China proper. As in the Islamic lands, during these centuries the presence of European powers became an issue in East Asia, though the details were quite different. Although one of the commodities that the British most wanted was the tea produced in China, Britain did not extend political control in China the way it did in India. Japan managed to refuse entry to most European traders after finding their presence and their support for missionary activity disturbing. The next chapter takes up these developments in East Asia.

ONLINE DOCUMENT PROJECT

Impressions of the Ottoman Empire

How did Europeans view the Ottoman Empire?

Examine a Habsburg ambassador's impressions of the Ottoman Empire, and then complete a quiz and writing assignment based on the evidence and details from this chapter. *See inside the front cover to learn more.*

| How did Christians, Jews, Hindus, and other non-Muslims fare under these Islamic states? | How were the Islamic empires affected by trade routes that bypassed their lands? | What common factors led to the decline of central power in the Islamic empires? | ✔ **LearningCurve** Check what you know. |

CHAPTER 17 STUDY GUIDE

STEP 1 **GET STARTED ONLINE**

LearningCurve

Now that you've read the chapter, make it stick by completing the LearningCurve activity.

STEP 2 **EXPLAIN WHY IT MATTERS**

Put your reading into practice. Identify each term below, and then explain why it matters in world history.

TERM	WHO OR WHAT & WHEN	WHY IT MATTERS
Ottomans (p. 487)		
Anatolia (p. 487)		
sultan (p. 488)		
viziers (p. 489)		
devshirme (p. 490)		
janissaries (p. 490)		
concubine (p. 490)		
shah (p. 490)		
Safavid (p. 490)		
Qizilbash (p. 490)		
ulama (p. 492)		
Mughal (p. 493)		
jizya (p. 500)		
factory-forts (p. 502)		
sepoys (p. 505)		

STEP 3 **MOVE BEYOND THE BASICS**

To demonstrate a more advanced understanding of the empires of the Ottomans, Safavids, and Mughals, fill in the chart below with descriptions of key aspects of each empire. What role did military expansion play in all three empires?

	Government and Military	Culture and Religion	Relations with Non-Muslims	Role of Slaves
Ottomans				
Safavids				
Mughals				

PUT IT ALL TOGETHER

Now, take a step back and try to explain the big picture. Remember to use specific examples from the chapter in your answers.

ORIGINS AND ORGANIZATION OF THE ISLAMIC EMPIRES

▶ How did Turkish culture and practices shape each of the empires?

▶ What common factors help explain the success of all three empires?

CULTURE AND SOCIETY OF THE ISLAMIC EMPIRES

▶ What role did religion play in the expansion and rule of each of the empires?

▶ What values and beliefs were reflected in the culture of the Islamic empires?

THE ISLAMIC EMPIRES IN THE SEVENTEENTH AND EIGHTEENTH CENTURIES

▶ What impact did European incursions have on the economies of the Islamic empires?

▶ What internal factors contributed to the decline of the Islamic empires? What about external factors?

LOOKING BACK, LOOKING AHEAD

▶ What connections can you make between the Islamic empires described in this chapter and the first Islamic empire established in the centuries following the death of Muhammad?

▶ What connections between the peoples of the Islamic empires would you expect to persist long after the onset of imperial decline? Why?

> IN YOUR OWN WORDS

Imagine that you must give an oral report to the class answering the following question: **What were the strengths and weaknesses of the three great Islamic empires?** What would be the most important points and why?

18
EUROPEAN POWER AND EXPANSION
1500–1750

> **How did European central governments consolidate and expand their power in the early modern period?** Chapter 17 examines the European struggle for stability in the early modern period. This struggle originated with conflicts sparked by the Protestant and Catholic Reformations in the early sixteenth century and continued with economic and social breakdown into the late seventeenth century. Between roughly 1589 and 1715 two basic patterns of government emerged from these conflicts: absolute monarchy and the constitutional state. Whether a government was constitutional or absolutist, an important foundation of state power was empire and colonialism. Jealous of Iberian overseas holdings, England, France, and the Netherlands vied for new acquisitions in Asia and the Americas, while Russia pushed its borders east to the Pacific.

Louis XIV In this painting, King Louis XIV receives foreign ambassadors to celebrate a peace treaty. The king grandly occupied the center of his court, which in turn served as the pinnacle for the French people and, at the height of his glory, for all of Europe. (Erich Lessing/Art Resource, NY)

> How did the Protestant and Catholic Reformations change power structures in Europe and shape European colonial expansion?

> How did seventeenth-century European states overcome social and economic crisis to build strong states?

> How did absolutism evolve in the seventeenth century in Spain, France, and Austria?

> Why and how did the constitutional state triumph in England and the Dutch Republic?

> How did European nations compete for global trade and empire in the Americas and Asia?

> How did Russian rulers build a distinctive absolutist monarchy and expand into a vast and powerful empire?

✓ LearningCurve

After reading the chapter, use LearningCurve to retain what you've read.

How did the Protestant and Catholic Reformations change power structures in Europe and shape European colonial expansion?

Jesuits in China

This European image depicts early Jesuit missionaries baptizing converts in South China. (Archiv Gerstenberg — ullstein bild/The Granger Collection, NYC — All rights reserved.)

Protestant Reformation

▶ A religious reform movement that began in the early sixteenth century and split the Western Christian Church.

AS A RESULT OF A MOVEMENT of religious reform known as the **Protestant Reformation**, Western Christendom broke into many divisions in the sixteenth century. This splintering happened not only for religious reasons but also because of political and social factors. Religious transformation provided a source of power for many rulers and shaped European colonial expansion.

The Protestant Reformation

In early-sixteenth-century western Europe, calls for reform in the church came from many quarters, both within and outside the church. Critics of the church concentrated their attacks on clerical immorality, ignorance, and absenteeism. Charges of immorality were aimed at a number of priests who were drunkards, neglected the rule of celibacy, gambled, or indulged in fancy dress. Charges of ignorance applied to barely literate priests who delivered poor-quality sermons.

In regard to absenteeism, many clerics, especially higher ecclesiastics, held several benefices (offices) simultaneously. However, they seldom visited the com-

CHAPTER LOCATOR | **How did the Protestant and Catholic Reformations shape colonial expansion?** | How did seventeenth-century European states overcome social and economic crisis? | How did absolutism evolve in in Spain, France, and Austria?

514 CHAPTER 18 EUROPEAN POWER AND EXPANSION

ca. 1500–1650 Consolidation of serfdom in eastern Europe	**1660** Restoration of English monarchy under Charles II
1533–1584 Reign of Ivan the Terrible in Russia	**1665–1683** Jean-Baptiste Colbert applies mercantilism to France
1589–1610 Reign of Henry IV in France	**1670–1671** Cossack revolt led by Stenka Razin
1598–1613 Time of Troubles in Russia	**1682** Louis XIV moves court to Versailles
1612–1697 Caribbean islands colonized by France, England, and the Netherlands	**1682–1725** Reign of Peter the Great in Russia
ca. 1620–1740 Growth of absolutism in Austria and Prussia	**1683–1718** Habsburgs push the Ottoman Turks from Hungary
1642–1649 English civil war, ending with the execution of Charles I	**1685** Edict of Nantes revoked
1643–1715 Reign of Louis XIV in France	**1688–1689** Glorious Revolution in England
1651 First of the Navigation Acts	**1701–1713** War of the Spanish Succession
1653–1658 Oliver Cromwell's military rule in England (the Protectorate)	

munities served by the benefices. Instead, they collected revenues from all the benefices assigned to them and hired a poor priest to fulfill their spiritual duties.

There was also local resentment of clerical privileges and immunities. Priests, monks, and nuns were exempt from civic responsibilities, such as defending the city and paying taxes. Yet religious orders frequently held large amounts of urban property. City governments were increasingly determined to integrate the clergy into civic life. This brought city leaders into opposition with bishops and the papacy, which for centuries had stressed the independence of the church from lay control.

This range of complaints helps explain why the ideas of Martin Luther (1483–1546), a priest and professor of theology from the German University of Wittenberg, found a ready audience. Luther and other Protestants—the word comes from a "protest" drawn up by a group of reforming princes in 1529—developed a new understanding of Christian doctrine that emphasized faith, the power of God's grace, and the centrality of the Bible. Protestant ideas were attractive to educated people and urban residents, and they spread rapidly through preaching, hymns, and the printing press.

Luther lived in the Holy Roman Empire, a loose collection of largely independent states in which the emperor had far less authority than did the monarchs of western Europe. The Habsburg emperor, Charles V, was a staunch supporter of Catholicism, but the ruler of the territory in which Luther lived protected the

Why and how did the constitutional state triumph in England and the Dutch Republic?	How did European nations compete for trade and empire in the Americas and Asia?	How did Russian rulers build an absolutist monarchy and expand into a powerful empire?	✔ LearningCurve Check what you know.

reformer. Although Luther appeared before Charles V when he was summoned, he was not arrested and continued to preach and write.

Luther's ideas appealed to the local rulers of the empire for a variety of reasons. Though Germany was not a nation, people did have an understanding of being German because of their language and traditions. Luther frequently used the phrase "we Germans" in his attacks on the papacy, and his appeal to national feeling influenced many rulers. Also, while some German rulers were sincerely attracted to Lutheran ideas, material considerations swayed many others. The adoption of Protestantism would mean the legal confiscation of church properties. Thus many political authorities in the empire used the religious issue to extend their power and to enhance their independence from the emperor. Luther worked closely with political authorities, viewing them as fully justified in reforming the church in their territories. Thus, just as in the Ottoman and Safavid Empires (see Chapter 17), rulers drew their legitimacy in part from their support for religion. By 1530 many parts of the Holy Roman Empire and Scandinavia had broken with the Catholic Church.

In England the issue of the royal succession triggered that country's break with Rome, and a Protestant Church was established during the 1530s under King Henry VIII (r. 1509–1547) and reaffirmed under his daughter Elizabeth I (r. 1558–1603). Church officials were required to sign an oath of loyalty to the monarch, and people were required to attend services at the state church, which became known as the Anglican Church.

Protestant ideas also spread into France, the Netherlands, Scotland, and eastern Europe. In all these areas, a second generation of reformers built on earlier ideas to develop their own theology and plans for institutional change. The most important of the second-generation reformers was the Frenchman John Calvin (1509–1564), who reformed the city of Geneva, Switzerland. Calvin believed that God was absolutely sovereign and omnipotent and that humans had no free will. Thus men and women could not actively work to achieve salvation, because God had decided at the beginning of time who would be saved and who damned, a theological principle called predestination.

The church in Geneva served as the model for the Presbyterian Church in Scotland, the Huguenot (HYOO-guh-naht) Church in France, and the Puritan Churches in England and New England. Calvinism became the compelling force in international Protestantism, first in Europe and then in many Dutch and English colonies around the world. Calvinism was also the dominant form of Protestantism in France (Map 18.1).

The Catholic Reformation

In response to the Protestant Reformation, by the 1530s the papacy was leading a movement for reform within the Roman Catholic Church. Many historians see the developments within the Catholic Church after the Protestant Reformation as two interrelated movements, one a drive for internal reform linked to earlier reform efforts and the other a Counter-Reformation that opposed Protestantism spiritually, politically, and militarily.

Pope Paul III (pontificate 1534–1549) established the Supreme Sacred Congregation of the Roman and Universal Inquisition, often called the Holy Office, with judicial authority over all Catholics and the power to imprison and execute.

CHAPTER LOCATOR | **How did the Protestant and Catholic Reformations shape colonial expansion?** | How did seventeenth-century European states overcome social and economic crisis? | How did absolutism evolve in in Spain, France, and Austria?

CHAPTER 18
516 EUROPEAN POWER AND EXPANSION

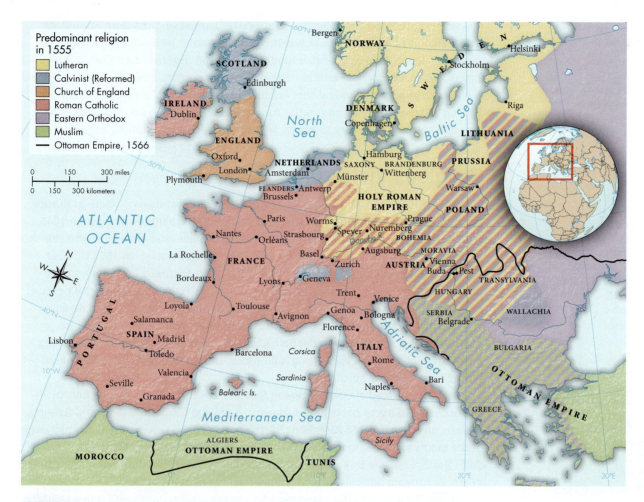

MAP 18.1 ■ Religious Divisions, ca. 1555

In the mid-sixteenth century, much of Europe remained Catholic. The Peace of Augsburg (1555) allowed the ruler of each territory in the Holy Roman Empire to determine the religion of its people. The northern territories of the empire became Lutheran, as did Scandinavia, while much of the southern empire remained Catholic. Sizable Calvinist populations existed in Scotland, the Netherlands and central Europe. Eastern Europe was dominated by Orthodox Christianity and the Ottoman Empire to the south and southeast was Muslim.

He also called a general council of the church, which met intermittently from 1545 to 1563 at the city of Trent. The Council of Trent laid a solid basis for the spiritual renewal of the Catholic Church. It gave equal validity to the Scriptures and to tradition as sources of religious truth and tackled problems that had disillusioned many Christians. Bishops were required to live in their dioceses and to establish a seminary for educating and training clergy. Finally, it placed great emphasis on preaching to and instructing the laity.

Just as seminaries provided education, so did new religious orders, which aimed to raise the moral and intellectual level of the clergy and people. The Ursuline (UHR-suh-luhn) order of nuns, founded by Angela Merici (1474–1540), attained enormous prestige for its education of women.

Another important new order was the Society of Jesus, or **Jesuits**. Founded by Ignatius Loyola (1491–1556) in 1540, this order played a powerful international

Jesuits

▶ Members of the Society of Jesus, founded by Ignatius Loyola and approved by the papacy in 1540, whose goal was the spread of the Roman Catholic faith through humanistic schools and missionary activity.

| Why and how did the constitutional state triumph in England and the Dutch Republic? | How did European nations compete for trade and empire in the Americas and Asia? | How did Russian rulers build an absolutist monarchy and expand into a powerful empire? | ✓ LearningCurve Check what you know. |

role in strengthening Catholicism in Europe and spreading the faith around the world. Recruited primarily from wealthy merchant and professional families, the Society of Jesus developed into a highly centralized organization. They established well-run schools to educate the sons of the nobility as well as the poor. The Jesuits achieved phenomenal success for the papacy and the reformed Catholic Church, carrying Christianity to the Americas, Asia, and Africa. Also, as confessors and spiritual directors to kings, Jesuits exerted great political influence.

Religious Violence

Religious differences led to riots, civil wars, and international conflicts in Europe during the sixteenth century. In the Holy Roman Empire fighting began in 1546. The initial success of Emperor Charles V led to French intervention on the side of the Protestants, lest the emperor acquire even more power. In 1555 Charles agreed to the Peace of Augsburg, which officially recognized Lutheranism and ended religious war in Germany for many decades. Under this treaty, the political authority in each territory of the Holy Roman Empire was permitted to decide whether the territory would be Catholic or Lutheran. His hope of uniting his empire under a single church dashed, Charles V abdicated in 1556, transferring power over his Spanish and Dutch holdings to his son Philip II and his imperial power to his brother Ferdinand.

In France armed clashes between Catholic royalists and Calvinist antiroyalists occurred in many parts of the country. A savage Catholic attack on Calvinists in Paris on August 24, 1572—Saint Bartholomew's Day—occurred at the marriage of the king's sister Margaret of Valois to the Protestant Henry of Navarre. The Saint Bartholomew's Day massacre initiated a civil war that dragged on for fifteen years, destroying agriculture and commercial life in many areas.

In the Netherlands the movement for church reform developed into a struggle for Dutch independence. In the 1560s Spanish authorities attempted to suppress Calvinist worship and raised taxes. Civil war broke out from 1568 to 1578 between Catholics and Protestants in the Netherlands and between the provinces of the Netherlands and Spain. Eventually the ten southern provinces came under the control of the Spanish Habsburg forces. The seven northern provinces, led by Holland, formed the Union of Utrecht (United Provinces of the Netherlands) and in 1581 declared their independence from Spain. The north was Protestant, and the south remained Catholic. Hostilities continued until 1609, when Spain agreed to a truce that recognized the independence of the northern provinces.

The era of religious wars was also the time of the most extensive witch persecutions in European history. Both Protestants and Catholics tried and executed those accused of being witches, with church officials and secular authorities acting together. The heightened sense of God's power and divine wrath in the Reformation era was an important factor in the witch-hunts, as were new demonological ideas, legal procedures involving torture, and neighborhood tensions.

> ### > Witchcraft Trials: 1450–1650
>
> - Between 100,000 and 200,000 people tried for witchcraft
> - Between 40,000 and 60,000 executed
> - Between 75 and 85 percent of those tried and executed were women

> QUICK REVIEW

How did the Reformation lead to an increase in personal and state violence in the sixteenth and seventeenth centuries?

CHAPTER LOCATOR | How did the Protestant and Catholic Reformations shape colonial expansion? | **How did seventeenth-century European states overcome social and economic crisis?** | How did absolutism evolve in in Spain, France, and Austria?

518 CHAPTER 18 EUROPEAN POWER AND EXPANSION

How did seventeenth-century European states overcome social and economic crisis to build strong states?

HISTORIANS OFTEN REFER TO THE seventeenth century as an "age of crisis" because Europe was challenged by population losses, economic decline, and social and political unrest. These difficulties were partially due to climate changes that reduced agricultural productivity. But they also resulted from military competition among European powers, the religious divides of the Reformations, increased taxation, and war.

The atmosphere of crisis encouraged governments to take emergency measures to restore order, measures that they successfully turned into long-term reforms that strengthened the power of the state. In the long run, European states proved increasingly able to impose their will on the populace.

The Social Order and Peasant Life

Peasants occupied the lower tiers of a society organized in hierarchical levels. In much of Europe, the monarch occupied the summit, celebrated as a semidivine being chosen by God to embody the state. In Catholic countries, the clergy constituted the first order of society, followed by the nobles. Christian prejudices against commerce and money meant that merchants could never lay claim to the highest honors. However, many prosperous mercantile families had bought their

| Why and how did the constitutional state triumph in England and the Dutch Republic? | How did European nations compete for trade and empire in the Americas and Asia? | How did Russian rulers build an absolutist monarchy and expand into a powerful empire? | ✔ LearningCurve Check what you know. |

way into the nobility through service to the monarchy in the fifteenth and sixteenth centuries, and they constituted a second tier of nobles. Those lower on the social scale, the peasants and artisans who formed the vast majority of the population, were expected to show deference to their betters.

In addition to being rigidly hierarchical, European societies were patriarchal. Religious and secular law commanded a man's wife, children, servants, and apprentices to respect and obey him. Fathers were entitled to use physical violence, imprisonment, and other forceful measures to impose their authority. These powers were balanced by expectations that a good father would care benevolently for his dependents.

In the seventeenth century the vast majority of Europeans lived in the countryside, as was the case in most parts of the world. The hub of the rural world was the small peasant village centered on a church and a manor.

In western Europe a small number of peasants owned enough land to feed themselves and possessed the livestock and plows necessary to work their land. Independent farmers were leaders of the peasant village. Below them were small landowners and tenant farmers who did not have enough land to be self-sufficient. At the bottom were villagers who worked as dependent laborers and servants. Private landowning among peasants was a distinguishing feature of western Europe. In central and eastern Europe the vast majority of peasants toiled as serfs for noble landowners, while in the Ottoman Empire all land belonged to the sultan.

Famine and Economic Crisis

In the seventeenth century a period of colder and wetter climate throughout Europe, dubbed the "little ice age" by historians, meant a shorter farming season with lower yields. A bad harvest created food shortages; a series of bad harvests could lead to famine. Recurrent famines significantly reduced the population of early modern Europe through reduced fertility, susceptibility to disease, and outright starvation.

Industry also suffered. The output of woolen textiles declined sharply in the first half of the seventeenth century. Food prices were high, wages stagnated, and unemployment soared. This economic crisis was not universal: it struck various regions at different times and to different degrees. In the middle decades of the century, for example, Spain, France, Germany, and England all experienced great economic difficulties, but these years were the golden age of the Netherlands (see page 535).

The urban poor and peasants were the hardest hit. When the price of bread rose beyond their capacity to pay, they frequently expressed their anger by rioting. Women often led these actions, since their role as mothers gave them some impunity in authorities' eyes. Historians have used the term **moral economy** for this vision of a world in which community needs predominate over competition and profit.

moral economy
▶ The early modern European view that community needs predominated over competition and profit and that necessary goods should thus be sold at a fair price.

Thirty Years' War
▶ A large-scale conflict extending from 1618 to 1648 that pitted Protestants against Catholics in central Europe, but also involved dynastic interests, notably of Spain and France.

The Thirty Years' War

Harsh economic conditions in the seventeenth century were greatly exacerbated by the decades-long conflict known as the **Thirty Years' War** (1618–1648). Shifts in the balance between the population of Protestants and Catholics in the Holy Roman Empire led to the deterioration of the Peace of Augsburg. Lutheran princes

CHAPTER LOCATOR | How did the Protestant and Catholic Reformations shape colonial expansion? | **How did seventeenth-century European states overcome social and economic crisis?** | How did absolutism evolve in in Spain, France, and Austria?

520 CHAPTER 18 EUROPEAN POWER AND EXPANSION

felt compelled to form the Protestant Union (1608), and Catholics retaliated with the Catholic League (1609). Dynastic interests were also involved; the Spanish Habsburgs strongly supported the goals of their Austrian relatives: the unity of the empire and the preservation of Catholicism within it.

The war began with a conflict in Bohemia (part of the present-day Czech Republic) between the Catholic League and the Protestant Union but soon spread through the Holy Roman Empire, drawing in combatants from across Europe. After a series of initial Catholic victories, the tide of the conflict turned due to the intervention of Sweden, under its king Gustavus Adolphus (r. 1594–1632), and then France, whose prime minister, Cardinal Richelieu, intervened on the side of the Protestants to undermine Habsburg power.

The 1648 Peace of Westphalia that ended the Thirty Years' War marked a turning point in European history. The treaties that established the peace not only ended conflicts fought over religious faith but also recognized the independent authority of more than three hundred German princes (Map 18.2, see page 522), reconfirming the emperor's severely limited authority. The Augsburg agreement of 1555 became permanent, adding Calvinism to Catholicism and Lutheranism as legally permissible creeds. The United Provinces of the Netherlands, known as the Dutch Republic, won official freedom from Spain.

The Thirty Years' War was probably the most destructive event in central Europe prior to the world wars of the twentieth century. Perhaps one-third of urban residents and two-fifths of the rural population died.

European Achievements in State-Building

In this context of warfare, economic crisis, and demographic decline, European monarchs took urgent measures to restore order and rebuild their states. In some states absolutist models of government prevailed. In others, constitutionalist forces dominated. Despite their political differences, all these states sought to protect and expand their frontiers, raise new taxes, consolidate central control, and compete for colonies and trade in the New and Old Worlds. In so doing, they followed a broad pattern of state-building and consolidation of power found across Eurasia in this period.

Rulers who wished to increase their authority encountered formidable obstacles, including poor communications, entrenched local power structures, and ethnic and linguistic diversity. Nonetheless, over the course of the seventeenth century both absolutist and constitutional governments achieved new levels of power and national unity. They did so by transforming emergency measures of wartime into permanent structures of government and by subduing privileged groups through the combined use of force and economic and social incentives. Increased state authority may be seen in four areas in particular: a tremendous growth in the size and professionalism of armies; much higher taxes; larger and more efficient bureaucracies; and territorial expansion both within Europe and overseas.

Over time, centralized power added up to something close to **sovereignty**. A state may be termed sovereign when it possesses a monopoly over the instruments of justice and the use of force within clearly defined boundaries. In a sovereign state, no nongovernmental system of courts competes with state courts in the dispensation of justice. Also, private armies present no threat to central authority. While seventeenth-century states did not acquire full sovereignty, they made important strides toward that goal.

sovereignty

▶ Authority of states that possess a monopoly over the instruments of justice and the use of force within clearly defined boundaries and in which private armies present no threat to central control; seventeenth-century European states made important advances toward sovereignty.

Why and how did the constitutional state triumph in England and the Dutch Republic?

How did European nations compete for trade and empire in the Americas and Asia?

How did Russian rulers build an absolutist monarchy and expand into a powerful empire?

☑ LearningCurve
Check what you know.

MAP 18.2 ■ **Europe After the Thirty Years' War**

Which country emerged from the Thirty Years' War as the strongest European power? What dynastic house was that country's major rival in the early modern period?

> QUICK REVIEW

How did war and famine contribute to the seventeenth-century crisis?

CHAPTER LOCATOR | How did the Protestant and Catholic Reformations shape colonial expansion? | How did seventeenth-century European states overcome social and economic crisis? | **How did absolutism evolve in in Spain, France, and Austria?**

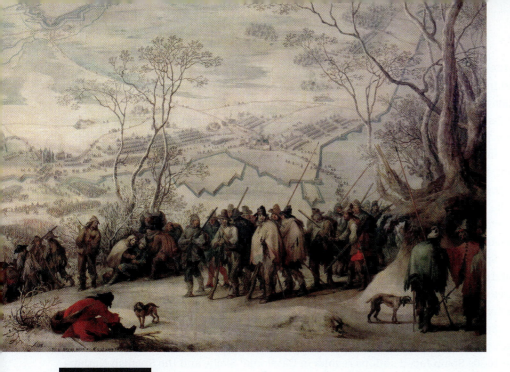

Spanish Troops

The long wars that Spain fought over Dutch independence, in support of Habsburg interests in Germany, and against France left the country militarily exhausted and financially drained by the mid-1600s. In this detail from a painting by Peeter Snayers, Spanish troops — thin, emaciated, and probably unpaid — straggle away from battle. (detail, *Troops at the Siege of Aire Sur La Lys*, 1658, by Peeter Snayers [1592–1667]/Prado, Madrid, Spain/Index/The Bridgeman Art Library)

How did absolutism evolve in the seventeenth century in Spain, France, and Austria?

RULERS IN ABSOLUTIST STATES asserted that, because they were chosen by God, they were responsible to God alone. Under the rule of **absolutism**, monarchs claimed exclusive power to make and enforce laws, denying any other institution or group the authority to check their power. Spain, France, and Austria provide three key examples of the development of the absolutist state.

Spain

The discovery of silver at Potosí in 1541 (see page 476) had produced momentous wealth for Spain, allowing it to dominate Europe militarily. Yet Spain had inherent weaknesses that the vast wealth of empire had hidden. It was a combination of different kingdoms with their own traditions and loyalties. Spanish silver had created great wealth but also dependency. While Creoles undertook new industries in the colonies and European nations targeted Spanish colonial trade, industry and finance in Spain itself remained undeveloped.

The impact of these developments became apparent during the first half of the seventeenth century. Between 1610 and 1650 Spanish trade with the colonies

absolutism

▶ A political system common to early modern Europe in which monarchs claimed exclusive power to make and enforce laws, without checks by other institutions; this system was limited in practice by the need to maintain legitimacy and compromise with elites.

Why and how did the constitutional state triumph in England and the Dutch Republic?

How did European nations compete for trade and empire in the Americas and Asia?

How did Russian rulers build an absolutist monarchy and expand into a powerful empire?

✓ **LearningCurve**
Check what you know.

in the New World fell 60 percent due to competition from colonial industries and from Dutch and English traders. At the same time, disease decimated the enslaved workers who toiled in South American silver mines. Moreover, the mines started to run dry, and the quantity of metal produced steadily declined after 1620.

In Madrid royal expenditures constantly exceeded income. To meet state debt, the Spanish crown repeatedly devalued the coinage and declared bankruptcy, which resulted in the collapse of national credit and steep inflation. Meanwhile, commerce and manufacturing shrank. To make matters worse, in 1609 the Crown expelled some three hundred thousand Moriscos, or former Muslims, significantly reducing the pool of skilled workers and merchants.

Spanish aristocrats, attempting to maintain an extravagant lifestyle they could no longer afford, increased the rents on their estates. High rents and heavy taxes drove the peasants from the land, leading to a decline in agricultural productivity. In cities wages and production stagnated.

Spain's situation worsened with internal conflicts and fresh military defeats during the Thirty Years' War and the remainder of the seventeenth century. In the 1640s Spain faced serious revolts in Catalonia, Sicily, and the Spanish Netherlands. The Treaty of Westphalia, which ended the Thirty Years' War, compelled Spain to recognize the independence of the Dutch Republic, and another treaty in 1659 granted extensive territories to France. Finally, in 1688 the Spanish crown reluctantly recognized the independence of Portugal. With these losses, the era of Spanish dominance in Europe ended.

The Foundations of French Absolutism

At the beginning of the seventeenth century France's position appeared extremely weak. Struggling to recover from decades of religious civil war, France posed little threat to Spain's predominance in Europe. By the end of the century the countries' positions were reversed.

Henry IV (r. 1589–1610) inaugurated a remarkable recovery by defusing religious tensions and rebuilding France's economy. He issued the Edict of Nantes in 1598, allowing Huguenots (French Protestants) the right to worship in 150 traditionally Protestant towns throughout France. He invested in infrastructure and raised revenue by selling royal offices instead of charging high taxes. Despite his efforts at peace, Henry was murdered in 1610 by a Catholic zealot.

Cardinal Richelieu (1585–1642) became first minister of the French crown on behalf of Henry's young son Louis XIII (r. 1610–1643). Richelieu designed his domestic policies to strengthen royal control. He extended the use of intendants, commissioners for each of France's thirty-two districts who were appointed by and were responsible to the monarch. As the intendants' power increased under Richelieu, so did the power of the centralized French state.

Cardinal Jules Mazarin (1602–1661) succeeded Richelieu as chief minister for the next child-king, the four-year-old Louis XIV who inherited the throne from his father in 1643. Mazarin's struggle to increase royal revenues led to the uprisings of 1648–1653 known as the Fronde. In Paris magistrates of the Parlement of Paris, the nation's most important law court, were outraged by the Crown's autocratic measures. These so-called robe nobles (named for the robes they wore in court) encouraged violent protest by the common people. As rebellion spread outside

CHAPTER LOCATOR | How did the Protestant and Catholic Reformations shape colonial expansion? | How did seventeenth-century European states overcome social and economic crisis? | **How did absolutism evolve in in Spain, France, and Austria?**

524 CHAPTER 18
EUROPEAN POWER AND EXPANSION

Paris and to the sword nobles (the traditional warrior nobility), civil order broke down completely, and young Louis XIV had to flee Paris.

Much of the rebellion faded, however, when Louis XIV was declared king in his own right in 1651. The French people were desperate for peace and stability after the disorders of the Fronde and were willing to accept a strong monarch who could restore order. Louis pledged to do just that.

Louis XIV and Absolutism

During the long reign of Louis XIV (r. 1643–1715), the French monarchy reached the peak of absolutist development. Louis believed in the **divine right of kings**: God had established kings as his rulers on earth, and they were answerable ultimately to him alone. However, he also recognized that kings could not simply do as they pleased. They had to obey God's laws and rule for the good of the people.

divine right of kings

▶ The belief propagated by absolutist monarchs that they derived their power from God and were only answerable to him.

Like his counterpart, the Kangxi emperor of China, who inherited his realm only two decades after the Sun King did (see page 622), Louis XIV impressed his subjects with his discipline and hard work. He ruled his realm through several councils of state and insisted on taking a personal role in many of the councils' decisions.

Although personally tolerant, Louis hated division. He insisted that religious unity was essential to the security of the state. In 1685 Louis revoked the Edict of Nantes. Around two hundred thousand Protestants, including some of the kingdom's most highly skilled artisans, fled France. Louis's insistence on "one king, one law, one religion" contrasts sharply with the religious tolerance exhibited by the Ottoman Empire (see page 499).

Despite his claims to absolute authority, there were multiple constraints on Louis's power. As a representative of divine power, he was obliged to rule in a way that seemed consistent with virtue and benevolent authority. He had to uphold the laws issued by his royal predecessors. Moreover, he also relied on the collaboration of nobles. Without their cooperation, it would have been impossible for Louis to extend his power throughout France or wage his many foreign wars.

Expansion Within Europe

Louis XIV kept France at war for thirty-three of the fifty-four years of his personal rule. Under the leadership of François le Tellier, marquis de Louvois, Louis's secretary of state for war, France acquired a huge professional army. The French army almost tripled in size. Uniforms and weapons were standardized, and a system of training and promotion was devised. As in so many other matters, Louis's model was emulated across Europe.

During this long period of warfare, Louis's goal was to expand France to what he considered its natural borders. His results were mixed. During the 1660s and 1670s, French armies won a number of important victories. The wars of the 1680s and 1690s, however, brought no additional territories and placed unbearable strains on French resources.

Louis's last war, the War of the Spanish Succession (1701–1713), was endured by a French people suffering high taxes, crop failure, and widespread malnutrition and death. This war was the result of Louis's unwillingness to abide by a previous

Why and how did the constitutional state triumph in England and the Dutch Republic?

How did European nations compete for trade and empire in the Americas and Asia?

How did Russian rulers build an absolutist monarchy and expand into a powerful empire?

✔️ LearningCurve
Check what you know.

525

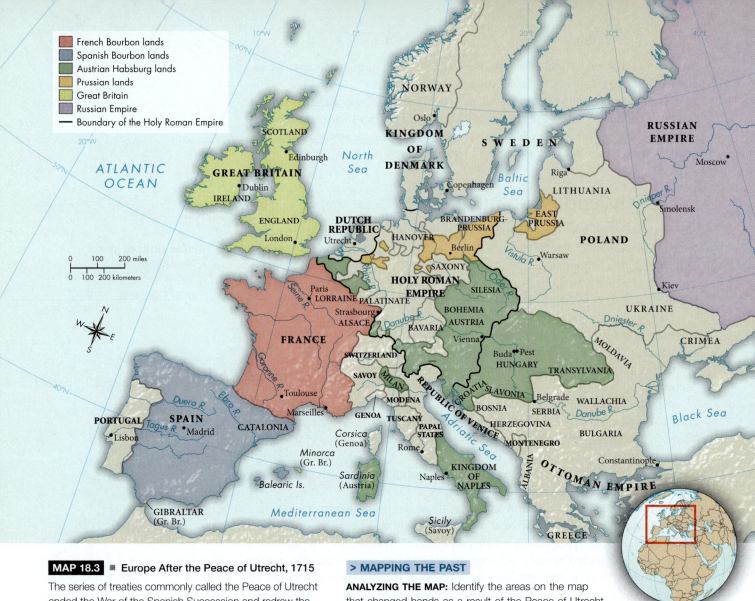

Legend:
- French Bourbon lands
- Spanish Bourbon lands
- Austrian Habsburg lands
- Prussian lands
- Great Britain
- Russian Empire
- — Boundary of the Holy Roman Empire

MAP 18.3 ■ Europe After the Peace of Utrecht, 1715

The series of treaties commonly called the Peace of Utrecht ended the War of the Spanish Succession and redrew the map of Europe. A French Bourbon king succeeded to the Spanish throne. France surrendered the Spanish Netherlands (later Belgium), then in French hands, to Austria and recognized the Hohenzollern rulers of Prussia. Spain ceded Gibraltar to Great Britain, for which it has been a strategic naval station ever since. Spain also granted Britain the *asiento*, the contract for supplying African slaves to America.

> **MAPPING THE PAST**

ANALYZING THE MAP: Identify the areas on the map that changed hands as a result of the Peace of Utrecht. How did these changes affect the balance of power in Europe?

CONNECTIONS: How and why did so many European countries possess scattered or discontiguous territories? What does this suggest about European politics in this period? Does this map suggest potential for future conflict?

agreement to divide Spanish possessions between France and the Holy Roman Emperor upon the death of the childless Spanish king Charles II (r. 1665–1700). In 1701 the English, Dutch, Austrians, and Prussians formed the Grand Alliance against Louis XIV. War dragged on until 1713, when it was ended by the Peace of Utrecht (Map 18.3).

The Peace of Utrecht marked the end of French expansion. Thirty-three years of war had given France the rights to all of Alsace and some commercial centers in the north. But at what price? At the time of Louis's death in 1715, an exhausted France hovered on the brink of bankruptcy.

CHAPTER LOCATOR | How did the Protestant and Catholic Reformations shape colonial expansion? | How did seventeenth-century European states overcome social and economic crisis? | **How did absolutism evolve in in Spain, France, and Austria?**

526 CHAPTER 18 EUROPEAN POWER AND EXPANSION

The Economic Policy of Mercantilism

France's ability to build armies and fight wars depended on a strong economy. Fortunately for Louis, his controller general, Jean-Baptiste Colbert (1619–1683), proved to be a financial genius. Colbert's central principle was that the wealth and the economy of France should serve the state. To this end, Colbert rigorously applied mercantilist policies to France.

Mercantilism is a collection of governmental policies for the regulation of economic activities by and for the state. It derives from the idea that a nation's international power is based on its wealth, specifically its supply of gold and silver. To accumulate wealth, a country always had to sell more goods abroad than it bought from foreign countries.

To increase exports, Colbert supported old industries and created new ones. He enacted new production regulations, created guilds to boost quality standards, and encouraged foreign craftsmen to immigrate to France. To encourage the purchase of French goods, he abolished many domestic tariffs and raised tariffs on foreign products. In 1664 Colbert founded the Company of the East Indies with hopes of competing with the Dutch for Asian trade. Colbert also sought to increase France's control over and presence in New France (Canada) (see page 835).

During Colbert's tenure as controller general, Louis was able to pursue his goals without massive tax increases and without creating a stream of new offices. The constant pressure of warfare after Colbert's death, however, undid many of his economic achievements.

mercantilism
▶ A system of economic regulations aimed at increasing the power of the state derived from the belief that a nation's international power was based on its wealth, specifically its supply of gold and silver.

The Austrian Habsburgs

Like all of central Europe, the Austrian Habsburgs emerged from the Thirty Years' War impoverished and exhausted. Their efforts to destroy Protestantism in the German lands and to turn the weak Holy Roman Empire into a real state had failed. Defeat in central Europe encouraged the Austrian Habsburgs to turn away from a quest for imperial dominance and to focus inward and eastward in an attempt to unify their diverse holdings.

Habsburg victory over Bohemia during the Thirty Years' War was an important step in this direction. Ferdinand II (r. 1619–1637) drastically reduced the power of the Bohemian Estates, the largely Protestant representative assembly. He also confiscated the landholdings of Protestant nobles and gave them to his supporters. After 1650 a large portion of the Bohemian nobility was of recent origin and owed its success to the Habsburgs.

With the support of this new nobility, the Habsburgs established direct rule over Bohemia. Under their rule, the condition of the serfs worsened substantially. The Habsburgs also successfully eliminated Protestantism in Bohemia. These changes were important steps in creating absolutist rule.

Ferdinand III (r. 1637–1657) continued to build state power. He centralized the government in the empire's German-speaking provinces, which formed the core Habsburg holdings, and established a permanent standing army. Between 1683 and 1699 the Habsburgs pushed the Ottomans from most of Hungary and Transylvania. The recovery of all the former kingdom of Hungary was completed in 1718.

Austrian Expansion, to 1699

■ Austrian Habsburg territory in 1648
■ Lands taken from Ottomans by Austrian Habsburgs, to 1699

Why and how did the constitutional state triumph in England and the Dutch Republic?

How did European nations compete for trade and empire in the Americas and Asia?

How did Russian rulers build an absolutist monarchy and expand into a powerful empire?

✓ LearningCurve
Check what you know.

Despite its reduced strength, the Hungarian nobility effectively thwarted the full development of Habsburg absolutism. Throughout the seventeenth century Hungarian nobles periodically rose in revolt against the Habsburgs. In 1703, with the Habsburgs bogged down in the War of the Spanish Succession, the Hungarians rose in one last patriotic rebellion under Prince Francis Rákóczy (RAH-coht-see). Rákóczy and his forces were eventually defeated, but the Habsburgs agreed to restore many of the traditional privileges of the Hungarian aristocracy in return for the country's acceptance of Habsburg rule.

Elsewhere, the Habsburgs made significant achievements in state-building by forging consensus with the church and the nobility. A sense of common identity and loyalty to the monarchy grew among elites in Habsburg lands. German became the language of the state, and Vienna became the political and cultural center of the empire.

The Absolutist Palace

In 1682 Louis moved his court and government to the newly renovated palace at Versailles, in the countryside southwest of Paris. The palace quickly became the center of political, social, and cultural life. The king required all great nobles to spend at least part of the year in attendance on him there.

Louis further revolutionized court life by establishing an elaborate set of etiquette rituals to mark every moment of his day, from waking up and dressing in the morning to removing his clothing and retiring at night. These rituals were far from meaningless or trivial. The king controlled immense resources and privileges; access to him meant favored treatment for government offices, military and religious posts, state pensions, honorary titles, and a host of other benefits.

A system of patronage—in which a higher-ranked individual protected a lower-ranked one in return for loyalty and services—flowed from the court to the provinces. Through this mechanism Louis gained cooperation from powerful nobles. Although they were denied public offices and posts, women played a central role in the patronage system. At court the king's wife, mistresses, and other female relatives recommended individuals for honors, advocated policy decisions, and brokered alliances between noble factions.

With Versailles as the center of European politics, French culture grew in international prestige. French became the language of polite society and international diplomacy. France inspired a cosmopolitan European culture in the late seventeenth century that looked to Versailles as its center. Moreover, Louis's rival European monarchs soon followed his example and palace building became a Europe-wide phenomenon.

> **QUICK REVIEW**

Why did Spain's situation deteriorate over the course of the seventeenth century? Why did France's improve?

CHAPTER LOCATOR | How did the Protestant and Catholic Reformations shape colonial expansion? | How did seventeenth-century European states overcome social and economic crisis? | How did absolutism evolve in in Spain, France, and Austria?

528 CHAPTER 18
EUROPEAN POWER AND EXPANSION

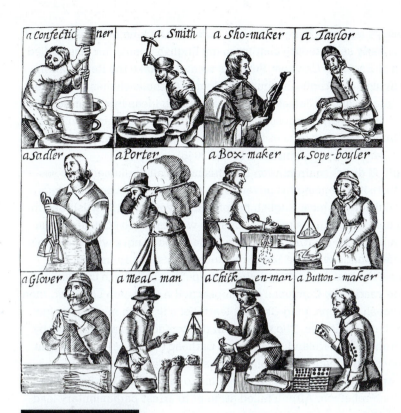

Puritan Occupations

These twelve engravings depict typical Puritan occupations and show that the Puritans came primarily from the artisan and lower middle classes. The governing classes and peasants made up a much smaller percentage of Puritans, and most generally adhered to the traditions of the Church of England. (Visual Connection Archive)

Why and how did the constitutional state triumph in England and the Dutch Republic?

WHILE MOST EUROPEAN NATIONS developed absolutist states in the seventeenth century, England and the Netherlands evolved toward **constitutionalism**, which is the limitation of government by law. Constitutionalism also implies a balance between the authority and power of the government, on the one hand, and the rights and liberties of the subjects, on the other.

Religious Divides and Civil War

In 1603 beloved Queen Elizabeth was succeeded by her Scottish cousin James Stuart, who ruled England as James I (r. 1603–1625). Like Louis XIV, James believed that a monarch had a divine right to his authority and was responsible only to God. James I and his son Charles I (r. 1625–1649) considered any legislative constraint on their power a threat to their divine-right prerogative. Consequently, at every meeting of Parliament between 1603 and 1640, bitter squabbles erupted between the Crown and the House of Commons.

constitutionalism

▶ A form of government in which power is limited by law and balanced between the authority and power of the government, on the one hand, and the rights and liberties of the subject or citizen, on the other; it includes constitutional monarchies and republics.

Why and how did the constitutional state triumph in England and the Dutch Republic?	How did European nations compete for trade and empire in the Americas and Asia?	How did Russian rulers build an absolutist monarchy and expand into a powerful empire?	✓ LearningCurve Check what you know.

Puritans

▶ Members of a sixteenth- and seventeenth-century reform movement within the Church of England that advocated purifying it of Roman Catholic elements, such as bishops, elaborate ceremonials, and wedding rings.

The English Civil War, 1642–1649

SCOTLAND

IRELAND
Irish Sea
North Sea
Manchester
ENGLAND
Naseby 1645
London
Langport 1645
Canterbury
English Channel

☐ Parliamentarians
☐ Royalists
✸ Major battle

Religious issues also embittered relations between the king and the House of Commons. In the early seventeenth century many English people felt dissatisfied with the Church of England. Calvinist **Puritans** wanted to take the Reformation further by "purifying" the Anglican Church of Roman Catholic elements, including crown-appointed bishops. James I responded to such ideas by declaring, "No bishop, no king." His son and successor, Charles I, further antagonized subjects by marrying a French Catholic princess and supporting the high-handed policies of archbishop of Canterbury William Laud (1573–1645).

Charles avoided direct confrontation by refusing to call Parliament into session from 1629 to 1640, financing his government through extraordinary stopgap levies considered illegal by most English people. However, when Scottish Calvinists revolted against his religious policies, Charles was forced to summon Parliament to obtain funding for an army to put down the revolt. Angry with the king's behavior and sympathetic with the Scots' religious beliefs, the House of Commons passed the Triennial Act in 1641, which compelled the king to call Parliament every three years. The Commons also impeached Archbishop Laud and then threatened to abolish bishops. King Charles, fearful of a Scottish invasion, reluctantly accepted these measures. The next act in the conflict was precipitated by the outbreak of rebellion in Ireland. In 1641 the Catholic gentry of Ireland led an uprising in response to a feared invasion by British anti-Catholic forces.

Without an army, Charles I could neither come to terms with the Scots nor respond to the Irish rebellion. After a failed attempt to arrest parliamentary leaders, Charles left London and began to raise an army. In response, Parliament formed its own army, the New Model Army.

The English civil war (1642–1649) pitted the power of the king against that of Parliament. After three years of fighting, Parliament's army defeated the king's forces at the Battles of Naseby and Langport in the summer of 1645. Charles refused to concede defeat, and both sides waited for a decisive event. This arrived in the form of the army under the leadership of Oliver Cromwell, a member of the House of Commons and a devout Puritan. In 1647 Cromwell's troops captured the king and dismissed members of the Parliament who opposed Cromwell's actions. In 1649 the remaining representatives, known as the Rump Parliament, put Charles on trial for high treason. Charles was found guilty and beheaded on January 30, 1649.

The Puritan Protectorate

With the execution of Charles, the monarchy was abolished and a commonwealth, or republican government, was proclaimed. Theoretically, legislative power rested in the surviving members of Parliament, and executive power was lodged in a council of state. In fact, the army that had defeated the king controlled the government, and Oliver Cromwell controlled the army. Though called the Protectorate, the rule of Cromwell (1653–1658) was a form of military dictatorship. Reflecting Puritan ideas of morality, Cromwell's state forbade sports, kept the theaters closed, and rigorously censored the press.

On the issue of religion, Cromwell favored some degree of tolerance, and all Christians except Roman Catholics had the right to practice their faiths. Cromwell had long associated Catholicism in Ireland with sedition and heresy, and he led an army there to reconquer the country in August 1649. Following Cromwell's recon-

CHAPTER LOCATOR | How did the Protestant and Catholic Reformations shape colonial expansion? | How did seventeenth-century European states overcome social and economic crisis? | How did absolutism evolve in in Spain, France, and Austria?

530 CHAPTER 18 EUROPEAN POWER AND EXPANSION

quest, the English banned Catholicism in Ireland, executed priests, and confiscated land from Catholics for English and Scottish settlers.

The Protectorate collapsed when Cromwell died in 1658 and his ineffectual son succeeded him. Fed up with military rule, the English longed for a return to civilian government. By 1660 they were ready to restore the monarchy.

Constitutional Monarchy

The Restoration of 1660 brought to the throne Charles II (r. 1660–1685), the eldest son of Charles I. Both houses of Parliament were also restored, as was the Anglican Church. However, Charles was succeeded by his Catholic brother James II, arousing fears of a return of Catholicism. A group of eminent persons in Parliament and the Church of England offered the English throne to James's Protestant daughter Mary and her Dutch husband, Prince William of Orange. In December 1688 James II, his queen, and their infant son fled to France. Early in 1689 William and Mary were crowned king and queen of England.

In England these events, known as the Glorious Revolution, represented the final destruction of the idea of divine-right monarchy. The men who brought about the revolution framed their intentions in the **Bill of Rights of 1689**, which was formulated in direct response to Stuart absolutism. Law was to be made in Parliament; once made, it could not be suspended by the Crown. Parliament had to be called at least once every three years. The Bill of Rights also established the independence of the judiciary and mandated that there be no standing army in peacetime. Protestants could possess arms, but the Catholic minority could not. Catholics could not inherit the throne. Additional legislation granted freedom of worship to Protestant dissenters but not to Catholics.

The Glorious Revolution and the concept of representative government found its best defense in political philosopher John Locke's *Second Treatise of Civil Government* (1690). Locke (1632–1704) maintained that a government that oversteps its proper function—protecting the natural rights of life, liberty, and property—becomes a tyranny. Under a tyrannical government, he argued, the people have the natural right to rebellion.

Although the events of 1688 and 1689 brought England closer to Locke's ideal, they did not constitute a democratic revolution. The Glorious Revolution placed sovereignty in Parliament, and Parliament represented the upper classes.

Bill of Rights of 1689
▶ A bill passed by Parliament and accepted by William and Mary that limited the powers of British monarchs and affirmed those of Parliament.

The Dutch Republic

The independence of the Republic of the United Provinces of the Netherlands was recognized in 1648 in the treaty that ended the Thirty Years' War. Rejecting the rule of a monarch, the Dutch adopted a system of **republicanism**, whereby power rested in the hands of the people and was exercised through elected representatives. An oligarchy of wealthy businessmen called regents handled domestic affairs in each province's Estates, or assemblies. The provincial Estates held virtually all the power. A federal assembly, or States General, handled foreign affairs and war, but all issues had to be referred back to the local Estates for approval, and each of the seven provinces could veto any proposed legislation. Holland, the province with the largest navy and the most wealth, usually dominated the republic and the States General.

republicanism
▶ A form of government in which there is no monarch and power rests in the hands of the people as exercised through elected representatives.

Why and how did the constitutional state triumph in England and the Dutch Republic?

How did European nations compete for trade and empire in the Americas and Asia?

How did Russian rulers build an absolutist monarchy and expand into a powerful empire?

✓ LearningCurve
Check what you know.

> PICTURING THE PAST

ANALYZING THE IMAGE: What social and cultural values does this painting seem to celebrate? What insight does the painter offer into masculine and feminine roles in this society? Why do you think the husband and wife are standing separately and not together, as they probably would in a modern family portrait?

CONNECTIONS: Based on your reading in this chapter, how might the portrait of a more typical European family of 1640 differ from this one? Why would a family in the Netherlands have a different lifestyle from many families in other European countries?

In each province, the Estates appointed an executive officer, known as the stadholder. Although in theory freely chosen by the Estates, in practice the reigning prince of Orange usually held the office of stadholder in several of the seven provinces of the republic. Tensions persisted between supporters of the House of Orange and those of the staunchly republican Estates, who suspected the princes of harboring monarchical ambitions.

Global trade and commerce brought the Dutch the highest standard of living in Europe, perhaps in the world. Salaries were high, and all classes of society ate well. The moral and ethical bases of Dutch commercial wealth were thrift, frugality, and religious tolerance. Jews enjoyed a level of acceptance and assimilation in Dutch business and general culture unique in early modern Europe. (See "Individuals in Society: Glückel of Hameln," page 533.) Tolerance contributed to profits by attracting a great deal of foreign capital and investment.

> **QUICK REVIEW**

What limits had been put in place on the power of English kings by the end of the seventeenth century?

CHAPTER LOCATOR | How did the Protestant and Catholic Reformations shape colonial expansion? | How did seventeenth-century European states overcome social and economic crisis? | How did absolutism evolve in in Spain, France, and Austria?

CHAPTER 18

532 EUROPEAN POWER AND EXPANSION

Glückel of Hameln

In 1690 a Jewish widow in the small German town of Hameln in Lower Saxony sat down to write her autobiography. She wanted to distract her mind from the terrible grief she felt over the death of her husband and to provide her twelve children with a record. She told them that she was writing her memoirs "so you will know from what sort of people you have sprung, lest today or tomorrow your beloved children or grandchildren came and know naught of their family." Out of her pain and heightened consciousness, Glückel (1646–1724) produced an invaluable source for scholars.

She was born in Hamburg two years before the end of the Thirty Years' War. In 1649 the merchants of Hamburg expelled the Jews, who moved to nearby Altona, then under Danish rule. When the Swedes overran Altona in 1657–1658, the Jews returned to Hamburg "purely at the mercy of the Town Council." Glückel's narrative unfolds against a background of the constant harassment to which Jews were subjected — special papers, permits, bribes — and in Hameln she wrote, "And so it has been to this day and, I fear, will continue in like fashion."

When Glückel was "barely twelve," her father betrothed her to Chayim Hameln, and they married when she was fourteen. She describes him as "the perfect pattern of the pious Jew," a man who stopped his work every day for study and prayer, fasted, and was scrupulously honest in his business dealings. Only a few years older than Glückel, Chayim earned his living dealing in precious metals and in making small loans on pledges (pawned goods). This work required constant travel to larger cities, markets, and fairs, often in bad weather, always over dangerous roads. Chayim consulted his wife about all his business dealings. As he lay dying, a friend asked if he had any last wishes.

"None," he replied. "My wife knows everything. She shall do as she has always done." For thirty years Glückel had been his friend, full business partner, and wife. They had thirteen children, twelve of whom survived their father, eight then unmarried. As Chayim had foretold, Glückel succeeded in launching the boys in careers and in providing dowries for the girls.

Glückel's world was her family, the Jewish community of Hameln, and the Jewish communities into which her children married. Her social and business activities took her across Europe, from Amsterdam to Berlin, from Danzig to Vienna; thus her world was far from narrow or provincial. She took great pride that Prince Frederick of Cleves, later king of Prussia, danced at the wedding of her eldest daughter. The rising prosperity of Chayim's businesses allowed the couple to maintain up to six servants.

Glückel was deeply religious, and her culture was steeped in Jewish literature, legends, and mystical and secular works. Above all, she relied on the Bible. Her language, heavily sprinkled with scriptural references, testifies to a rare familiarity with the Scriptures.

Students who wish to learn about seventeenth-century business practices, the importance of the dowry in marriage, childbirth, Jewish life, birthrates, family celebrations, and even the meaning of life can gain a good deal from the memoirs of this extraordinary woman who was, in the words of one of her descendants, the poet Heinrich Heine, "the gift of a world to me."

Source: *The Memoirs of Glückel of Hameln* (New York: Schocken Books, 1977).

QUESTIONS FOR ANALYSIS

1. Consider the ways in which Glückel of Hameln was both an ordinary and an extraordinary woman of her times. Would you call her a marginal or a central person in her society? Why?
2. How might Glückel's successes be attributed to the stabilizing force of absolutism in the seventeenth century?

Although no images of Glückel exist, Rembrandt's *The Jewish Bride* suggests the mutual devotion of Glückel and her husband. (Rijksmuseum, Amsterdam, The Netherlands/The Bridgeman Art Library)

LaunchPad

ONLINE DOCUMENT PROJECT

What factors shaped life for European Jews in the early modern era? Read excerpts from Glückel of Hameln's memoirs and other accounts of Jewish life, and then complete a quiz and writing assignment based on the evidence and details from this chapter. *See inside the front cover to learn more.*

> How did European nations compete for global trade and empire in the Americas and Asia?

The Fur Trade

In the early seventeenth century, European fur traders relied on Native Americans' expertise and experience, leading to the equal relations depicted in this scene from the colony of New Sweden (in modern-day Pennsylvania). The action in the background shows violence among indigenous groups, rivalries exacerbated by contact with Europeans and their trade goods. Hudson's Bay Company, the English colonial trading company, issued its own tokens as currency in the fur trade. This token, dating from the mid-nineteenth century, displays the company's crest, which says "a skin for a skin" in Latin. Two stags face each other, with a fox at the top and four beavers on the shield. Traders received tokens for the pelts they sold and could use them to purchase goods from the company's store. European demand for beaver hats, made from the felted pelts of beavers, drove the tremendous expansion of the North American fur trade in the beginning of the seventeenth century. (engraving: From *Geographia Americae with An Account of the Delaware Indians, Based on Surveys and Notes Made 1654–1656,* by Peter Lindestrom, published by The Swedish Colonial Society/Visual Connection Archive; token: © National Maritime Museum, London, UK/The Image Works)

FOR MUCH OF THE SIXTEENTH CENTURY, the Spanish and Portuguese dominated European overseas trade and colonization (see Chapter 16). In the early seventeenth century, however, England, France, and the Netherlands challenged Spain's monopoly.

| How did the Protestant and Catholic Reformations shape colonial expansion? | How did seventeenth-century European states overcome social and economic crisis? | How did absolutism evolve in in Spain, France, and Austria? |

The Dutch Trading Empire

The so-called golden age of the Dutch Republic in the seventeenth century was built on its commercial prosperity and its highly original republican system of government. The Dutch came to dominate the European shipping business by putting profits from their original industry — herring fishing — into shipbuilding. They then took aim at Portugal's immensely lucrative Asian trade empire.

In 1599 a Dutch fleet returned to Amsterdam from a voyage to South East Asia carrying a huge cargo of spices. Those who had invested in the expedition received a 100 percent profit. The voyage led to the establishment in 1602 of the Dutch East India Company, founded with the stated intention of capturing the spice trade from the Portuguese.

In return for assisting Indonesian princes in local squabbles and disputes with the Portuguese, the Dutch won broad commercial concessions. Through agreements, seizures, and outright military aggression, they gained control of the western access to the Indonesian archipelago in the first half of the seventeenth century. Gradually, they acquired political domination over the archipelago itself. The Dutch were willing to use force more ruthlessly than the Portuguese and had superior organizational efficiency. These factors allowed them to expel the Portuguese from Ceylon and other East Indian islands in the 1660s and henceforth dominate the production and trade of spices. The company also established the colony of Cape Town on the southern tip of Africa as a provisioning point for its Asian fleets.

The Dutch also aspired to a role in the Americas (Map 18.4). Founded in 1621, the Dutch West India Company aggressively sought to open trade with North and South America and capture Spanish territories there. The company captured or destroyed hundreds of Spanish ships, seized the Spanish silver fleet in 1628, and claimed portions of Brazil and the Caribbean. The Dutch also successfully interceded in the transatlantic slave trade, establishing a large number of trading stations on the west coast of Africa. Ironically, the nation that was known as a bastion of tolerance and freedom came to be one of the principal operators of the slave trade starting in the 1640s.

Colonial Empires of England and France

England and France followed the Dutch in challenging Iberian dominance overseas. Unlike the Iberian powers, whose royal governments financed exploration and directly ruled the colonies, England, France, and the Netherlands conducted the initial phase of colonization through chartered companies with monopolies over settlement and trade in a given area.

After an unsuccessful first colony at Roanoke (in what is now North Carolina), the English colony of Virginia, founded at Jamestown in 1607, gained a steady hold by producing tobacco for a growing European market. In the 1670s English colonists from the Caribbean island of Barbados settled Carolina, where conditions were suitable for large rice plantations. During the late seventeenth century enslaved Africans replaced indentured servants as laborers on tobacco and rice plantations, and a harsh racial divide was imposed.

For the first settlers on the coast of New England, the reasons for seeking a new life in the colonies were more religious than economic. Many of these

Why and how did the constitutional state triumph in England and the Dutch Republic?

How did European nations compete for trade and empire in the Americas and Asia?

How did Russian rulers build an absolutist monarchy and expand into a powerful empire?

✓ LearningCurve
Check what you know.

535

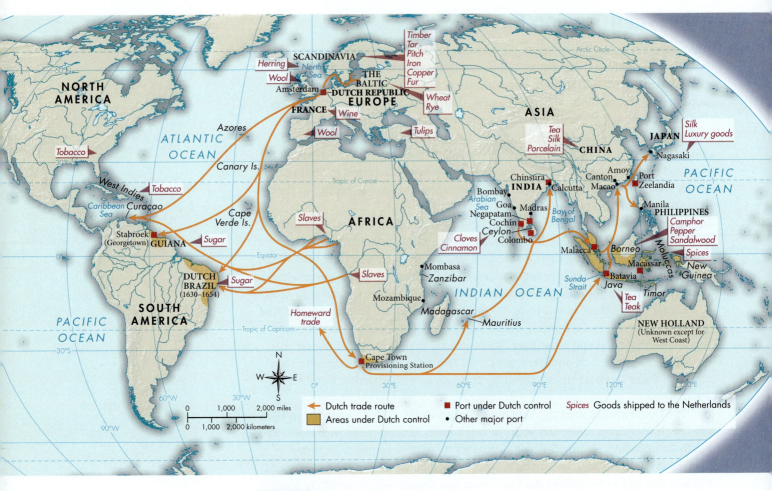

MAP 18.4 ■ Seventeenth-Century Dutch Commerce

Dutch wealth rested on commerce, and commerce depended on the huge Dutch merchant marine, manned by perhaps forty-eight thousand sailors. The fleet carried goods from all parts of the globe to the port of Amsterdam.

colonists were radical Protestants escaping Anglican repression. The small and struggling outpost of Plymouth Colony (1620) was followed by Massachusetts Bay Colony (1630), which grew into a prosperous settlement. Religious disputes in Massachusetts led to the dispersion of settlers into the new communities of Providence, Connecticut, Rhode Island, and New Haven. Because New England lacked the conditions for plantation agriculture, slavery was always a minor factor there.

As the English crown grew more interested in colonial expansion, efforts were made to acquire the territory between New England in the north and Virginia in the south. The goal was to unify English holdings and minimize French and Dutch competition on the Atlantic seaboard. The results of these efforts were the mid-Atlantic colonies: the Catholic settlement of Maryland (1632); New York, captured from the Dutch in 1664; and the Quaker colony of Pennsylvania (1681).

Whereas English settlements were largely agricultural, the French established trading factories in present-day Canada, much like those in Asia and Africa. Louis XIV's capable controller general, Jean-Baptiste Colbert, established direct

CHAPTER LOCATOR | How did the Protestant and Catholic Reformations shape colonial expansion? | How did seventeenth-century European states overcome social and economic crisis? | How did absolutism evolve in in Spain, France, and Austria?

CHAPTER 18
536 EUROPEAN POWER AND EXPANSION

royal control over New France (Canada) and tried to enlarge its population by sending colonists.

French immigration to New Canada remained small compared with the stream of settlers who came to British North America; nevertheless, the French were energetic and industrious traders and explorers. Following the waterways of the St. Lawrence River, the Great Lakes, and the Mississippi River, they ventured into much of North America in the 1670s and 1680s. In 1673 the Jesuit Jacques Marquette and the merchant Louis Joliet sailed down the Mississippi as far as present-day Arkansas. In 1682 Robert de La Salle traveled the Mississippi to the Gulf of Mexico, opening the way for French occupation of Louisiana.

In the first decades of the seventeenth century, English and French captains also challenged Spain's hold over the Caribbean (see Map 19.2, page 574), seizing a number of islands. These islands acquired new importance after 1640, when the Portuguese brought sugar plantations to Brazil. Sugar and slaves quickly followed in the West Indies (see pages 475–476), making the Caribbean plantations the most lucrative of all colonial possessions.

The northern European powers also expanded in Africa and Asia. In the 1600s France and England—along with Denmark and other northern European powers—established fortified trading posts, or factories, in West Africa as bases for purchasing slaves and in India and the Indian Ocean for spices and other luxury goods. Thus, by the end of the seventeenth century, a handful of European powers possessed overseas empires that truly spanned the globe.

European Claims in North America, 1714

Mercantilism and Colonial Wars

Trade to and among European overseas possessions was governed by mercantilist economic policy (see page 527). The mercantilist notion of a "zero-sum game," in which any country's gain must come from another country's loss, led to hostile competition and outright warfare among European powers over their colonial possessions.

In England Oliver Cromwell established the first of a series of **Navigation Acts** in 1651, and the restored monarchy of Charles II extended them in 1660 and 1663. The acts required most goods imported into England and Scotland (Great Britain after 1707) to be carried on British-owned ships with British crews or on ships of the country producing the article. Moreover, these laws gave British merchants and shipowners a virtual monopoly on trade with British colonies. These economic regulations were intended to eliminate foreign competition and to encourage the development of a British shipping industry whose seamen could serve when necessary in the Royal Navy.

The Navigation Acts were a form of economic warfare against the Dutch, who were far ahead of the English in shipping and foreign trade in the mid-seventeenth century. In conjunction with three Anglo-Dutch wars between 1652 and 1674, the Navigation Acts seriously damaged Dutch shipping and commerce. By the late seventeenth century the Netherlands was falling behind England in shipping, trade, and settlement.

Thereafter France was England's most serious rival in the competition for overseas empire. France was continental Europe's leading military power. It was already building a powerful fleet and a worldwide system of rigidly monopolized colonial trade. But the War of the Spanish Succession, the last of Louis XIV's many

Navigation Acts
▶ Mid-seventeenth-century English mercantilist laws that greatly restricted other countries' rights to trade with England and its colonies.

Why and how did the constitutional state triumph in England and the Dutch Republic?

How did European nations compete for trade and empire in the Americas and Asia?

How did Russian rulers build an absolutist monarchy and expand into a powerful empire?

☑ LearningCurve
Check what you know.

537

wars (see page 525), tilted the balance in favor of England. The 1713 Peace of Utrecht forced France to cede its North American holdings in Newfoundland, Nova Scotia, and the Hudson Bay territory to Britain. Spain was compelled to give Britain control of its West African slave trade and to let Britain send one ship of merchandise into the Spanish colonies annually. These acquisitions primed Britain to take a leading role in the growing Atlantic trade of the eighteenth century, including the transatlantic slave trade (discussed in Chapter 19).

People Beyond Borders

As they seized new territories, European nations produced maps proudly outlining their possessions. The situation on the ground, however, was often much more complicated than the lines on those maps would suggest. Many groups of people lived in the contested frontiers between empires, habitually crisscrossed their borders, or carved out niches within empires where they carried out their own lives in defiance of the official rules.

Restricted from owning land and holding many occupations in Europe, Jews were eager participants in colonial trade and established closely linked mercantile communities scattered across many different empires. Similarly, a community of Christian Armenians in Isfahan in the Safavid Empire formed the center of a trade network extending from London to Manila and Acapulco. Family ties and trust within these minority groups was a tremendous advantage in generating the financial credit and cooperation necessary for international commerce. Yet Jews and Armenians were minorities where they settled and vulnerable to persecution.

The nomadic Cossacks and Tartars who inhabited the steppes of the Don River basin that bordered the Russian and Ottoman Empires are yet another example of "in-between" peoples. The Cossacks and the Tartars maintained considerable political and cultural autonomy through the seventeenth century and enjoyed a degree of peaceful interaction. By the eighteenth century, however, both Ottoman and Russian rulers had expanded state control in their frontiers and had reined in the raiding and migration of nomadic steppe peoples. As their example suggests, the assertion of state authority in the seventeenth and eighteenth centuries made it progressively harder for all of these groups to retain autonomy from the grip of empire.

> ## QUICK REVIEW

What steps did England take toward the acquisition of an overseas empire in the seventeenth century?

CHAPTER LOCATOR | How did the Protestant and Catholic Reformations shape colonial expansion? | How did seventeenth-century European states overcome social and economic crisis? | How did absolutism evolve in in Spain, France, and Austria?

538 CHAPTER 18 EUROPEAN POWER AND EXPANSION

Russian Peasants

An eighteenth-century French artist visiting Russia recorded his impressions of the daily life of the Russian people in this etching of a fish merchant pulling his wares through a snowy village on a sleigh. Two caviar vendors behind him make a sale to a young mother standing at her doorstep with her baby in her arms. (From Jean-Baptiste Le Prince's second set of Russian etchings, 1765. Private Collection/Gérard PIERSON/www.amis-paris-petersbourg.org)

How did Russian rulers build a distinctive absolutist monarchy and expand into a vast and powerful empire?

RUSSIA OCCUPIED A UNIQUE POSITION among Eurasian states. With borders straddling eastern Europe and northwestern Asia, its development into a strong imperial state drew on elements from both continents.

Mongol Rule in Russia and the Rise of Moscow

In the thirteenth century the Mongols had conquered Kievan Rus, the medieval Slavic state that included most of present-day Ukraine, Belarus, and part of northwest Russia. For two hundred years the Mongols forced the Slavic princes to submit to their rule. The princes of the Grand Duchy of Moscow, a principality within Kievan Rus, became particularly adept at serving the Mongols. Eventually the Muscovite princes were able to destroy the other princes who were their rivals for power. Ivan III (r. 1462–1505), known as Ivan the Great, greatly expanded the principality of Moscow, claiming large territories in the north and east to the Siberian frontier.

| Why and how did the constitutional state triumph in England and the Dutch Republic? | How did European nations compete for trade and empire in the Americas and Asia? | **How did Russian rulers build an absolutist monarchy and expand into a powerful empire?** | ☑ LearningCurve Check what you know. |

By 1480 Ivan III was strong enough to refuse to pay tribute to the Mongols and declare the autonomy of Moscow. To legitimize his new position, Ivan and his successors borrowed elements of Mongol rule. They forced weaker Slavic principalities to render tribute and adopted Mongol institutions such as the tax system, postal routes, and census. Loyalty from the highest-ranking nobles, or boyars, helped the Muscovite princes consolidate their power.

Another source of legitimacy lay in Moscow's claim to the political and religious inheritance of the Byzantine Empire. After the empire's capital, Constantinople, fell to the Ottomans in 1453, the princes of Moscow saw themselves as heirs of the Byzantine caesars (emperors) and guardians of the Orthodox Christian Church.

Building the Russian Empire

Developments in Russia took a chaotic turn with the reign of Ivan IV (r. 1533–1584), the famous Ivan the Terrible, who ascended to the throne at age three. His mother died when he was eight, leaving Ivan to suffer insults and neglect from the boyars at court. At age sixteen he pushed aside his hated advisers and crowned himself tsar.

After the sudden death of his wife, however, Ivan began a campaign of persecution against those he suspected of opposing him. He executed members of leading boyar families, along with their families, friends, servants, and peasants. To replace them, Ivan created a new service nobility, whose loyalty was guaranteed by their dependence on the state for land and titles.

As landlords demanded more from the serfs who survived the persecutions, growing numbers of peasants fled toward recently conquered territories to the east and south. There they joined free groups and warrior bands known as **Cossacks**. Ivan responded by tying serfs ever more firmly to the land. Simultaneously, he ordered that urban dwellers be bound to their towns and jobs so that he could tax them more heavily. These restrictions checked the growth of the Russian middle classes and stood in sharp contrast to economic and social developments in western Europe.

Ivan's reign was successful in defeating the remnants of Mongol power, adding vast new territories to the realm, and laying the foundations for the huge multiethnic Russian empire. In the 1550s, strengthened by an alliance with Cossack bands, he conquered the Muslim khanates of Kazan and Astrakhan and brought the fertile steppe region around the Volga River under Russian control. In the 1580s Cossacks fighting for the Russian state crossed the Ural Mountains and began the long conquest of Siberia.

Following Ivan's death, Russia entered a chaotic period known as the Time of Troubles (1598–1613). While Ivan's relatives struggled for power, the Cossacks and peasants rebelled against nobles and officials. This social explosion from below brought the nobles together. They crushed the Cossack rebellion and elected Ivan's grandnephew, Michael Romanov (r. 1613–1645), the new hereditary tsar.

Despite the turbulence of the period, the Romanov tsars, like their western European counterparts, made further achievements in territorial expansion and state-building. After a long war, Russia gained land to the west in Ukraine in 1667. By the end of the century it had completed the conquest of Siberia to the east. This vast territorial expansion brought Russian power to the Pacific Ocean

Cossacks

▶ Free groups and outlaw armies living on the borders of Russian territory from the fourteenth century onward. By the end of the sixteenth century they had formed an alliance with the Russian state.

CHAPTER LOCATOR | How did the Protestant and Catholic Reformations shape colonial expansion? | How did seventeenth-century European states overcome social and economic crisis? | How did absolutism evolve in in Spain, France, and Austria?

540 CHAPTER 18 EUROPEAN POWER AND EXPANSION

and was only checked by the powerful Qing Dynasty. The basis of Russian wealth in Siberia was furs, which the state collected by forced annual tribute payments from local peoples. Profits from furs and other natural resources, especially mining in the eighteenth century, funded expansion of the Russian bureaucracy and the army.

The growth of state power did nothing to improve the lot of the common people. In 1649 a new law code extended serfdom to all peasants in the realm, giving lords unrestricted rights over their serfs and establishing penalties for harboring runaways. The new code also removed the privileges that non-Russian elites had enjoyed within the empire and required conversion to Russian orthodoxy. Henceforth, Moscow maintained strict control of trade and administration throughout the empire.

The peace imposed by harsh Russian rule was disrupted in 1670 by a failed rebellion led by the Cossack Stenka Razin, who attracted a great army of urban poor and peasants. The ease with which Moscow crushed the rebellion testifies to the success of the Russian state in unifying and consolidating its empire.

Peter the Great and Russia's Turn to the West

Heir to his predecessors' efforts at state-building, Peter the Great (r. 1682–1725) embarked on a tremendous campaign to accelerate and complete these processes. Peter built on the service obligations of Ivan the Terrible and his successors and continued their tradition of territorial expansion. Peter's ambitions hinged on gaining access to the sea by extending Russia's borders to the Black Sea (controlled by the Ottomans) and to the Baltic Sea (dominated by Sweden).

Peter embarked on his first territorial goal by conquering the Ottoman fort of Azov in 1696 and quickly built Russia's first navy base nearby. In 1697 the tsar went on an eighteen-month tour of western European capitals. Peter was fascinated by foreign technology, and he hoped to forge an anti-Ottoman alliance to strengthen his hold on the Black Sea. Peter failed to secure a military alliance, but he did learn his lessons from the growing power of the Dutch and the English.

To realize his second goal, Peter entered the Great Northern War (1700–1721) against Sweden. After a humiliating defeat at the Battle of Narva in 1700, Peter responded with measures designed to increase state power, strengthen his military, and gain victory. He required all nobles to serve in the army or in the civil administration — for life. Peter also created schools and universities to produce skilled technicians and experts. Furthermore, he established an interlocking military-civilian bureaucracy with fourteen ranks, and he decreed that all had to start at the bottom and work toward the top. He sought talented foreigners and placed them in his service. These measures gradually combined to make the army and government more powerful and efficient.

Peter also greatly increased the service requirements of commoners. He established a regular standing army of peasant-soldiers, drafted for life. In addition, he created special regiments of Cossacks and foreign mercenaries. To fund the army, taxes on peasants increased threefold during Peter's reign. Serfs were also arbitrarily assigned to work in the growing number of factories and mines that supplied the military.

Why and how did the constitutional state triumph in England and the Dutch Republic?

How did European nations compete for trade and empire in the Americas and Asia?

How did Russian rulers build an absolutist monarchy and expand into a powerful empire?

✓ LearningCurve
Check what you know.

541

Peter the Great

This compelling portrait by Grigory Musikiysky captures the strength and determination of the warrior-tsar in 1723, after more than three decades of personal rule. In his hand Peter holds the scepter, symbol of royal sovereignty, and across his breastplate is draped an ermine fur, a mark of honor. In the background are the battleships of Russia's new Baltic fleet and the famous St. Peter and St. Paul Fortress that Peter built in St. Petersburg. Peter the Great commissioned this magnificent new crown (left) for himself for his 1682 joint coronation with his half brother Ivan. (crown: bpk, Berlin/Kremlin Museum, Moscow, Russia/Art Resource, NY; portrait: Hermitage, St. Petersburg, Russia/The Bridgeman Art Library)

In 1709 Peter's new war machine was able to crush Sweden's army in Ukraine at Poltava (Map 18.5). Russia's victory against Sweden was conclusive in 1721, and Estonia and present-day Latvia came under Russian rule for the first time. As a result, Russia became the dominant power in the Baltic and very much a great European power.

After his victory at Poltava, Peter channeled enormous resources into building a new Western-style capital on the Baltic. The city of St. Petersburg was designed to reflect modern urban planning with wide, straight avenues; buildings set in a uniform line; and large parks. Each summer, twenty-five thousand to forty thousand peasants were sent to provide construction labor in St. Petersburg without pay.

There were other important consequences of Peter's reign. For Peter, modernization meant westernization, and both Westerners and Western ideas flowed into Russia for the first time. He required nobles to shave their heavy beards and wear Western clothing. He also required them to attend parties where young men and women would mix together and freely choose their own spouses. From these efforts a new elite class of Western-oriented Russians began to emerge.

CHAPTER LOCATOR | How did the Protestant and Catholic Reformations shape colonial expansion? | How did seventeenth-century European states overcome social and economic crisis? | How did absolutism evolve in in Spain, France, and Austria?

542   CHAPTER 18
EUROPEAN POWER AND EXPANSION

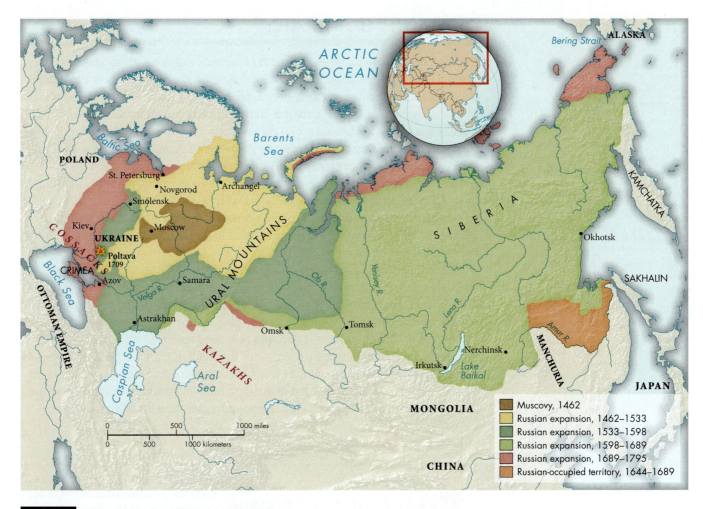

MAP 18.5 ■ The Expansion of Russia, 1462–1689

In little more than two centuries, Russia expanded from the small principality of Muscovy to an enormous multiethnic empire, stretching from the borders of western Europe through northern Asia to the Pacific.

Peter's reforms were unpopular with many Russians. For nobles, one of Peter's most detested reforms was the imposition of unigeniture—inheritance of land by one son alone. For peasants, the reign of the tsar saw a significant increase in the bonds of serfdom. Nonetheless, Peter's modernizing and westernizing of Russia paved the way for it to move somewhat closer to the European mainstream in its thought and institutions during the Enlightenment, especially under Catherine the Great (see page 568).

QUICK REVIEW

What were Peter the Great's primary goals?
How did he go about achieving them?

| Why and how did the constitutional state triumph in England and the Dutch Republic? | How did European nations compete for trade and empire in the Americas and Asia? | **How did Russian rulers build an absolutist monarchy and expand into a powerful empire?** | ✔ LearningCurve Check what you know. |

543

CHAPTER SUMMARY

Most parts of Europe experienced the first centuries of the early modern era as a time of crisis. Following the religious divides of the sixteenth-century Protestant and Catholic Reformations, Europeans in the seventeenth century suffered from economic stagnation, social upheaval, and renewed military conflict. Despite these obstacles, both absolutist and constitutional European states emerged from the seventeenth century with increased powers and more centralized control.

Monarchs in Spain, France, and Austria used divine right to claim they possessed absolute power and were not responsible to any representative institutions. Absolute monarchs overcame the resistance of the nobility both through military force and by affirming existing economic and social privileges. England and the Netherlands defied the general trend toward absolute monarchy, adopting distinctive forms of constitutional rule.

As Spain's power weakened in the early seventeenth century, the Netherlands, England, and France competed for access to overseas trade and territory. Mercantilist competition among these powers led to hostility and war. England emerged in the early eighteenth century with a distinct advantage over its rivals.

In Russia, Mongol conquest and rule set the stage for a harsh tsarist autocracy that was firmly in place by the time of the reign of Ivan the Terrible in the sixteenth century. The reign of Ivan and his successors saw a great expansion of Russian territory, laying the foundations for a huge multiethnic empire. Peter the Great forcibly turned Russia toward the West by adopting Western technology and culture.

 **CONNECTIONS** With the re-establishment of order in the second half of the century, maintaining stability was of paramount importance to European rulers. While a few nations placed their trust in constitutionally limited governments, many more were ruled by monarchs proclaiming their absolute and God-given authority. The ability to assume such power depended on cooperation from local elites, who acquiesced to state authority in exchange for privileges and payoffs. In this way, both absolutism and constitutionalism relied on political compromises forged from decades of strife.

As Spain's power weakened, other European nations bordering the Atlantic Ocean sought their own profits and glory from overseas empires. Henceforth, war among European powers would include conflicts over territories and trade in the colonies. European rulers' increased control over their own subjects thus went hand in glove with the expansion of European power in the world.

The eighteenth century was to see these power politics thrown into question by new Enlightenment aspirations for human society, which themselves derived from the inquisitive and self-confident spirit of the Scientific Revolution. These movements are explored in the next chapter. By the end of the eighteenth century demands for real popular sovereignty, colonial self-rule, and slave emancipation challenged the very bases of order so painfully achieved in the seventeenth century. Chapter 22 recounts the revolutionary movements that swept the late-eighteenth-century Atlantic world, while Chapters 25, 26, and 27 follow the story of European imperialism and the resistance of colonized peoples into the nineteenth century.

CHAPTER LOCATOR | How did the Protestant and Catholic Reformations shape colonial expansion? | How did seventeenth-century European states overcome social and economic crisis? | How did absolutism evolve in in Spain, France, and Austria?

544 CHAPTER 18 EUROPEAN POWER AND EXPANSION

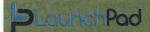

ONLINE DOCUMENT PROJECT

Jewish Life in the Early Modern Era

What factors shaped life for European Jews in the early modern era?

Read excerpts from Glückel of Hameln's memoirs and other accounts of Jewish life, and then complete a quiz and writing assignment based on the evidence and details from this chapter. *See inside the front cover to learn more.*

Why and how did the constitutional state triumph in England and the Dutch Republic?	How did European nations compete for trade and empire in the Americas and Asia?	How did Russian rulers build an absolutist monarchy and expand into a powerful empire?	✔ **LearningCurve** Check what you know.

CHAPTER 18 STUDY GUIDE

STEP 1 **GET STARTED ONLINE**

 **LearningCurve**

Now that you've read the chapter, make it stick by completing the LearningCurve activity.

STEP 2 **EXPLAIN WHY IT MATTERS**

Put your reading into practice. Identify each term below, and then explain why it matters in world history.

TERM	WHO OR WHAT & WHEN	WHY IT MATTERS
Protestant Reformation (p. 514)		
Jesuits (p. 517)		
moral economy (p. 520)		
Thirty Years' War (p. 520)		
sovereignty (p. 521)		
absolutism (p. 523)		
divine right of kings (p. 525)		
mercantilism (p. 527)		
constitutionalism (p. 529)		
Puritans (p. 530)		
Bill of Rights of 1689 (p. 531)		
republicanism (p. 531)		
Navigation Acts (p. 537)		
Cossacks (p. 540)		

STEP 3 **MOVE BEYOND THE BASICS**

To demonstrate a more advanced understanding of the growth of state power in France, Prussia, Austria, Russia, and England, fill in the chart below by describing developments in each state in four areas where seventeenth-century governments achieved new levels of control: taxation, the armed forces, bureaucracies, and the ability to compel obedience from subjects. How did the growth of the state in England differ from the growth of the state in absolutist France, Prussia, Russia, and Austria?

	Taxation	Armed Forces	Bureaucracies	Control over Subjects
France				
Prussia				
Austria				
Russia				
England				

PUT IT ALL TOGETHER

Now, take a step back and try to explain the big picture. Remember to use specific examples from the chapter in your answers.

ABSOLUTIST MONARCHIES AND THE SEVENTEENTH-CENTURY CRISIS

▶ How did life for Europe's peasants change during the seventeenth century? Why was peasant life harder in eastern Europe than in western Europe?

▶ How and why did Louis XIV try to co-opt and control the French aristocracy? In practice, how "absolute" was his rule?

▶ Compare and contrast absolutism in Austria, Prussia, and Russia. What common problems and challenges did would-be absolutist rulers face in each of these three states?

CONSTITUTIONAL STATES AND THE SEVENTEENTH-CENTURY CRISIS

▶ Why did the efforts of English monarchs to build an absolutist state fail? What groups and institutions in English society were most responsible for the triumph of constitutionalism?

▶ Compare and contrast the constitutional governments of England and the Netherlands. What role did merchant elites and commercial interests play in each state?

COMPETITION FOR EMPIRE

▶ Why did northern European powers enter the competition for New World land and resources in the seventeenth century?

▶ How did England come to dominate the Atlantic economy over the course of the seventeenth century?

LOOKING BACK, LOOKING AHEAD

▶ How did the strong, centralized states of the second half of the seventeenth century differ from their fifteenth- and sixteenth-century counterparts? What new powers and responsibilities did seventeenth-century states take on?

▶ How might the state-building efforts of European powers in the seventeenth century have contributed to the acceleration of globalization that characterized the eighteenth and nineteenth centuries?

> ## IN YOUR OWN WORDS

Imagine that you must give an oral report to the class answering the following question: **How did European central governments consolidate and expand their power in the early modern period?** What would be the most important points and why?

19

NEW WORLDVIEWS AND WAYS OF LIFE

1540–1790

> **How and why did Europeans' understanding of the natural world and human society change in the early modern period?** Chapter 19 examines the impact of the Scientific Revolution and the Enlightenment on European life. From the mid-sixteenth century on, age-old patterns of knowledge and daily life were disrupted by a fundamental shift in the basic framework for understanding the natural world and the methods for examining it known collectively as the "Scientific Revolution." In the eighteenth century self-proclaimed members of an "Enlightenment" movement extended the use of reason from nature to human society. The expression of new ideas was encouraged by changes in the material world. During the eighteenth century ships crisscrossing the Atlantic circulated commodities, ideas, and people to all four continents bordering the ocean. As trade became more integrated and communication intensified, an Atlantic world of mixed identities and vivid debates emerged.

Free People of Color A sizable mixed-race population emerged in many European colonies in the Americas, including descendants of unions between masters and enslaved African women. The wealthiest of the free people of color, as they were called, were plantation owners with slaves of their own. (Unknown artist, *Portrait of a Young Woman*, pastel on paper, previously attributed to Jean-Etienne Liotard [1702–1789]/Saint Louis Art Museum, Missouri, USA/The Bridgeman Art Library)

> What revolutionary discoveries were made in the sixteenth and seventeenth centuries, and why did they occur in Europe?

> What intellectual and social changes occurred as a result of the Scientific Revolution?

> What new ideas about society and human relations emerged in the Enlightenment, and what new practices and institutions enabled these ideas to take hold?

> How did economic and social change and the rise of Atlantic trade interact with Enlightenment ideas?

LearningCurve
After reading the chapter, use LearningCurve to retain what you've read.

What revolutionary discoveries were made in the sixteenth and seventeenth centuries, and why did they occur in Europe?

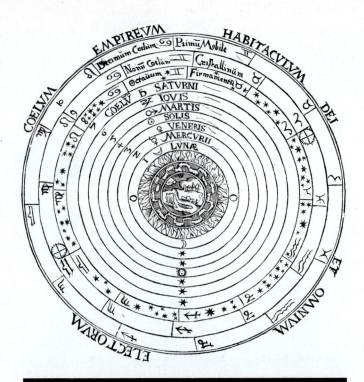

The Aristotelian Universe as Imagined in the Sixteenth Century

A round earth is at the center, surrounded by spheres of water, air, and fire. Beyond this small nucleus, the moon, the sun, and the five planets were embedded in their own rotating crystal spheres, with the stars sharing the surface of one enormous sphere. Beyond, the heavens were composed of unchanging ether. (Image Select/Art Resource, NY)

BUILDING ON DEVELOPMENTS in the Middle Ages and the Renaissance, tremendous advances in Europeans' knowledge of the natural world and techniques for establishing such knowledge took place between 1500 and 1700. Collectively known as the "Scientific Revolution," these developments were the result of many more people studying the natural world, who used new methods to answer fundamental questions about the universe and how it operated.

Why Europe?

In 1500 scientific activity flourished in many parts of the world. With the expansion of Islam into the lands of the Byzantine Empire in the seventh and eighth centuries, Muslim scholars inherited ancient Greek learning, which itself was built on centuries of borrowing from older civilizations in Egypt, Babylonia, and India. The interaction of peoples and cultures across the vast Muslim world, facilitated by religious tolerance and the common scholarly language of Arabic, was highly favorable to advances in learning.

In a great period of cultural and intellectual flourishing from 1000 to 1500, Muslim scholars thrived in cultural centers such as Baghdad and Córdoba. They established the world's first universities. In this fertile atmosphere, scholars

CHAPTER LOCATOR | **What revolutionary discoveries were made in the sixteenth and seventeenth centuries?** | What intellectual and social changes occurred as a result of the Scientific Revolution?

CHAPTER 19
550 NEW WORLDVIEWS AND WAYS OF LIFE

ca. 1500–1700 Scientific Revolution	**1762–1796** Reign of Catherine the Great of Russia
ca. 1690–1789 Enlightenment	**1765** Philosophes publish *Encyclopedia: The Rational Dictionary of the Sciences, the Arts, and the Crafts*
ca. 1700–1789 Growth of book publishing	**1780–1790** Reign of Joseph II of Austria
1720–1780 Rococo style in art and decoration	**1791** Establishment of the Pale of Settlement
1740–1786 Reign of Frederick the Great of Prussia	**1792** Establishment of mining school in Mexico City as part of reforms
ca. 1740–1789 French salons led by elite women	

surpassed the texts they had inherited in areas such as mathematics, physics, astronomy, and medicine. Arab and Persian mathematicians, for example, invented algebra, the concept of the algorithm, and decimal point notation, while Arab astronomers improved on measurements recorded in ancient works.

China was also a vital center of scientific activity, which reached a peak in the mid-fourteenth century. Among its many achievements, papermaking, gunpowder, and the use of the compass in navigation would be the most influential for the West. In Mesoamerica, civilizations such as the Maya and the Aztecs, devised complex calendar systems based on astronomical observations and developed mathematics and writing.

Given the multiple world sites of learning and scholarship, it was by no means inevitable that Europe would take the lead in scientific thought. In world history, periods of advancement produced by intense cultural interaction, such as those that occurred after the spread of Islam, are often followed by stagnation and decline during times of conflict and loss of authority. This is what happened in western Europe after the fall of the Western Roman Empire in the fifth century and in the Maya civilization after the collapse of its cultural and political centers around 900.

The re-establishment of stronger monarchies and the growth of trade in the High Middle Ages contributed to a renewal of learning in western Europe. As Europeans began to encroach on Islamic lands in Iberia, Sicily, and the eastern Mediterranean, they became aware of the rich heritage of Greek learning in these regions and the ways scholars had improved upon ancient knowledge. In the twelfth century many ancient Greek texts were translated into Latin, along with the commentaries of Arab scholars. A number of European cities created universities in which Aristotle's works dominated the curriculum.

As Europe recovered from the ravages of the Black Death in the late fourteenth and fifteenth centuries, the intellectual and cultural movement known as the Renaissance provided a crucial foundation for the Scientific Revolution. Scholars called humanists emphasized the value of acquiring knowledge for the practical purposes of life. The quest to restore the glories of the ancient past led to the rediscovery of a host of important classical texts.

What new ideas about society and human relations emerged in the Enlightenment?	How did economic and social change interact with Enlightenment ideas?	✓ **LearningCurve** Check what you know.

In this period, western European universities established new professorships of mathematics, astronomy, and natural philosophy. The prestige of the new fields was low, especially mathematics, which was reserved for practical problems but not used as a tool to understand the functioning of the physical world itself. Nevertheless, these professorships eventually enabled the union of mathematics with natural philosophy that was to be a hallmark of the Scientific Revolution.

European overseas expansion in the fifteenth and sixteenth centuries provided another catalyst for new thought about the natural world. In particular, the navigational problems of long oceanic voyages in the age of expansion stimulated scientific research and invention. To help solve these problems, inventors developed many new scientific instruments. Better instruments, which permitted more accurate observations, often led to important new knowledge. Another crucial technology in this period was printing, which provided a faster and less expensive way to circulate knowledge.

Political and social conflicts were widespread in Eurasia in the sixteenth and early seventeenth centuries, but they had different results. The three large empires of the Muslim world (see Chapter 17) that arose in the wake of the Mongol Empire sought to restore order and assert legitimacy in part by imposing Islamic orthodoxy. Their failure to adopt the printing press (see page 497) can be seen as part of a wider reaction against earlier traditions of innovation. Similarly, in China after the Manchu invasion of 1644, the new Qing Dynasty legitimized its authority through stricter adherence to Confucian tradition. By contrast, western Europe remained politically fragmented into smaller competitive nations, divisions that were augmented by the religious fracturing of the Protestant Reformation. These conditions made it impossible for authorities to impose one orthodox set of ideas and thus allowed individuals to question dominant patterns of thinking.

Scientific Thought to 1550

For medieval scholars, philosophy was the path to true knowledge about the world, and its proofs consisted of the authority of ancients (as interpreted by Christian theologians) and their techniques of logical argumentation. Questions about the physical nature of the universe and how it functioned belonged to a minor branch of philosophy, called natural philosophy. Natural philosophy was based primarily on the ideas of Aristotle, the great Greek philosopher of the fourth century B.C.E. According to the Christianized version of Aristotle, a motionless earth stood at the center of the universe and was encompassed by ten separate concentric crystal spheres in which were embedded the moon, sun, planets, and stars. Beyond the spheres was Heaven with the throne of God and the souls of the saved.

Aristotle's views also dominated thinking about physics and motion on earth. Aristotle had distinguished between the world of the celestial spheres and that of the earth—the sublunar world. The sublunar realm was made up of four imperfect, changeable elements: air, fire, water, and earth. Aristotle and his followers also believed that a uniform force moved an object at a constant speed and that the object would stop as soon as that force was removed.

The work of the ancient Greek scholar Ptolemy provided the basic foundation of knowledge about the earth. Rediscovered around 1410, his *Geography* presented crucial advances on medieval cartography by representing a round earth divided into 360 degrees with the major latitude marks. However, Ptolemy's map

CHAPTER LOCATOR | What revolutionary discoveries were made in the sixteenth and seventeenth centuries? | What intellectual and social changes occurred as a result of the Scientific Revolution?

CHAPTER 19
552 NEW WORLDVIEWS AND WAYS OF LIFE

reflected the limits of ancient knowledge, showing only the continents of Europe, Africa, and Asia, with land covering three-quarters of the world.

Astronomy and Physics

The first great departure from the medieval understanding of cosmology was the work of the Polish cleric Nicolaus Copernicus (1473–1543). Without questioning the Aristotelian belief in crystal spheres, Copernicus theorized that the stars and planets, including the earth, revolved around a fixed sun. Fearing the ridicule of other astronomers, Copernicus did not publish his *On the Revolutions of the Heavenly Spheres* until 1543, the year of his death.

One astronomer who agreed with the **Copernican hypothesis** was the Danish astronomer Tycho Brahe (TEE-koh BRAH-hee) (1546–1601). Brahe established himself as Europe's leading astronomer with his detailed observations of a new star that appeared suddenly in 1572 and shone very brightly for almost two years. The new star, which was actually a distant exploding star, challenged the idea that the heavenly spheres were unchanging and therefore perfect. For twenty years Brahe observed the stars and planets with his naked eye in order to create new and improved tables of planetary motions.

Brahe's assistant, Johannes Kepler (1571–1630), used Brahe's data to develop three revolutionary laws of planetary motion. First, he demonstrated that the orbits of the planets around the sun are elliptical rather than circular. Second, he demonstrated that the planets do not move at a uniform speed in their orbits. When a planet is close to the sun it accelerates, and it slows as it moves farther away from the sun. Finally, Kepler's third law stated that the time a planet takes to make its complete orbit is precisely related to its distance from the sun. Kepler's contribution was monumental. Whereas Copernicus had speculated, Kepler used mathematics to prove the precise relations of a sun-centered (solar) system.

While Kepler was unraveling planetary motion, a young Florentine named Galileo Galilei (1564–1642) was challenging Aristotelian ideas about motion on earth. Galileo focused on deficiencies in Aristotle's theories of motion. He measured the movement of a rolling ball across a surface, repeating the action again and again to verify his results. In his famous acceleration experiment, he showed that a uniform force—in this case, gravity—produced a uniform acceleration. Through another experiment, he formulated the **law of inertia**. He found that rest was not the natural state of objects. Rather, an object continues in motion forever unless stopped by some external force. His discoveries proved Aristotelian physics wrong.

On hearing details about the invention of the telescope in Holland, Galileo made one for himself in 1609. He quickly discovered the first four moons of Jupiter, which clearly demonstrated that Jupiter could not possibly be embedded in an impenetrable crystal sphere as Aristotle and Ptolemy maintained. This discovery provided concrete evidence for the Copernican theory.

Newton's Synthesis

By about 1640 the work of Brahe, Kepler, and Galileo had been largely accepted by the scientific community despite opposition from religious leaders (see page 559). But the new findings failed to explain what forces controlled the movement of the planets and objects on earth. That challenge was taken up by English scientist Isaac Newton (1642–1727).

Copernican hypothesis
▶ The idea that the sun, not the earth, was the center of the universe.

law of inertia
▶ A law formulated by Galileo stating that motion, not rest, is the natural state of an object and that an object continues in motion forever unless stopped by some external force.

What new ideas about society and human relations emerged in the Enlightenment?	How did economic and social change interact with Enlightenment ideas?	☑ LearningCurve Check what you know.

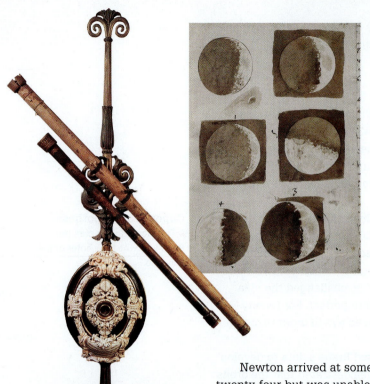

Newton arrived at some of his most basic ideas about physics in 1666 at age twenty-four but was unable to prove them mathematically. In 1684, after years of studying optics, Newton returned to physics for eighteen intensive months. The result was his towering accomplishment, a single explanatory system that integrated the astronomy of Copernicus, as corrected by Kepler's laws, with the physics of Galileo and his predecessors. Newton did this through a set of mathematical laws that explain motion and mechanics. These laws were published in 1687 in Newton's *Mathematical Principles of Natural Philosophy* (also known as the *Principia*).

The key feature of the Newtonian synthesis was the **law of universal gravitation**. According to this law, each body in the universe attracts every other body in a precise mathematical relationship, whereby the force of attraction is proportional to the quantity of matter of the objects and inversely proportional to the square of the distance between them. The whole universe was unified in one majestic system. Matter moved on earth and throughout the heavens according to the same laws, which could be understood and expressed in mathematical terms.

law of universal gravitation

▶ Newton's law that all objects are attracted to one another and that the force of attraction is proportional to the object's quantity of matter and inversely proportional to the square of the distance between them.

Natural History and Empire

At the same time that they made advances in astronomy and physics, Europeans embarked on the pursuit of knowledge about unknown geographical regions. Because they were the first to acquire a large overseas empire, the Spanish pioneered these efforts. The Spanish crown sponsored many scientific expeditions to gather information and specimens, out of which emerged new discoveries that reshaped the fields of botany, zoology, cartography, and metallurgy, among others.

Plants were a particular source of interest because they offered tremendous profits in the form of spices, medicines, dyes, and cash crops. King Philip II of Spain sent his personal physician, Francisco Hernández, to New Spain for seven years in the 1560s. Hernández filled fifteen volumes with illustrations of three

CHAPTER LOCATOR | **What revolutionary discoveries were made in the sixteenth and seventeenth centuries?** | What intellectual and social changes occurred as a result of the Scientific Revolution?

thousand plants previously unknown in Europe. He interviewed local healers about the plants' medicinal properties, thereby benefiting from centuries of Meso-american botanical knowledge.

Other countries followed the Spanish example as their global empires expanded, relying both on official expeditions and the private initiative of merchants, missionaries, and settlers. The stream of new information about plant and animal species overwhelmed existing intellectual frameworks. Carl Linnaeus (1707–1778) of Sweden sent his students on exploratory voyages around the world and, based on their observations and the specimens they collected, devised a system of naming and classifying living organisms still used today (with substantial revisions).

Magic and Alchemy

Recent historical research on the Scientific Revolution has focused on the contribution of ideas and practices that no longer belong to the realm of science, such as astrology and alchemy. Many of the most celebrated astronomers were also astrologers. Used as a diagnostic tool in medicine, astrology formed a regular part of the curriculum of medical schools.

Centuries-old practices of magic and alchemy also remained important traditions for natural philosophers. Early modern practitioners of magic strove to understand and control hidden connections they perceived among different elements of the natural world, such as that between a magnet and iron. The idea that objects possessed hidden or "occult" qualities that allowed them to affect other objects was a particularly important legacy of the magical tradition.

Johannes Kepler exemplifies the interaction among these different strands of interest in the natural world. His duties as court mathematician included casting horoscopes for the royal family, and he based his own life on astrological principles. He also wrote at length on cosmic harmonies and explained elliptical motion through ideas about the beautiful music created by the combined motion of the planets. Another example of the interweaving of ideas and beliefs is Sir Isaac Newton, who was both intensely religious and also fascinated by alchemy, whose practitioners believed (among other things) that base metals could be turned into gold.

QUICK REVIEW

In what ways did the work of Isaac Newton represent the culmination of the Scientific Revolution?

What new ideas about society and human relations emerged in the Enlightenment?

How did economic and social change interact with Enlightenment ideas?

LearningCurve
Check what you know.

> What intellectual and social changes occurred as a result of the Scientific Revolution?

Frontispiece to *De Humani Corporis Fabrica* (*On the Structure of the Human Body*)

The frontispiece to Vesalius's pioneering work, published in 1543, shows him dissecting a corpse before a crowd of students. This was a revolutionary new hands-on approach for physicians, who usually worked from a theoretical, rather than a practical, understanding of the body. Based on direct observation, Vesalius replaced ancient ideas drawn from Greek philosophy with a much more accurate account of the structure and function of the body. (© SSPL/Science Museum/The Image Works)

THE SCIENTIFIC REVOLUTION was not accomplished by a handful of brilliant individuals working alone. Advancements occurred in many fields as scholars developed new methods to seek answers to long-standing problems with the collaboration and assistance of skilled craftsmen who invented new instruments and helped conduct experiments. These results circulated in an international intellectual community from which women were usually excluded.

The Methods of Science

The English politician and writer Francis Bacon (1561–1626) was the greatest early propagandist for the experimental method. Rejecting the Aristotelian and medieval method of using speculative reasoning to build general theories, Bacon

CHAPTER LOCATOR

What revolutionary discoveries were made in the sixteenth and seventeenth centuries?

What intellectual and social changes occurred as a result of the Scientific Revolution?

556 CHAPTER 19
NEW WORLDVIEWS AND WAYS OF LIFE

argued that new knowledge had to be pursued through empirical research. The researcher who wants to learn more about leaves or rocks, for example, should not speculate about the subject but should rather collect a multitude of specimens and then compare and analyze them to derive general principles. Bacon's contribution was to formalize the empirical method, which had already been used by Brahe and Galileo, into the general theory of inductive reasoning known as empiricism.

On the continent more speculative methods retained support. In 1619 the French philosopher René Descartes (day-KAHRT) (1596–1650) experienced a life-changing intellectual vision. Descartes saw that there was a perfect correspondence between geometry and algebra and that geometrical spatial figures could be expressed as algebraic equations and vice versa. A major step forward in mathematics, Descartes's discovery of analytic geometry provided scientists with an important new tool.

Descartes used mathematics to elaborate a highly influential vision of the workings of the cosmos. Drawing on ancient Greek atomist philosophies, Descartes developed the idea that matter was made up of identical "corpuscles"

empiricism

▶ A theory of inductive reasoning that calls for acquiring evidence through observation and experimentation rather than reason and speculation.

MAJOR CONTRIBUTORS TO THE SCIENTIFIC REVOLUTION

Nicolaus Copernicus (1473–1543)	Published *On the Revolutions of the Heavenly Spheres* (1543); theorized that the sun, rather than the earth, was the center of the galaxy
Paracelsus (1493–1541)	Pioneered the use of chemicals and drugs to address perceived chemical imbalances
Andreas Vesalius (1514–1564)	Published *On the Structure of the Human Body* (1543)
Tycho Brahe (1546–1601)	Built observatories and compiled data for the *Rudolphine Tables*, a new table of planetary data
Francis Bacon (1561–1626)	Advocated experimental method, formalizing theory of inductive reasoning known as empiricism
Galileo Galilei (1564–1642)	Used telescopic observation to provide evidence for Copernican hypothesis; experimented to formulate laws of physics, such as inertia
Johannes Kepler (1571–1630)	Used Brahe's data to mathematically prove the Copernican hypothesis; his new laws of planetary motion united for the first time natural philosophy and mathematics; completed the *Rudolphine Tables* in 1627
William Harvey (1578–1657)	Discovered blood circulation (1628)
René Descartes (1596–1650)	Used deductive reasoning to formulate theory of Cartesian dualism
Robert Boyle (1627–1691)	Founded the modern science of chemistry; created the first vacuum; discovered Boyle's law on the properties of gases
Isaac Newton (1642–1727)	Introduced the law of universal gravitation, synthesizing the theories of Copernicus and Galileo

What new ideas about society and human relations emerged in the Enlightenment?

How did economic and social change interact with Enlightenment ideas?

✔ LearningCurve
Check what you know.

(tiny particles) that collided together in an endless series of motions, akin to the working of a machine. All occurrences in nature could be analyzed as matter in motion, and, according to Descartes, the total "quantity of motion" in the universe was constant. Descartes's mechanistic philosophy of the universe depended on the idea that a vacuum was impossible, which meant that every action had an equal reaction, continuing in an eternal chain reaction.

Descartes's greatest achievement was to develop his initial vision into a whole philosophy of knowledge and science. When experiments proved that sensory impressions could be wrong, Descartes decided it was necessary to doubt them and everything that could reasonably be doubted, and then, as in geometry, to use deductive reasoning from self-evident truths, which he called "first principles," to ascertain scientific laws. Descartes's reasoning ultimately reduced all substances to "matter" and "mind"—that is, to the physical and the spiritual. His view of the world as consisting of two fundamental entities is known as Cartesian dualism.

Both Bacon's inductive experimentalism and Descartes's deductive mathematical reasoning had flaws. Bacon's inability to appreciate the importance of mathematics and his obsession with practical results illustrated the limitations of antitheoretical empiricism. Likewise, some of Descartes's positions demonstrated the inadequacy of rigid, dogmatic rationalism. He believed, for example, that it was possible to deduce the whole science of medicine from first principles. Although insufficient on their own, Bacon's and Descartes's extreme approaches are combined in the modern scientific method, which began to crystallize in the late seventeenth century.

Medicine, the Body, and Chemistry

The Scientific Revolution, which began with the study of the cosmos, soon transformed understanding of the human body. For many centuries the ancient Greek physician Galen's explanation of the body carried the same authority as Aristotle's account of the universe. According to Galen, the body contained four humors: blood, phlegm, black bile, and yellow bile. Illness was believed to result from an imbalance of these humors.

Swiss physician and alchemist Paracelsus (1493–1541) was an early proponent of the experimental method in medicine and pioneered the use of chemicals and drugs to address what he saw as chemical, rather than humoral, imbalances. Another experimentalist, Flemish physician Andreas Vesalius (1514–1564), studied anatomy by dissecting human bodies. In 1543, Vesalius issued *On the Structure of the Human Body*. Its two hundred precise drawings revolutionized the understanding of human anatomy, disproving Galen. The experimental approach also led English royal physician William Harvey (1578–1657) to discover the circulation of blood through the veins and arteries in 1628.

The work of Irishman Robert Boyle (1627–1691) led to the development of modern chemistry. Following Paracelsus's lead, he undertook experiments to discover the basic elements of nature, which he believed was composed of infinitely small atoms. Boyle was the first to create a vacuum, thus disproving Descartes's belief that a vacuum could not exist in nature, and he discovered Boyle's law (1662), which states that the pressure of a gas varies inversely with volume.

CHAPTER LOCATOR | What revolutionary discoveries were made in the sixteenth and seventeenth centuries? | What intellectual and social changes occurred as a result of the Scientific Revolution?

558 CHAPTER 19 NEW WORLDVIEWS AND WAYS OF LIFE

Science and Religion

It is sometimes assumed that the relationship between science and religion is fundamentally hostile and that the pursuit of knowledge based on reason and proof is incompatible with faith. Yet during the Scientific Revolution most practitioners were devoutly religious and saw their work as contributing to the celebration of God's glory. However, the concept of heliocentrism, which displaced the earth from the center of the universe, threatened the understanding of the place of mankind in creation as stated in Genesis. All religions derived from the Old Testament thus faced difficulties accepting the Copernican system. The Catholic Church was initially less hostile than Protestant and Jewish religious leaders, but in the first decades of the sixteenth century its attitude changed. In 1616 the Holy Office placed the works of Copernicus and his supporters, including Kepler, on a list of books Catholics were forbidden to read.

Out of caution Galileo Galilei silenced his views on heliocentrism for several years, until 1623 saw the ascension of Pope Urban VIII, a man sympathetic to the new science. However, Galileo's 1632 *Dialogue on the Two Chief Systems of the World* went too far. Published in Italian and widely read, it openly lampooned the Aristotelian view and defended Copernicus. In 1633 Galileo was tried for heresy by the papal Inquisition. Imprisoned and threatened with torture, the aging Galileo recanted.

Science and Society

The rise of modern science had many consequences. First, it led to the rise of a new and expanding social group—the international scientific community. Members of this community were linked together by common interests and values as well as by journals and scientific societies. The personal success of scientists and scholars depended on making new discoveries, and as a result science became competitive. Second, as governments intervened to support and sometimes direct research, the new scientific community became closely tied to the state and its agendas. National academies of science were created under state sponsorship in London in 1662, Paris in 1666, Berlin in 1700, and later across Europe.

It was long believed that the Scientific Revolution was the work of exceptional geniuses. More recently, historians have emphasized the importance of skilled craftsmen in the rise of science, particularly in the

Popularizing Science

The frontispiece illustration of Fontenelle's *Conversations on the Plurality of Worlds* (1686) invites the reader to share the pleasures of astronomy with an elegant lady and an entertaining teacher. The drawing shows the planets revolving around the sun. (© Roger-Viollet/ The Image Works)

What new ideas about society and human relations emerged in the Enlightenment?	How did economic and social change interact with Enlightenment ideas?	✓ LearningCurve Check what you know.

development of the experimental method. Many artisans developed a strong interest in emerging scientific ideas, and, in turn, the practice of science in the seventeenth century relied heavily on artisans' expertise in making instruments and conducting precise experiments.

Some things did not change in the Scientific Revolution. For example, scholars willing to challenge received ideas about the natural universe did not question traditional inequalities between the sexes. Instead, the emergence of professional science may have worsened the inequality in some ways. When Renaissance courts served as centers of learning, talented noblewomen could find niches in study and research. But the rise of a scientific community raised barriers for women because the universities and academies that furnished professional credentials refused them entry.

There were, however, a number of noteworthy exceptions. In Italy universities and academies did accept women. Across Europe women worked as makers of wax anatomical models and as botanical and zoological illustrators. They were also very much involved in informal scientific communities, attending salons (see page 575), conducting experiments, and writing learned treatises.

> **QUICK REVIEW**

What contributions did Francis Bacon and René Descartes make to the development of the scientific method?

CHAPTER LOCATOR | What revolutionary discoveries were made in the sixteenth and seventeenth centuries? | What intellectual and social changes occurred as a result of the Scientific Revolution?

CHAPTER 19
560 NEW WORLDVIEWS AND WAYS OF LIFE

Voltaire in Conversation

The French philosopher Voltaire is depicted here with his long-time companion, writer and mathematician Gabrielle-Emilie Le Tonnelier de Breteuil, marquise du Châtelet. (Château de Breteuil/Gianni Dagli Orti/ The Art Archive at Art Resource, NY)

What new ideas about society and human relations emerged in the Enlightenment, and what new practices and institutions enabled these ideas to take hold?

THE POLITICAL, INTELLECTUAL, AND religious developments of the early modern period that gave rise to the Scientific Revolution further contributed to a series of debates about key issues in eighteenth-century Europe and the wider world that came to be known as the **Enlightenment**. Proponents of the Enlightenment came to believe that answers to all social, political, and economic questions could be found through observation and the use of reason. Progress was possible in human society as well as science.

The Early Enlightenment

Loosely united by certain key questions and ideas, the European Enlightenment (ca. 1690–1789) was a broad intellectual and cultural movement that gained strength gradually and did not reach its maturity until about 1750. Its origins in the late seventeenth century lie in a combination of developments, including political opposition to absolutist rule, religious conflicts between Protestants

Enlightenment
▶ An intellectual and cultural movement in late seventeenth- and eighteenth-century Europe and its colonies that used rational and critical thinking to debate issues such as political sovereignty, religious tolerance, gender roles, and racial difference.

What new ideas about society and human relations emerged in the Enlightenment?	How did economic and social change interact with Enlightenment ideas?	✓ LearningCurve Check what you know.

and Catholics and within Protestantism, and the attempt to apply principles and practices from the Scientific Revolution to human society.

A key crucible for Enlightenment thought was the Dutch Republic, with its proud commitments to religious tolerance and republican rule. When Louis XIV demanded that all Protestants convert to Catholicism, many Huguenots fled the country and resettled in the Dutch Republic. From this haven of tolerance, French Huguenots and their supporters began to publish tracts denouncing religious intolerance and suggesting that only a despotic monarch would deny religious freedom. Their challenge to authority thus combined religious and political issues.

These dual concerns drove the career of one important early Enlightenment writer, Pierre Bayle (1647–1706), a Huguenot who took refuge from government persecution in the Dutch Republic. Bayle critically examined the religious beliefs and persecutions of the past in his *Historical and Critical Dictionary* (1697). Demonstrating that human beliefs had been extremely varied and very often mistaken, he concluded that nothing can ever be known beyond all doubt, a view known as skepticism.

The Dutch Jewish philosopher Baruch Spinoza (1632–1677) was a key figure in the transition from the Scientific Revolution to the Enlightenment. Deeply inspired by advances in the Scientific Revolution Spinoza sought to apply natural philosophy to thinking about human society. He borrowed Descartes's emphasis on rationalism and his methods of deductive reasoning but rejected the French thinker's mind-body dualism. Instead Spinoza came to espouse monism, the idea that mind and body are united in one substance and that God and nature were merely two names for the same thing. He envisioned a deterministic universe in which good and evil were merely relative values, and human actions were shaped by outside circumstances, not free will.

German philosopher and mathematician Gottfried Wilhelm von Leibniz (1646–1716), who had developed calculus independently of Isaac Newton, refuted both Cartesian dualism and Spinoza's monism. Instead he adopted the idea of an infinite number of substances, or "monads," from which all matter is composed according to a harmonious divine plan.

Out of this period of intellectual turmoil came John Locke's *Essay Concerning Human Understanding* (1690), perhaps the most important text of the early Enlightenment. In this work Locke (1632–1704) set forth a new theory about how human beings learn and form their ideas. Whereas Descartes based his deductive logic on the conviction that certain first principles, or innate ideas, are imbued

CHAPTER LOCATOR | What revolutionary discoveries were made in the sixteenth and seventeenth centuries? | What intellectual and social changes occurred as a result of the Scientific Revolution?

CHAPTER 19

562 NEW WORLDVIEWS AND WAYS OF LIFE

in humans by God, Locke insisted that all ideas are derived from experience. According to Locke, the human mind at birth is like a blank tablet, or tabula rasa, on which understanding and beliefs are inscribed by experience. Human development is therefore determined by external forces, like education and social institutions, not innate characteristics. Locke's essay contributed to the theory of **sensationalism**, the idea that all human ideas and thoughts are produced as a result of sensory impressions.

The Influence of the Philosophes

Divergences among the early thinkers of the Enlightenment show that, while they shared many of the same premises and questions, the answers they found differed widely. The spread of this spirit of inquiry and debate owed a great deal to the work of the **philosophes**, a group of influential French intellectuals.

To appeal to the public and get around the censors, the philosophes wrote novels and plays, histories and philosophies, and dictionaries and encyclopedias, all filled with satire and double meanings to spread their message. One of the greatest philosophes, the baron de Montesquieu (mahn-tuhs-KYOO) (1689–1755) pioneered this approach in *The Persian Letters* (1721). This work consists of letters supposedly written by two Persian travelers, Usbek and Rica, who as outsiders see European customs in unique ways and thereby allow Montesquieu a vantage point for criticizing existing practices and beliefs.

Disturbed by the growth in royal power under Louis XIV and inspired by the example of the physical sciences, Montesquieu set out to apply the critical method to the problem of government in *The Spirit of Laws* (1748). Arguing that forms of governments were shaped by history, geography, and customs, Montesquieu identified three main types: monarchies, republics, and despotisms. A great admirer of the English parliamentary system, Montesquieu argued for a separation of powers, with political power divided among different classes and legal estates holding unequal rights and privileges. Decades later, his theory of separation of powers had a great impact on the constitutions of the United States in 1789 and of France in 1791.

The most famous philosophe was François-Marie Arouet, known by the pen name Voltaire (1694–1778). Early in his career he was arrested twice for insulting noblemen. To avoid a prison term, Voltaire moved to England for three years, and there he came to share Montesquieu's enthusiasm for English liberties and institutions.

Returning to France, Voltaire met Gabrielle-Emilie Le Tonnelier de Breteuil, marquise du Châtelet (1706–1749), a gifted noblewoman. Madame du Châtelet invited Voltaire to live in her country house at Cirey in Lorraine. Passionate about science, she studied physics and mathematics and published the first French translation of Newton's *Principia*.

While living at Cirey, Voltaire wrote works praising England and popularizing English scientific progress. Yet, like almost all the philosophes, Voltaire was a reformer, not a revolutionary. He pessimistically concluded that the best form of government was a good monarch, since human beings "are very rarely worthy to govern themselves." Nor did Voltaire believe in social and economic equality. The only realizable equality, Voltaire thought, was that "by which the citizen

sensationalism
▶ An idea, espoused by John Locke, that all human ideas and thoughts are produced as a result of sensory impressions.

philosophes
▶ A group of French intellectuals who proclaimed that they were bringing the light of knowledge to their fellow creatures in the Age of Enlightenment.

What new ideas about society and human relations emerged in the Enlightenment?

How did economic and social change interact with Enlightenment ideas?

✓ LearningCurve
Check what you know.

563

only depends on the laws which protect the freedom of the feeble against the ambitions of the strong."[1]

Voltaire's philosophical and religious positions were much more radical. Voltaire believed in God, but he rejected Catholicism in favor of **deism**, belief in a distant, noninterventionist deity. Above all, Voltaire and most of the philosophes hated religious intolerance, which they believed led to fanaticism and cruelty.

The strength of the philosophes lay in their number, dedication, and organization. Their greatest achievement was a group effort—the seventeen-volume *Encyclopedia: The Rational Dictionary of the Sciences, the Arts, and the Crafts*, edited by Denis Diderot (1713–1784) and Jean le Rond d'Alembert (1717–1783). Completed in 1765 despite opposition from the French state and the Catholic Church, the *Encyclopedia* contained hundreds of thousands of articles by leading scientists, writers, skilled workers, and progressive priests. Science and the industrial arts were exalted, religion and immortality questioned. Intolerance, legal injustice, and out-of-date social institutions were openly criticized.

After about 1770 a number of thinkers and writers began to attack the philosophes' faith in reason and progress. The most famous of these was the Swiss intellectual Jean-Jacques Rousseau (1712–1778). Like other Enlightenment think-

deism

► Belief in a distant, noninterventionist deity, shared by many Enlightenment thinkers.

MAJOR FIGURES OF THE ENLIGHTENMENT

Baruch Spinoza (1632–1677)	Early Enlightenment thinker excommunicated from the Jewish community for his concept of a deterministic universe
John Locke (1632–1704)	*Essay Concerning Human Understanding* (1690)
Gottfried Wilhelm von Leibniz (1646–1716)	Early German rational philosopher and scientist
Pierre Bayle (1647–1706)	*Historical and Critical Dictionary* (1697)
Montesquieu (1689–1755)	*The Persian Letters* (1721); *The Spirit of Laws* (1748)
Voltaire (1694–1778)	Renowned French philosopher and author of more than seventy works
Gabrielle-Emilie Le Tonnelier de Breteuil, marquise du Châtelet (1706–1749)	French scholar and supporter of equal education for women
David Hume (1711–1776)	Central figure of the Scottish Enlightenment
Jean-Jacques Rousseau (1712–1778)	*The Social Contract* (1762)
Denis Diderot (1713–1784) and Jean le Rond d'Alembert (1717–1783)	Editors of *Encyclopedia: The Rational Dictionary of the Sciences, the Arts, and the Crafts* (1765)
Adam Smith (1723–1790)	Pioneering political economist and author of *An Inquiry into the Nature and Causes of the Wealth of Nations* (1776)
Immanuel Kant (1724–1804)	*What Is Enlightenment?* (1784); *On the Different Races of Man* (1775)

CHAPTER LOCATOR | What revolutionary discoveries were made in the sixteenth and seventeenth centuries? | What intellectual and social changes occurred as a result of the Scientific Revolution?

564 CHAPTER 19 NEW WORLDVIEWS AND WAYS OF LIFE

ers, Rousseau was passionately committed to individual freedom. Unlike them, however, he attacked rationalism and civilization as destroying, rather than liberating, the individual. Warm, spontaneous feeling, Rousseau believed, had to complement and correct cold intellect. Rousseau's ideals greatly influenced the early romantic movement, which rebelled against the culture of the Enlightenment in the late eighteenth century.

Rousseau also called for a rigid division of gender roles, arguing that women and men were radically different beings. According to Rousseau, because women were destined by nature to assume a passive role in sexual relations, they should also be passive in social life and devote themselves to taking care of their husbands and children. Additionally, he believed that women's love for displaying themselves in public, attending salons, and pulling the strings of power was unnatural and had a corrupting effect on both politics and society.

Rousseau's contribution to political theory in *The Social Contract* (1762) was based on two fundamental concepts: the general will and popular sovereignty. According to Rousseau, the **general will** is sacred and absolute, reflecting the common interests of all people, who have displaced the monarch as the holder of sovereign power. The general will is not necessarily the will of the majority, however. At times the general will may be the authentic, long-term needs of the people as correctly interpreted by a farseeing minority.

general will
▶ A concept associated with Rousseau, referring to the common interests of all the people, who have replaced the power of the monarch.

Cultural Contacts and Race

The Scientific Revolution and the political and religious conflicts of the late seventeenth century were not the only developments that influenced European thinkers. Europeans' increased interactions with non-European peoples and cultures also helped produce the Enlightenment spirit. In the wake of the great discoveries of the fifteenth and sixteenth centuries, the rapidly growing travel literature taught Europeans that the peoples of China, India, Africa, and the Americas had very different beliefs and customs. Educated Europeans began to look at truth and morality in relative, rather than absolute, terms.

The powerful and advanced nations of Asia were obvious sources of comparison with the West. During the eighteenth century Enlightenment opinion on China was divided. Voltaire and some other philosophes revered China—without ever visiting or seriously studying it—as an ancient culture replete with wisdom and learning, ruled by benevolent absolutist monarchs. They enthusiastically embraced Confucianism as a natural religion in which universal moral truths were uncovered by reason. By contrast, Montesquieu and Diderot criticized China as a despotic land ruled by fear.

Attitudes toward Islam and the Muslim world were similarly mixed. As the Ottoman military threat receded at the end of the seventeenth century, some Enlightenment thinkers assessed Islam favorably. Others, including Spinoza, saw Islamic culture as superstitious and favorable to despotism. In most cases, writing about Islam and Muslim cultures served primarily as a means to reflect on Western values and practices.

One writer with considerable personal experience in a Muslim country was Lady Mary Wortley Montagu, wife of the English ambassador to the Ottoman Empire. Her letters challenged prevailing ideas by depicting Turkish people as

What new ideas about society and human relations emerged in the Enlightenment?

How did economic and social change interact with Enlightenment ideas?

✓ LearningCurve
Check what you know.

565

sympathetic and civilized. Montagu also disputed the notion that women were oppressed in Ottoman society.

Apart from debates about Asian and Muslim lands, the "discovery" of the New World and subsequent explorations in the Pacific Ocean also destabilized existing norms and values in Europe. One popular idea, among Rousseau and others, was that indigenous peoples of the Americas were living examples of "natural man," who embodied the essential goodness of humanity uncorrupted by decadent society.

As scientists developed taxonomies of plant and animal species in response to discoveries in the Americas, they also began to classify humans into hierarchically ordered "races" and to speculate on the origins of such races. The French naturalist Georges-Louis Leclerc, comte de Buffon (1707–1788), argued that humans originated with one species that then developed into distinct races due largely to climatic conditions.

Using the word *race* to designate biologically distinct groups of humans was new in European thought. Previously, Europeans had grouped other peoples into "nations" based on their historical, political, and cultural affiliations, rather than on supposedly innate physical differences. Unsurprisingly, when thinkers drew up a hierarchical classification of human species, their own "race" was placed at the top. Europeans had long believed they were culturally superior. The new idea that racial difference was physical and innate rather than cultural taught them they were biologically superior as well. In turn, scientific racism helped legitimate and justify the tremendous growth of slavery that occurred during the eighteenth century by depicting Africans as belonging to a biologically inferior race that was naturally fit for enslavement.

Racist ideas did not go unchallenged. The abbé Raynal's *History of the Two Indies* (1770) fiercely attacked slavery and the abuses of European colonization. *Encyclopedia* editor Denis Diderot adopted Montesquieu's technique of criticizing European attitudes through the voice of outsiders in his dialogue between Tahitian villagers and their European visitors. Former slaves, like Olaudah Equiano (see Chapter 20) and Ottobah Cugoana published eloquent memoirs testifying to the horrors of slavery and the innate equality of all humans. These challenges to racism, however, were in the minority. More often, Enlightenment thinkers, Thomas Jefferson among them, supported racial inequality.

The International Enlightenment

The Enlightenment was a movement of international dimensions, with thinkers traversing borders in a constant exchange of visits, letters, and printed materials. The Republic of Letters, as this international group of scholars and writers was called, was a truly cosmopolitan set of networks stretching from western Europe to its colonies in the Americas, to Russia and eastern Europe, and along the routes of trade and empire to Africa and Asia.

Within this broad international conversation, scholars have identified regional and national particularities. Outside of France, many strains of Enlightenment thought sought to reconcile reason with faith, rather than emphasizing the errors of religious fanaticism and intolerance. Some scholars point to a distinctive "Catholic Enlightenment" that aimed to renew and reform the church from within, looking to divine grace rather than human will as the source of social progress.

CHAPTER LOCATOR | What revolutionary discoveries were made in the sixteenth and seventeenth centuries? | What intellectual and social changes occurred as a result of the Scientific Revolution?

CHAPTER 19

566 NEW WORLDVIEWS AND WAYS OF LIFE

Enlightenment Culture

An actor performs the first reading of a new play by Voltaire at the salon of Madame Geoffrin in this painting from 1755. Voltaire, then in exile, is represented by a bust statue. (Painting by Gabriel Lemonnier [1743–1824], oil on canvas/De Agonstini Picture Library/Gianni Dagli Orti/The Bridgeman Art Library)

> **PICTURING THE PAST**

ANALYZING THE IMAGE: Which of these people do you think is the hostess, Madame Geoffrin, and why? Using details from the painting to support your answer, how would you describe the status of the people shown?
CONNECTIONS: What does this image suggest about the reach of Enlightenment ideas to common people? To women? Does the painting of the bookstore on page 572 suggest a broader reach? Why?

The Scottish Enlightenment, centered in Edinburgh, was marked by an emphasis on common sense and scientific reasoning. A central figure in Edinburgh was David Hume (1711–1776). Building on Locke's writings on learning, Hume argued that the human mind is really nothing but a bundle of impressions. These impressions originate only in sensory experiences and our habits of joining these experiences together. Since our ideas ultimately reflect only our sensory experiences, our reason cannot tell us anything about questions that cannot be verified by sensory experience (in the form of controlled experiments or mathematics), such as the origin of the universe or the existence of God. Hume further argued, in opposition to Descartes, that reason alone could not supply moral principles but that they derived instead from emotions and desires, such as feelings of approval or shame. Hume's rationalistic inquiry thus ended up undermining the Enlightenment's faith in the power of reason by emphasizing the superiority of the passions over reason in driving human behavior.

What new ideas about society and human relations emerged in the Enlightenment?

How did economic and social change interact with Enlightenment ideas?

 LearningCurve
Check what you know.

Hume's ideas had a formative influence on another major figure of the Scottish Enlightenment, Adam Smith (1723–1790). In his *Theory of Moral Sentiments* (1759), Smith argued that social interaction produced feelings of mutual sympathy that led people to behave in ethical ways, despite inherent tendencies toward self-interest. Smith believed that the thriving commercial life of the eighteenth century was likely to produce civic virtue through the values of competition, fair play, and individual autonomy. In *An Inquiry into the Nature and Causes of the Wealth of Nations* (1776), Smith attacked the laws and regulations created by mercantilist governments that, he argued, prevented commerce from reaching its full capacity (see Chapter 18). For Smith, ordinary people were capable of forming correct judgments based on their own experience and should therefore not be hampered by government regulations. Smith's **economic liberalism** became the dominant form of economic thought in the early nineteenth century.

Inspired by philosophers of moral sentiments, like Hume and Smith, as well as by physiological studies of the role of the nervous system in human perception, the celebration of sensibility became an important element of eighteenth-century culture. Sensibility referred to an acute sensitivity of the nerves and brains to outside stimulus that produced strong emotional and physical reactions. Novels, plays, and other literary genres depicted moral and aesthetic sensibility as a particular characteristic of women and the upper classes. The proper relationship between reason and the emotions became a key question.

After 1760 Enlightenment ideas were hotly debated in the German-speaking states, often in dialogue with Christian theology. Immanuel Kant (1724–1804) was the greatest German philosopher of his day. Kant posed the question of the age when he published a pamphlet in 1784 titled *What Is Enlightenment?* He answered, "*Sapere Aude* (dare to know)! 'Have the courage to use your own understanding' is therefore the motto of enlightenment." He argued that if intellectuals were granted the freedom to exercise their reason publicly in print, enlightenment would surely follow. Kant was no revolutionary; he also insisted that in their private lives, individuals must obey all laws, no matter how unreasonable. Like other Enlightenment figures in central and east-central Europe, Kant thus tried to reconcile absolutism and religious faith with a critical public sphere.

Important developments in Enlightenment thought also took place in the Italian peninsula. After achieving independence from Habsburg rule (1734), the kingdom of Naples entered a period of intellectual flourishing. In northern Italy a central figure was Cesare Beccaria (1738–1794). His *On Crimes and Punishments* (1764) was a passionate plea for reform of the penal system that decried the use of torture, arbitrary imprisonment, and capital punishment and advocated the prevention of crime over its punishment.

Enlightened Absolutism and Its Limits

Some absolutist rulers tried to reform their governments in accordance with Enlightenment ideals. The result was what historians have called the **enlightened absolutism** of the later eighteenth century. (Similar programs of reform in France and Spain will be discussed in Chapter 22.) Influenced by the philosophes, Frederick II (r. 1740–1786) of Prussia, known as Frederick the Great, and Catherine the Great of Russia (r. 1762–1796) set out to rule in an enlightened manner. Frederick promoted religious tolerance and free speech and improved the educational system.

economic liberalism
▶ The theory, associated with Adam Smith, that the pursuit of self-interest in a competitive market suffices to improve living conditions, rendering government intervention unnecessary and undesirable.

enlightened absolutism
▶ Term coined by historians to describe the rule of eighteenth-century monarchs who, without renouncing their own absolute authority, adopted Enlightenment ideals of rationalism, progress, and tolerance.

CHAPTER LOCATOR | What revolutionary discoveries were made in the sixteenth and seventeenth centuries? | What intellectual and social changes occurred as a result of the Scientific Revolution?

CHAPTER 19
568 NEW WORLDVIEWS AND WAYS OF LIFE

Under his reign, Prussia's laws were simplified, torture of prisoners was abolished, and judges decided cases quickly and impartially. However, Frederick did not free the serfs of Prussia; instead he extended the privileges of the nobility over them.

Frederick's reputation as an enlightened prince was rivaled by that of Catherine the Great of Russia. Catherine pursued three major goals. First, she worked hard to continue Peter the Great's efforts to bring the culture of western Europe to Russia (see page 541). Catherine's second goal was domestic reform. Like Frederick, she restricted the practice of torture, allowed limited religious tolerance, and tried to improve education and local government. The philosophes applauded these measures and hoped more would follow.

These hopes were dashed by a massive uprising of serfs in 1733 under the leadership of a Cossack soldier named Emelian Pugachev. Although Pugachev was ultimately captured and executed, his rebellion shocked Russian rulers. After 1775 Catherine gave nobles absolute control of their serfs and extended serfdom into new areas. In 1785 she formally freed nobles from taxes and state service. Under Catherine the Russian nobility thus attained its most exalted position, and serfdom entered its most oppressive phase.

Catherine's third goal was territorial expansion. Her armies subjugated the last descendants of the Mongols and the Crimean Tartars and began the conquest of the Caucasus on the border between Europe and Asia. Her greatest coup was the partition of Poland, which took place in stages from 1772 to 1795 (Map 19.1).

Joseph II (r. 1780–1790), the Austrian Habsburg emperor, was perhaps the most sincere proponent of enlightened absolutism. Joseph abolished serfdom in 1781, and in 1789 he decreed that peasants could pay landlords in cash rather than through compulsory labor. When Joseph died at forty-nine, the Habsburg empire was in turmoil. His brother Leopold II (r. 1790–1792) canceled Joseph's radical edicts in order to re-establish order.

Perhaps the best examples of the limitations of enlightened absolutism are the debates surrounding the possible emancipation of the Jews. For the most part, Jews in Europe were confined to tiny, overcrowded ghettos; were excluded by law from most occupations; and could be ordered out of a kingdom at a moment's notice.

In the eighteenth century an Enlightenment movement known as the **Haskalah** emerged from within the European Jewish community, led by the Prussian philosopher Moses Mendelssohn (1729–1786). Christian and Jewish Enlightenment philosophers, including Mendelssohn, began to advocate for freedom and civil rights for European Jews. (See "Individuals in Society: Moses Mendelssohn and the Jewish Enlightenment," page 571.)

Arguments for tolerance won some ground, especially under Joseph II of Austria. Most monarchs, however, refused to entertain the idea of emancipation. In 1791 Catherine the Great established the Pale of Settlement, a territory encompassing modern-day Belarus, Lithuania, Latvia, Moldova, Ukraine, and parts of Poland, in which most Jews were required to live until the Russian Revolution of 1917.

The Pale of Settlement, 1791

Haskalah

▶ A Jewish Enlightenment movement led by Prussian philosopher Moses Mendelssohn.

What new ideas about society and human relations emerged in the Enlightenment?

How did economic and social change interact with Enlightenment ideas?

☑ LearningCurve
Check what you know.

569

INDIVIDUALS IN SOCIETY
Moses Mendelssohn and the Jewish Enlightenment

In 1743 a small, humpbacked Jewish boy with a stammer left his poor parents in Dessau in central Germany and walked eighty miles to Berlin, the capital of Frederick the Great's Prussia. According to one story, when the boy reached the Rosenthaler Gate, the only one through which Jews could pass, he told the inquiring watchman that his name was Moses and that he had come to Berlin "to learn." The watchman laughed and waved him through. "Go Moses, the sea has opened before you."*

In Berlin the young Mendelssohn studied Jewish law and eked out a living copying Hebrew manuscripts in a beautiful hand. But he was soon fascinated by an intellectual world that had been closed to him in the Dessau ghetto. There, like most Jews throughout central Europe, he had spoken Yiddish — a mixture of German, Polish, and Hebrew. Now, working mainly on his own, he mastered German; learned Latin, Greek, French, and English; and studied mathematics and Enlightenment philosophy. Word of his exceptional abilities spread in Berlin's Jewish community (the dwelling of 1,500 of the city's 100,000 inhabitants). He began tutoring the children of a wealthy Jewish silk merchant, and he soon became the merchant's clerk and later his partner. But his great passion remained the life of the mind and the spirit, which he avidly pursued in his off-hours.

Gentle and unassuming in his personal life, Mendelssohn was a bold thinker. Reading eagerly in works of Western philosophy dating back to antiquity, he was, as a pious Jew, soon convinced that Enlightenment teachings need not be opposed to Jewish thought and religion. He concluded that reason could complement and strengthen religion, although each would retain its integrity as a separate sphere.† Developing this idea in his first great work, "On the Immortality of the Soul" (1767), Mendelssohn used the neutral setting of a philosophical dialogue between Socrates and his followers in ancient Greece to argue that the human soul lived forever. In refusing to bring religion and critical thinking into conflict, he was strongly influenced by contemporary German philosophers who argued similarly on behalf of Christianity. His thoughts reflected the way the German Enlightenment generally supported established religion, in contrast to the French Enlightenment, which attacked it.

Mendelssohn's treatise on the human soul captivated the educated German public, which marveled that a Jew could have written a philosophical mas-

Lavater (right) attempts to convert Mendelssohn, in a painting of an imaginary encounter by Moritz Oppenheim. (Oil on canvas painting by Daniel Moritz Oppenheim (1800–1882)/Judah L. Magnes Memorial Museum/akg-images)

terpiece. In the excitement, a Christian zealot named Lavater challenged Mendelssohn in a pamphlet to accept Christianity or to demonstrate how the Christian faith was not "reasonable." Replying politely but passionately, the Jewish philosopher affirmed that his studies had only strengthened him in his faith, although he did not seek to convert anyone not born into Judaism. Rather, he urged tolerance in religious matters and spoke up courageously against Jewish oppression.

An Orthodox Jew and a German philosophe, Moses Mendelssohn serenely combined two very different worlds. He built a bridge from the ghetto to the dominant culture over which many Jews would pass, including his novelist daughter Dorothea and his famous grandson, the composer Felix Mendelssohn.

QUESTIONS FOR ANALYSIS

1. How did Mendelssohn seek to influence Jewish religious thought in his time?
2. How do Mendelssohn's ideas compare with those of the French Enlightenment?

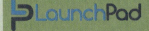

ONLINE DOCUMENT PROJECT

How did Moses Mendelssohn fit into the larger Enlightenment debate about religious tolerance? Examine primary sources written by Mendelssohn and his contemporaries, and then complete a quiz and writing assignment based on the evidence and details from this chapter. *See inside the front cover to learn more.*

---

*H. Kupferberg, *The Mendelssohns: Three Generations of Genius* (New York: Charles Scribner's Sons, 1972), p. 3.

†D. Sorkin, *Moses Mendelssohn and the Religious Enlightenment* (Berkeley: University of California Press, 1996), pp. 8ff.

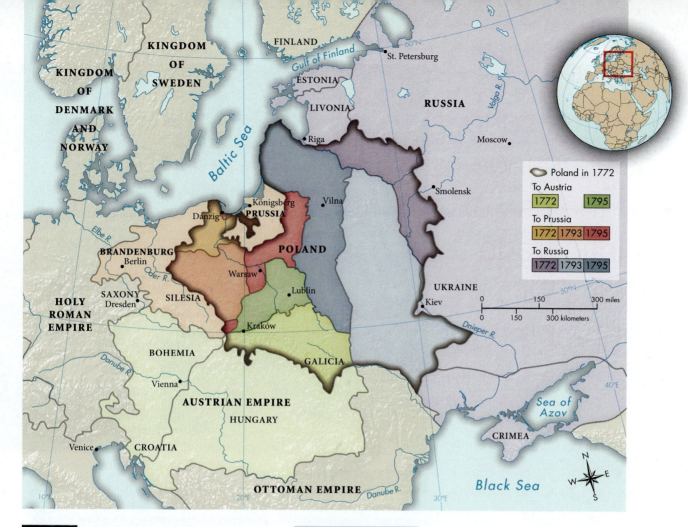

MAP 19.1 ■ **The Partition of Poland, 1772–1795**

In 1772 the threat of war between Russia and Austria arose over Russian gains from the Ottoman Empire. To satisfy desires for expansion without fighting, Prussia's Frederick the Great proposed dividing parts of Poland among Austria, Prussia, and Russia. In 1793 and 1795 the three powers partitioned the remainder, and Poland ceased to exist as an independent nation.

> MAPPING THE PAST

ANALYZING THE MAP: Of the three powers that divided the kingdom of Poland, which benefited the most? How did the partition affect the geographical boundaries of each state, and what was the significance? What border with the former Poland remained unchanged? Why do you think this was the case?

CONNECTIONS: Why was Poland vulnerable to partition in the later half of the eighteenth century? What does it say about European politics at the time that a country could simply cease to exist on the map? Could that happen today?

QUICK REVIEW

How did participants in the Enlightenment build on the accomplishments of the Scientific Revolution?

What new ideas about society and human relations emerged in the Enlightenment?	How did economic and social change interact with Enlightenment ideas?	✓ LearningCurve Check what you know.

How did economic and social change and the rise of Atlantic trade interact with Enlightenment ideas?

The French Book Trade

Book consumption surged in the eighteenth century and along with it, new bookstores. This appealing bookshop in France with its intriguing ads for the latest works offers to put customers "Under the Protection of Minerva," the Roman goddess of wisdom. Large packets of books sit ready for shipment to foreign countries. (Musée des Beaux-Arts, Dijon, France/Art Resource, NY)

ENLIGHTENMENT DEBATES TOOK PLACE within a rapidly evolving material world. Agricultural reforms contributed to a rise in population that in turned fueled substantial economic growth in eighteenth-century Europe. A new public sphere emerged in the growing cities in which people exchanged opinions in cafés, bookstores, and other spaces. A consumer revolution brought fashion and imported foods into the reach of common people for the first time.

These economic and social changes were fed by an increasingly integrated Atlantic economy. Over time, the peoples, goods, and ideas that crisscrossed the ocean created distinctive Atlantic communities and identities.

Economic and Demographic Change

The seventeenth century saw important gains in agricultural productivity in northwestern Europe that slowly spread throughout the continent. Using new scientific techniques of observation and experimentation, a group of scientists, government

CHAPTER LOCATOR | What revolutionary discoveries were made in the sixteenth and seventeenth centuries? | What intellectual and social changes occurred as a result of the Scientific Revolution?

572 CHAPTER 19 NEW WORLDVIEWS AND WAYS OF LIFE

officials, and a few big landowners devised agricultural practices and tools that raised crop yields dramatically, especially in England and the Netherlands. These included new forms of crop rotation, better equipment, and selective breeding of livestock. The controversial process of **enclosure**, fencing off common land to create privately owned fields, allowed a break with traditional methods but at the cost of reducing poor farmers' access to land.

Colonial plants also provided new sources of calories and nutrition. Introduced into Europe from the Americas—along with corn, squash, tomatoes, and many other useful plants—the potato provided an excellent new food source and offset the lack of fresh vegetables and fruits in common people's winter diet. The potato had become an important dietary supplement in much of Europe by the end of the eighteenth century.

Increases in agricultural productivity and better nutrition, combined with the disappearance of bubonic plague after 1720 and improvements in sewage and water supply, contributed to the tremendous growth of the European population in the eighteenth century. The explosion of population was a major phenomenon in all European countries, leading to a doubling of the number of Europeans between 1700 and 1835.

Population growth increased the number of rural workers with little or no land, and this in turn contributed to the development of industry in rural areas. The poor in the countryside increasingly needed to supplement their agricultural earnings with other types of work. **Cottage industry**, which consisted of manufacturing with hand tools in peasant cottages and work sheds, grew markedly in the eighteenth century and became a crucial feature of the European economy.

Despite the rise in rural industry, life in the countryside was insufficient to support the rapidly growing population. Many people thus left their small villages to join the tide of migration to the cities, especially after 1750.

The Atlantic Economy

European economic growth in the eighteenth century was spurred by the expansion of trade across the Atlantic Ocean. Commercial exchange in the Atlantic is often referred to as the triangle trade, designating a three-way transport of goods: European commodities to Africa; enslaved Africans to the colonies; and colonial goods back to Europe. This model highlights some of the most important flows of trade but significantly oversimplifies the picture. For example, a brisk intercolonial trade existed, with the Caribbean slave colonies importing food from other American colonies in exchange for sugar and slaves (Map 19.2).

Moreover, the Atlantic economy was inextricably linked to trade with the Indian and Pacific Oceans. The rising economic and political power of Europeans in the eighteenth century thus drew on the connections they established between the long-standing Asian and Atlantic trade worlds.

Over the course of the eighteenth century the economies of European nations bordering the Atlantic Ocean relied more and more on colonial exports. In England sales to the mainland colonies of North America and the West Indian sugar islands soared from £500,000 to £4 million (Figure 19.1). Exports to England's colonies in Ireland and India also rose substantially from 1700 to 1800.

At the core of this Atlantic world was the misery and profit of the Atlantic slave trade (see pages 598–603). The brutal practice intensified dramatically after

enclosure
▶ The controversial process of fencing off common land to create privately owned fields that increased agricultural production at the cost of reducing poor farmers' access to land.

cottage industry
▶ Manufacturing with hand tools in peasant cottages and work sheds, a form of economic activity that became important in eighteenth-century Europe.

What new ideas about society and human relations emerged in the Enlightenment?

How did economic and social change interact with Enlightenment ideas?

✓ LearningCurve
Check what you know.

573

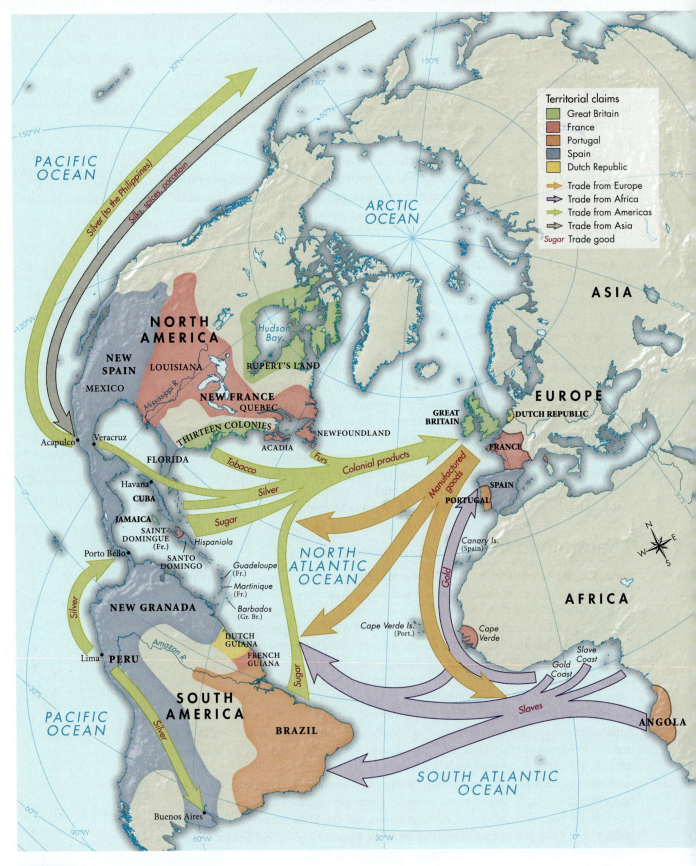

Territorial claims
- Great Britain
- France
- Portugal
- Spain
- Dutch Republic

→ Trade from Europe
→ Trade from Africa
→ Trade from Americas
→ Trade from Asia
Sugar Trade good

PACIFIC OCEAN

ARCTIC OCEAN

ASIA

Silver (to the Philippines)

Silks, spices, porcelain

NORTH AMERICA

NEW SPAIN

MEXICO

LOUISIANA

Mississippi R.

NEW FRANCE

QUEBEC

Hudson Bay

RUPERT'S LAND

EUROPE

DUTCH REPUBLIC

GREAT BRITAIN

FRANCE

THIRTEEN COLONIES

NEWFOUNDLAND

ACADIA

FLORIDA

Tobacco

Furs

Colonial products

Veracruz

Acapulco

Havana

CUBA

JAMAICA

SAINT DOMINGUE (Fr.)

Porto Bello

SANTO DOMINGO

Hispaniola

Silver

Sugar

Manufactured goods

SPAIN

PORTUGAL

Canary Is. (Spain)

Gold

NORTH ATLANTIC OCEAN

Guadeloupe (Fr.)

Martinique (Fr.)

Barbados (Gr. Br.)

Cape Verde Is. (Port.)

Cape Verde

AFRICA

NEW GRANADA

Amazon R.

DUTCH GUIANA

FRENCH GUIANA

Sugar

Silver

Lima

PERU

Slave Coast

Gold Coast

Slaves

ANGOLA

SOUTH AMERICA

BRAZIL

PACIFIC OCEAN

Silver

Buenos Aires

SOUTH ATLANTIC OCEAN

MAP 19.2 ■ The Atlantic Economy, 1701

The growth of trade encouraged both economic development and military conflict in the Atlantic basin. Four continents were linked together by the exchange of goods and slaves.

CHAPTER LOCATOR | What revolutionary discoveries were made in the sixteenth and seventeenth centuries? | What intellectual and social changes occurred as a result of the Scientific Revolution?

1700 and especially after 1750 with the growth of trade and demand for slave-produced goods. English dominance of the slave trade provided another source of large profits to the home country.

The French also profited enormously from colonial trade in the eighteenth century, even after losing their vast North American territories to England in 1763. The Caribbean colonies of Saint-Domingue (modern-day Haiti), Martinique, and Guadeloupe provided immense fortunes from slave-based plantation agriculture. The wealth generated from colonial trade fostered the confidence of the merchant classes in Nantes, Bordeaux, and other large cities, and merchants soon joined other elite groups clamoring for more political power.

The third major player in the Atlantic economy, Spain, also saw its colonial fortunes improve during the eighteenth century. Its mercantilist goals were boosted by a recovery in silver production. Spanish territory in North America expanded significantly in the second half of the eighteenth century. At the close of the Seven Years' War (1756–1763) (see page 647), Spain gained Louisiana from the French, and its influence extended westward all the way to northern California through the efforts of Spanish missionaries and ranchers.

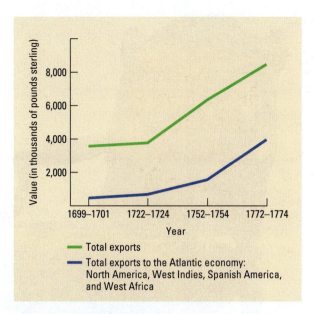

FIGURE 19.1 ■ Exports of English Manufactured Goods, 1700–1774

While trade between England and Europe stagnated after 1700, English exports to Africa and the Americas boomed and greatly stimulated English economic development. (Source: Data from R. Davis, "English Foreign Trade, 1700–1774," *Economic History Review*, 2nd ser., 15 [1962]: 302–303.)

Urban Life and the Public Sphere

Urban life in the Atlantic world gave rise to new institutions and practices that encouraged the spread of Enlightenment thought. From about 1700 to 1789 the production and consumption of books grew significantly. Lending libraries, bookshops, cafés, and Masonic lodges provided spaces in which urban people debated new ideas. Together these spaces and institutions helped create a new **public sphere** that celebrated open debate informed by critical reason.

Another important Enlightenment institution was the salon. In Paris from about 1740 to 1789, a number of talented, wealthy women presided over regular social gatherings named after their elegant private drawing rooms, or **salons**. There they encouraged the exchange of observations on literature, science, and philosophy with great aristocrats, wealthy middle-class financiers, high-ranking officials, and noteworthy foreigners.

Elite women also exercised great influence on artistic taste. Soft pastels, ornate interiors, sentimental portraits, and starry-eyed lovers protected by hovering cupids were all hallmarks of the rococo style they favored. Women were also closely associated with the rise of the novel as a literary genre, both as authors and readers. The novel helped popularize the cult of sensibility, which celebrated strong emotions and intimate family love.

Economic growth in the second half of the eighteenth century also enabled a significant rise in the consumption of finished goods and new foodstuffs that historians have labeled a "consumer revolution." A boom in textile production and cheap reproductions of luxury items meant that the common people could afford to follow fashion for the first time. Colonial trade made previously expensive and rare foodstuffs, such as sugar, tea, coffee, chocolate, and tobacco, widely available.

public sphere
▶ An idealized intellectual space that emerged in Europe during the Enlightenment. Here, the public came together to discuss important social, economic, and political issues.

salons
▶ Regular social gatherings held by talented and rich Parisian women in their homes, where philosophes and their followers met to discuss literature, science, and philosophy.

What new ideas about society and human relations emerged in the Enlightenment?

How did economic and social change interact with Enlightenment ideas?

✓ LearningCurve
Check what you know.

The Consumer Revolution

From the mid-eighteenth century on, the cities of western Europe witnessed a new proliferation of consumer goods. Items once limited to the wealthy few — such as fans (above), watches, snuffboxes, umbrellas, ornamental containers, and teapots — were now reproduced in cheaper versions for middling and ordinary people. The fashion for wide hoopskirts was so popular that the armrests of the chairs of the day, known as Louis XV chairs (left), were specially designed to accommodate them. (fan: Musée Conde, Chantilly, France/ Scala/White Images/Art Resource, NY; chair: © RMN–Grand Palais/ Art Resource, NY)

Culture and Community in the Atlantic World

As contacts among the Atlantic coasts of the Americas, Africa, and Europe became more frequent, and as European settlements grew into well-established colonies, new identities and communities emerged. The term *Creole* referred to people of Spanish or other European ancestry born in the Americas. Wealthy Creoles throughout the Atlantic colonies prided themselves on following European ways of life.

Over time, however, the colonial elite came to feel that their circumstances gave them different interests and characteristics from people of their home countries. Creoles adopted native foods, like chocolate, chili peppers, and squash, and sought relief from tropical disease in native remedies. Also, they began to turn against restrictions from their home countries: Creole traders and planters, along with their counterparts in English colonies, increasingly resented the regulations and taxes imposed by colonial bureaucrats, and such resentment would eventually lead to revolutions against colonial powers (discussed in Chapter 22).

CHAPTER LOCATOR | What revolutionary discoveries were made in the sixteenth and seventeenth centuries? | What intellectual and social changes occurred as a result of the Scientific Revolution?

CHAPTER 19
576 NEW WORLDVIEWS AND WAYS OF LIFE

Not all Europeans in the colonies were wealthy or well educated. Numerous poor and lower-middle-class whites worked as clerks, shopkeepers, craftsmen, and laborers. With the exception of the English colonies of North America, white Europeans made up a minority of the population, outnumbered by indigenous peoples in Spanish America and, in the Caribbean, by the growing numbers of enslaved people of African descent. Since most European migrants were men, much of the colonial population of the Atlantic world descended from unions—forced or through consent—of European men and indigenous or African women. Colonial attempts to identify and control racial categories greatly influenced developing Enlightenment thought on racial differences.

In the Spanish and French Caribbean, as in Brazil, many slave masters acknowledged and freed their mixed-race children, leading to sizable populations of free people of color. In the second half of the eighteenth century the prosperity of some free people of color brought a backlash from the white population of Saint-Domingue in the form of new race laws prohibiting nonwhites from marrying whites and forcing them to adopt distinctive attire. In the British colonies of the Caribbean and the southern mainland, by contrast, masters tended to leave their mixed-race progeny in slavery, maintaining a stark discrepancy between free whites and enslaved people of color.[2]

Restricted from owning land and holding many occupations in Europe, Jews were eager participants in the new Atlantic economy and established a network of mercantile communities along its trade routes. As in the Old World, Jews in European colonies faced discrimination. Jews were considered to be white Europeans and thus ineligible to be slaves, but they did not enjoy equal status with Christians. The status of Jews adds one more element to the complexity of Atlantic identities.

The Atlantic Enlightenment

The colonies of British North America were deeply influenced by the Scottish Enlightenment, with its emphasis on pragmatic approaches to the problems of life. Following the Scottish model, leaders in the colonies adopted a moderate, "commonsense" version of the Enlightenment that emphasized self-improvement and ethical conduct. In most cases, this version of the Enlightenment was perfectly compatible with religion and was chiefly spread through the growing colleges and universities of the colonies.

Northern Enlightenment thinkers often depicted Spain and its American colonies as the epitome of the superstition and barbarity they contested. Nonetheless, the dynasty that took power in Spain in the early eighteenth century followed its own course of enlightened absolutism, just like its counterparts in the rest of Europe. Under King Carlos III (r. 1759–1788) and his son Carlos IV (r. 1788–1808), Spanish administrators attempted to strengthen colonial rule and improve government efficiency. Enlightened administrators debated the status of indigenous peoples and whether it would be better for these peoples if they maintained their distinct legal status or were integrated into Spanish society.

Educated Creoles were well aware of the new currents of thought, and the universities, newspapers, and salons of Spanish America produced their own

What new ideas about society and human relations emerged in the Enlightenment?

How did economic and social change interact with Enlightenment ideas?

✓ LearningCurve
Check what you know.

577

reform ideas. As in other European colonies, one effect of Enlightenment thought was to encourage Creoles to criticize the policies of the mother country and aspire toward greater autonomy.

> **QUICK REVIEW**

How did the relationship between the Americas and the rest of the world change in the seventeenth and eighteenth centuries?

CHAPTER SUMMARY

Decisive breakthroughs in astronomy and physics in the seventeenth century demolished the medieval synthesis of Aristotelian philosophy and Christian theology. The impact of these scientific breakthroughs on intellectual life was enormous, nurturing a new critical attitude in many disciplines. In addition, an international scientific community arose, and state-sponsored academies, which were typically closed to women, advanced scientific research.

Believing that all aspects of life were open to debate and skepticism, Enlightenment thinkers asked challenging questions about religious tolerance, representative government, and racial and sexual difference. Enlightenment thinkers drew inspiration from the new peoples and cultures encountered by Europeans and devised new ideas about race as a scientific and biological category. The ideas of the Enlightenment inspired absolutist rulers in central and eastern Europe, but real reforms were limited.

In the second half of the eighteenth century agricultural reforms helped produce tremendous population growth. Economic growth and urbanization favored the spread of Enlightenment thought by producing a public sphere in which ideas could be debated. The expansion of transatlantic trade made economic growth possible, as did the lowering of prices on colonial goods due to the growth of slave labor. Atlantic trade involved the exchange of commodities among Europe, Africa, and the Americas, but it was also linked with trade in the Indian and Pacific Oceans. The movement of people and ideas across the Atlantic helped shape the identities of colonial inhabitants.

 **CONNECTIONS** Hailed as the origin of modern thought, the Scientific Revolution must also be seen as a product of its past. Borrowing from Islamic cultural achievements, medieval universities gave rise to important new scholarship in mathematics and natural philosophy. In turn, the ambition and wealth of Renaissance patrons nurtured intellectual curiosity and encouraged scholarly research and foreign exploration. Natural philosophers

CHAPTER LOCATOR | What revolutionary discoveries were made in the sixteenth and seventeenth centuries? | What intellectual and social changes occurred as a result of the Scientific Revolution?

pioneered new methods of explaining and observing nature while drawing on centuries-old traditions of astrology, alchemy, and magic. A desire to control and profit from empire led the Spanish, followed by their European rivals, to explore and catalogue the flora and fauna of their American colonies. These efforts resulted in new frameworks in natural history.

Enlightenment ideas of the eighteenth century were a similar blend of past and present, progressive and traditional, homegrown and foreign-inspired. Enlightenment thinkers advocated universal rights and liberties but also preached the biological inferiority of non-Europeans and women. Their principles often served as much to bolster absolutist regimes as to inspire revolutionaries to fight for human rights.

New notions of progress and social improvement would drive Europeans to embark on world-changing revolutions in politics and industry (see Chapters 22 and 23) at the end of the eighteenth century. These revolutions provided the basis for modern democracy and unprecedented scientific advancement. Yet some critics have seen a darker side. For them, the mastery over nature enabled by the Scientific Revolution now threatens to overwhelm the earth's fragile equilibrium, and the Enlightenment belief in the universal application of reason can lead to intolerance of other people's spiritual, cultural, and political values.

As the era of European exploration and conquest gave way to empire building, the eighteenth century witnessed increased consolidation of global markets and bitter competition among Europeans. The eighteenth-century Atlantic world thus tied the shores of Europe, the Americas, and Africa in a web of commercial and human exchange, including the tragedy of slavery, discussed in Chapter 20. The Atlantic world maintained strong ties with trade in the Pacific and the Indian Ocean.

ONLINE DOCUMENT PROJECT

Moses Mendelssohn

How did Moses Mendelssohn fit into the larger Enlightenment debate about religious tolerance?

Examine primary sources written by Mendelssohn and his contemporaries, and then complete a quiz and writing assignment based on the evidence and details from this chapter. *See inside the front cover to learn more.*

What new ideas about society and human relations emerged in the Enlightenment?

How did economic and social change interact with Enlightenment ideas?

✔️ **LearningCurve**
Check what you know.

CHAPTER 19 STUDY GUIDE

GET STARTED ONLINE

 **LearningCurve**

Now that you've read the chapter, make it stick by completing the LearningCurve activity.

EXPLAIN WHY IT MATTERS

Put your reading into practice. Identify each term below, and then explain why it matters in world history.

TERM	WHO OR WHAT & WHEN	WHY IT MATTERS
Copernican hypothesis (p. 553)		
law of inertia (p. 553)		
law of universal gravitation (p. 554)		
empiricism (p. 557)		
Enlightenment (p. 561)		
sensationalism (p. 563)		
philosophes (p. 563)		
deism (p. 564)		
general will (p. 565)		
economic liberalism (p. 568)		
enlightened absolutism (p. 568)		
Haskalah (p. 569)		
enclosure (p. 573)		
cottage industry (p. 573)		
public sphere (p. 575)		
salons (p. 575)		

MOVE BEYOND THE BASICS

To demonstrate a more advanced understanding of key figures of the Scientific Revolution, fill in the chart below with descriptions of the scientific discoveries of the figures listed. Be sure to include both concrete discoveries and contributions to the development of the scientific method. How did these thinkers build off of each other's discoveries and insights? What common goals did they share?

	Discoveries and Contributions
Nicolaus Copernicus	
Tycho Brahe	
Johannes Kepler	
Francis Bacon	
René Descartes	
Galileo Galilei	
Isaac Newton	

STEP 4 PUT IT ALL TOGETHER

Now, take a step back and try to explain the big picture. Remember to use specific examples from the chapter in your answers.

THE SCIENTIFIC REVOLUTION

▶ What was revolutionary about the Scientific Revolution? How did the study of nature in the sixteenth century differ from the study of nature in the Middle Ages?

▶ What role did religion play in the Scientific Revolution? How did religious belief both stimulate and hinder scientific inquiry?

THE ENLIGHTENMENT AND ENLIGHTENED ABSOLUTISM

▶ How did the Scientific Revolution contribute to the emergence of the Enlightenment? What new ideas about the power and potential of human reason were central to both developments?

▶ What connections can you make between the state-building ambitions of central and eastern European absolute monarchs and their embrace of Enlightenment reforms?

CONSUMERISM AND THE ATLANTIC WORLD

▶ How did the growth and consolidation of the Atlantic economy shape the everyday lives of eighteenth-century Europeans?

▶ How did Enlightenment thinkers deal with issues of gender and race? How did New World encounters shape their thinking?

LOOKING BACK, LOOKING AHEAD

▶ How did medieval and Renaissance developments contribute to the Scientific Revolution? Should the Scientific Revolution be seen a sharp break with the past, or the culmination of long-term, gradual change?

▶ A noted historian has said that the Scientific Revolution was "the real origin both of the modern world and the modern mentality." Do you agree or disagree with this characterization? Why?

> IN YOUR OWN WORDS

Imagine that you must give an oral report to the class answering the following question: **How and why did Europeans' understanding of the natural world and human society change in the early modern period?** What would be the most important points and why?

20

AFRICA AND THE WORLD

1400–1800

> **What were the short-term and long-term consequences of the transatlantic slave trade for African societies?** Chapter 20 examines early modern Africa. Early modern African states and societies included a wide variety of languages, cultures, political systems, and levels of economic development. African societies of this period were connected to each other and to the outside world by extensive trade networks. Modern European intrusion into Africa beginning in the fifteenth century profoundly affected these diverse societies and ancient trading networks. Most important, the intrusion led to the transatlantic slave trade, one of the greatest forced migrations in world history, through which Africa made a substantial, though involuntary, contribution to the building of the West's industrial civilization.

Waist Pendant of Benin Worn by Royalty European intrusion in Africa during the early modern period deeply affected the diverse societies of Africa. The facial features, the beard, and the ruffled collar on this Edo peoples' artifact dating from the sixteenth to the nineteenth centuries are clearly Portuguese, but the braided hair is distinctly African, probably signifying royalty. (Hip Ornament: Portuguese Face, 16th–19th century. Brass, iron. Gift of Mr. and Mrs. Klaus G. Perls, 1991 [1991.162.9]. The Metropolitan Museum of Art, New York, NY, USA/Image copyright © The Metropolitan Museum of Art/Image source: Art Resource, NY)

> What different types of economic, social, and political structures were found in the kingdoms and states along the west coast and in the Sudan?

> How did the arrival of Europeans and other foreign cultures affect the East African coast, and how did Ethiopia and the Swahili city-states respond to these incursions?

> What role did slavery play in African societies before the transatlantic slave trade began, and what was the effect of European involvement?

 **LearningCurve**

After reading the chapter, use LearningCurve to retain what you've read.

What different types of economic, social, and political structures were found in the kingdoms and states along the west coast and in the Sudan?

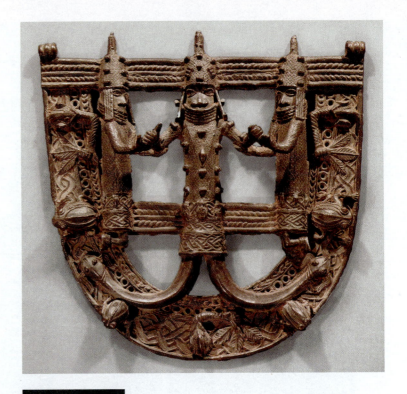

The Oba of Benin

The oba's palace walls were decorated with bronze plaques that date from about the sixteenth to eighteenth centuries. This plaque vividly conveys the oba's power, majesty, and authority. The two attendants holding his arms also imply that the oba needs the support of his people. The oba's legs are mudfish, which represent fertility, peace, well-being, and prosperity, but their elongation, suggesting electric eels, relates the oba's terrifying and awesome power to the eel's jolting shock. (National Museum, Lagos, Nigeria/photo: André Held/akg-images)

IN MID-FIFTEENTH-CENTURY AFRICA, Benin and a number of other kingdoms flourished along the two-thousand-mile west coast between Senegambia and the northeastern shore of the Gulf of Guinea. Further inland, in the region of the Sudan, the kingdoms of Songhai, Kanem-Bornu, and Hausaland benefited from the trans-Saharan caravan trade. Stateless societies such as those in the region of Senegambia existed alongside these more centralized states. Despite their political differences and whether they were agricultural, pastoral, or a mixture of both, West African cultures all faced the challenges presented by famine, disease, and the slave trade.

The West Coast: Senegambia and Benin

The Senegambian states possessed a homogeneous culture and a common history. For centuries Senegambia served as an important entrepôt for desert caravan contact with North African and Middle Eastern Islamic civilizations. Through the

CHAPTER LOCATOR | What different types of economic, social, and political structures were found in the kingdoms and states along the west coast and in the Sudan? | How did the arrival of Europeans and other foreign cultures affect the East African coast, and how did Ethiopia and the Swahili city-states respond to these incursions?

584 CHAPTER 20 AFRICA AND THE WORLD

1400–1600s Salt trade dominates West African economy	**1543** Joint Ethiopian and Portuguese force defeat Muslims in Ethiopia
ca. 1464–1591 Songhai kingdom dominates the western Sudan	**1571–1603** Idris Alooma governs kingdom of Kanem-Bornu
1485 Portuguese and other Europeans first appear in Benin	**1591** Moroccan army defeats Songhai
1493–1528 Muhammad Toure governs and expands kingdom of Songhai	**1658** Dutch East India Company allows importation of slaves into Cape Colony
1498 Portuguese explorer Vasco da Gama sails around Africa	**1680s** Famine from Senegambian coast to Upper Nile
ca. 1500–1900 Era of transatlantic slave trade	**1738–1756** Major famine in West Africa
1502–1507 Portuguese erect forts at Kilwa, Zanzibar, and Sofala on Swahili coast	**1789** Olaudah Equiano publishes autobiography
1529 Adal defeats Ethiopian emperor and begins systematic devastation of Ethiopia	

transatlantic slave trade, Senegambia came into contact with Europe and the Americas. Thus Senegambia felt the impact of Islamic culture to the north and of European influences from the maritime West.

The Senegambian peoples spoke Wolof, Serer, and Pulaar, which all belong to the West African language group. Both the Wolof-speakers and the Serer-speakers had clearly defined social classes: royalty, nobility, warriors, peasants, low-caste artisans such as blacksmiths and leatherworkers, and enslaved persons. The enslaved class consisted of individuals who were pawned for debt, house servants who could not be sold, and people who were acquired through war or purchase. Senegambian slavery varied from society to society. In some places slaves were considered chattel property and were treated as harshly as they would be later in the Western Hemisphere.

The word **chattel** originally comes from a Latin word meaning "head," as in "so many head of cattle." It reflects the notion that enslaved people are not human, but subhuman, like beasts of burden or other animals. Thus they can be treated like animals. But in Senegambia and elsewhere in Africa, many enslaved people were not considered chattel property and could not be bought and sold. Some even served as royal advisers and enjoyed great power and prestige.[1] Unlike in the Americas, where slave status passed forever from one generation to the next, in Africa the enslaved person's descendants were sometimes considered free.

Senegambia was composed of stateless societies, culturally homogeneous ethnic populations living in small groups of villages without a central capital. Among these stateless societies, **age-grade systems** evolved. Age-grades were groups of teenage males and females whom the society initiated into adulthood

chattel
▶ An item of personal property; a term used in reference to enslaved people that conveys the idea that they are subhuman, like animals, and therefore may be treated like animals.

age-grade systems
▶ Among the societies of Senegambia, groups of men and women whom the society initiated into adulthood at the same time.

What role did slavery play in African societies before the transatlantic slave trade began, and what was the effect of European involvement?

☑ LearningCurve
Check what you know.

at the same time. Age-grades cut across family ties, created community-wide loyalties, and provided a means of local law enforcement, because each age-grade was responsible for the behavior of all its members.

The typical Senegambian community was a small, self-supporting agricultural village of closely related families. The average six- to eight-acre farm supported a moderate-size family. Millet and sorghum were the staple grains in northern Senegambia; farther south, forest dwellers cultivated yams as a staple. Social life centered on the family, and government played a limited role, interceding mostly to resolve family disputes and conflicts between families.

Alongside West African stateless societies like Senegambia were kingdoms and states ruled by kings who governed defined areas through bureaucratic hierarchies. The great forest kingdom of Benin emerged in the fifteenth and sixteenth centuries in what is now southern Nigeria (see Map 20.1). Over time, the position

MAP 20.1 ■ **West African Societies, ca. 1500–1800**

The coastal region of West Africa witnessed the rise of a number of kingdoms in the sixteenth century.

> MAPPING THE PAST

ANALYZING THE MAP: What geographical features defined each of the kingdoms shown here? Consider rivers, lakes, oceans, deserts, and forests. How might they have affected the size and shape of these kingdoms?

CONNECTIONS: Compare this map to the spot map of the slave coast of West Africa on page 590. Consider the role that rivers and other geographical factors played in the development of the West African slave trade. Why were Luanda and Benguela the logical Portuguese sources for slaves?

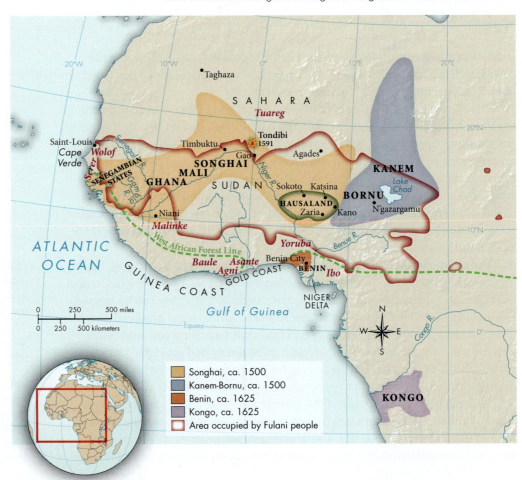

CHAPTER LOCATOR

What different types of economic, social, and political structures were found in the kingdoms and states along the west coast and in the Sudan?

How did the arrival of Europeans and other foreign cultures affect the East African coast, and how did Ethiopia and the Swahili city-states respond to these incursions?

of its oba, or king, was exalted, bringing stability to the state. In the later fifteenth century the oba Ewuare strengthened his army and pushed Benin's borders as far as the Niger River in the east, westward into Yoruba country, and south to the Gulf of Guinea. During the late sixteenth and seventeenth centuries the office of the oba evolved from a warrior-kingship to a position of spiritual leadership.

At its height in the late sixteenth century, Benin controlled a vast territory, and European visitors described a sophisticated society. A Dutch visitor in the early 1600s, possibly Dierick Ruiters, described the capital, Benin City, as possessing a great, wide, and straight main avenue down the middle, with many side streets crisscrossing it. Visitors noted that Benin City was kept scrupulously clean and had no beggars and that public security was so effective that theft was unknown. The period also witnessed remarkable artistic creativity in ironwork, carved ivory, and especially bronze portrait busts. Over nine hundred brass plaques survive, providing important information about Benin court life, military triumphs, and cosmological ideas.

In 1485 Portuguese and other Europeans began to appear in Benin in pursuit of trade, and over the next couple of centuries Benin grew rich from the profits made through the slave trade and the export of tropical products. Its main European trading partners along this stretch of the so-called slave coast were the Dutch and Portuguese.

The Sudan: Songhai, Kanem-Bornu, and Hausaland

The Songhai kingdom, a successor state of the kingdoms of Ghana (ca. 900–1100) and Mali (ca. 1200–1450), dominated the whole Niger region of the western and central Sudan (see Map 20.1). The imperial expansion of Songhai (song-GUY) began during the reign of the Songhai king Sonni Ali (r. ca. 1464–1492) and continued under his eventual successor, Muhammad Toure (r. 1493–1528). From his capital at Gao, Toure extended his rule as far north as the salt-mining center at Taghaza in the western Sahara and as far east as Agades and Kano. A convert to Islam, Toure tried to bring about greater centralization in his own territories by building a strong army, improving taxation procedures, and replacing local Songhai officials with more efficient Arabs in an effort to substitute royal institutions for ancient kinship ties.

When the scholar Leo Africanus (ca. 1465–1550) visited Timbuktu, the second-largest city of the empire, in 1513 he was impressed by its intellectual climate. "Here [is] a great store of doctors, judges, priests, and other learned men, that are bountifully maintained at the King's court," he reported.[2] Many of these Islamic scholars had studied in Cairo and other Muslim learning centers. They gave Timbuktu a reputation for intellectual sophistication, religious piety, and moral justice.

Songhai under Muhammad Toure seems to have enjoyed economic prosperity. The elite had immense wealth, and expensive North African and European luxuries were much in demand. The existence of many shops and markets implies the development of an urban culture. In Timbuktu merchants, scholars, judges, and artisans constituted a distinctive bourgeoisie, or middle class. The presence of

oba
► The title of the king of Benin.

Taghaza
► A settlement in the western Sahara, the site of the main salt-mining center.

What role did slavery play in African societies before the transatlantic slave trade began, and what was the effect of European involvement?

✓ LearningCurve
Check what you know.

many foreign merchants, including Jews and Italians, gave the city a cosmopolitan atmosphere.

Slavery played an important role in Songhai's economy. On the royal farms scattered throughout the kingdom, enslaved people produced rice for the royal granaries. Slaves could possess their own slaves, land, and cattle, but they could not bequeath any of this property. Muhammad Toure greatly increased the number of royal slaves. He bestowed slaves on favorite Muslim scholars, who thus gained a steady source of income. Slaves were also sold at the large market at Gao, where traders from North Africa bought them to resell later in Cairo, Constantinople, Lisbon, Naples, Genoa, and Venice.

Despite its considerable economic and cultural strengths, Songhai had serious internal problems. Islam never took root in the countryside, and Muslim officials alienated the king from his people. Muhammad Toure's reforms were a failure. He governed diverse peoples who were often hostile to one another, and no cohesive element united them. Moreover, revolts, conspiracies, and palace intrigues followed the death of every king, and only three of the nine rulers in the dynasty begun by Muhammad Toure died natural deaths. Muhammad Toure himself was murdered by one of his sons. His death began a period of political instability that led to the kingdom's slow disintegration. The empire came to an end in 1591 when a Moroccan army of three thousand soldiers—many of whom were slaves of European origin equipped with European muskets—crossed the Sahara and inflicted a crushing defeat on the Songhai at Tondibi.

East of Songhai lay the kingdoms of Kanem-Bornu and Hausaland (see Map 20.1). Under the dynamic military leader Idris Alooma (r. 1571–1603), Kanem-Bornu gained jurisdiction over an extensive area. Well drilled and equipped with firearms, his standing army and camel-mounted cavalry decimated warriors fighting with spears and arrows. Idris Alooma perpetuated a form of feudalism by granting land to able fighters in return for loyalty and the promise of future military assistance. Kanem-Bornu shared in the trans-Saharan trade, shipping eunuchs and young girls to North Africa in return for horses and firearms.

A devote Muslim, Idris Alooma built mosques at his capital city of N'gazargamu and substituted Muslim courts and Islamic law for African tribunals and ancient customary law. His eighteenth-century successors lacked his vitality and military skills, however, and the empire declined.

Between Songhai and Kanem-Bornu were the lands of the Hausa, an agricultural people who lived in small villages. Hausa merchants carried on a sizable trade in slaves and kola nuts with North African communities across the Sahara. Trading posts evolved into important Hausa city-states like Kano and Katsina, through which Islamic influences entered the region. Kano and Katsina became Muslim intellectual centers and in the fifteenth century attracted scholars from Timbuktu. As in Songhai and Kanem-Bornu, however, Islam made no strong imprint on the Hausa masses until the nineteenth century.

The Lives of the People of West Africa

Wives and children were highly desired in African societies because they could clear and cultivate the land and because they brought prestige, social support, and security in old age. The results were intense competition for women, inequal-

CHAPTER LOCATOR | **What different types of economic, social, and political structures were found in the kingdoms and states along the west coast and in the Sudan?** | How did the arrival of Europeans and other foreign cultures affect the East African coast, and how did Ethiopia and the Swahili city-states respond to these incursions?

588 CHAPTER 20 AFRICA AND THE WORLD

ity of access to them, an emphasis on male virility and female fertility, and serious tension between male generations. Polygyny was almost universal.

Men acquired wives in two ways. In some cases, couples simply eloped and began their union. More commonly, a man's family gave bride wealth to the bride's family. Because it took time for a young man to acquire the bride wealth, all but the richest men delayed marriage until about age thirty. Women married at about the onset of puberty.

The easy availability of land in Africa reduced the kinds of generational conflict that occurred in western Europe, where land was scarce. Competition for wives between male generations, however, was fierce. On the one hand, myth and folklore stressed respect for the elderly, and the older men in a community imposed their authority over the younger ones. On the other hand, young men possessed the powerful asset of their labor, which could easily be turned into independence where so much land was available.

Children were the primary goal of marriage. A woman might have six widely spaced pregnancies in her fertile years; the universal practice of breast-feeding infants for two, three, or even four years may have inhibited conception. Long intervals between births due to food shortages also may have limited pregnancies and checked population growth.

Both nuclear and extended families were common in West Africa. Nuclear families averaged only five or six members, but the household of a Big Man (a local man of power) included his wives, married and unmarried sons, unmarried daughters, poor relations, dependents, and scores of children. Extended families were common among the Hausa and Mandinka peoples. On the Gold Coast in the seventeenth century, a well-to-do man's household might number 150 people, in the Kongo region in west-central Africa, several hundred.

In agriculture men did the heavy work of felling trees and clearing the land; women then planted, weeded, and harvested. Between 1000 and 1400, cassava (manioc), bananas, and plantains came to West Africa from Asia. In the sixteenth century the Portuguese introduced maize (corn), sweet potatoes, and new varieties of yams from the Americas. Fish supplemented the diets of people living near bodies of water.

Disease posed perhaps the biggest obstacle to population growth. Malaria, spread by mosquitoes and rampant in West Africa, was the greatest killer, especially of infants. West Africans developed a relatively high degree of immunity to malaria and other parasitic diseases. Acute strains of smallpox introduced by Europeans certainly did not help population growth, nor did venereal syphilis, which possibly originated in Latin America. As in Chinese and European communities in the early modern period, the sick depended on folk medicine. African medical specialists administered a variety of treatments. Still, disease was common where the diet was poor and lacked adequate vitamins.

The devastating effects of famine represented another major check on population growth. Drought, excessive rain, swarms of locusts, and rural wars that

Queen Mother and Attendants

As in Ottoman, Chinese, and European societies, the mothers of African rulers sometimes exercised considerable political power because of their influence on their sons. African kings granted the title Queen Mother as a badge of honor. In this figure, the long beaded cap, called "chicken's beak," symbolizes the mother's rank, as do her elaborate neck jewelry and attendants. (Culture: Edo peoples. Culture: Court of Benin. Altar Tableau: Queen Mother and Attendants, 18th century. Brass. Front, view #1. Gift of Mr. and Mrs. Klaus G. Perls, 1991 [1991.17.111]. The Metropolitan Museum of Art, New York, NY, USA/Image copyright © The Metropolitan Museum of Art/Image source: Art Resource, NY)

What role did slavery play in African societies before the transatlantic slave trade began, and what was the effect of European involvement?

LearningCurve
Check what you know.

prevented land cultivation all meant later food shortages. In the 1680s famine extended from the Senegambian coast to the Upper Nile, and many people sold themselves into slavery for food. In the eighteenth century "slave exports" reached their peak in times of famine.

Because the Americas had been isolated from the Eurasian-African landmass for thousands of years, parasitic diseases common in Europe, Africa, and Asia were unknown in the Americas before the Europeans' arrival. Enslaved Africans taken to the Americas brought with them the diseases common to tropical West Africa. Thus the hot, humid disease environment in the American tropics, where the majority of enslaved Africans lived and worked, became more "African." On the other hand, cold-weather European diseases, such as chicken pox, mumps, measles, and influenza, prevailed in the northern temperate zone in North America and the southern temperate zone in South America. This difference in disease environment partially explains why Africans made up the majority of the unskilled labor force in the tropical areas of the Americas, and Europeans made up the majority of the unskilled labor force in the Western Hemisphere temperate zones, such as the northern United States and Canada.

Trade and Industry

As in all premodern societies, West African economies rested on agriculture. There was some trade and industry, but population shortages encouraged local self-sufficiency, slowed transportation, and hindered exchange. There were very few large markets, and their relative isolation from the outside world and failure to attract large numbers of foreign merchants limited technological innovation.

For centuries black Africans had exchanged goods with North African merchants in centers such as Gao and Timbuktu. This long-distance trans-Saharan trade was conducted and controlled by Muslim-Berber merchants using camels. The two primary goods exchanged were salt, which came from salt mines in North Africa, and gold, which came mainly from gold mines in modern-day Mali, and later, modern Ghana.

As elsewhere around the world, water was the cheapest method of transportation, and many small dugout canoes and larger trading canoes plied the Niger and its delta region (see Map 20.1). On land West African peoples used pack animals rather than wheeled vehicles; only a narrow belt of land in the Sudan was suitable for animal-drawn carts. When traders reached an area infested with tsetse flies, they transferred each animal's load to human porters. Such difficulties in transport severely restricted long-distance trade, so most people relied on the regional exchange of local specialties.

West African communities had a well-organized market system. At informal markets on riverbanks, fishermen bartered fish for local specialties. More formal markets existed within towns and villages or on neutral ground between them. Markets also rotated among neighboring villages on certain days. Local sellers were usually women; traders from afar were men.

The salt trade dominated the West African economies in the fifteenth, sixteenth, and seventeenth centuries. The main salt-mining center was at Taghaza (see Map 20.1) in the western Sahara. In the most wretched conditions, slaves dug the salt from desiccated lakes and loaded heavy blocks onto camels' backs. **Tuareg** warriors and later Moors (peoples of Berber and Arab descent) traded

West African Trade Routes

Tuareg

▶ Along with the Moors, warriors who controlled the north-south trans-Saharan trade in salt.

CHAPTER LOCATOR | **What different types of economic, social, and political structures were found in the kingdoms and states along the west coast and in the Sudan?** | How did the arrival of Europeans and other foreign cultures affect the East African coast, and how did Ethiopia and the Swahili city-states respond to these incursions?

CHAPTER 20
590 AFRICA AND THE WORLD

Salt Making in the Central Sahara

For centuries camel caravans transported salt south across the Sahara to the great West African kingdoms, where it was exchanged for gold. Here at Tegguida-n-Tessum, Niger, in the central Sahara, salt is still collected by pouring spring water into small pools dug out of the saline soil. The water leaches out the salt before evaporating in the desert sun, leaving deposits of pure salt behind, which are then shaped into blocks for transport. (Afrique Photo, Cliché Naud/Visual Connection Archive)

their salt south for gold, grain, slaves, and kola nuts. **Cowrie shells**, imported from the Maldives in the Indian Ocean by way of Gujarat (see page 502) and North Africa, served as the medium of exchange. Gold continued to be mined and shipped from Mali until South American bullion flooded Europe in the sixteenth century. Thereafter, its production in Africa steadily declined.

West African peoples engaged in many crafts, such as basket weaving and potterymaking. Ironworking became hereditary in individual families; such expertise was regarded as family property. The textile industry had the greatest level of specialization. The earliest fabric in West Africa was made of vegetable fiber. Muslim traders introduced cotton and its weaving in the ninth century.

cowrie shells
▶ Imported from the Maldives, they served as the medium of exchange in West Africa.

QUICK REVIEW

What role did trade play in West African society?

What role did slavery play in African societies before the transatlantic slave trade began, and what was the effect of European involvement?

✓ LearningCurve
Check what you know.

How did the arrival of Europeans and other foreign cultures affect the East African coast, and how did Ethiopia and the Swahili city-states respond to these incursions?

Chinese Porcelain Plates

Embedded in an eighteenth-century Kunduchi pillar tomb, these Chinese plates testify to the enormous Asian-African trade that flourished in the fourteenth to sixteenth centuries. Kunduchi, whose ruins lie north of Dar es Salaam in present-day Tanzania, was one of the Swahili city-states. (Werner Forman Archive/The Bridgeman Art Library)

> **PICTURING THE PAST**

ANALYZING THE IMAGE: How many Chinese plates can you identify? What features identify this as a tomb?
CONNECTIONS: Why would a Muslim African want a Chinese plate embedded in his tomb? What does this suggest about his status, occupation, and wealth?

EAST AFRICA IN THE EARLY modern period faced repeated incursions from foreign powers. At the beginning of the sixteenth century Ethiopia faced challenges from the Muslim state of Adal, and then from Europeans. Jesuit attempts to impose Roman Catholic practices met with fierce resistance and ushered in a centuries-long period of hostility to foreigners. The wealthy Swahili city-states along the southeastern African coast also resisted European intrusions in the sixteenth century, with even more disastrous results.

CHAPTER LOCATOR | What different types of economic, social, and political structures were found in the kingdoms and states along the west coast and in the Sudan? | How did the arrival of Europeans and other foreign cultures affect the East African coast, and how did Ethiopia and the Swahili city-states respond to these incursions?

592 CHAPTER 20 AFRICA AND THE WORLD

Muslim and European Incursions in Ethiopia, ca. 1500–1630

At the beginning of the sixteenth century the powerful East African kingdom of Ethiopia extended from Massawa in the north to several tributary states in the south (Map 20.2), but the ruling Solomonic dynasty in Ethiopia, in power since the thirteenth century, faced serious external threats. Alone among the states in northeast and eastern Africa, Ethiopia was a Christian kingdom that practiced **Coptic Christianity**, an orthodox form of the Christian faith that originated in Egypt in 451. By the early 1500s Ethiopia was an island of Christianity surrounded by a sea of Muslim states.

Adal, a Muslim state along the southern base of the Red Sea, began incursions into Ethiopia, and in 1529 the Adal general Ahmad ibn-Ghazi inflicted a disastrous defeat on the Ethiopian emperor Lebna Dengel (r. 1508–1540). Ibn-Ghazi followed up his victory with systematic devastation of the land; destruction of many Ethiopian artistic and literary works, churches, and monasteries; and the forced conversion of thousands to Islam. Lebna Dengel fled to the mountains and appealed to Portugal for assistance. The Portuguese came to his aid, but Dengel was killed in battle before the Portuguese arrived. The Muslim occupation of Christian Ethiopia, which began around 1531, ended in 1543, after a joint Ethiopian and Portuguese force defeated a larger Muslim army at the Battle of Wayna Daga.

In the late twelfth century tales of Prester John, rumored to be a powerful Christian monarch ruling a vast and wealthy African empire, reached western Europe. The search for Prester John, as well as for gold and spices, spurred the Portuguese to undertake a series of trans-African expeditions that reached Timbuktu and Mali in the 1480s and the Ethiopian court by 1508. It was their desire to convert Ethiopians from Coptic Christianity to Roman Catholicism that motivated the Portuguese to aid the Ethiopians in defeating Adal's Muslim forces.

No sooner had the Muslim threat ended than Ethiopia encountered three more dangers. The Galla moved northward in great numbers in the 1530s, occupying portions of Harar, Shoa, and Amhara. The Ethiopians could not defeat

Coptic Christianity

▶ Orthodox form of Christianity from Egypt practiced in Ethiopia.

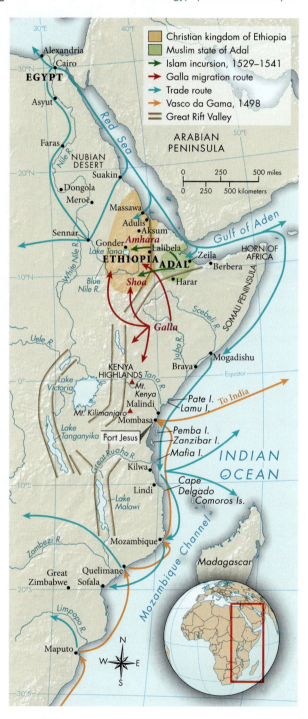

MAP 20.2 ■ East Africa in the Sixteenth Century

In early modern times, the Christian kingdom of Ethiopia, first isolated and then subjected to Muslim and European pressures, played an insignificant role in world affairs. But the East African city-states, which stretched from Sofala in the south to Mogadishu in the north, had powerfully important commercial relations with Mughal India, China, the Ottoman world, and southern Europe.

What role did slavery play in African societies before the transatlantic slave trade began, and what was the effect of European involvement?

 LearningCurve
Check what you know.

This wall painting of Saint George slaying a dragon resides in the stone-carved Church of Saint George in Lalibela, Ethiopia, and attests to the powerful and pervasive Christian influence on Ethiopian culture. (Galen R. Frysinger)

them militarily, and the Galla were not interested in assimilation. For the next two centuries the two peoples lived together in an uneasy truce. Simultaneously, the Ottoman Turks seized Massawa and other coastal cities. Then the Jesuits arrived and attempted to force Roman Catholicism on the Ethiopian people. Since Ethiopian national sentiment was closely tied to Coptic Christianity, violent rebellion and anarchy ensued.

In 1633 the Jesuit missionaries were expelled. For the next two centuries hostility to foreigners, weak political leadership, and regionalism characterized Ethiopia. Civil conflicts between Galla and Ethiopians erupted continually. The Coptic Church, though lacking strong authority, survived as the cornerstone of Ethiopian national identity.

The Swahili City-States and the Arrival of the Portuguese, ca. 1500–1600

Swahili
▶ Meaning "People of the Coast," the term used for the people living along the East African coast and on nearby islands.

The word **Swahili** means "People of the Coast" and refers to the people living along the East African coast and on the nearby islands. Although predominantly a Bantu-speaking people, the Swahili have incorporated significant aspects of Arab culture. The Arabic alphabet was used for the first written works in Swahili and

CHAPTER LOCATOR | What different types of economic, social, and political structures were found in the kingdoms and states along the west coast and in the Sudan? | How did the arrival of Europeans and other foreign cultures affect the East African coast, and how did Ethiopia and the Swahili city-states respond to these incursions?

CHAPTER 20
594 AFRICA AND THE WORLD

roughly 35 percent of Swahili words come from Arabic. By the eleventh century the Swahili had accepted Islam, which provided a common identity and unifying factor for all the peoples along coastal East Africa. Living on the Indian Ocean coast, the Swahili also felt the influences of Indians, Indonesians, Persians, and even the Chinese.

Swahili civilization was overwhelmingly maritime. A fertile, well-watered, and intensely cultivated stretch of land extending down the coast yielded valuable crops. The region's considerable prosperity, however, rested on trade and commerce. The Swahili acted as middlemen in an Indian Ocean–East African economy that might be described as early capitalism. In the fifteenth century the cosmopolitan city-states of Mogadishu, Pate, Lamu, Mombasa, and especially Kilwa enjoyed a worldwide reputation for commercial prosperity and high living standards.[3]

The arrival of the Portuguese explorer Vasco da Gama (see Map 16.2, page 465) in 1498 spelled the end of the Swahili cities' independence. Lured by the spice trade, da Gama wanted to build a Portuguese maritime empire in the Indian Ocean. Some Swahili rulers quickly agreed to a trading alliance with the Portuguese. Others were tricked into commercial agreements. Swahili rulers who rejected Portuguese overtures saw their cities bombarded and attacked. To secure alliances made between 1502 and 1507, the Portuguese erected forts at the southern port cities of Kilwa, Zanzibar, and Sofala. These fortified markets and trading posts served as the foundation of Portuguese commercial power on the Swahili coast. The better-fortified northern cities, such as Mogadishu, survived as important entrepôts for goods to India.

The Portuguese presence in the south did not yield the expected commercial fortunes. Rather than accept Portuguese commercial restrictions, the residents deserted the towns, and the town economies crumbled. Large numbers of Kilwa's people, for example, immigrated to northern cities. The gold flow from inland mines to Sofala slowed to a trickle. Swahili noncooperation successfully prevented the Portuguese from gaining control of the local coastal trade.

In the late seventeenth century pressures from the northern European maritime powers—the Dutch, French, and English, aided greatly by Omani Arabs—combined with local African rebellions to bring about the collapse of Portuguese influence in Africa. A Portuguese presence remained only at Mozambique in the far south and Angola on the west coast.

QUICK REVIEW

What distinctive features characterized East African coastal societies?

What role did slavery play in African societies before the transatlantic slave trade began, and what was the effect of European involvement?

☑ LearningCurve
Check what you know.

What role did slavery play in African societies before the transatlantic slave trade began, and what was the effect of European involvement?

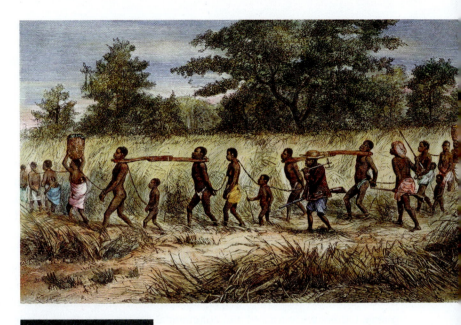

The African Slave Trade

Enslaved African men, women, and children, captured in the interior, are marched to the coast by their African captors. The guards carry guns obtained from Europeans in the slave trade. The enslaved men are linked together by heavy wooden yokes, making it impossible to escape.

THE ENSLAVEMENT OF HUMAN BEINGS was practiced in some form or another all over Africa—indeed, all over the world. Sanctioned by law and custom, enslaved people served critical and well-defined roles in the social, political, and economic organization of many African societies.

Over time, the trans-Saharan slave trade became less important than the transatlantic trade, which witnessed an explosive growth during the seventeenth and eighteenth centuries. The millions of enslaved Africans forcibly exported to the Americas had a lasting impact on African society and led ultimately to a wider use of slaves within Africa itself.

The Institution of Slavery in Africa

Islamic practices strongly influenced African slavery. African rulers justified enslavement with the Muslim argument that prisoners of war could be sold and that captured people were considered chattel. Between 650 and 1600 Muslims transported perhaps as many as 4.82 million black slaves across the trans-Saharan

CHAPTER LOCATOR

What different types of economic, social, and political structures were found in the kingdoms and states along the west coast and in the Sudan?

How did the arrival of Europeans and other foreign cultures affect the East African coast, and how did Ethiopia and the Swahili city-states respond to these incursions?

596 CHAPTER 20 AFRICA AND THE WORLD

trade route.[4] In the fourteenth and fifteenth centuries the rulers and elites of Mali and Benin imported thousands of white Slavic slave women, symbols of wealth and status, who had been seized in slave raids from the Balkans and Caucasus regions of the eastern Mediterranean by Turks, Mongols, and others.[5]

Meanwhile, the flow of black people to Europe, begun during the Renaissance, continued. In the seventeenth and eighteenth centuries as many as two hundred thousand Africans entered European societies. Some arrived as slaves, others as servants; the legal distinction was not always clear. Eighteenth-century London, for example, had more than ten thousand blacks, most of whom arrived as sailors on Atlantic crossings or as personal servants brought from the West Indies. London's black population constituted a well-organized, self-conscious subculture, with black pubs, black churches, and black social groups assisting the black poor and unemployed. Some black people attained wealth and position.

In 1658 the Dutch East India Company (see page 476) began to allow the importation of slaves into the Cape Colony, which the company had founded on the southern tip of Africa in 1652. Over the next century and a half about 75 percent of the slaves brought into the colony came from Dutch East India Company colonies in India and Southeast Asia or from Madagascar; the remaining 25 percent came from Africa. Most worked long and hard as field hands and at any other menial or manual forms of labor needed by their European masters. The Dutch East India Company was the single largest slave owner in the Cape Colony, employing its slaves on public works and company farms.

Although in the seventeenth and eighteenth centuries Holland enjoyed a Europe-wide reputation for religious tolerance and intellectual freedom (see page 535), in the Cape Colony the Dutch used a strict racial hierarchy and heavy-handed paternalism to maintain control over enslaved native and foreign-born peoples. In Muslim society the offspring of a free man and an enslaved woman were free, but in southern Africa such children remained enslaved. Because enslaved males greatly outnumbered enslaved females in the Cape Colony, marriage and family life were almost nonexistent. Because there were few occupations requiring special skills, those enslaved in the colony lacked opportunities to earn manumission, or freedom. And in contrast with North and South America and with Muslim societies, in the Cape Colony only a very small number of those enslaved won manumission.[6]

The slave trade expanded greatly in East Africa's savanna and Horn regions in the late eighteenth century and the first half of the nineteenth century. Why this increased demand? Merchants and planters wanted slaves to work the sugar plantations on the Mascarene Islands, located east of Madagascar; the clove plantations on Zanzibar and Pemba; and the food plantations along the Kenyan coast. The eastern coast also exported enslaved people to the Americas, particularly to

KITCHIN STUFF.

Below Stairs

The prints and cartoons of Thomas Rowlandson (1756–1827) testify to the sizable numbers of blacks in eighteenth-century London, where they worked in naval and military service as well as domestic service. Here the household cook, maid, and footman relax before the kitchen fire. Interracial marriages were not uncommon. (© The Trustees of The British Museum/Art Resource, NY)

Cape Colony, ca. 1750

What role did slavery play in African societies before the transatlantic slave trade began, and what was the effect of European involvement?

✓ LearningCurve
Check what you know.

Brazil. In the late eighteenth and early nineteenth centuries, precisely when the slave trade to North America and the Caribbean declined, the Arabian and Asian markets expanded.

The Transatlantic Slave Trade

Although the trade in African people was a worldwide phenomenon, the transatlantic slave trade involved the largest number of enslaved Africans. This forced migration of millions of human beings, extending from the early sixteenth to the late nineteenth centuries, represents one of the most inhumane, unjust, and shameful tragedies in human history. It also immediately provokes a troubling question: why, in the seventeenth and eighteenth centuries, did enslavement in the Americas become exclusively African?

European settlers first enslaved indigenous peoples, the Amerindians, to mine the silver and gold discovered in the New World (see page 476). When they proved ill suited to the harsh rigors of mining, the Spaniards brought in Africans.

Why did the Spaniards turn to Africa to solve their labor problem? One theory holds that in the Muslim and Arab worlds by the tenth century, an association had developed between blackness and menial slavery. Although the great majority of enslaved persons in the Islamic world were white, a racial element existed in Muslim perceptions: not all slaves were black, but blacks were identified with slavery. In Europe, after the arrival of tens of thousands of sub-Saharan Africans in the Iberian Peninsula during the fifteenth century, Christian Europeans also began to make a strong association between slavery and black Africans. Therefore, Africans seemed the "logical" solution to the labor shortage in the Americas.[7]

Another important question relating to the African slave trade is this: why were African peoples enslaved in a period when serfdom was declining in western Europe, and when land was so widely available and much of the African continent had a labor shortage? The answer seems to lie in a technical problem related to African agriculture. African conditions were unsuitable for plowing with draft animals, and most work had to be done by hand with the hoe. Productivity, therefore, was low. Thus, in precolonial Africa the individual's agricultural productivity was low, so his or her economic value to society was less than the economic value of a European peasant in Europe. Enslaved persons in the Americas were more productive than free producers in Africa. And European slave dealers were very willing to pay a price higher than the value of an African's productivity in Africa.

The incidence of disease in the Americas also helps explain African enslavement. Smallpox took a terrible toll on Native Americans, and between 30 and 50 percent of Europeans exposed to malaria succumbed to that sickness. Africans had developed some immunity to both diseases, and in the Americas they experienced the lowest mortality rate of any people, making them, ironically, the most suitable workers for the environment.

Portuguese colonization of Brazil began in the early 1530s, and in 1551 the Portuguese founded a sugar colony at Bahia. Between 1551 and 1575, before the North American slave traffic began, the Portuguese delivered more African slaves to Brazil than ever reached British North America (Figure 20.1). Portugal essentially monopolized the slave trade until 1600 and continued to play a significant

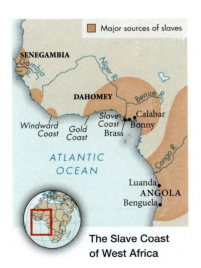

The Slave Coast
of West Africa

CHAPTER LOCATOR | What different types of economic, social, and political structures were found in the kingdoms and states along the west coast and in the Sudan? | How did the arrival of Europeans and other foreign cultures affect the East African coast, and how did Ethiopia and the Swahili city-states respond to these incursions?

598
CHAPTER 20
AFRICA AND THE WORLD

role in the seventeenth century, though the trade was increasingly taken over by the Dutch, French, and English. From 1690 until the British House of Commons abolished the slave trade in 1807, England was the leading carrier of African slaves.

Population density and supply conditions along the West African coast and the sailing time to New World markets determined the sources of slaves. As the demand for slaves rose, slavers moved down the West African coast from Senegambia to the more densely populated hinterlands of the Bight of Benin and the Bight of Biafra. The abundant supply of Africans to enslave in Angola, the region south of the Congo River, and the quick passage from Angola to Brazil and the Caribbean established that region as the major coast for Portuguese slavers.

Transatlantic wind patterns partly determined exchange routes. Shippers naturally preferred the swiftest crossing—that is, from the African port nearest the latitude of the intended American destination. Thus Portuguese shippers carried their cargoes from Angola to Brazil, and British merchants sailed from the Bight of Benin to the Caribbean. The great majority of enslaved Africans were intended for the sugar and coffee plantations extending from the Caribbean islands to Brazil. Angola produced 26 percent of all African slaves and 70 percent of all Portuguese slaves. Trading networks extending deep into the interior culminated at two major ports on the Angolan coast, Luanda and Benguela. The Portuguese acquired a few slaves through warfare but secured the vast majority through trade with African dealers. Whites did not participate in the inland markets, which were run solely by Africans.

Almost all Portuguese shipments went to satisfy the virtually insatiable Brazilian demand for slaves. The so-called **Middle Passage** was the horrific journey experienced by Africans from freedom to enslavement in the Americas. Packed tightly into nearly airless holds, enslaved Africans were treated as animals, with large numbers succumbing to disease, malnutrion, and despair before they reached their destination.

Olaudah Equiano (see "Individuals in Society: Olaudah Equiano," page 600) describes the experience of his voyage as a captured slave from Benin to Barbados in the Caribbean:

> The stench of the hold while we were on the coast was so intolerably loathsome that it was dangerous to remain there for any time, and some of us had been permitted to stay on the deck for the fresh air; but now that the whole

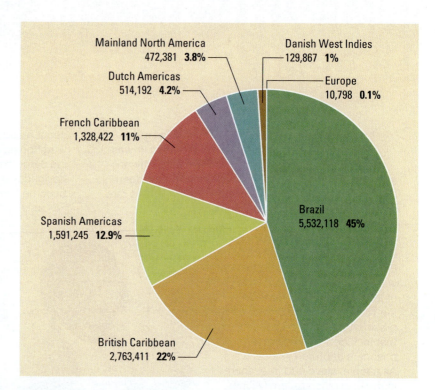

FIGURE 20.1 ■ Estimated Slave Imports by Destination, 1501–1866

Brazil was the single largest importer of African slaves from 1501 to 1866. But when taken cumulatively, the British, French, Dutch, and Danish colonies of the Caribbean rivaled the much larger colony of Brazil for numbers of slaves imported from Africa.
(Source: Data from Emory University. "Assessing the Slave Trade: Estimates," in *Voyages: The Trans-Atlantic Slave Trade Database*. 2009. http://www.slavevoyages.org.)

Middle Passage

▶ African slaves' voyage across the Atlantic to the Americas, a long and treacherous journey during which slaves endured appalling and often deadly conditions.

What role did slavery play in African societies before the transatlantic slave trade began, and what was the effect of European involvement?

 LearningCurve
Check what you know.

The transatlantic slave trade was a mass movement involving millions of human beings. It was also the sum of individual lives spent partly or entirely in slavery. Most of those lives remain hidden to us. Olaudah Equiano (1745–1797) represents a rare window into the slaves' obscurity; he is probably the best-known African slave.

In his autobiography, *The Interesting Narrative of the Life of Olaudah Equiano* (1789), Equiano says that he was born in Benin (modern Nigeria) of Ibo ethnicity.* His father, one of the village elders (or chieftains), presided over a large household that included "many slaves," prisoners captured in local wars. All people, slave and free, shared in the cultivation of family lands. One day, when all the adults were in the fields, two strange men and a woman broke into the family compound, kidnapped the eleven-year-old Olaudah and his sister, tied them up, and dragged them into the woods. Brother and sister were separated, and Olaudah was sold several times to various dealers before reaching the coast. As it took six months to walk there, his home must have been far inland. The sea, the slave ship, and the strange appearance of the white crew terrified the boy (see page 599). Equiano's master took him to Jamaica, to Virginia, and then to England, where he placed him in the custody of a kind family. They gave him the rudiments of an education, and he was baptized a Christian.

Equiano soon went to sea as a captain's boy (servant), serving in the Royal Navy during the Seven Years' War (see page 647). On shore at Portsmouth, England, after one battle, Equiano was urged by his master to read, study, and learn basic mathematics. This education served him well, for after a voyage to the West Indies, his master sold him to a Philadelphia Quaker, Robert King, who was a rum and sugar merchant. Equiano worked as a clerk in King's warehouse, as a longshoreman loading and unloading cargo ships, and at sea where he developed good navigational skills; King paid him for his work. Equiano became an entrepreneur himself, buying and selling small goods in the islands and mainland ports.

Determined to buy his freedom, Equiano had amassed enough money by 1766, and King signed the deed of manumission. Equiano was twenty-one years old; he had been a slave for ten years.

Equiano returned to London and used his remaining money to hire tutors to teach him hairdressing, mathematics, and how to play the French horn. When money was scarce, he found work as a merchant seaman, traveling to Portugal, Nice, Genoa, Naples, and Turkey. He even participated in an Arctic expedition.

Equiano's *Narrative* reveals a complex and sophisticated man. He had a strong constitution and an equally strong character. His Christian faith undoubtedly sustained him. On the title page of his book, he cited a verse from Isaiah (12:2): "The Lord Jehovah is my strength and my song." The very first thought that came to his mind the day he was freed was a passage from Psalm 126: "I glorified God in my heart, in whom I trusted."

Equiano loathed the brutal slavery he saw in the West Indies and the vicious racism he experienced in the North American colonies. He respected the fairness of Robert King, admired British navigational and industrial technologies, and had many close white friends. He once described himself as "almost an Englishman." He was also involved in the black communities in the West Indies and in London. Equiano's *Narrative* is a well-documented argument for the abolition of slavery and a literary classic that went through nine editions before his death.

Olaudah Equiano's *Narrative*, with its horrific descriptions of slavery, proved influential, and after its publication Equiano became active in the abolition movement. He spoke to large crowds in the industrial cities of Manchester and Birmingham in England, arguing that it was in the business interests of manufacturers to support abolition, as Africa was a huge,

In this 1789 portrait, Olaudah Equiano holds his Bible, open to the book of Acts. (1789 mezzotint, British Library, London, UK/© British Library Board. All Rights Reserved./The Bridgeman Art Library)

*Recent scholarship has re-examined Equiano's life and raised some questions about his African origins and his experience of the Middle Passage. To explore the debate over Equiano's authorship of the African and Middle Passage portions of his autobiography, see Vincent Carretta, *Equiano, the African: Biography of a Self-Made Man* (New York: Penguin, 2007).

virtually untapped market for English cloth. Though he died in 1797, ten years before its passage, Equiano significantly advanced the abolitionist cause that led to the Slave Trade Act of 1807.

Source: *Equiano's Travels: The Interesting Narrative of the Life of Olaudah Equiano*, ed. Paul Edwards (Portsmouth, N.H.: Heinemann, 1996).

QUESTIONS FOR ANALYSIS

1. How typical was Olaudah Equiano's life as a slave? How atypical?
2. Describe Equiano's culture and his sense of himself.

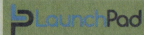

ONLINE DOCUMENT PROJECT

What role did slave accounts play in antislavery activism? Read several first-person accounts of slavery, and then complete a quiz and writing assignment based on the evidence and details from this chapter. *See inside the front cover to learn more.*

ship's cargo were confined together it became absolutely pestilential. The closeness of the place and the heat of the climate, added to the number in the ship, which was so crowded that each had scarcely room to turn himself, almost suffocated us. This produced copious perspirations, so that the air soon became unfit for respiration from a variety of loathsome smells, and brought on a sickness among the slaves, of which many died. . . . This wretched situation was again aggravated by the galling of the chains, now become insupportable, and the filth of the necessary tubs [of human waste], into which the children often fell and were almost suffocated. The shrieks of the women and the groans of the dying rendered the whole a scene of horror almost inconceivable.[8]

Although the demand was great, Portuguese merchants in Angola and Brazil sought to maintain only a steady trickle of slaves from the African interior to Luanda and across the ocean to Bahia and Rio de Janeiro: a flood of slaves would have depressed the American market. Planters and mine operators from the provinces traveled to Rio to buy slaves. Between 1795 and 1808 approximately 10,000 Angolans per year stood in the Rio slave market. In 1810 the figure rose to 18,000; in 1828 it reached 32,000.[9]

The English ports of London, Bristol, and particularly Liverpool dominated the British slave trade. In the eighteenth century Liverpool was the world's greatest slave-trading port. In all three cities, small and cohesive merchant classes exercised great public influence. The cities also had huge stores of industrial products for export, growing shipping industries, and large amounts of ready cash for investment abroad.

Slaving ships from Bristol plied back and forth along the Gold Coast, the Bight of Benin, Bonny, and Calabar looking for African traders who were willing to supply them with slaves. Liverpool's ships drew enslaved people from Gambia, the Windward Coast, and the Gold Coast. British ships carried textiles, gunpowder and flint, beer and spirits, British and Irish linens, and woolen cloth to Africa. A collection of goods was grouped together

Peddlers in Rio de Janeiro

A British army officer sketched this early-nineteenth-century scene of everyday life in Rio de Janeiro, Brazil. The ability to balance large burdens on the head meant that the person's hands were free for other use. Note the player (on the left) of a musical instrument originating in the Congo. On the right a woman gives alms to the man with the holy image in return for being allowed to kiss the image as an act of devotion. We do not know whether the peddlers were free and self-employed or were selling for their owners. (From "Views and Costumes of the City and Neighborhood of Rio de Janeiro, Brazil," in *Drawings Taken by Lieutenant Henry Chamberlain, During the Years 1819 and 1820* [London: Columbian Press, 1822]/ Visual Connection Archive)

sorting

▶ A collection or batch of British goods that would be traded for a slave or for a quantity of gold, ivory, or dyewood.

shore trading

▶ A process for trading goods in which European ships sent boats ashore or invited African dealers to bring traders and slaves out to the ships.

into what was called the **sorting**. An English sorting might include bolts of cloth, firearms, alcohol, tobacco, and hardware; this batch of goods was traded for an enslaved individual or a quantity of gold, ivory, or dyewood.[10]

European traders had two systems for exchange. First, especially on the Gold Coast, they established factory-forts. (For more on factory-forts, see page 502.) These fortified trading posts were expensive to maintain but proved useful for fending off European rivals. Second, they used **shore trading**, in which European ships sent boats ashore or invited African dealers to bring traders and enslaved Africans out to the ships.

The shore method of buying slaves allowed the ship to move easily from market to market. The final prices of those enslaved depended on their ethnic origin, their availability when the shipper arrived, and their physical health when offered for sale in the West Indies or the North or South American colonies.

The supply of slaves for the foreign market was controlled by a small, wealthy African merchant class or by a state monopoly. By contemporary standards, slave raiding was a costly operation, and only black African entrepreneurs with sizable capital and labor could afford to finance and direct raiding drives.

The transatlantic slave trade that the British, as well as the Dutch, Portuguese, French, Americans, and others, participated in was part of a much larger trading network that is known as the triangle trade. European merchants sailed to Africa on the first leg of the voyage to trade European manufactured goods for enslaved Africans. When they had filled their ships' holds with enslaved peoples,

CHAPTER LOCATOR | What different types of economic, social, and political structures were found in the kingdoms and states along the west coast and in the Sudan? | How did the arrival of Europeans and other foreign cultures affect the East African coast, and how did Ethiopia and the Swahili city-states respond to these incursions?

602 CHAPTER 20 AFRICA AND THE WORLD

they headed across the Atlantic on the second leg of the voyage, the Middle Passage. When they reached the Americas, the merchants unloaded and sold their human cargoes and used the profits to purchase raw materials—such as cotton, sugar, and indigo—that they then transported back to Europe, completing the third leg of the commercial triangle.

> **The Triangle Trade:**

- Africa: Europeans trade manufactured goods for enslaved Africans
- The Americas: Enslaved Africans are sold and raw materials are purchased
- Europe: Raw materials are sold and manufactured goods are purchased

Enslaved African people had an enormous impact on the economies and cultures of the Portuguese and Spanish colonies of South America and the Dutch, French, and British colonies of the Caribbean and North America. For example, on the sugar plantations of Mexico and the Caribbean; on the North American cotton, rice, and tobacco plantations; and in Peruvian and Mexican silver and gold mines, enslaved Africans not only worked in the mines and fields but also filled skilled, supervisory, and administrative positions and performed domestic service. In the United States enslaved Africans and their descendants influenced many facets of American culture, such as language, music (ragtime and jazz), dance, and diet. But the importance of the slave trade extended beyond the Atlantic world. Both the expansion of capitalism and the industrialization of Western societies; Egypt; and the nations of West, Central, and South Africa were related in one way or another to the traffic in African people.

Impact on African Societies

What economic impact did European trade have on African societies? Africans possessed technology well suited to their environment. Over the centuries they had cultivated a wide variety of plant foods; developed plant and animal husbandry techniques; and mined, smelted, and otherwise worked a great variety of metals. Apart from a handful of items, most notably firearms, European goods presented no novelty to Africans. Africans exchanged slaves, ivory, gold, pepper, and animal skins for those goods. African states eager to expand or to control commerce bought European firearms, although the difficulty of maintaining guns often gave gun owners only marginal superiority over skilled bowmen.[11]

The African merchants who controlled the production of exports gained the most from foreign trade. Slave-trading entrepôts, which provided opportunities for traders and for farmers who supplied foodstuffs to towns, caravans, and slave ships, prospered. But such economic returns did not spread very far.[12] International trade did not lead to Africa's economic development. Africa experienced neither technological growth nor the gradual spread of economic benefits in early modern times.

As in the Islamic world, women in sub-Saharan Africa also engaged in the slave trade. In Guinea these women slave merchants and traders were known as *nhara*. They acquired considerable riches, often by marrying the Portuguese merchants and serving as go-betweens for these outsiders who were not familiar with the customs and languages of the African coast.

What role did slavery play in African societies before the transatlantic slave trade began, and what was the effect of European involvement?

 LearningCurve
Check what you know.

Sapi-Portuguese Saltcellar

Contact with the Sapi people of present-day Sierra Leone in West Africa led sixteenth-century Portuguese traders to commission this ivory saltcellar, for which they brought Portuguese designs. But the object's basic features — a spherical container and separate lid on a flat base, with men and/or women supporting, or serving as, beams below — are distinctly African. Here a Portuguese caravel sits on top with a man in the crow's nest. Four men stand below: two finely carved, regally dressed, and fully armed noblemen facing forward and two attendants in profile. (© akg-images/The Image Works)

The intermarriage of French traders and Wolof women in Senegambia created a métis, or mulatto, class. In the emerging urban centers at Saint-Louis, members of this small class adopted the French language, the Roman Catholic faith, and a French manner of life, and they exercised considerable political and economic power. However, European cultural influences did not penetrate West African society beyond the seacoast.

The political consequences of the slave trade varied from place to place. The trade enhanced the power and wealth of some kings and warlords in the short run but promoted conditions of instability and collapse over the long run. In the Kongo kingdom the perpetual Portuguese search for Africans to enslave undermined the monarchy, destroyed political unity, and led to constant disorder and warfare; power passed to the village chiefs. Likewise in Angola, the slave trade decimated and scattered the population and destroyed the local economy. By contrast, the military kingdom of Dahomey, which entered into the slave trade in the eighteenth century and made it a royal monopoly, prospered enormously. Dahomey's economic strength rested on the slave trade. The royal army raided deep into the interior, and in the late eighteenth century Dahomey became one of the major West African sources of slaves. When slaving expeditions failed to yield sizable catches and when European demand declined, the resulting depression in the Dahomean economy caused serious political unrest. Iboland, inland from the Niger Delta, from whose great port cities of Bonny and Brass the British drained tens of thousands of enslaved Africans, experienced minimal political effects. A high birthrate kept pace with the incursions of the slave trade, and Ibo societies remained demographically and economically strong.

What demographic impact did the slave trade have on Africa? Between approximately 1501 and 1866 more than 12 million Africans were forcibly exported to the Americas, 6 million were traded to Asia, and 8 million were retained as slaves within Africa. Figure 20.2 shows the estimated number of slaves shipped to the Americas in the transatlantic slave trade. Export figures do not include the

CHAPTER LOCATOR | What different types of economic, social, and political structures were found in the kingdoms and states along the west coast and in the Sudan?

How did the arrival of Europeans and other foreign cultures affect the East African coast, and how did Ethiopia and the Swahili city-states respond to these incursions?

CHAPTER 20

604 AFRICA AND THE WORLD

approximately 10 to 15 percent who died during procurement or in transit.

The early modern slave trade involved a worldwide network of relationships among markets in the Middle East, Africa, Asia, Europe, and the Americas. But Africa was the crucible of the trade. There is no small irony in the fact that Africa, which of all the continents was most desperately in need of population because of its near total dependence on labor-intensive agriculture and pastoralism, lost so many millions to the trade. Although the British Parliament abolished the slave trade in 1807 and traffic in Africans to Brazil and Cuba gradually declined, within Africa the trade continued at the levels of the peak years of the transatlantic trade, 1780–1820. In the later nineteenth century developing African industries, using slave labor, produced a variety of products for domestic consumption and export. Again, there is irony in the fact that in the eighteenth century European demand for slaves expanded the trade (and wars) within Africa, yet in the nineteenth century European imperialists defended territorial aggrandizement by arguing that they were "civilizing" Africans by abolishing slavery. But after 1880 European businessmen (and African governments) did not push abolition; they wanted cheap labor.

Markets in the Americas generally wanted young male slaves. Asian and African markets preferred young females. Women were sought for their reproductive value, as sex objects, and because their economic productivity was not threatened by the possibility of physical rebellion, as might be the case with young men. Consequently, two-thirds of those exported to the Americas were male, one-third female. As a result, the population on Africa's western coast became predominantly female; the population in the East African savanna and Horn regions was predominantly male. The slave trade therefore had significant consequences for the institutions of marriage, the local trade in enslaved people (as these local populations became skewed with too many males or too many females), and the sexual division of labor. Although Africa's overall population may have shown modest growth from roughly 1650 to 1900, that growth was offset by declines in the Horn and on the eastern and western coasts. While Europe and Asia experienced considerable demographic and economic expansion in the eighteenth century, Africa suffered a decline.[13]

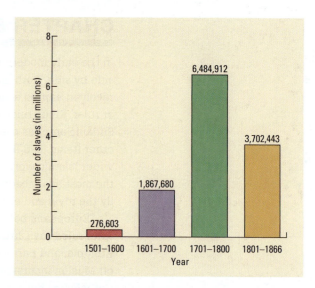

FIGURE 20.2 ▪ The Transatlantic Slave Trade, 1501–1866

The volume of slaves involved in the transatlantic slave trade peaked during the eighteenth century. These numbers show the slaves who embarked from Africa and do not reflect the 10 to 15 percent of enslaved Africans who died in transit. (Source: Data from Emory University. "Assessing the Slave Trade: Estimates," in *Voyages: The Trans-Atlantic Slave Trade Database.* 2009. http://www.slavevoyages.org.)

QUICK REVIEW ❮

How did the transatlantic slave trade shape African demographic trends?

What role did slavery play in African societies before the transatlantic slave trade began, and what was the effect of European involvement?

 LearningCurve
Check what you know.

CHAPTER SUMMARY

In the early modern world, West African kingdoms and stateless societies existed side by side. Both had predominantly agricultural economies. Stateless societies revolved around a single village or group of villages without a central capital or ruler. Kings ruled over defined areas through bureaucratic hierarchies. The Sudanic empires controlled the north-south trans-Saharan trade in gold, salt, and other items. Led by predominantly Muslim rulers, these kingdoms belonged to a wider Islamic world, allowing them access to vast trade networks and some of the most advanced scholarship in the world. Still, Muslim culture affected primarily the royal and elite classes, seldom reaching the masses.

Europeans believed a wealthy (mythical) Christian monarch named Prester John ruled the Christian kingdom of Ethiopia. This fable attracted Europeans to Ethiopia, and partly explains why the Portuguese helped the Ethiopians fight off Muslim incursions. Jesuit missionaries tried to convert Ethiopians to Roman Catholicism but were fiercely resisted and expelled in 1633.

Swahili city-states on Africa's southeastern coast possessed a Muslim and mercantile culture. The Swahili acted as middlemen in the East African–Indian Ocean trade network, which, in the late fifteenth and early sixteenth centuries, Portugal sought to conquer and control. Swahili rulers who refused to form trading alliances with the Portuguese were attacked. The Portuguese presence caused the economic decline and death of many Swahili cities.

Slavery existed across Africa before Europeans arrived. Enslaved people were treated relatively benignly in some societies but elsewhere as chattel possessions, suffering harsh and brutal treatment. European involvement in the slave trade began around 1550, when the Portuguese purchased Africans to work in Brazil. The Dutch East India Company used enslaved Africans and southeast Asians in their Cape Colony. African entrepreneurs and merchants partnered in the trade, capturing people in the interior and exchanging them for firearms, liquor, and other goods with European slave ships. Though some kingdoms experienced a temporary rise of wealth and power, over time the slave trade was largely destabilizing. The individual suffering and social disruption in Africa caused by the enslavement of millions of Africans is impossible to estimate.

 **CONNECTIONS** During the period from 1400 to 1800 many parts of Africa experienced a profound transition with the arrival of Europeans all along Africa's coasts. Ancient trade routes, such as those across the Sahara Desert or up and down the East African coast, were disrupted. In West Africa trade routes that had been purely internal now connected with global trade networks at European coastal trading posts. Along Africa's east coast the Portuguese attacked Swahili city-states in their effort to take control of the Indian Ocean trade nexus.

The most momentous consequence of the European presence along Africa's coast, however, was the introduction of the transatlantic slave trade. For more than three centuries Europeans, with the aid of African slave traders, enslaved millions of African men and women. Although many parts of Africa were untouched by the

CHAPTER LOCATOR | What different types of economic, social, and political structures were found in the kingdoms and states along the west coast and in the Sudan?

How did the arrival of Europeans and other foreign cultures affect the East African coast, and how did Ethiopia and the Swahili city-states respond to these incursions?

606 CHAPTER 20 AFRICA AND THE WORLD

transatlantic slave trade, at least directly, areas where Africans were enslaved experienced serious declines in agricultural production, little progress in technological development, and significant increases in violence.

As we saw in Chapter 17 and will see in Chapter 21, early European commercial contacts with the empires of the Middle East and of South and East Asia were similar in many ways to those with Africa. Initially, the Portuguese, and then the English, Dutch, and French, did little more than establish trading posts at port cities and had to depend on the local people to bring them trade goods from the interior. Tropical diseases, particularly in India and Southeast Asia, took heavy death tolls on the Europeans, as they did in tropical Africa. What is more, while it was possible for the Portuguese to attack and conquer the individual Swahili city-states, Middle Eastern and Asian empires were, like the West African kingdoms, economically and militarily powerful enough to dictate terms of trade with the Europeans.

Resistance to enslavement took many forms on both sides of the Atlantic. In Haiti, as discussed in Chapter 22, resistance led to revolution and independence, marking the first successful uprising of non-Europeans against a colonial power. At the end of the nineteenth century, as described in Chapter 25, Europeans used the ongoing Arab-Swahili slave raids from Africa's eastern coast far into the interior as an excuse to invade and eventually colonize much of central and eastern Africa. The racial discrimination that accompanied colonial rule in Africa set the stage for a struggle for equality that led to eventual independence after World War II.

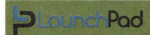

ONLINE DOCUMENT PROJECT

African Voices in the Antislavery Movement

What role did slave accounts play in antislavery activism?

Read several first-person accounts of slavery, and then complete a quiz and writing assignment based on the evidence and details from this chapter. *See inside the front cover to learn more.*

What role did slavery play in African societies before the transatlantic slave trade began, and what was the effect of European involvement?

LearningCurve
Check what you know.

CHAPTER 20 STUDY GUIDE

STEP 1 **GET STARTED ONLINE**

LearningCurve
Now that you've read the chapter, make it stick by completing the LearningCurve activity.

STEP 2 **EXPLAIN WHY IT MATTERS**

Put your reading into practice. Identify each term below, and then explain why it matters in world history.

TERM	WHO OR WHAT & WHEN	WHY IT MATTERS
chattel (p. 585)		
age-grade systems (p. 585)		
oba (p. 587)		
Taghaza (p. 587)		
Tuareg (p. 590)		
cowrie shells (p. 591)		
Coptic Christianity (p. 593)		
Swahili (p. 594)		
Middle Passage (p. 599)		
sorting (p. 602)		
shore trading (p. 602)		

STEP 3 **MOVE BEYOND THE BASICS**

To demonstrate a more advanced understanding of early modern West and East Africa, fill in the chart below with descriptions of key aspects of each region. What were the most important differences between West African and East African states?

	Political Organization	Economy and Commerce	Relationship to Europe and the Muslim World	Slavery and the Slave Trade
West Africa				
East Africa				

STEP 4 **PUT IT ALL TOGETHER** Now, take a step back and try to explain the big picture. Remember to use specific examples from the chapter in your answers.

WEST AFRICA

▶ What was the relationship between stateless societies and the dominant states of West Africa?

▶ How did the slave trade shape marriage patterns and family structure in West Africa?

EAST AFRICA

▶ What was the legacy for Ethiopia of early modern conflicts among Muslims, Coptic Christians, and Roman Catholics?

▶ Why was the arrival of the Portuguese an economic disaster for East Africa?

THE AFRICAN SLAVE TRADE

▶ What economic forces, both inside Africa and in the larger Atlantic world, contributed to the growth of the transatlantic slave trade?

▶ How and why did enslavement in the Americas become exclusively African?

LOOKING BACK, LOOKING AHEAD

▶ How did the transatlantic slave trade build on earlier African labor practices and commercial connections? How were older patterns of trade and exchange disrupted by the demand for African slaves in the Americas?

▶ What connections can you make between the colonization and exploitation of Africa by industrialized nations in the nineteenth and twentieth centuries and the transatlantic slave trade?

> **IN YOUR OWN WORDS**

Imagine that you must give an oral report to the class answering the following question: **What were the short-term and long-term consequences of the transatlantic slave trade for African societies?** What would be the most important points and why?

21
CONTINUITY AND CHANGE IN EAST ASIA

1400–1800

> **What fueled population and economic growth in East Asia between 1400 and 1800?** Chapter 21 examines major developments in China and Japan from 1400 to 1800. Under the Ming (1368–1644), China saw agricultural reconstruction, commercial expansion, and the rise of a vibrant urban culture. In the early seventeenth century, after the Ming Dynasty fell into disorder, the non-Chinese Manchus founded the Qing Dynasty (1644–1911) and added Taiwan, Mongolia, Tibet, and Xinjiang to their realm. In Japan the fifteenth century saw the start of a long period of civil war. At the end of the sixteenth century, Hideyoshi (HEE-deh-YOH-shee) became the supreme ruler. After his death, power was seized by Tokugawa Ieyasu (toh-koo-GAH-wuh ee-eh-YAH-soo). Under the Tokugawa Shogunate (1603–1867), Japan restricted contact with the outside world and social mobility among its own people. Yet Japan thrived, as agricultural productivity increased and a lively urban culture developed.

Kabuki Actor Urban entertainment flourished in Japan under the rule of the Tokugawa shoguns. This late-eighteenth-century woodblock print was made for the many fans of the Kabuki actor Matsumoto Yonesaburo, who specialized in performing female roles. (Private Collection/Photo © Boltin Picture Library/The Bridgeman Art Library)

> What sort of state and society developed in China after the Mongols were ousted?

> Did the return of alien rule with the Manchus have any positive consequences for China?

> How did Japan change during this period of political instability?

> What was life like in Japan during the Tokugawa peace?

> How did the sea link the countries of East Asia, and what happened when Europeans entered this maritime sphere?

LearningCurve
After reading the chapter, use LearningCurve to retain what you've read.

What sort of state and society developed in China after the Mongols were ousted?

Portrait of a Scholar-Official

The official Jiang Shunfu arranged to have his portrait painted wearing an official robe and hat and followed by two boy attendants, one holding a lute wrapped in cloth. During Ming and Qing times, the rank of an official was made visible by the badges he wore on his robes. The pair of cranes on Jiang's badge shows he held a first-rank post in the civil service hierarchy. (From *Mingqing renwuxiaoxiang huaxuan* [Nanjing: Nanjing Bowuguan], pl 16/Visual Connection Archive)

THE OVERTHROW OF THE MONGOLS and the establishment of the Ming Dynasty ushered in an era of peace, prosperity, and lively urban culture. By the beginning of the seventeenth century, however, the Ming government was beset by fiscal, military, and political problems.

Ming Dynasty

▶ The Chinese dynasty in power from 1368 to 1644; it marked a period of agricultural reconstruction, foreign expeditions, commercial expansion, and vibrant urban culture.

The Rise of Zhu Yuanzhang and the Founding of the Ming Dynasty

The founder of the **Ming Dynasty**, Zhu Yuanzhang (1328–1398) (JOO yoowan-JAHNG), began life in poverty during the last decades of the Mongol Yuan Dynasty. His home region was hit by drought and then plague in the 1340s, and when he

CHAPTER LOCATOR | What sort of state and society developed in China after the Mongols were ousted? | Did the return of alien rule with the Manchus have any positive consequences for China?

612 CHAPTER 21 CONTINUITY AND CHANGE IN EAST ASIA

1368–1644 Ming Dynasty in China	**1603–1867** Tokugawa Shogunate in Japan
1405–1433 Zheng He's naval expeditions	**1615** Battle of Osaka leads to persecution of Christians in Japan
1407–1420 Construction of Beijing as Chinese capital	**1629** Tokugawa government bans actresses from the stage
1467–1600 Period of civil war in Japan	**1639** Japan closes its borders
ca. 1500–1600 Increased availability of books for general audiences in China	**1644–1911** Qing Dynasty in China
1549 First Jesuit missionaries land in Japan	**1793** Lord Macartney's diplomatic visit to China
1557 Portuguese set up trading base at Macao	

was only sixteen years old, his father, oldest brother, and that brother's wife all died. With no relatives to turn to, Zhu Yuanzhang asked a monastery to accept him as a novice. The monks soon sent Zhu out to beg for food, and for three or four years he wandered through central China. Only after he returned to the monastery did he learn to read.

In 1351 members of a religious sect known as the Red Turbans rose in rebellion against the government. Red Turban teachings drew on Manichaean ideas about the incompatibility of the forces of good and evil as well as on the cult of the Maitreya Buddha, who according to believers would in the future bring his paradise to earth to relieve human suffering. When the temple where Zhu Yuanzhang was living was burned down in the fighting, Zhu joined the rebels and rose rapidly.

Zhu and his followers developed into brilliant generals, and gradually they defeated one rival after another. In 1356 Zhu took the city of Nanjing and made it his base. In 1368 his armies took Beijing, and Zhu Yuanzhang declared himself emperor of the Ming (Bright) Dynasty. As emperor, he is known as Taizu (TIGH-dzoo) or the Hongwu emperor.

Taizu started his reign wanting to help the poor. To lighten the weight of government taxes and compulsory labor, he ordered a full-scale registration of cultivated land and population so that these burdens could be assessed more fairly.

Although in many ways anti-Mongol, Taizu retained some Yuan practices. One was setting up provinces as the administrative layer between the central government and the prefectures (local governments a step above counties). Another was the hereditary service obligation for both artisan and military households.

Garrisons were concentrated along the northern border and near the capital at Nanjing. Each garrison was allocated a tract of land that the soldiers took turns cultivating to supply their own food. Although in theory this system should have provided the Ming with a large but inexpensive army, the reality was less satisfactory. Garrisons were rarely self-sufficient. Furthermore, men compelled to

Ming China, ca. 1600

How did Japan change during this period of political instability?	What was life like in Japan during the Tokugawa peace?	How did the sea link the countries of East Asia, and what happened when Europeans entered this maritime sphere?	✓ LearningCurve Check what you know.

613

become soldiers did not necessarily make good fighting men, and desertion was difficult to prevent. Consequently, like earlier dynasties, the Ming turned to non-Chinese northerners for much of its armed forces.

Taizu had deeply ambivalent feelings about men of education and sometimes brutally humiliated them in open court. His behavior was so erratic that it is most likely that he suffered from some form of mental illness. When literary men began to avoid official life, Taizu made it illegal to turn down appointments or to resign from office. In 1376 Taizu had thousands of officials killed because they were found to have taken shortcuts in their handling of paperwork for the grain tax. In 1380 Taizu concluded that his chancellor was plotting to assassinate him, and thousands only remotely connected to the chancellor were executed. From then on, Taizu acted as his own chancellor, dealing directly with the heads of departments and ministries.

The next important emperor, called Chengzu or the Yongle emperor (r. 1403–1425), was also a military man. One of Taizu's younger sons, he took the throne by force from his nephew and often led troops into battle against the Mongols. Like his father, Chengzu was willing to use terror to keep government officials in line.

Early in his reign, Chengzu decided to move the capital from Nanjing to Beijing, which had been his own base as a prince and the capital during Mongol times. Constructed between 1407 and 1420, Beijing was a planned city. Like Chang'an in Sui-Tang times (581–907), it was arranged like a set of boxes within boxes and built on a north-south axis. The main outer walls were forty feet high and nearly fifteen miles around. Inside was the Imperial City, with government offices, and within that the palace itself, called the Forbidden City.

The areas surrounding Beijing were not nearly as agriculturally productive as those around Nanjing. To supply Beijing with grain, the Yuan Grand Canal connecting the city to the rice basket of the Yangzi River regions was broadened, deepened, and supplied with more locks and dams.

Forbidden City

The palace complex in Beijing, commonly called the Forbidden City, was built in the early fifteenth century when the capital was moved from Nanjing to Beijing. Audience halls and other important state buildings are arranged on a north-south axis with huge courtyards between them, where officials would stand during ceremonies. (sinopictures/Wenxiao–ullstein bild/The Granger Collection, NYC — All rights reserved)

CHAPTER LOCATOR | **What sort of state and society developed in China after the Mongols were ousted?** | Did the return of alien rule with the Manchus have any positive consequences for China?

Problems with the Imperial Institution

Taizu had decreed that succession should go to the eldest son of the empress or to the son's eldest son if the son predeceased his father, the system generally followed by earlier dynasties. In Ming times, the flaws in this system became apparent as one mediocre, obtuse, or erratic emperor followed another.

Because Taizu had abolished the position of chancellor, emperors turned to secretaries and eunuchs to manage the paperwork. Eunuchs were essentially slaves. Society considered eunuchs the basest of servants, and Confucian scholars heaped scorn on them. Yet Ming emperors, like rulers in earlier dynasties, often preferred the always-compliant eunuchs to high-minded, moralizing civil service officials.

In Ming times, the eunuch establishment became huge. By the late fifteenth century the eunuch bureaucracy had grown as large as the civil service. After 1500 the eunuch bureaucracy grew even more rapidly, and by the mid-sixteenth century seventy thousand eunuchs were in service throughout the country, with ten thousand in the capital. Tension between the two bureaucracies was high. In 1420 Chengzu set up a eunuch-run secret service to investigate cases of suspected corruption and sedition in the regular bureaucracy. Eunuch control over vital government processes became a severe problem.

In hope of persuading emperors to make reforms, many Ming officials risked their careers and lives by speaking out and engaging in public protests. The Confucian tradition celebrated these acts of political protest as heroic. Rarely, however, did they succeed in moving an emperor to change his mind.

Although the educated public complained about the performance of emperors, no one proposed or even imagined alternatives to imperial rule. High officials were forced to find ways to work around uncooperative emperors, but they were not able to put in place institutions that would limit the damage an emperor could do. Knowing that strong emperors often acted erratically, many high officials came to prefer weak emperors who let them take care of the government.

The Mongols and the Great Wall

The early Ming emperors feared the formation of another great Mongol military machine of the sort Chinggis Khan (ca. 1162–1227) had put together two centuries earlier. Although in Ming times the Mongols were never united in a pan-Mongol federation, groups of Mongols could and did raid. Twice they threatened the dynasty: in 1449 the khan of the western Mongols captured the Chinese emperor, and in 1550 Beijing was surrounded by the forces of the khan of the Mongols in Inner Mongolia. Fearful of anything that might strengthen the Mongols, Ming officials were reluctant to grant any privileges to Mongol leaders, such as trading posts along the borders. Instead they wanted the different groups of Mongols to trade only through the formal tribute system. When trade was finally liberalized in 1570, friction was reduced.

Two important developments shaped Ming-Mongol relations: the construction of the Great Wall, and closer relations between Mongolia and Tibet. The Great Wall extends about 1,500 miles from northeast of Beijing into Gansu province. In the eastern 500 miles, the wall averages about 35 feet high and 20 feet across, with lookout towers every half mile.

Whether the wall did much to protect Ming China from the Mongols is still debated. Perhaps of more significance was the spread of Tibetan Buddhism

| How did Japan change during this period of political instability? | What was life like in Japan during the Tokugawa peace? | How did the sea link the countries of East Asia, and what happened when Europeans entered this maritime sphere? | ✔ LearningCurve Check what you know. |

among the Mongols. The Tibetan Buddhist Tsong-kha-pa (1357–1419) founded the Yellow Hat, or Gelug-pa, sect, whose heads later became known as the Dalai Lamas. In 1577 the third Dalai Lama accepted the invitation of Altan Khan to visit Mongolia, and the khan declared Tibetan Buddhism to be the official religion of all the Mongols. The Dalai Lama gave the khan the title "King of Religion," and the khan swore that the Mongols would renounce blood sacrifice. When the third Dalai Lama's reincarnation was found to be the great-grandson of Altan Khan, the ties between Tibet and Mongolia, not surprisingly, became even stronger. From the perspective of Ming China, the growing influence of Buddhism among the Mongols seemed a positive development, as Buddhist emphasis on nonviolence was expected to counter the Mongols' love of war.

The Examination Life

In sharp contrast to Europe in this era, Ming China had few social barriers. It had no hereditary aristocracy that could have limited the emperor's absolute power. Although China had no titled aristocracy, it did have an elite whose status was based above all on government office acquired through education. Unlike in many European countries of the era, China's merchants did not become a politically articulate bourgeoisie. Instead the politically active class was that of the scholars who Confucianism taught should aid the ruler in running the state. Merchants tried to marry into the scholar class in order to rise in the world.

Thus, despite the harsh and arbitrary ways in which the Ming emperors treated their civil servants, educated men were eager to enter the government. Reversing the policies of the Mongol Yuan Dynasty, the Ming government recruited almost all its officials through **civil service examinations**. To become officials, candidates had to pass examinations at the prefectural, the provincial, and the capital levels. To keep the wealthiest areas from dominating the exams, quotas were established for the number of candidates that each province could send on to the capital.

Of course, boys from well-to-do families had a significant advantage because their families could start their education with tutors at age four or five, though less costly schools were becoming increasingly available as well. Families that for generations had pursued other careers—for example, as merchants or physicians—had more opportunities than ever for their sons to become officials through the exams. (See "Individuals in Society: Tan Yunxian, Woman Doctor," page 617.) Clans sometimes operated schools for their members. Most of those who attended school stayed only a few years, but students who seemed most promising moved on to advanced schools where they practiced essay writing and studied the essays of men who had succeeded in the exams.

The examinations at the prefecture level lasted a day and drew hundreds if not thousands of candidates. The provincial and capital examinations were given in three sessions spread out over a week. In the first session, candidates wrote essays on passages from the classics. In the second and third sessions, candidates had to write essays on practical policy issues and on a passage from the *Classic of Filial Piety* (a brief text celebrating devotion to parents and other superiors). In addition, they had to show that they could draft state papers such as edicts, decrees, and judicial rulings. Reading the dynastic histories was a good way to prepare for policy questions and state paper exercises.

civil service examinations
▶ A highly competitive series of written tests held at the prefecture, province, and capital levels to select men to become officials.

CHAPTER LOCATOR | What sort of state and society developed in China after the Mongols were ousted? | Did the return of alien rule with the Manchus have any positive consequences for China?

CHAPTER 21
616 CONTINUITY AND CHANGE IN EAST ASIA

INDIVIDUALS IN SOCIETY
Tan Yunxian, Woman Doctor

The grandmother of Tan Yunxian (1461–1554) was the daughter of a physician, and her husband had married into her home to learn medicine himself. At least two of their sons — including Yunxian's father — passed the civil service examination and became officials, raising the social standing of the family considerably. The grandparents wanted to pass their medical knowledge down to someone, and because they found Yunxian very bright, they decided to teach it to her.

Tan Yunxian married and raised four children but also practiced medicine, confining her practice to women. At age fifty she wrote an autobiographical account, *Sayings of a Female Doctor*. In the preface she described how, under her grandmother's tutelage, she had first memorized the *Canon of Problems* and the *Canon of the Pulse*. Then when her grandmother had time, she asked her granddaughter to explain particular passages in these classic medical treatises.

Tan Yunxian began the practice of medicine by treating her own children, asking her grandmother to check her diagnoses. When her grandmother was old and ill, she gave Yunxian her notebook of prescriptions and her equipment for making medicines, telling her to study them carefully. Later, Yunxian herself became seriously ill and dreamed of her grandmother telling her on what page of which book to find the prescription that would cure her. When she recovered, she began her medical career in earnest.

Tan Yunxian's book records the cases of thirty-one patients she treated, most of them women with chronic complaints rather than critical illnesses. Many of the women had what the Chinese classed as women's complaints, such as menstrual irregularities, repeated miscarriages, barrenness, and postpartum fatigue. Some had ailments that men too could suffer, such as coughs, nausea, insomnia, diarrhea, rashes, and swellings. Like other literati physicians, Yunxian regularly prescribed herbal medications. She also practiced moxibustion, the technique of burning moxa (dried artemisia) at specified points on the body with the goal of stimulating the circulation of qi (life energy). Because the physician applying the moxa had to touch the patient, male physicians could not perform moxibustion on women.

Yunxian's patients included working women, and Yunxian seems to have thought that their problems often sprang from overwork. One woman came to her because she had had vaginal bleeding for three years. When questioned, the woman told Yunxian that she worked all day with her husband at their kiln making bricks and tiles. Yunxian's diagnosis was overwork, and she gave the woman pills to replenish her yin energies. A boatman's wife came to her complaining of numbness in her hands. When the woman told Yunxian that she worked in the wind and rain handling the boat,

Tan Yunxian would have consulted traditional herbals, like this one, with sketches of plants of medicinal value and descriptions of their uses. (Wellcome Trust, London)

the doctor advised some time off. In another case Yunxian explained to a servant girl that she had gone back to work too soon after suffering a wind damage fever.

By contrast, when patients came from upper-class families, Tan Yunxian believed negative emotions were the source of their problems, particularly if a woman reported that her mother-in-law had scolded her or that her husband had recently brought a concubine home. Yunxian told two upper-class women who had miscarried that they lost their babies because they had hidden their anger, causing fire to turn inward and destabilize the fetus.

Tan Yunxian herself lived a long life, dying at age ninety-three.

Source: Based on Charlotte Furth, *A Flourishing Yin: Gender in China's Medical History, 960–1665* (Berkeley: University of California Press, 1999), pp. 285–295.

QUESTIONS FOR ANALYSIS

1. Why do you think Tan Yunxian treated only women? Why might she have been more effective with women patients than a male physician would have been?
2. What do you think of Yunxian's diagnoses? Do you think she was able to help many of her patients?

ONLINE DOCUMENT PROJECT

What kinds of treatments did Chinese doctors employ? Examine artwork depicting Chinese medical practices, and then complete a quiz and writing assignment based on the evidence and details from this chapter. *See inside the front cover to learn more.*

Everyday Life in Ming China

For civil servants and almost everyone else, everyday life in Ming China followed patterns established in earlier periods. The family remained central to most people's lives, and almost everyone married. Beyond the family, people's lives were shaped by the type of work they did and where they lived.

Large towns and cities proliferated in Ming times. In these urban areas small businesses manufactured textiles, paper, and luxury goods such as silks and porcelains. The southeast became a center for the production of cotton and silks; other areas specialized in the grain and salt trades and in silver.

Printing was invented in Tang times (618–907) and had a great impact on the life of the educated elite in Song times (960–1279), but not until Ming times did it transform the culture of the urban middle classes. By the late Ming period, publishing houses were putting out large numbers of books aimed at general audiences. To make their books attractive in the marketplace, entrepreneurial book publishers commissioned artists to illustrate them. By the sixteenth century more and more books were being published in the vernacular language (the language people spoke), especially short stories, novels, and plays. Ming vernacular short stories depicted a world much like that of their readers, full of shop clerks and merchants, monks and prostitutes, students and matchmakers.

The full-length novel made its first appearance during the Ming period. The plots of the early novels were heavily indebted to story cycles developed by oral storytellers over the course of several centuries. Competing publishers brought out their own editions of popular novels, sometimes adding new illustrations or commentaries.

> ## > Popular Ming Novels:

- *Water Margin*: an episodic tale of a band of bandits
- *The Romance of the Three Kingdoms*: a work of historical fiction based on the exploits of the generals and statesmen contending for power at the end of the Han Dynasty
- *The Journey to the West*: a fantastic account of the Tang monk Xuanzang's travels to India
- *Plum in the Golden Vase*: novel of manners about a lustful merchant with a wife and five concubines

The Chinese found recreation and relaxation in many ways besides reading. The affluent indulged in an alcoholic drink made from fermented and distilled rice, and once tobacco was introduced from the Americas, both men and women took up pipes. Plays were also very popular, and people not only enjoyed play performances but also avidly read the play scripts.

Rice supplied most of the calories of the population in central and south China. (In north China, wheat, made into steamed or baked bread or into noodles, served as the dietary staple.) In the south, terracing and irrigation of mountain slopes, introduced in the eleventh century, had increased rice harvests. Other innovations also brought good results. Farmers began to stock the rice paddies with fish, which continuously fertilized the rice fields, destroyed malaria-bearing mosquitoes, and enriched the diet. Farmers also grew cotton, sugarcane, and indigo as commercial crops. New methods of crop rotation allowed for continuous cultivation and for more than one harvest per year from a single field.

CHAPTER LOCATOR | **What sort of state and society developed in China after the Mongols were ousted?** | Did the return of alien rule with the Manchus have any positive consequences for China?

The Ming rulers promoted the repopulation and colonization of war-devastated regions through reclamation of land and massive transfers of people. Immigrants to these areas received large plots and exemption from taxation for many years. Reforestation played a dramatic role in the agricultural revolution. In 1391 the Ming government ordered 50 million trees planted in the Nanjing area to produce lumber for the construction of a maritime fleet. In 1392 each family holding a land grant in Anhui province had to plant two hundred mulberry, jujube, and persimmon trees. In 1396 peasants in the present-day provinces of Hunan and Hubei in central China planted 84 million fruit trees. Historians have estimated that 1 billion trees were planted during Taizu's reign.

Increased food production led to steady population growth and the multiplication of markets, towns, and small cities. Larger towns had permanent shops; smaller towns had periodic markets. Tradesmen carrying their wares on their backs and craftsmen—carpenters, barbers, joiners, locksmiths—moved constantly from market to market.

Ming Decline

Beginning in the 1590s the Ming government was beset by fiscal, military, and political problems. The government went nearly bankrupt helping defend Korea against a Japanese invasion (see pages 634–635). Then came a series of natural disasters: floods, droughts, locusts, and epidemics ravaged one region after another. At the same time, a "little ice age" brought a drop in average temperatures that shortened the growing season and reduced harvests. In areas of serious food shortages, gangs of army deserters and laid-off soldiers began scouring the countryside in search of food. Once the gangs had stolen all their grain, hard-pressed farmers joined them just to survive. The Ming government had little choice but to try to increase taxes to deal with these threats, but the last thing people needed was heavier taxes.

Adding to the hardship was a sudden drop in the supply of silver. In place of the paper money that had circulated in Song and Yuan times, silver ingots came into general use as money in Ming times. Much of this silver originated in either Japan or the New World and entered China as payment for the silk and porcelains exported from China. When events in Japan and the Philippines led to disruption of trade, silver imports dropped. This led to deflation in China, which caused real rents to rise. Soon there were riots among urban workers and tenant farmers. In 1642 a group of rebels cut the dikes on the Yellow River, causing massive flooding. A smallpox epidemic soon added to the death toll. In 1644 the last Ming emperor, in despair, took his own life when rebels entered Beijing, opening the way for the start of a new dynasty.

QUICK REVIEW

What were the defining characteristics of Ming government?

How did Japan change during this period of political instability?

What was life like in Japan during the Tokugawa peace?

How did the sea link the countries of East Asia, and what happened when Europeans entered this maritime sphere?

LearningCurve
Check what you know.

Did the return of alien rule with the Manchus have any positive consequences for China?

Presenting a Horse to the Emperor

This detail from a 1757 hand scroll shows the Qianlong emperor, seated, receiving envoys from the Kazakhs. Note how the envoy, presenting a pure white horse, is kneeling to the ground performing the kowtow, which involved lowering his head to the ground as an act of reverence. The artist was Guiseppe Castiglione, an Italian who worked as a painter in Qianlong's court. (by Father Guiseppe Castiglione [1688–1766]; Musée des Arts Asiatiques-Guimet/© RMN–Grand Palais/Art Resource, NY)

Qing Dynasty

▶ The dynasty founded by the Manchus that ruled China from 1644 to 1911.

THE NEXT DYNASTY, THE Qing Dynasty (1644–1911), was founded by the Manchus, a non-Chinese people who were descended from the Jurchens. In the late sixteenth century the Manchus began expanding their territories, and in 1644 they founded the Qing Dynasty, which brought peace and in time prosperity. Successful Qing military campaigns extended the borders into Mongol, Tibetan, and Uighur regions, creating a multiethnic empire that was larger than any earlier Chinese dynasty.

The Rise of the Manchus

In the Ming period, the Manchus lived in dispersed communities in what is loosely called Manchuria (the northeast of modern-day China). In the more densely populated southern part of Manchuria, the Manchus lived in close contact with Mon-

CHAPTER LOCATOR | What sort of state and society developed in China after the Mongols were ousted? | **Did the return of alien rule with the Manchus have any positive consequences for China?**

620
CHAPTER 21
CONTINUITY AND CHANGE IN EAST ASIA

MAP 21.1 ■ The Qing Empire, ca. 1800

The sheer size of the Qing Empire in China almost inevitably led to its profound cultural influence on the rest of Asia.

> MAPPING THE PAST

ANALYZING THE MAP: How many different cultural groups are depicted? Which occupied the largest territories? Where was crop agriculture most prevalent?

CONNECTIONS: What geographical and political factors limited the expansion of the Qing Empire?

---

gols, Koreans, and Chinese (Map 21.1). They were not nomads but rather hunters, fishers, and farmers. Like the Mongols, they also were excellent horsemen and archers and had a strongly hierarchical social structure, with elites and slaves. Slaves, often Korean or Chinese, were generally acquired through capture. Manchu villages were generally small and often at odds with each other over resources. Interspersed among these Manchu settlements were groups of nomadic Mongols who lived in tents.

The Manchus credited their own rise to Nurhaci (1559–1626). Over several decades, he united the Manchus and expanded their territories. Like Chinggis Khan, who had reorganized the Mongol armies to reduce the importance of tribal affiliations, Nurhaci created a new social basis for his armies in units called **banners**. Each banner was made up of a set of military companies and included the families and slaves of the soldiers. Each company had a hereditary captain, often from Nurhaci's own lineage. When new groups were defeated, their members were distributed among several banners to lessen their potential for subversion.

banners

▶ Units of the Qing army, composed of soldiers, their families, and slaves.

How did Japan change during this period of political instability?

What was life like in Japan during the Tokugawa peace?

How did the sea link the countries of East Asia, and what happened when Europeans entered this maritime sphere?

✓ LearningCurve
Check what you know.

The Manchus entered China by invitation of the distinguished Ming general Wu Sangui, who was near the eastern end of the Great Wall when he heard that the rebels had captured Beijing. The Manchus proposed to Wu that they join forces and liberate Beijing. Wu opened the gates of the Great Wall to let the Manchus in, and within a couple of weeks they occupied Beijing. When the Manchus made clear that they intended to conquer the rest of the country and take the throne themselves, Wu and many other Chinese generals joined forces with them. Before long, China was again under alien rule.

Once securely in power, the Qing put in place policies and institutions that gave China a respite from war and disorder. Most of the political institutions of the Ming Dynasty were taken over relatively unchanged, including the examination system.

After peace was achieved, population growth took off. Between 1700 and 1800 the Chinese population seems to have nearly doubled, from about 150 million to over 300 million. Population growth during the eighteenth century has been attributed to many factors: global warming that extended the growing season, expanded use of New World crops, slowing of the spread of new diseases that had accompanied the sixteenth-century expansion of global traffic, and the efficiency of the Qing government in providing relief in times of famine.

Competent and Long-Lived Emperors

For more than a century, China was ruled by only three rulers, each of them hardworking, talented, and committed to making the Qing Dynasty a success. Two, the Kangxi and Qianlong emperors, had exceptionally long reigns.

Kangxi (r. 1661–1722) proved adept at meeting the expectations of both the Chinese and the Manchu elites. Kangxi (KAHNG-shee) could speak, read, and write Chinese and made efforts to persuade educated Chinese that the Manchus had a legitimate claim to rule, even trying to attract Ming loyalists who had been unwilling to serve the Qing. He undertook a series of tours of the south, where Ming loyalty had been strongest, and he held a special exam to select men to compile the official history of the Ming Dynasty.

Qianlong (chyan-loong) (r. 1722–1735) understood that the Qing's capacity to hold the multiethnic empire together rested on their ability to appeal to all those they ruled. Besides speaking Manchu and Chinese, Qianlong learned to converse in Mongolian, Uighur, Tibetan, and Tangut, and he addressed envoys in their own languages. He became as much a patron of Tibetan Buddhism as of Chinese Confucianism. He initiated a massive project to translate the Tibetan Buddhist canon into Mongolian and Manchu and had huge multilingual dictionaries compiled.

To demonstrate to the Chinese scholar-official elite that he was a sage emperor, Qianlong worked on affairs of state from dawn until early afternoon and then turned to reading, painting, and calligraphy. He was ostentatious in his devotion to his mother, visiting her daily and tending to her comfort with all the devotion of the most filial Chinese son.

Through Qianlong's reign, China remained an enormous producer of manufactured goods and led the way in assembly-line production. The government operated huge textile factories, but some private firms were even larger. Hangzhou had a textile firm that gave work to 4,000 weavers, 20,000 spinners, and 10,000

CHAPTER LOCATOR | What sort of state and society developed in China after the Mongols were ousted? | **Did the return of alien rule with the Manchus have any positive consequences for China?**

dyers and finishers. The porcelain kilns at Jingdezhen employed the division of labor on a large scale and were able to supply porcelain to much of the world. The growth of the economy benefited the Qing state, and the treasury became so full that the Qianlong emperor was able to cancel taxes on several occasions.

Imperial Expansion

The Qing Dynasty put together a multiethnic empire that was larger than any earlier Chinese dynasty. Taiwan was acquired in 1683. In 1696 Kangxi led an army of eighty thousand men into Mongolia, and within a few years Manchu supremacy was accepted there. Cannon and muskets gave Qing forces military superiority over the Mongols, who were armed only with bows and arrows. Thus the Qing could dominate the steppe cheaply, effectively ending two thousand years of Inner Asian military advantage.

In the 1720s the Qing established a permanent garrison of banner soldiers in Tibet. By this time, the expanding Qing and Russian Empires were nearing each other. In 1689 the Manchu and the Russian rulers approved a treaty defining their borders in Manchuria and regulating trade. Another treaty in 1727 allowed a Russian ecclesiastical mission to reside in Beijing and a trade caravan to make a trip from Russia to Beijing once every three years.

The last region to be annexed was Chinese Turkestan (the modern province of Xinjiang). Both the Han and the Tang Dynasties had stationed troops in the region, exercising loose overlordship, but neither the Song nor the Ming had tried to control the area. The Qing won the region in the 1750s through a series of campaigns against Uighur and Dzungar Mongol forces.

QUICK REVIEW

What factors and developments help explain Qing success?

| How did Japan change during this period of political instability? | What was life like in Japan during the Tokugawa peace? | How did the sea link the countries of East Asia, and what happened when Europeans entered this maritime sphere? | ✓ LearningCurve Check what you know. |

How did Japan change during this period of political instability?

Matsumoto Castle

Hideyoshi built Matsumoto Castle between 1594 and 1597. Designed to be impregnable, it was surrounded by a moat and had a base constructed of huge stones. In the sixteenth and early seventeenth centuries Spanish and Portuguese missionaries compared Japanese castles favorably to European castles of the period. (Adina Tovy/Robert Harding World Imagery)

IN THE TWELFTH CENTURY Japan entered an age that can be compared to Europe's feudal age. The Kamakura Shogunate (1185–1333) had its capital in the east, at Kamakura. It was succeeded by the Ashikaga Shogunate (1338–1573), which returned the government to Kyoto (KYOH-toh) and helped launch, during the fifteenth century, the great age of Zen-influenced Muromachi culture. The sixteenth century brought civil war over succession to the shogunate, leading to the building of massive castles and the emergence of rulers of obscure origins who eventually unified the realm.

Muromachi Culture

The headquarters of the Ashikaga shoguns were on Muromachi Street in Kyoto, and the refined and elegant style that they promoted is often called Muromachi culture. The shoguns patronized Zen Buddhism, the school of Buddhism associated with meditation and mind-to-mind transmission of truth.

CHAPTER LOCATOR | What sort of state and society developed in China after the Mongols were ousted? | Did the return of alien rule with the Manchus have any positive consequences for China?

Zen ideas of simplicity permeated the arts. The Silver Pavilion built by the shogun Yoshimasa (r. 1449–1473) epitomizes Zen austerity. A white sand cone constructed in the temple garden was designed to reflect moonlight. Yoshimasa was also influential in the development of the tea ceremony. Aesthetes celebrated the beauty of imperfect objects, such as plain or misshapen cups or pots. Spare monochrome paintings fit into this aesthetic, as did simple asymmetrical flower arrangements.

The shoguns were also patrons of the **Nō theater**. Nō drama originated in popular forms of entertainment, including comical skits and dances directed to the gods. It was transformed into high art by Zeami (1363–1443), an actor and playwright. Nō was performed on a bare stage with a pine tree painted across the backdrop. One or two actors wearing brilliant brocade robes performed, using stylized gestures and stances. The actors were accompanied by a chorus and a couple of musicians playing drums and flute. Many of the stories concerned ghosts consumed by jealous passions or the desire for revenge. Zeami argued that the most meaningful moments came during silence, when the actor's spiritual presence allowed the audience to catch a glimpse of the mysterious and inexpressible.

Nō theater
▶ A type of Japanese theater in which performers convey emotions and ideas as much through gestures, stances, and dress as through words.

Civil War

Civil war began in Kyoto in 1467 as a struggle over succession to the shogunate. Rival claimants and their followers burned down temples and mansions, destroying much of the city and its treasures. Once Kyoto was laid waste, war spread to outlying areas. When the shogun could no longer protect cities, merchants banded together to hire mercenaries. In the political vacuum, the Lotus League, a commoner-led religious sect united by faith in the saving power of the Lotus Sutra, set up a commoner-run government that collected taxes and settled disputes. In 1536, during eight days of fighting, the powerful Buddhist monastery Enryakuji attacked the League and its temples; burned much of the city; and killed men, women, and children thought to be believers.

In these confused and violent circumstances, power devolved to the local level, where warlords, called **daimyo** (DIGH-myoh), built their power bases. To raise revenues, they surveyed the land and promoted irrigation and trade. Many of the most successful daimyo were self-made men who rose from obscurity.

daimyo
▶ Regional lords in Japan, many of whom were self-made men.

The violence of the period encouraged castle building. The castles were built not on mountaintops but on level plains, and they were surrounded by moats and walls made from huge stones. Inside a castle was a many-storied keep. Though relatively safe from incendiary missiles, the keeps were vulnerable to Western-style cannon, introduced in the 1570s.

The Victors: Nobunaga and Hideyoshi

The first daimyo to gain a predominance of power was Oda Nobunaga (1534–1582). A samurai of the lesser daimyo class, he recruited followers from masterless samurai. After he won control of his native province in 1559, he immediately set out to extend his power through central Japan. A key step was destroying the military power of the great monasteries. To increase revenues, he minted coins

How did Japan change during this period of political instability? | What was life like in Japan during the Tokugawa peace? | How did the sea link the countries of East Asia, and what happened when Europeans entered this maritime sphere? | ✓ LearningCurve Check what you know.

625

Hideyoshi's Campaigns in
Japan and Korea, 1592–1598

and promoted trade by eliminating customs barriers and opening the little fishing village of Nagasaki to foreign commerce; it soon became Japan's largest port.

In 1582, in an attempted coup, Nobunaga was forced by one of his vassals to commit suicide. His general and staunchest adherent, Toyotomi Hideyoshi (1537–1598), avenged him and continued the drive toward unification of the daimyo-held lands.

Like the Ming founder, Hideyoshi was a peasant's son who rose to power through military talent. A series of campaigns brought all of Japan under Hideyoshi's control. Hideyoshi soothed the vanquished daimyo as Nobunaga had done—with lands and military positions—but he also required them to swear allegiance and to obey him down to the smallest particular. For the first time in over two centuries, Japan had a single ruler.

Hideyoshi did his best to ensure that future peasants' sons would not be able to rise as he had. His great sword hunt of 1588 collected weapons from farmers, who were no longer allowed to wear swords. Restrictions were also placed on samurai; they were prohibited from leaving their lord's service or switching occupations. To improve tax collection, Hideyoshi ordered a survey of the entire country. His surveys not only tightened tax collection, but also registered each peasant household and tied the peasants to the land. With the country pacified, Hideyoshi embarked on an ill-fated attempt to conquer Korea and China that ended only with his death, discussed later in the chapter (see page 634).

> ## QUICK REVIEW

Who held power during Japan's Middle Ages?
How did they wield it?

CHAPTER LOCATOR | What sort of state and society developed in China after the Mongols were ousted? | Did the return of alien rule with the Manchus have any positive consequences for China?

Daimyo Procession

The system of alternate residence meant that some daimyo were always on the road. The constant travel of daimyo with their attendants between their domains and Edo, the shogun's residence, stimulated construction of roads, inns, and castle-towns. (*Daimyo's Processions Passing Along the Tokaido*, by Utagawa Sadahide [1807–1873]/triptych of polychrome woodblock prints; ink and color on paper, Edo period [1615–1868]. Bequest of William S. Lieberman, 2005, accession 2007.49.290a–c/Metropolitan Museum of Art, New York, NY, USA/Image copyright © The Metropolitan Museum of Art/Image source: Art Resource, NY)

ON HIS DEATHBED, Hideyoshi set up a council of regents to govern during the minority of his infant son. The strongest regent was Hideyoshi's long-time supporter Tokugawa Ieyasu (1543–1616). In 1600 at Sekigahara, Ieyasu smashed a coalition of daimyo defenders of the heir and began building his own government. In 1603 he took the title "shogun." The **Tokugawa Shogunate** that Ieyasu fashioned lasted until 1867. This era is also called the Edo period after the location of the shogunate, starting Tokyo's history as Japan's most important city (Map 21.2).

Tokugawa Shogunate
▶ The Japanese government in Edo founded by Tokugawa Ieyasu. It lasted from 1603 to 1867.

Tokugawa Government

Over the course of the seventeenth century the Tokugawa shoguns worked to consolidate relations with the daimyo. In a scheme resembling the later residency requirements imposed by Louis XIV in France (see page 528) and Peter the Great in Russia (see page 541), Ieyasu set up the **alternate residence system**, which compelled the lords to live in Edo every other year and to leave their wives and sons there—essentially as hostages.

The peace imposed by the Tokugawa Shogunate brought a steady rise in population to about 30 million people by 1800. To maintain stability, the early

alternate residence system
▶ Arrangement in which lords lived in Edo every other year and left their wives and sons there as hostages.

How did Japan change during this period of political instability?	**What was life like in Japan during the Tokugawa peace?**	How did the sea link the countries of East Asia, and what happened when Europeans entered this maritime sphere?	 LearningCurve Check what you know.

Tokugawa shoguns froze social status. Laws rigidly prescribed what each class could and could not do. Daimyo, for example, were prohibited from moving troops outside their frontiers, making alliances, and coining money. As intended, these rules protected the Tokugawa shoguns from daimyo attack and helped ensure a long era of peace.

The early Tokugawa shoguns also restricted the construction and repair of castles—symbols, in Japan as in medieval Europe, of feudal independence. Continuing Hideyoshi's policy, the Tokugawa regime enforced a policy of complete separation of samurai and peasants. Samurai were defined as those permitted to carry swords. They had to live in castles, and they depended on stipends from their lords, the daimyo. Samurai were effectively prevented from establishing ties to the land, so they could not become landholders. Likewise, merchants and artisans had to live in towns and could not own land.

After 1639 Japan limited its contacts with the outside world because of concerns about both the loyalty of subjects converted to Christianity by European missionaries and about the imperialist ambitions of European powers (discussed below). However, China remained an important trading partner and source of ideas. The Edo period also saw the development of a school of native learning that rejected Buddhism and Confucianism as alien and tried to identify a distinctly Japanese sensibility.

MAP 21.2 ■ Tokugawa Japan, 1603–1867

The lands that the shogunate directly controlled were concentrated near its capital at Edo. The daimyo of distant places, such as the island of Kyushu, were required to make long journeys to and from Edo every year.

What sort of state and society developed in China after the Mongols were ousted?

Did the return of alien rule with the Manchus have any positive consequences for China?

Commercialization and the Growth of Towns

During the civil war period, warfare seems to have promoted social and economic change, much as it had in China during the Warring States Period (403–221 B.C.E.). Trade grew, and greater use was made of coins imported from Ming China. Markets began appearing at river crossings, at the entrances to temples and shrines, and at other places where people congregated. Towns and cities sprang up all around the country, some of them around the new castles. Traders and artisans dealing in a specific product began forming guilds. Foreign trade also flourished, despite chronic problems with pirates who raided the Japanese, Korean, and Chinese coasts (see pages 634–635).

In most cities, merchant families with special privileges from the government controlled the urban economy. Frequently, a particular family dominated the trade in a particular product and then branched out into other businesses. Japanese merchant families also devised distinct patterns and procedures for their business operations. What today is called "family-style management principles" determined the age of apprenticeship (between eleven and thirteen); the employee's detachment from past social relations and adherence to the norms of a particular family business; salaries; seniority as the basis of promotion, although job performance at the middle rungs determined who reached the higher ranks; and the time for retirement. All employees in a family business were expected to practice frugality, resourcefulness, self-denial, and careful accounting. These values formed the basis of what has been called the Japanese "industrious revolution." They help to explain how, after the Meiji (MAY-jee) Restoration of 1867 (see page 796), Japan was able to industrialize rapidly and compete successfully with the West.

In the seventeenth century underemployed farmers and samurai thronged to the cities. As a result, Japan's cities grew tremendously. Kyoto became the center for the manufacture of luxury goods like lacquer, brocade, and fine porcelain. Osaka was the chief market, especially for rice. Edo was a center of consumption by the daimyo, their vassals, and government bureaucrats. Both Osaka and Edo reached about a million residents.

Two hundred fifty towns came into being in this period. Most ranged in size from 3,000 to 20,000 people, but a few, such as Hiroshima, Kagoshima, and Nagoya, had populations of between 65,000 and 100,000. In addition, perhaps two hundred towns along the main road to Edo emerged to meet the needs of men traveling on the alternate residence system. In the eighteenth century perhaps 4 million people, 15 percent of the Japanese population, resided in cities or towns.

The Life of the People in the Edo Period

The Tokugawa shoguns brought an end to civil war by controlling the military. Stripped of power and required to spend alternate years at Edo, many of the daimyo and samurai passed their lives in idle pursuit of pleasure. They spent extravagantly on fine silks, paintings, concubines, boys, the theater, and the redecoration of their castles. These temptations, as well as more sophisticated pleasures and the heavy costs of maintaining alternate residences at Edo, gradually bankrupted the warrior class.

All major cities contained places of amusement for men—teahouses, theaters, restaurants, and houses of prostitution. Desperately poor parents sometimes sold

How did Japan change during this period of political instability?

What was life like in Japan during the Tokugawa peace?

How did the sea link the countries of East Asia, and what happened when Europeans entered this maritime sphere?

☑ LearningCurve Check what you know.

629

Interior View of a Theater

Complex kabuki plays, which dealt with heroes, loyalty, and tragedy and included music and dance, became the most popular form of entertainment in Tokugawa Japan for all classes. Movable scenery and lighting effects made possible the staging of storms, fires, and hurricanes. (woodblock print by Okumura Masanobu, 18th century/Private Collection/J.T. Vintage/The Bridgeman Art Library)

> PICTURING THE PAST

ANALYZING THE IMAGE: How many people are performing in this scene? Are there more men or women in the audience? How do you distinguish them? Are any of the men samurai?
CONNECTIONS: What connections do you see between the popularity of kabuki plays and other aspects of Japanese life in this period?

kabuki theater

▶ A popular form of Japanese drama that brings together dialogue, dance, and music to tell stories. The actors wear colorful costumes and dramatic makeup.

their daughters to entertainment houses (as they did in China and medieval Europe), and the most attractive or talented girls, trained in singing, dancing, and conversational arts, became courtesans, later called geishas (GAY-shahz), "accomplished persons."

Another form of entertainment in the cities was **kabuki theater**, patronized by both merchants and samurai. An art form created by townspeople, kabuki originated in crude, bawdy skits dealing with love and romance. Because actresses were thought to corrupt public morals, the Tokugawa government banned them from the stage in 1629. From that time on, men played all the parts. Homosexuality, long accepted in Japan, was widely practiced among the samurai, who pursued the actors and spent profligately on them. Some moralists and bureaucrats complained from time to time, but the Tokugawa government decided to accept kabuki and prostitution as necessary evils.

Cities were also the center for commercial publishing. As in contemporary China, the reading public eagerly purchased fiction and the scripts for plays. The art of color woodblock printing also was perfected during this period. Many of the surviving prints, made for a popular audience, depict the theater and women of the entertainment quarters.

CHAPTER LOCATOR | What sort of state and society developed in China after the Mongols were ousted? | Did the return of alien rule with the Manchus have any positive consequences for China?

CHAPTER 21
630   CONTINUITY AND CHANGE IN EAST ASIA

Almost as entertaining as attending the theater was watching the long processions of daimyo, their retainers, and their luggage as they passed back and forth to and from Edo twice a year. The shogunate prohibited travel by commoners, but they could get passports to take pilgrimages, visit relatives, or seek the soothing waters of medicinal hot springs. Setting out on foot, groups of villagers would travel to such shrines as Ise, often taking large detours to visit Osaka or Edo to sightsee or attend the theater.

According to Japanese tradition, farmers deserved respect. In practice, however, peasants were often treated callously. Government regulations described them as "people without sense or forethought," a characterization used to justify strict control over almost every aspect of their lives.

During the seventeenth and eighteenth centuries daimyo and upper-level samurai paid for their extravagant lifestyles by raising taxes on their subordinate peasants from 30 or 40 percent of the rice crop to 50 percent. Not surprisingly, this angered peasants, and peasant protests became chronic during the eighteenth century. Natural disasters also added to the peasants' misery. In 1783 Mount Asama erupted, spewing volcanic ash that darkened the skies all summer; the resulting crop failures led to famine. When famine recurred again in 1787, commoners rioted for five days in Edo. The shogunate responded by trying to control the floating population of day laborers without families in the city. At one point they were rounded up and transported to work the gold mines in an island off the north coast, where most of them died within two or three years.

This picture of peasant hardship tells only part of the story. Agricultural productivity increased substantially during the Tokugawa period. Peasants who improved their lands and increased their yields continued to pay the same assessed tax and could pocket the surplus as profit. As those without land drifted to the cities, peasants left in the countryside found ways to improve their livelihoods. At Hirano near Osaka, for example, 61.7 percent of all arable land was sown in cotton. In many rural places, as many peasants worked in the manufacture of silk, cotton, or vegetable oil as in the production of rice.

In comparison to farmers, merchants had a much easier life, even if they had no political power. By contemporary standards anywhere in the world, the Japanese mercantile class lived well. In 1705 the shogunate confiscated the property of a merchant in Osaka at the urging of influential daimyo and samurai who owed the merchant gigantic debts. The government seized 50 pairs of gold screens, 360 carpets, several mansions, 48 granaries and warehouses scattered around the country, and hundreds of thousands of gold pieces. Few merchants possessed such fabulous wealth, but many lived very comfortably.

Within a village, some families would be relatively well-off, others barely able to get by. The village headman generally came from the richest family, but he consulted a council of elders on important matters. Women in better-off families were much more likely to learn to read than women in poor families. Daughters of wealthy peasants studied penmanship, the Chinese classics, poetry, and the proper forms of correspondence, and they rounded out their education with

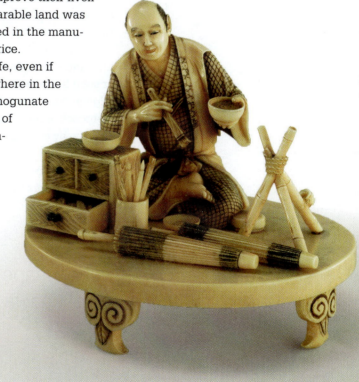

Edo Craftsman at Work

Less than 3 inches tall, this ivory figure shows a parasol maker seated on the floor (the typical Japanese practice) eating his lunch, his tools by his side. (Photo © Boltin Picture Library/The Bridgeman Art Library)

How did Japan change during this period of political instability?

What was life like in Japan during the Tokugawa peace?

How did the sea link the countries of East Asia, and what happened when Europeans entered this maritime sphere?

☑ LearningCurve
Check what you know.

631

travel. By contrast, girls from middle-level peasant families might have had from two to five years of formal schooling focused on moral instruction intended to instill virtue.

By the fifteenth and sixteenth centuries Japan's family and marriage systems had evolved in the direction of a patrilocal, patriarchal system more like China's, and Japanese women had lost the prominent role in high society that they had occupied during the Heian period. It became standard for women to move into their husbands' homes, where they occupied positions subordinate to both their husbands and their mothers-in-law. In addition, elite families stopped dividing their property among all their children; instead they retained it for the sons alone or increasingly for a single son who would continue the family line. Wedding rituals involved both the exchange of betrothal gifts and the movement of the bride from her parents' home to her husband's home. She brought with her a trousseau that provided her with clothes and other items she would need for daily life, but not with land, which would have given her economic autonomy. On the other hand, her position within her new family was more secure, for it became more difficult for a husband to divorce his wife. She also gained authority within the family. If her husband was away, she managed family affairs. If her husband fathered children with concubines, she was their legal mother.

A peasant wife shared responsibility for the family's economic well-being with her husband. If of poor or middling status, she worked alongside her husband in the fields. If they were farm hands and worked for wages, the wife invariably earned a third or a half less than her husband. Wives of prosperous farmers never worked in the fields, but they reeled silk, wove cloth, helped in any family business, and supervised the maids. When cotton growing spread to Japan in the sixteenth century, women took on the jobs of spinning and weaving it. Whatever their economic status, Japanese women, like women everywhere in the world, tended the children. Families were growing smaller in this period in response to the spread of single-heir inheritance.

How was divorce initiated, and how frequent was it? Among the elite, the husband alone could initiate divorce; all he had to do was order his wife to leave or send her possessions to her parents' home. For the wife, divorce carried a stigma, but she could not prevent it or insist on keeping her children. Widows and divorcées of the samurai elite were not expected to remarry. Among the peasant classes, by contrast, divorce seems to have been fairly common. A poor woman wanting a divorce could simply leave her husband's home. It was also possible to secure divorce through a temple. If a married woman entered the temple and performed rites there for three years, her marriage bond was dissolved.

> **QUICK REVIEW**

How did government policy shape social and economic development under the Tokugawa Shogunate?

CHAPTER LOCATOR | What sort of state and society developed in China after the Mongols were ousted? | Did the return of alien rule with the Manchus have any positive consequences for China?

632 CHAPTER 21 CONTINUITY AND CHANGE IN EAST ASIA

How did the sea link the countries of East Asia, and what happened when Europeans entered this maritime sphere?

Dutch in Japan

The Japanese were curious about the appearance, dress, and habits of the Dutch who came to the enclave of Deshima to trade. In this detail from a long hand scroll, Dutch traders are shown interacting with a Japanese samurai in a room with Japanese tatami mats on the floor. Note also the Western musical instrument. (Private Collection/The Bridgeman Art Library)

IN THE PERIOD 1400–1800 maritime trade and piracy connected China and Japan to each other and also to Korea, Southeast Asia, and Europe. Both Korea and Japan relied on Chinese coinage, and China relied on silver from Japan. During the fifteenth century China launched overseas expeditions. Japan was a major base for pirates. In the sixteenth century European traders appeared, eager for Chinese porcelains and silks. Christian missionaries followed. Political changes in Europe changed the international makeup of the European traders in East Asia, with the dominant groups first the Portuguese, next the Dutch, and then the British.

Zheng He's Voyages

Early in the Ming period, the Chinese government tried to revive the tribute system of the Han (206–220 C.E.) and Tang (618–907) Dynasties, when China had dominated East Asia and envoys had arrived from dozens of distant lands. To invite more countries to send missions, the third Ming emperor (Chengzu, or

How did Japan change during this period of political instability?

What was life like in Japan during the Tokugawa peace?

How did the sea link the countries of East Asia, and what happened when Europeans entered this maritime sphere?

LearningCurve
Check what you know.

633

Yongle) authorized a series of voyages to the Indian Ocean under the command of the Muslim eunuch Zheng He (1371–1433).

Zheng He's father had made the trip to Mecca, and the seven voyages that Zheng led between 1405 and 1433 followed old Arab trade routes. The first of the seven was made by a fleet of 317 ships. Each expedition involved from twenty thousand to thirty-two thousand men. Their itineraries included stops in Vietnam, Malaysia, Indonesia, Sri Lanka, India, and, in the later voyages, Hormuz (on the coast of Persia) and East Africa. At each stop Zheng He went ashore to visit rulers, transmit messages of China's peaceful intentions, and bestow lavish gifts. Rulers were invited to come to China or send envoys and were offered accommodation on the return voyages. Near the Straits of Malacca, Zheng He's fleet battled Chinese pirates, bringing them under control. Zheng He made other shows of force as well, deposing rulers deemed unacceptable in Java, Sumatra, and Sri Lanka.

Why were these voyages abandoned? Officials complained about their cost and modest returns. As a consequence, after 1474 all the remaining ships with three or more masts were broken up and used for lumber. China did not pull back from trade in the South China Sea and Indian Ocean, but the government no longer promoted trade, leaving the initiative to private merchants and migrants.

Piracy and Japan's Overseas Adventures

One goal of Zheng He's expeditions was to suppress piracy, which had become a problem all along the China coast. Already in the thirteenth century social disorder and banditry in Japan had expanded into seaborne banditry, some of it within the Japanese islands around the Inland Sea (Map 21.3), but also in the straits between Korea and Japan. Although the pirates were called the "Japanese pirates" by both the Koreans and the Chinese, pirate gangs in fact recruited from all countries. The Ryūkyū (ryoo-kyoo) Islands and Taiwan became major bases.

Possibly encouraged by the exploits of these bandits, Hideyoshi, after his victories in unifying Japan, decided to extend his territory across the seas. In 1590, after receiving congratulations from Korea on his victories, Hideyoshi sent a letter asking the Koreans to allow his armies to pass through their country, declaring that his real target was China. He also sent demands for submission to countries of Southeast Asia and to the Spanish governor of the Philippines.

In 1592 Hideyoshi mobilized 158,000 soldiers and 9,200 sailors for his invasion and equipped them with muskets and cannon, which had recently been introduced into Japan. His forces overwhelmed Korean defenders and reached Seoul within three weeks and Pyongyang in two months. A few months later, in the middle of winter, Chinese armies arrived to help defend Korea, and Japanese forces were pushed back from Pyongyang. A stalemate lasted till 1597, when Hideyoshi sent new troops. This time the Ming army and the Korean navy were more successful in resisting the Japanese. In 1598, after Hideyoshi's death, the Japanese army withdrew, but Korea was left devastated.

After recovering from the setbacks of these invasions, Korea began to advance socially and economically. During the Chosŏn Dynasty (1392–1910), the Korean elite (the yangban) turned away from Buddhism and toward strict Neo-Confucian orthodoxy. As agricultural productivity improved, the population began to grow. With economic advances, slavery declined. When slaves ran away, land-

CHAPTER LOCATOR

What sort of state and society developed in China after the Mongols were ousted?

Did the return of alien rule with the Manchus have any positive consequences for China?

634 CHAPTER 21
CONTINUITY AND CHANGE IN EAST ASIA

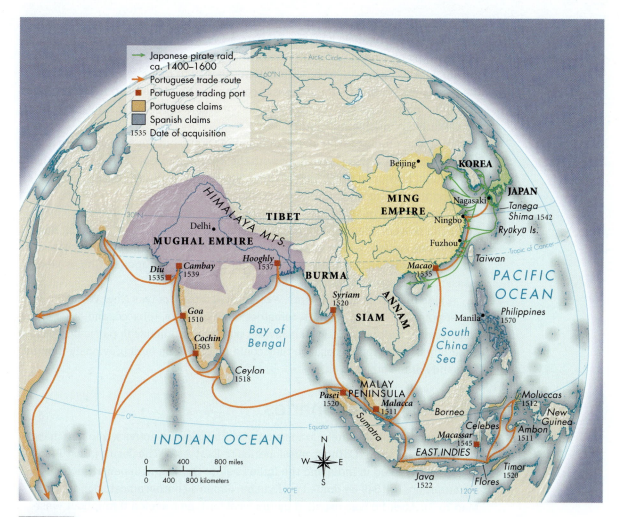

Japanese pirate raid, ca. 1400–1600
→ Portuguese trade route
■ Portuguese trading port
▨ Portuguese claims
▨ Spanish claims
1535 Date of acquisition

MAP 21.3 ■ East Asia, ca. 1600

Pirates and traders often plied the same waters as seaborne trade grew in the sixteenth century. The Portuguese were especially active in setting up trading ports.

owners found that it was less expensive to replace them with sharecroppers than to recapture them. Between 1750 and 1790 the slave population dropped from 30 percent to 5 percent of the population. The hold of the yangban elite, however, remained strong.

Europeans Enter the Scene

In the sixteenth century Portuguese, Spanish, and Dutch merchants and adventurers began to participate in the East Asian maritime world (see Chapter 16). The trade between Japan, China, and Southeast Asia was very profitable, and the European traders wanted a share of it. They also wanted to develop trade between Asia and Europe.

The Portuguese and Dutch were not reluctant to use force to gain control of trade, and they seized many outposts along the trade routes. Moreover, they made little distinction between trade, smuggling, and piracy. In 1521 the Ming tried to

How did Japan change during this period of political instability?

What was life like in Japan during the Tokugawa peace?

How did the sea link the countries of East Asia, and what happened when Europeans entered this maritime sphere?

✓ LearningCurve
Check what you know.

ban the Portuguese from China. Two years later an expeditionary force commissioned by the Portuguese king to negotiate a friendship treaty defeated its mission by firing on Chinese warships near Guangzhou. In 1557, without informing Beijing, local Chinese officials decided that the way to regulate trade was to allow the Portuguese to build a trading post near the mouth of the Pearl River. The city they built there—Macao—became the first destination for Europeans going to China until the nineteenth century.

European products were not in demand in China, but silver was. Japan had supplied much of China's silver, but with the development of silver mines in the New World, European traders began supplying large quantities of silver to China, allowing the expansion of China's economy.

Chinese were quick to take advantage of the new trading ports set up by European powers. Manila, under Spanish control, and Taiwan and Batavia, both under Dutch control, all attracted thousands of Chinese colonists. Local people felt the intrusion of Chinese more than of Europeans, and riots against Chinese led to massacres on several occasions.

A side benefit of the appearance of European traders was New World crops. Sweet potatoes, maize, peanuts, tomatoes, chili peppers, tobacco, and other crops were quickly adopted in East Asia. Sweet potatoes and maize in particular facilitated population growth because they could be grown on land previously thought too sandy or too steep to cultivate.

Christian Missionaries

The Spanish and Portuguese kings supported missionary activity, and merchant vessels soon brought Catholic missionaries to East Asia. The Jesuit priest Francis Xavier had worked in India and the Indies before China and Japan attracted his attention. In 1549 he landed on Kyushu, Japan's southernmost island (see Map 21.2). After he was expelled by the local lord, he traveled throughout western Japan as far as Kyoto, proselytizing wherever warlords allowed. He soon made many converts among the poor and even some among the daimyo. Xavier then set his sights on China but died on an uninhabited island off the China coast in 1552.

Other missionaries carried on his work, and by 1600 there were three hundred thousand baptized Christians in Japan. Most of them lived on Kyushu, where the shogun's power was weakest and the loyalty of the daimyo most doubtful. In 1615 bands of Christian samurai supported Tokugawa Ieyasu's enemies at the Battle of Osaka. A couple of decades later, thirty thousand peasants in the heavily Catholic area of northern Kyushu revolted. The Tokugawa shoguns thus came to associate Christianity with domestic disorder and insurrection. Accordingly, what had been mild persecution of Christians became ruthless repression after 1639.

Meanwhile, in China the Jesuits concentrated on gaining the linguistic and scholarly knowledge they would need to convert the educated class. The Jesuit Matteo Ricci studied for years in Macao before setting himself up in Nanjing and trying to win over members of the educated class. In 1601 he was given permission to reside in Beijing, where he made several high-placed conversions. He also interested educated Chinese men in Western geography, astronomy, and Euclidean mathematics.

Ricci and his Jesuit successors believed that Confucianism was compatible with Christianity. The Jesuits thought that both faiths shared similar concerns

CHAPTER LOCATOR | What sort of state and society developed in China after the Mongols were ousted? | Did the return of alien rule with the Manchus have any positive consequences for China?

636   CHAPTER 21   CONTINUITY AND CHANGE IN EAST ASIA

Among the objects produced in China that were in high demand in Europe in the seventeenth and eighteenth centuries were colorful porcelains. In this period Chinese potters perfected the use of overglaze enamels, which allowed the application of many colors to a single object. Blue, green, yellow, orange, and red all appear on this 18-inch-tall vase. (Vase, Qing dynasty, Kangxi period [1662–1722], late 17th–early 18th century. Porcelain painted in overglaze famille verte enamels and gold. Bequest of John D. Rockefeller Jr., 1960 [61.200.66], The Metropolitan Museum of Art, New York, NY, USA/Image copyright © The Metropolitan Museum of Art/Image Source: Art Resource, NY)

for morality and virtue. The Franciscan and Dominican friars disagreed with the Jesuit position. In 1715 religious and political quarrels in Europe led the pope to decide that the Jesuits' accommodating approach was heretical. Angry at this insult, the Kangxi emperor forbade all Christian missionary work in China.

Learning from the West

Although both China and Japan ended up prohibiting Christian missionary work, other aspects of Western culture were seen as impressive and worth learning. The closed-country policy that Japan instituted in 1639 restricted Japanese from leaving the country and kept European merchants in small enclaves. Still, Japanese interest in Europe did not disappear. Through the Dutch enclave of Deshima on a tiny island in Nagasaki harbor, a stream of Western ideas and inventions trickled into Japan in the eighteenth century.

In China, too, both scholars and rulers showed an interest in Western learning. The Kangxi emperor frequently discussed scientific and philosophical questions with the Jesuits at court. In addition, he had translations made of a collection of Western works on mathematics and the calendar. The court was impressed with the Jesuits' skill in astronomy and quickly appointed them to the Board of Astronomy. In 1674 the emperor asked them to re-equip the observatory with European instruments. Firearms and mechanical clocks were also widely admired. The court established its own clock and watch factory, and in 1673 the emperor insisted that the Jesuits manufacture cannon for him and supervise gunnery practice.

Admiration was not one-sided. In the early eighteenth century China enjoyed a positive reputation in Europe. Voltaire wrote of the rationalism of Confucianism and saw advantages to the Chinese political system. Chinese medical practice also drew European interest. One Chinese practice that Europeans adopted was "variolation," an early form of smallpox inoculation.

The Shifting International Environment in the Eighteenth Century

The East Asian maritime world underwent many changes from the sixteenth to the eighteenth centuries. As already noted, the Japanese pulled back their own traders and limited opportunities for Europeans to trade in Japan. In China the Qing government limited trading contacts with Europe to Guangzhou in the far

How did Japan change during this period of political instability? | What was life like in Japan during the Tokugawa peace? | **How did the sea link the countries of East Asia, and what happened when Europeans entered this maritime sphere?** | ☑ LearningCurve Check what you know.

637

south in an attempt to curb piracy. Portugal lost many of its bases to the Dutch, and by the eighteenth century the British had become as active as the Dutch.

By the late eighteenth century Britain had become a great power and did not see why China should be able to dictate the terms of trade. Wanting to renegotiate relations, King George III sent Lord George Macartney to China with six hundred cases of British goods. The Qianlong emperor was, however, not impressed. The Qing court was as intent on maintaining the existing system of regulated trade as Britain was intent on doing away with it.

> QUICK REVIEW

How did the governments of China and Japan respond to the arrival of Europeans in East Asia in the sixteenth and seventeenth centuries?

CHAPTER SUMMARY

After the fall of the Mongols, China was ruled by the native Ming Dynasty for nearly three centuries. Despite the poor quality of most Ming emperors, China thrived in many ways. Population grew as food production increased. Educational levels were high as more and more men prepared for the civil service examinations. Urban culture was lively, and publishing houses put out novels, short stories, and plays in the vernacular language for large audiences.

In 1644 the Ming Dynasty fell to the non-Chinese Manchus. The Manchu rulers proved more competent than the Ming emperors and were able to both maintain peace and expand the empire. Population grew steadily under Manchu rule.

During the fifteenth and sixteenth centuries Japan was fragmented by civil war. As daimyo attacked and defeated each other, power was gradually consolidated, until Hideyoshi gained control of most of the country. Japan also saw many cultural developments during this period, including the increasing influence of Zen ideas on the arts and the rise of Nō theater.

After Hideyoshi's death, power was seized by Tokugawa Ieyasu, the founder of the Tokugawa Shogunate. The early rulers tried to create stability by freezing the social structure and limiting foreign contact to the city of Nagasaki. As the wealth of the business classes grew, the samurai, now dependent on fixed stipends, became progressively poorer. Samurai and others in search of work and pleasure streamed into the cities.

Between 1400 and 1800 maritime trade connected the countries of Asia, but piracy was a perpetual problem. Early in this period China sent out naval expeditions looking to promote diplomatic contacts, reaching as far as Africa. In the sixteenth century European traders arrived in China and Japan and soon developed profitable trading relationships. The Chinese economy became so dependent on huge imports of silver acquired through this trade that a cutoff in supplies caused severe hardship. Trade with Europe also brought New World crops and new ideas. The Catholic missionaries who began to arrive in Asia introduced

CHAPTER LOCATOR | What sort of state and society developed in China after the Mongols were ousted? | Did the return of alien rule with the Manchus have any positive consequences for China?

638   CHAPTER 21   CONTINUITY AND CHANGE IN EAST ASIA

Western science and learning as well as Christianity, until they were banned in both Japan and China. Although the shogunate severely restricted trade, some Western scientific ideas and technology entered Japan through the port of Nagasaki. Chinese, too, took an interest in Western painting, astronomy, and firearms. Because Europeans saw much to admire in East Asia in this period, ideas also flowed from East to West.

 **CONNECTIONS** During the four centuries from 1400 to 1800, the countries of East Asia became increasingly connected. At the same time, their cultures and social structures were in no sense converging. The elites of the three countries were very different: in both Korea and Japan elite status was hereditary, while in China the key route to status and power involved doing well on a written examination. In Japan the samurai elite were expected to be skilled warriors, but in China and Korea the highest prestige went to men of letters.

By the end of this period, East Asian countries found themselves in a rapidly changing international environment, mostly because of revolutions occurring far from their shores. The next two chapters take up the story of these revolutions, first the political ones in America, France, and Haiti, and then the Industrial Revolution that began in Britain. In time, these revolutions would profoundly alter East Asia as well.

ONLINE DOCUMENT PROJECT
Chinese Medicine
What kinds of treatments did Chinese doctors employ?

Examine artwork depicting Chinese medical practices, and then complete a quiz and writing assignment based on the evidence and details from this chapter. *See inside the front cover to learn more.*

How did Japan change during this period of political instability?

What was life like in Japan during the Tokugawa peace?

How did the sea link the countries of East Asia, and what happened when Europeans entered this maritime sphere?

LearningCurve
Check what you know.

CHAPTER 21 STUDY GUIDE

GET STARTED ONLINE

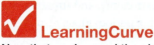

Now that you've read the chapter, make it stick by completing the LearningCurve activity.

EXPLAIN WHY IT MATTERS

Put your reading into practice. Identify each term below, and then explain why it matters in world history.

TERM	WHO OR WHAT & WHEN	WHY IT MATTERS
Ming Dynasty (p. 612)		
civil service examinations (p. 616)		
Qing Dynasty (p. 620)		
banners (p. 621)		
Nō theater (p. 625)		
daimyo (p. 625)		
Tokugawa Shogunate (p. 627)		
alternate residence system (p. 627)		
kabuki theater (p. 630)		

MOVE BEYOND THE BASICS

To demonstrate a more advanced understanding of Qing China and Tokugawa Japan, fill in the chart below with descriptions of key aspects of each empire: social and economic developments, nature and role of elites, and relations with Europeans. How and why did Japanese and Chinese society and culture diverge in this period?

	Social and Economic Developments	Nature and Role of Elites	Relations with Europeans
Qing China			
Tokugawa Japan			

STEP 4 · PUT IT ALL TOGETHER

Now, take a step back and try to explain the big picture. Remember to use specific examples from the chapter in your answers.

CHINA UNDER THE MING AND THE QING

▶ How did Ming officials manage the government when emperors were incompetent? How did this ultimately contribute to the Ming's decline?

▶ How did the Qing respond to the challenge of ruling a multiethnic empire?

WAR AND PEACE IN JAPAN

▶ How did the role of the samurai in Japanese society and government change between 1400 and 1800?

▶ What explains the emergence of a vibrant urban culture during the Tokugawa Shogunate?

THE ASIAN MARITIME SPHERE

▶ What do Zheng He's voyages tell us about Chinese attitudes toward overseas trade, expansion, and international relations?

▶ Why did both the Japanese and Chinese have mixed feelings about European culture? What did they admire? What did they dislike and fear?

LOOKING BACK, LOOKING AHEAD

▶ What explains the cultural divergence between China and Japan in this period?

▶ What trends in the relationship between Asia and Europe were emerging by the end of this period? How did Asian governments respond to the changes that were beginning to take place?

> IN YOUR OWN WORDS

Imagine that you must give an oral report to the class answering the following question: **What fueled population and economic growth in East Asia between 1400 and 1800?** What would be the most important points and why?

22
REVOLUTIONS IN THE ATLANTIC WORLD

1775–1825

> **How did revolution change the Atlantic world? What aspects of Atlantic society and politics were left unchanged?** Chapter 22 examines the wave of revolutions that rocked the Atlantic world from 1775 to 1825. The revolutionary era began in North America in 1775, where the United States of America won freedom from Britain in 1783. Then in 1789 France became the leading revolutionary nation. It established first a constitutional monarchy, then a radical republic, and finally a new empire under Napoleon that would last until 1815. Inspired both by the ideals of the revolution on the continent and by internal colonial conditions, the slaves in the French colony of Saint Domingue rose up in 1791, followed by colonial settlers, indigenous people, and slaves in Spanish America. In Europe and its colonies abroad, the world of modern politics was born.

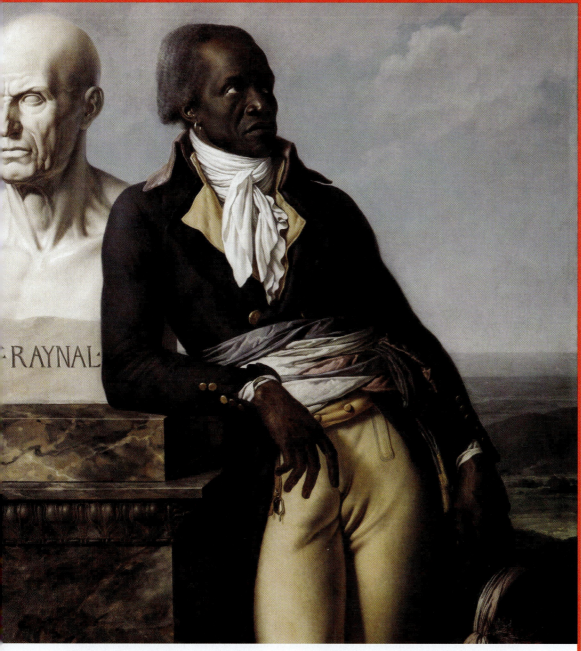

Jean-Baptiste Belley Born in Senegal and enslaved in the colony of Saint-Domingue, Jean-Baptiste Belley fought in the American War of Independence and was elected as a deputy to the French National Convention. His career epitomizes the transnational connections of the era of Atlantic revolutions. (*Jean-Baptiste Belley* [1747–1805], Deputy of Santo Domingo at the French Convention, by Anne-Louis Girodet de Roussy-Trioson [1767–1824], 1797, oil on canvas. Inv. MV4616. Photo: Gérard Blot/Châteaux de Versailles et de Trianon, Versailles, France/© RMN–Grand Palais/Art Resource, NY)

LearningCurve
After reading the chapter, use LearningCurve to retain what you've read.

> What were the factors behind the age of revolution in the Atlantic world?

> Why and how did American colonists forge a new, independent nation?

> How did the events of 1789 result in a constitutional monarchy in France, and what were the consequences?

> How did Napoleon Bonaparte assume control of France and much of Europe, and what factors led to his downfall?

> How did slave revolt on colonial Saint-Domingue lead to the creation of the independent nation of Haiti in 1804?

> Why and how did the Spanish and Portuguese colonies of North and South America shake off European domination and develop into national states?

> What were the factors behind the age of revolution in the Atlantic world?

The Three Estates

French inhabitants were legally divided into three orders, or estates: the clergy, the nobility, and everyone else. In this political cartoon from 1789 a peasant of the third estate struggles under the weight of a happy clergyman and a plumed nobleman. The caption — "Let's hope this game ends soon" — sets forth a program of reform that any peasant could understand. (Musée de la Ville de Paris, Musée Carnavalet, Paris, France/The Bridgeman Art Library)

THE ORIGINS OF REVOLUTIONS in the Atlantic world were complex, and no one cause lay behind them. However, a series of shared factors helped set the stage for reform. They included: fundamental social and economic changes and political crises that eroded state authority; the impact of political ideas derived from the Enlightenment; and, perhaps most important, imperial competition and financial crises generated by the expenses of imperial warfare.

Social Change

Eighteenth-century European society was legally divided into groups with special privileges, such as the nobility and the clergy, and groups with special burdens, such as the peasantry. Nobles were the largest landowners. They enjoyed exemption from many taxes and exclusive rights such as hunting and bearing swords.

CHAPTER LOCATOR | **What were the factors behind the age of revolution in the Atlantic world?** | Why and how did American colonists forge a new, independent nation?

1715–1774 Reign of Louis XV in France	**1775–1783** American Revolution
1743–1803 Life of Toussaint L'Ouverture	**1789–1799** French Revolution
1756–1763 Seven Years' War	**1790** Edmund Burke publishes *Reflections on the Revolution in France*
1763 Treaty of Paris	**1791–1804** Haitian Revolution
1774–1792 Reign of Louis XVI in France	**1799–1814** Reign of Napoleon Bonaparte in France
1775 Thomas Paine publishes *Common Sense*	

In most countries, various middle-class groups—professionals, merchants, and guild masters—enjoyed privileges that allowed them to monopolize all sorts of economic activity.

Traditional prerogatives persisted in societies undergoing dramatic change. Due to increased agricultural production, Europe's population rose rapidly after 1750, and its cities and towns swelled in size. Inflation kept pace with demography, making it increasingly difficult for urban people to find affordable food and living space. One way they kept up, and even managed to participate in the new consumer revolution (see page 575), was by working harder and for longer hours. More positive developments were increased schooling and a rise in literacy rates, particularly among urban men.

Economic growth created new inequalities between rich and poor. While the poor struggled with rising prices, investors grew rich from the spread of rural manufacture and overseas trade. Old distinctions between landed aristocracy and city merchant began to fade as enterprising nobles put money into trade and rising middle-class bureaucrats and merchants bought landed estates and noble titles. Marriages between nobles and wealthy, educated commoners (called the *bourgeoisie* [boorzh-wah-ZEE] in France) served both groups' interests, and a mixed-caste elite began to take shape.

Another social change involved the racial regimes established in European colonies. By the late eighteenth century European law accepted that only Africans and people of African descent were subject to slavery. Even free people of color—a term for nonslaves of African or mixed African-European descent—were subject to significant restrictions on their legal rights. Racial privilege conferred a new dimension of entitlement on European settlers in the colonies, and they used extremely brutal methods to enforce it.

In Spanish America and Brazil, people of European and African descent intermingled with the very large indigenous population. Until the reforms of Charles III, indigenous people and Spaniards were required by law to live in separate communities, although many of the former secretly fled to Spanish cities and

How did the events of 1789 result in a constitutional monarchy in France?	How did Napoleon Bonaparte assume control of France and much of Europe?	How did slave revolt on colonial Saint-Domingue lead to the creation of Haiti in 1804?	How did the Spanish and Portuguese colonies of the Americas shake off European domination?	✔ **LearningCurve** Check what you know.

haciendas to escape forced labor obligations. Mestizos (meh-STEE-zohz), people of mixed European and indigenous descent, held a higher social status than other nonwhites, but a lower status than Europeans.

Demands for Liberty and Equality

In addition to destabilizing social changes, the ideals of liberty and equality helped fuel revolutions in the Atlantic world. The call for liberty was first of all a call for individual human rights. Supporters of the cause of individual liberty (who became known as "liberals" in the early nineteenth century) demanded freedom to worship according to the dictates of their consciences, an end to censorship, and freedom from arbitrary laws and from judges who simply obeyed orders from the government.

The call for liberty was also a call for a new kind of government. Reformers believed that the people had sovereignty—that is, that the people alone had the authority to make laws limiting an individual's freedom of action. In practice, this system of government meant choosing legislators who represented the people and were accountable to them. Monarchs might retain their thrones, but their rule should be constrained by the will of the people.

Equality was a more ambiguous idea. Eighteenth-century liberals argued that, in theory, all citizens should have identical rights and liberties. However, they accepted a number of distinctions. First, most male eighteenth-century liberals believed that equality between men and women was neither practical nor desirable. Second, few questioned the superiority of people of European descent over those of indigenous or African origin.

Finally, liberals never believed that everyone should be equal economically. Great differences in wealth and income between rich and poor were perfectly acceptable, so long as every free white male had a legally equal chance at economic gain. However limited they appear to modern eyes, these demands for liberty and equality were revolutionary, given that a privileged elite had long existed with little opposition.

The two most important Enlightenment references for late-eighteenth-century liberals were John Locke and the baron de Montesquieu. Locke maintained that England's long political tradition rested on "the rights of Englishmen" and on representative government through Parliament. He argued that if a government oversteps its proper function of protecting the natural rights of life, liberty, and private property, it becomes a tyranny. Montesquieu was also an admirer of England's Parliament. He believed that powerful "intermediary groups"—such as the judicial nobility of which he was a proud member—offered the best defense of liberty against despotism.

The Atlantic revolutions began with aspirations for equality and liberty among the social elite. Soon, however, dissenting voices emerged as some revolutionaries became frustrated with the limitations of liberal notions of equality and liberty and clamored for a fuller realization of these concepts. Depending on location, their demands included political rights for women and free people of color, the emancipation of slaves, better treatment of indigenous people, and government regulations to reduce economic inequality. The age of revolution was thus characterized by bitter conflicts over how far reform should go and to whom it should apply.

CHAPTER LOCATOR | **What were the factors behind the age of revolution in the Atlantic world?** | Why and how did American colonists forge a new, independent nation?

646 CHAPTER 22 REVOLUTIONS IN THE ATLANTIC WORLD

The Seven Years' War

The roots of revolutionary ideology could be found in Enlightenment texts, but it was by no means inevitable that such ideas would result in revolution. Instead events—political, economic, and military—created crises that opened the door for radical action. One of the most important was the global conflict known as the Seven Years' War (1756–1763).

The war's battlefields stretched from central Europe to India to North America, pitting a new alliance of England and Prussia against the French, Austrians, and, later, Spanish. Its origins were in conflicts left unresolved at the end of the War of the Austrian Succession in 1748, during which Prussia had seized the Austrian territory of Silesia. In central Europe, Austria's monarch Maria Theresa vowed to win back Silesia, and to crush Prussia. By the end of the Seven Years' War, Maria Theresa had almost succeeded, but Prussia survived with its boundaries intact.

In North America the encroachment of English settlers into territory claimed by the French in the Ohio Valley resulted in skirmishes that soon became war. French forces achieved major victories until 1758, but the tide of the conflict turned when the British diverted resources from the war in Europe, using superior sea power to destroy the French fleet and choke French commerce around the world.

British victory on all colonial fronts was ratified in the 1763 **Treaty of Paris**. Canada and all French territory east of the Mississippi River passed to Britain, and France ceded Louisiana to Spain as compensation for Spain's loss of Florida to Britain. France also gave up most of its holdings in India, opening the way to British dominance on the subcontinent (Map 22.1).

The war was costly for all participants and, in its aftermath, British, French, and Spanish governments had to increase taxes to repay loans, raising a storm of protest and demands for political reform. Since the Caribbean colony of Saint-Domingue remained French, revolutionary turmoil in the mother country would directly affect its population. The seeds of revolutionary conflict in the Atlantic world were thus sown.

Treaty of Paris

▶ The 1763 peace treaty that ended the Seven Years' War, according vast French territories in North America and India to Britain and Louisiana to Spain.

How did the events of 1789 result in a constitutional monarchy in France?

How did Napoleon Bonaparte assume control of France and much of Europe?

How did slave revolt on colonial Saint-Domingue lead to the creation of Haiti in 1804?

How did the Spanish and Portuguese colonies of the Americas shake off European domination?

☑ LearningCurve
Check what you know.

647

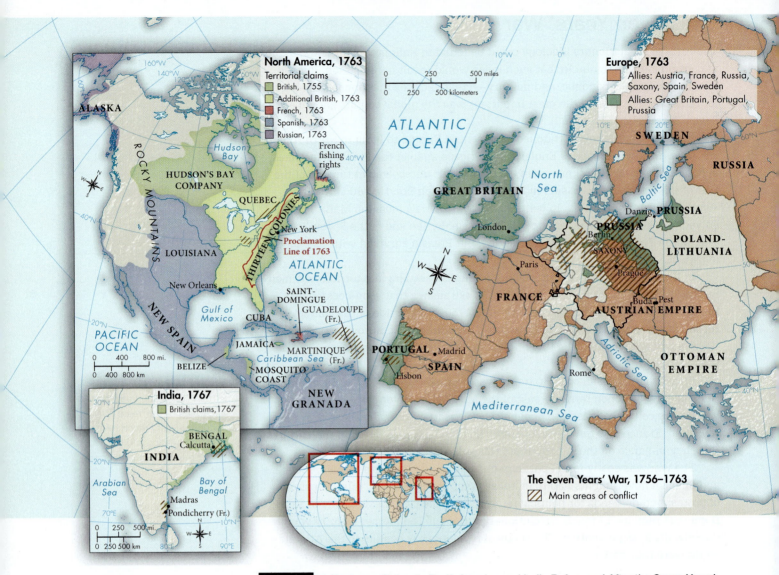

MAP 22.1 ■ European Claims in North America and India Before and After the Seven Years' War, 1755–1763

As a result of the war, France lost its vast territories in North America and India. In an effort to avoid costly conflicts with Native Americans living in the newly conquered territory, the British government in 1763 prohibited colonists from settling west of the Appalachian Mountains. One of the few remaining French colonies in the Americas, Saint-Domingue (on the island of Hispaniola) was the most profitable plantation in the New World.

> **QUICK REVIEW**

How did imperial rivalries contribute to the outbreak of revolutions across the Atlantic world?

CHAPTER LOCATOR | What were the factors behind the age of revolution in the Atlantic world? | Why and how did American colonists forge a new, independent nation?

648 CHAPTER 22
REVOLUTIONS IN THE ATLANTIC WORLD

The Signing of the Declaration of Independence, July 4, 1776

John Trumbull's famous painting shows the dignity and determination of America's revolutionary leaders. An extraordinarily talented group, they succeeded in rallying popular support without losing power to more radical forces in the process. (Photo © Boltin Picture Library/The Bridgeman Art Library)

Why and how did American colonists forge a new, independent nation?

INCREASED TAXES AND GOVERNMENT control sparked colonial protests in the New World, where the era of liberal political revolution began. Participants in the revolution believed they were demanding only the traditional rights of English men and women. But those traditional rights were liberal rights, and in the American context they had strong democratic and popular overtones.

The Origins of the Revolution

The high cost of the Seven Years' War doubled the British national debt. Anticipating further expenses to defend newly conquered territories, the British government broke with tradition and announced that it would maintain a large army in North America and tax the colonies directly. In 1765 Parliament passed the Stamp Act, which levied taxes on a long list of commercial and legal documents, diplomas, newspapers, almanacs, and playing cards. These measures seemed perfectly reasonable to the British, for a much heavier stamp tax already existed in Britain,

How did the events of 1789 result in a constitutional monarchy in France?

How did Napoleon Bonaparte assume control of France and much of Europe?

How did slave revolt on colonial Saint-Domingue lead to the creation of Haiti in 1804?

How did the Spanish and Portuguese colonies of the Americas shake off European domination?

☑ **LearningCurve**
Check what you know.

and proceeds from the tax were to fund the defense of the colonies. Nonetheless, the colonists vigorously protested the Stamp Act by rioting and by boycotting British goods. Thus Parliament reluctantly repealed it.

This dispute raised an important political issue. The British government believed that Americans were represented in Parliament, albeit indirectly (like most British people), and that Parliament ruled throughout the empire. Many Americans felt otherwise, and came to see British colonial administration and parliamentary supremacy as grave threats to existing American liberties.

Americans' resistance to these threats was fed by the great degree of independence they had long enjoyed. In British North America, unlike in England and Europe, religious freedom was taken for granted. Colonial assemblies made the important laws, which were seldom overturned by the British government. Also, the right to vote was much more widespread than in England.

Moreover, greater political equality was matched by greater social and economic equality, at least for the free population. There was no hereditary nobility, and independent farmers dominated colonial society. This was particularly true in the northern colonies, where the revolution originated.

In 1773 disputes over taxes and representation flared up again. Under the Tea Act of that year, the East India Company secured a profitable monopoly on the tea trade, and colonial merchants were excluded. The price on tea was actually lowered for colonists, but the act generated a great deal of opposition because of its impact on local merchants.

In protest, Boston men disguised as Native Americans held a rowdy Tea Party in which they boarded East India Company ships and threw tea from them into the harbor. In response, the so-called Coercive Acts of 1774 instated a series of harsh measures. County conventions in Massachusetts urged that the acts be "rejected as the attempts of a wicked administration to enslave America." Other colonial assemblies joined in the denunciations. In September 1774 the First Continental Congress met in Philadelphia. The more radical members of this assembly argued successfully against concessions to the English crown. The British Parliament also rejected compromise, and in April 1775 fighting between colonial and British troops began at Lexington and Concord.

Independence from Britain

As fighting spread, the colonists moved slowly toward open calls for independence. The uncompromising attitude of the British government and its use of German mercenaries did much to dissolve loyalties to the home country and to unite the separate colonies. *Common Sense* (1775), a brilliant attack by the recently arrived English radical Thomas Paine (1737–1809), also mobilized public opinion in favor of independence.

Declaration of Independence

▶ The 1776 document in which the American colonies declared independence from Great Britain and recast traditional English rights as universal human rights.

On July 4, 1776, the Second Continental Congress adopted the **Declaration of Independence**. Written by Thomas Jefferson and others, this document listed the tyrannical acts committed by George III (r. 1760–1820) and proclaimed the natural rights of mankind and the sovereignty of the American states. The Declaration of Independence in effect universalized the traditional rights of English people and made them the rights of all mankind.

After the Declaration of Independence, the conflict often took the form of a civil war pitting patriots against Loyalists, those who maintained an allegiance

CHAPTER LOCATOR | What were the factors behind the age of revolution in the Atlantic world? | **Why and how did American colonists forge a new, independent nation?**

650 CHAPTER 22 REVOLUTIONS IN THE ATLANTIC WORLD

to the Crown. The Loyalists were few in number in New England and Virginia, but more common in the Deep South and on the western frontier. British commanders also recruited Loyalists from enslaved people by promising freedom to any slave who left his master to fight for the mother country.

On the international scene, the French wanted revenge against the British for the humiliating defeats of the Seven Years' War. Thus they sympathized with the rebels and supplied guns and gunpowder from the beginning of the conflict. In 1778 the French government offered the Americans a formal alliance, and in 1779 and 1780 the Spanish and Dutch declared war on Britain. Catherine the Great of Russia helped organize the League of Armed Neutrality to protect neutral shipping rights and succeeded in hampering Britain's naval power.

Thus by 1780 Britain was engaged in an imperial war against most of Europe as well as the thirteen colonies. In these circumstances, and in the face of severe reverses in India, in the West Indies, and at Yorktown in Virginia, a new British government decided to cut its losses and end the war. Under the Treaty of Paris of 1783, Britain recognized the independence of the thirteen colonies and ceded all its territory between the Allegheny Mountains and the Mississippi River to the Americans.

Loyalist Strength in the Colonies, ca. 1774–1776

KEY EVENTS OF THE AMERICAN REVOLUTION

1765	Britain passes the Stamp Act
1773	Britain passes the Tea Act
1774	Britain passes the Coercive Acts in response to the Tea Party in the colonies; the First Continental Congress refuses concessions to the English crown
April 1775	Fighting begins between colonial and British troops
July 4, 1776	The Second Continental Congress adopts the Declaration of Independence
1777–1780	The French, Spanish, and Dutch side with the colonists against Britain
1783	The Treaty of Paris recognizes the independence of the American colonies
1787	The U.S. Constitution is signed
1791	The first ten amendments to the Constitution are ratified (the Bill of Rights)

Framing the Constitution

The liberal program of the American Revolution was consolidated by the federal Constitution, the Bill of Rights, and the creation of a national republic. Assembling in Philadelphia in the summer of 1787, the delegates to the Constitutional Convention were determined to end the period of economic depression, social uncertainty, and leadership under a weak central government that had followed independence. The delegates thus decided to grant the federal, or central, government important powers: regulation of domestic and foreign trade, the right to tax, and the means to enforce its laws.

When the results of the Constitutional Convention were presented to the states for ratification, a great public debate began. The opponents of the proposed

How did the events of 1789 result in a constitutional monarchy in France? | How did Napoleon Bonaparte assume control of France and much of Europe? | How did slave revolt on colonial Saint-Domingue lead to the creation of Haiti in 1804? | How did the Spanish and Portuguese colonies of the Americas shake off European domination? | LearningCurve Check what you know.

651

Antifederalists

▶ Opponents of the American Constitution who felt it diminished individual rights and accorded too much power to the federal government at the expense of the states.

Constitution—the **Antifederalists**—charged that the framers of the new document had taken too much power from the individual states and made the federal government too strong. Moreover, many Antifederalists feared for the individual freedoms for which they had fought. To overcome these objections, the Federalists promised to spell out these basic freedoms as soon as the new Constitution was adopted. The result was the first ten amendments to the Constitution, which the first Congress passed shortly after it met in New York in March 1789. These amendments, ratified in 1791, formed an effective Bill of Rights to safeguard the individual.

Limitations of Liberty and Equality

The American Constitution and the Bill of Rights exemplified the strengths and the limits of what came to be called classical liberalism. Liberty meant individual freedoms and political safeguards. Liberty also meant representative government, but it did not mean democracy, with its principle of one person, one vote. Equality meant equality before the law, not equality of political participation or wealth. It did not mean equal rights for slaves, Native Americans, or women.

A vigorous abolitionist movement during the 1780s led to the passage of emancipation laws in all northern states, but slavery remained prevalent in the South, and discord between pro- and antislavery delegates roiled the Constitutional Convention of 1787. The result was a set of compromises that ensured that slavery would endure in the United States for the foreseeable future.

The new republic also failed to protect the Native American tribes whose lands fell within or alongside the territory ceded by Britain at the Treaty of Paris. The 1787 Constitution promised protection to Native Americans and guaranteed that their land would not be taken without consent. Nonetheless, the rights and interests of Native Americans were generally ignored as a growing colonial population pushed westward.

Women played a vital role in the American Revolution. Women were essential participants in boycotts of British goods, which squeezed profits from British merchants and fostered the revolutionary spirit. After the outbreak of war, women raised funds for the Continental Army and took care of homesteads, workshops, and other businesses when their men went off to fight. Women did not, however, receive the right to vote in the new Constitution, an omission confirmed by a clause added in 1844.

> **QUICK REVIEW**

What did proponents of the American Revolution mean by the terms "liberty" and "equality"?

CHAPTER LOCATOR | What were the factors behind the age of revolution in the Atlantic world? | Why and how did American colonists forge a new, independent nation?

652 CHAPTER 22
REVOLUTIONS IN THE ATLANTIC WORLD

The Tennis Court Oath, June 20, 1789

Painted two years after the event shown, this dramatic painting by Jacques-Louis David depicts a crucial turning point in the early days of the Revolution. On June 20 delegates of the third estate arrived at their meeting hall in the Versailles palace to find the doors closed and guarded. Fearing the king was about to dissolve their meeting by force, the deputies reassembled at a nearby indoor tennis court and swore a solemn oath not to disperse until they had been recognized as the National Assembly. (Musée de la Ville de Paris, Musée Carnavalet, Paris, France/Giraudon/The Bridgeman Art Library)

ALTHOUGH INSPIRED IN PART by events in North America, the French Revolution did not mirror the American example. It was more radical and more complex, more influential and more controversial. For Europeans and most of the rest of the world, it was the great revolution of the eighteenth century, the revolution that opened the modern era in politics.

Breakdown of the Old Order

As did the American Revolution, the French Revolution had its immediate origins in the financial difficulties of the government. The efforts of the ministers of King Louis XV (r. 1715–1774) to raise taxes to meet the expenses of the War of the Austrian Succession and the Seven Years' War were thwarted by the high courts, known as the parlements. The noble judges of the parlements resented this threat to their exemption from taxation and decried the government's actions as a form of royal despotism.

How did the events of 1789 result in a constitutional monarchy in France? | How did Napoleon Bonaparte assume control of France and much of Europe? | How did slave revolt on colonial Saint-Domingue lead to the creation of Haiti in 1804? | How did the Spanish and Portuguese colonies of the Americas shake off European domination? | ☑ LearningCurve Check what you know.

653

When renewed efforts to reform the tax system similarly failed in 1776, the government was forced to finance its enormous expenditures during the American war with borrowed money. As a result, the national debt soared. In 1786 the finance minister informed King Louis XVI (r. 1774–1792) that the nation was on the verge of bankruptcy.

> **> France's Annual Budget (1786):**
>
> - 50 percent: Interest payments on the national debt
> - 25 percent: Maintenance of the military
> - 6 percent: Expenses of the royal family and the court
> - Less than 20 percent: Productive functions of the state, such as transportation and general administration

Louis XVI's minister of finance convinced the king to call an assembly of notables in 1787 to gain support for major fiscal reforms. The assembled notables declared that sweeping tax changes required the approval of the **Estates General**, the representative body of all three estates. Louis XVI's efforts to reject their demands failed, and in July 1788 he reluctantly called the Estates General into session.

Estates General

▶ Traditional representative body of the three estates of France that met in 1789 in response to imminent state bankruptcy.

The National Assembly

The Estates General was a legislative body with representatives from the three orders of society: the clergy, nobility, and commoners. On May 5, 1789, the twelve hundred newly elected delegates of the three estates gathered in Versailles for the opening session of the Estates General. They met in an atmosphere of deepening economic crisis, triggered by a poor grain harvest in 1788.

The Estates General was almost immediately deadlocked by arguments about voting procedures. The government insisted that each estate should meet and vote separately. Critics had demanded instead a single assembly dominated by the third estate. In his famous pamphlet "What Is the Third Estate?" the abbé Emmanuel Joseph Sieyès argued that the nobility was a tiny, overprivileged minority and that commoners constituted the true strength of the French nation. The issue came to a crisis in June 1789 when delegates of the third estate refused to meet until the king ordered the clergy and nobility to sit with them in a single body. On June 20 the delegates of the third estate moved to a large indoor tennis court where they swore the famous Oath of the Tennis Court, pledging not to disband until they had been recognized as a **National Assembly** and had written a new constitution.

National Assembly

▶ French representative assembly formed in 1789 by the delegates of the third estate and some members of the clergy, the second estate.

The king's response was disastrously ambivalent. Although he made a conciliatory speech accepting the deputies' demands, he called a large army toward the capital to bring the Assembly under control, and on July 11 he dismissed his finance minister and other liberal ministers. On July 14, 1789, several hundred common people, angered by the king's actions, stormed the Bastille (ba-STEEL), a royal prison. Ill-judged severity on the part of the Crown thus led to the first episodes of popular violence.

Uprisings also rocked the countryside. In the summer of 1789 throughout France peasants began to rise in insurrection against their lords. Fear of maraud-

CHAPTER LOCATOR | What were the factors behind the age of revolution in the Atlantic world? | Why and how did American colonists forge a new, independent nation?

654 CHAPTER 22 REVOLUTIONS IN THE ATLANTIC WORLD

ers and vagabonds hired by vengeful landlords—called the Great Fear by contemporaries—seized the rural poor and fanned the flames of rebellion.

The National Assembly responded to the swell of popular anger with a surprise maneuver on the night of August 4, 1789. By a decree of the Assembly, all the old noble privileges were abolished along with tithes paid to the church. On August 27, 1789, the Assembly further issued the Declaration of the Rights of Man and of the Citizen, guaranteeing equality before the law, representative government for a sovereign people, and individual freedom.

The National Assembly's declaration had little practical effect for the poor and hungry people of Paris. The economic crisis worsened after the fall of the Bastille, as aristocrats fled the country and the luxury market collapsed. Foreign markets also shrank, and unemployment among the urban working class grew.

Constitutional Monarchy

The next two years, until September 1791, saw the consolidation of the liberal revolution. In June 1790 the National Assembly abolished the nobility, and in July the king swore to uphold the as-yet-unwritten constitution. The king remained the head of state, but all lawmaking power now resided in the National Assembly, elected by the wealthiest half of French males. The constitution finally passed in September 1791 was the first in French history. It legalized divorce and broadened women's rights to inherit property and to obtain financial support for illegitimate children from fathers, but excluded women from political office and voting.

In addition to ruling on women's rights, the National Assembly replaced the patchwork of historic provinces with eighty-three departments of approximately equal size. The deputies prohibited monopolies, guilds, and workers' associations and abolished barriers to trade within France. Thus the National Assembly applied the spirit of the Enlightenment in a thorough reform of France's laws and institutions.

The National Assembly also imposed a radical reorganization on religious life. It granted religious freedom to the small minority of French Jews and Protestants. Furthermore, in November 1789 it nationalized the property of the Catholic Church and abolished monasteries.

In July 1790 the Civil Constitution of the Clergy established a national church with priests chosen by voters. The National Assembly then forced the Catholic clergy to take an oath of loyalty to the new government. The pope formally condemned this measure, and only half the priests of France swore the oath. Many sincere Christians, especially those in the countryside, were also upset by these changes in the religious order. The attempt to remake the Catholic Church, like the abolition of guilds and workers' associations, sharpened the conflict between the educated classes and the common people that had been emerging in the eighteenth century.

The National Convention

The outbreak and progress of revolution in France produced great excitement and a sharp division of opinion in Europe and the United States. Liberals and radicals saw a triumph of liberty over despotism, while conservative leaders were deeply troubled by the aroused spirit of reform.

How did the events of 1789 result in a constitutional monarchy in France?

How did Napoleon Bonaparte assume control of France and much of Europe?

How did slave revolt on colonial Saint-Domingue lead to the creation of Haiti in 1804?

How did the Spanish and Portuguese colonies of the Americas shake off European domination?

✓ LearningCurve
Check what you know.

655

Jacobin club

▶ A political club during the French Revolution to which many of the deputies of the Legislative Assembly belonged.

Mountain

▶ Led by Robespierre, the French National Convention's radical faction, which led the Convention in 1793.

Girondists

▶ A moderate group that fought for control of the French National Convention in 1793.

sans-culottes

▶ The laboring poor of Paris, so called because the men wore trousers instead of the knee breeches of the aristocracy and middle class; the term came to refer to the militant radicals of the city.

The kings and nobles of continental Europe, who had at first welcomed the revolution in France as weakening a competing power, now feared its impact. In June 1791 the royal family was arrested and returned to Paris after a failed attempt to escape France. To the monarchs of Austria and Prussia, the arrest of a crowned monarch was unacceptable. Two months later they issued the Declaration of Pillnitz, proclaiming their willingness to intervene in France to restore Louis XVI's rule, if necessary.

The new French representative body, called the Legislative Assembly, was dominated by members of the **Jacobin club**. The Jacobins and other deputies reacted with patriotic fury to the Declaration of Pillnitz, and in April 1792 France declared war on Francis II of Austria, the Habsburg monarch.

France's crusade against tyranny went poorly at first. Prussian forces joined Austria against the French, who broke and fled at their first military encounter with this First Coalition of antirevolutionary foreign powers. The Legislative Assembly declared the country in danger, and volunteers rallied to the capital. In August the Assembly suspended the king from all his functions and imprisoned him.

The fall of the monarchy marked a rapid radicalization of the Revolution. In late September 1792 a new assembly, called the National Convention, was elected by universal manhood suffrage. The Convention proclaimed France a republic, a nation in which the people, instead of a monarch, held sovereign power. Under the leadership of the **Mountain**, the radical faction of the Jacobin club led by Maximilien Robespierre and Georges Jacques Danton, the Convention tried and convicted the king for treason. On January 21, 1793, Louis was executed. His wife, Marie Antoinette, suffered the same fate later that year.

In February 1793 the National Convention declared war on Britain, the Dutch Republic, and Spain. Republican France was now at war with almost all of Europe, and it faced mounting internal opposition. Peasants in western France revolted against being drafted into the army, with the Vendée region of Brittany emerging as the epicenter of revolt. Devout Catholics, royalists, and foreign agents encouraged their rebellion.

By March 1793 the National Convention was locked in struggle between two factions of the Jacobin club, the radical Mountain and the more moderate **Girondists**. With the middle-class delegates so bitterly divided, the laboring poor of Paris once again emerged as the decisive political factor. The laboring poor and the petty traders were often known as the **sans-culottes** (san-koo-LAHT; "without breeches") because their men wore trousers instead of the knee breeches of the wealthy. They demanded radical political action to guarantee them their daily bread. The Mountain, sensing an opportunity to outmaneuver the Girondists, joined with sans-culotte activists to engineer a popular uprising. On June 2, 1793, armed sans-culottes invaded the Convention and forced its deputies to arrest twenty-nine Girondist deputies for treason. All power passed to the Mountain.

This military and political crisis led to the most radical period of the Revolution, which lasted from spring 1793 until summer 1794. To deal with threats from within and outside France, the Convention formed the Committee of Public Safety in April 1793. Led by Robespierre, the Committee advanced on several fronts in 1793 and 1794. First, in September 1793 Robespierre and his coworkers established a planned economy. Rather than let supply and demand determine prices, the government set maximum allowable prices for key products. Though the state was too weak to enforce all its price regulations, it did fix the price of bread in Paris at levels the poor could afford.

Areas of French Insurrection, 1793

CHAPTER LOCATOR | What were the factors behind the age of revolution in the Atlantic world? | Why and how did American colonists forge a new, independent nation?

Des Tetes! — du Sang! — la Mort! — à la Lanterne! — à la Guillotine. — point de Reine! — Je suis la Deesse de la Liberté! — l'egalité! — que Londres soit brulé! — que Paris soit Libre! — Vive la Guillotine!

Contrasting Visions of the Sans-Culottes

These two images offer profoundly different representations of a sans-culotte woman. The image on the left was created by a French artist, while the image on the right is English. The French words above the image on the right read in part, "Heads! Blood! Death! . . . I am the Goddess of Liberty! . . . Long Live the Guillotine!" (left: Musée de la Ville de Paris, Musée Carnavalet, Paris, France/ Archives Charmet/The Bridgeman Art Library; right: by James Gillray [1757–1815]. © Courtesy of the Warden and Scholars of New College, Oxford, UK/The Bridgeman Art Library)

> **PICTURING THE PAST**

ANALYZING THE IMAGE: How would you describe the woman on the left? What qualities does the artist seem to ascribe to her, and how do you think these qualities relate to the sans-culottes and the French Revolution? How would you characterize the facial expression and attire of the woman on the right? How does the inclusion of the text contribute to your impressions of her?

CONNECTIONS: What does the contrast between these two images suggest about differences between French and English perceptions of the sans-culottes and of the French Revolution? Why do you think the artists have chosen to depict women?

The government also put the people to work producing arms, munitions, and uniforms for the war effort. The government told craftsmen what to produce, nationalized many small workshops, and requisitioned raw materials and grain. These economic reforms amounted to an emergency form of socialism, which thoroughly frightened Europe's propertied classes and greatly influenced the subsequent development of socialist ideology.

Second, the **Reign of Terror** (1793–1794) enforced compliance with republican beliefs and practices. Special revolutionary courts tried "enemies of the nation" for political crimes. As a result, some forty thousand French men and women were executed or died in prison. Presented as a necessary measure to save the republic, the Terror was a weapon directed against all suspected of opposing the revolutionary government.

In their efforts to impose unity, the Jacobins also took actions to suppress women's participation in political debate, which they perceived as disorderly and a distraction from women's proper place in the home. On October 30, 1793, the National Convention declared, "The clubs and popular societies of women, under whatever denomination are prohibited."

The third element of the Committee's program was to bring about a cultural revolution that would transform former royal subjects into republican citizens.

Reign of Terror

▶ The period from 1793 to 1794, during which Robespierre's Committee of Public Safety tried and executed thousands suspected of treason and a new revolutionary culture was imposed.

How did the events of 1789 result in a constitutional monarchy in France?

How did Napoleon Bonaparte assume control of France and much of Europe?

How did slave revolt on colonial Saint-Domingue lead to the creation of Haiti in 1804?

How did the Spanish and Portuguese colonies of the Americas shake off European domination?

☑ LearningCurve
Check what you know.

KEY EVENTS OF THE FRENCH REVOLUTION

May 5, 1789	Estates General meets at Versailles
June 20, 1789	Oath of the Tennis Court
July 14, 1789	Storming of the Bastille
July–August 1789	Great Fear
August 4, 1789	National Assembly abolishes feudal privileges
August 27, 1789	National Assembly issues Declaration of the Rights of Man and of the Citizen
July 1790	Civil Constitution of the Clergy establishes a national church; Louis XVI agrees to a constitutional monarchy
June 1791	Royal family is arrested while attempting to flee France
August 1791	Austria and Prussia issue the Declaration of Pillnitz
April 1792	France declares war on Austria
August 1792	Legislative Assembly takes Louis XVI prisoner and suspends him from functions
September 1792	National Convention declares France a republic and abolishes monarchy
January 21, 1793	Louis XVI is executed
February 1793	France declares war on Britain, the Dutch Republic, and Spain; revolts take place in some provinces
March 1793	Struggle between Girondists and the Mountain
June 1793	Sans-culottes invade the National Convention; Girondist leaders are arrested
September 1793	Price controls are instituted to aid the poor
1793–1794	Reign of Terror
Spring 1794	French armies are victorious on all fronts
July 1794	Robespierre is executed; Thermidorian reaction begins
1795	Economic controls are abolished, and suppression of the sans-culottes begins
1795–1799	Directory rules
1798–1799	Austria, Britain, and Russia form the Second Coalition against France
1799	Napoleon Bonaparte overthrows the Directory and seizes power

The government sponsored revolutionary art and songs as well as secular holidays and open-air festivals to celebrate republican virtues. It also attempted to rationalize daily life by adopting the decimal system for weights and measures and a new calendar based on ten-day weeks. A campaign of de-Christianization aimed to eliminate Catholic symbols and beliefs. Fearful of the hostility aroused in rural France, however, Robespierre called for a halt to de-Christianization measures in mid-1794.

The final element in the program of the Committee of Public Safety was its appeal to a new sense of national identity and patriotism. With a common language and a common tradition reinforced by the revolutionary ideals of popular sovereignty and democracy, many French people developed an intense emotional attachment to the nation. This was the birth of modern nationalism, the strong identification with one's nation, which would have a profound effect on subsequent European history.

CHAPTER LOCATOR | What were the factors behind the age of revolution in the Atlantic world? | Why and how did American colonists forge a new, independent nation?

658 CHAPTER 22 REVOLUTIONS IN THE ATLANTIC WORLD

To defend the nation, a decree of August 1793 imposed a draft on all unmarried young men. By January 1794 French armed forces outnumbered those of their enemies almost four to one. By spring 1794 French armies were victorious on all fronts and domestic revolt was largely suppressed. The republic was saved.

The Directory

The success of French armies led the Committee of Public Safety to relax emergency economic controls, but they extended the political Reign of Terror. The revolutionary tribunals sent many critics to the guillotine, including long-standing collaborators whom Robespierre believed had turned against him. A group of radicals and moderates in the Convention, knowing that they might be next, organized a conspiracy. They howled down Robespierre when he tried to speak to the National Convention on July 27, 1794—a date known as 9 Thermidor according to France's newly adopted republican calendar. The next day it was Robespierre's turn to be guillotined.

The respectable middle-class lawyers and professionals who had led the liberal Revolution of 1789 then reasserted their authority. This period of **Thermidorian reaction**, as it was called, harkened back to the moderate beginnings of the Revolution. In 1795 the National Convention abolished many economic controls and severely restricted local political organizations. In addition, the middle-class members of the National Convention wrote a new constitution restricting eligibility to serve as a deputy to men of substantial means. Real power lay with a new five-man executive body, called the Directory. France's new rulers continued to support military expansion abroad, but war was no longer so much a crusade as a response to economic problems. Large, victorious armies reduced unemployment at home. However, the French people quickly grew weary of the corruption and ineffectiveness that characterized the Directory. This general dissatisfaction revealed itself clearly in the national elections of 1797, which returned a large number of conservative and even monarchist deputies. Fearing for their survival, the Directory used the army to nullify the elections and began to govern dictatorially. Two years later Napoleon Bonaparte ended the Directory in a coup d'état (koo day-TAH) and substituted a strong dictatorship for a weak one. While claiming to uphold revolutionary values, Napoleon would install authoritarian rule.

Thermidorian reaction

▶ A reaction in 1794 to the violence of the Reign of Terror, resulting in the execution of Robespierre and the loosening of economic controls.

The Execution of Robespierre

Completely wooden except for the heavy iron blade, the guillotine was devised by a French revolutionary doctor named Guillotin as a humane method of execution. The guillotine was painted red for Robespierre's execution. Large crowds witnessed the execution in a majestic public square in central Paris, then known as the Place de la Revolution and now called the Place de la Concorde (Harmony Square). (Musée de la Ville de Paris, Musée Carnavalet, Paris, France/Giraudon/The Bridgeman Art Library)

QUICK REVIEW <

How and why did the French Revolution change between 1789 and 1799?

How did the events of 1789 result in a constitutional monarchy in France?	How did Napoleon Bonaparte assume control of France and much of Europe?	How did slave revolt on colonial Saint-Domingue lead to the creation of Haiti in 1804?	How did the Spanish and Portuguese colonies of the Americas shake off European domination?	☑ LearningCurve Check what you know.

How did Napoleon Bonaparte assume control of France and much of Europe, and what factors led to his downfall?

The Coronation of Napoleon, 1804

In this detail from a grandiose painting by Jacques-Louis David, Napoleon, instead of the pope, prepares to crown his wife, Josephine, in an elaborate ceremony in Notre Dame Cathedral. Napoleon, the ultimate upstart, also crowned himself. Pope Pius VII, seated glumly behind the emperor, is reduced to being a spectator. (Photo by Jacques-Louis David [1748–1825]/Louvre, Paris, France/ The Bridgeman Art Library)

NAPOLEON BONAPARTE (1769–1821) sought to put an end to civil strife in France in order to create unity and consolidate his rule. And he did. But Napoleon saw himself as a man of destiny, and the glory of war and the dream of universal empire proved irresistible.

Napoleon's Rule of France

Born on the Mediterranean island of Corsica, Napoleon left home and became a lieutenant in the French artillery in 1785. Rising rapidly in the new army, Napoleon was placed in command of French forces in Italy and won brilliant victories there in 1796 and 1797. His next campaign, in Egypt, was a failure, but Napoleon returned to France before the fiasco was generally known. French aggression in Egypt and elsewhere provoked the British to organize a new alliance in 1798, the Second Coalition, which included Austria and Russia.

Napoleon soon learned that some prominent members of the legislature were plotting against the Directory. The dissatisfaction of these plotters stemmed not

CHAPTER LOCATOR | What were the factors behind the age of revolution in the Atlantic world? | Why and how did American colonists forge a new, independent nation?

so much from the fact that the Directory was a dictatorship as from the fact that it was a weak dictatorship.

The young Napoleon, nationally revered for his heroism, was an ideal figure of authority. On November 9, 1799, Napoleon and his conspirators ousted the Directors, and the following day soldiers disbanded the legislature. Napoleon was named first consul of the republic, and a new constitution consolidating his position was overwhelmingly approved in a plebiscite in December 1799. Republican appearances were maintained, but Napoleon became the real ruler of France.

Napoleon worked to maintain order and end civil strife by appeasing powerful groups in France, offering them favors in return for loyal service. Napoleon's bargain with the middle class was codified in the Civil Code of March 1804, also known as the **Napoleonic Code**, which reasserted two of the fundamental principles of the Revolution of 1789: equality of all male citizens before the law and absolute security of wealth and private property. Napoleon and the leading bankers of Paris established the privately owned Bank of France in 1800, which served the interests of both the state and the financial oligarchy. Napoleon won over peasants by defending the gains in land and status they had won during the Revolution.

At the same time, Napoleon consolidated his rule by recruiting disillusioned revolutionaries for the network of government officials. Nor were members of the old nobility slighted. In 1800 and again in 1802 Napoleon granted amnesty to noble émigrés on the condition that they return to France and take a loyalty oath. Members of this returning elite soon occupied high posts in the expanding centralized state. Napoleon also created a new imperial nobility to reward his most talented generals and officials.

Furthermore, Napoleon sought to restore the Catholic Church in France so that it could serve as a bulwark of social stability. Napoleon and Pope Pius VII (pontificate 1800–1823) signed the Concordat of 1801. Under this agreement the pope gained the right for French Catholics to practice their religion freely, but Napoleon's government now nominated bishops, paid the clergy, and exerted great influence over the church in France.

Order and unity had a price: authoritarian rule. Women lost many of the gains they had made in the 1790s. Under the Napoleonic Code, women were dependents of either their fathers or their husbands, and they could not make contracts or have bank accounts in their own names. Napoleon also curtailed free speech and freedom of the press and manipulated voting in the occasional elections. After 1810 political suspects were held in state prisons, as they had been during the Terror.

Napoleonic Code
▶ French civil code promulgated in 1804 that reasserted the 1789 principles of the equality of all male citizens before the law and the absolute security of wealth and private property.

Napoleon's Expansion in Europe

After coming to power in 1799, Napoleon sent peace feelers to Austria and Britain, the dominant powers of the Second Coalition. When these overtures were rejected, French armies led by Napoleon decisively defeated the Austrians. Subsequent treaties with Austria in 1801 and Britain in 1802 consolidated France's hold on the territories its armies had won up to that point.

In 1802 Napoleon was secure but still driven to expand his power. Aggressively redrawing the map of German-speaking lands so as to weaken Austria and encourage the secondary states of southwestern Germany to side with France,

How did the events of 1789 result in a constitutional monarchy in France? | **How did Napoleon Bonaparte assume control of France and much of Europe?** | How did slave revolt on colonial Saint-Domingue lead to the creation of Haiti in 1804? | How did the Spanish and Portuguese colonies of the Americas shake off European domination? | ✔ LearningCurve Check what you know.

661

German Confederation of the Rhine, 1806

Napoleon tried to restrict British trade with all of Europe. He then plotted to attack Britain, but his Mediterranean fleet was destroyed by Lord Nelson at the Battle of Trafalgar on October 21, 1805.

Austria, Russia, and Sweden joined with Britain to form the Third Coalition against France shortly before the Battle of Trafalgar. Yet the Austrians and the Russians were no match for Napoleon, who scored a brilliant victory over them at the Battle of Austerlitz in December 1805. Russia decided to pull back, and Austria accepted large territorial losses in return for peace as the Third Coalition collapsed.

Napoleon then reorganized the German states to his liking. In 1806 he abolished many tiny German states as well as the Holy Roman Empire and established by decree the German Confederation of the Rhine, a union of fifteen German states minus Austria, Prussia, and Saxony.

Napoleon's intervention in German affairs alarmed the Prussians, who mobilized their armies. In October 1806 Napoleon attacked them and won two more victories at Jena and Auerstädt. The war with Prussia, now joined by Russia, continued into the following spring. After Napoleon won another victory, Alexander I of Russia was ready to negotiate for peace. In the treaties of Tilsit in 1807, Prussia lost half its population through land concessions, while Russia accepted Napoleon's reorganization of western and central Europe and promised to enforce Napoleon's economic blockade against British goods.

The Grand Empire and Its End

Grand Empire
▶ The empire over which Napoleon and his allies ruled, encompassing virtually all of Europe except Great Britain.

Continental System
▶ A blockade imposed by Napoleon to halt all trade between continental Europe and Britain, thereby weakening the British economy and military.

Napoleon's so-called **Grand Empire** had three parts. The core, or first part, was an ever-expanding France (Map 22.2). The second part consisted of a number of dependent satellite kingdoms. The third part comprised the independent but allied states of Austria, Prussia, and Russia. After 1806 both satellites and allies were expected to support Napoleon's **Continental System**, a blockade in which no ship coming from Britain or her colonies was permitted to dock at any port that was controlled by the French. The blockade was intended to destroy the British economy and, thereby, its ability to wage war.

In the areas incorporated into France and in the satellites, French rule sparked patriotic upheavals and encouraged the growth of reactive nationalism. The first great revolt occurred in Spain. In 1808 Napoleon deposed Spanish king Ferdinand VII and placed his own brother Joseph on the throne. A coalition of Catholics, monarchists, and patriots rebelled against this attempt to turn Spain into a satellite of France. French armies occupied Madrid, but the foes of Napoleon fled to the hills and waged guerrilla warfare. Events in Spain sent a clear warning: resistance to French imperialism was growing.

Yet Napoleon pushed on. In 1810, when the Grand Empire was at its height, Britain still remained at war with France, helping the guerrillas in Spain and Portugal. The Continental System was a failure. Instead of harming Britain, the system provoked the British to set up a counter-blockade, which created hard times for French consumers. Perhaps looking for a scapegoat, Napoleon turned on Alexander I of Russia, who in 1811 openly repudiated Napoleon's prohibitions against British goods.

Napoleon's invasion of Russia began in June 1812 with a force that eventually numbered 600,000. Originally planning to winter in the Russian city of Smolensk,

MAP 22.2 ■ Napoleonic Europe in 1812

At the height of the Grand Empire in 1810, Napoleon had conquered or allied with every major European power except Britain. But in 1812, angered by Russian repudiation of his ban on trade with Britain, Napoleon invaded Russia with disastrous results. Compare this map with Map 18.3 (page 526), which shows the division of Europe in 1715.

> MAPPING THE PAST

ANALYZING THE MAP: How had the balance of power shifted in Europe from 1715 to 1812? What changed, and what remained the same? What was the impact of Napoleon's wars on Germany, the Italian peninsula, and Russia?
CONNECTIONS: Why did Napoleon achieve vast territorial gains where Louis XIV did not?

Napoleon recklessly pressed on toward Moscow (see Map 22.2). The Battle of Borodino that followed was a draw. Alexander ordered the evacuation of Moscow, which the Russians then burned in part, and he refused to negotiate. Finally, after five weeks in the scorched city, Napoleon ordered a disastrous retreat. When the

| How did the events of 1789 result in a constitutional monarchy in France? | **How did Napoleon Bonaparte assume control of France and much of Europe?** | How did slave revolt on colonial Saint-Domingue lead to the creation of Haiti in 1804? | How did the Spanish and Portuguese colonies of the Americas shake off European domination? | ✓ LearningCurve Check what you know. |

frozen remnants of Napoleon's army staggered into Poland and Prussia in December, 370,000 men had died and another 200,000 had been taken prisoner.

Leaving his troops to their fate, Napoleon raced to Paris to raise another army. Meanwhile, Austria and Prussia deserted Napoleon and joined Russia and Britain in the Treaty of Chaumont in March 1814, by which the four powers formed the Quadruple Alliance to defeat the French emperor. Less than a month later, on April 4, 1814, a defeated Napoleon abdicated his throne. The victorious allies then exiled Napoleon to the island of Elba off the coast of Italy.

In February 1815 Napoleon staged a daring escape from Elba. Landing in France, he issued appeals for support and marched on Paris. But Napoleon's gamble was a desperate long shot, for the allies were united against him. At the end of a frantic period known as the Hundred Days, they crushed his forces at Waterloo on June 18, 1815, and imprisoned him on the island of St. Helena, off the western coast of Africa. The restored Bourbon dynasty took power under Louis XVIII, a younger brother of Louis XVI.

> **QUICK REVIEW**

What kind of state did Napoleon create?
From which social groups did he draw his support?

CHAPTER LOCATOR | What were the factors behind the age of revolution in the Atlantic world? | Why and how did American colonists forge a new, independent nation?

664 CHAPTER 22 REVOLUTIONS IN THE ATLANTIC WORLD

How did slave revolt on colonial Saint-Domingue lead to the creation of the independent nation of Haiti in 1804?

Saint-Domingue Slave Life

Although the brutal conditions of plantation slavery left little time or energy for leisure, slaves on Saint-Domingue took advantage of their day of rest on Sunday to engage in social and religious activities. The law officially prohibited slaves of different masters from mingling together, but such gatherings were often tolerated if they remained peaceful. This image depicts a fight between two slaves, precisely the type of unrest and violence feared by authorities. (Musée du Nouveau Monde, La Rochelle, France/Scala/White Images/Art Resource, NY)

PRIOR TO 1789 SAINT-DOMINGUE, the French colony that was to become Haiti, reaped huge profits through a ruthless system of slave-based plantation agriculture. News of revolution in France lit a powder keg of contradictory aspirations among white planters, free people of color, and slaves. Free people of color and, later, the enslaved rose up to claim their freedom. They succeeded, despite invasion by the British and Spanish and Napoleon Bonaparte's bid to reimpose French control. In 1804 Haiti became the only nation in history to claim its freedom through slave revolt.

Revolutionary Aspirations in Saint-Domingue

On the eve of the French Revolution, Saint-Domingue was inhabited by a variety of social groups who resented and mistrusted one another. The European population included French colonial officials, wealthy plantation owners and merchants,

How did the events of 1789 result in a constitutional monarchy in France? | How did Napoleon Bonaparte assume control of France and much of Europe? | **How did slave revolt on colonial Saint-Domingue lead to the creation of Haiti in 1804?** | How did the Spanish and Portuguese colonies of the Americas shake off European domination? | ✔ **LearningCurve** Check what you know.

665

and poor artisans and clerks. Vastly outnumbering the white population were the colony's five hundred thousand enslaved people, along with a sizable population of some forty thousand free people of African and mixed African and European descent. Members of this last group referred to themselves as "free people of color."

Most of the island's enslaved population performed grueling toil in the island's sugar plantations. The highly outnumbered planters used extremely harsh methods, such as beating, maiming, and executing slaves, to maintain their control. The 1685 Code Noir (Black Code) that legally regulated slavery was intended to provide minimal standards of humane treatment, but its tenets were rarely enforced. Masters calculated that they could earn more by working slaves ruthlessly and purchasing new ones when they died than by providing the food, rest, and medical care needed to allow the enslaved population to reproduce naturally. This meant that a constant inflow of newly enslaved people from Africa was necessary to work the plantations.

Despite their brutality, slaveholders on Saint-Domingue freed a certain number of their slaves, mostly their own mixed-race children, thereby producing one of the largest populations of free people of color in any slaveholding colony. The Code Noir had originally granted free people of color the same legal status as whites. From the 1760s on, however, colonial administrators began rescinding these rights, and by the time of the French Revolution free people of color were subject to many discriminatory laws.

The political and intellectual turmoil of the 1780s, with its growing rhetoric of liberty, equality, and fraternity, raised new challenges and possibilities for each of Saint-Domingue's social groups. For enslaved people, news of abolitionist movements in France led to hopes that the mother country might grant them freedom. Free people of color looked to reforms in Paris as a means of gaining political enfranchisement and reasserting equal status with whites. The white elite, however, was determined to protect its way of life, including slaveholding. They hoped to gain control of their own affairs, as had the American colonists before them.

The National Assembly frustrated the hopes of all these groups. Cowed by colonial representatives who claimed that support for free people of color would result in slave insurrection, the Assembly refused to extend French constitutional safeguards to the colonies. At the same time, however, the Assembly also reaffirmed French monopolies over colonial trade, thereby angering planters as well.

In July 1790 Vincent Ogé (aw-ZHAY) (ca. 1750–1791), a free man of color, returned to Saint-Domingue from Paris determined to win rights for his people. He raised an army and sent letters to the new Provincial Assembly of Saint-Domingue demanding political rights for all free citizens. When Ogé's demands were refused, he and his followers turned to armed insurrection. After initial victories, his army was defeated, and Ogé was executed by colonial officials. Revolutionary leaders in Paris were more sympathetic to Ogé's cause. In May 1791 the National Assembly granted political rights to free people of color born to two free parents who possessed sufficient property. When news of this legislation arrived in Saint-Domingue, the colonial governor refused to enact it. Violence then erupted between groups of whites and free people of color in parts of the colony.

CHAPTER LOCATOR | What were the factors behind the age of revolution in the Atlantic world? | Why and how did American colonists forge a new, independent nation?

CHAPTER 22
666 REVOLUTIONS IN THE ATLANTIC WORLD

The Outbreak of Revolt

Just as the sans-culottes helped push forward more radical reforms in France, the second stage of revolution in Saint-Domingue also resulted from decisive action from below. In August 1791 slaves took events into their own hands. Revolts began on a few plantations on the night of August 22. As the uprising spread, rebels joined together in an ever-growing slave army. During the next month enslaved combatants attacked and destroyed hundreds of sugar and coffee plantations.

On April 4, 1792, as war loomed with the European states, the National Assembly issued a decree extending full citizenship rights to free men of color. The Assembly hoped this measure would win the loyalty of free men of color and their aid in defeating the slave rebellion.

Warfare in Europe soon spread to Saint-Domingue (Map 22.3). Since the beginning of the slave insurrection, the Spanish colony of Santo Domingo, on the eastern side of the island of Hispaniola, had supported rebel slaves. In early 1793

MAP 22.3 ■ The War of Haitian Independence, 1791–1804

Neighbored by the Spanish colony of Santo Domingo, Saint-Domingue was the most profitable European colony in the Caribbean. In 1791 slave revolts erupted in the north near Le Cap, which had once been the capital. In 1770 the French had transferred the capital to Port-au-Prince, which in 1804 became capital of the newly independent Haiti.

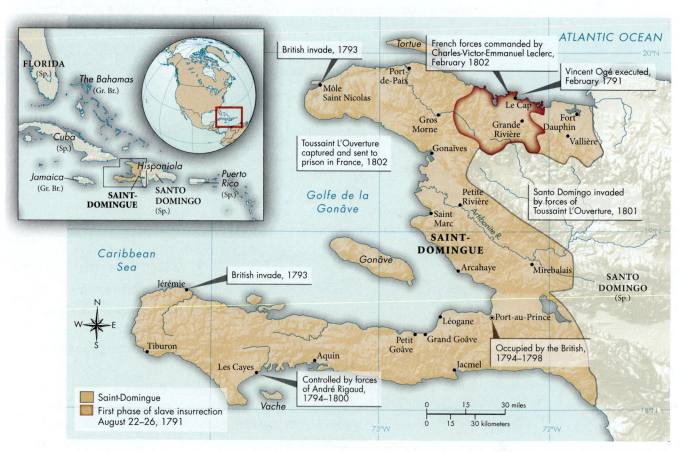

| How did the events of 1789 result in a constitutional monarchy in France? | How did Napoleon Bonaparte assume control of France and much of Europe? | **How did slave revolt on colonial Saint-Domingue lead to the creation of Haiti in 1804?** | How did the Spanish and Portuguese colonies of the Americas shake off European domination? | ✓ LearningCurve Check what you know. |

the Spanish began to bring slave leaders and their soldiers into the Spanish army. Toussaint L'Ouverture (TOO-sahn LOO-vair-toor) (1743–1803), a freed slave who had joined the revolt, was named a Spanish officer. In September the British navy blockaded the colony, and invading British troops captured French territory on the island. For the Spanish and British, revolutionary chaos provided a tempting opportunity to capture a profitable colony.

Desperate for forces to oppose France's enemies, commissioners sent by the newly elected National Convention promised freedom to slaves who fought for France. By October 1793 the commissioners had abolished slavery throughout the colony. On February 4, 1794, the Convention ratified the abolition of slavery and extended it to all French territories.

The tide of battle began to turn when Toussaint L'Ouverture switched sides. By 1796 the French had regained control of the colony, and L'Ouverture had emerged as a key military leader. (See "Individuals in Society: Toussaint L'Ouverture," page 669.) In May 1796 he was named commander of the western province of Saint-Domingue (see Map 22.3).

The War of Haitian Independence

With Toussaint L'Ouverture acting increasingly as an independent ruler of the western province of Saint-Domingue, another general, André Rigaud (1761–1811), set up his own government in the southern peninsula. Tensions mounted between L'Ouverture and Rigaud. While L'Ouverture was a freed slave of African

KEY EVENTS OF THE HAITIAN REVOLUTION

1760s	Colonial administrators begin rescinding the rights of free people of color
July 1790	Vincent Ogé leads a failed rebellion to gain rights for free people of color
August 1791	Slave revolts begin
April 4, 1792	National Assembly enfranchises all free blacks and free people of color
September 1793	British troops invade Saint-Domingue
February 4, 1794	National Convention ratifies the abolition of slavery and extends it to all French territories
May 1796	Toussaint L'Ouverture is named commander of Saint-Domingue
1800	After invading the south of Saint-Domingue, L'Ouverture gains control of the entire colony
1802	French general Charles-Victor-Emmanuel Leclerc arrests L'Ouverture and deports him to France
1803	L'Ouverture dies
1804	After defeating French forces, Jean Jacques Dessalines declares the independence of Saint-Domingue and the creation of the sovereign nation of Haiti

CHAPTER LOCATOR | What were the factors behind the age of revolution in the Atlantic world? | Why and how did American colonists forge a new, independent nation?

668 CHAPTER 22 REVOLUTIONS IN THE ATLANTIC WORLD

INDIVIDUALS IN SOCIETY
Toussaint L'Ouverture

Little is known of the early life of Saint-Domingue's brilliant military and political leader Toussaint L'Ouverture. He was born in 1743 on a plantation outside Le Cap owned by the Count de Bréda. According to tradition, L'Ouverture was the eldest son of a captured African prince from modern-day Benin. Toussaint Bréda, as he was then called, occupied a privileged position among slaves. Instead of performing backbreaking labor in the fields, he served his master as a coachman and livestock keeper. He also learned to read and write French and some Latin, but he was always more comfortable with the Creole dialect.

During the 1770s the plantation manager emancipated L'Ouverture, who subsequently leased his own small coffee plantation, worked by slaves. He married Suzanne Simone, who already had one son, and the couple had another son during their marriage. In 1791 he joined the slave uprisings that swept Saint-Domingue, and he took on the *nom de guerre* (war name) L'Ouverture, meaning "the opening." L'Ouverture rose to prominence among rebel slaves allied with Spain and by early 1794 controlled his own army. A devout Catholic who led a frugal and ascetic life, L'Ouverture impressed others with his enormous physical energy, intellectual acumen, and air of mystery. In 1794 he defected to the French side and led his troops to a series of victories against the Spanish. In 1795 the National Convention promoted L'Ouverture to brigadier general.

Over the next three years L'Ouverture successively eliminated rivals for authority on the island. First he freed himself of the French commissioners sent to govern the colony. With a firm grip on power in the northern province, L'Ouverture defeated General André Rigaud in 1800 to gain control in the south. His army then marched on the capital of Spanish Santo Domingo on the eastern half of the island, meeting little resistance. The entire island of Hispaniola was now under his command.

With control in his hands, L'Ouverture was confronted with the challenge of building a post-

Equestrian portrait of Toussaint L'Ouverture.
(Bibliothèque Nationale, Paris, France/Archives Charmet/ The Bridgeman Art Library)

emancipation society, the first of its kind. The task was made even more difficult by the chaos wreaked by war, the destruction of plantations, and bitter social and racial tensions. For L'Ouverture the most pressing concern was to re-establish the plantation economy. Without revenue to pay his army, the gains of the rebellion could be lost. He therefore encouraged white planters to return and reclaim their property. He also adopted harsh policies toward former slaves, forcing them back to their plantations and restricting their ability to acquire land. When they resisted, he sent troops across the island to enforce submission. L'Ouverture's 1801 constitution reaffirmed his draconian labor policies and named L'Ouverture governor for life, leaving Saint-Domingue as a colony in name alone. In June 1802 French forces arrested L'Ouverture and jailed him at Fort de Joux in France's Jura Mountains near the Swiss border. He died of pneumonia on April 7, 1803, leaving his lieutenant, Jean Jacques Dessalines, to win independence for the new Haitian nation.

QUESTIONS FOR ANALYSIS

1. Toussaint L'Ouverture was both slave and slave owner. How did each experience shape his life and actions?
2. What did L'Ouverture and Napoleon Bonaparte have in common? How did they differ?

▷LaunchPad

ONLINE DOCUMENT PROJECT

How did the French Revolution affect France's Caribbean colonies? Examine reactions of slaves and free men of color to the French Revolution, and then complete a quiz and writing assignment based on the evidence and details from this chapter. *See inside the front cover to learn more.*

descent, Rigaud belonged to the elite group of free people of color. This elite resented the growing power of former slaves like L'Ouverture, who in turn accused the elite of adopting the prejudices of white settlers. Civil war broke out between the two sides in 1799, when L'Ouverture's forces, led by his lieutenant, Jean Jacques Dessalines (1758–1806), invaded the south. Victory over Rigaud in 1800 gave L'Ouverture control of the entire colony.

This victory was soon challenged by Napoleon, who had his own plans for using the profits from a re-established system of plantation slavery as a basis for expanding the French empire. In 1802 Toussaint L'Ouverture was arrested and deported to France, along with his family, where he died in 1803.

It was left to L'Ouverture's lieutenant, Jean Jacques Dessalines, to unite the resistance, and he led it to a crushing victory over French forces. On January 1, 1804, Dessalines formally declared the independence of Saint-Domingue and the creation of the new sovereign nation of Haiti, the name used by the pre-Columbian inhabitants of the island.

> **QUICK REVIEW**

How did tensions between slaves and free people of color shape the Haitian Revolution?

CHAPTER LOCATOR | What were the factors behind the age of revolution in the Atlantic world? | Why and how did American colonists forge a new, independent nation?

670   CHAPTER 22
REVOLUTIONS IN THE ATLANTIC WORLD

Why and how did the Spanish and Portuguese colonies of North and South America shake off European domination and develop into national states?

Triumph of Bolívar

Bolívar was treated as a hero everywhere he went in South America. (akg-images)

THE LATIN AMERICAN MOVEMENTS for independence drew strength from unfair taxation and trade policies, Spain's declining control over its Latin American colonies, racial and class discrimination, and the spread of revolutionary ideas. Between 1806 and 1825 the Spanish colonies in Latin America were convulsed by upheavals that ultimately resulted in their separation from Spain.

The Origins of the Revolutions Against Colonial Powers

Spain's humiliating defeat in the War of the Spanish Succession (1701–1713; see page 537) prompted demands for sweeping reform of all of Spain's institutions, including its colonial policies and practices. The new Bourbon dynasty initiated

How did the events of 1789 result in a constitutional monarchy in France?	How did Napoleon Bonaparte assume control of France and much of Europe?	How did slave revolt on colonial Saint-Domingue lead to the creation of Haiti in 1804?	**How did the Spanish and Portuguese colonies of the Americas shake off European domination?**	☑ LearningCurve Check what you know.

a decades-long effort known as the Bourbon reforms, which aimed to improve administrative efficiency and increase central control. Under Charles III (r. 1759–1788), Spanish administrators drew on Enlightenment ideals of rationalism and progress to strengthen colonial rule and thereby increase the fortunes and power of the Spanish state. They created a permanent standing army and enlarged colonial militias, sought to bring the church under tighter control, and dispatched intendants (government commissioners) with extensive new powers to oversee the colonies.

Additionally, Spain ended its policy of insisting on monopoly over trade with its colonies. Instead it adopted a policy of free trade in order to compete with Great Britain and Holland in the struggle for empire. In Latin America these actions stimulated the production and export of agricultural commodities that were in demand in Europe. Colonial manufacturing, however, which had been growing steadily, suffered a heavy blow under free trade. Colonial textiles and china, for example, could not compete with cheap Spanish products.

Madrid's tax reforms also aggravated discontent. Like Great Britain, Spain believed its colonies should bear some of the costs of their own defense. Accordingly, Madrid raised the prices of its monopoly products—tobacco and liquor—and increased sales taxes on many items. War with revolutionary France in the 1790s led to additional taxes and forced loans, all of which were widely resented. Moreover, new taxes took a heavy toll on indigenous communities, which bore the brunt of all forms of taxation and suffered from the corruption and brutality of tax collectors. Riots and protest movements met with harsh repression.

Political conflicts beyond the colonies also helped drive aspirations for independence. The French Revolution and the Napoleonic Wars, which involved France's occupation of Spain and Britain's domination of the seas, isolated Spain from Latin America. As a result, Spain's control over its Latin American colonies diminished.

Creoles

▶ People of Spanish or other European descent born in the Americas.

peninsulares

▶ A term for natives of Spain and Portugal.

Racial, ethnic, and class privileges also fueled discontent. The **Creoles**—people of Spanish or other European descent born in the Americas (see page 576)—resented the economic and political dominance of the **peninsulares** (puh-nihn-suh-LUHR-ayz), as the colonial officials and other natives of Spain or Portugal were called. The Creoles wanted to free themselves from Spain and Portugal and to rule the colonies themselves. They had little interest in improving the lot of the Indians, the mestizos of mixed Spanish and Indian background, or the mulattos of mixed Spanish and African heritage.

As in Saint-Domingue, a racial backlash against the growing numbers and social prominence of people of mixed racial origin occurred in the last quarter of the eighteenth century. In 1776 King Charles III outlawed marriages between whites and any person with Indian or African blood. A number of cities issued ordinances prohibiting nonwhites from joining guilds, serving in the militia, and mixing with whites in public.

A final factor contributing to rebellion was cultural and intellectual ideas. One set of such ideas was Enlightenment thought, which had been trickling into Latin America for decades (see Chapter 19). By 1800 the Creole elite throughout Latin America was familiar with liberal Enlightenment political thought and its role in inspiring colonial revolt.

Another important set of ideas consisted of indigenous traditions of justice and political rule, which often looked back to an idealized precolonial past. During

CHAPTER LOCATOR | What were the factors behind the age of revolution in the Atlantic world? | Why and how did American colonists forge a new, independent nation?

672 CHAPTER 22 REVOLUTIONS IN THE ATLANTIC WORLD

the eighteenth century these ideas served as a rallying point for Indians and non-Indians alike. Creoles took advantage of indigenous symbols, but this did not mean they were prepared to view Indians and mestizos as equals.

Resistance, Rebellion, and Independence

The mid-eighteenth century witnessed frequent Andean Indian rebellions. In 1780, under the leadership of a descendant of the Inca rulers who took the name Túpac Amaru II, a massive insurrection exploded. Creoles joined forces with Spaniards and Indian nobles to crush the rebellion, shocked by the radical social and economic reforms promised by its leaders.

As news of the rebellion of Túpac Amaru II trickled northward, it helped stimulate the 1781 Comuneros Revolt in the New Granada viceroyalty (see Map 22.4). In this uprising, an Indian and mestizo peasant army commanded by Creole captains marched on Bogotá. Dispersed by the ruling Spanish, who made promises they did not intend to keep, the revolt in the end did little to improve the Indians' lives.

While these revolts shook authorities, two events outside of Spanish America did more to shape the ensuing struggle for independence. First, the revolution on Saint-Domingue and the subsequent independence of the nation of Haiti in 1804 convinced Creole elites, many of whom were slaveholders, of the dangers of slave revolt and racial warfare (see Map 22.3). Their plans and strategies would henceforth be shaped by their determination to avoid a similar outcome in Spanish America.

Second, in 1808 Napoleon Bonaparte deposed Spanish king Ferdinand VII and placed his own brother on the Spanish throne (see page 662). The Creoles in Latin America claimed that the removal of the legitimate king shifted sovereignty to the people—that is, to themselves.

The great hero of the movement for independence was Simón Bolívar (1783–1830). Under his leadership, a regional congress in Caracas declared the independence of the United States of Venezuela in July 1811 and quickly drafted a constitution guaranteeing freedom of the press and racial equality. The republic failed after only one year, but Bolívar continued to fight royalist forces for the next eight years, with assistance from the newly formed Haitian republic. His victories over Spanish armies won him the presidency of the new republic of Gran Colombia (formerly the New Granada viceroyalty) in 1819. The territories of Gran Colombia, however, soon splintered (see Map 22.4), and a sadly disillusioned Bolívar went into exile.

In 1808, after Napoleon's coup, the Spanish viceroy assumed control of the government of New Spain from its capital in Mexico City. Meanwhile, groups of rebels plotted to overthrow royalist power. Under the leadership of two charismatic priests, poor Creoles and indigenous peasants rose up against the Spanish. This movement from below fell to royalist forces, but in 1821 a new movement commanded by Creole elites succeeded in winning independence from Spain.

Although Creole officers dominated rebel armies, their success depended on a rank and file largely composed of nonwhites. These included many blacks and free people of color. In Mexico many indigenous people also fought for the patriots, but elsewhere Indians were often indifferent to independence or felt their status was more secure with the royal government than with the Creoles.

How did the events of 1789 result in a constitutional monarchy in France?

How did Napoleon Bonaparte assume control of France and much of Europe?

How did slave revolt on colonial Saint-Domingue lead to the creation of Haiti in 1804?

How did the Spanish and Portuguese colonies of the Americas shake off European domination?

✔ LearningCurve
Check what you know.

673

MAP 22.4 ■ Latin America
ca. 1780 and 1830

By 1830 almost all of Central
America, South America, and
the Caribbean islands had won
independence. Note that the
many nations that now make
up Central America were unified
when they first won independence
from Mexico. Similarly, modern
Venezuela, Colombia, and
Ecuador were still joined in Gran
Colombia.

Before independence

Spanish colonies

- Viceroyalty of New Spain
- Viceroyalty of New Granada
- Viceroyalty of Peru and Audiencia of Chile
- Viceroyalty of Rio de la Plata

Portuguese colonies

- Viceroyalty of Brazil

✕ Silver mine

In 1830

1811 Year independence gained

Colony

CHAPTER LOCATOR | What were the factors behind the age of revolution in the Atlantic world? | Why and how did American colonists forge a new, independent nation?

In the 1830s regional separatism resulted in New Spain's breakup into five separate countries. The failure of political union in New Spain and Gran Colombia isolated individual countries, prevented collective action, and later paved the way for the political and economic intrusion of the United States and other powers.

Brazil followed a different path to independence. When Napoleon's troops entered Portugal, the royal family fled to Brazil and made Rio de Janeiro the capital of the Portuguese Empire. The king returned to Portugal in 1821, leaving his son Pedro in Brazil as regent. Under popular pressure, Pedro proclaimed Brazil's independence in 1822, issued a constitution, and even led resistance against Portuguese troops. He accepted the title Emperor Pedro I (r. 1822–1831). Even though Brazil was a monarchy, Creole elites dominated society as they did elsewhere in Latin America.

KEY EVENTS IN EARLY LATIN AMERICAN REVOLUTIONS

1759–1788	Reign of Charles III, who instituted administrative and economic reforms
1794	Colombian Antonio Nariño publishes the French Declaration of the Rights of Man and of the Citizen
July 1811	Regional congress in Caracas declares independence of the United States of Venezuela
1822	Proclamation of Brazil's independence from Portugal
1826	Call by Simón Bolívar for Panama conference on Latin American union
1830s	New Spain breaks up into five separate countries
1888	Emancipation of slaves in Brazil

The Aftermath of Revolution in the Atlantic World

The aftermath of the Atlantic revolutions brought extremely different fortunes to the new nations that emerged from them. France returned to royal rule with the restoration of the Bourbon monarchy in 1815. A series of revolutionary crises ensued in the nineteenth century as succeeding generations struggled over the legacies of monarchicalism, republicanism, and Bonapartism. It was not until 1871 that republicanism finally prevailed (see Chapter 24). The transition to an independent republic was permanent and relatively smooth in the United States. Nevertheless, the unresolved conflict over slavery would lead to catastrophic civil war in 1860. The independent nation of Haiti was built on the only successful slave revolt in history, but the need for revenue from plantation agriculture soon led to the return of coercive labor requirements, if not outright slavery.

The newly independent nations of Latin America had difficulty achieving political stability when the wars of independence ended. The economic lives of most Latin American countries were disrupted during the years of war. Mexico and Venezuela in particular suffered great destruction of farmland and animals.

How did the events of 1789 result in a constitutional monarchy in France?

How did Napoleon Bonaparte assume control of France and much of Europe?

How did slave revolt on colonial Saint-Domingue lead to the creation of Haiti in 1804?

How did the Spanish and Portuguese colonies of the Americas shake off European domination?

✓ LearningCurve
Check what you know.

Between 1836 and 1848 Mexico lost half its territory to the United States, and other countries, too, had difficulty defending themselves from their neighbors. The Creole leaders of the revolutions had little experience in government, and the wars left a legacy of military, not civilian, leadership.

> QUICK REVIEW

How did events and developments in Europe influence revolutionary struggles in Latin America?

CHAPTER SUMMARY

From 1775 to 1825 a wave of revolution sweep through the Atlantic world. Its origins included long-term social and economic changes, Enlightenment ideals of liberty and equality, and the costs of colonial warfare. British efforts to raise taxes after the Seven Years' War aroused violent protest in the American colonies. In 1776 the Second Continental Congress issued the Declaration of Independence, and by 1783 Britain had recognized the independence of the thirteen colonies.

In 1789 delegates to the Estates General defied royal authority to declare themselves a National Assembly, which promulgated France's first constitution in 1791. Led by the Jacobin club, the Assembly waged war on Austria and Prussia and proclaimed France a republic. From the end of 1793, under the Reign of Terror, the Revolution pursued internal and external enemies ruthlessly and instituted economic controls to aid the poor. The weakness of the Directory government after the fall of Robespierre enabled Napoleon Bonaparte to claim control of France. Napoleon's relentless military ambitions allowed him to spread French power through much of Europe but ultimately led to his downfall.

After a failed uprising by free men of color, slaves rose in revolt in the French colony of Saint-Domingue in August 1791. Their revolt, combined with the outbreak of war and the radicalization of the French Revolution, led to a sequence of conflicts and rebellions that culminated in independence for the new Haitian nation in 1804.

Latin American independence movements drew strength from Spain's unpopular policies. Under the leadership of Simón Bolívar, the United States of Venezuela claimed independence in 1811. Led by Creole officers but reliant on nonwhite soldiers, rebel armies successfully fought Spanish forces over the next decade. Despite Bolivar's efforts to build a unified state, in the1830s New Spain split into five separate countries. In Brazil the royal regent proclaimed independence in 1822 and reigned as emperor of the new state.

CHAPTER LOCATOR | What were the factors behind the age of revolution in the Atlantic world? | Why and how did American colonists forge a new, independent nation?

CHAPTER 22
676 REVOLUTIONS IN THE ATLANTIC WORLD

CONNECTIONS The Atlantic world formed an essential context for a great revolutionary wave in the late eighteenth and early nineteenth centuries. The movement of peoples, commodities, and ideas across the Atlantic Ocean in the eighteenth century created a world of common debates, conflicts, and aspirations. Moreover, the high stakes of colonial empire heightened competition among European states, leading to a series of wars that generated crushing costs for overburdened treasuries. For both the British in their North American colonies and the French at home, the desperate need for new taxes weakened government authority and opened the door to revolution. In turn, the ideals of the French Revolution inspired slaves and free people of color in Saint-Domingue to rise up and claim the promise of liberty, equality, and fraternity for people of all races.

The chain reaction did not end with the liberation movements in Spanish America that followed the Haitian Revolution. Throughout the nineteenth and early twentieth centuries periodic convulsions occurred in Europe, the Americas, and elsewhere as successive generations struggled over political rights first proclaimed by late-eighteenth-century revolutionaries. Meanwhile, as dramatic political events unfolded, a parallel economic revolution was gathering steam. This was the Industrial Revolution, originating around 1780 and accelerating through the end of the eighteenth century (see Chapter 23). After 1815 the twin forces of industrialization and democratization would combine to transform Europe and the world.

ONLINE DOCUMENT PROJECT

The Rights of Which Men?

How did the French Revolution affect France's Caribbean colonies?

Examine reactions of slaves and free men of color to the French Revolution, and then complete a quiz and writing assignment based on the evidence and details from this chapter. *See inside the front cover to learn more.*

How did the events of 1789 result in a constitutional monarchy in France?

How did Napoleon Bonaparte assume control of France and much of Europe?

How did slave revolt on colonial Saint-Domingue lead to the creation of Haiti in 1804?

How did the Spanish and Portuguese colonies of the Americas shake off European domination?

✔ LearningCurve
Check what you know.

CHAPTER 22 STUDY GUIDE

 **GET STARTED ONLINE**

 **LearningCurve**
Now that you've read the chapter, make it stick by completing the LearningCurve activity.

 **EXPLAIN WHY IT MATTERS**

Put your reading into practice. Identify each term below, and then explain why it matters in world history.

TERM	WHO OR WHAT & WHEN	WHY IT MATTERS
Treaty of Paris (p. 647)		
Declaration of Independence (p. 650)		
Antifederalists (p. 652)		
Estates General (p. 654)		
National Assembly (p. 656)		
Jacobin club (p. 656)		
Mountain (p. 656)		
Girondists (p. 656)		
sans-culottes (p. 656)		
Reign of Terror (p. 657)		
Thermidorian reaction (p. 659)		
Napoleonic Code (p. 661)		
Grand Empire (p. 662)		
Continental System (p. 662)		
Creoles (p. 672)		
peninsulares (p. 672)		

 **MOVE BEYOND THE BASICS**

To demonstrate a more advanced understanding of the four main phases of the French Revolution, fill in the chart below with descriptions of the leaders and key groups that shaped important developments, the policies and reforms initiated during each phase, and the groups that gained and lost the most as a result of those policies. What role did violence play in the transition between each phase of the Revolution?

	Leaders and Key Groups	Policies and Reforms	Winners and Losers
The First Revolution: 1789–1791			
The Second Revolution: 1791–1794			
The Directory: 1795–1799			
Napoleonic France: 1799–1815			

PUT IT ALL TOGETHER

Now, take a step back and try to explain the big picture. Remember to use specific examples from the chapter in your answers.

THE AGE OF REVOLUTIONS BEGINS

▶ How did social, economic, ideological, and fiscal problems combine to spark the age of revolutions?

▶ How did the relative social and political equality enjoyed by white inhabitants of the British North American colonies shape the American Revolution?

THE FRENCH REVOLUTION

▶ What role did the poor people of France play in shaping the French Revolution? At what points did they take control of events from elite and middle-class leaders?

▶ How was violence used as a political tool during the period of the Second Revolution? What justifications were offered for its use? In your opinion, how valid were these justifications?

THE NAPOLEONIC ERA AND THE HAITIAN REVOLUTION

▶ Should Napoleon be considered a "revolutionary"? Why or why not?

▶ How did the people of Saint-Domingue react to the news of revolution in France? How would you explain their reaction? How did the French Revolution contribute to increasing social and political tensions in Saint-Domingue?

LOOKING BACK, LOOKING AHEAD

▶ What was revolutionary about the age of revolution? How did the states that emerged out of the eighteenth-century revolutions differ from the states that predominated in previous centuries?

▶ In what sense did the age of revolution mark the beginning of modern politics in Europe and the Americas?

> IN YOUR OWN WORDS

Imagine that you must give an oral report to the class answering the following question: **How did revolution change the Atlantic world? What aspects of Atlantic society and politics were left unchanged?** What would be the most important points and why?

23
THE REVOLUTION IN ENERGY AND INDUSTRY

1760–1850

> What were the social, cultural, and economic consequences of the Industrial Revolution?

Chapter 23 examines the Industrial Revolution. The Industrial Revolution began in Great Britain around 1780 and soon began to influence continental Europe and the United States. Industrialization profoundly modified human experience. It changed patterns of work, transformed the social structure, and eventually altered the international balance of political power in favor of the most rapidly industrialized nations, especially Great Britain. What was most remarkable about the Industrial Revolution was that it inaugurated a period of sustained economic and demographic growth that has continued to the present.

LearningCurve

After reading the chapter, use LearningCurve to retain what you've read.

Young Factory Worker Children composed a substantial element of the workforce in early factories, where they toiled long hours in dangerous and unsanitary conditions. Until a mechanized process was invented at the end of the nineteenth century, boys working in glass-bottle factories, like the youth pictured here, stoked blazing furnaces with coal and learned to blow glass. (Detail, *Interior of a Furnace*, 1865, oil on canvas by Charles Housez [1822–1888]/© Boume Gallery, Reigate, Surrey, UK/The Bridgeman Art Library)

> Why did the Industrial Revolution begin in Britain, and how did it develop between 1780 and 1850?

> How did countries in Europe and around the world respond to the challenge of industrialization after 1815?

> How did work evolve during the Industrial Revolution, and how did daily life change for working people?

> How did the changes brought about by the Industrial Revolution lead to new social classes, and how did people respond to the new structure?

Why did the Industrial Revolution begin in Britain, and how did it develop between 1780 and 1850?

Woman Working a Spinning Jenny

The loose cotton strands on the slanted bobbins shown in this illustration of Hargreaves's spinning jenny passed up to the sliding carriage and then on to the spindles (inset) in back for fine spinning. The worker, almost always a woman, regulated the sliding carriage with one hand, and with the other she turned the crank on the wheel to supply power. By 1783 one woman could spin a hundred threads at a time. (spinning jenny: © Mary Evans Picture Library/The Image Works; spindle: Picture Research Consultants & Archives)

THE INDUSTRIAL REVOLUTION ORIGINATED from a unique combination of possibilities and constraints in late-eighteenth-century Britain. With no models to copy and no idea of what to expect, Britain pioneered not only in industrial technology but also in social relations and urban living.

Why Britain?

Why did the Industrial Revolution originate in western Europe, and Britain in particular, rather than in other parts of the world, such as Asia? The best answer seems to be that Britain possessed a unique set of possibilities and constraints—abundant coal, high wages, a relatively peaceful and centralized government, well-developed financial systems, innovative culture, highly skilled craftsmen, and a strong position in empire and global trade—that spurred its people to adopt a capital-intensive, machine-powered system of production.

CHAPTER LOCATOR | **Why did the Industrial Revolution begin in Britain, and how did it develop?** | How did countries respond to the challenge of industrialization?

ca. 1765
Hargreaves invents spinning jenny; Arkwright creates water frame

1769
Watt patents modern steam engine

ca. 1780–1850
Industrial Revolution and accompanying population boom in Great Britain

1799
Combination Acts passed in England

1805
Egypt begins process of modernization

1810
Strike of Manchester, England, cotton spinners

1824
British Combination Acts repealed

1829
Stephenson's *Rocket*; first important railroad

1830s
Industrial banks promote rapid industrialization of Belgium

1833
Factory Act passed in England

1834
Creation of a *Zollverein* (customs union) among many German states

1842
Mines Act passed in England

1844
Engels, *The Condition of the Working Class in England*

1850s
Japan begins to adopt Western technologies; industrial gap widens between the West and the rest of the world

1851
Great Exhibition held at Crystal Palace in London

1860s
Germany and the United States begin to industrialize rapidly

Thus a number of factors came together over the long term to give rise to the Industrial Revolution in Britain. The Scientific Revolution and the Enlightenment fostered a new worldview that embraced progress and the role of research and experimentation in understanding and mastering the natural world. Moreover, Britain's intellectual culture emphasized the public sharing of knowledge, including that of scientists and technicians from other countries.

In the economic realm, the seventeenth-century expansion of rural industry produced a surplus of English woolen cloth. Exported throughout Europe, English cloth brought commercial profits and high wages. By the eighteenth century the expanding Atlantic economy and trade with India and China were also serving Britain well. The mercantilist colonial empire Britain aggressively built, augmented by a strong position in Latin America and in the transatlantic slave trade, provided raw materials like cotton and a growing market for British manufactured goods (see Chapter 19). Strong demand for British manufacturing meant that British workers earned high wages compared to the rest of the world's laborers.

Agriculture also played an important role in bringing about the Industrial Revolution. English farmers were second only to the Dutch in productivity in 1700, and they were continually adopting new methods of farming (see page 572). Because of increasing efficiency, landowners were able to produce more food with a smaller workforce. The enclosure movement had deprived many small landowners of their land, leaving the landless poor to work as hired agricultural laborers or in rural industry. These groups created a pool of potential laborers for the new factories.

How did work evolve during the Industrial Revolution, and how did daily life change for working people?

How did the changes brought about by the Industrial Revolution lead to new social classes, and how did people respond to the new structure?

✓ LearningCurve
Check what you know.

Cottage Industry and Transportation in Great Britain in the 1700s

Industrial areas
- ■ Coal deposit
- ○ Metal goods
- ■ Woolen cloth
- — Canals, 1800
- — Navigable rivers

Industrial Revolution

▶ A term first coined in the 1830s to describe the burst of major inventions and economic expansion that took place in certain industries, such as cotton textiles and iron, between 1780 and 1850.

Abundant food and high wages in turn meant that the ordinary English family no longer had to spend almost everything it earned just to buy bread. Thus the family could spend more on manufactured goods. They could also pay to send their children to school. Britain's populace enjoyed high levels of education compared to the rest of Europe. Moreover, in the eighteenth century the members of the average British family—including women and girls—were redirecting their labor away from unpaid work for household consumption and toward work for wages that they could spend on goods.

Britain also benefited from rich natural resources and a well-developed infrastructure. In an age when it was much cheaper to ship goods by water than by land, no part of England was more than fifty miles from navigable water. Beginning in the 1770s a canal-building boom enhanced this advantage. Rivers and canals provided easy movement of England and Wales's enormous deposits of iron and coal. The abundance of coal combined with high wages in manufacturing placed Britain in a unique position among the nations of the world: its manufacturers had extremely strong incentives to develop technologies to draw on the power of coal to increase workmen's productivity. In regions with lower wages, such as India and China, the costs of mechanization outweighed potential gains in productivity.

A final factor favoring British industrialization was the British state and its policies. Britain's parliamentary system taxed its population aggressively and spent the money on a navy to protect imperial commerce and on an army that could be used to quell uprisings by disgruntled workers. Starting with the Navigation Acts under Oliver Cromwell (see Chapter 18), the British state also adopted aggressive tariffs, or duties, on imported goods to protect its industries.

All these factors combined to initiate the **Industrial Revolution**, a term first coined to describe the burst of major inventions and technical changes that took place in certain industries. This technical revolution went hand in hand with an impressive quickening in the annual rate of industrial growth in Britain. Whereas industry had grown at only 0.7 percent between 1700 and 1760 (before the Industrial Revolution), it grew at the much higher rate of 3 percent between 1801 and 1831, when industrial transformation was in full swing.[1]

Technological Innovations and Early Factories

The pressure to produce more goods for a growing market and to reduce the labor costs of manufacturing was directly related to the first decisive breakthrough of the Industrial Revolution: the creation of the world's first machine-powered factories in the British cotton textile industry. Technological innovations in the manufacture of cotton cloth led to a new system of production and social relationships.

The putting-out system that developed in the seventeenth-century textile industry involved a merchant who loaned, or "put out," raw materials to cottage workers who processed the raw materials in their own homes and returned the finished products to the merchant. There was always a serious imbalance in textile production based on cottage industry: the work of four or five spinners was needed to keep one weaver steadily employed. During the eighteenth century the putting-out system grew across Europe, but most extensively in Britain. The growth of demand only increased pressures on the supply of thread.

CHAPTER LOCATOR | **Why did the Industrial Revolution begin in Britain, and how did it develop?** How did countries respond to the challenge of industrialization?

CHAPTER 23

684 THE REVOLUTION IN ENERGY AND INDUSTRY

Many a tinkering worker knew that devising a better spinning wheel promised rich rewards. It proved hard to spin the traditional raw materials — wool and flax — with improved machines, but cotton was different. Cotton textiles had first been imported into Britain from India by the East India Company. By 1760 a tiny domestic cotton industry had emerged in northern England based on imported raw materials, but it could not compete with cloth produced by workers in India and other parts of Asia. International competition thus drove English entrepreneurs to invent new technologies to bring down labor costs.

After many experiments over a generation, a carpenter and jack-of-all-trades, James Hargreaves, invented his cotton-spinning jenny about 1765. At almost the same moment, a barber-turned-manufacturer named Richard Arkwright invented (or possibly pirated) another kind of spinning machine, the water frame. These breakthroughs produced an explosion in the infant cotton textile industry in the 1780s. By 1790 the new machines were producing ten times as much cotton yarn as had been made in 1770.

Hargreaves's **spinning jenny** was simple, inexpensive, and powered by hand. In early models from six to twenty-four spindles were mounted on a sliding carriage, and each spindle spun a fine, slender thread. Arkwright's **water frame** employed a different principle. It quickly acquired a capacity of several hundred spindles driven by waterpower. The water frame required large specialized mills located beside rivers and factories that employed as many as one thousand workers from the very beginning. The major drawback of the water frame was that it could spin only a coarse, strong thread. Around 1790 a hybrid machine invented by Samuel Crompton proved capable of spinning very fine and strong thread in large quantities. Gradually, all cotton spinning was concentrated in large-scale factories.

These revolutionary developments in the textile industry allowed British manufacturers to produce vast quantities of both fine and coarse cotton thread. Families using cotton in cottage industry were freed from their constant search for adequate yarn from scattered part-time spinners, because all the thread needed could be spun in the cottage on the jenny or obtained from a nearby factory. The income of weavers, now hard-pressed to keep up with the spinners, rose markedly until about 1792. In response, mechanics and capitalists sought to invent a power loom to save on labor costs. This Edmund Cartwright achieved in 1785. But the power looms of the factories worked poorly at first and did not fully replace handlooms until the 1820s.

Working conditions in the early cotton factories were so poor that adult workers were reluctant to work in them. Factory owners often turned to orphans and abandoned children instead. By placing them in "apprenticeship" with factory owners, parish officers charged with caring for such children saved money. The owners gained workers over whom they exercised almost the authority of slave owners. Housed, fed, and locked up nightly in factory dormitories, the young workers labored thirteen or fourteen hours a day, six days a week, for little or no pay.

The Steam Engine Breakthrough

Well into the eighteenth century, Europe, like other areas of the world, relied mainly on wood for energy, and human beings and animals performed most work. This dependence meant that Europe and the rest of the world remained poor in energy and power.

spinning jenny

▶ A simple, inexpensive, hand-powered spinning machine created by James Hargreaves in 1765.

water frame

▶ A spinning machine created by Richard Arkwright that had a capacity of several hundred spindles and used waterpower; it therefore required a larger and more specialized mill — a factory.

How did work evolve during the Industrial Revolution, and how did daily life change for working people?

How did the changes brought about by the Industrial Revolution lead to new social classes, and how did people respond to the new structure?

☑ LearningCurve
Check what you know.

By the eighteenth century wood was in ever-shorter supply in Britain. Processed wood (charcoal) was mixed with iron ore in blast furnaces to produce pig iron that could be processed into steel, cast iron, or wrought iron. The iron industry's appetite for wood was enormous, and by 1740 the British iron industry was stagnating. As wood became ever more scarce, the British looked to coal as an alternative. The real breakthrough came when industrialists began to use coal to produce mechanical energy and to power machinery.

To produce more coal, mines had to be dug deeper and deeper and were constantly filling with water. Mechanical pumps, usually powered by animals walking in circles at the surface, had to be installed. Animal power was expensive and bothersome. In an attempt to overcome these disadvantages, Thomas Savery in 1698 and Thomas Newcomen in 1705 invented the first primitive **steam engines**. Both engines burned coal to produce steam that drove the water pumps.

In 1763 a gifted young Scot named James Watt (1736–1819) was drawn to a critical study of the steam engine. Watt worked at the University of Glasgow as a skilled craftsman making scientific instruments. In 1763 Watt was called on to repair a Newcomen engine being used in a physics course. Watt discovered that the Newcomen engine could be significantly improved by adding a separate condenser. This invention, patented in 1769, greatly increased the efficiency of the steam engine.

To make his invention a practical success, Watt needed skilled workers, precision parts, and capital, and the relatively advanced nature of the British economy proved essential. A partnership in 1775 with Matthew Boulton, a wealthy English industrialist, provided Watt with adequate capital and exceptional skills in salesmanship that equaled those of the renowned pottery king, Josiah Wedgwood. (See "Individuals in Society: Josiah Wedgwood.) Among Britain's highly skilled locksmiths, tinsmiths, and millwrights, Watt found mechanics who could install, regulate, and repair his sophisticated engines. From ingenious manufacturers, Watt was gradually able to purchase precision parts. By the late 1780s the firm of Boulton and Watt had made the steam engine a practical and commercial success in Britain.

The coal-burning steam engine of Watt and his followers was the Industrial Revolution's most fundamental advance in technology. For the first time in history, humanity had, at least for a few generations, almost unlimited power at its disposal. Steam power began to replace waterpower in cotton-spinning mills during the 1780s, contributing greatly to that industry's phenomenal rise. Steam also took the place of waterpower in flour mills, in the malt mills used in breweries, in the flint mills supplying the pottery industry, and in the mills exported by Britain to the West Indies to crush sugarcane.

The British iron industry was also radically transformed. After 1770 the adoption of steam-driven bellows in blast furnaces allowed for great increases in the quantity of pig iron produced by British ironmakers. In the 1780s Henry Cort developed the puddling furnace, which allowed pig iron to be refined with coke, a smokeless and hot-burning fuel produced by heating coal to rid it of impurities.

Cort also developed steam-powered rolling mills, which were capable of spewing out finished iron in every shape and form. The economic consequence of these technical innovations was a great boom in the British iron industry. Once scarce and expensive, iron became the cheap, basic, indispensable building block of the British economy.

steam engines

▶ A breakthrough invention by Thomas Savery in 1698 and Thomas Newcomen in 1705 that burned coal to produce steam, which was then used to operate a pump; the early models were superseded by James Watt's more efficient steam engine, patented in 1769.

CHAPTER LOCATOR | Why did the Industrial Revolution begin in Britain, and how did it develop? | How did countries respond to the challenge of industrialization?

CHAPTER 23

686 THE REVOLUTION IN ENERGY AND INDUSTRY

INDIVIDUALS IN SOCIETY
Josiah Wedgwood

As the making of cloth and iron was revolutionized by technical change and factory organization, so, too, were the production and consumption of pottery. Acquiring beautiful tableware became a craze for eighteenth-century consumers, and continental monarchs often sought prestige in building royal china works. But the grand prize went to Josiah Wedgwood, who wanted to "astonish the world."

The twelfth child of a poor potter, Josiah Wedgwood (1730–1795) grew up in the pottery district of Staffordshire in the English Midlands, where many tiny potteries made simple earthenware utensils for sale in local markets. Having grown up as an apprentice in the family business inherited by his oldest brother, Wedgwood struck off on his own in 1752. Soon manager of a small pottery, Wedgwood learned that new products recharged lagging sales. Studying chemistry and determined to succeed, Wedgwood spent his evenings experimenting with different chemicals and firing conditions.

In 1759, after five years of tireless efforts, Wedgwood perfected a beautiful new green glaze. Now established as a master potter, he opened his own factory and began manufacturing teapots and tableware finished in his green and other unique glazes, or adorned with printed scenes far superior to those being produced by competitors. Wedgwood's products caused a sensation among consumers, and his business quickly earned substantial profits. Subsequent breakthroughs, including ornamental vases imitating classical Greek models and jasperware for jewelry, contributed greatly to Wedgwood's success.

Competitors were quick to copy Wedgwood's new products and sell them at lower prices. Thus Wedgwood and his partner, Thomas Bentley, sought to cultivate an image of superior fashion, taste, and quality in order to develop and maintain a dominant market position. They did this by first capturing the business of the trendsetting elite. In one brilliant coup the partners first sold a very large cream-colored dinner set to Britain's queen, which they quickly christened "Queen's ware" and sold as a very expensive, must-have luxury to English aristocrats. Equally brilliant was Bentley's suave expertise in the elegant London showroom selling Wedgwood's imitation Greek vases, which became the rage after the rediscovery of the cities of Pompeii and Herculaneum in the mid-eighteenth century.

Josiah Wedgwood perfected jasperware, a fine-grained pottery usually made in "Wedgwood blue" with white decoration. This elegant cylindrical vase, decorated in the form of a miniature Roman household altar, was destined for the luxury market. (Josiah Wedgwood [1730–1795]. Vase, 18th century. Jasperware. Vase [09.194.7]: English [Staffordshire, Etruria]. Rogers Fund, 1909 [09.194.7-9], designed by John Flaxman [1755–1826]. Metropolitan Museum of Art, New York, NY, USA/ Image copyright © The Metropolitan Museum of Art/Image source: Art Resource, NY)

Above all, once Wedgwood had secured his position as the luxury market leader, he was able to successfully extend his famous brand to the growing middle class, capturing an enormous mass market for his "useful ware." Thus, when sales of a luxury good grew "stale," Wedgwood made tasteful modifications and sold it to the middling classes for twice the price his competitors could charge. This unbeatable combination of mass appeal and high prices brought Wedgwood great fame all across Europe and enormous wealth.

A workaholic with an authoritarian streak, Wedgwood contributed substantially to the development of the factory system. In 1769 he opened a model factory on a new canal he had promoted. With two hundred workers in several departments, Wedgwood exercised tremendous control over his workforce, imposing fines for many infractions, such as being late, drinking on the job, or wasting material. He wanted, he said, to create men who would be like "machines" that "cannot err." Yet Wedgwood also recognized the value in treating workers well. He championed a division of labor that made most workers specialists who received ongoing training. He also encouraged employment of family groups, who were housed in company row houses with long, narrow backyards suitable for raising vegetables and chickens. Paying relatively high wages and providing pensions and some benefits, Wedgwood developed a high-quality labor force that learned to accept his rigorous discipline and carried out his ambitious plans.

QUESTIONS FOR ANALYSIS

1. How and why did Wedgwood succeed?
2. Was Wedgwood a good boss or a bad one? Why?
3. How did Wedgwood exemplify the new class of factory owners?

LaunchPad

ONLINE DOCUMENT PROJECT
How were social and economic change connected in nineteenth-century England? Read sources on early industrial manufacturing, and then complete a quiz and writing assignment based on the evidence and details from this chapter. *See inside the front cover to learn more.*

Steam-Powered Transportation

Rocket

▶ The name given to George Stephenson's effective locomotive that was first tested in 1829 on the Liverpool and Manchester Railway and reached a maximum speed of 35 miles per hour.

The first steam locomotive was built by Richard Trevithick after much experimentation. George Stephenson's locomotive named **Rocket** sped down the track of the just-completed Liverpool and Manchester Railway at a maximum speed of 35 miles per hour in 1829. The line from Liverpool to Manchester was a financial as well as a technical success, and many private companies were organized to build more rail lines. Within twenty years they had completed the main trunk lines of Great Britain (Map 23.1). Other countries were quick to follow, with the first steam-powered trains operating in the United States in the 1830s and in Brazil, Chile, Argentina, and the British colonies of Canada, Australia, and India in the 1850s (Figure 23.1).

The arrival of the railroad had many significant consequences. It dramatically reduced the cost and uncertainty of shipping freight over land. Previously, markets had tended to be small and local; as the barrier of high transportation costs was lowered, markets became larger and even nationwide. Larger markets encouraged larger factories with more sophisticated machinery in a growing number of industries. Such factories could make goods more cheaply and gradually subjected most cottage workers and many urban artisans to severe competitive pressures. In all countries, the construction of railroads created a strong demand for unskilled labor and contributed to the growth of a class of urban workers.

The railroad also had a tremendous impact on cultural values and attitudes. The last and culminating invention of the Industrial Revolution, the railroad dramatically revealed the power and increased the speed of the new age. Some great painters, notably Joseph M. W. Turner (1775–1851) and Claude Monet (1840–1926), succeeded in expressing the sense of power and awe railroads inspired. So did the massive new train stations, the cathedrals of the industrial age.

The steam engine also transformed water travel. French engineers completed the first steamships in the 1770s, and the first commercial steamships came into use in North America several decades later. The steamship brought the advantages of the railroad—speed, reliability, efficiency—to water travel.

Towns with over 20,000 people are shown

50 400   2.4
Thousand   Million

Cities with over 100,000 people are labeled

- Exposed coal deposit
- Industrial area
- Principal railroad

SCOTLAND

North Sea

Cotton and woolen textiles Machinery, Iron — Bradford

Manchester
Liverpool
Leeds
Sheffield

Irish Sea

Iron Hardware

ENGLAND   Norwich

WALES

Iron Machinery Pottery — Birmingham

Iron

Bristol   London
Bath

Tin and copper mining — Exeter

Machinery Consumer goods

English Channel

MAP 23.1 ■ The Industrial Revolution in Great Britain, ca. 1850

Industry concentrated in the rapidly growing cities of the north and the center of England, where rich coal and iron deposits were close to one another.

CHAPTER LOCATOR | **Why did the Industrial Revolution begin in Britain, and how did it develop?** | How did countries respond to the challenge of industrialization?

The International Sleeping-Car Company was founded in 1872, inspired by the model of the American Pullman night trains. It quickly became the most important operator of sleeping and dining cars in Europe. The company's posters, like the one pictured here, appealed to wealthy and middle-class customers by emphasizing the luxury and spaciousness of its accommodations. The company's most famous line was the Orient Express (1883–2009), which ran from Paris to Istanbul. (Kharbine-Tapabor/The Art Archive at Art Resource, NY)

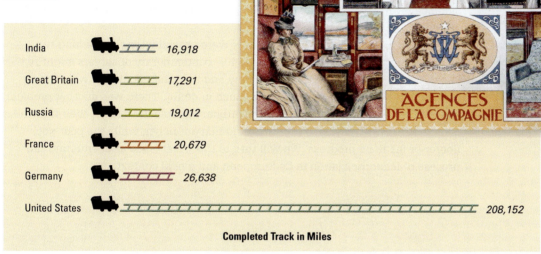

Country	Completed Track in Miles
India	16,918
Great Britain	17,291
Russia	19,012
France	20,679
Germany	26,638
United States	208,152

Completed Track in Miles

FIGURE 23.1 ■ Railroad Track Mileage, 1890

Steam railroads were first used by the general public for shipping in England in the 1820s, and they quickly spread to other countries. The United States was an early adopter of railroads and by 1890 had surpassed all other countries in miles of track, as shown in this figure.

Industry and Population

In 1851 London hosted an industrial fair called the Great Exhibition in the newly built **Crystal Palace**. The building was made entirely of glass and iron, both of which were now cheap and abundant. Sponsored by the British royal family, the exhibition celebrated the new era of industrial technology and the kingdom's role as world economic leader.

As the British economy significantly increased its production of manufactured goods, the gross national product (GNP) rose roughly fourfold at constant prices between 1780 and 1851. At the same time, the population of Britain boomed, growing from about 9 million in 1780 to almost 21 million in 1851. Thus growing numbers consumed much of the increase in total production.

Rapid population growth in Great Britain was key to industrial development. More people meant a more mobile labor force, with a wealth of young workers in need of employment and ready to go where the jobs were. Sustaining the dramatic increase in population, in turn, was only possible through advances in agriculture

Crystal Palace

▶ The location of the Great Exhibition in 1851 in London, an architectural masterpiece made entirely of glass and iron.

How did work evolve during the Industrial Revolution, and how did daily life change for working people?　｜　How did the changes brought about by the Industrial Revolution lead to new social classes, and how did people respond to the new structure?　 LearningCurve Check what you know.

689

and industry. Many contemporaries feared that the rapid growth in population would inevitably lead to disaster. In his *Essay on the Principle of Population* (1798), Thomas Malthus (1766–1834) argued that population would always tend to grow faster than the food supply. Malthus concluded that the only hope of warding off such "positive checks" to population growth as war, famine, and disease was "prudential restraint." That is, young men and women had to limit the growth of population by marrying late in life. But Malthus was not optimistic about this possibility. The powerful attraction of the sexes would cause most people to marry early and have many children.

Economist David Ricardo (1772–1823) spelled out the pessimistic implications of Malthus's thought. Ricardo's depressing **iron law of wages** posited that, because of the pressure of population growth, wages would always sink to subsistence level. That is, wages would be just high enough to keep workers from starving.

Malthus, Ricardo, and their followers were proved wrong in the long run. However, until the 1820s, or even the 1840s, contemporary observers might reasonably have concluded that the economy and the total population were racing neck and neck, with the outcome very much in doubt. There was another problem as well. Perhaps workers, farmers, and ordinary people did not get their rightful share of the new wealth. Perhaps only the rich got richer, while the poor got poorer or made no progress. We will turn to this great issue after situating the process of industrialization in its European and global context.

iron law of wages

▶ Theory proposed by English economist David Ricardo suggesting that the pressure of population growth prevents wages from rising above the subsistence level.

> **QUICK REVIEW**

What role did technology play in the early phases of the Industrial Revolution?

CHAPTER LOCATOR | Why did the Industrial Revolution begin in Britain, and how did it develop? | **How did countries respond to the challenge of industrialization?**

CHAPTER 23

690   THE REVOLUTION IN ENERGY AND INDUSTRY

How did countries in Europe and around the world respond to the challenge of industrialization after 1815?

A German Ironworks, 1845

The Borsig ironworks in Berlin mastered the new British method of smelting iron ore with coke. Germany, especially the state of Prussia, was well endowed with both iron and coal, and the rapid exploitation of these resources after 1840 transformed a poor agricultural country into an industrial powerhouse. (Stiftung Stadtmuseum/akg-images)

AS NEW TECHNOLOGIES and a new organization of labor began to revolutionize production in Britain, other countries took notice and began to emulate its example. With the end of the Napoleonic Wars, the nations of the European continent quickly adopted British inventions and achieved their own pattern of technological innovation and economic growth. By the last decades of the nineteenth century, western European countries as well as the United States and Japan had industrialized their economies to a considerable, albeit varying, degree.

National and International Variations

Comparative data on industrial production in different countries over time help give us an overview of what happened. One set of data, the work of a Swiss scholar, compares the level of industrialization on a per capita basis in several countries from 1750 to 1913. These data are far from perfect, but they reflect basic trends and are presented in Table 23.1 for closer study.

Table 23.1 presents a comparison of how much industrial product was produced, on average, for each person in a given country in a given year. All the numbers are expressed in terms of a single index number of 100, which equals the per capita level of industrial goods in Great Britain and Ireland in 1900. Every number in the table is thus a percentage of the 1900 level in Britain and is directly

How did work evolve during the Industrial Revolution, and how did daily life change for working people?

How did the changes brought about by the Industrial Revolution lead to new social classes, and how did people respond to the new structure?

 LearningCurve
Check what you know.

TABLE 23.1 ■ Per Capita Levels of Industrialization, 1750–1913

	1750	1800	1830	1860	1880	1900	1913
Great Britain	10	16	25	64	87	100	115
Belgium	9	10	14	28	43	56	88
United States	4	9	14	21	38	69	126
France	9	9	12	20	28	39	59
Germany	8	8	9	15	25	52	85
Austria-Hungary	7	7	8	11	15	23	32
Italy	8	8	8	10	12	17	26
Russia	6	6	7	8	10	15	20
China	8	6	6	4	4	3	3
India	7	6	6	3	2	1	2

Note: All entries are based on an index value of 100, equal to the per capita level of industrialization in Great Britain in 1900. Data for Great Britain include Ireland, England, Wales, and Scotland.

Source: P. Bairoch, "International Industrialization Levels from 1750 to 1980," *Journal of European Economic History* 11 (Spring 1982): 294, U.S. Journals at Cambridge University Press. Reprinted by permission.

comparable with other numbers. The countries are listed in roughly the order that they began to use large-scale, power-driven technology.

What does this overview tell us? First, one sees in the first column that in 1750 all countries were fairly close together, including non-Western areas such as China and India. However, the column headed 1800 shows that Britain had opened up a noticeable lead over all countries by 1800, and that gap progressively widened as the British Industrial Revolution accelerated through 1830 and reached full maturity by 1860.

Second, the table shows that Western countries began to emulate the British model successfully over the nineteenth century, with significant variations in the timing and in the extent of industrialization. Belgium led in adopting Britain's new technology, and it experienced a truly revolutionary surge between 1830 and 1860. France developed factory production more gradually and did not experience "revolutionary" acceleration in the growth of overall industrial output. Slow but steady economic growth in France was overshadowed by the spectacular rise of Germany and the United States after 1860 in what has been termed the "Second Industrial Revolution." In general, eastern and southern Europe began the process of industrialization later than northwestern and central Europe. Nevertheless, these regions made real progress in the late nineteenth century, as growth after 1880 in Austria-Hungary, Italy, and Russia suggests. This meant that all European states as well as the United States managed to raise per capita industrial levels in the nineteenth century.

These increases stood in stark contrast to the decreases that occurred at the same time in many non-Western countries, most notably in China and India as Table 23.1 shows. European countries industrialized to a greater or lesser extent even as most of the non-Western world stagnated. Japan, which is not included in this table, stands out as an exceptional area of non-Western industrial growth in

CHAPTER LOCATOR | Why did the Industrial Revolution begin in Britain, and how did it develop?

How did countries respond to the challenge of industrialization?

692

CHAPTER 23
THE REVOLUTION IN ENERGY AND INDUSTRY

the second half of the nineteenth century. After the forced opening of the country to the West in the 1850s, Japanese entrepreneurs began to adopt Western technology and manufacturing methods, resulting in a production boom by the late nineteenth century (see Chapter 26). Differential rates of wealth- and power-creating industrial development, which heightened disparities within Europe, also greatly magnified existing inequalities between Europe and the rest of the world (see Chapter 25).

Industrialization in Continental Europe

Throughout Europe the eighteenth century was an era of agricultural improvement, population increase, expanding foreign trade, and growing cottage industry. Thus, when the pace of British industry began to accelerate in the 1780s, continental businesses began to adopt the new methods as they proved their profitability. During the period of the revolutionary and Napoleonic Wars, from 1793 to 1815, however, western Europe experienced tremendous political and social upheaval that temporarily halted economic development. With the return of peace in 1815, however, western European countries again began to play catch-up.

They faced significant challenges. In the newly mechanized industries, British goods were being produced very economically, and these goods had come to dominate world markets. In addition, British technology had become so advanced that very few engineers or skilled technicians outside England understood it. Moreover, the technology of steam power involved large investments in the iron and coal industries and, after 1830, required the existence of railroads. Continental business people had great difficulty amassing the large sums of money the new methods demanded, and laborers bitterly resisted the move to working in factories. All these factors slowed the spread of mechanization (Map 23.2).

Nevertheless, western European nations possessed a number of advantages that helped them respond to these challenges. First, most had rich traditions of putting-out enterprise, merchant capitalism, and skilled urban trades. These assets gave their firms the ability to adapt and survive in the face of new market conditions. Second, continental capitalists did not need to develop their own advanced technology. Instead, they could "borrow" the new methods developed in Great Britain, as well as the engineers and some of the financial resources they lacked. Finally, European countries had strong, independent governments that were willing to use the power of the state to promote industry and catch up with Britain.

Agents of Industrialization

Western European success in adopting British methods took place despite the best efforts of the British to prevent it. The British realized the great value of their technical discoveries and tried to keep their secrets to themselves. Until 1825 it was illegal for artisans and skilled mechanics to leave Britain; until 1843 the export of textile machinery and other equipment was forbidden. Many talented, ambitious workers, however, slipped out of the country illegally and introduced the new methods abroad.

Thus British technicians and skilled workers were a powerful force in the spread of early industrialization. A second agent of industrialization consisted of talented European entrepreneurs such as Fritz Harkort (1793–1880). Serving in England as a Prussian army officer during the Napoleonic Wars, Harkort was impressed with what he saw. Harkort set up shop building steam engines in the

How did work evolve during the Industrial Revolution, and how did daily life change for working people?

How did the changes brought about by the Industrial Revolution lead to new social classes, and how did people respond to the new structure?

☑ LearningCurve
Check what you know.

693

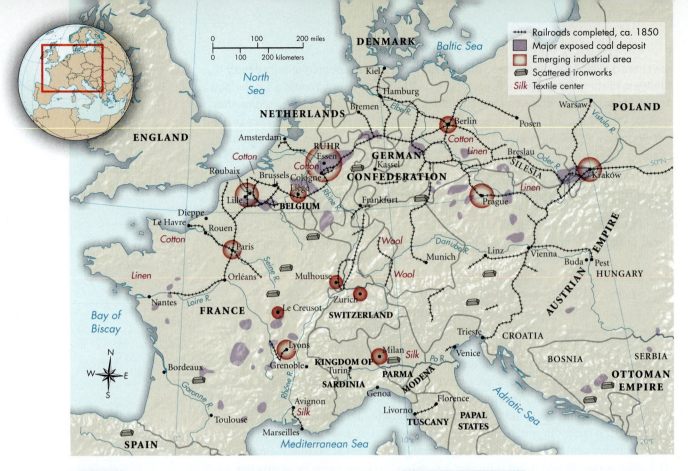

MAP 23.2 ■ Continental Industrialization, ca. 1850

Although continental countries were beginning to make progress by 1850, they still lagged far behind Britain. For example, continental railroad building was still in an early stage, whereas the British rail system was essentially complete (see Map 23.1). Coal played a critical role in nineteenth-century industrialization, both as a power source for steam engines and as a raw material for making iron and steel.

> MAPPING THE PAST

ANALYZING THE MAP: Locate the major exposed (that is, known) coal deposits in 1850. Which countries and areas appear rich in coal resources, and which appear poor? Is there a difference between northern and southern Europe? **CONNECTIONS:** What is the relationship between known coal deposits and emerging industrial areas in continental Europe? In England (see Map 23.1)?

Ruhr Valley, on the western border with France. In spite of problems obtaining skilled workers and machinery, Harkort succeeded in building and selling engines. However, his ambitious efforts failed to turn a profit. His career illustrates both the great efforts of a few important business leaders to duplicate the British achievement and the difficulty of the task.

National governments played an even more important role in supporting industrialization in continental Europe than in Britain. **Tariff protection** was one such support. The French, for example, responded to a flood of cheap British goods in 1815, after the Napoleonic Wars, by laying high taxes on imported goods. Customs agreements emerged among some German states starting in 1818, and in 1834 a number of states signed a treaty creating a customs union, or *Zollverein*. The treaty allowed goods to move between member states without tariffs, while erecting a single uniform tariff against other nations.

After 1815 continental governments also bore the cost of building roads, canals, and railroads to improve transportation. Belgium led the way in the 1830s and 1840s, building a state-owned railroad network that stimulated the development of heavy industry and made the country an early industrial leader. In France

tariff protection

▶ A government's way of supporting and aiding its own economy by laying high taxes on imported goods from other countries, as when the French responded to the flood of cheaper British goods in their country by imposing high tariffs on some imported products.

CHAPTER LOCATOR | Why did the Industrial Revolution begin in Britain, and how did it develop? | **How did countries respond to the challenge of industrialization?**

the state shouldered all the expense of acquiring and laying roadbed, including bridges and tunnels.

Finally, banks, like governments, also played a larger and more creative role on the continent than in Britain. Previously, almost all banks in Europe had been private. Because of the possibility of unlimited financial loss, the partners of private banks generally avoided industrial investment as being too risky.

In the 1830s two important Belgian banks pioneered in a new direction. They received permission from the growth-oriented government to establish themselves as corporations enjoying limited liability. That is, if the bank went bankrupt, stockholders would lose only their original investments in the bank's common stock, and they could not be forced to pay for additional losses out of other property they owned. Limited liability helped these banks attract investors. They mobilized impressive resources for investment in big companies, became industrial banks, and successfully promoted industrial development. Similar corporate banks became important in France and Germany in the 1850s and 1860s.

The combined efforts of skilled workers, entrepreneurs, governments, and industrial banks meshed successfully between 1850 and the financial crash of 1873. In Belgium, France, and the German states key indicators of modern industrial development increased at average annual rates of 5 to 10 percent. As a result, rail networks were completed in western Europe and much of central Europe, and the leading continental countries mastered the industrial technologies that had first been developed in Great Britain. In the early 1870s Britain was still Europe's most industrial nation, but a select handful of countries were closing the gap.

The Global Picture

The Industrial Revolution did not extend outside of Europe prior to the 1860s, with the exception of the United States and Japan. In many countries, national governments and pioneering entrepreneurs promoted industrialization, but fell short of transitioning to an industrial economy. For example, in Russia the

Press for Packing Indian Cotton, 1864

British industrialization destroyed a thriving Indian cotton textile industry, whose weavers could not compete with cheap British imports. India continued to supply raw cotton to British manufacturers. (English wood engraving, 1864/The Granger Collection, NYC — All rights reserved.)

How did work evolve during the Industrial Revolution, and how did daily life change for working people?

How did the changes brought about by the Industrial Revolution lead to new social classes, and how did people respond to the new structure?

✓ LearningCurve
Check what you know.

imperial government brought steamships to the Volga River and a railroad to the capital, St. Petersburg, in the first decades of the nineteenth century. By mid-century ambitious entrepreneurs had established steam-powered cotton factories using imported British machines. However, these advances did not lead to overall industrialization of the country. Instead Russia confirmed its role as provider of raw materials, especially timber and grain, to the hungry West.

Egypt, a territory of the Ottoman empire, similarly began an ambitious program of modernization after a reform-minded viceroy took power in 1805. This program included the use of imported British technology and experts in textile manufacture and other industries (see page 731). These industries, however, could not compete with lower-priced European imports. Like Russia, Egypt fell back on agricultural exports, such as sugar and cotton, to European markets.

Such examples of faltering efforts at industrialization could be found in many other places in the Middle East, Asia, and Latin America. Where European governments maintained direct or indirect control, they acted to maintain colonial markets as both sources of raw materials and consumers for their own products, rather than encouraging the spread of industrialization. In India millions of poor textile workers lost their livelihood because they could not compete with industrially produced British cotton. The British charged stiff import duties on Indian cottons entering the kingdom, but prohibited the Indians from doing the same to British imports. The arrival of railroads in India in the mid-nineteenth century served the purpose of agricultural rather than industrial development.

Latin American economies were disrupted by the early-nineteenth-century wars of independence (see Chapter 22). As these countries' economies recovered in the mid-nineteenth century, they increasingly adopted steam power for sugar and coffee processing and for transportation. Like elsewhere, this technology first supported increased agricultural production for export and only later drove domestic industrial production.

The rise of industrialization in Britain, western Europe, and the United States thus caused other regions of the world to become increasingly economically dependent. Instead of industrializing, many territories underwent a process of deindustrialization or delayed industrialization. In turn, relative economic weakness made them vulnerable to the new wave of imperialism undertaken by industrialized nations in the second half of the nineteenth century (see Chapters 25 and 26).

As for China, it did not adopt mechanized production until the end of the nineteenth century, but continued as a market-based, commercial society with a massive rural sector and industrial production based on traditional methods. In the 1860s and 1870s, when Japan was successfully adopting industrial methods, the Chinese government showed similar interest in Western technology and science. However, China faced widespread uprisings in the mid-nineteenth century, which drained attention and resources to the military; moreover, after the Boxer Rebellion of 1898–1900 (see page 794), Western powers forced China to pay massive indemnities, further reducing its capacity to promote industrialization.

> **QUICK REVIEW**

Why did British practices spread to continental Europe, but not to most of the rest of the world?

CHAPTER LOCATOR | Why did the Industrial Revolution begin in Britain, and how did it develop? | How did countries respond to the challenge of industrialization?

CHAPTER 23

696 THE REVOLUTION IN ENERGY AND INDUSTRY

How did work evolve during the Industrial Revolution, and how did daily life change for working people?

Workers at a U.S. Mill

Female workers at a U.S. cotton mill in 1890 take a break from operating belt-driven weaving machines to pose for this photograph, accompanied by their male supervisor. The first textile mills, established in the 1820s in Massachusetts, employed local farm girls. As competition intensified, conditions deteriorated and the mills increasingly relied on immigrant women who had few alternatives to the long hours, noise, and dangers of factory work. By 1900 more than 1 million women worked in factories in the United States. (Courtesy of George Eastman House, International Museum of Photography and Film, accession number 1966:0039:0013)

HAVING FIRST EMERGED in the British countryside in the late eighteenth century, factories and industrial labor began migrating to cities by the early nineteenth century. For some people, the Industrial Revolution brought improvements, but living and working conditions for the poor stagnated or even deteriorated until around 1850, especially in overcrowded industrial cities.

Work in Early Factories

The first factories of the Industrial Revolution were cotton mills, which began functioning in the 1770s along fast-running rivers and streams and were often located in sparsely populated areas. Cottage workers, accustomed to the putting-out system, were reluctant to work in the new factories even when they received relatively good wages. In a factory, workers had to keep up with the machine and follow its relentless tempo. Moreover, they had to show up every day, on time, and work long, monotonous hours under the constant supervision of demanding overseers.

| **How did work evolve during the Industrial Revolution, and how did daily life change for working people?** | How did the changes brought about by the Industrial Revolution lead to new social classes, and how did people respond to the new structure? | ✓ LearningCurve Check what you know. |

Cottage workers were not used to that way of life. All members of the family worked hard and long, but in spurts, setting their own pace. Women and children could break up their long hours of spinning with other tasks. On Saturday afternoon the head of the family delivered the week's work to the merchant manufacturer and got paid. Saturday night was a time of relaxation and drinking, especially for men.

Also, early factories resembled English poorhouses, where totally destitute people went to live at public expense. The similarity between large brick factories and large stone poorhouses increased the cottage workers' fear of factories and their hatred of factory discipline. It was cottage workers' reluctance to work in factories that prompted early cotton mill owners to turn to pauper children.

Working Families and Children

By the 1790s the early labor pattern was rapidly changing. The use of pauper apprentices was in decline, and in 1802 it was forbidden by Parliament. Many more textile factories were being built, mainly in urban areas, where they could use steam power rather than waterpower and attract a workforce more easily than in the countryside. People came from near and far to work in the cities. Collectively, these wage laborers came to be known as the "working class," a term first used in the late 1830s.

In some cases, workers accommodated to the system by carrying over familiar working traditions. Some came to the mills and the mines as family units, as they had worked on farms and in the putting-out system. The mill or mine owner bargained with the head of the family and paid him or her for the work of the whole family.

Ties of kinship were particularly important for newcomers, who often traveled great distances to find work. Many urban workers in Great Britain were from Ireland. They were forced out of rural Ireland by population growth and deteriorating economic conditions from 1817. Their numbers increased dramatically during the desperate years of the potato famine, from 1845 to 1851. Like many other immigrant groups held together by ethnic and religious ties, the Irish worked together, formed their own neighborhoods, and maintained their cultural traditions.

In the early decades of the nineteenth century, however, technical changes made it less and less likely that workers could continue to labor in family groups. As control and discipline passed into the hands of impersonal managers and overseers, adult workers began to protest against inhuman conditions on behalf of their children. Some enlightened employers and social reformers in Parliament agreed that more humane standards were necessary, and they used widely circulated parliamentary reports to influence public opinion.

Factory Act of 1833

▶ English law that led to a sharp decline in the employment of children by limiting the hours that children over age nine could work and banning employment of children younger than nine.

These efforts resulted in a series of British Factory Acts from 1802 to 1833 that progressively limited the workday of child laborers and set minimum hygiene and safety requirements. The **Factory Act of 1833** installed a system of full-time professional inspectors to enforce the provisions of previous acts. The Factory Acts constituted significant progress in preventing the exploitation of children. One unintended drawback of restrictions on child labor, however, was that they broke the pattern of whole families working together in the factory, because efficiency required standardized shifts for all workers. After 1833 the number of children employed in industry declined rapidly.

CHAPTER LOCATOR | Why did the Industrial Revolution begin in Britain, and how did it develop? | How did countries respond to the challenge of industrialization?

698   CHAPTER 23   THE REVOLUTION IN ENERGY AND INDUSTRY

The Sexual Division of Labor

With the restriction of child labor and the collapse of the family work pattern in the 1830s came a new sexual division of labor. By 1850 the man was emerging as the family's primary wage earner, while the married woman found only limited job opportunities. Generally denied good jobs at high wages in the growing urban economy, wives were expected to concentrate on their duties at home. Evolving gradually, but largely in place by 1850, this new pattern of **separate spheres** in Britain constituted a major development in the history of women and of the family.

> **The Sexual Division of Labor:**

- Married women from the working classes were much less likely to work full-time for wages outside the house after the first child arrived
- Married women who did work for wages outside the house usually came from the poorest families
- Poor married or widowed women had to compete with young unmarried women for the limited employment opportunities available to women
- All women were generally confined to low-paying, dead-end jobs

Several factors combined to create this new sexual division of labor. First, the new and unfamiliar discipline of the clock and the machine was especially hard on married women of the laboring classes. Factory discipline conflicted with child care in a way that labor on the farm or in the cottage had not.

Second, running a household in conditions of urban poverty was an extremely demanding job in its own right. There were no supermarkets or public transportation. Shopping and feeding the family constituted a never-ending challenge. Taking on a brutal job outside the house had limited appeal for the average married woman from the working class. Thus many women might well have accepted the emerging division of labor as the best available strategy for family survival in the industrializing society.[2]

Third, to a large degree the young, generally unmarried women who did work for wages outside the home were segregated from men and confined to certain "women's jobs" because the new sexual division of labor replicated long-standing patterns of gender segregation and inequality. In the preindustrial economy, a small sector of the labor market had always been defined as "women's work," especially tasks involving needlework, spinning, food preparation, child care, and nursing. This traditional sexual division of labor took on new overtones, however, in response to the factory system. The growth of factories and mines brought unheard-of opportunities for girls and boys to mix on the job, free of familial supervision. Such opportunities led to more unplanned pregnancies and fueled the illegitimacy explosion that had begun in the late eighteenth century and that gathered force until at least 1850. Thus segregation of jobs by gender was partly an effort by older people to help control the sexuality of working-class youths.

Investigations into the British coal industry before 1842 provide a graphic example of this concern. The middle-class men leading the inquiry professed horror at the sight of girls and women working without shirts, which was a common

How did work evolve during the Industrial Revolution, and how did daily life change for working people? | How did the changes brought about by the Industrial Revolution lead to new social classes, and how did people respond to the new structure? | ✓ LearningCurve Check what you know.

699

practice because of the heat, and they quickly assumed the prevalence of licentious sex with the male miners. In fact, most girls and married women worked for related males in a family unit that provided considerable protection and restraint. Yet many witnesses from the working class also believed that the mines were inappropriate and dangerous places for women and girls. Some miners stressed particularly the danger of sexual aggression for girls working past puberty. The Mines Act of 1842 prohibited underground work for all women and girls as well as for boys under ten.

A final factor encouraging working-class women to withdraw from paid labor was the domestic ideals emanating from middle-class women, who had largely embraced the "separate spheres" ideology. Middle-class reformers published tracts and formed societies to urge poor women to devote more care and attention to their homes and families.

Mines Act of 1842
▶ English law prohibiting underground work for all women and girls as well as for boys under ten.

Living Standards for the Working Class

Although the evidence is complex and sometimes contradictory, most historians now agree that overall living standards for the working class did not rise substantially until the 1840s at least. Factory wages began to rise after 1815, but these gains were modest and were offset by a decline in married women's and children's participation in the labor force, meaning that many households had less total income than before. Moreover, many people still worked outside the factories as cottage workers or rural laborers, and in those sectors wages declined. Thus the increase in the productivity of industry did not lead to an increase in the purchasing power of the British working classes. Only after 1830, and especially after 1840, did real wages rise substantially, so that the average worker earned roughly 30 percent more in real terms in 1850 than in 1770.[3] Up to that point, the harshness of labor in the new industries probably outweighed their benefits as far as working people were concerned.

As the factories moved to urban areas, workers followed them in large numbers, leading to an explosion in the size of cities, especially in the north of England. Life in the new industrial cities, such as Manchester and Glasgow, was grim. Given extremely high rates of infant mortality, average life expectancy was around only twenty-five to twenty-seven years, some fifteen years less than the national average.[4] Migrants to the booming cities found expensive, hastily constructed, overcrowded apartments and inadequate sanitary systems.

Another way to consider the workers' standard of living is to look at the goods they purchased, which also suggest stagnant or declining living standards until the middle of the nineteenth century. One important area of improvement was in the consumption of cotton goods, which became much cheaper and could be enjoyed by all classes. However, in other areas, food in particular, the modest growth in factory wages was not enough to compensate for rising prices.

From the 1840s onward, matters improved considerably as wages made substantial gains and the prices of many goods dropped. A greater variety of foods became available, including the first canned goods. Some of the most important advances were in medicine. Smallpox vaccination became routine, and surgeons began to use anesthesia in the late 1840s. By 1850 trains and steamships had revolutionized transportation for the masses, while the telegraph made instant

CHAPTER LOCATOR | Why did the Industrial Revolution begin in Britain, and how did it develop? | How did countries respond to the challenge of industrialization?

700 CHAPTER 23 THE REVOLUTION IN ENERGY AND INDUSTRY

communication possible for the first time in human history. Gaslights greatly expanded the possibilities of nighttime activity.

In addition to the technical innovations that resulted from industrialization, other, less tangible changes were also taking place. As young men and women migrated away from their villages to seek employment in urban factories, many close-knit rural communities were destroyed. The loss of skills and work autonomy, along with the loss of community, must be included in the assessment of the Industrial Revolution's impact on the living conditions of the poor.

QUICK REVIEW

How did industrialization change European family life?

How did work evolve during the Industrial Revolution, and how did daily life change for working people?   How did the changes brought about by the Industrial Revolution lead to new social classes, and how did people respond to the new structure?   ☑ LearningCurve Check what you know.

701

How did the changes brought about by the Industrial Revolution lead to new social classes, and how did people respond to the new structure?

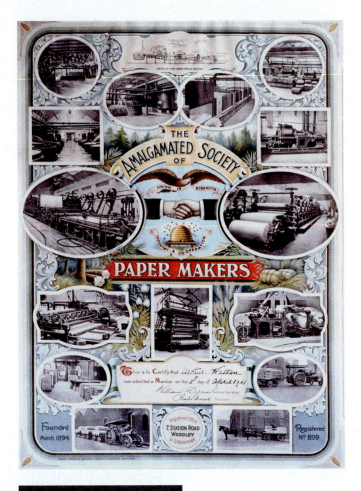

This handsome membership certificate belonged to Arthur Watton, a properly trained and certified papermaker of Kings Norton in Birmingham, England. Members of such unions proudly framed their certificates and displayed them in their homes, showing that they were skilled workers. (Courtesy, Sylvia Waddell)

IN GREAT BRITAIN industrial development led to the creation of new social groups and intensified long-standing problems between capital and labor. A new class of factory owners and industrial capitalists arose. The demands of modern industry regularly brought the interests of the middle-class industrialists into conflict with those of the people who worked for them—the working class. As observers took note of these changes, they raised new questions about how industrialization affected social relationships. Meanwhile, enslaved labor in European colonies contributed to the industrialization process in multiple ways.

CHAPTER LOCATOR | Why did the Industrial Revolution begin in Britain, and how did it develop? | How did countries respond to the challenge of industrialization?

The New Class of Factory Owners

Early industrialists operated in a highly competitive economic system. There were countless production problems, and success and large profits were by no means certain. Manufacturers therefore waged a constant battle to cut their production costs and stay afloat. Much of the profit had to go back into the business for new and better machinery.

Most early industrialists drew upon their families and friends for labor and capital, but they came from a variety of backgrounds. Many were from well-established merchant families with rich networks of contacts and support. Others were of modest means, especially in the early days. Artisans and skilled workers of exceptional ability had unparalleled opportunities. Members of ethnic and religious groups who had been discriminated against in the traditional occupations controlled by the landed aristocracy jumped at the new chances and often helped each other.

As factories and firms grew larger, and opportunities declined, it became harder for a gifted but poor young mechanic to start a small enterprise and end up as a wealthy manufacturer. Expensive, formal education became more important for young men as a means of success and advancement. In Britain by 1830 and in France and Germany by 1860, leading industrialists were more likely to have inherited their well-established enterprises, and they were financially much more secure than their struggling parents had been.

Just like working-class women, the wives and daughters of successful businessmen also found fewer opportunities for active participation in Europe's business world. Rather than contributing as vital partners in a family-owned enterprise, as so many middle-class women had done before, these women were increasingly valued for their ladylike gentility.

Responses to Industrialization

From the beginning, the British Industrial Revolution had its critics. Among the first were the romantic poets, including William Blake (1757–1827) and William Wordsworth (1770–1850). Some handicraft workers—notably the **Luddites**, who attacked factories in northern England in 1811 and later—smashed the new machines, which they believed were putting them out of work. Doctors and reformers wrote of problems in the factories and new towns, while Malthus and Ricardo concluded that workers would earn only enough to stay alive.

This pessimistic view was accepted and reinforced by Friedrich Engels (1820–1895), the future revolutionary and colleague of Karl Marx (see Chapter 24). After studying conditions in northern England, this young son of a wealthy Prussian cotton manufacturer published in 1844 *The Condition of the Working Class in England*, a blistering indictment of the capitalist classes. Engels's extremely influential account of capitalist exploitation and increasing worker poverty was embellished by Marx and later socialists (see Chapter 24).

Analysis of industrial capitalism, often combined with reflections on the French Revolution, led to the development of a new overarching interpretation— a new paradigm—regarding social relationships. Briefly, this paradigm argued that individuals were members of separate classes based on their relationship to

Luddites
▶ Group of handicraft workers who attacked factories in northern England in 1811 and after, smashing the new machines that they believed were putting them out of work.

How did work evolve during the Industrial Revolution, and how did daily life change for working people?

How did the changes brought about by the Industrial Revolution lead to new social classes, and how did people respond to the new structure?

✓ LearningCurve
Check what you know.

703

Ford Maddox Brown, *Work*

This midcentury painting provides a rich and realistic visual representation of the new concepts of social class that had become common by 1850. (Birmingham Museums and Art Gallery, Birmingham, UK/ The Bridgeman Art Library)

> PICTURING THE PAST

ANALYZING THE IMAGE: Describe the different types of work shown. What different social classes are depicted, and what kinds of work and leisure are the members of the different social classes engaged in? **CONNECTIONS:** What does this painting and its title suggest about the artist's opinion of the work of common laborers?

the means of production, that is, the machines and factories that dominated the new economy. As owners of expensive industrial machinery and as dependent laborers in their factories, the two main groups of society had separate and conflicting interests. Accordingly, the comfortable, well-educated "public" of the eighteenth century came increasingly to be defined as the middle class and the "people" gradually began to perceive themselves as composing a modern working class. And while the new class interpretation was open to criticism, it appealed to many because it seemed to explain what was happening. Therefore, conflicting classes existed, in part, because many individuals came to believe they existed and developed an awareness that they belonged to a particular social class—what Karl Marx called **class-consciousness**.

class-consciousness

▶ An individual's sense of class differentiation, a term introduced by Karl Marx.

The Early Labor Movement in Britain

Not everyone worked in large factories and coal mines during the Industrial Revolution. In 1850 more British people still worked on farms than in any other single occupation. The second-largest occupation was domestic service, with more than 1 million household servants, 90 percent of whom were women.

CHAPTER LOCATOR | Why did the Industrial Revolution begin in Britain, and how did it develop? | How did countries respond to the challenge of industrialization?

704   CHAPTER 23   THE REVOLUTION IN ENERGY AND INDUSTRY

Within industry itself, the pattern of artisans working with hand tools in small shops remained unchanged in many trades, even as others were revolutionized by technological change. For example, the British iron industry was completely dominated by large-scale capitalist firms by 1850. Yet the firms that fashioned iron into small metal goods employed on average fewer than ten wage workers who used handicraft skills.

Working-class solidarity and class-consciousness developed in small workshops as well as in large factories. In the northern factory districts, anticapitalist sentiments were frequent by the 1820s. Commenting in 1825 on a strike in the woolen center of Bradford and the support it had gathered from other regions, one newspaper claimed with pride that "it is all the workers of England against a few masters of Bradford."[5]

Such sentiments ran contrary to the liberal tenets of economic freedom. Liberal economic principles were embraced by statesmen and middle-class business owners in the late eighteenth century and continued to gather strength in the early nineteenth century. In 1799 Parliament passed the **Combination Acts**, which outlawed unions and strikes. In 1813 and 1814 Parliament repealed an old law regulating the wages of artisans and the conditions of apprenticeship. As a result of these and other measures, certain skilled artisan workers found aggressive capitalists ignoring traditional work rules and trying to flood their trades with unorganized women workers and children to beat down wages.

The capitalist attack on artisan guilds and work rules was bitterly resented by many craftworkers, who subsequently played an important part in Great Britain and in other countries in gradually building a modern labor movement. The Combination Acts were widely disregarded by workers. Craftsmen continued to take collective action, and societies of skilled factory workers also organized unions. Unions sought to control the number of skilled workers, to limit apprenticeship to members' own children, and to bargain with owners over wages. In the face of widespread union activity, Parliament repealed the Combination Acts in 1824, and unions were tolerated, though not fully accepted, after 1825.

The next stage in the development of the British trade-union movement was the attempt to create a single large national union. This effort was led not so much by working people as by social reformers such as Robert Owen. Owen, a self-made cotton manufacturer, had pioneered in industrial relations by combining firm discipline with concern for the health, safety, and hours of his workers. After 1815 he experimented with cooperative and socialist communities. Then in 1834 Owen organized one of the largest and most visionary of the early national unions, the Grand National Consolidated Trades Union.

When Owen's and other grandiose schemes collapsed, the British labor movement moved once again after 1851 in the direction of craft unions. These unions won real benefits for members by fairly conservative means and thus became an accepted part of the industrial scene.

British workers also engaged in direct political activity in defense of their interests. After the collapse of Owen's national trade union, many working people went into the Chartist movement, which fought for universal manhood suffrage. Workers were also active in campaigns to limit the workday in factories to ten hours and to permit duty-free importation of wheat into Great Britain to secure cheap bread. Thus working people developed a sense of their own identity and

Combination Acts
▶ English laws passed in 1799 that outlawed unions and strikes, favoring capitalist business owners over skilled artisans. Bitterly resented and widely disregarded by many craft guilds, the acts were repealed by Parliament in 1824.

How did work evolve during the Industrial Revolution, and how did daily life change for working people?

How did the changes brought about by the Industrial Revolution lead to new social classes, and how did people respond to the new structure?

✓ LearningCurve
Check what you know.

705

played an active role in shaping the new industrial system. They were neither helpless victims nor passive beneficiaries.

The Impact of Slavery

Another mass labor force of the Industrial Revolution was composed of the millions of enslaved men, women, and children who toiled in European colonies in the Caribbean and in North and South America. Historians have long debated the extent to which revenue from slavery contributed to Britain's achievements in the Industrial Revolution.

Most now agree that profits from colonial plantations and slave trading were a small portion of British national income in the eighteenth century. Nevertheless, the impact of slavery on Britain's economy was much broader than direct profits alone. In the mid-eighteenth century the need for items to exchange for colonial cotton, sugar, tobacco, and slaves stimulated demand for British manufactured goods in the Caribbean, North America, and West Africa. Britain's dominance in the slave trade also led to the development of finance and credit institutions that would help early industrialists obtain capital for their businesses.

The British Parliament abolished the slave trade in 1807 and freed all slaves in British territories in 1833, but by 1850 most of the cotton processed by British mills was supplied by the coerced labor of slaves in the southern United States. Thus the Industrial Revolution cannot be detached from the Atlantic world and the misery of slavery it included.

> **QUICK REVIEW**

What steps did working-class people take to shape the conditions under which they labored?

CHAPTER SUMMARY

As markets for manufactured goods increased both domestically and overseas, Britain was able to respond with increased production, largely because of its stable government, abundant natural resources, and flexible labor force. The first factories arose as a result of innovations in the textile industry. The demand for improvements in energy led to innovations and improvements in the steam engine, which transformed the iron industry, among others. In the early nineteenth century transportation of goods was greatly enhanced with the adoption of steam-powered trains and ships.

After 1815 continental European countries gradually built on England's technical breakthroughs. Newly established corporate banks worked in conjunction with government interventions in finance and tariff controls to promote railroads and other industries. Beginning around 1850 Japan and the United States also

CHAPTER LOCATOR | Why did the Industrial Revolution begin in Britain, and how did it develop? | How did countries respond to the challenge of industrialization?

CHAPTER 23
706 THE REVOLUTION IN ENERGY AND INDUSTRY

began to rapidly industrialize, but generally the Industrial Revolution spread more slowly outside of Europe, as many countries were confined to producing agricultural goods and other raw materials to serve European markets.

The rise of modern industry had a profound impact on society, beginning in Britain in the late eighteenth century. Industrialization led to the growing size and wealth of the middle class and the rise of a modern industrial working class. Improvements in the standard of living came slowly, but they were substantial by 1850. Married women withdrew increasingly from wage work and concentrated on child care and household responsibilities. The era of industrialization also fostered new attitudes toward child labor, encouraged protective factory legislation, and called forth a new sense of class feeling and an assertive labor movement. Slave labor in European colonies contributed to the rise of the Industrial Revolution.

 **CONNECTIONS** For much of its history, Europe lagged behind older and more sophisticated civilizations in China and the Middle East. And yet by 1800 Europe had broken ahead of the other regions of the world in terms of wealth and power.

One important prerequisite for the rise of Europe was its growing control over world trade, first in the Indian Ocean in the sixteenth and seventeenth centuries and then in the eighteenth-century Atlantic world. A second crucial factor in the rise of Europe was the Industrial Revolution, which dramatically increased the pace of production and distribution while reducing their cost, thereby allowing Europeans to control other countries first economically and then politically. By the middle of the nineteenth century the gap between Western industrial production and standards of living and those of the non-West had grown dramatically, bringing with it the economic dependence of non-Western nations, meager wages for their largely impoverished populations, and increasingly aggressive Western imperial ambitions (see Chapter 25).

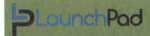

ONLINE DOCUMENT PROJECT

Inventing a New Workforce

How were social and economic change connected in nineteenth-century England?

Read sources on early industrial manufacturing, and then complete a quiz and writing assignment based on the evidence and details from this chapter. *See inside the front cover to learn more.*

How did work evolve during the Industrial Revolution, and how did daily life change for working people?

How did the changes brought about by the Industrial Revolution lead to new social classes, and how did people respond to the new structure?

✔ **LearningCurve**
Check what you know.

CHAPTER 23 STUDY GUIDE

STEP 1 **GET STARTED ONLINE**

LearningCurve

Now that you've read the chapter, make it stick by completing the LearningCurve activity.

STEP 2 **EXPLAIN WHY IT MATTERS**

Put your reading into practice. Identify each term below, and then explain why it matters in world history.

TERM	WHO OR WHAT & WHEN	WHY IT MATTERS
Industrial Revolution (p. 684)		
spinning jenny (p. 685)		
water frame (p. 685)		
steam engines (p. 686)		
Rocket (p. 688)		
Crystal Palace (p. 689)		
iron law of wages (p. 690)		
tariff protection (p. 694)		
Factory Act of 1833 (p. 698)		
separate spheres (p. 699)		
Mines Act of 1842 (p. 700)		
Luddites (p. 703)		
class-consciousness (p. 704)		
Combination Acts (p. 705)		

STEP 3 **MOVE BEYOND THE BASICS**

To demonstrate a more advanced understanding of the changes brought on by the process of industrialization, fill in the chart below with descriptions of key aspects of work and home life for cottage and factory workers. How did industrialization change the way that workers thought about themselves and their communities?

	Cottage Industry	Factory Work
Nature of Work		
Work and Gender		
Work and Children		
Relationship to Home Life		
Identity/Class-Consciousness		

PUT IT ALL TOGETHER

Now, take a step back and try to explain the big picture. Remember to use specific examples from the chapter in your answers.

THE INDUSTRIAL REVOLUTION IN BRITAIN

▶ What advantages help explain Britain's early industrialization? How did those advantages combine to spark the Industrial Revolution?

▶ How did British innovators solve the eighteenth-century energy crisis? How did their solution help transform the British economy?

INDUSTRIALIZATION IN CONTINENTAL EUROPE

▶ Compare and contrast conditions in Continental Europe before and after 1815. What made conditions after 1815 more favorable to industrialization than conditions before 1815?

▶ What role did government play in continental industrialization? How did continental governments work with private individuals and companies to promote economic development?

RELATIONS BETWEEN CAPITAL AND LABOR

▶ How did ideas about "women's work" change as a result of industrialization?

▶ What is class-consciousness? How did industrialization help produce a new sense among workers of their own social identity?

LOOKING BACK, LOOKING AHEAD

▶ How did developments between 1600 and 1800 contribute to the rise of Europe to world dominance in the nineteenth century?

   ▶ Argue for or against the following proposition: "Given contemporary trends, the dominance of the West in the nineteenth and twentieth centuries should be seen as a temporary aberration, rather than as a fundamental and permanent shift in the global balance of power."

> ## IN YOUR OWN WORDS

Imagine that you must give an oral report to the class answering the following question: **What were the social, cultural, and economic consequences of the Industrial Revolution?** What would be the most important points and why?

24
IDEOLOGIES OF CHANGE IN EUROPE
1815–1914

> **What role did social conflict play in nineteenth-century European politics?** Chapter 25 examines political and ideological conflict in nineteenth-century Europe. After 1815 the powers that defeated Napoleon united under a revived conservatism to stamp out the spread of liberal and democratic reforms. In response, powerful ideologies — liberalism, nationalism, and socialism — emerged to oppose conservatism. All played critical roles in the great popular upheaval that eventually swept across Europe in the revolutions of 1848. These revolutions failed, however, and gave way to more sober — and more successful — nation building in the 1860s. European political leaders and middle-class nationalists also began to deal effectively with the challenges of the emerging urban society. One way they did so was through nationalism — mass identification with a nation-state that was increasingly responsive to the needs of its people.

Christabel Pankhurst, Militant Suffragette Christabel Pankhurst led the British Women's Social and Political Union, whose motto was "deeds, not words." This photo was taken in 1912 in Paris, where Pankhurst was living to avoid arrest for her increasingly violent actions to obtain the vote for women, including bombing the home of the future prime minister. Women in Britain and many other countries gained the right to vote in the years immediately after World War I. (© Hulton-Deutsch Collection/Corbis)

> How did the allies fashion a peace settlement in 1815, and what radical ideas emerged between 1815 and 1848?

> Why did revolutions triumph briefly throughout most of Europe in 1848, and why did they fail?

> How did strong leaders and nation building transform Italy, Germany, and Russia?

> What was the impact of urban growth on cities, social classes, families, and ideas?

> How did nationalism and socialism shape European politics in the decades before the Great War?

LearningCurve

After reading the chapter, use LearningCurve to retain what you've read.

How did the allies fashion a peace settlement in 1815, and what radical ideas emerged between 1815 and 1848?

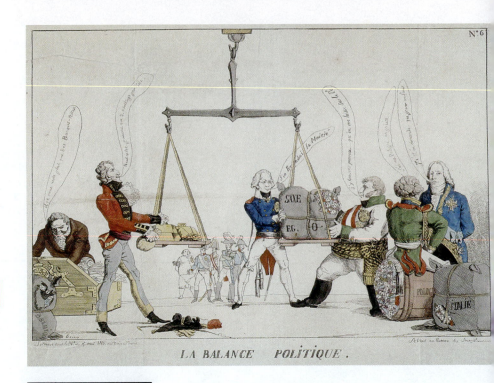

LA BALANCE POLITIQUE.

Adjusting the Balance

The Englishman on the left uses his money to counterbalance the people that the Prussian and the fat Metternich are gaining in Saxony and Italy. Alexander I sits happily on his prize, Poland. This cartoon captures the essence of how the educated public thought about the balance-of-power diplomacy resulting in the Treaty of Vienna. ("*La Balance Politique,*" 1815, colored etching/Deutsches Historisches Museum, Berlin, Germany/© DHM/The Bridgeman Art Library)

Congress of Vienna

▶ A meeting of the Quadruple Alliance (Russia, Prussia, Austria, Great Britain) and France held in 1814–1815 to fashion a general peace settlement that attempted to redraw Europe's political map after the defeat of Napoleonic France.

conservatism

▶ A political philosophy that stressed retaining traditional values and institutions, including hereditary monarchy and a strong landowning aristocracy.

AFTER FINALLY DEFEATING NAPOLEON, the conservative aristocratic monarchies of Russia, Prussia, Austria, and Great Britain—known as the Quadruple Alliance (see Chapter 22)—agreed to meet at the **Congress of Vienna** to fashion a lasting peace settlement. By carefully managing the European balance of power and embracing conservative restoration, they brokered an agreement that contributed to fifty years without major warfare in Europe (see Map 24.1, page 714).

In the years following the peace settlement, intellectuals and social observers sought to harness the radical ideas of the revolutionary age to new political movements. Many rejected **conservatism**, a political philosophy that stressed retaining traditional values and institutions. Radical thinkers developed alternative ideologies and tried to convince society to act on them.

The Political and Social Situation after 1815

When the Quadruple Alliance, along with representatives of minor powers, met together at the Congress of Vienna they combined leniency toward France with strong defensive measures. The Low Countries—Belgium and Holland—were

CHAPTER LOCATOR | **How did the allies fashion a peace settlement in 1815?** | Why did revolutions throughout Europe in 1848 triumph and why did they fail?

ca. 1790s–1840s Romantic movement in literature and the arts	**1861** Freeing of Russian serfs
1814–1815 Congress of Vienna	**1866–1871** Unification of Germany
1832 Reform Bill in Britain	**1873** Stock market crash spurs renewed anti-Semitism in central and eastern Europe
ca. 1840s–1890s Realism is dominant in Western literature	**1883** First social security laws to help workers in Germany
1845–1851 Great Famine in Ireland	**1889–1914** Second Socialist International
1848 Revolutions in France, Austria, and Prussia; Marx and Engels, *The Communist Manifesto*; first public health law in Britain	**1890–1900** Massive industrialization surge in Russia
1854 Pasteur studies fermentation and develops pasteurization	**1904–1905** Russo-Japanese War
1854–1870 Development of germ theory	**1905** Revolution in Russia
1859 Darwin, *On the Origin of Species by the Means of Natural Selection*	**1906–1914** Social reform in Britain
1859–1870 Unification of Italy	

united under an enlarged Dutch monarchy capable of opposing France more effectively. Prussia received considerably more territory along France's eastern border to stand as a "sentinel on the Rhine" against renewed French aggression. At the same time, France did not have to pay any war reparations and it did not lose large amounts of territory.

In their moderation toward France, the allies were motivated by self-interest and traditional ideas about the balance of power. To the peacemakers, especially to Klemens von Metternich (1773–1859), Austria's foreign minister, the balance of power meant an international equilibrium of political and military forces that would discourage aggression by any state or combination of states. The Quadruple Alliance members, therefore, agreed to meet periodically to discuss their common interests and to consider appropriate measures to maintain peace in Europe. This agreement marked the beginning of the European "congress system," which lasted long into the nineteenth century.

Conservatism After 1815

The peace settlement's domestic side was much less moderate. In 1815, under Metternich's leadership, Austria, Prussia, and Russia formed the Holy Alliance, dedicated to crushing the ideas and politics of the revolutionary era. Metternich's

How did strong leaders and nation building transform Italy, Germany, and Russia?	What was the impact of urban growth on cities, social classes, families, and ideas?	How did nationalism and socialism shape politics in the decades before the Great War?	✓ LearningCurve Check what you know.

MAP 24.1 ■ Europe in 1815

In 1815 Europe contained many different states, but after the defeat of Napoleon international politics was dominated by the five Great Powers: Russia, Prussia, Austria, Great Britain, and France. (The number rises to six if one includes the Ottoman Empire.)

> **MAPPING THE PAST**

ANALYZING THE MAP: Trace the political boundaries of each Great Power, and compare their geographical strengths and weaknesses. What territories did Prussia and Austria gain as a result of the war with Napoleon?

CONNECTIONS: How did Prussia's and Austria's territorial gains contribute to the balance of power established at the Congress of Vienna? What other factors enabled the Great Powers to achieve such a long-lasting peace?

policies dominated the entire German Confederation of thirty-eight independent German states (Map 24.1). It was through the German Confederation that Metternich had the repressive Karlsbad Decrees issued in 1819. These decrees required the member states to root out radical ideas in their universities and newspapers, and a permanent committee was established to investigate and punish any liberal or radical organizations.

CHAPTER LOCATOR | **How did the allies fashion a peace settlement in 1815?** | Why did revolutions throughout Europe in 1848 triumph and why did they fail?

Adhering to a conservative political philosophy, Metternich believed that strong governments were needed to protect society from its worst instincts. Like many European conservatives of his time, Metternich believed that liberalism (see below), as embodied in revolutionary America and France, had been responsible for a generation of war with untold bloodshed and suffering.

Another belief that Metternich opposed, which was often allied with liberalism, was nationalism, the idea that each national group had a right to establish its own independent government. The Habsburg's Austrian Empire was a dynastic state dominated by Germans but containing many other national groups. This multinational state was both strong and weak. It was strong because of its large population and vast territories, but weak because of its many and potentially dissatisfied nationalities. In these circumstances, Metternich opposed both liberalism and nationalism, for Austria could not accommodate those ideologies and remain a powerful empire.

Liberalism and the Middle Class

The principal ideas of liberalism—liberty and equality—were by no means defeated in 1815. Liberalism demanded representative government and equality before the law. The idea of liberty also meant specific individual freedoms: freedom of the press, freedom of speech, freedom of assembly, and freedom from arbitrary arrest.

Liberalism faced more radical ideological competitors in the early nineteenth century. Opponents of liberalism especially criticized its economic principles, which called for unrestricted private enterprise and no government interference in the economy. This philosophy was popularly known as the doctrine of laissez faire (lay-say FEHR). In early-nineteenth-century Britain economic liberalism was embraced most enthusiastically by business groups and thus became a doctrine associated with business interests.

In the early nineteenth century liberal political ideals also became more closely associated with narrow class interests. Early-nineteenth-century liberals favored representative government, but they generally wanted property qualifications attached to the right to vote and to serve in Parliament.

As liberalism became increasingly identified with the middle class after 1815, some intellectuals and foes of conservatism felt that liberalism did not go nearly far enough. They called for replacing monarchical rule with republics, for democracy through universal male suffrage, and for greater economic and social equality. These democrats and republicans were more radical than the liberals, and they were more willing to endorse violence to achieve goals. As a result, liberals and radical republicans could join forces against conservatives only up to a point.

The Growing Appeal of Nationalism

Nationalism was a second radical ideology that emerged in the years after 1815. Early advocates of the "national idea" argued that the members of what we would call today an ethnic group had its own genius and its own cultural unity, which were manifested especially in a common language, history, and territory.

liberalism
▶ A philosophy whose principal ideas were equality and liberty; liberals demanded representative government and equality before the law as well as such individual freedoms as freedom of the press, freedom of speech, freedom of assembly, and freedom from arbitrary arrest.

laissez faire
▶ A doctrine of economic liberalism advocating unrestricted private enterprise and no government interference in the economy.

nationalism
▶ The idea that each people had its own genius and its own cultural unity, which manifested itself especially in a common language and history and could serve as the basis for an independent political state.

| How did strong leaders and nation building transform Italy, Germany, and Russia? | What was the impact of urban growth on cities, social classes, families, and ideas? | How did nationalism and socialism shape politics in the decades before the Great War? | ✓ LearningCurve Check what you know. |

In fact, such cultural unity was more a dream than a reality as local dialects abounded, historical memory divided the inhabitants of the different states as much as it unified them, and a variety of ethnic groups shared the territory of most states.

Nevertheless, many European nationalists sought to make the territory of each people coincide with well-defined boundaries in an independent nation-state. It was this political goal that made nationalism so explosive in central and eastern Europe after 1815, when there were either too few states (Austria, Russia, and the Ottoman Empire) or too many (the Italian peninsula and the German Confederation), and when different peoples overlapped and intermingled.

Between 1815 and 1850 most people who believed in nationalism also believed in either liberalism or radical democratic republicanism. A common faith in the creativity and nobility of the people was perhaps the single most important reason for the linking of these two concepts. Liberals and especially democrats saw the people as the ultimate source of all good government. They agreed that the benefits of self-government would only be possible if the people were united by common traditions that transcended class and local interests. Thus individual liberty and love of a free nation overlapped greatly.

Yet early nationalists also stressed the differences among peoples, and they developed a strong sense of "we" and "they." Thus, while European nationalism's main thrust was liberal and democratic, below the surface lurked ideas of national superiority and national mission.

The Birth of Socialism

socialism

▶ A radical political doctrine that opposed individualism and the fragmentation of society and that advocated international cooperation and a sense of community; key ideas were economic planning, greater economic equality, and state regulation of property.

Socialism, the new radical doctrine after 1815, began in France. Early French socialists shared a sense of disappointment in the outcome of the French Revolution. They were also alarmed by the rise of laissez faire and the emergence of modern industry, which they saw as fostering inequality and selfish individualism. There was, they believed, an urgent need for a further reorganization of society to establish cooperation and a new sense of community.

Early French socialists felt an intense desire to help the poor, and they preached greater economic equality between the rich and the poor. Inspired by the economic planning implemented in revolutionary France (see Chapter 22), they argued that the government should rationally organize the economy to control prices and prevent unemployment. Socialists also believed that government should regulate private property or that private property should be abolished and replaced by state or community ownership.

> **> Early French Socialists:**

- Henri de Saint-Simon (1760–1825): Believed that the key to progress was technocratic government and economic planning
- Charles Fourier (1772–1837): Envisaged a socialist utopia of self-sufficient communities; called for the abolition of marriage, free unions based only on love, and sexual freedom
- Pierre-Joseph Proudhon (1809–1865): Argued that property was profit stolen from the workers who actually produced all wealth

CHAPTER LOCATOR | How did the allies fashion a peace settlement in 1815? | Why did revolutions throughout Europe in 1848 triumph and why did they fail?

CHAPTER 24
716   IDEOLOGIES OF CHANGE IN EUROPE

Up to the 1840s France was the center of socialism, as it had been the center of revolution in Europe, but in the following decades the German intellectual Karl Marx (1818–1883) would weave the diffuse strands of social thought into a distinctly modern ideology. In 1848 the thirty-year-old Karl Marx and the twenty-eight-year-old Friedrich Engels (see page 703) published *The Communist Manifesto*, which became the guiding text of socialism.

Marx argued that middle-class interests and those of the industrial working class were inevitably opposed to each other. According to the *Manifesto*, the "history of all previously existing society is the history of class struggles." In Marx's view, one class had always exploited the other, and, with the advent of modern industry, society was split more clearly than ever before: between the middle class—the **bourgeoisie**—and the modern working class—the **proletariat**.

Just as the bourgeoisie had triumphed over the feudal aristocracy in the French Revolution, Marx predicted that the proletariat would conquer the bourgeoisie in a new revolution. While a tiny majority owned the means of production and grew richer, the ever-poorer proletariat was constantly growing in size and in class-consciousness. Marx believed that the critical moment when class conflict would result in revolution was very near.

bourgeoisie
▶ The well-educated, prosperous, middle-class groups.

proletariat
▶ The Marxist term for the modern working class.

QUICK REVIEW

What connections were there between liberalism and nationalism in the first half of the nineteenth century?

How did strong leaders and nation building transform Italy, Germany, and Russia?

What was the impact of urban growth on cities, social classes, families, and ideas?

How did nationalism and socialism shape politics in the decades before the Great War?

✓ LearningCurve
Check what you know.

Why did revolutions triumph briefly throughout most of Europe in 1848, and why did they fail?

Das merkwürdige Jahr 1848. ___ Eine neue Bilderzeitung.

Street Fighting in Berlin, 1848

This contemporary lithograph portrays a street battle on March 18, 1848, between Prussian troops loyal to King Frederick William IV and civilian men and women demonstrators. The king withdrew his troops the following day rather than kill anymore of his "beloved Berliners." Revolutionaries across Europe often dug up paving stones and used them as weapons. The tricolor flag achieved prominence during the revolution as the symbol of a united and democratic Germany. (akg-images)

AS LIBERAL, NATIONALIST, AND SOCIALIST FORCES battered the conservatism of 1815, social and economic conditions continued to deteriorate for many Europeans, adding to the mounting pressures. In some countries, such as Great Britain, change occurred gradually and largely peacefully, but in 1848 radical political and social ideologies combined with economic crisis to produce revolutionary movements that demanded an end to repressive government.

Social and Economic Conflict

The slow and uneven spread of industrialization in Europe after 1815 (see Chapter 23) meant that the benefits of higher productivity were not felt by many. In Great Britain, the earliest adopter of industrial methods, living standards did not rise until the 1840s, and this trend took longer to spread to the continent. Most of

CHAPTER LOCATOR | How did the allies fashion a peace settlement in 1815? | **Why did revolutions throughout Europe in 1848 triumph and why did they fail?**

718 CHAPTER 24 IDEOLOGIES OF CHANGE IN EUROPE

the continent remained agricultural, and the traditional social hierarchy, dominated by a landowning aristocracy, persisted. In the early nineteenth century the pressures of a rapidly growing population, the adoption of new forms of agriculture, and the spread of exploitative rural industry destabilized these existing patterns.

Many of the social conflicts that ensued resembled those of the eighteenth century. Peasants resented the demands of their noble landlords and state tax collectors. Many lost access to collective land due to enclosure and the adoption of more efficient farming techniques. The growing number of cottage workers resisted exploitation by merchant capitalists, and journeymen battled masters in urban industries. Serfdom still existed in the Hungarian provinces of the Austrian Empire, Prussian Silesia, and Russia.[1]

What transformed these conflicts was the political ideologies born from the struggles and unfulfilled hopes of the French Revolution—liberalism, nationalism, and socialism—as well as the newly invigorated conservatism that stood against them. These ideologies helped turn economic and social conflicts into the revolutions of 1848.

Liberal Reform in Great Britain

The English parliamentary system guaranteed basic civil rights, but only about 8 percent of the population could vote for representatives to Parliament. By the 1780s there was growing interest in reform, but the French Revolution threw the British aristocracy into a panic. After 1815 the British government put down popular protests over unemployment and the high cost of grain caused by the Napoleonic Wars with repressive legislation and military force.

By the early 1830s the social and economic changes created by industrialization began to be felt in politics. In 1832 continuous pressure from the liberal middle classes and popular unrest convinced the king and the House of Lords that they needed to act. The Reform Bill of 1832 moved British politics in a more democratic direction by giving new industrial areas increased representation in the House of Commons and by increasing the number of voters by about 50 percent. Two years later, the New Poor Law called for unemployed and indigent families to be placed in harsh workhouses rather than receiving aid from local parishes to remain in their own homes. With this act, Britain's rulers sought to relieve middle-class taxpayers of the burden of poor relief and to encourage unemployed rural workers to migrate to cities and take up industrial work.

Thus limited democratic reform was counterbalanced by harsh measures against the poor, both linked to the new social and economic circumstances of the Industrial Revolution. Many working people protested their exclusion from voting and the terms of the New Poor Law. Between 1838 and 1848 they joined the Chartist movement (see page 704), which demanded universal male suffrage. In 1847 the ruling conservative party, known as the Tories, sought to appease working people with the Ten Hours Act, which limited the workday for women and young people in factories to ten hours. Tory aristocrats championed such legislation in order to compete with the middle class for working-class support.

This competition meant that the Parliamentary state functioned well in eliciting support from its people and thereby managed unrest without the outbreak of revolution. Another factor favoring Great Britain's largely peaceful evolution in

How did strong leaders and nation building transform Italy, Germany, and Russia?

What was the impact of urban growth on cities, social classes, families, and ideas?

How did nationalism and socialism shape politics in the decades before the Great War?

✓ LearningCurve
Check what you know.

719

the nineteenth century was the fact that living standards had begun to rise significantly by the 1840s, as the benefits of industrialization finally began to be felt. Thus England avoided the violence and turmoil of the revolutions of 1848 that shook continental Europe.

The people of Ireland did not benefit from these circumstances. Long ruled as a conquered people, the population was mostly composed of Irish Catholic peasants who rented their land from a tiny minority of Protestant landowners, many of whom resided in England. Ruthlessly exploited and growing rapidly in numbers, the rural population around 1800 lived under abominable conditions.

In spite of terrible conditions, Ireland's population doubled from 4 million to 8 million between 1780 and 1840, fueled in large part by the calories and nutritive qualities of the potato. However, the potato crop failed in 1845, 1846, 1848, and 1851 in Ireland and throughout much of Europe. Many suffered in Europe, but in Ireland, where dependency on the potato was much more widespread, the result was starvation and death. The British government, committed to laissez-faire economic policies, reacted slowly and utterly inadequately. One and a half million died, while another million fled between 1845 and 1851, primarily to the United States and Great Britain. The Great Famine, as this tragedy came to be known, intensified anti-British feeling and promoted Irish nationalism.

Revolutions in France

Louis XVIII's Constitutional Charter of 1814 was essentially a liberal constitution. It protected economic and social gains made by the middle class and the peasantry in the French Revolution, recognized intellectual and artistic freedom, and created a parliament with upper and lower houses. The charter was anything but democratic, however. Only a tiny minority of males had the right to vote for the legislative deputies who, with the king and his ministers, made the nation's laws.

Louis's conservative successor, Charles X (r. 1824–1830), wanted to re-establish the old order in France. To rally French nationalism and gain popular support, he exploited a long-standing dispute with Muslim Algeria. In June 1830 a French force crossed the Mediterranean and took the capital of Algiers. Buoyed by this success, Charles overplayed his hand and repudiated the Constitutional Charter. After three days of uprisings in Paris, which sparked a series of revolts by frustrated liberals and democrats across Europe, Charles fled. His cousin Louis Philippe (r. 1830–1848) accepted the Constitutional Charter of 1814 and assumed the title of the "king of the French people." Still, the situation in France remained fundamentally unchanged. Political and social reformers and the poor of Paris were bitterly disappointed.

During the 1840s this sense of disappointment was worsened by bad harvests and the slow development of industrialization. Similar conditions prevailed across continental Europe, which was soon rocked by insurrections. In February full-scale revolution broke out in France, and its shock waves ripped across the continent.

Louis Philippe had refused to approve social legislation or consider electoral reform. Frustrated desires for change, high-level financial scandals, and crop failures in 1845 and 1846 united diverse groups of the king's opponents, including merchants, intellectuals, shopkeepers, and workers. In February 1848, as popular revolt broke out, barricades went up, and Louis Philippe abdicated.

CHAPTER LOCATOR | How did the allies fashion a peace settlement in 1815? | Why did revolutions throughout Europe in 1848 triumph and why did they fail?

CHAPTER 24

720   IDEOLOGIES OF CHANGE IN EUROPE

The Triumph of Democratic Republics

This French illustration offers an opinion of the initial revolutionary breakthrough in 1848. The peoples of Europe, joined together around their respective national banners, are achieving republican freedom, which is symbolized by the Statue of Liberty and the discarded crowns. The woman wearing pants at the base of the statue — very radical attire — represents feminist hopes for liberation. (Lithograph by Frederic Sorrieu [1807–ca. 1861]. Musée de la Ville de Paris, Musée Carnavalet, Paris, France/Giraudon/The Bridgeman Art Library)

> **PICTURING THE PAST**

ANALYZING THE IMAGE: How many different flags can you count and/or identify? How would you characterize the types of people marching and the mood of the crowd?
CONNECTIONS: What do the angels, Statue of Liberty, and discarded crowns suggest about the artist's view of the events of 1848? Do you think this illustration was created before or after the collapse of the revolution in France? Why?

The revolutionaries quickly drafted a democratic, republican constitution for France's Second Republic, granting the right to vote to every adult male. Slaves in the French colonies were freed, the death penalty was abolished, and national workshops were established for unemployed Parisian workers.

Yet there were profound differences within the revolutionary coalition in Paris. The socialism promoted by radical republicans frightened not only the liberal middle and upper classes but also the peasants, many of whom owned land. When the French masses voted for delegates to the new Constituent Assembly in late April 1848, the monarchists won a clear majority. When the new government dissolved the national workshops in Paris, workers rose in a spontaneous insurrection. After three terrible "June Days" and the death or injury of more than ten thousand people, the republican army stood triumphant in a sea of working-class blood and hatred.

The revolution in France thus ended in failure. The middle and working classes had turned against each other. In place of a generous democratic republic,

How did strong leaders and nation building transform Italy, Germany, and Russia?

What was the impact of urban growth on cities, social classes, families, and ideas?

How did nationalism and socialism shape politics in the decades before the Great War?

☑ **LearningCurve**
Check what you know.

the Constituent Assembly completed a constitution featuring a strong executive. This allowed Louis Napoleon, nephew of Napoleon Bonaparte, to win a landslide victory in the December 1848 election based on promises to lead a strong government in favor of popular interests.

President Louis Napoleon at first shared power with a conservative National Assembly. But in 1851 Louis Napoleon dismissed the Assembly and seized power in a coup d'état. A year later he called on the French to make him hereditary emperor, and 97 percent voted to do so in a national plebiscite. Louis Napoleon then ruled France's Second Empire as Napoleon III, initiating policies favoring economic growth and urban development to appease the populace.

The Revolutions of 1848 in Central Europe

Throughout central Europe, social conflicts were exacerbated by the economic crises of 1845 to 1846. News of the upheaval in France in 1848 provoked the outbreak of revolution. Liberals demanded written constitutions, representative government, and greater civil liberties from authoritarian regimes. When governments hesitated, popular revolts followed. Urban workers and students allied with middle-class liberals and peasants. In the face of these coalitions, monarchs made hasty concessions. Soon, however, popular revolutionary fronts broke down as they had in France.

Compared with the situation in France, where political participation by working people reached its peak, revolts in central Europe tended to be dominated by social elites. They were also more sharply divided between moderate constitutionalists and radical republicans. The revolution in the Austrian Empire began in 1848 in Hungary, when nationalistic Hungarians demanded national autonomy, full civil liberties, and universal suffrage. When Viennese students and workers also took to the streets and peasant disorders broke out, the Habsburg emperor Ferdinand I (r. 1835–1848) capitulated and promised reforms and a liberal constitution. The coalition of revolutionaries was not stable, however. When the monarchy abolished serfdom, the newly free peasants lost interest in the political and social questions agitating the cities.

The revolutionary coalition was also weakened and ultimately destroyed by conflicting national aspirations. In March the Hungarian revolutionary leaders pushed through an extremely liberal constitution, but they also sought to create a unified Hungarian nation. The minority groups that formed half the population objected that such unification would hinder their own political autonomy and cultural independence. Likewise, Czech nationalists based in Bohemia and the city of Prague came into conflict with German nationalists. Thus nationalism within the Austrian Empire enabled the monarchy to play off one ethnic group against the other.

The monarchy's first breakthrough came in June when the army crushed a working-class revolt in Prague. In October the predominantly peasant troops of the regular Austrian army attacked the student and working-class radicals in Vienna and retook the city. When Ferdinand I abdicated in favor of his young nephew, Franz Joseph (see page 741), only Hungary had yet to be brought under control. Nicholas I of Russia (r. 1825–1855) obligingly lent his support. In June 1849, 130,000 Russian troops poured into Hungary and subdued the country. For a number of years the Habsburgs ruled Hungary as a conquered territory.

CHAPTER LOCATOR | How did the allies fashion a peace settlement in 1815? | **Why did revolutions throughout Europe in 1848 triumph and why did they fail?**

CHAPTER 24
722 IDEOLOGIES OF CHANGE IN EUROPE

After Austria, Prussia was the largest and most influential kingdom in the German Confederation. Prior to 1848, middle-class Prussian liberals had sought to reshape Prussia into a liberal constitutional monarchy, which would lead the confederation's thirty-eight states into a unified nation. When artisans and factory workers in Berlin exploded in revolt in March 1848 and joined with middle-class liberals against the monarchy, Prussian king Frederick William IV (r. 1840–1861) caved in. On March 21 he promised to grant Prussia a liberal constitution and to merge Prussia into a new national German state.

Elections were held across the German Confederation for a national parliament, which convened to write a federal constitution for a unified German state. Members of the new parliament completed drafting a liberal constitution in March 1849 and elected King Frederick William of Prussia emperor of the new German national state. By early 1849, however, Frederick William had reasserted his royal authority, contemptuously refusing to accept the "crown from the gutter." When Frederick William tried to get the small monarchs of Germany to elect him emperor on his own terms, with authoritarian power, Austria balked. Supported by Russia, Austria forced Prussia to renounce all its unification schemes in late 1850.

Thus, across Europe, the uprisings of 1848, which had been inspired by the legacy of the late-eighteenth-century revolutionary era, were unsuccessful. Reform movements splintered into competing factions, while the forces of order proved better organized and more united, on both a domestic and international level.

QUICK REVIEW

How did Britain avoid the waves of revolutionary
upheaval that struck the continent?

| How did strong leaders and nation building transform Italy, Germany, and Russia? | What was the impact of urban growth on cities, social classes, families, and ideas? | How did nationalism and socialism shape politics in the decades before the Great War? | ✓ LearningCurve Check what you know. |

How did strong leaders and nation building transform Italy, Germany, and Russia?

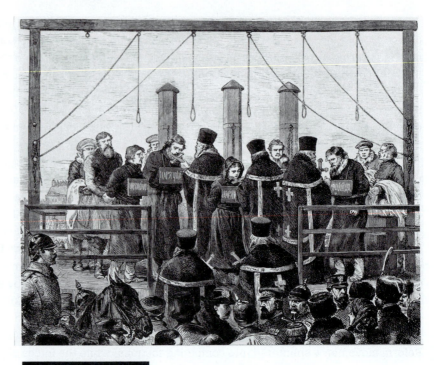

The Fruits of Terrorism

In the late 1870s a small group of revolutionaries believed that killing the tsar could destroy the Russian state. Succeeding in blowing up the reforming Alexander II after several near misses, the five assassins, including one woman, were quickly caught and hanged. Russia entered an era of reaction and harsh authoritarian rule. (Visual Connection Archive)

modernization
▶ The changes that enable a country to compete effectively with the leading countries at a given time.

LOUIS NAPOLEON'S TRIUMPH IN 1848 and his authoritarian rule in the 1850s provided Europe's victorious forces of order with a new political model. To what extent might the expanding urban middle classes and even portions of the working classes rally to a strong and essentially conservative national state that also promised change? In central Europe a resounding answer came with the national unification of Italy and Germany.

The Russian empire also experienced profound political crises in this period, but they were unlike those in Italy or Germany because Russia was already a vast multinational state. It became clear to Russian leaders that they had to embrace the process of **modernization**, defined narrowly as the changes that enable a country to compete effectively with the leading countries at a given time.

Cavour, Garibaldi, and the Unification of Italy

Italy had never been a united nation prior to 1850. A battleground for the Great Powers after 1494, Italy was reorganized in 1815 at the Congress of Vienna. Austria received the northern provinces of Lombardy and Venetia. Sardinia and

Piedmont fell under the rule of an Italian monarch, and Tuscany shared north-central Italy with several smaller states. The papacy ruled over central Italy and Rome, while a branch of the Bourbons ruled Naples and Sicily (Map 24.2).

After 1815 the goal of a unified Italian nation captivated many Italians, but there was no agreement on how it could be achieved. In 1848 the idealistic nationalist Giuseppe Mazzini's efforts to form a democratic Italian republic were crushed by Austrian forces. Temporarily driven from Rome during the upheavals of 1848, a frightened Pope Pius IX (pontificate 1846–1878) turned against most modern trends, including national unification. At the same time, Victor Emmanuel, king of independent Sardinia, retained the moderate liberal constitution granted under duress in March 1848. To the Italian middle classes, Sardinia (see Map 24.2) appeared to be a liberal, progressive state ideally suited to drive Austria out of northern Italy and achieve the goal of national unification.

Sardinia had the good fortune of being led by Count Camillo Benso di Cavour. Cavour's national goals were limited and realistic. Until 1859 he sought unity only for the states of northern and perhaps central Italy in a greatly expanded kingdom of Sardinia.

MAP 24.2 ■ The Unification of Italy, 1859–1870

The leadership of Sardinia-Piedmont, nationalist fervor, and Garibaldi's attack on the Kingdom of the Two Sicilies were decisive factors in the unification of Italy.

How did strong leaders and nation building transform Italy, Germany, and Russia?

What was the impact of urban growth on cities, social classes, families, and ideas?

How did nationalism and socialism shape politics in the decades before the Great War?

LearningCurve
Check what you know.

In the 1850s Cavour worked to consolidate Sardinia as a liberal constitutional state capable of leading northern Italy. He worked out a secret alliance with Napoleon III, and in July 1858 he goaded Austria into attacking Sardinia. The combined Franco-Sardinian forces were victorious, but Napoleon III decided on a compromise peace with the Austrians in July 1859 to avoid offending French Catholics by supporting an enemy of the pope. Sardinia would receive only Lombardy, the area around Milan. Cavour resigned in protest.

Popular revolts and Italian nationalism salvaged Cavour's plans. While the war against Austria raged in the north, dedicated nationalists in central Italy had risen and driven out their rulers. Cavour returned to power in early 1860, and the people of central Italy voted overwhelmingly to join a greatly enlarged kingdom of Sardinia. Cavour had achieved his original goal of a north Italian state (see Map 24.2).

For superpatriots such as Giuseppe Garibaldi (1807–1882), the job of unification was still only half done. Having led a unit of volunteers to several victories over Austrian troops in 1859, Garibaldi emerged in 1860 as an independent force in Italian politics. (See "Individuals in Society: Giuseppe Garibaldi," page 727.)

Secretly supported by Cavour, Garibaldi landed on the shores of Sicily in May 1860. His guerrilla band captured the imagination of the Sicilian peasantry, which rose in rebellion. Garibaldi captured Palermo and crossed to the mainland. When Garibaldi and Victor Emmanuel rode through Naples to cheering crowds, they symbolically sealed the union of north and south, of monarch and people.

The new kingdom of Italy, which did not include Venice until 1866 or Rome until 1870, was a parliamentary monarchy under Victor Emmanuel, neither radical nor democratic. Only a small minority of Italian males could vote. Despite political unity, the propertied classes and the common people were divided. A great social and cultural gap separated the industrializing north from the agrarian south.

Bismarck and German Unification

In the aftermath of 1848 the German states, particularly Austria and Prussia, were locked in a political stalemate, each seeking to block the power of the other within the German Confederation. At the same time, powerful economic forces were undermining the political status quo. Modern industry was growing rapidly within the German customs union, or *Zollverein*. By 1853 all the German states except Austria had joined the customs union, and a new Germany excluding Austria was becoming an economic reality. Rising prosperity from the rapid growth of industrialization after 1850 gave new impetus to middle-class liberals.

By 1859 liberals had assumed control of the parliament that emerged from the upheavals of 1848 in Prussia. The national uprising in Italy in 1859, however, convinced Prussia's tough-minded William I (r. 1861–1888) that political change and even war with Austria or France was possible. William I pushed to raise taxes and increase the defense budget to double the army's size. The Prussian parliament, reflecting the middle class's desire for a less militaristic society, rejected the military budget in 1862, and the liberals triumphed in new elections. King William then called on Count Otto von Bismarck to head a new ministry and defy the parliament.

When Otto von Bismarck (1815–1898) took office as chief minister in 1862, he declared that government would rule without parliamentary consent. Bismarck

CHAPTER LOCATOR | How did the allies fashion a peace settlement in 1815? | Why did revolutions throughout Europe in 1848 triumph and why did they fail?

726 CHAPTER 24 IDEOLOGIES OF CHANGE IN EUROPE

INDIVIDUALS IN SOCIETY
Giuseppe Garibaldi

When Giuseppe Garibaldi visited England in 1864, he received the most triumphant welcome ever given to any foreigner. Honored and feted by politicians and high society, he also captivated the masses. An unprecedented crowd of a half-million people cheered his carriage through the streets of London. These ovations were no fluke. In his time, Garibaldi was probably the most famous and most beloved figure in the world.* How could this be?

A rare combination of wild adventure and extraordinary achievement partly accounted for his demigod status. Born in Nice, Garibaldi went to sea at fifteen and sailed the Mediterranean for twelve years. At seventeen his travels took him to Rome, and he was converted in an almost religious experience to the "New Italy, the Italy of all the Italians." As he later wrote in his best-selling *Autobiography*, "The Rome that I beheld with the eyes of youthful imagination was the Rome of the future — the dominant thought of my whole life."

Sentenced to death in 1834 for his part in a revolutionary uprising in Genoa, Garibaldi barely escaped to South America. For twelve years he led a guerrilla band in Uruguay's struggle for independence from Argentina. "Shipwrecked, ambushed, shot through the neck," he found in a tough young woman, Anna da Silva, a mate and companion in arms. Their first children nearly starved in the jungle while Garibaldi, clad in his long red shirt, fashioned a legend as a fearless freedom fighter.

After he returned to Italy in 1848, the campaigns of his patriotic volunteers against the Austrians in 1848 and 1859 mobilized democratic nationalists. The stage was set for his volunteer army to liberate Sicily against enormous odds, astonishing the world and creating a large Italian state. Garibaldi's achievement matched his legend.

A brilliant fighter, the handsome and inspiring leader was an uncompromising idealist of absolute integrity. He never drew personal profit from his exploits, continuing to milk his goats and rarely possessing more than one change of clothing. When Victor Emmanuel offered him lands and titles after his great victory in 1860, even as the left-leaning volunteers were disbanded and humiliated, Garibaldi declined, saying he could not be bought off. Returning to his farm on a tiny rocky island, he denounced the government without hesitation when he concluded that it was betraying the dream of unification with its ruthless rule in the south. Yet even after a duplicitous Italian government caused two later attacks on Rome

Giuseppe Garibaldi, the charismatic leader, shown in a portrait painted in 1850. (1850 oil on canvas painting by Auguste Etienne [1794–1865]. Musée de l'Armee/akg-images)

to fail, his faith in the generative power of national unity never wavered. Garibaldi showed that ideas and ideals count in history.

Above all, millions of ordinary men and women identified with Garibaldi because they believed that he was fighting for them. They recognized him as one of their own and saw that he remained true to them in spite of his triumphs, thereby ennobling their own lives and aspirations. Welcoming runaway slaves as equals in Latin America, advocating the emancipation of women, introducing social reforms in the south, and pressing for free education and a broader suffrage in the new Italy, Garibaldi the national hero fought for freedom and human dignity. The common people understood and loved him for it.

QUESTIONS FOR ANALYSIS

1. Why was Garibaldi so famous and popular?
2. Nationalism evolved and developed in the nineteenth century. How did Garibaldi fit into this evolution? What kind of a nationalist was he?

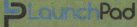

ONLINE DOCUMENT PROJECT

How did Italian nationalists respond to unification? Examine evidence from the period following Italian unification, and then complete a quiz and writing assignment based on the evidence and details from this chapter. *See inside the front cover to learn more.*

*Denis Mack Smith, *Garibaldi: A Great Life in Brief* (New York: Alfred A. Knopf, 1956), pp. 136–147; Denis Mack Smith, "Giuseppe Garibaldi," *History Today*, August 1991, pp. 20–26.

MAP 24.3 ■ The Unification of Germany, 1866–1871

This map shows how Prussia expanded and a new German Empire was created through two wars, the Austro-Prussian War of 1866 and the Franco-Prussian War of 1870–1871.

had the Prussian bureaucracy continue to collect taxes even though the parliament refused to approve the budget, and he reorganized the army. For their part, the voters of Prussia continued to express their opposition by sending large liberal majorities to the parliament from 1862 to 1866.

In 1866 Bismarck launched the Austro-Prussian War with the intent of expelling Austria from German politics. The war lasted only seven weeks, as the reorganized Prussian army defeated Austria decisively. Bismarck forced Austria to withdraw from German affairs and dissolved the existing German Confederation. The mainly Protestant states north of the Main River were grouped in the new North German Confederation, led by an expanded Prussia (Map 24.3). Each state retained its own local government, but the federal government—William I and Bismarck—controlled the army and foreign affairs.

CHAPTER LOCATOR | How did the allies fashion a peace settlement in 1815? | Why did revolutions throughout Europe in 1848 triumph and why did they fail?

To make peace with the liberal middle class and the nationalist movement, Bismarck asked the Prussian parliament to approve after the fact all the government's "illegal" spending between 1862 and 1866. Overawed by Bismarck's achievements, middle-class liberals now jumped at the chance to cooperate, opting for national unity and military glory over the battle for truly liberal institutions. Bismarck also followed Napoleon III's example by creating a legislature with members of the lower house elected by universal male suffrage, allowing him to bypass the middle class and appeal directly to the people if necessary.

The final act in the drama of German unification followed quickly with a patriotic war against France. The apparent issue—whether a distant relative of Prussia's William I might become king of Spain—was only a diplomatic pretext. By 1870, alarmed by Prussia's growing power, French leaders had decided on a war to teach Prussia a lesson.

As soon as war against France began in 1870, Bismarck had the wholehearted support of the south German states. The Germans quickly defeated Louis Napoleon's armies at Sedan on September 1, 1870. Three days later French patriots in Paris proclaimed yet another French republic and vowed to continue fighting. But after five months, in January 1871, a starving Paris surrendered, and France accepted Bismarck's harsh peace terms. By this time the south German states had agreed to join a new German Empire.

The Franco-Prussian War released an enormous surge of patriotic feeling in Germany. The new German Empire had become Europe's most powerful state, and most Germans were enormously proud. Semi-authoritarian nationalism and a "new conservatism," which was based on an alliance of the propertied classes and sought the active support of the working classes, had triumphed in Germany.

The Modernization of Russia

In the 1850s Russia was a poor agrarian society with a rapidly growing population. Almost 90 percent of the population lived off the land, and serfdom was still the basic social institution. Then the Crimean War of 1853 to 1856 arose from the breakdown of the balance of power established at the Congress of Vienna, European competition over influence in the Middle East, and Russian desires to expand into European territories held by the Ottoman Empire. France and Great Britain, aided by Sardinia and the Ottoman Empire, inflicted a humiliating defeat on Russia.

Russia's military defeat showed that it had fallen behind the industrializing nations of western Europe. Moreover, the war had caused hardship and raised the specter of massive peasant rebellion. Military disaster thus forced the new tsar, Alexander II (r. 1855–1881), and his ministers along the path of rapid social change and general modernization.

The first and greatest of the reforms was the freeing of the serfs in 1861. The emancipated peasants received, on average, about half of the land, which was to be collectively owned by peasant villages. The prices for the land were high, and collective ownership limited the possibilities of agricultural improvement and migration to urban areas. Thus the effects of the reform were limited. More successful was reform of the legal system, which established independent courts and equality before the law. The government also relaxed censorship and partially liberalized policies toward Russian Jews.

The Crimean War, 1853–1856

How did strong leaders and nation building transform Italy, Germany, and Russia?

What was the impact of urban growth on cities, social classes, families, and ideas?

How did nationalism and socialism shape politics in the decades before the Great War?

☑ LearningCurve
Check what you know.

729

Russia's greatest strides toward modernization were economic rather than political. Rapid, government-subsidized railroad construction to 1880 enabled agricultural Russia to export grain and thus earn money for further industrialization. Russia began seizing territory in far eastern Siberia, on the border with China; in Central Asia, north of Afghanistan; and in the Islamic lands of the Caucasus.

In 1881 an anarchist assassinated Alexander II, and the reform era came to an abrupt end. Political modernization remained frozen until 1905, but economic modernization sped forward in the massive industrial surge of the 1890s. The key leader was Sergei Witte (suhr-GAY VIH-tuh), the energetic minister of finance. Under Witte's leadership, the government doubled Russia's railroad network by the end of the century and promoted Russian industry with high protective tariffs.

By 1900 Russia was catching up with western Europe and expanding its empire in Asia. By 1903 Russia had established a sphere of influence in Chinese Manchuria and was eyeing northern Korea. When the protests of equally imperialistic Japan were ignored, the Japanese launched a surprise attack on Russian forces in Manchuria in February 1904. After Japan scored repeated victories Russia was forced in September 1905 to accept a humiliating defeat.

Military disaster in East Asia brought political upheaval at home. On January 22, 1905, workers peacefully protesting for improved working conditions and higher wages were attacked by the tsar's troops outside the Winter Palace. This event, known as Bloody Sunday, set off a wave of strikes, peasant uprisings, and troop mutinies across Russia. The revolutionary surge culminated in October 1905 in a paralyzing general strike, which forced the government to capitulate. The tsar, Nicholas II (r. 1894–1917), issued the **October Manifesto**, which granted full civil rights and promised a popularly elected Duma (DOO-muh; parliament) with real legislative power.

Under the new constitution, Nicholas II retained great powers and the Duma had only limited authority. The middle-class liberals, the largest group in the newly elected Duma, were badly disappointed, and efforts to cooperate with the tsar's ministers soon broke down. In 1907 Nicholas II and his reactionary advisers rewrote the electoral law so as to increase greatly the weight of the propertied classes. On the eve of World War I, Russia was partially modernized, a conservative constitutional monarchy with an agrarian but industrializing economy.

The Russian Revolution of 1905

- ▢ Area of peasant unrest
- ● Major strikes and mutinies

St. Petersburg
Moscow
RUSSIA
Warsaw

Black Sea

October Manifesto

▶ The result of a great general strike in Russia in October 1905, it granted full civil rights and promised a popularly elected Duma (parliament) with real legislative power.

> **QUICK REVIEW**

What role did war play in Italian and German unification?

CHAPTER LOCATOR | How did the allies fashion a peace settlement in 1815? | Why did revolutions throughout Europe in 1848 triumph and why did they fail?

Madrid in 1900

This wistful painting of a Spanish square on a rainy day, by Enrique Martínez Cubells y Ruiz (1874–1917), includes a revealing commentary on how scientific discoveries transformed urban life. Coachmen wait atop their expensive hackney cabs for a wealthy clientele, while modern electric streetcars that carry the masses converge on the square from all directions. In this way the development of electricity brought improved urban transportation and enabled the city to expand to the suburbs. (Museo Muncipal, Madrid, Spain/Giraudon/The Bridgeman Art Library)

BY 1900 WESTERN EUROPE WAS urban and industrial as surely as it had been rural and agrarian in 1800. Rapid urban growth in the nineteenth century worsened long-standing overcrowding and unhealthy living conditions, lending support to voices calling for revolutionary change. In response, government leaders, city planners, reformers, and scientists urgently sought solutions to these challenges.

Urban Development

Since the Middle Ages, European cities had been congested, dirty, and unhealthy. Industrialization greatly worsened these conditions. The steam engine freed industrialists from dependence on the energy of streams and rivers so that by 1800 there was every incentive to build new factories in cities, which had better shipping facilities and a large and ready workforce. Therefore, as industry grew, overcrowded and unhealthy cities expanded rapidly.

How did strong leaders and nation building transform Italy, Germany, and Russia?

What was the impact of urban growth on cities, social classes, families, and ideas?

How did nationalism and socialism shape politics in the decades before the Great War?

✓ LearningCurve
Check what you know.

In the 1820s and 1830s people in Britain and France began to worry about the condition of their cities. Parks and open areas were almost nonexistent, and narrow houses were built wall to wall in long rows. Highly concentrated urban populations lived in extremely unsanitary conditions, with open drains and sewers flowing alongside or down the middle of unpaved streets.

The urban challenge—and the growth of socialist movements calling for radical change—eventually brought an energetic response from a generation of reformers. The most famous early reformer was Edwin Chadwick, a British official. Collecting detailed reports from local officials and publishing his findings in 1842, Chadwick concluded that the stinking excrement of communal outhouses could be carried off by water through sewers at less than one-twentieth the cost of removing it by hand. In 1848 Chadwick's report became the basis of Great Britain's first public health law, which created a national health board and gave cities broad authority to build modern sanitary systems. Such sanitary movements won dedicated supporters in the United States, France, and Germany from the 1840s on.

Early sanitary reformers were handicapped by the prevailing miasmatic theory of disease—the belief that people contract disease when they breathe foul odors. In the 1840s and 1850s keen observation by doctors and public health officials suggested that contagion spread through physical contact with filth and not by its odors, thus weakening the miasmatic idea. An understanding of how this occurred came out of the work of Louis Pasteur (1822–1895), who developed the **germ theory** of disease. By 1870 the work of Pasteur and others had demonstrated that specific living organisms caused specific diseases and that those organisms could be controlled. These discoveries led to the development of a number of effective vaccines. Surgeons also applied the germ theory in hospitals, sterilizing not only the wound but everything else that entered the operating room.

The achievements of the bacterial revolution coupled with the public health movement saved millions of lives, particularly after about 1890. In England, France, and Germany death rates declined dramatically, and diphtheria, typhoid, typhus, cholera, and yellow fever became vanishing diseases in the industrializing nations.

More effective urban planning after 1850 also improved the quality of urban life. France took the lead during the rule of Napoleon III (r. 1848–1870), who believed that rebuilding Paris would provide employment, improve living conditions, and glorify and strengthen his empire. Baron Georges Haussmann (1809–1884), whom Napoleon III placed in charge of Paris, destroyed the old medieval core of Paris to create broad tree-lined boulevards, long open vistas, monumental buildings, middle-class housing, parks, and improved sewers and aqueducts. The rebuilding of Paris stimulated urban development throughout Europe, particularly after 1870.

Mass public transportation was also of great importance in the improvement of urban living conditions. In the 1890s countries in North America and Europe adopted an American transit innovation, the electric streetcar. Millions of riders hopped on board during the workweek. On weekends and holidays streetcars carried city people on outings to parks and the countryside, racetracks, and music halls.[2] Electric streetcars also gave people of modest means access to improved housing, as the still-crowded city was able to expand and become less congested.

Industrialization and the growth of global trade also led to urbanization outside of Europe. The tremendous appetite of industrializing nations for raw materials, food, and other goods caused the rapid growth of port cities and mining

germ theory
▶ The idea that disease is caused by the spread of living organisms that can be controlled.

CHAPTER LOCATOR | How did the allies fashion a peace settlement in 1815? | Why did revolutions throughout Europe in 1848 triumph and why did they fail?

732 CHAPTER 24 IDEOLOGIES OF CHANGE IN EUROPE

centers across the world. Many of these new cities consciously emulated European urban planning. For example, from 1880 to 1910 the Argentine capital of Buenos Aires modernized rapidly. The development of Buenos Aires was greatly stimulated by the arrival of many Italian and Spanish immigrants, part of a much larger wave of European migration in this period (see Chapter 27).

Social Inequality and Class

By 1850 at the latest, the wages and living conditions of the working classes were finally improving. Greater economic rewards, however, did not significantly narrow the gap between rich and poor. In fact, economic inequality worsened in Europe over the course of the nineteenth century and reached its height on the eve of World War I.

Despite extreme social inequality, society had not split into two sharply defined opposing classes, as Marx had predicted. Instead economic specialization created an almost unlimited range of jobs, skills, and earnings; one group or subclass blended into another in a complex, confusing hierarchy.

Between the tiny elite of the very rich and the sizable mass of the dreadfully poor existed a range of subclasses, each filled with individuals struggling to rise or at least to hold their own in the social order. A confederation of middle classes was loosely linked by occupations requiring mental, rather than physical, skill. As the upper middle class, composed mainly of successful business families, gained in income and progressively lost all traces of radicalism after the trauma of 1848, they were drawn toward the aristocratic lifestyle.

One step below was a much larger group of moderately successful industrialists and merchants, professionals in law and medicine, and midlevel managers of large public and private institutions. The expansion of industry and technology called for experts with specialized knowledge, and the most valuable of the specialties became solid middle-class professions. Next came independent shopkeepers, small traders, and tiny manufacturers—the lower middle class. Industrialization and urbanization also diversified the lower middle class and expanded the number of white-collar employees. White-collar employees were propertyless, but generally they were fiercely committed to the middle class and to the ideal of moving up in society.

Food, housing, clothes, and behavior all expressed middle-class values. Employment of at least one full-time maid was the clearest sign that a family had crossed the divide from the working classes into the middle classes. Freed from domestic labor, the middle-class wife directed her servants, supervised her children's education, and used her own appearance and that of her home to display the family's status. The middle classes shared a code of expected behavior and morality, which stressed hard work, self-discipline, and personal achievement.

At the beginning of the twentieth century about four out of five Europeans belonged to the working classes, that is people whose livelihoods depended primarily on physical labor. Many of them were small landowning peasants and hired farm hands, especially in eastern Europe. The urban working classes were even less unified than the middle classes. Economic development and increased specialization during the nineteenth century expanded the traditional range of working-class skills, earnings, and experiences. Skilled, semiskilled, and unskilled workers accordingly developed widely divergent lifestyles and cultural values,

How did strong leaders and nation building transform Italy, Germany, and Russia?

What was the impact of urban growth on cities, social classes, families, and ideas?

How did nationalism and socialism shape politics in the decades before the Great War?

☑ LearningCurve
Check what you know.

733

and their differences contributed to a keen sense of social status and hierarchy within the working classes.

Highly skilled workers, who made up about 15 percent of the working classes, became known as the labor aristocracy. They were led by construction bosses and factory foremen. The labor aristocracy also included members of the traditional highly skilled handicraft trades that had not transitioned to mechanized production, as well as new kinds of skilled workers such as shipbuilders and railway locomotive engineers.

Below the labor aristocracy stood the complex world of semiskilled and unskilled urban workers. A large number of the semiskilled were factory workers who earned good wages and whose relative importance in the labor force was increasing. Below the semiskilled workers was a larger group of unskilled workers that included day laborers and domestic servants.

To make ends meet, many working-class wives had to join the ranks of working women in the "sweated industries." These industries resembled the old putting-out and cottage industries of earlier times, and they were similar to what we call sweatshops today. The women normally worked at home and were paid by the piece, often making clothing after the advent of the sewing machine in the 1850s.

Despite their harsh lives, the urban working classes found outlets for fun and recreation. Across Europe drinking remained a favorite working-class leisure-time activity along with sports and music halls. Religion continued to provide working people with solace and meaning, although church attendance among the urban working classes declined in the late nineteenth century, especially among men.

The Changing Family

Industrialization and the growth of modern cities also brought great changes to the lives of women and families. As economic conditions improved, only women in poor families tended to work outside the home. The ideal became separate

CHAPTER LOCATOR | How did the allies fashion a peace settlement in 1815? | Why did revolutions throughout Europe in 1848 triumph and why did they fail?

734 CHAPTER 24 IDEOLOGIES OF CHANGE IN EUROPE

spheres (see page 699), the strict division of labor by sex. This rigid division meant that married women faced great obstacles if they needed or wanted to move into the world of paid employment outside the home. Well-paying jobs were off-limits to women, and a woman's wage was almost always less than a man's, even for the same work.

Because they needed to be able to support their wives, middle-class men did not marry until they were well established in their careers. The system encouraged marriages between much older men and younger women, who had little experience with adult life. Men were encouraged to see themselves as the protectors of their fragile and vulnerable wives.

As the ideology and practice of rigidly separate spheres narrowed women's horizons, their control and influence in the home became increasingly strong throughout Europe in the late nineteenth century. The comfortable home run by the middle-class wife was idealized as a warm shelter in a hard and impersonal urban world. By 1900 working-class families had adopted many middle-class values, but they did not have the means to fully realize the ideals of domestic comfort or separate spheres. Nevertheless, the working-class wife generally determined how the family's money was spent and took charge of all major domestic decisions. The woman's guidance of the household went hand in hand with the increased emotional importance of home and family for all social groups.

Ideas about sexuality within marriage varied. Many French marriage manuals of the late 1800s stressed that women had legitimate sexual needs. In the more puritanical United States, however, sex manuals recommended sexual abstinence for unmarried men and limited sexual activity for married men. Respectable women were thought to experience no sexual pleasure at all from sexual activity.

Medical doctors in both Europe and the United States began to study sexual desires and behavior more closely, and to determine what was considered "normal" and "abnormal." Same-sex attraction, labeled "homosexuality" for the first time, was identified as a "perversion." Governments increasingly regulated prostitution, the treatment of venereal disease, and access to birth control in ways that were shaped by class and gender hierarchies. Medical science also turned its attention to motherhood, and a wave of books instructed middle-class women on how to be better mothers.

Ideas about sexuality and motherhood were inextricably tied up with ideas about race. As European nations embarked on imperialist expansion in the second half of the nineteenth century, the need to maintain the racial superiority that justified empire led to increased concerns about the possible dilution or weakening of the European races. Maintaining healthy bodies, restricting sexuality, preventing interracial marriages, and ensuring that women properly raised their children were all components of racial strength, in the eyes of many European thinkers.

Women in industrializing countries also began to limit the number of children they bore. This revolutionary reduction in family size, in which the comfortable and well-educated classes took the lead, was founded on parents' desire to improve their economic and social position and that of their children. By having fewer youngsters, parents could give those they had advantages, from music lessons to expensive university educations.

The ideal of separate spheres and the rigid gender division of labor meant that middle-class women lacked legal rights and faced discrimination in education and employment. Organizations founded by middle-class feminists campaigned

How did strong leaders and nation building transform Italy, Germany, and Russia?

What was the impact of urban growth on cities, social classes, families, and ideas?

How did nationalism and socialism shape politics in the decades before the Great War?

✓ LearningCurve
Check what you know.

735

for legal equality as well as for access to higher education and professional employment. In the late nineteenth century middle-class women scored some significant victories, such as the 1882 law giving British married women full property rights. Rather than contesting existing notions of women as morally superior guardians of the home, feminists drew on these ideas for legitimacy in speaking out about social issues.

Socialist women leaders usually took a different path. They argued that the liberation of working-class women would come only with the liberation of the entire working class. In the meantime, they championed the cause of working women and won some practical improvements. In a general way, these different approaches to women's issues reflected the diversity of classes and political views in urban society.

Science for the Masses

Breakthroughs in industrial technology stimulated basic scientific inquiry as researchers sought to explain how such things as steam engines and blast furnaces actually worked. The result from the 1830s onward was an explosive growth of fundamental scientific discoveries that were increasingly transformed into material improvements for the general population.

A perfect example of the translation of better scientific knowledge into practical human benefits was the development of the branch of physics known as thermodynamics, the study of the relationship between heat and mechanical energy. By midcentury physicists had formulated the fundamental laws of thermodynamics, which were then applied to mechanical engineering, chemical processes, and many other fields. Electricity was transformed from a curiosity in 1800 to a commercial form of energy. By 1890 the internal combustion engine fueled by petroleum was an emerging competitor to steam and electricity.

Everyday experience and innumerable articles in newspapers and magazines impressed the importance of science on the popular mind. The methods of science acquired unrivaled prestige after 1850. Many educated people came to believe that the union of careful experiment and abstract theory was the only reliable route to truth and objective reality. The Enlightenment idea that natural processes were determined by rigid laws, leaving little room for either divine intervention or human will, won broad acceptance.

Living in an era of rapid change, nineteenth-century thinkers in Europe were fascinated with the idea of evolution and dynamic development. The most influential of all nineteenth-century evolutionary thinkers was Charles Darwin (1809–1882). Darwin believed that all life had gradually evolved from a common ancestral origin in an unending "struggle for survival." Darwin's theory of **evolution** is summarized in the title of his work *On the Origin of Species by the Means of Natural Selection* (1859). He argued that small variations within individuals in one species enabled them to acquire more food and better living conditions and made them more successful in reproducing, thus allowing them to pass their genetic material to the next generation. When a number of individuals within a species became distinct enough that they could no longer interbreed successfully with others, they became a new species.

Darwin's theory of natural selection provoked resistance, particularly because he extended the theory to humans. His findings reinforced the teachings of secu-

evolution

▶ The idea, developed by Charles Darwin, that all life had gradually evolved from a common origin through a process of natural selection; as applied by thinkers in many fields, the idea stressed gradual change and continuous adjustment.

CHAPTER LOCATOR | How did the allies fashion a peace settlement in 1815? | Why did revolutions throughout Europe in 1848 triumph and why did they fail?

736 CHAPTER 24 IDEOLOGIES OF CHANGE IN EUROPE

larists such as Marx, who scornfully dismissed religious belief in favor of agnostic or atheistic materialism. Many writers also applied the theory of biological evolution to human affairs. Herbert Spencer (1820–1903), an English philosopher, saw the human race as driven forward to ever-greater specialization and progress by a brutal economic struggle that determines the "survival of the fittest." The idea that human society also evolves, and that the stronger will become powerful and prosperous while the weaker will be conquered or remain poor, became known as **Social Darwinism**. Powerful nations used this ideology to justify nationalism and expansion, and colonizers to justify imperialism.

Not only did science shape society, but society also shaped science. As nations asserted their differences from one another, they sought "scientific" proof for those differences, which generally meant proof of their own superiority. European and American scientists, anthropologists, and physicians sought to prove that whites were more intelligent than other races, and that northern Europeans were more advanced than southern Europeans. Africans were described and depicted as "missing links" between chimpanzees and Europeans. This scientific racism extended to Jews, who were increasingly described as a separate and inferior race, not a religious group.

Cultural Shifts

In part a revolt against what was perceived as the cold rationality of the Enlightenment, **romanticism** was characterized by a belief in emotional exuberance, unrestrained imagination, and spontaneity in both art and personal life. Preoccupied with emotional excess, romantic works explored the awesome power of love and desire and of hatred, guilt, and despair. Where Enlightenment thinkers embraced secularization and civic life, romantics delved into religious ecstasy and the hidden recesses of the self. The romantics were passionately moved by nature and decried the growth of modern industry and industrial cities.

The French romantic painter Eugène Delacroix (oo-ZHEHN deh-luh-KWAH) (1798–1863) depicted dramatic, colorful scenes that stirred the emotions. He frequently painted non-European places and people, whether lion hunts in Morocco or women in a sultan's harem. Like other romantic works, Delacroix's art reveals the undercurrents of desire and fascination within Europe's imperial ambitions in "exotic" and "savage" places in the nineteenth century.

It was in music that romanticism realized most fully and permanently its goals of free expression and emotional intensity. Abandoning well-defined structures, the great romantic composers used a wide range of forms to create musical landscapes and evoke powerful emotion. The first great romantic composer is among the most famous today, Ludwig van Beethoven (1770–1827).

Romanticism also found a distinctive voice in poetry. In 1798 William Wordsworth (1770–1850) and his fellow romantic poet Samuel Taylor Coleridge (1772–1834) published their *Lyrical Ballads*, which abandoned flowery classical conventions for the language of ordinary speech. Wordsworth described his conception of poetry as the "spontaneous overflow of powerful feeling recollected in tranquility."

Victor Hugo's (1802–1885) powerful novels exemplified the romantic fascination with fantastic characters, strange settings, and human emotions. The hero of Hugo's famous *Hunchback of Notre Dame* (1831) is the great cathedral's deformed

Social Darwinism
▶ The application of the theory of biological evolution to human affairs, it sees the human race as driven to ever-greater specialization and progress by an unending economic struggle that determines the survival of the fittest.

romanticism
▶ A movement in art, literature, and music characterized by a belief in emotional exuberance, unrestrained imagination, and spontaneity in both art and personal life.

How did strong leaders and nation building transform Italy, Germany, and Russia?

What was the impact of urban growth on cities, social classes, families, and ideas?

How did nationalism and socialism shape politics in the decades before the Great War?

✓ LearningCurve
Check what you know.

737

bell-ringer, a "human gargoyle" overlooking the teeming life of fifteenth-century Paris.

The study of history became a romantic passion. History was the key to a universe that was now perceived to be organic and dynamic, not mechanical and static as the Enlightenment thinkers had believed. Historical studies supported the development of national aspirations and encouraged entire peoples to seek in the past their special destinies.

In central and eastern Europe, in particular, literary romanticism and early nationalism reinforced each other. Romantics turned their attention to peasant life and transcribed the folk songs, tales, and proverbs that the cosmopolitan Enlightenment had disdained. The brothers Jacob and Wilhelm Grimm were particularly successful at rescuing German fairy tales from oblivion. In the Slavic lands romantics played a decisive role in converting spoken peasant languages into modern written languages.

Beginning in the 1840s romanticism gave way to a new artistic genre, realism. Influenced by the growing prestige of science in this period, realist writers believed that literature should depict life exactly as it is. Forsaking poetry for prose and the personal, emotional viewpoint of the romantics for strict scientific objectivity, the realists simply observed and recorded.

Realist writers focused on creating fiction based on contemporary everyday life. Beginning with a dissection of the middle classes, from which most of them sprang, many realists eventually focused on the working classes, especially the urban working classes, which had been neglected in literature before this time. The realists put a microscope to unexplored and taboo topics—sex, strikes, violence, alcoholism—shocking middle-class critics.

The realists' claims of objectivity did not prevent the elaboration of a definite worldview. Realists such as the famous French novelist Émile Zola (1840–1902) and English novelist Thomas Hardy (1840–1928) were determinists. They believed that human beings, like atoms, are components of the physical world and that all human actions are caused by unalterable natural laws: heredity and environment determine human behavior; good and evil are merely social conventions. They were also critical of the failures of industrial society; by depicting the plight of poor workers, they hoped to bring about positive social change.

> **QUICK REVIEW**

Why did growing economic inequality not lead to increasing class conflict in the second half of the nineteenth century?

CHAPTER LOCATOR | How did the allies fashion a peace settlement in 1815? | Why did revolutions throughout Europe in 1848 triumph and why did they fail?

Le Petit Journal

SUPPLÉMENT ILLUSTRÉ

Huit pages : CINQ centimes

DIMANCHE 13 JANVIER 1895

LE TRAITRE

How did nationalism and socialism shape European politics in the decades before the Great War?

The Traitor: Degradation of Alfred Dreyfus

After being arrested and convicted in a secret court martial for treason, Captain Dreyfus bravely stood at attention during a public degradation ceremony. While the officer on duty tore off his stripes, ripped off his honors, and broke his sword in two, Dreyfus shouted out, "You are degrading an innocent man! Long live France! Long live the army!" (Le Petit Journal, 13 January 1895/engraving by Henri Meyer [1844–99]/Private Collection/The Bridgeman Art Library)

AFTER 1871 NATIONALISM SERVED, for better or worse, as a new unifying political principle. At the same time, socialist parties grew rapidly. Governing elites manipulated national feeling to create a sense of unity to divert attention from underlying class conflicts, and increasingly channeled national sentiment in an antiliberal and militaristic direction, tolerating anti-Semitism and waging wars in non-Western lands. This policy helped manage domestic conflicts, but only at the expense of increasing the international tensions that erupted in World War I.

Trends in Suffrage

There were good reasons why ordinary people felt increasing loyalty to their governments in central and western Europe. More people could vote. By 1914 universal male suffrage had become the rule rather than the exception. Ordinary men felt they were becoming "part of the system."

| How did strong leaders and nation building transform Italy, Germany, and Russia? | What was the impact of urban growth on cities, social classes, families, and ideas? | **How did nationalism and socialism shape politics in the decades before the Great War?** | ✔ LearningCurve Check what you know. |

Women also began to demand the right to vote. The first important successes occurred in Scandinavia and Australia. In Sweden taxpaying single women and widows could vote in municipal elections after 1862. Australia and Finland gave women the right to vote in national elections and stand for parliament in 1902 and 1906, respectively. In the western United States, women could vote in twelve states by 1913.

As the right to vote spread, politicians and parties in national parliaments usually represented the people more responsively. The multiparty system prevailing in most countries meant that parliamentary majorities were built on shifting coalitions, which gave political parties leverage to obtain benefits for their supporters. Governments also passed laws to alleviate general problems, thereby acquiring greater legitimacy and appearing more worthy of support.

The German Empire

The new German Empire was a federal union of Prussia and twenty-four smaller states. Unifying the whole was a strong national government with a chancellor— Bismarck until 1890—and a popularly elected parliament called the Reichstag. Although Bismarck repeatedly ignored the wishes of the parliamentary majority, he nonetheless preferred to win the support of the Reichstag to lend legitimacy to his policy goals.

Bismarck was a fierce opponent of socialism. In 1878 he pushed through a law outlawing the German Social Democratic Party, but he was unable to force socialism out of existence. Bismarck then urged the Reichstag to enact new social welfare measures to gain the allegiance of the working classes. In 1883 the Reichstag created national health insurance, followed in 1884 by accident insurance and in 1889 by old-age pensions and retirement benefits. Together, these laws created a national social security system that was the first of its kind anywhere, funded by contributions from wage earners, employers, and the state.

Under Kaiser William I (r. 1861–1888), Bismarck had managed the domestic and foreign policies of the state. In 1890 the new emperor, William II (r. 1888–1918), eager to rule in his own right and to earn the workers' support, forced Bismarck to resign. Following Bismarck's departure, the Reichstag passed new laws to aid workers and to legalize socialist political activity.

Although William II was no more successful than Bismarck in getting workers to renounce socialism, in the years before World War I the Social Democratic Party broadened its base and adopted a more patriotic tone. German socialists identified increasingly with the German state and concentrated on gradual social and political reform.

Republican France

Although Napoleon III's reign made some progress in reducing antagonisms between classes, the Franco-Prussian war undid these efforts, and in 1871 France seemed hopelessly divided once again. The republicans who proclaimed the Third Republic in Paris refused to admit defeat. They defended Paris with great heroism for weeks, until they were starved into submission by German armies in January 1871. When national elections then sent a large majority of conservatives and mon-

CHAPTER LOCATOR | How did the allies fashion a peace settlement in 1815? | Why did revolutions throughout Europe in 1848 triumph and why did they fail?

archists to the National Assembly, France's leaders decided they had no choice but to surrender Alsace and Lorraine to Germany. The traumatized Parisians exploded in patriotic frustration and proclaimed the Paris Commune in March 1871.

Commune leaders wanted to govern Paris without interference from the conservative French countryside. The National Assembly, led by conservative politician Adolphe Thiers, ordered the French army into Paris and brutally crushed the Commune. Twenty thousand people died in the fighting. Out of this tragedy France slowly formed a new national unity, achieving considerable stability before 1914.

The moderate republicans who governed France sought to preserve their creation by winning the loyalty of the next generation. Trade unions were fully legalized, and France acquired a colonial empire (see Chapter 25). A series of laws between 1879 and 1886 established free compulsory elementary education for both girls and boys, thereby greatly reducing the role of parochial Catholic schools, which had long been hostile to republicanism. In France and throughout the world, the general expansion of public education served as a critical nation- and nationalism-building tool in the late nineteenth century.

Although the educational reforms of the 1880s disturbed French Catholics, many of them rallied to the republic in the 1890s, and tensions between church and state eased. Unfortunately, the **Dreyfus affair** changed all that. In 1894 Alfred Dreyfus, a Jewish captain in the French army, was falsely accused and convicted of treason. In 1898 and 1899 the case split France apart. On one side was the army, which had manufactured evidence against Dreyfus, joined by anti-Semites and most of the Catholic establishment. On the other side stood the civil libertarians and most of the more radical republicans.

This battle, which eventually led to Dreyfus's being declared innocent, revived militant republican feeling against the church. Between 1901 and 1905 the government severed all ties between the state and the Catholic Church after centuries of close relations.

Dreyfus affair

▶ A divisive case in which Alfred Dreyfus, a Jewish captain in the French army, was falsely accused and convicted of treason. The Catholic Church sided with the anti-Semites against Dreyfus; after Dreyfus was declared innocent, the French government severed all ties between the state and the church.

Great Britain and the Austro-Hungarian Empire

The development of Great Britain and Austria-Hungary, two leading but quite different powers, throws a powerful light on the dynamics of nationalism in Europe before 1914. At home Britain made more of its citizens feel a part of the nation by passing consecutive voting rights bills that culminated with the establishment of universal male suffrage in 1884. Moreover, extensive social welfare measures were passed in a spectacular rush between 1906 and 1914. The state was integrating the urban masses socially as well as politically.

On the eve of World War I, however, the unanswered question of Ireland brought Great Britain to the brink of civil war. The terrible Irish famine of the 1840s and early 1850s had fueled an Irish revolutionary movement. The English slowly granted concessions, and in 1913 the British Parliament passed a bill granting Ireland self-government, or home rule.

Irish Protestants in the northern counties of Ulster, however, vowed to resist home rule, fearing they would fall under the control of the majority Catholics. Unable to resolve the conflict as World War I started in August 1914, the British government postponed indefinitely the whole question of Irish home rule.

How did strong leaders and nation building transform Italy, Germany, and Russia?

What was the impact of urban growth on cities, social classes, families, and ideas?

How did nationalism and socialism shape politics in the decades before the Great War?

✓ LearningCurve
Check what you know.

741

The Irish dilemma helps one appreciate how desperate the situation in the Austro-Hungarian Empire had become by the early twentieth century. Following its defeat by Prussia in 1866, a weakened Austria was forced to establish the so-called dual monarchy. The empire was divided in two, and the nationalistic Magyars gained virtual independence for Hungary. The two states were joined only by a shared monarch and common ministries for finance, defense, and foreign affairs. Still, the disintegrating force of competing nationalisms continued unabated, and the Austro-Hungarian Empire was progressively weakened and eventually destroyed by the conflicting national aspirations of its different ethnic groups. It was these ethnic conflicts in the Balkans that touched off the Great War in 1914 (see Chapter 28).

Jewish Emancipation and Modern Anti-Semitism

Revolutionary changes in political principles and the triumph of the nation-state brought equally revolutionary changes in Jewish life in western and central Europe. Beginning in France in 1791, Jews gradually gained their civil rights. In the 1850s and 1860s liberals in Austria, Italy, and Prussia pressed successfully for legal equality. In 1871 the constitution of the new German Empire abolished all restrictions on Jewish marriage, choice of occupation, place of residence, and property ownership. Exclusion from government employment and discrimination in social relations remained, however, in central Europe.

By 1871 a majority of Jews in western and central Europe had improved their economic situations and entered the middle classes. Most Jews identified strongly with their respective nation-states and considered themselves patriotic citizens.

Vicious anti-Semitism reappeared after the stock market crash of 1873, beginning in central Europe. Drawing on long traditions of religious intolerance, this

"The Expulsion of the Jews from Russia"

So reads this postcard, correctly suggesting that Russian government officials often encouraged popular anti-Semitism and helped drive many Jews out of Russia in the late nineteenth century. The road signs indicate that these poor Jews are crossing into Germany, where they will find a grudging welcome and a meager meal at the Jolly Onion Inn. Other Jews from eastern Europe settled in France and Britain, thereby creating small but significant Jewish populations in both countries for the first time since they had expelled most of their Jews in the Middle Ages. (Alliance Israelite Universele, Paris, France/Archives Charmet/The Bridgeman Art Library)

CHAPTER LOCATOR | How did the allies fashion a peace settlement in 1815? | Why did revolutions throughout Europe in 1848 triumph and why did they fail?

hostility also drew on modern, supposedly scientific ideas about Jews as a separate race (see page 736). Anti-Semitic beliefs were particularly popular among conservatives, extremist nationalists, and people who felt threatened by Jewish competition.

Anti-Semites also created modern political parties. In Austrian Vienna in the early 1890s, Karl Lueger (LOO-guhr), the popular mayor of Vienna from 1897 to 1910, combined fierce anti-Semitic rhetoric with his support of municipal ownership of basic services. In response to spreading anti-Semitism, a Jewish journalist named Theodor Herzl (1860–1904) turned from German nationalism to advocate Jewish political nationalism, or **Zionism**, and the creation of a Jewish state.

Before 1914 anti-Semitism was most oppressive in eastern Europe, where Jews also suffered from terrible poverty. In the Russian empire officials used anti-Semitism to channel popular discontent away from the government. In 1881–1882 a wave of violent pogroms commenced in southern Russia. The police and the army stood aside for days while peasants assaulted Jews and looted and destroyed their property. Official harassment continued in the following decades, and many Russian Jews emigrated to western Europe and the United States.

Zionism
▶ The movement toward Jewish political nationhood started by Theodor Herzl.

The Socialist Movement

Socialism appealed to large numbers of working men and women in the late nineteenth century, and the growth of socialist parties after 1871 was phenomenal. By 1912 the German Social Democratic Party, which espoused Marxist principles, had millions of followers and was the Reichstag's largest party. Socialist parties also grew in other countries, and Marxist socialist parties were linked together in an international organization.

As socialist parties grew and attracted large numbers of members, they looked more and more toward gradual change and steady improvement for the working class and less and less toward revolution. Workers themselves were progressively less inclined to follow radical programs for several reasons. As workers gained the right to vote and won real benefits, their attention focused more on elections than on revolutions. Workers were also not immune to nationalistic patriotism. Nor were workers a unified social group. Perhaps most important of all, workers' standard of living rose steadily after 1850, and the quality of life improved substantially in urban areas.

The growth of labor unions reinforced this trend toward moderation. In Great Britain new unions that formed for skilled workers after 1850 avoided radical politics and concentrated on winning better wages and hours for their members through collective bargaining and compromise. After 1890 unions for unskilled workers developed in Britain.

German unions were not granted important rights until 1869, and until the Anti-Socialist Laws were repealed in 1890 the government frequently harassed them as socialist fronts. But after most legal harassment was eliminated, union membership skyrocketed.

The German trade unions and their leaders were thoroughgoing revisionists. **Revisionism** was an effort by various socialists to update Marxist doctrines to reflect the realities of the time. The socialist Eduard Bernstein (1850–1932) argued in his *Evolutionary Socialism* in 1899 that Marx's predictions of ever-greater poverty for workers had been proved false. Therefore, Bernstein suggested, socialists

revisionism
▶ An effort by various socialists to update Marxist doctrines to reflect the realities of the time.

How did strong leaders and nation building transform Italy, Germany, and Russia?   What was the impact of urban growth on cities, social classes, families, and ideas?   **How did nationalism and socialism shape politics in the decades before the Great War?**   ✓ LearningCurve Check what you know.

should reform their doctrines and win gradual evolutionary gains for workers through legislation, unions, and further economic development.

Socialist parties in other countries had clear-cut national characteristics. Russians and socialists in the Austro-Hungarian Empire tended to be the most radical. In Great Britain the socialist but non-Marxist Labour Party formally committed to gradual reform. In Spain and Italy anarchism, seeking to smash the state rather than the bourgeoisie, dominated radical thought and action.

In short, socialist policies and doctrines varied from country to country. Socialism itself was to a large extent "nationalized." This helps explain why almost all socialist leaders supported their governments when war came in 1914.

> **QUICK REVIEW**

How did political elites gain the loyalty of elements of the working classes in the late nineteenth century?

CHAPTER SUMMARY

In 1814 the victorious allied powers sought to restore peace and stability in Europe. The conservative powers used intervention and repression as they sought to prevent the spread of subversive ideas and radical changes in politics. After 1815 ideologies of liberalism, nationalism, and socialism all developed to challenge the new order. The growth of these forces culminated in the liberal and nationalistic revolutions of 1848, revolutions that were crushed by resurgent conservative forces. In the second half of the nineteenth century Italy and Germany became unified nation-states, while Russia undertook a modernization program and struggled with popular discontent.

Living conditions in rapidly growing industrial cities declined until the mid-nineteenth century, when governments undertook major urban development. Major changes in the class structure and family life occurred, as the separate spheres ideology strengthened, and the class structure became more complex and diversified. The prestige of science grew tremendously, and scientific discoveries challenged the traditional religious understanding of the world. In the realm of literature and the arts, the romantic movement reinforced the spirit of change. Romanticism gave way to realism in the 1840s.

Western society became increasingly nationalistic as well as urban and industrial in the late nineteenth century. Nation-states became more responsive to the needs of their people, and they enlisted widespread support as political participation expanded, educational opportunities increased, and social security systems took shape. Even socialism became increasingly national in orientation, gathering strength as a champion of working-class interests in domestic politics. Yet even though nationalism served to unite peoples, it also drove them apart and contributed to the tragic conflicts of the twentieth century.

CHAPTER LOCATOR | How did the allies fashion a peace settlement in 1815? | Why did revolutions throughout Europe in 1848 triumph and why did they fail?

 **CONNECTIONS** Much of world history in the past two centuries can be seen as a struggle over the unfinished legacies of the late-eighteenth-century revolutions in politics and economics. Although defeated in 1848, the new political ideologies associated with the French Revolution re-emerged decisively after 1850. Nationalism, with its commitment to the nation-state, became the most dominant of the new ideologies.

After 1870 nationalism and militarism, its frequent companion, touched off increased competition between the major European powers for raw materials and markets for manufactured goods. As discussed in the next two chapters, during the last decades of the nineteenth century Europe colonized nearly all of Africa and large areas in Asia. In Europe itself nationalism promoted bitter competition between states, threatening the very progress and unity it had helped to build. In 1914 the power of unified nation-states turned on itself, unleashing an unprecedented conflict among Europe's Great Powers. Chapter 28 tells the story of this First World War.

Nationalism also sparked worldwide challenges to European dominance by African and Asian leaders who fought to liberate themselves from colonialism, and it became a rallying cry in nominally independent countries like China and Japan, whose leaders sought freedom from European and American influence and a rightful place among the world's leading nations. Chapters 25, 26, and 33 explore these developments. Likewise, Chapter 33 discusses how the problems of rapid urbanization and the huge gaps between rich and poor caused by economic transformations in America and Europe in the 1800s are now the concern of policymakers in Africa, Asia, and Latin America.

Another important ideology of change, socialism, remains popular in Europe, which has seen socialist parties democratically elected to office in many countries. Marxist revolutions that took absolute control of entire countries, as in Russia, China, and Cuba, occurred in the twentieth century.

ONLINE DOCUMENT PROJECT
Competing Visions of a United Italy
How did Italian nationalists respond to unification?

Examine evidence from the period following Italian unification, and then complete a quiz and writing assignment based on the evidence and details from this chapter. *See inside the front cover to learn more.*

How did strong leaders and nation building transform Italy, Germany, and Russia?	What was the impact of urban growth on cities, social classes, families, and ideas?	How did nationalism and socialism shape politics in the decades before the Great War?	✔ **LearningCurve** Check what you know.

STEP 1 GET STARTED ONLINE

 **LearningCurve**

Now that you've read the chapter, make it stick by completing the LearningCurve activity.

STEP 2 EXPLAIN WHY IT MATTERS

Put your reading into practice. Identify each term below, and then explain why it matters in world history.

TERM	WHO OR WHAT & WHEN	WHY IT MATTERS
Congress of Vienna (p. 712)		
conservatism (p. 712)		
liberalism (p. 715)		
laissez faire (p. 715)		
nationalism (p. 715)		
socialism (p. 716)		
bourgeoisie (p. 717)		
proletariat (p. 717)		
modernization (p. 724)		
October Manifesto (p. 730)		
germ theory (p. 732)		
evolution (p. 736)		
Social Darwinism (p. 737)		
romanticism (p.737)		
Dreyfus affair (p. 741)		
Zionism (p. 743)		
revisionism (p. 743)		

STEP 3 MOVE BEYOND THE BASICS

To demonstrate a more advanced understanding of the new ideologies that shaped European history in the nineteenth century, fill in the chart below with the key characteristics and beliefs associated with liberalism, conservatism, nationalism, and socialism. How were each of these four ideologies shaped by memories of the French Revolution?

	Key Characteristics and Beliefs
Liberalism	
Conservatism	
Nationalism	
Socialism	

STEP 4

PUT IT ALL TOGETHER

Now, take a step back and try to explain the big picture. Remember to use specific examples from the chapter in your answers.

REACTION AND REVOLUTION

► What were the goals of the participants in the Congress of Vienna? How did their experience of the French Revolution and the Napoleonic Wars shape their vision of postwar Europe?

► What explains the near simultaneous eruption of revolution across Europe in 1848? How did revolution in one country help trigger revolution in another? Why did all of the revolutions of 1848 fail?

NATION BUILDING IN ITALY, GERMANY, AND RUSSIA

► How did Bismarck use war to promote German unification under Prussian leadership? How did he use war to tame his domestic opponents?

► What did Russian leaders mean by "modernization"? How successful were their modernization efforts?

LATE NINETEENTH-CENTURY SOCIETY, CULTURE, AND POLITICS

► What explains the increasing social diversity of nineteenth-century Europe? What were the economic and political implications of this diversity?

► How did governments across Europe work to cement the loyalty of their citizens in the late nineteenth century? How effective were their efforts?

LOOKING BACK, LOOKING AHEAD

► How did nineteenth-century nation-states differ from their eighteenth-century counterparts? What role did industrialization and new political ideologies play in producing the differences you note?

► In what sense were the societies and states that developed in nineteenth-century Europe "modern"? What fundamental features of contemporary nation-states emerged in the period covered in this chapter?

> **IN YOUR OWN WORDS**

Imagine that you must give an oral report to the class answering the following question: **What role did social conflict play in nineteenth-century European politics?** What would be the most important points and why?

25

AFRICA, THE OTTOMAN EMPIRE, AND THE NEW IMPERIALISM

1800–1914

> **How and why did Western nations strive for global dominance over the course of the nineteenth century?** Chapter 25 examines nineteenth-century Western imperialism in Africa and the Middle East. As the process of industrialization advanced, European commercial interests went in search of new sources of raw materials and markets for their manufactured goods. At the same time, millions of Europeans and Asians picked up stakes and emigrated abroad. What began as a relatively peaceful exchange of products with Africa and Asia in the early nineteenth century had transformed by century's end into a frenzy of imperialist occupation and domination that had a profound impact on both colonizer and colonized. The political annexation of territory in the 1880s — the "new imperialism," as it is often called by historians — was the capstone of Western society's underlying economic and technological transformation.

Sengbe Pieh Enslaved in 1839, Pieh (later known as Joseph Cinqué) led a famous revolt on the slave ship *Amistad*. He and his fellow slaves were charged with mutiny and murder, but in March 1840 the U.S. Supreme Court found them innocent because they had been illegally captured and sold. They returned to their native Sierra Leone as free men. (Oil on canvas by Nathaniel Jocelyn, 1839/The Granger Collection, New York — All rights reserved.)

LearningCurve
After reading the chapter, use LearningCurve to retain what you've read.

> What were the most significant changes in Africa during the nineteenth century, and why did they occur?

> What were the causes and consequences of European empire building after 1880?

> How did the Ottoman Empire and Egypt try to modernize themselves, and what were the most important results?

> What were the global consequences of European industrialization between 1800 and 1914?

> What fueled migration, and what was the general pattern of this unprecedented movement of people?

> What were the most significant changes in Africa during the nineteenth century, and why did they occur?

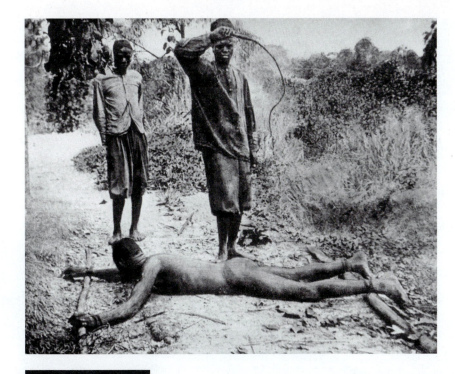

Brutality in the Congo

No Africans suffered more violent and brutal treatment under colonial rule than those living in Belgian king Leopold the II's Congo Free State. When not having their hands, feet, or heads cut off as punishment, Africans were whipped with *chicottes*, whips made of dried hippopotamus hide. Some Congolese were literally whipped to death. (© TopFoto/The Image Works)

FROM THE BEGINNING OF THE NINETEENTH CENTURY to the global depression of the 1930s, the different regions of Africa experienced gradual but monumental change. The transatlantic slave trade declined and practically disappeared by the late 1860s. In the early nineteenth century Islam expanded its influence south of the Sahara, but Africa generally remained free of European political control. After about 1880 Africa was divided and largely conquered by Europeans, and by 1900 the foreigners were consolidating their authoritarian empires.

Trade and Social Change

The most important development in West Africa before the European conquest was the decline of the Atlantic slave trade and the simultaneous rise in exports of **palm oil** and other commodities. This shift in African foreign trade marked the beginning of modern economic development in sub-Saharan Africa.

Although the trade in enslaved Africans was a global phenomenon, the transatlantic slave trade between Africa and the Americas became the most extensive

palm oil
▶ A West African tropical product often used to make soap; the British encouraged its cultivation as an alternative to the slave trade.

CHAPTER LOCATOR | **What were the most significant changes in Africa during the nineteenth century?** | What were the causes and consequences of European empire building after 1880?

750 CHAPTER 25 AFRICA, THE OTTOMAN EMPIRE, AND THE NEW IMPERIALISM

1805–1849 Muhammad Ali modernizes Egypt	**1880** Western and central Sudan unite under Islam
1808–1839 Mahmud II rules Ottoman state and enacts reforms	**1880–1900** Most of Africa falls under European rule
1809 Uthman dan Fodio founds Sokoto caliphate	**1880–1914** Height of new imperialism in Asia and Africa
1830 France begins conquest of Algeria	**1879–1882** Ahmed Arabi leads revolt against foreign control of Egypt
1839–1876 Western-style reforms (Tanzimat) in Ottoman Empire	**1884–1885** Berlin Conference
1860s Transatlantic slave trade declines rapidly	**1899** Kipling, "The White Man's Burden"; Amin, *The Liberation of Women*
1869 Completion of Suez Canal	
1875 Ottoman state declares partial bankruptcy; European creditors take over	**1899–1902** South African War
	1902 Conrad, *Heart of Darkness*; Hobson, *Imperialism*
1876 Europeans take financial control in Egypt	**1908** Young Turks seize power in Ottoman Empire

and significant portion of it (see pages 598–603). After 1775 a broad campaign to abolish slavery, in which British women played a critical role, developed in Britain and grew into one of the first peaceful mass political movements based on the mobilization of public opinion in British history. Abolitionists also argued for a transition to legitimate (nonslave) trade, to end both the transatlantic slave trade and the internal African slave systems. In 1807 Parliament declared the slave trade illegal. Britain then established the antislavery West Africa Squadron, using its navy to seize slave runners' ships, liberate the captives, and settle them in the British port of Freetown, in Sierra Leone, as well as in Liberia (see Map 25.1, page 755). Freed American slaves had established the colony of Liberia in 1821–1822.

British action had a limited impact at first. Britain's West Africa Squadron intercepted fewer than 10 percent of all slave ships, and the demand for slaves remained high on the expanding and labor-intensive sugar and coffee plantations of Cuba and Brazil until the 1850s and 1860s. In the United States, President Thomas Jefferson signed into law an act that banned slave importation from January 1, 1808. From that time on, natural increase (slaves having children) mainly accounted for the subsequent growth of the African American slave population before the Civil War. Strong financial incentives remained, however, for Portuguese and other European slave traders and for those African rulers who relied on profits from the trade for power and influence.

As more nations joined Britain in outlawing the slave trade, shipments of human cargo slackened along the West African coast (see Map 25.1, page 755).

How did the Ottoman Empire and Egypt try to modernize themselves?	What were the global consequences of European industrialization?	What fueled migration, and what was the pattern of this movement of people?	☑ **LearningCurve** Check what you know.

The first step towards lightening

The White Man's Burden

is through teaching the virtues of cleanliness.

Pears' Soap

is a potent factor in brightening the dark corners of the earth as civilization advances, while amongst the cultured of all nations it holds the highest place—it is the ideal toilet soap.

At the same time the ancient but limited shipment of slaves across the Sahara and from the East African coast into the Indian Ocean and through the Red Sea expanded dramatically. Only in the 1860s did this trade begin to decline rapidly. As a result of these shifting currents, total slave exports from all regions of sub-Saharan Africa declined only marginally. Abolitionists failed to achieve their vision of "legitimate" commerce in tropical products quickly replacing illegal slave exports.

Nevertheless, beginning in West Africa, trade in tropical products did make steady progress for several reasons. First, with Britain encouraging palm tree cultivation as an alternative to the slave trade, palm oil sales from West Africa to Britain surged. Second, the sale of palm oil admirably served the self-interest of industrializing Europe. Manufacturers used palm oil to lubricate their giant machines and to make cheap soap and other cosmetics. Third, peanut production for export also grew rapidly, in part because both small, independent African family farmers and large-scale enterprises could produce peanuts for the substantial American and European markets.

Finally, powerful West African rulers and warlords who had benefited from the Atlantic slave trade redirected some of their slaves' labor into the production of legitimate goods for world markets. This was possible because local warfare and slave raiding continued to enslave large numbers of people in sub-Saharan Africa, so slavery and slave markets remained strong. Although some enslaved captives might still be sold abroad, now women were often kept as wives, concubines, or servants, while men were used to transport goods, mine gold, grow crops, and serve in slave armies. Thus, the transatlantic slave trade's slow decline coincided with the most intensive use of slaves within Africa.

All the while, a new group of African merchants was emerging to handle legitimate trade, and some grew rich. Women were among the most successful

CHAPTER LOCATOR | **What were the most significant changes in Africa during the nineteenth century?** | What were the causes and consequences of European empire building after 1880?

CHAPTER 25
752 AFRICA, THE OTTOMAN EMPIRE, AND THE NEW IMPERIALISM

of these merchants. There is a long tradition of West African women being actively involved in trade (see pages 603–605), but the arrival of Europeans provided new opportunities. The African wife of a European trader served as her husband's interpreter and learned all aspects of his business. If the husband died, the African wife inherited his commercial interests, including his inventory and his European connections. Many such widows used their considerable business acumen to make small fortunes.

By the 1850s and 1860s legitimate African traders, flanked by Western-educated African lawyers, teachers, and journalists, had formed an emerging middle class in the West African coastal towns. Unfortunately for West Africans, in the 1880s and 1890s African business leadership gave way to imperial subordination.

Islamic Revival and Expansion in Africa

The Sudanic savanna is that vast belt of flat grasslands across Africa below the Sahara's southern fringe (the Sahel). By the early eighteenth century Islam had been practiced throughout this region for five hundred to one thousand years, depending on the area. City dwellers, political rulers, and merchants in many small states were Muslim. Yet the rural peasant farmers and migratory cattle raisers—the vast majority of the population—generally held onto traditional animist practices. Muslim rulers did not try to convert their subjects in the countryside or enforce Islamic law.

A powerful Islamic revival began in the eighteenth century and gathered strength in the early nineteenth century. In essence, Muslim scholars and fervent religious leaders arose to wage successful **jihads**, or religious wars, against both animist rulers and Islamic states they deemed corrupt. The new reformist rulers believed African cults and religious practice could no longer be tolerated, and they often effected mass conversions of animists to Islam.

The most important of these revivalist states, the **Sokoto caliphate**, illustrates the pattern of Islamic revival in Africa. It was founded by Uthman dan Fodio (1754–1817), a Muslim teacher who first won followers in the Muslim state of Gobir in the northern Sudan. After his religious community was attacked by Gobir's rulers, Uthman launched the jihad of 1804, one of the most important events in nineteenth-century West Africa. Uthman claimed the Hausa rulers of Muslim Gobir were idolaters who killed and plundered their subjects without any regard for Islamic law.[1] He recruited young religious students and discontented Fulani cattle raisers to form the backbone of his jihadi fighters and succeeded in overthrowing the Hausa rulers and expanding Islam into the Sudan. In 1809 Uthman established the new Sokoto caliphate (see Map 25.1, page 755).

The triumph of the Sokoto caliphate had profound consequences for Africa and the Sudan. First, the caliphate was governed by a sophisticated written constitution based on Islamic history and law. This government of laws, rather than men, provided stability and made Sokoto one of the most prosperous regions in tropical Africa. Second, because of Sokoto and other revivalist states, Islam became much more widely and deeply rooted in sub-Saharan Africa than ever before. Finally, as one historian explained, Islam had always approved of slavery for non-Muslims and Muslim heretics, and "the *jihads* created a new slaving frontier on the basis of rejuvenated Islam."[2] In 1900 the Sokoto caliphate had at least 1 million and perhaps as many as 2.5 million slaves.

jihad
▶ Religious war waged by Muslim scholars and religious leaders against both animist rulers and Islamic states that they deemed corrupt.

Sokoto caliphate
▶ Founded in 1809 by Uthman dan Fodio, this African state was based on Islamic history and law.

How did the Ottoman Empire and Egypt try to modernize themselves? | What were the global consequences of European industrialization? | What fueled migration, and what was the pattern of this movement of people? | ✔ LearningCurve Check what you know.

753

Islam also expanded in East Africa. From the 1820s on, Arab merchants and adventurers pressed far into the interior in search of slaves and ivory, converting and intermarrying with local Nyamwezi (nyahm-WAY-zee) elites and establishing small Muslim states. The Arab immigrants brought literacy, administrative skills, and increased trade and international contact, as well as the intensification of slavery, to East Africa. In 1870, before Christian missionaries and Western armies began to arrive in force and halt Islam's spread, it appeared that most of the East and Central African populations would accept Islam within a generation.[3]

The Scramble for Africa, 1880–1914

Between 1880 and 1914 Britain, France, Germany, Belgium, Spain, and Italy scrambled for African possessions as if their national livelihoods were at stake. In 1880 Europeans controlled barely 20 percent of the African continent, mainly along the coast; by 1914 they controlled over 90 percent. Only Ethiopia in northeast Africa and Liberia on the West African coast remained independent (Map 25.1).

In addition to the general causes underlying Europe's imperialist burst after 1880, certain events and individuals stand out. First, as the antislavery movement succeeded in shutting down the Atlantic slave trade by the late 1860s, slavery's persistence elsewhere attracted growing attention in western Europe and the Americas. Missionaries played a key role in publicizing the horrors of slave raids and the suffering of thousands of enslaved Africans. The public was led to believe that European conquest and colonization would end this human tragedy by bringing, in Scottish missionary David Livingstone's famous phrase, "Commerce, Christianity, and Civilization" to Africa.

King Leopold II (r. 1865–1909) of Belgium also played a crucial role. His agents signed treaties with African chiefs and planted Leopold's flag along the Congo River. By 1883 Europe had caught "African fever," and the race for territory was on. To lay down some rules for this imperialist competition, French premier Jules Ferry and German chancellor Otto von Bismarck arranged a European conference on Africa in Berlin in 1884–1885. The **Berlin Conference** established the principle that a nation could establish a colony only if it had effectively taken possession of the territory through signed treaties with local leaders and had begun to develop it economically.

In addition to developing rules for imperialist competition, participants at the Berlin Conference also promised to stop black and Islamic slave dealers and to bring Christianity and civilization to Africa. In truth, however, these ideals ran a distant second to, and were not allowed to interfere with, the nations' primary goal of commerce—holding on to their old markets and exploiting new ones.

The Berlin Conference coincided with Germany's emergence as an imperial power. In 1884 and 1885 Bismarck's Germany established **protectorates** over a number of small African kingdoms and societies (see Map 25.1). In acquiring colonies, Bismarck cooperated with France's Jules Ferry against the British. The French expanded into West Africa and also formed a protectorate on the Congo River. Meanwhile, the British began enlarging their West African enclaves and pushed northward from the Cape Colony and westward from the East African coast.

The British also moved southward from Egypt, which they had seized in 1882 (see page 767), but were blocked in the eastern Sudan by fiercely independent

Berlin Conference

▶ A meeting of European leaders held in 1884–1885 to lay down basic rules for imperialist competition in sub-Saharan Africa.

protectorate

▶ An autonomous state or territory partly controlled and protected by a stronger outside power.

CHAPTER LOCATOR | What were the most significant changes in Africa during the nineteenth century? | What were the causes and consequences of European empire building after 1880?

CHAPTER 25
754 AFRICA, THE OTTOMAN EMPIRE, AND THE NEW IMPERIALISM

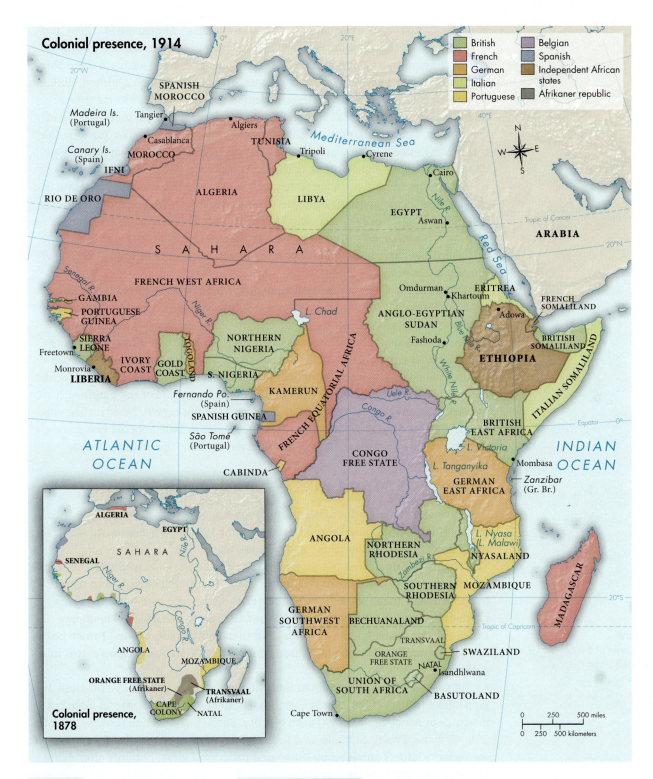

Colonial presence, 1914

Legend:
- British
- French
- German
- Italian
- Portuguese
- Belgian
- Spanish
- Independent African states
- Afrikaner republic

SPANISH MOROCCO
Madeira Is. (Portugal)
Tangier
Canary Is. (Spain)
IFNI
RIO DE ORO
Casablanca
MOROCCO
Algiers
TUNISIA
Tripoli
Cyrene
Mediterranean Sea
Cairo
ALGERIA
LIBYA
EGYPT
Aswan
SAHARA
Tropic of Cancer
ARABIA
FRENCH WEST AFRICA
Senegal R.
GAMBIA
PORTUGUESE GUINEA
SIERRA LEONE
Freetown
Monrovia
LIBERIA
IVORY COAST
GOLD COAST
TOGOLAND
Niger R.
NORTHERN NIGERIA
L. Chad
S. NIGERIA
KAMERUN
Fernando Po. (Spain)
SPANISH GUINEA
São Tomé (Portugal)
FRENCH EQUATORIAL AFRICA
Uele R.
Congo R.
CABINDA
Omdurman
Khartoum
ANGLO-EGYPTIAN SUDAN
Fashoda
Blue Nile R.
White Nile R.
Nile R.
Red Sea
ERITREA
Adowa
FRENCH SOMALILAND
BRITISH SOMALILAND
ETHIOPIA
ITALIAN SOMALILAND
BRITISH EAST AFRICA
L. Victoria
Mombasa
Zanzibar (Gr. Br.)
Equator
INDIAN OCEAN
ATLANTIC OCEAN
CONGO FREE STATE
GERMAN EAST AFRICA
L. Tanganyika
ANGOLA
NORTHERN RHODESIA
Zambezi R.
L. Nyasa (L. Malawi)
NYASALAND
MOZAMBIQUE
SOUTHERN RHODESIA
GERMAN SOUTHWEST AFRICA
BECHUANALAND
MADAGASCAR
Tropic of Capricorn
TRANSVAAL
SWAZILAND
ORANGE FREE STATE
NATAL
Isandhlwana
UNION OF SOUTH AFRICA
BASUTOLAND
Cape Town

Inset map — Colonial presence, 1878

ALGERIA
EGYPT
SAHARA
Nile R.
SENEGAL
Niger R.
Congo R.
ANGOLA
MOZAMBIQUE
ORANGE FREE STATE (Afrikaner)
TRANSVAAL (Afrikaner)
CAPE COLONY
NATAL

0 250 500 miles
0 250 500 kilometers

MAP 25.1 ■ The Partition of Africa

The European powers carved up Africa after 1880 and built vast political empires.

> MAPPING THE PAST

ANALYZING THE MAP: What European countries were leading imperialist states in Africa, and what lands did they hold? What countries maintained political independence?

CONNECTIONS: The late nineteenth century was the high point of European imperialism. What were the motives behind the rush for land and empire in Africa?

How did the Ottoman Empire and Egypt try to modernize themselves?

What were the global consequences of European industrialization?

What fueled migration, and what was the pattern of this movement of people?

✔ LearningCurve
Check what you know.

Muslims. In 1881 a pious Sudanese leader, Muhammad Ahmad (1844–1885), proclaimed himself the "Mahdi" (a messianic redeemer of Islam) and led a revolt against foreign control of Egypt. In 1885 his army massacred a British force, forcing the British to retreat to Cairo. Ten years later a British force returned, building a railroad to supply arms and reinforcements as it went. In 1898 these troops, under the command of Field Marshal Horatio Hubert Kitchener, met their foe at Omdurman, where Sudanese Muslims armed with spears were cut down by the recently invented machine gun. In the end eleven thousand Muslim fighters lay dead. Only twenty-eight Britons had been killed.

All European nations resorted to some violence in their colonies to retain control, subdue the population, appropriate land, and force African laborers to work long hours at physically demanding, and often dangerous, jobs. In no colony, however, was the violence and brutality worse than in Leopold II's Congo Free State. The European companies operating in the Congo Free State introduced slavery, unimaginable savagery, and terror.

Profits in the Congo Free State came first from the ivory trade, but in the 1890s, after many of the Congo's elephant herds had been decimated, rubber surpassed ivory as the colony's major income producer. Violence and brutality increased exponentially as industrial demand for rubber increased. Europeans and their well-armed mercenaries terrorized entire regions, cutting off hands, feet, and heads and wiping out whole villages to send the message that Africans must either work for the Europeans or die. In the first years of the nineteenth century, human rights activists such as Edmund Morel exposed the truth about the horrific conditions in the Congo Free State, and in 1908 Leopold was forced to turn over his private territory to Belgium as a colony, the Belgian Congo.

Southern Africa in the Nineteenth Century

The development of southern Africa diverged from the rest of sub-Saharan Africa in important ways. Whites settled in large numbers, modern capitalist industry took off, and British imperialists had to wage all-out war.

When the British took possession of the Dutch Cape Colony during the Napoleonic Wars, there were about twenty thousand free Dutch citizens and twenty-five thousand African slaves, with substantial mixed-race communities on the northern frontier of white settlement. After 1815 powerful African chiefdoms, Dutch settlers—first known as Boers, and then as **Afrikaners**—and British colonial forces waged a complicated three-cornered battle to build strong states in southern Africa.

Afrikaners

▶ Descendants of the Dutch settlers in the Cape Colony in southern Africa.

While the British consolidated their rule in the Cape Colony, the talented Zulu king Shaka (r. 1818–1828) was creating the largest and most powerful kingdom in southern Africa in the nineteenth century. Shaka's wars led to the creation of Zulu, Tswana, Swazi, Ndebele, and Sotho states in southern Africa. By 1890 these states were largely subdued by Dutch and British invaders, but only after many hard-fought frontier wars.

Between 1834 and 1838 the British abolished slavery in the Cape Colony and introduced racial equality before the law to protect African labor. In 1836 about ten thousand Afrikaner cattle ranchers and farmers, resentful of equal treatment of blacks by British colonial officials and missionaries after the abolition of slavery, began to make their so-called Great Trek northward into the interior. In 1845

CHAPTER LOCATOR | What were the most significant changes in Africa during the nineteenth century? | What were the causes and consequences of European empire building after 1880?

CHAPTER 25

756 AFRICA, THE OTTOMAN EMPIRE, AND THE NEW IMPERIALISM

Diamond Mining in South Africa

At first, both black and white miners could own and work claims at the diamond diggings, as this early photo suggests. However, as the industry expanded and was monopolized by European financial interests, white workers claimed the supervisory jobs, and blacks were limited to dangerous low-wage labor. (Robert Harvey/© Hulton-Deutsch Collection/Corbis)

another group of Afrikaners joined them north of the Orange River. Over the next thirty years Afrikaner and British settlers reached a mutually advantageous division of southern Africa. The British ruled the strategically valuable colonies of Cape Colony and Natal (nuh-TAL) on the coast, and the Afrikaners controlled the ranch-land republics of Orange Free State and the Transvaal in the interior.

The discovery of incredibly rich deposits of diamonds in 1867 near Kimberley, and of gold in 1886 in the Afrikaners' Transvaal Republic around modern Johannesburg, revolutionized the southern African economy, making possible large-scale industrial capitalism and transforming the lives of all its peoples. The extraction of these minerals, particularly the deep-level gold deposits, required big foreign investment, European engineering expertise, and an enormous labor force. Thus small-scale miners soon gave way to powerful financiers, particularly Cecil Rhodes (1853–1902). Rhodes came from a large middle-class British family and at seventeen went to southern Africa to seek his fortune. By 1888 Rhodes's firm, the De Beers mining company, monopolized the world's diamond industry and earned him fabulous profits.

How did the Ottoman Empire and Egypt try to modernize themselves?

What were the global consequences of European industrialization?

What fueled migration, and what was the pattern of this movement of people?

✓ LearningCurve
Check what you know.

The mining bonanza whetted the appetite of British imperialists led by the powerful Rhodes. Between 1888 and 1893 Rhodes used missionaries and his British South Africa Company, chartered by the British government, to force African chiefs to accept British protectorates, and he managed to add Southern and Northern Rhodesia (modern-day Zimbabwe and Zambia) to the British Empire.

Southern Rhodesia is one of the most egregious examples of Europeans misleading African rulers to take their land. In 1888 the Ndebele (or Matabele) king, Lobengula (1845–1894), ruler over much of modern southwestern Zimbabwe, met with three of Rhodes's men, led by Charles Rudd, and signed the Rudd Concession. Lobengula believed he was simply allowing a handful of British fortune hunters a few years of gold prospecting in Matabeleland. Lobengula had been misled, however, by the resident London Missionary Society missionary (and Lobengula's supposed friend), the Reverend Charles Helm, as to the document's true meaning and Rhodes's hand behind it. Even though Lobengula soon repudiated the agreement, he opened the way for Rhodes's seizure of the territory.

The Transvaal gold fields still remained in Afrikaner hands, however, so Rhodes and the imperialist clique initiated a series of events that sparked the South African War of 1899–1902 (also known as the Anglo-Boer War). Often considered the first "total war," this conflict witnessed the British use of a scorched-earth strategy to destroy Afrikaner property, and concentration camps to detain Afrikaner families and their servants, thousands of whom died of illness.

The long and bitter war divided whites in South Africa, but South Africa's blacks were the biggest losers. The British had promised the Afrikaners representative government in return for surrender in 1902, and they made good on their pledge. In 1910 the Cape Colony, Natal, the Orange Free State, and the Transvaal formed a new self-governing Union of South Africa. After the peace settlement, because the white minority held almost all political power in the new union, and because Afrikaners outnumbered English-speakers, the Afrikaners began to regain what they had lost on the battlefield. South Africa, under a joint British-Afrikaner government within the British Empire, began the creation of a modern segregated society that culminated in an even harsher system of racial separation, or apartheid, after World War II.

Colonialism's Impact After 1900

By 1900 much of Africa had been conquered and a system of colonial administration was taking shape. In general, this system weakened or shattered the traditional social order and challenged accepted values.

The self-proclaimed political goal of the French and the British—the principal colonial powers—was to provide good government for their African subjects, especially after World War I. "Good government" meant, above all, law and order. It meant strong, authoritarian government, which maintained a small army, built up an African police force, and included a modern bureaucracy capable of taxing and governing the population. Many African leaders and their peoples had chosen not to resist the invaders' superior force, and others stopped fighting and turned to other, less violent means of resisting colonial rule. Thus the goal of law and order was widely achieved.

Colonial governments demonstrated much less interest in providing basic social services. Education, public health, hospital, and other social service

The Struggle for South Africa, 1878

Boer republics
British territory
Battle

KALAHARI DESERT

TRANSVAAL

ZULULAND

ORANGE FREE STATE

NATAL

CAPE COLONY

Cape Town

ATLANTIC OCEAN

INDIAN OCEAN

CHAPTER LOCATOR | What were the most significant changes in Africa during the nineteenth century? | What were the causes and consequences of European empire building after 1880?

758 CHAPTER 25 AFRICA, THE OTTOMAN EMPIRE, AND THE NEW IMPERIALISM

expenditures increased after the Great War but still remained small. Europeans feared the political implications of mass education and typically relied instead on the modest efforts of state-subsidized mission schools. Moreover, they tried to make even their poorest colonies pay for themselves. Thus government workers' salaries normally absorbed nearly all tax revenues.

Economically, the colonial goal was to draw the African interior into the world economy on terms favorable to the dominant Europeans. The key was railroads linking coastal trading centers to interior outposts. Cheap, dependable transportation facilitated easy shipment of raw materials out and manufactured goods in. Railroads had two other important outcomes: they allowed quick troop movements to put down local unrest, and they allowed many African peasants to earn wages for the first time.

The focus on economic development and low-cost rule explains why colonial governments were reluctant to move decisively against slavery within Africa. Officials feared that an abrupt abolition of slavery where it existed would disrupt production and lead to costly revolts by powerful slaveholding elites, especially in Muslim areas. Thus colonial regimes settled for halfway measures designed to satisfy humanitarian groups in Europe and also make all Africans, free or enslaved, participate in a market economy and work for wages. Even this cautious policy emboldened many slaves to run away, thereby facilitating a rapid decline of slavery within Africa.

Colonial governments also often imposed head or hut taxes. Payable only in labor or European currency, these taxes compelled Africans to work for their white overlords. In some regions, particularly in West Africa, African peasants continued to respond freely to the new economic opportunities by voluntarily shifting to export crops on their own farms. Overall, the result of these developments was an increase in wage work and production geared to the world market and a decline in nomadic herding and traditional self-sufficient farming of sustainable crops. In sum, the imposition of bureaucratic Western rule and the gradual growth of a world-oriented cash economy after 1900 had a revolutionary impact on large parts of Africa.

QUICK REVIEW

How and why did European nations engage in the "scramble for Africa"?

How did the Ottoman Empire and Egypt try to modernize themselves?

What were the global consequences of European industrialization?

What fueled migration, and what was the pattern of this movement of people?

☑ LearningCurve
Check what you know.

What were the causes and consequences of European empire building after 1880?

Tools for Empire Building

Western technological advances aided imperialist ambitions in Africa. The Maxim gun was highly mobile and could lay down a continuous barrage that decimated charging enemies, as in the slaughter of Muslim tribesman at the Battle of Omdurman in Sudan. Quinine, first taken around 1850 to prevent the contraction of malaria, enabled Europeans to move safely into the African interior and overwhelm native peoples. And the development of the electromagnetic telegraph in the 1840s permitted rapid long-distance communications for the first time in history. (gun: Private Collection/Peter Newark Military Pictures/The Bridgeman Art Library; quinine: Wellcome Library, London; telegraph: John D. Jenkins, www.sparksmuseum.com)

WESTERN EXPANSION INTO AFRICA AND ASIA reached its apex between about 1880 and 1914. In those years the leading European nations sent streams of money and manufactured goods to both continents and also rushed to create or enlarge vast overseas political empires. This frantic activity differed sharply with the limited economic penetration of non-Western territories between 1816 and 1880, which, albeit by naked military force, had left a China or a Japan "opened" but politically independent (see Chapter 26). By contrast,

CHAPTER LOCATOR | What were the most significant changes in Africa during the nineteenth century? | **What were the causes and consequences of European empire building after 1880?**

760 CHAPTER 25
AFRICA, THE OTTOMAN EMPIRE, AND THE NEW IMPERIALISM

late-nineteenth-century empires recalled the old European colonial empires of the seventeenth and eighteenth centuries and led contemporaries to speak of the **new imperialism**.

Causes of the New Imperialism

Economic motives played an important role in the extension of political empires, especially of the British Empire. By the 1870s France, Germany, and the United States were rapidly industrializing. For a century Great Britain had been the "workshop of the world," the dominant modern industrial power. Now it was losing its industrial leadership, as its share of global manufacturing output dropped from 33 percent to just 14 percent between 1870 and 1914, and facing increasingly tough competition in foreign markets. In this changing environment of widening economic internationalism, the world experienced one of the worse economic depressions in history, the Long Depression, which lasted from 1873 to 1879. To protect home industries, America and Europe (except for Britain and the Netherlands) raised tariff barriers, abandoning the century-long practice of free trade and laissez-faire capitalism (see page 715). Unable to export their goods and faced with excess production, market saturation, and high unemployment, Britain, the other European powers, and the United States turned to imperial expansion, seeking African and Asian colonies to sell their products and acquire cheap raw materials. The Long Depression was arguably the single most important spark touching off the age of new imperialism.

Economic gains from the new imperialism proved limited, however, before 1914. The new colonies were too poor to buy much, and they offered few immediately profitable investments. Nonetheless, colonies became important for political and diplomatic reasons. Each leading European country considered them crucial to national security, military power, and international prestige.

Colonial rivalries reflected the increasing aggressiveness of Social Darwinian theories of brutal competition among races (see page 736). From a Social Darwinist perspective, European nations, considered as racially distinct parts of the dominant white race, had to seize colonies to prove their strength and virility. Moreover, since racial struggle was nature's inescapable law, the conquest of "inferior" peoples was just. Social Darwinism and harsh racial doctrines fostered imperialist expansion.

So, too, did the industrial world's unprecedented technological and military superiority. Three developments were crucial. First, the rapidly firing machine gun was an ultimate weapon in many unequal battles. Second, newly discovered **quinine** effectively controlled malaria attacks, which had previously decimated Europeans in the tropics. Third, the introduction of steam power (see page 688) strengthened the Western powers in two ways. Militarily, they could swiftly transport their armies by sea or rail where they were most needed. Economically, steamships with ever-larger cargoes now made round-trip journeys to far-flung colonies much more quickly and economically. Small steamboats could travel back and forth along the coast and also carry goods up and down Africa's great rivers. Likewise, freight cars pulled by powerful steam engines replaced the thousands of African porters hitherto responsible for carrying raw materials from the interior to the coast. Never before—and never again after 1914—would the

new imperialism
▶ The late-nineteenth-century drive by European countries to create vast political empires abroad.

quinine
▶ An agent that proved effective in controlling attacks of malaria, which had previously decimated Europeans in the tropics.

How did the Ottoman Empire and Egypt try to modernize themselves?

What were the global consequences of European industrialization?

What fueled migration, and what was the pattern of this movement of people?

✓ LearningCurve
Check what you know.

technological gap between the West and the non-Western regions of the world be so great.

Domestic political and class conflicts also contributed to overseas expansion. Conservative political leaders often manipulated colonial issues in order to divert popular attention from domestic problems and to create a false sense of national unity. Imperial propagandists relentlessly stressed that colonies benefited workers as well as capitalists, and they encouraged the masses to savor foreign triumphs and imperial glory.

Finally, special-interest groups in each country were powerful agents of expansion. Shipping companies wanted lucrative subsidies. White settlers wanted more land. Missionaries and humanitarians wanted to spread religion and stop the slave trade. Military men and colonial officials foresaw rapid advancement and high-paid positions in growing empires. The actions of such groups pushed the course of empire forward.

A "Civilizing Mission"

To rationalize imperialist expansion, Europeans and Americans argued they could and should "civilize" supposedly primitive non-Western peoples. According to this view, Africans and Asians would benefit from Western educations, modern economies, cities, advanced medicine, and higher living standards and eventually might be ready for self-government and Western democracy.

Another argument was that imperial government protected colonized peoples from ethnic warfare, the slave trade within Africa, and other forms of exploitation by white settlers and business people. Thus the French spoke of their sacred "civilizing mission." In 1899 Rudyard Kipling (1865–1936), perhaps the most influential British writer of the 1890s, exhorted Westerners to unselfish service in distant lands (while warning of the high costs involved) in his poem "The White Man's Burden." Kipling's poem, written in response to America's seizure of the Philippines after the Spanish-American War, and his concept of a **white man's burden** won wide acceptance among American imperialists. This principle was an important factor in the decision to rule, rather than liberate, the Philippines after the Spanish-American War (see page 838). Like their European counterparts, these Americans believed their civilization had reached unprecedented heights, enabling them to bestow unique benefits on all "less advanced" peoples.

Imperialists also claimed that peace and stability under European or American dominion permitted the spread of Christianity. In Africa Catholic and Protestant missionaries competed with Islam south of the Sahara, seeking converts and building schools. Many Africans' first real contact with Europeans and Americans was in mission schools. Some peoples, such as the Ibo in Nigeria, became highly Christianized. Such successes in black Africa contrasted with the general failure of missionary efforts in the Islamic world and in much of Asia.

Critics of Imperialism

Imperial expansion aroused sharp, even bitter, critics. One forceful attack was delivered in 1902, after the unpopular South African War, by radical English economist J. A. Hobson (1858–1940) in his *Imperialism*. Hobson contended that the

white man's burden

▶ The idea that Europeans could and should civilize more primitive nonwhite peoples and that imperialism would eventually provide nonwhites with modern achievements and higher standards of living.

CHAPTER LOCATOR | What were the most significant changes in Africa during the nineteenth century? | **What were the causes and consequences of European empire building after 1880?**

762 CHAPTER 25 AFRICA, THE OTTOMAN EMPIRE, AND THE NEW IMPERIALISM

rush to acquire colonies resulted from the economic needs of unregulated (by governments) capitalism. Moreover, Hobson argued, the quest for empire diverted popular attention away from domestic reform and the need to reduce the great gap between rich and poor at home. These and similar arguments had limited appeal because most people fervently believed imperialism was economically profitable for the homeland. Both Hobson and public opinion were wrong, however. Most British and European investors put the bulk of their money in the United States, Canada, Russia and other industrializing countries. Sub-Saharan Africa accounted for less than 5 percent of British exports in 1890, and British investments in Africa flowed predominantly to the mines in southern African. Thus, while some sectors of the British economy did profit from imperial conquests, and trade with these conquests was greater just before the Great War than in 1870, overall profits from imperialism were marginal at best.

Hobson and many Western critics struck home, however, with their moral condemnation of whites imperiously ruling nonwhites. Kipling and his kind were lampooned as racist bullies whose rule rested on brutality, racial contempt, and the Maxim machine gun. Polish-born novelist Joseph Conrad (1857–1924), in *Heart of Darkness* (1902), castigated the "pure selfishness" of Europeans in "civilizing" Africa.

Critics charged Europeans with applying a degrading double standard and failing to live up to their own noble ideals. At home Europeans had won or were winning representative government, individual liberties, and a certain equality of opportunity. In their empires Europeans imposed military dictatorships on Africans and Asians, forced them to work involuntarily, and discriminated against them shamelessly.

African and Asian Resistance

Initially African and Asian rulers often responded to imperialist incursions by trying to drive the unwelcome foreigners away, as in China and Japan (see Chapter 26). Violent antiforeign reactions exploded elsewhere again and again, but the industrialized West's superior military technology almost invariably prevailed. In addition, Europeans sought to divide and conquer by giving special powers and privileges to some individuals and groups from among the local population, including traditional leaders such as chiefs, landowners, and religious figures, and Western-educated professionals and civil servants, including police officers and military officers. These local elites recognized the imperial power realities in which they were enmeshed, and manipulated them to maintain or gain authority over the masses. Some concluded that the West was superior in certain ways and that they needed to reform and modernize their societies by copying some European achievements. By ruling indirectly through a local elite, a relatively small number of Europeans could maintain control over much larger populations without constant rebellion and protest. European empires were won by force, but they were maintained by cultural as well as military and political means.

Nevertheless, imperial rule was in many ways an imposing edifice built on sand. Acceptance of European rule was shallow and weak among the colonized masses. They were often quick to follow determined charismatic personalities who came to oppose the Europeans. Such leaders always arose, both when

How did the Ottoman Empire and Egypt try to modernize themselves? | What were the global consequences of European industrialization? | What fueled migration, and what was the pattern of this movement of people? | ✓ LearningCurve Check what you know.

763

Europeans ruled directly, or indirectly through native governments, for at least two basic reasons.

First, the nonconformists—the eventual anti-imperialist leaders—developed a burning desire for human dignity. They felt such dignity was incompatible with, and impossible under, foreign rule. Second, potential leaders found in the Western world the necessary ideologies and justification for their protest. Above all, they found themselves attracted to the nineteenth-century Western ideology of nationalism, which asserted that every people had the right to control their own destiny (see Chapter 24). After 1917 anti-imperialist revolt found another weapon in Lenin's version of Marxist socialism.

> **QUICK REVIEW**

What were the defining characteristics of the "new imperialism"?

CHAPTER LOCATOR | What were the most significant changes in Africa during the nineteenth century? | What were the causes and consequences of European empire building after 1880?

CHAPTER 25
764 AFRICA, THE OTTOMAN EMPIRE, AND THE NEW IMPERIALISM

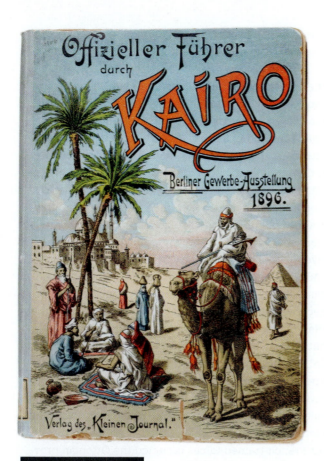

Egyptian Travel Guide

Ismail's efforts to transform Cairo were fairly successful. As a result, European tourists could more easily visit the country that their governments dominated. Ordinary Europeans were lured to exotic lands by travel books like this colorful "Official Guide" to an exhibition on Cairo held in Berlin. (Private Collection/Archives Charmet/The Bridgeman Art Library)

How did the Ottoman Empire and Egypt try to modernize themselves, and what were the most important results?

STRETCHING FROM WEST AFRICA into southeastern Europe and across Southwest Asia to the East Indies, Islamic civilization competed successfully with western Europe for centuries. Beginning in the late seventeenth century, however, the rising absolutist states of Austria and Russia began to challenge the Ottoman Empire and gradually to reverse Ottoman rule in southeastern Europe. In the nineteenth century European industrialization and nation building further altered the long-standing balance of power, and Western expansion eventually posed a serious challenge to Muslims everywhere.

Decline and Reform in the Ottoman Empire

Although the Ottoman Empire began a slow decline after Suleiman the Magnificent in the sixteenth century, the relationship between the Ottomans and the Europeans in about 1750 was still one of roughly equal strength. This parity

How did the Ottoman Empire and Egypt try to modernize themselves? | What were the global consequences of European industrialization? | What fueled migration, and what was the pattern of this movement of people? | ✓ LearningCurve Check what you know.

765

began to change quickly and radically, however, in the later eighteenth century, as the Ottomans fell behind western Europe in science, industrial skill, and military technology.

A transformation of the army was absolutely necessary to battle the Europeans more effectively and enhance the sultanate's authority within the empire. There were two primary obstacles to change, however. First, Ottoman military weakness reflected the decline of the sultan's "slave army," the so-called janissary corps (see page 490). With time, the janissaries—boys and other slaves raised in Turkey as Muslims, then trained to serve in the Ottoman infantry's elite corps—became a corrupt and privileged hereditary caste, absolutely opposed to any military innovations that might undermine their high status. Second, the empire was no longer a centralized military state. Instead local governors were becoming increasingly independent, pursuing their own interests and even seeking to establish their own governments and hereditary dynasties.

Sultan Selim III (r. 1789–1807) understood these realities, but when he tried to reorganize the army, the janissaries refused to use any "Christian" equipment. In 1807 they revolted and executed Selim in a palace revolution, one of many that plagued the Ottoman state. Selim's successor, the reform-minded Mahmud II (r. 1808–1839), proceeded cautiously, picking loyal officers and building his dependable artillery corps. In 1826 his council ordered the janissaries to drill in the European manner. As expected, the janissaries revolted and charged the palace, where they were mowed down by the waiting artillery.

The destruction and abolition of the janissaries cleared the way for building a new army, but it came too late to stop the rise of Muhammad Ali, the Ottoman governor in Egypt. In 1831 his French-trained forces occupied the Ottoman province of Syria and appeared ready to depose Mahmud II. The Ottoman sultan survived, but only with help from Britain, Russia, and Austria. The Ottomans were saved again in 1839, after their forces were routed trying to drive Muhammad Ali from Syria. In the last months of 1840 Russian diplomatic efforts, British and Austrian naval blockades, and threatened military action convinced Muhammad Ali to return Syria to the Ottomans. European powers preferred a weak and dependent Ottoman state to a strong and revitalized Muslim entity under a leader such as Muhammad Ali.

Tanzimat

▶ A set of radical reforms designed to remake the Ottoman Empire on a western European model.

In 1839, realizing their precarious position, liberal Ottoman statesmen launched an era of radical reforms, which lasted until 1876 and culminated in a constitution and a short-lived parliament. Known as the **Tanzimat**, these reforms were designed to remake the empire on a western European model. The new decrees called for Muslim, Christian, and Jewish equality before the law and in business, security of life and property, and a modernized administration and military. New commercial laws allowed free importation of foreign goods, as British advisers demanded, and permitted foreign merchants to operate freely throughout an economically dependent empire. Under British pressure, slavery in the empire was drastically curtailed, though not abolished completely. Of great significance, growing numbers among the elite and the upwardly mobile embraced Western education, adopted Western manners and artistic styles, and accepted secular values to some extent.

The Tanzimat achieved only partial success. The Ottoman state and society failed to regain its earlier power and authority for several reasons. First, implementation of the reforms required a new generation of well-trained and trust-

CHAPTER LOCATOR | What were the most significant changes in Africa during the nineteenth century? | What were the causes and consequences of European empire building after 1880?

CHAPTER 25

766 AFRICA, THE OTTOMAN EMPIRE, AND THE NEW IMPERIALISM

worthy officials, and that generation did not exist. Second, the liberal reforms failed to halt the growth of nationalism among Christian subjects in the Balkans (see below and Chapter 28), which resulted in crises and defeats that undermined all reform efforts. Third, the Ottoman initiatives did not curtail the appetite of Western imperialism, and European bankers gained a stranglehold on Ottoman finances. In 1875 the Ottoman state had to declare partial bankruptcy and place its finances in the hands of European creditors.

Finally, the elaboration of equal rights for citizens and religious communities failed to create greater unity within the state. Religious disputes increased, worsened by the Great Powers' relentless interference. This development embittered relations between religious communities, distracted the government from its reform mission, and split Muslims into secularists and religious conservatives. Islamic conservatives became the most dependable supporters of Sultan Abdülhamid II (r. 1876–1909), who abandoned the model of European liberalism in his long and repressive reign.

Ottoman Decline in the Balkans, 1818–1830

Meanwhile, the Ottoman Empire gradually lost control of its vast territories. Serbian nationalists rebelled and forced the Ottomans to grant Serbia local autonomy in 1816. The Greeks revolted against Ottoman rule in 1821 and won their national independence in 1830. As the Ottomans dealt with these uprisings by their Christian subjects in Europe, they failed to defend their Islamic provinces in North Africa. In 1830 French armies began their conquest of the Arabic-speaking province of Algeria.

Finally, during the Russo-Turkish War (1877–1878), absolutist Russia and a coalition of Balkan countries pushed southward into Ottoman lands and won a decisive victory. At the Congress of Berlin in 1878, the European Great Powers and the Ottoman Empire met to formally recognize Bulgarian, Romanian, Serbian, and Montenegrin independence. The Ottomans also lost territory to the Russians in the Caucasus, Austria-Hungary occupied the Ottoman provinces of Bosnia-Herzegovina and Novi Pazar, and Great Britain took over Cyprus.

The combination of declining international power and conservative tyranny eventually led to a powerful resurgence of the modernizing impulse among idealistic Turkish exiles in Europe and young army officers in Istanbul. These fervent patriots, the so-called **Young Turks**, seized power in the 1908 revolution, overthrowing Sultan Abdülhamid II. They made his brother Mehmed V (r. 1909–1918) the figurehead sultan and forced him to implement reforms. Though they failed to stop the rising tide of anti-Ottoman nationalism in the Balkans, the Young Turks did help prepare the way for the birth of modern secular Turkey after the defeat and collapse of the Ottoman Empire in World War I (see pages 864–866).

Young Turks

▶ Fervent patriots who seized power in the revolution of 1908, forcing the conservative sultan to implement reforms; they helped pave the way for the birth of modern secular Turkey.

Egypt: From Reform to British Occupation

Egypt had been ruled by a succession of foreigners from 525 B.C.E. to the Ottoman conquest in the early sixteenth century. In 1798, as France and Britain prepared for war in Europe, Napoleon Bonaparte invaded Egypt, thereby threatening British access to India, and occupied the territory for three years. Into the power vacuum left by the French withdrawal stepped an extraordinary Albanian-born Turkish general, Muhammad Ali (1769–1849).

Appointed Egypt's governor in 1805, Muhammad Ali set out to build his own state on the strength of a large, powerful army organized along European lines.

How did the Ottoman Empire and Egypt try to modernize themselves?	What were the global consequences of European industrialization?	What fueled migration, and what was the pattern of this movement of people?	✔ LearningCurve Check what you know.

He also reformed the government and promoted modern industry. (See "Individuals in Society: Muhammad Ali," page 769.) For a time Muhammad Ali's ambitious strategy seemed to work, but it eventually foundered when his armies occupied Syria and he threatened the Ottoman sultan, Mahmud II. In the face of European military might and diplomatic entreaties, Muhammad Ali agreed to peace with his Ottoman overlords and withdrew. In return he was given unprecedented hereditary rule over Egypt and Sudan. By his death in 1849, Muhammad Ali had established a strong and virtually independent Egyptian state within the Ottoman Empire.

To pay for a modern army and industrialization, Muhammad Ali encouraged the development of commercial agriculture geared to the European market, which had profound social implications. Egyptian peasants had been largely self-sufficient, growing food on state-owned land allotted to them by tradition. High-ranking officials and members of Muhammad Ali's family began carving private landholdings out of the state domain, and they forced the peasants to grow cash crops for European markets.

Muhammad Ali's modernization policies attracted growing numbers of Europeans to the banks of the Nile. Europeans served as army officers, engineers, doctors, government officials, and police officers. Others worked in trade, finance, and shipping. Above all, Europeans living in Egypt combined with landlords and officials to continue steering commercial agriculture toward exports. As throughout the Ottoman Empire, Europeans enjoyed important commercial and legal privileges and formed an economic elite.

Following in his grandfather's footsteps, Ismail (r. 1863–1879) was a westernizing autocrat. He promoted cotton production, and exports to Europe soared. Ismail also borrowed large sums, and with his support the Suez Canal was completed by a French company in 1869, shortening the voyage from Europe to Asia by thousands of miles. Cairo acquired modern boulevards and Western hotels.

Major cultural and intellectual changes accompanied the political and economic ones. The Arabic of the masses, rather than the conqueror's Turkish, became the official language, and young, European-educated Egyptians helped spread new skills and ideas in the bureaucracy. A host of writers, intellectuals, and religious thinkers responded to the novel conditions with innovative ideas that had a powerful impact in Egypt and other Muslim societies.

Three influential figures who represented broad families of thought were especially significant. The teacher and writer Jamal al-Din al-Afghani (1838/39–1897) argued for the purification of Islamic religious belief, Muslim unity, and a revolutionary overthrow of corrupt Muslim rulers and foreign exploiters. The more moderate Muhammad Abduh (1849–1905) launched the modern Islamic reform movement. Abduh concluded that Muslims should adopt a flexible, reasoned approach to change, modernity, science, social questions, and foreign ideas and not reject these out of hand.

Finally, the writer Qasim Amin (1863–1908) represented those who found inspiration in the West in the late nineteenth century. In his influential book *The Liberation of Women* (1899), Amin argued forcefully that superior education for European women had contributed greatly to the Islamic world's falling far behind the West. In his view, the rejuvenation of Muslim societies required greater equality for women.

The Suez Canal, 1869

CHAPTER LOCATOR | What were the most significant changes in Africa during the nineteenth century? | What were the causes and consequences of European empire building after 1880?

CHAPTER 25
768   AFRICA, THE OTTOMAN EMPIRE, AND THE NEW IMPERIALISM

INDIVIDUALS IN SOCIETY
Muhammad Ali

The dynamic leader Muhammad Ali stands across the history of modern Egypt like a colossus. Yet the essence of the man remains a mystery, and historians vary greatly in their interpretations of him. Sent by the Ottomans, with Albanian troops, to oppose the French occupation of Egypt in 1799, Muhammad Ali maneuvered skillfully after the French withdrawal in 1802. In 1805 he was named pasha, or Ottoman governor, of Egypt. Only the Mamluks remained as rivals. Originally an elite corps of Turkish slave soldiers, the Mamluks had become a semifeudal military ruling class living off the Egyptian peasantry. In 1811 Muhammad Ali offered to make peace, and he invited the Mamluk chiefs and their retainers to a banquet in Cairo's Citadel. As the unsuspecting guests processed through a narrow passage, his troops opened fire, slaughtering all the Mamluk leaders.

Muhammad Ali, the Albanian-born ruler of Egypt, in 1839. (© Mary Evans Picture Library/The Image Works)

After eliminating his foes, Muhammad Ali embarked on a program of radical reforms. He reorganized agriculture and commerce, reclaiming most of the cultivated land for the state domain, which he controlled. He also established state agencies to monopolize, for his own profit, the sale of agricultural goods. Commercial agriculture geared to exports to Europe developed rapidly, especially after the successful introduction of high-quality cotton in 1821. Canals and irrigation systems along the Nile were rebuilt and expanded.

Muhammad Ali used his growing revenues to recast his army along European lines. He recruited French officers to train the soldiers. As the military grew, so did the need for hospitals, schools of medicine and languages, and secular education. Young Turks and some Egyptians were sent to Europe for advanced study. The ruler boldly financed factories to produce uniforms and weapons, and he prohibited the importation of European goods so as to protect Egypt's infant industries. In the 1830s state factories were making one-fourth of Egypt's cotton into cloth. Above all, Muhammad Ali drafted Egyptian peasants into the military for the first time, thereby expanding his army to one hundred thousand men. It was this force that conquered the Ottoman province of Syria, threatened the sultan in Istanbul, and triggered European intervention. Grudgingly recognized by his Ottoman overlord as Egypt's hereditary ruler in 1841, Muhammad Ali nevertheless had to accept European and Ottoman demands to give up Syria and

abolish his monopolies and protective tariffs. The old ruler then lost heart; his reforms languished, and his factories disappeared.

In the attempt to understand Muhammad Ali and his significance, many historians have concluded that he was a national hero, the "founder of modern Egypt." His ambitious state-building projects — hospitals, schools, factories, and the army — were the basis for an Egyptian reawakening and eventual independence from the Ottomans' oppressive foreign rule. Similarly, state-sponsored industrialization promised an escape from poverty and Western domination, which was foiled only by European intervention and British insistence on free trade.

A growing minority of historians question these views. They see Muhammad Ali primarily as an Ottoman adventurer. In their view, he did not aim for national independence for Egypt, but rather "intended to carve out a small empire for himself and for his children after him."* Paradoxically, his success, which depended on heavy taxes and brutal army service, led to Egyptian nationalism among the Arabic-speaking masses, but that new nationalism was directed against Muhammad Ali and his Turkish-speaking entourage. Continuing research into this leader's life will help resolve these conflicting interpretations.

*K. Fahmy, *All the Pasha's Men: Mehmed Ali, His Army, and the Making of Modern Egypt* (Cambridge: Cambridge University Press, 1997), p. 310.

QUESTIONS FOR ANALYSIS

1. Which of Muhammad Ali's actions support the interpretation that he was the founder of modern Egypt? Which actions support the opposing view?
2. After you have studied Chapter 26, compare Muhammad Ali and the Meiji reformers in Japan. What accounts for the similarities and differences?

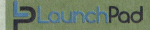

ONLINE DOCUMENT PROJECT

How did reformers address the challenges facing the Ottoman Empire in the nineteenth century? Read excerpts from Ottoman reformers, and then complete a quiz and writing assignment based on the evidence and details from this chapter. *See inside the front cover to learn more.*

Egypt changed rapidly during Ismail's rule, but his projects were reckless and enormously expensive. By 1876 the Egyptian government could not pay the interest on its debt. Rather than let Egypt go bankrupt and repudiate its loans, France and Great Britain intervened, forcing Ismail to appoint French and British commissioners to oversee Egyptian finances. This meant that Europeans would determine the state budget and in effect rule Egypt.

Foreign financial control evoked a violent nationalistic reaction. Continuing diplomatic pressure, which forced Ismail to abdicate in favor of his weak son, Tewfiq (r. 1879–1892), resulted in bloody anti-European riots in Alexandria in 1882. In response, the British fleet bombarded Alexandria, and a British expeditionary force occupied all of Egypt. British armies remained in Egypt until 1956.

Initially the British maintained the fiction that Egypt was an autonomous province of the Ottoman Empire. In reality, British consul, General Evelyn Baring, later Lord Cromer, ruled the country after 1883. Baring was a paternalistic reformer. He initiated tax reforms and made some improvements to conditions for peasants. Foreign bondholders received their interest payments, while Egyptian nationalists chafed under foreign rule.

> **QUICK REVIEW**

How did European nations undermine reform efforts in the Ottoman Empire and in Egypt?

CHAPTER LOCATOR | What were the most significant changes in Africa during the nineteenth century?   What were the causes and consequences of European empire building after 1880?

CHAPTER 25
770   AFRICA, THE OTTOMAN EMPIRE, AND THE NEW IMPERIALISM

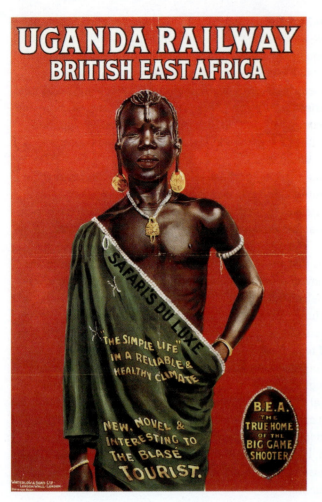

What were the global consequences of European industrialization between 1800 and 1914?

British East African Railway Poster

Europeans constructed railroads in most of their African colonies to haul raw materials from the interior to coastal ports and to transport colonial officials, white settlers, and foreign tourists. Britain's East African railroad line from Kampala, Uganda, to the Kenyan port city of Mombasa was one of the most famous and most romanticized. Indians from British India did much of the construction and then remained in Kenya to form substantial Indian communities. President Theodore Roosevelt rode this train while on his 1909 African safari. (Advertising Archive/Courtesy The Everett Collection)

OVER THE COURSE OF THE NINETEENTH CENTURY the Industrial Revolution expanded and transformed economic relations across the face of the earth. As a result, the world's total income grew as never before, and international trade boomed. Western nations used their superior military power to force non-Western nations to open their doors to Western economic interests. Consequently, the largest share of the ever-increasing gains from trade flowed to the West, resulting in a stark division between rich and poor countries.

The Rise of Global Inequality

A gap between the industrializing regions (Europe, North America, Japan) and the nonindustrializing regions (mainly Africa, Asia, and Latin America) opened and grew steadily throughout the nineteenth century (Figure 25.1). Moreover, this pattern of uneven global development became institutionalized, built into the structure of the world economy.

How did the Ottoman Empire and Egypt try to modernize themselves?

What were the global consequences of European industrialization?

What fueled migration, and what was the pattern of this movement of people?

 LearningCurve
Check what you know.

771

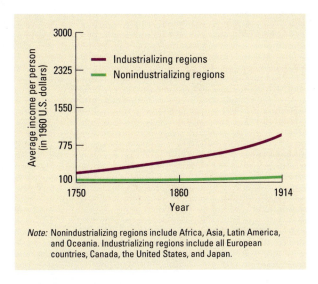

FIGURE 25.1 ■ The Growth of Average Income per Person Worldwide, 1750–1914

(Source of data: P. Bairoch and M. Lévy-Leboyer, eds., *Disparities in Economic Development Since the Industrial Revolution*, published 1981, Macmillan Publishers.)

In 1750 the average living standard was no higher in Europe as a whole than in the rest of the world. By 1914 the average person in the wealthiest countries had an income four or five times as great (and in Great Britain nine or ten times as great) as an average person's income in the poorest countries of Africa and Asia. The rise in average income and well-being reflected the rising level of industrialization in Great Britain and then in the other developed countries before World War I.

The reasons for these enormous income disparities have generated a great deal of debate. One school of interpretation stresses that the West used science, technology, capitalist organization, and even its critical worldview to create its wealth and greater physical well-being. An opposing school argues that the West used its political, economic, and military power to steal much of its riches through its rapacious colonialism in the nineteenth and twentieth centuries.

These issues are complex, and there are few simple answers. As noted in Chapter 23, the wealth-creating potential of technological improvement and more intensive capitalist organization was great. At the same time, the initial breakthroughs in the late eighteenth century rested in part on Great Britain's having already used political force to dominate a substantial part of the world economy. In the nineteenth century other industrializing countries joined with Britain to extend Western dominion over the entire world economy. Unprecedented wealth was created, but the lion's share of that new wealth flowed to the West and its propertied classes and to a tiny indigenous elite of cooperative rulers, landowners, and merchants.

The World Market

World trade was a powerful stimulus to economic development in the nineteenth century. In 1913 the value of world trade was about twenty-five times what it had been in 1800, even though prices of manufactured goods and raw materials were lower in 1913 than in 1800. In a general way, this enormous increase in international commerce summed up the growth of an interlocking world economy centered in Europe.

Great Britain played a key role in using trade to tie the world together economically. In 1815 Britain already possessed a colonial empire. The technological breakthroughs of the Industrial Revolution encouraged British manufacturers to seek export markets around the world. After Parliament repealed laws restricting grain importation in 1846, Britain also became the world's leading importer of foreign goods. Free access to Britain's market stimulated the development of mines and plantations in Africa and Asia.

The conquest of distance facilitated the growth of trade. Wherever railroads were built, they drastically reduced transportation costs, opened new economic opportunities, and called forth new skills and attitudes. Much of the railroad construction undertaken in Africa, Asia, and Latin America connected seaports with inland cities and regions, as opposed to linking and developing cities and regions

CHAPTER LOCATOR | What were the most significant changes in Africa during the nineteenth century?

What were the causes and consequences of European empire building after 1880?

CHAPTER 25

772   AFRICA, THE OTTOMAN EMPIRE, AND THE NEW IMPERIALISM

within a country. Thus railroads dovetailed with Western economic interests, facilitating the inflow and sale of Western manufactured goods and the export and development of local raw materials.

Steam power also revolutionized transportation by sea. Steam power was first used to supplant sails on the world's oceans in the late 1860s. Passenger and freight rates tumbled, and the shipment of low-priced raw materials from one continent to another became feasible.

The revolution in land and sea transportation helped European settlers seize vast, thinly populated territories and produce agricultural products and raw materials for sale in Europe. Improved transportation enabled Asia, Africa, and Latin America to export agricultural commodities and industrial raw materials.

Intercontinental trade was enormously facilitated by the Suez Canal and the Panama Canal (see page 839). Of great importance, too, was large and continual investment in modern port facilities. Finally, transoceanic telegraph cables inaugurated rapid communications among the world's financial centers and linked world commodity prices in a global network.

The growth of trade and the conquest of distance encouraged Europeans to make massive foreign investments beginning about 1840, but not to European colonies or protectorates in Asia and Africa. About three-quarters of total European investment went to other European countries, the United States and Canada, Australia and New Zealand, and Latin America. Much of this investment was peaceful and mutually beneficial for lenders and borrowers. The victims were Native Americans, Australian Aborigines, New Zealand Maoris, and other native peoples who were displaced and decimated by an aggressively expanding Western society (see Chapter 27).

QUICK REVIEW

What role did technology play in late nineteenth-century globalization?

How did the Ottoman Empire and Egypt try to modernize themselves?

What were the global consequences of European industrialization?

What fueled migration, and what was the pattern of this movement of people?

LearningCurve
Check what you know.

What fueled migration, and what was the general pattern of this unprecedented movement of people?

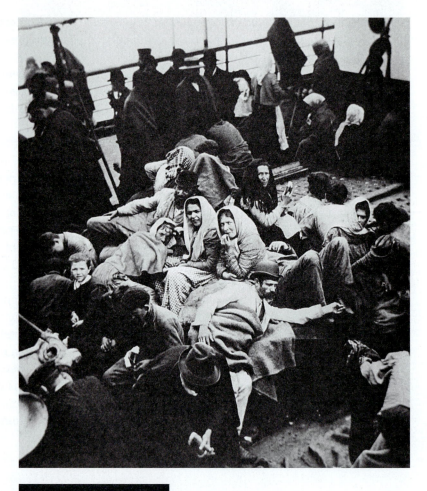

Steerage Passengers, 1902

Conditions for steerage passengers traveling from Europe to the Americas were cramped, as evidenced by this photo from 1902.
(Private Collection/Peter Newark American Pictures/The Bridgeman Art Library)

great migration

▶ The mass movement of people from Europe in the nineteenth century, one reason that the West's impact on the world was so powerful and complex.

A POIGNANT HUMAN DRAMA WAS INTERWOVEN with this worldwide economic expansion: millions of people left their ancestral lands in one of history's greatest migrations, the so-called **great migration**. In the early eighteenth century the world's population entered a period of rapid growth that continued unabated through the nineteenth and twentieth centuries. Europe's population (including Asiatic Russia) more than doubled during the nineteenth century. Since African and Asian populations increased more slowly than those in Europe, Europeans and peoples of predominantly European origin jumped from about 22 percent of the world's total in 1850 to a high of about 38 percent in 1930.

CHAPTER LOCATOR | What were the most significant changes in Africa during the nineteenth century? | What were the causes and consequences of European empire building after 1880?

Rapid population growth led to relative overpopulation in area after area in Europe and was a driving force behind emigration and Western expansion. Millions of country folk moved to nearby cities, and the more adventuresome went abroad, in search of work and economic opportunity. Wars, famine, poverty, and, particularly in the case of Russian and eastern European Jews, bigotry and discrimination were also leading causes for emigrants to leave their ancestral homelands. More than 60 million people left Europe over the course of the nineteenth century, primarily for the rapidly growing "areas of European settlement" — North and South America, Australia, New Zealand, and Siberia (see Chapter 27).

The European migrant was most often a small peasant landowner or a village craftsman whose traditional way of life was threatened by too little land, estate agriculture, and cheap factory-made goods. Determined to maintain or improve their precarious status, the vast majority of migrants were young and often unmarried. Many European migrants returned home after some time abroad.

Ties of family and friendship played a crucial role in the movement of peoples. Over several years a given province or village might lose significant numbers of its inhabitants to migration. These then settled together in rural enclaves or tightly knit urban neighborhoods in foreign lands thousands of miles away. Very often a strong individual—a businessman, a religious leader—blazed the way, and others followed, forming a **migration chain**.

A substantial number of Asians—especially Chinese, Japanese, Indians, and Filipinos—also responded to population pressure and rural hardship with temporary or permanent migration. At least 3 million Asians moved abroad before 1920. Most went as indentured laborers to work on the plantations or in the gold mines of Latin America, southern Asia, Africa, California, Hawaii, and Australia (see Chapter 26). White estate owners often used Asians to replace or supplement black Africans after the suppression of the Atlantic slave trade.

Asian migration would undoubtedly have been much greater if planters and mine owners desiring cheap labor had had their way. But usually they did not. Asians fled the plantations and gold mines as soon as possible, seeking greater opportunities in trade and towns. Here, however, they came into conflict with white settlers, who demanded a halt to Asian immigration. By the 1880s Americans and Australians were building **great white walls**—discriminatory laws designed to keep Asians out.

The general policy of "whites only" in the lands of large-scale European settlement meant that Europeans and people of European ancestry reaped the main benefits of the great migration. By 1913 people in Australia, Canada, and the United States all had higher average incomes than did people in Great Britain, still Europe's wealthiest nation. This, too, contributed to Western dominance in the increasingly lopsided world.

Within Asia and Africa the situation was different. Migrants from south China frequently settled in Dutch, British, and French colonies of Southeast Asia, where they established themselves as peddlers and small shopkeepers (see Chapter 26). These "overseas Chinese" gradually emerged as a new class of entrepreneurs and office workers. Traders from India and modern-day Lebanon performed the same function in much of sub-Saharan Africa after European colonization in the

migration chain
▶ The movement of peoples in which one strong individual blazes the way and others follow.

great white walls
▶ Discriminatory laws built by Americans and Australians to keep Asians from settling in their countries in the 1880s.

How did the Ottoman Empire and Egypt try to modernize themselves?   What were the global consequences of European industrialization?   **What fueled migration, and what was the pattern of this movement of people?**   ☑ LearningCurve Check what you know.

775

late nineteenth century. Thus in some parts of Asia and Africa the business class was both Asian and foreign, protected and tolerated by Western imperialists who found these business people useful.

> **QUICK REVIEW**

Why did so many Europeans leave their homelands and settle overseas in the late nineteenth and early twentieth centuries?

CHAPTER SUMMARY

Following Europe's Industrial Revolution in the late eighteenth and early nineteenth centuries, European demands for raw materials and new markets reoriented Africa's economy. The transatlantic slave trade declined dramatically as Africans began producing commodities for export. This legitimate trade in African goods proved profitable and led to the emergence of a small black middle class. Islam revived and expanded until about 1870.

After 1880 a handful of Western nations seized most of Africa and parts of Asia and rushed to build authoritarian empires. The reasons for this empire building included trade rivalries, competitive nationalism in Europe, and self-justifying claims of a civilizing mission.

The Ottoman Empire and Egypt prepared to become modern nation-states in the twentieth century by introducing reforms to improve the military, provide technical and secular education, and expand personal liberties. They failed, however, to defend themselves from Western imperialism. The Ottoman Empire lost territory but survived in a weakened condition. Egypt's Muhammad Ali reformed the government and promoted modern industry, but Egypt went bankrupt and was conquered and ruled by Britain.

Population pressures at home and economic opportunities abroad caused millions of European emigrants to resettle in the sparsely populated areas of European settlement in North and South America, Australia, and Asiatic Russia. Migration from Asia was much more limited, mainly because European settlers raised high barriers to prevent the settlement of Asian immigrants.

CHAPTER LOCATOR | What were the most significant changes in Africa during the nineteenth century? | What were the causes and consequences of European empire building after 1880?

776 CHAPTER 25
AFRICA, THE OTTOMAN EMPIRE, AND THE NEW IMPERIALISM

 **CONNECTIONS** By the end of the nineteenth century broader industrialization across Europe increased the need for raw materials and markets, and with it came a rush to create or enlarge vast political empires abroad. The new imperialism was aimed primarily at Africa and Asia, and in the years before 1914 the leading European nations not only created empires abroad, but also continued to send massive streams of migrants, money, and manufactured goods around the world. (The impact of this unprecedented migration is taken up in the next two chapters.)

European influence also grew in the Middle East. Threatened by European military might, modernization, and Christianity, Turks and Arabs tried to implement reforms that would assure their survival and independence but also endeavored to retain key aspects of their cultures, particularly Islam. Although they made important advances in the modernization of their economies and societies, their efforts were not enough to overcome Western imperialism. With the end of World War I and the collapse of the Ottoman Empire, England and France divided much of the Middle East into colonies and established loyal surrogates as rulers in other, nominally independent, countries. Chapter 29 will take up the story of these developments.

As European imperialism was dividing the world after the 1880s, the leading European states were also dividing themselves into two opposing military alliances. As Chapter 28 will show, when the two armed camps stumbled into war in 1914, the results were disastrous. World War I set the stage for a new anti-imperialist struggle in Africa and Asia for equality and genuine independence (see Chapters 32 and 33).

ONLINE DOCUMENT PROJECT

Reform Movements in the Late Ottoman Empire

How did reformers address the challenges facing the Ottoman Empire in the nineteenth century?

Read excerpts from Ottoman reformers, and then complete a quiz and writing assignment based on the evidence and details from this chapter. *See inside the front cover to learn more.*

How did the Ottoman Empire and Egypt try to modernize themselves?

What were the global consequences of European industrialization?

What fueled migration, and what was the pattern of this movement of people?

LearningCurve Check what you know.

CHAPTER 25 STUDY GUIDE

STEP 1

GET STARTED ONLINE

 **LearningCurve**

Now that you've read the chapter, make it stick by completing the LearningCurve activity.

STEP 2

EXPLAIN WHY IT MATTERS

Put your reading into practice. Identify each term below, and then explain why it matters in world history.

TERM	WHO OR WHAT & WHEN	WHY IT MATTERS
palm oil (p. 750)		
jihad (p. 753)		
Sokoto caliphate (p. 753)		
Berlin Conference (p. 754)		
protectorate (p. 754)		
Afrikaners (p. 756)		
new imperialism (p. 761)		
quinine (p. 761)		
white man's burden (p. 762)		
Tanzimat (p. 766)		
Young Turks (p. 767)		
great migration (p. 774)		
migration chain (p. 775)		
great white walls (p. 775)		

STEP 3

MOVE BEYOND THE BASICS

To demonstrate a more advanced understanding of the "New Imperialism" of the late nineteenth century, fill in the chart below with descriptions of the causes, motives, and characteristics of Western expansion before and after 1880. How did the nature of Western domination change after 1880? How would you explain the changes you note?

	Causes and Motives	Key Characteristics
Western Expansion Before 1880		
Western Expansion After 1880		

STEP 4 — PUT IT ALL TOGETHER

Now, take a step back and try to explain the big picture. Remember to use specific examples from the chapter in your answers.

THE NEW IMPERIALISM

▶ How did Western pressure shape African development before 1880? How about after 1880?

▶ How did Westerners justify imperialism? How did Western critics of imperialism challenge such justifications?

MODERNIZATION AND REFORM IN THE ISLAMIC HEARTLAND

▶ How did Ottoman and Egyptian leaders use Western ideas and culture to resist Western domination?

▶ Should the modernization efforts of the Ottomans and Egyptian be deemed "failures"? Why or why not?

GLOBALIZATION, INDUSTRIALIZATION, AND MIGRATION

▶ Who benefitted the most from the economic growth and globalization of the nineteenth century? Why?

▶ Compare and contrast European and Asian migration during the nineteenth century. What important differences do you note? What common factors help explain the movements of both groups of migrants?

LOOKING BACK, LOOKING AHEAD

▶ What place did Europe have in the world economy in 1750? What about 1900? How would you explain the differences you note?

▶ What connections might one make between nineteenth-century European imperialism and the disastrous wars that befell Europe if the first half of the twentieth century?

> IN YOUR OWN WORDS

Imagine that you must give an oral report to the class answering the following question: **How and why did Western nations strive for global dominance over the course of the nineteenth century?** What would be the most important points and why?

26

ASIA AND THE PACIFIC IN THE ERA OF IMPERIALISM

1800–1914

> **> How did Asian leaders respond to the challenges posed by Western imperialism?**

Chapter 26 examines the impact of nineteenth-century Western imperialism on Asia. At the beginning of the century Spain, the Netherlands, and Britain had colonies in the Philippines, modern Indonesia, and India, respectively. By the end of the century most of the southern tier of Asia, from India to the Philippines, had been colonized. Not all the countries in Asia were reduced to colonies. Although Western powers put enormous pressures on China, it remained politically independent. Much more impressively, Japan became the first non-Western nation to meet successfully the many-sided challenge of Western expansion. By the end of this period Japan had become an industrialized, imperialist power itself.

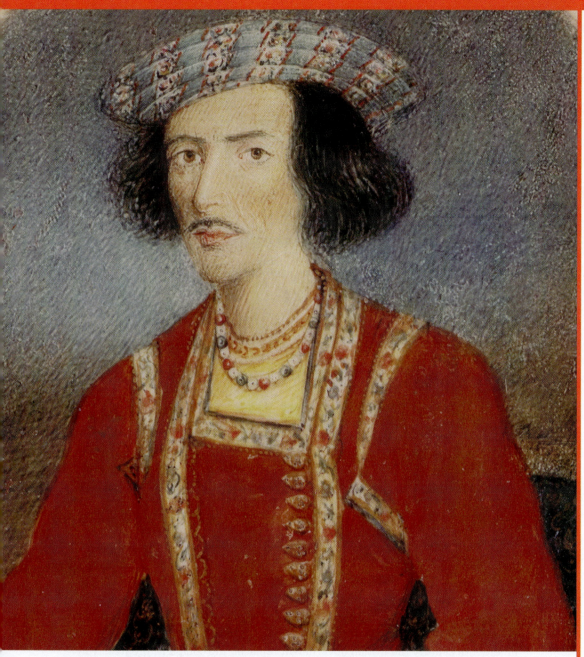

Rammohun Roy The expansion of British power in India posed intellectual and cultural challenges to the native elite. Among those who rose to this challenge was writer and reformer Rammohun Roy, depicted here. (V&A Images, London, UK/Art Resource, NY)

> In what ways did India change as a consequence of British rule?

> Why were most but not all Southeast Asian societies reduced to colonies?

> Was China's decline in the nineteenth century due more to internal problems or to Western imperialism?

> How was Japan able to quickly master the challenges posed by the West?

> What were the causes and consequences of the vast movement of people in the Pacific region?

> What explains the similarities and differences in the experiences of Asian countries in this era?

LearningCurve
After reading the chapter, use LearningCurve to retain what you've read.

In what ways did India change as a consequence of British rule?

British and Sikh Leaders at Lahore

The Sikh kingdom in the Punjab fell to the British in a brief war in 1845–1846. This painting depicts the British and Sikh representatives who negotiated the resulting treaty, which gave Britain control of the region. (© The Trustees of the British Museum/Art Resource, NY)

ARRIVING IN INDIA IN THE SEVENTEENTH CENTURY, the British East India Company outmaneuvered French and Dutch rivals and was there to pick up the pieces as the Mughal Empire decayed during the eighteenth century (see pages 506–508). By 1757 the company had gained control over much of India. During the nineteenth century the British government replaced the company, progressively unified the subcontinent, and harnessed its economy to British interests.

The Evolution of British Rule

In India the British ruled with the cooperation of local princely allies, whom they could not afford to offend. To assert their authority, the British disbanded and disarmed local armies, introduced simpler private property laws, and enhanced the powers of local princes and religious leaders, both Hindu and Muslim. The British administrators were on the whole competent and concerned about the welfare of the Indian peasants. Slavery was outlawed and banditry suppressed, and new laws designed to improve women's position in society were introduced.

CHAPTER LOCATOR | **In what ways did India change as a consequence of British rule?** | Why were most but not all Southeast Asian societies reduced to colonies?

782 CHAPTER 26
ASIA AND THE PACIFIC IN THE ERA OF IMPERIALISM

1825 King Minh Mang outlaws teaching of Christianity in Vietnam	**1869** Suez Canal opens
1830 Dutch institute Culture System in Indonesia	**1872** Universal public schools established in Japan
1839–1842 Opium War	**1885** Foundation of Indian National Congress
1851–1864 Taiping Rebellion in China	**1894–1895** Japan defeats China in Sino-Japanese War and gains control of Taiwan
1853 Commodore Perry opens Japanese ports to foreign trade	**1898** United States takes control of Philippines from Spain
1857 Great Mutiny / Great Revolt by Indian sepoys against British rule	**1900** Boxer Rebellion in China
1858 British Parliament begins to rule India	**1904** Japan attacks Russia and starts Russo-Japanese War
1859–1885 Vietnam becomes a colony of France	**1910** Korea becomes a province of Japan
1867 Meiji Restoration in Japan	**1912** China's monarchy is replaced by a republic

The last armed resistance to British rule occurred in 1857. By that date the British military presence in India had grown to include two hundred thousand Indian sepoy troops and thirty-eight thousand British officers. In 1857 groups of sepoys, especially around Delhi, revolted in what the British called the **Great Mutiny** and the Indians called the **Great Revolt**. The sepoys' grievances were many, ranging from the use of fat from cows (sacred to Hindus) and pigs (regarded as filthy by Muslims) to grease rifle cartridges to high tax rates and the incorporation of low-caste soldiers into the army. The insurrection spread rapidly throughout northern and central India before it was finally crushed. Thereafter, although princely states were allowed to continue, Britain ruled India much more tightly. Moreover, the British in India acted more like an occupying power and mixed less with the Indian elite.

After 1858 India was ruled by the British Parliament in London and administered by a civil service in India, the upper echelons of which were all white. In 1900 this elite consisted of fewer than 3,500 top officials for a population of 300 million.

The Socioeconomic Effects of British Rule

The impact of British rule on the Indian economy was multifaceted. In the early stages, the British East India Company expanded agricultural production, creating large plantations. Early crops were opium to export to China (see page 791) and

Great Mutiny / Great Revolt

▶ The terms used by the British and the Indians, respectively, to describe the last armed resistance to British rule in India, which occurred in 1857.

The Great Revolt / Great Mutiny, 1857

Was China's decline due more to internal problems or to Western imperialism?	How was Japan able to quickly master the challenges posed by the West?	What were the causes and consequences of the vast movement of people in the Pacific region?	What explains the similarities and differences between Asian countries in this era?	✓ **LearningCurve** Check what you know.

tea to substitute for imports from China. India gradually replaced China as the leading exporter of tea to Europe. Clearing land for tea and coffee plantations, along with massive commercial logging operations, led to extensive deforestation.

To aid the transport of goods, people, and information, the colonial administration invested heavily in India's infrastructure. By 1855 India's major cities had all been linked by telegraph and railroads, and postal service was being extended to local villages. Irrigation also received attention, and by 1900 India had the world's most extensive irrigation system.

At the same time, Indian production of textiles suffered a huge blow. Britain imported India's raw cotton but exported machine-spun yarn and machine-woven cloth, displacing millions of Indian hand-spinners and hand-weavers. By 1900 India was buying 40 percent of Britain's cotton exports. Not until 1900 were small steps taken toward industrializing India.

Although the economy expanded, the poor did not see much improvement in their standard of living. Tenant farming and landlessness increased with the growth in plantation agriculture. Increases in production were eaten up by increases in population. There was also a negative side to improved transportation. As Indians traveled more widely on the convenient trains, disease spread, especially cholera, which is transmitted by exposure to contaminated water.

The British and the Indian Educated Elite

The Indian middle class probably gained more than the poor from British rule, because they were the ones to benefit from the English-language educational system Britain established in India. Missionaries also established schools with Western curricula High-caste Hindus came to form a new elite profoundly influenced by Western thought and culture.

By creating a well-educated, English-speaking Indian elite and a bureaucracy aided by a modern communication system, the British laid the groundwork for a unified, powerful state. Britain placed under the same general system of law and administration the various Hindu and Muslim peoples of the subcontinent who had resisted one another for centuries. University graduates tended to look on themselves as Indians more than as residents of separate states and kingdoms, a necessary step for the development of Indian nationalism.

CHAPTER LOCATOR | **In what ways did India change as a consequence of British rule?** | Why were most but not all Southeast Asian societies reduced to colonies?

Some Indian intellectuals sought to reconcile the values of the modern West and their own traditions. Rammohun Roy (1772–1833) founded a college that offered instruction in Western languages and subjects. He also founded a society to reform traditional customs, especially child marriage, the caste system, and restrictions on widows. He espoused a modern Hinduism founded on the *Upani-shads* (oo-PAH-nih-shadz), the ancient sacred texts of Hinduism.

The more that Western-style education was developed in India, the more the inequalities of the system became apparent to educated Indians. Indians were eligible to take the examinations for entry into the elite **Indian Civil Service**, the bureaucracy that administered the Indian government, but the exams were given in England. Since few Indians could travel such a long distance to take the test, in 1870 only 1 of the 916 members of the service was Indian. In other words, no matter how Anglicized educated Indians became, they could never become the white rulers' equals. The top jobs, the best clubs, the modern hotels, and even certain railroad compartments were sealed off to brown-skinned men and women. Most of the British elite considered all Indians to be racially inferior.

The peasant masses might accept such inequality as the latest version of age-old class and caste hierarchies, but the well-educated, English-speaking elite eventually could not. They had studied not only Milton and Shakespeare but also English traditions of democracy, liberty, and national pride.

In the late nineteenth century the colonial ports of Calcutta, Bombay, and Madras, now all linked by railroads, became centers of intellectual ferment. In these and other cities, newspapers in English and in regional languages gained influence. Lawyers trained in English law began agitating for Indian independence. By 1885, when a group of educated Indians came together to found the **Indian National Congress**, demands were increasing for equality and self-government. The Congress Party called for more opportunities for Indians in the Indian Civil Service and reallocation of the government budget from military expenditures to the alleviation of poverty. The party advocated unity across religious and caste lines, but most members were upper-caste, Western-educated Hindus.

Defending British possessions in India became a key element of Britain's foreign policy during the nineteenth century and led to steady expansion of the territory Britain controlled in Asia. By 1852, the British had annexed all of the kingdom of Burma, administering it as a province of India. The establishment of a British base in Singapore was followed by expansion into Malaya (now Malaysia) in the 1870s and 1880s. In both Burma and Malaya, Britain tried to foster economic development, building railroads and promoting trade. Burma became a major exporter of timber and rice, Malaya of tin and rubber. So many laborers were brought into Malaya for the expanding mines and plantations that its population came to be approximately one-third Malay, one-third Chinese, and one-third Indian.

Indian Civil Service
▶ The bureaucracy that administered the government of India. Entry into its elite ranks was through examinations that Indians were eligible to take, but these tests were offered only in England.

Indian National Congress
▶ A political association formed in 1885 that worked for Indian self-government.

QUICK REVIEW

Why did opposition to British rule among Indian elites increase in the late nineteenth century?

| Was China's decline due more to internal problems or to Western imperialism? | How was Japan able to quickly master the challenges posed by the West? | What were the causes and consequences of the vast movement of people in the Pacific region? | What explains the similarities and differences between Asian countries in this era? | ✓ LearningCurve Check what you know. |

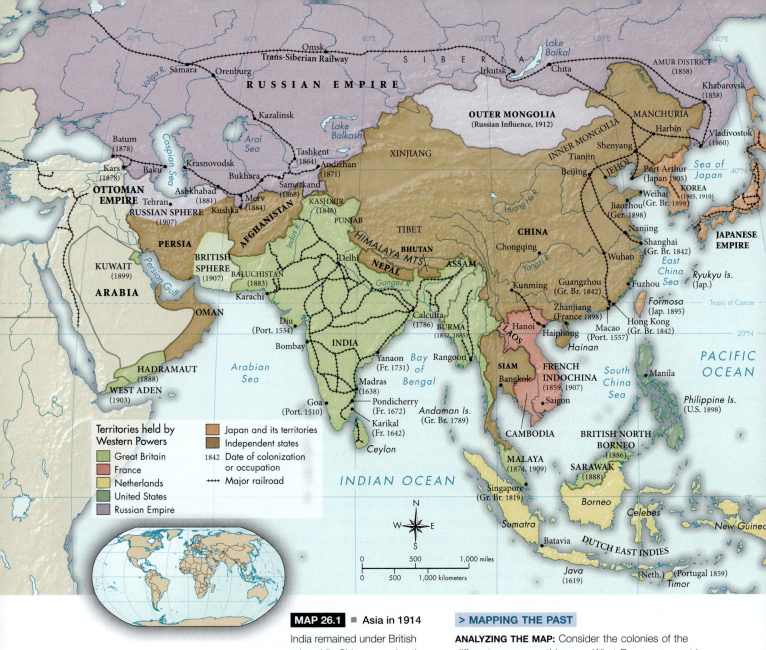

Territories held by
Western Powers

- Great Britain
- France
- Netherlands
- United States
- Russian Empire
- Japan and its territories
- Independent states

1842 Date of colonization or occupation
++++ Major railroad

MAP 26.1 ■ Asia in 1914

India remained under British rule, while China precariously preserved its political independence. The Dutch Empire in modern-day Indonesia was old, but French control of Indochina was a product of the new imperialism.

> MAPPING THE PAST

ANALYZING THE MAP: Consider the colonies of the different powers on this map. What European countries were leading imperialist states, and what lands did they hold? Can you see places where colonial powers were likely to come into conflict with each other?

CONNECTIONS: Do the sizes of the various colonial territories as seen on this map adequately reflect their importance to the countries that possessed them? If not, what else should be taken into account in thinking about the value of these sorts of colonial possessions?

CHAPTER LOCATOR | In what ways did India change as a consequence of British rule?

Why were most but not all Southeast Asian societies reduced to colonies?

786

CHAPTER 26
ASIA AND THE PACIFIC IN THE ERA OF IMPERIALISM

The Philippir

The United States bec
Philippines from Spain
colonize the Philippine
who had served the C
right to control public
pines. A local Filipino
private ownership of l
galleon trade between
Chinese community, w

In the late ninetee
study abroad, and a m
who had been abroad.
erupted in 1896. (See

In 1898 war betwe
838), and in May the A
into Manila Bay and sa
Filipino rebels to help
independence, the U.S
the Filipino rebels, and
the lives of five thousa
In the following years
included public works
and medicine, and, in

The French Governor General and the Vietnamese Emperor

The twelfth emperor of the Nguyen Dynasty, Khai Dinh (1885–1925),
had to find ways to get along with the French governor general (in this
picture, Albert Sarraut) if he wished to preserve his dynasty. Seen here
in 1917 or 1918, he had adopted Western leather shoes but otherwise
tried to keep a distinct Vietnamese identity in his dress. (© Maurice-Louis
Branger/Roger-Viollet/Getty Images)

Why were most but not all Southeast Asian societies reduced to colonies?

AT THE BEGINNING OF THE NINETEENTH CENTURY only a small part of Southeast Asia was under direct European control. By the end of the century most of
the region would be in foreign hands.

The Dutch East Indies

Although Dutch forts and trading posts in the East Indies dated back to the seventeenth century, in 1816 the Dutch ruled little more than the island of Java.
Thereafter they gradually brought almost all of the 3,000-mile-long archipelago
under their political authority. In extending their rule, the Dutch, like the British
in India, brought diverse peoples with different languages and distinct cultural
traditions into a single political entity (see Map 26.1).

Taking over the Dutch East India Company in 1799, the Dutch government
modified the company's loose control of Java and gradually built a modern

Was China's decline
due more to internal
problems or to Western
imperialism?

Was China's decline
due more to internal
problems or to Western
imperialism?

How was Japan able
to quickly master the
challenges posed by the
West?

What were the causes
and consequences of the
vast movement of people
in the Pacific region?

What explains the
similarities and differences
between Asian countries
in this era?

✓ LearningCurve
Check what you know.

787

Java War
► The 1825–1830 war bet[ween] the Dutch government an[d] the Javanese, fought over [the] extension of Dutch contro[l over] the island.

Nguyen Dynasty
► The last Vietnamese rulin[g] house, which lasted from 1[...] to 1945.

In the mid-seventeenth century a Chinese merchant immigrated to the Philippines and married a woman who was half Chinese, half Filipino. Because of anti-Chinese animosity, he changed his name to Mercado, Spanish for "merchant."

Mercado's direct patrilineal descendant, José Rizal (1861–1896), was born into a well-to-do family that leased a plantation from Dominican friars. Both of his parents were educated, and he was a brilliant student himself. In 1882, after completing his studies at the Jesuit-run college in Manila, he went to Madrid to study medicine. During his ten years in Europe he not only earned a medical degree in Spain and a Ph.D. in Germany but he also found time to learn several European languages and make friends with scientists, writers, and political radicals.

While in Europe, Rizal became involved with Filipino revolutionaries and contributed numerous articles to their newspaper, *La Solidaridad*, published in Barcelona. Rizal advocated making the Philippines a province of Spain, giving it representation in the Spanish parliament, replacing Spanish friars with Filipino priests, and making Filipinos and Spaniards equal before the law. He spent a year at the British Museum doing research on the early phase of the Spanish colonization of the Philippines. He also wrote two novels.

The first novel, written in Spanish, was fired by the passions of nationalism. In satirical fashion, it depicts a young Filipino of mixed blood who studies for several years in Europe before returning to the Philippines to start a modern secular school in his hometown and to marry his childhood sweetheart. The church stands in the way of his efforts, and the colonial administration proves incompetent. The novel ends with the hero being gunned down after the friars falsely implicate him in a revolutionary conspiracy. Rizal's own life ended up following this narrative surprisingly closely.

In 1892 Rizal left Europe, stopped briefly in Hong Kong, and then returned to Manila to help his family with a lawsuit. Though he secured his relatives' release from jail, he ran into trouble himself.

José Rizal. (Courtesy of the Library of Congress, LC-USZ62-43453)

Because his writings were critical of the power of the church, he made many enemies, some of whom had him arrested. He was sent into exile to a Jesuit mission town on the relatively primitive island of Mindanao. There he founded a school and a hospital, and the Jesuits tried to win him back to the church. He kept busy during his four years in exile, not only teaching English, science, and self-defense, but also maintaining his correspondence with scientists in Europe. When a nationalist secret society rose in revolt in 1896, Rizal, in an effort to distance himself, volunteered to go to Cuba to help in an outbreak of yellow fever. Although he had no connections with the secret society and was on his way across the ocean, Rizal was arrested and shipped back to Manila.

Tried for sedition by the military, Rizal was found guilty. When handed his death certificate, Rizal struck out the words "Chinese half-breed" and wrote "pure native." He was publicly executed by a firing squad in Manila at age thirty-five, making him a martyr of the nationalist cause.

QUESTIONS FOR ANALYSIS

1. How did Rizal's comfortable family background contribute to his becoming a revolutionary?
2. How would Rizal's European contemporaries have reacted to his opposition to the Catholic Church?

▷ LaunchPad

ONLINE DOCUMENT PROJECT

How did Filipinos and Americans respond to Spanish and American imperialism? Examine documents about the Philippines during the Spanish-American war, and then complete a quiz and writing assignment based on the evidence and details from this chapter. *See inside the front cover to learn more.*

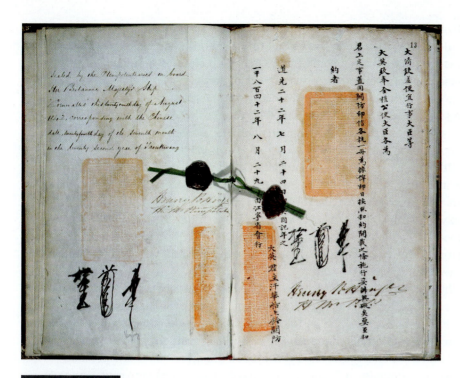

Treaty of Nanjing

The settlement reached by Britain and China in 1842 was written in both English and Chinese. The chief negotiators of both sides signed the document, and the seals of both countries were placed on it. The Chinese seal was impressed with red ink in the traditional way, while the British used wax. (© Mary Evans Picture Library/National Archives, UK/The Image Works)

Was China's decline in the nineteenth century due more to internal problems or to Western imperialism?

IN 1800 MOST CHINESE HAD NO REASON to question the concept of China as the central kingdom. A century later China's world standing had sunk precipitously. In 1900 foreign troops marched into China's capital to protect foreign nationals, and more and more Chinese had come to think that their government, society, and cultural values needed to be radically changed.

The Opium War

Seeing little to gain from trade with European countries, the Qing (Manchu) emperors, who had been ruling China since 1644 (see pages 620–622), permitted Europeans to trade only at the port of Guangzhou (Canton) and only through licensed Chinese merchants. Initially, the balance of trade was in China's favor. Great Britain and the other Western nations used silver to pay for tea, because they had not been able to find anything the Chinese wanted to buy. By the 1820s, however, the British had found something the Chinese would buy: opium. Grown

| Was China's decline due more to internal problems or to Western imperialism? | How was Japan able to quickly master the challenges posed by the West? | What were the causes and consequences of the vast movement of people in the Pacific region? | What explains the similarities and differences between Asian countries in this era? | ✓ LearningCurve Check what you know. |

791

legally in British-occupied India, opium was smuggled into China, where its use and sale were illegal. Huge profits and the cravings of addicts led to rapid increases in sales. At this point it was China that suffered a drain of silver because it was importing more than it was exporting.

To deal with this crisis, the Chinese government dispatched Lin Zexu to Guangzhou in 1839. He dealt harshly with Chinese who purchased opium and seized the opium stores of British merchants. Lin even wrote to Queen Victoria, calling on her to intervene.

Although for years foreign merchants had accepted Chinese rules, by 1839 the British, the dominant group, were ready to flex their muscles. British merchants wanted to create a market for their goods in China and get tea more cheaply by trading closer to its source in central China. They also wanted a European-style diplomatic relationship with China. With the encouragement of their merchants in China, the British sent an expeditionary force from India with forty-two warships.

With its control of the seas, the British easily shut down key Chinese ports and forced the Chinese to negotiate. Dissatisfied with the resulting agreement, the British sent a second, larger force, which took even more coastal cities. This **Opium War** was settled at gunpoint in 1842. The resulting treaties opened five ports to international trade, fixed the tariff on imported goods at 5 percent, imposed an indemnity of 21 million ounces of silver on China to cover Britain's war expenses, and ceded the island of Hong Kong to Britain. Through the clause on **extraterritoriality**, British subjects in China became answerable only to British law, even in disputes with Chinese. The treaties also had a "most-favored nation" clause, which meant that whenever one nation extracted a new privilege from China, it was extended automatically to Britain.

The treaties satisfied neither side. China continued to refuse to accept foreign diplomats at its capital in Beijing, and the expansion of trade fell far short of Western expectations. Between 1856 and 1860 Britain and France renewed hostilities with China. British and French troops occupied Beijing and set the emperor's summer palace on fire. Another round of harsh treaties gave European merchants and missionaries greater privileges and forced the Chinese to open several more cities to foreign trade.

Internal Problems

China's problems in the nineteenth century were not all of foreign origin. By 1850 China had a population of more than 400 million. As the population grew, farm size shrank, surplus labor suppressed wages, and conflicts over rights to water and tenancy increased. Hard times also led to increased female infanticide, as families felt that they could not afford to raise more than two or three children and saw sons as necessities.

These economic and demographic circumstances led to some of the most destructive rebellions in China's history. The worst was the **Taiping Rebellion** (1851–1864), in which some 20 million people lost their lives.

The Taiping (TIGH-ping) Rebellion was initiated by Hong Xiuquan (hong show-chwan) (1814–1864). Hong believed he was Jesus's younger brother and that he had a mission to wipe out evil in China. He soon gathered followers, whom he instructed to destroy idols and ancestral temples, give up opium and alcohol,

Opium War

▶ The 1839–1842 war between the British and the Chinese over limitations on trade and the importation of opium into China.

extraterritoriality

▶ The legal principle that exempts individuals from local law, applicable in China because of the agreements reached after China's loss in the Opium War.

Taiping Rebellion

▶ A massive rebellion by believers in the religious teachings of Hong Xiuquan, begun in 1851 and not suppressed until 1864.

CHAPTER LOCATOR | In what ways did India change as a consequence of British rule? | Why were most but not all Southeast Asian societies reduced to colonies?

792 CHAPTER 26 ASIA AND THE PACIFIC IN THE ERA OF IMPERIALISM

and renounce foot binding and prostitution. In 1851 he declared himself king of the Heavenly Kingdom of Great Peace (Taiping), an act of open insurrection.

By 1853 the Taiping rebels, as Hong's followers were known, had moved north and established their capital at the major city of Nanjing, which they held onto for a decade. There, they set about creating a utopian society based on the equalization of landholdings and the equality of men and women. To suppress the Taipings, the Manchus had to turn to Chinese scholar-officials, who raised armies on their own, revealing the Manchus' military weakness.

The Self-Strengthening Movement

After the various rebellions were suppressed, forward-looking reformers began addressing the Western threat. Under the slogan "self-strengthening," they set about modernizing the military along Western lines. Some of the most progressive reformers also initiated new industries, which in the 1870s and 1880s included railway lines, steam navigation companies, coal mines, telegraph lines, and cotton spinning and weaving factories.

Despite the enormous effort put into trying to catch up, China was humiliated yet again at the end of the nineteenth century. First came the discovery that Japan had so successfully modernized that it posed a threat to China. Then in 1894 Japanese efforts to separate Korea from Chinese influence led to the brief Sino-Japanese War in which China was decisively defeated. China's helplessness in the face of aggression led to a scramble among the European powers for

Chinese Rebellions, 1851–1911

Taiping Rebellion, 1851–1864
Boxer uprising, 1900
Revolt of 1911

China's First Railroad

Soon after this 15-mile-long railroad was constructed near Shanghai in 1876 by the British firm of Jardine, Matheson, and Company, the provincial governor bought it in order to tear it out. Many Chinese of the period saw the introduction of railroads as harmful not only to the balance of nature but also to people's livelihoods, because the railroads eliminated jobs in transport like dragging boats along canals or driving pack horses. (Private Collection/Visual Connection Archive)

Was China's decline due more to internal problems or to Western imperialism?

How was Japan able to quickly master the challenges posed by the West?

What were the causes and consequences of the vast movement of people in the Pacific region?

What explains the similarities and differences between Asian countries in this era?

✓ LearningCurve
Check what you know.

concessions and protectorates in China. At the high point of this rush in 1898, it appeared that the European powers might actually divide China among themselves, the way they had recently divided Africa.

Republican Revolution

China's humiliating defeat in the Sino-Japanese War in 1895 led to a renewed drive for reform. In 1898 a group of educated young reformers gained the support of the twenty-seven-year-old Qing emperor. They proposed redesigning China as a constitutional monarchy with modern financial and educational systems. For three months the emperor issued a series of reform decrees. But the Manchu establishment and the empress dowager felt threatened and not only suppressed the reform movement but imprisoned the emperor as well. Hope for reform from the top was dashed.

A period of violent reaction swept the country, reaching its peak in 1900 with the uprising of a secret society that foreigners dubbed the **Boxers**. The Boxers blamed China's ills on foreigners, especially Christian missionaries. After the Boxers laid siege to the foreign legation quarter in Beijing, a dozen nations including Japan sent twenty thousand troops to lift the siege. In the negotiations that followed, China had to accept a long list of harsh penalties.

After this defeat, gradual reform lost its appeal. More and more Chinese were studying abroad and learning about Western political ideas, including democracy and revolution. The most famous was Sun Yatsen (1866–1925). Sent by his peasant family to Hawaii, he learned English and then continued his education in Hong Kong. From 1894 on, he spent his time abroad organizing revolutionary societies. He joined forces with Chinese student revolutionaries studying in Japan, and together they sparked the **1911 Revolution**, which brought China's monarchy to an end in 1912, to be replaced by a Western-style republic. China had escaped direct foreign rule but would never be the same.

Boxers
▶ A Chinese secret society that blamed the country's ills on foreigners, especially missionaries, and rose in rebellion in 1900.

1911 Revolution
▶ The uprising that brought China's monarchy to an end.

> **QUICK REVIEW**

Why were Chinese efforts at modernization and reform largely ineffective?

CHAPTER LOCATOR | In what ways did India change as a consequence of British rule? | Why were most but not all Southeast Asian societies reduced to colonies?

CHAPTER 26
794   ASIA AND THE PACIFIC IN THE ERA OF IMPERIALISM

How was Japan able to quickly master the challenges posed by the West?

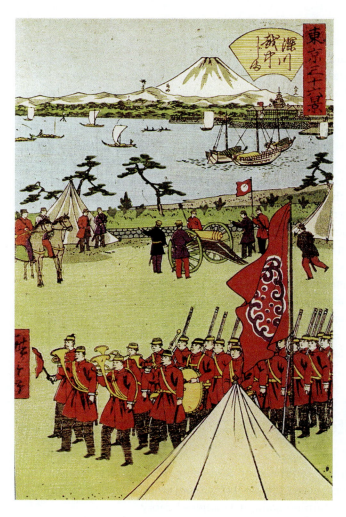

Japan's Modernized Army

A set of woodblock prints depicting the new sights of Tokyo included this illustration of a military parade ground. The soldiers' brightly colored Western-style uniforms undoubtedly helped make this a sight worth seeing.

DURING THE NINETEENTH CENTURY, while China's standing in the world plummeted, Japan's was rising. During the eighteenth century Japan (much more effectively than China) kept foreign merchants and missionaries at bay. It limited trade to a single port (Nagasaki), where only the Dutch were allowed, and forbade Japanese to travel abroad. Because Japan's land and population were so much smaller than China's, the Western powers never expected much from Japan as a trading partner and did not press it as urgently. Still, the European threat was part of what propelled Japan to modernize.

The "Opening" of Japan

Wanting to play a greater role in the Pacific, the United States decided to force the Japanese to open their ports to trade. In 1853 Commodore Matthew Perry steamed into Edo (now Tokyo) Bay and demanded diplomatic negotiations with

Was China's decline due more to internal problems or to Western imperialism?

How was Japan able to quickly master the challenges posed by the West?

What were the causes and consequences of the vast movement of people in the Pacific region?

What explains the similarities and differences between Asian countries in this era?

✔ **LearningCurve**
Check what you know.

gunboat diplomacy
▶ The imposition of treaties
and agreements under threat
of military violence, such as the
opening of Japan to trade after
Commodore Perry's demands.

the emperor. Under threat of **gunboat diplomacy**, and after consulting with the daimyo (major lords), Japanese officials signed a treaty with the United States that opened two ports and permitted trade.

Japan at this time was a complex society. The emperor in Kyoto had no effective powers. For more than two hundred years real power had been in the hands of the Tokugawa shogun in Edo (see pages 627–628). The country was divided into numerous domains, each under a daimyo. Each daimyo had under him samurai, who had hereditary stipends and privileges, such as the right to wear a sword. Peasants and merchants were also legally distinct classes, and in theory social mobility from peasant to merchant or merchant to samurai was impossible. After two centuries of peace, there were many more samurai than were needed to administer or defend the country, and many lived very modestly. They were proud, however, and felt humiliated by the sudden American intrusion and the unequal treaties that the Western countries imposed. Some began agitating against the shogunate under the slogan "Revere the emperor and expel the barbarians."

When foreign diplomats and merchants began to settle in Yokohama after 1858, radical samurai reacted with a wave of antiforeign terrorism and antigovernment assassinations. The Western response was swift and unambiguous. They sent an allied fleet of American, British, Dutch, and French warships to demolish key Japanese forts, further weakening the power and prestige of the shogun's government.

The Meiji Restoration

In 1867 a coalition of reform-minded daimyo led a coup that ousted the Tokugawa Shogunate. The samurai who led this coup declared a return to direct rule by the emperor. This emperor was called the Meiji (MAY-jee) emperor and this event the **Meiji Restoration**, a great turning point in Japanese history.

The domain leaders who organized the coup, called the Meiji Oligarchs, moved the boy emperor to Tokyo castle. They used the young sovereign to win over both the lords and the commoners. Real power, however, remained in the hands of the oligarchs.

The battle cry of the Meiji reformers had been "strong army, rich nation." How were these goals to be accomplished? Convinced that they could not beat the West until they had mastered the secrets of its military and industrial might, they dropped their antiforeign attacks and initiated a series of measures to reform Japan along modern Western lines. Within four years a delegation was traveling the world to learn what made the Western powers strong. Its members examined everything from the U.S. Constitution to the factories, shipyards, and railroads that made the European landscape so different from Japan's.

Japan under the shoguns had been decentralized, with most of the power over the population in the hands of the many daimyo. By elevating the emperor, the oligarchs were able to centralize the government. In 1871 they abolished the domains and merged the domain armies. Following the example of the French Revolution, they dismantled the four-class legal system and declared everyone equal. This amounted to stripping the samurai (7 to 8 percent of the population) of their privileges. Not surprisingly, some samurai rose up against their loss of privileges. None of these uncoordinated uprisings made any difference.

Meiji Restoration
▶ The 1867 ousting of the
Tokugawa Shogunate that
"restored" the power of the
Japanese emperors.

CHAPTER LOCATOR | In what ways did India change as a consequence of British rule? | Why were most but not all Southeast Asian societies reduced to colonies?

796 CHAPTER 26
ASIA AND THE PACIFIC IN THE ERA OF IMPERIALISM

Several leaders of the Meiji Restoration, in France on a fact-finding mission during the Franco-Prussian War of 1870–1871, were impressed by the active participation of French citizens in the defense of Paris. For Japan to survive in the hostile international environment, they concluded, ordinary people had to be trained to fight. Consequently, a conscription law, modeled on the French law, was issued in 1872. To improve the training of soldiers, the new War College was organized along German lines, and German instructors were recruited to teach there. Young samurai were trained to form the new professional officer corps.

Many of the new institutions established in the Meiji period reached down to the local level. Schools open to all were rapidly introduced beginning in 1872. Teachers were trained in newly established teachers' colleges. Another modern institution that reached the local level was a national police force. In 1884 police training schools were established in every prefecture, and within a few years police stations were set up throughout the country. Policemen came to act as local agents of the central government. They not only dealt with crime but also enforced public health rules, conscription laws, and codes of behavior.

In 1889 Japan became the first non-Western country to adopt the constitutional form of government. A commission sent abroad to study European constitutional governments had come to the conclusion that the German constitutional monarchy would provide the best model for Japan, rather than the more democratic governments of the British, French, and Americans. Japan's new government had a two-house parliament, called the Diet. The upper house of lords was drawn largely from former daimyo and nobles, and the lower house was elected by a limited electorate (about 5 percent of the adult male population in 1890). Although Japan now had a government based on laws, it was authoritarian rather than democratic. The emperor had the right to appoint the prime minister and cabinet. He did not have to ask the Diet for funds because wealth assigned to the imperial house was entrusted to the Imperial Household Ministry, which was outside the government's control.

> **Japan's 1889 Constitution:**

- Based on the German constitutional monarchy
- Two-house parliament (Diet)
- Upper house drawn largely from former daimyo and nobles
- Lower house elected by limited electorate
- Emperor remained outside of Diet's control

Cultural change during the Meiji period was as profound as political change. For more than a thousand years China had been the major source of ideas and technologies introduced into Japan. But in the late nineteenth century China, beset by Western pressure, had become an object lesson on the dangers of stagnation. The influential author Fukuzawa Yukichi began urging Japan to pursue "civilization and enlightenment," by which he meant Western civilization. Soon Japanese were being told to conform to Western taste, eat meat, wear Western-style clothes, and drop customs that Westerners found odd.

| Was China's decline due more to internal problems or to Western imperialism? | **How was Japan able to quickly master the challenges posed by the West?** | What were the causes and consequences of the vast movement of people in the Pacific region? | What explains the similarities and differences between Asian countries in this era? | ✓ LearningCurve Check what you know. |

797

Industrialization

The leaders of the Meiji Restoration, wanting to strengthen Japan's military capacity, promoted industrialization. The government paid foreign experts to help with industrialization, and Japanese were encouraged to go abroad to study science and engineering.

The government played an active role in getting railroads, mines, and factories started. Early on, the Japanese government decided to compete with China in the export of tea and silk to the West. Introducing the mechanical reeling of silk gave Japan a strong price advantage in the sale of silk, and Japan's total foreign trade increased tenfold from 1877 to 1900. The next stage was to develop heavy industry. The huge indemnity exacted from China in 1895 was used to establish the Yawata Iron and Steel Works. The third stage of Japan's industrialization would today be called import substitution. Factories such as cotton mills were set up to help cut the importation of Western consumer goods.

Most of the great Japanese industrial conglomerates known as *zaibatsu* (zigh-BAHT-dzoo), such as Mitsubishi, got their start in this period, often founded by men with government connections. Sometimes the government set up plants that it then sold to private investors at bargain prices. Successful entrepreneurs were treated as patriotic heroes.

As in Europe, the early stages of industrialization brought hardship to the countryside. Farmers often rioted as their incomes failed to keep up with prices or as their tax burdens grew. Workers in modern industries were no happier, and in 1898 railroad workers went on strike for better working conditions and overtime pay. Still, rice production increased, death rates dropped as public health was improved, and the population grew from about 33 million in 1868 to about 45 million in 1900.

Japan's First Skyscraper

Meiji Japan's fascination with things Western led to the construction of Western-style buildings. Japan's first elevator made possible this twelve-story tower built in Tokyo in 1890. Situated in the entertainment district, it was filled with shops, theaters, bars, and restaurants. ("Pavilion Above the Clouds," Sugoroku 1890, Utagawa Kunimasa IV [1848–1920]/Mead Art Museum, Amherst College, MA, USA/The Bridgeman Art Library)

> **PICTURING THE PAST**

ANALYZING THE IMAGE: Locate all the people in this picture. How are they dressed? What are they doing?

CONNECTIONS: Keeping in mind that the building in this picture was built in 1890, what connections can you draw between the politics of the period and this visual celebration of a new style of architecture?

CHAPTER LOCATOR | In what ways did India change as a consequence of British rule? | Why were most but not all Southeast Asian societies reduced to colonies?

798 CHAPTER 26 ASIA AND THE PACIFIC IN THE ERA OF IMPERIALISM

Japan as an Imperial Power

During the course of the Meiji period, Japan became an imperial power, making Taiwan and Korea into its colonies. The conflicts that led to Japanese acquisition of both of them revolved around Korea.

In the second half of the nineteenth century Korea found itself caught between China, Japan, and Russia, each trying to protect or extend its sphere of influence. Westerners also began demanding that Korea be "opened." Matters were complicated by the rise in the 1860s of a religious cult, the Tonghak movement, that had strong xenophobic elements. Although the government executed the cult founder in 1864, this cult continued to gain support, especially among impoverished peasants. Thus, like China in the same period, the Korean government faced simultaneous internal and external threats.

In 1871 the U.S. minister to China took five warships to try to open Korea, but left after exchanges of fire resulted in 250 Koreans dead without any progress in getting the Korean government to make concessions. Japan tried next and in 1876 forced the Korean government to sign an unequal treaty and open three ports to Japanese trade. On China's urging, Korea also signed treaties with the European powers in an effort to counterbalance Japan.

Over the next couple of decades reformers in China and Japan tried to encourage Korea to adopt its own self-strengthening movement, but Korean conservatives did their best to undo reform efforts. In 1894, when the religious cult rose in a massive revolt, both China and Japan sent military forces, claiming to come to the Korean government's aid. They ended up fighting each other instead in what is known as the Sino-Japanese War (see page 793). With Japan's decisive victory, it gained Taiwan from China and was able to make Korea a protectorate. In 1910 Korea was formally annexed as a province of Japan.

Japan also competed aggressively with the leading European powers for influence and territory in China, particularly in the northeast (Manchuria). There Japanese and Russian imperialism met and collided. In 1904 Japan attacked Russian forces and, after its 1905 victory in the bloody **Russo-Japanese War**, emerged with a foothold in China—Russia's former protectorate over Port Arthur (see Map 26.1).

Japan's victories over China and Russia changed the way European nations looked at Japan. Through negotiations Japan was able to eliminate extraterritoriality in 1899 and gain control of its own tariffs in 1911. Within Japan, the success of the military in raising Japan's international reputation added greatly to its political influence.

Japanese Expansion, 1875–1914

Russo-Japanese War

▶ The 1904–1905 war between Russia and Japan fought over imperial influence and territory in northeast China (Manchuria).

QUICK REVIEW <

What kind of government and society did Japanese leaders seek to create during the Meiji period?

Was China's decline due more to internal problems or to Western imperialism?	**How was Japan able to quickly master the challenges posed by the West?**	What were the causes and consequences of the vast movement of people in the Pacific region?	What explains the similarities and differences between Asian countries in this era?	LearningCurve Check what you know.

799

What were the causes and consequences of the vast movement of people in the Pacific region?

The "Life of Emigration" Puzzle, ca. 1840

Some of the advertising designed to attract people to move to Australia was aimed at children, such as this wooden puzzle depicting the life of a family moving from Britain to Australia. (Photograph courtesy of the State Library of South Australia, S.A. Memory website)

THE NINETEENTH CENTURY WAS MARKED by extensive movement of people into, across, and out of Asia and the broad Pacific region. Many of these migrants moved from one Asian country to another, but there was also a growing presence of Europeans in Asia, a consequence of the increasing integration of the world economy (see pages 771–772).

Settler Colonies in the Pacific: Australia and New Zealand

The largest share of the Europeans who moved to the Pacific region in the nineteenth century went to the settler colonies in Australia and New Zealand (Map 26.2). In the 1770s the English explorer James Cook visited New Zealand, Australia, and Hawaii. All three of these places in time became destinations for migrants.

CHAPTER LOCATOR | In what ways did India change as a consequence of British rule? | Why were most but not all Southeast Asian societies reduced to colonies?

As discussed in Chapter 12, between 200 and 1300 C.E. Polynesians settled numerous islands of the Pacific, from New Zealand in the south to Hawaii in the north and Easter Island in the east. Thus most of the lands that explorers like Cook encountered were occupied by societies with chiefs, crop agriculture, domestic animals, excellent sailing technology, and often considerable experience in warfare. Australia had been settled millennia earlier by a different population. When Cook arrived in Australia, it was occupied by about three hundred thousand Aborigines who lived entirely by food gathering, fishing, and hunting. Like the Indians of Central and South America, the people in all these lands fell victim to Eurasian diseases and died in large numbers.

Australia was first developed by Britain as a penal colony. Between 1787 and 1869, when the penal colony system was abolished, a total of 161,000 convicts were transported to Australia. After the end of the Napoleonic Wars in 1815, a

MAP 26.2 ■ Australia

Because of the vast deserts in western Australia, cities and industries developed mainly in the east. Australia's early geographical and cultural isolation bred a sense of inferiority. Air travel, the communications revolution, and the massive importation of Japanese products and American popular culture have changed that.

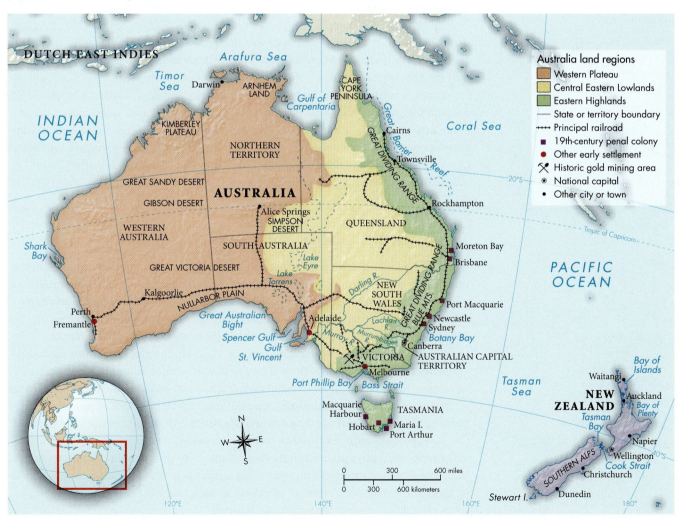

Was China's decline due more to internal problems or to Western imperialism?

How was Japan able to quickly master the challenges posed by the West?

What were the causes and consequences of the vast movement of people in the Pacific region?

What explains the similarities and differences between Asian countries in this era?

✓ LearningCurve
Check what you know.

steady stream of non-convicts voluntarily immigrated to Australia. Raising sheep proved suitable to Australia's climate, and wool exports steadily increased. To encourage migration, the government offered free passage and free land to immigrants. By 1850 Australia had five hundred thousand inhabitants. The discovery of gold in Victoria in 1851 quadrupled that number in a few years. The gold rush also provided the financial means for cultural development. Public libraries, museums, art galleries, and universities opened in the thirty years after 1851. These institutions dispensed a distinctly British culture.

Not everyone in Australia was of British origin, however. Chinese and Japanese built the railroads and ran the shops in the towns and the market gardens nearby. Filipinos and Pacific Islanders did the hard work in the sugarcane fields. Afghans and their camels controlled the carrying trade in some areas. But fear that Asian labor would lower living standards and undermine Australia's distinctly British culture led to efforts to keep Australia white.

Australia gained independence in stages. In 1850 the British Parliament passed the Australian Colonies Government Act, which allowed the four most populous colonies—New South Wales, Tasmania, Victoria, and South Australia—to establish colonial legislatures, determine the franchise, and frame their own constitutions. In 1902 Australia became one of the first countries in the world to give women the vote.

By 1900 New Zealand's population had reached 750,000, only a fifth of Australia's. One major reason more people had not settled these fertile islands was the resistance of the native Maori people. They quickly mastered the use of muskets and tried for decades to keep the British from taking their lands.

Foreign settlement in Hawaii began gradually. Initially, whalers stopped there for supplies, as they did at other Pacific Islands. Missionaries and businessmen came next, and soon other settlers followed, both whites and Asians. A plantation economy developed centered on sugarcane. In the 1890s leading settler families overthrew the native monarchy, set up a republic, and urged the United States to annex Hawaii, which it did in 1898.

Asian Emigration

Like Europeans, Asians left their native countries in unprecedented numbers in the nineteenth century (Map 26.3). As in Europe, both push and pull factors prompted people to leave home. China and India were extremely densely populated countries—China with more than 400 million people in the mid-nineteenth century, India with more than 200 million. Not surprisingly, these two giants were the leading exporters of people in search of work or land. On the pull side were the new opportunities created by the flow of development capital into previously underdeveloped areas. In many of the European colonies in Asia the business class came to consist of both Asian and European migrants. Asian diasporas formed in many parts of the world, with the majority in Asia itself, especially Southeast Asia.

By the nineteenth century the Chinese formed key components of mercantile communities throughout Southeast Asia. Chinese often assimilated in Siam and Vietnam, but they rarely did so in Muslim areas such as Java, Catholic areas such as the Philippines, and primitive tribal areas such as northern Borneo. In these places distinct Chinese communities emerged.

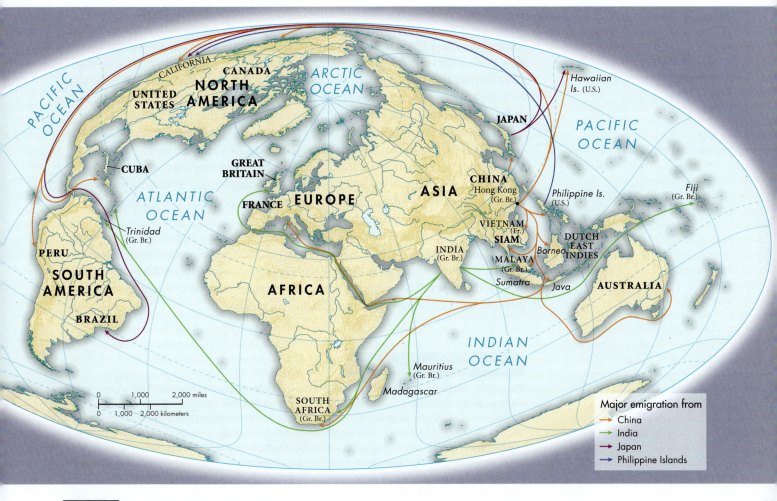

Major emigration from
— China
— India
— Japan
— Philippine Islands

MAP 26.3 ■ Emigration out of Asia, 1820–1914

As steamships made crossing oceans quicker and more reliable, many people in Asia left their home countries to find new opportunities elsewhere. European imperialism contributed to this flow, especially by recruiting workers for newly established plantations or mines. Many emigrants simply wanted to work a few years to build their savings and planned to return home. Often, however, they ended up staying in their new countries and forming families there.

With the growth in trade that accompanied the European imperial expansion, Chinese began to settle in the islands of Southeast Asia in larger numbers. After Singapore was founded by the British in 1819, Chinese rapidly poured in, soon becoming the dominant ethnic group. In British-controlled Malaya, some Chinese built great fortunes in the tin business, while others worked in the mines. Chinese also settled in the Spanish-controlled Philippines and in Dutch-controlled Indonesia.

Discovery of gold in California in 1848, Australia in 1851, and Canada in 1858 encouraged Chinese to book passage to those places. In California few arrived soon enough to strike gold, but thousands found work building railroads, and others took up mining in Wyoming and Idaho.

Indian entrepreneurs were similarly attracted by the burgeoning commerce of the growing British Empire. The bulk of Indian emigrants were **indentured laborers**,

indentured laborers

▶ Laborers who, in exchange for passage, agreed to work for a number of years, specified in a contract.

Was China's decline due more to internal problems or to Western imperialism?

How was Japan able to quickly master the challenges posed by the West?

What were the causes and consequences of the vast movement of people in the Pacific region?

What explains the similarities and differences between Asian countries in this era?

✓ LearningCurve
Check what you know.

803

recruited under contract. The rise of indentured labor from Asia was a direct result of the outlawing of the African slave trade in the early nineteenth century by Britain and the United States. Sugar plantations in the Caribbean and elsewhere needed new sources of workers, and planters in the British colonies discovered that they could recruit Indian laborers to replace blacks. After the French abolished slavery in 1848, they recruited workers from India as well. Later in the century many Indians emigrated to British colonies in Africa, the largest numbers to South Africa.

Indentured laborers secured as substitutes for slaves were often treated little better than slaves. In response to such abuse, the Indian colonial government established regulations stipulating a maximum indenture period of five years, after which the migrant would be entitled to passage home. Even though government "protectors" were appointed at the ports of embarkation, exploitation of indentured workers continued largely unchecked.

In areas outside the British Empire, China offered the largest supply of ready labor. Starting in the 1840s contractors arrived at Chinese ports to recruit labor for plantations and mines in Cuba, Peru, Hawaii, Sumatra, South Africa, and elsewhere. Chinese laborers did not have the British government to protect them and seem to have suffered even more than Indian workers.

Canadian Immigration Certificate

This certificate proved that the eleven-year-old boy in the photograph had a legal right to be in Canada, as the $500 head tax required for immigration of Chinese had been paid. The head tax on Chinese immigrants introduced in 1885 started at $50, but it was raised to $100 in 1900 and to $500 in 1903. Equal to about what a laborer could earn in two years, the tax succeeded in its goal of slowing the rate of Asian immigration to Canada. (Head tax certificate for Jung Bak Hun, issued January 3, 1919/© Government of Canada. Reproduced with the permission of the Minister of Public Works and Government Services Canada [2013]/Library and Archives Canada/Canada. Department of Employment and Immigration fonds/RG76-D-2-g, Vol. 712, C.I.5 certificate #88103)

CHAPTER LOCATOR | In what ways did India change as a consequence of British rule? | Why were most but not all Southeast Asian societies reduced to colonies?

804   CHAPTER 26
ASIA AND THE PACIFIC IN THE ERA OF IMPERIALISM

India and China sent more people abroad than any other Asian countries during this period, but they were not alone. As Japan started to industrialize, its cities could not absorb all those forced off the farms, and people began emigrating in significant numbers, many to Hawaii and later to South America. Emigration from the Philippines also was substantial, especially after it became a U.S. territory in 1898.

Asian migration to the United States, Canada, and Australia would undoubtedly have been greater if it had not been so vigorously resisted by the white settlers in those regions. In 1882 Chinese were barred from becoming American citizens, and the immigration of Chinese laborers was suspended. Australia also put a stop to Asian immigration with the Commonwealth Immigration Restriction Act of 1901, which established the "white Australia policy" that remained on the books until the 1970s.

Most of the Asian migrants discussed so far were illiterate peasants or business people, not members of traditional educated elites. By the beginning of the twentieth century, however, another group of Asians was going abroad in significant numbers: students. Most of these students traveled abroad to learn about Western science, law, and government in the hope of strengthening their own countries. On their return they contributed enormously to the intellectual life of their societies, increasing understanding of the modern Western world and also becoming the most vocal advocates of overthrowing the old order and driving out the colonial masters.

Among the most notable of these foreign-educated radicals were Mohandas Gandhi (1869–1948) and Sun Yatsen (see page 794). Sun developed his ideas about the republican form of government while studying in Hawaii and Hong Kong. Gandhi, after studying law in Britain, took a job in South Africa, where he became involved in trying to defend the interests of the Indians who lived and worked there. It was there that he gradually elaborated his idea of passive resistance.

QUICK REVIEW

Why did so many Asians migrate during this period?
Where did they most often go?

Was China's decline due more to internal problems or to Western imperialism?

How was Japan able to quickly master the challenges posed by the West?

What were the causes and consequences of the vast movement of people in the Pacific region?

What explains the similarities and differences between Asian countries in this era?

LearningCurve
Check what you know.

What explains the similarities and differences in the experiences of Asian countries in this era?

AT THE START OF THE NINETEENTH CENTURY the societies of Asia varied much more than those of any other part of the world. In the temperate zones of East Asia, the old established monarchies of China, Japan, and Korea were all densely populated and boasted long literary traditions and traditions of unified governments. They had ties to each other that dated back many centuries and shared many elements of their cultures. South of them, in the tropical and subtropical regions, cultures were more diverse. India was just as densely populated as China, Japan, and Korea, but politically and culturally less unified. In both India and Southeast Asia, Islam was much more important than it was in East Asia. All the countries with long written histories and literate elites were at a great remove from the thinly populated and relatively primitive areas without literate cultures and sometimes even without agriculture, such as Australia and some of the islands of the Philippines and Indonesia.

The nineteenth century gave the societies of Asia more in common in that all of them in one way or another had come into contact with the expanding West. Still, the Western powers did not treat all the countries the same way. Western powers initially wanted manufactured goods from the more developed Asian societies, especially Indian cotton textiles and Chinese porcelains. At the beginning of the nineteenth century Britain had already gained political control over large parts of India and was intent on forcing China to trade on terms more to its benefit. It paid virtually no attention to Korea and Japan, not seeing in them the same potential for profit. The less developed parts of Asia also attracted increasing Western interest, not because they could provide manufactured goods, but because they offered opportunities for Western development, much as the Americas had earlier.

The West that the societies of Asia faced during the nineteenth century was itself rapidly changing, and the steps taken by Western nations to gain power in

CHAPTER LOCATOR | In what ways did India change as a consequence of British rule? | Why were most but not all Southeast Asian societies reduced to colonies?

Asia naturally also changed over time. Western science and technology were making rapid advances, which gave European armies progressively greater advantages in weaponry. The Industrial Revolution made it possible for countries that industrialized early, such as Britain, to produce huge surpluses of goods for which they had to find markets; this development shifted their interest in Asia from a place to buy goods to a place to sell goods. Britain had been able to profit from its colonization of India, and this profit both encouraged it to consolidate its rule and invited its European rivals to look for their own colonies.

There were some commonalities in the ways Asian countries responded to pressure from outside. In the countries with long literary traditions, often the initial response of the established elite was to try to drive the unwelcome foreigners away. This was the case in China, Japan, and Korea in particular. Violent antiforeign reactions exploded again and again, but the superior military technology of the industrialized West almost invariably prevailed. Some Asian leaders insisted on the need to preserve their cultural traditions at all costs. Others came to the opposite conclusion that the West was indeed superior in some ways and that they would have to adopt European ideas or techniques for their own purposes. The struggles between the traditionalists and the westernizers were often intense. As nationalism took hold in the West, it found a receptive audience among the educated elites in Asia. How could the assertion that every people had the right to control its own destiny not appeal to the colonized?

Whether they were colonized or not, most countries in Asia witnessed the spread of new technologies between 1800 and 1914. Railroads, telegraphs, modern sanitation, and a wider supply of inexpensive manufactured goods brought fundamental changes in everyday life not only to lands under colonial rule, such as India and Vietnam, but also, if less rapidly, to places that managed to remain independent, such as China and Japan. In fact, the transformation of Japan between 1860 and 1900 was extraordinary. By 1914 Japan had urban conveniences and educational levels comparable to those in Europe.

QUICK REVIEW

What common factor shaped the development of all Asian societies in the nineteenth century?

Was China's decline due more to internal problems or to Western imperialism?

How was Japan able to quickly master the challenges posed by the West?

What were the causes and consequences of the vast movement of people in the Pacific region?

What explains the similarities and differences between Asian countries in this era?

✓ LearningCurve
Check what you know.

CHAPTER SUMMARY

In the nineteenth century the countries of Asia faced new challenges. In India Britain extended its rule to the whole subcontinent, though often the British ruled indirectly through local princes. Britain brought many modern advances to India, such as railroads and schools. Slavery was outlawed, as was widow suicide and infanticide. Resistance to British rule took several forms. In 1857 Indian soldiers in the employ of the British rose in a huge revolt, and after Britain put down this rebellion it ruled India much more tightly. Indians who received English education turned English ideas of liberty and representative rule against the British and founded the Indian National Congress, which called for Indian independence.

In Southeast Asia by the end of the nineteenth century most countries had been made colonies of Western powers, which developed them as exporters of agricultural products or raw materials. The principal exception was Siam (Thailand), whose king was able to play the English and French off against each other and institute centralizing reforms. In the Philippines more than three centuries of Spanish rule ended in 1898, but Spain was replaced by another colonial power: the United States.

In the nineteenth century China's world standing declined as a result of both foreign intervention and internal unrest. The government's efforts to suppress opium imports from Britain led to military confrontation with the British and to numerous concessions that opened China to trade on Britain's terms. Within its borders, China faced unprecedented population pressure and worsening economic conditions that resulted in uprisings in several parts of the country. Further humiliations by the Western powers led to concerted efforts to modernize, but China never quite caught up. Inspired by Western ideas of republican government, revolutionaries tried to topple the dynasty, finally succeeding in 1911–1912.

Japan was the one Asian country to quickly transform itself when confronted by the military strength of the West. It did this by overhauling its power structure. The Meiji centralized and strengthened Japan's power by depriving the samurai of their privileges, writing a constitution, instituting universal education, and creating a modern army. At the same time they guided Japan toward rapid industrialization. By the early twentieth century Japan had become an imperialist power with colonies in Korea and Taiwan.

The nineteenth century was also a great age of migration. Citizens of Great Britain came east in large numbers. Subjects of Asian countries also went abroad, often leaving one Asian country for another. Asian students traveled to Europe, Japan, or the United States to continue their educations. Millions more left in search of work. With the end of the African slave trade, recruiters from the Americas and elsewhere went to India and China to secure indentured laborers. Asian diasporas formed in many parts of the world.

By the turn of the twentieth century the countries in the Asia and Pacific region varied greatly in wealth and power. There are several reasons for this. The countries did not start with equivalent circumstances. Some had long traditions of unified rule; others did not. Some had manufactured goods that Western powers wanted; others offered raw materials or cheap labor. The timing of the arrival of Western powers also made a difference, especially because Western military superiority increased over time. European Great Power rivalry had a

CHAPTER LOCATOR | In what ways did India change as a consequence of British rule? | Why were most but not all Southeast Asian societies reduced to colonies?

CHAPTER 26

808   ASIA AND THE PACIFIC IN THE ERA OF IMPERIALISM

major impact, especially after 1860. Similarities in the experiences of Asian countries are also notable and include many of the benefits (and costs) of industrialization seen elsewhere in the world, such as modernizations in communication and transportation, extension of schooling, and the emergence of radical ideologies.

 **CONNECTIONS** The nineteenth century brought Asia change on a much greater scale than did any earlier century. Much of the change was political—old political orders were ousted or reduced to tokens by new masters, often European colonial powers. Old elites found themselves at a loss when confronted by the European powers with their modern weaponry and modern armies. Cultural change was no less dramatic as the old elites pondered the differences between their traditional values and the ideas that seemed to underlie the power of the European states. In several places ordinary people rose in rebellion, probably in part because they felt threatened by the speed of cultural change. Material culture underwent major changes as elites experimented with Western dress and architecture and ordinary people had opportunities to travel on newly built railroads.

In the Americas, too, the nineteenth century was an era of unprecedented change and movement of people. Colonial empires were being overturned there, not imposed as they were in Asia in the same period. The Americas were on the receiving end of the huge migrations taking place, while Asia, like Europe, was much more an exporter of people. The Industrial Revolution brought change to all these areas, both by making available inexpensive machine-made products and by destroying some old ways of making a living. Intellectually, in both Asia and the Americas the ideas of nationalism and nation building shaped how people, especially the more educated, thought about the changes they were experiencing.

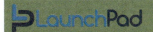 LaunchPad

ONLINE DOCUMENT PROJECT

Imperialism in the Philippines

How did Filipinos and Americans respond to Spanish and American imperialism?

Examine documents about the Philippines during the Spanish-American war, and then complete a quiz and writing assignment based on the evidence and details from this chapter. *See inside the front cover to learn more.*

Was China's decline due more to internal problems or to Western imperialism?

How was Japan able to quickly master the challenges posed by the West?

What were the causes and consequences of the vast movement of people in the Pacific region?

What explains the similarities and differences between Asian countries in this era?

✔ LearningCurve
Check what you know.

CHAPTER 26 STUDY GUIDE

 GET STARTED ONLINE

 **LearningCurve**

Now that you've read the chapter, make it stick by completing the LearningCurve activity.

STEP 2 EXPLAIN WHY IT MATTERS

Put your reading into practice. Identify each term below, and then explain why it matters in world history.

TERM	WHO OR WHAT & WHEN	WHY IT MATTERS
Great Mutiny / Great Revolt (p. 783)		
Indian Civil Service (p. 785)		
Indian National Congress (p. 785)		
Java War (p. 788)		
Nguyen Dynasty (p. 788)		
Opium War (p. 792)		
extraterritoriality (p. 792)		
Taiping Rebellion (p. 792)		
Boxers (p. 794)		
1911 Revolution (p. 794)		
gunboat diplomacy (p. 796)		
Meiji Restoration (p. 796)		
Russo-Japanese War (p. 799)		
indentured laborers (p. 803)		

STEP 3 MOVE BEYOND THE BASICS

To demonstrate a more advanced understanding of the experiences of India, China, and Japan in the era of imperialism, fill in the chart below with descriptions of the nature and extent of Western intervention, the economic impact of the Western presence, and the efforts of the peoples of each society to respond to and resist Western expansion. What connections can you make between the nature of Western intervention and its economic impact in each society?

	Nature of Western Intervention	Economic Impact	Response and Resistance
India			
China			
Japan			

PUT IT ALL TOGETHER

Now, take a step back and try to explain the big picture. Remember to use specific examples from the chapter in your answers.

INDIA AND SOUTHEAST ASIA

► What motives underlay British efforts to shape India's society and economy? What role did Indians play in implementing British policy?

► Why was Siam able to resist colonization while much of the rest of Southeast Asia was not?

CHINA AND JAPAN

► Why was Japan so much more successful than China at resisting Western domination?

► Argue for or against the following statement. "By the end of the nineteenth century, Japan had become, for all intents and purposes, a Western imperial power."

REGIONAL TRENDS

► How did global economic and political developments influence Asian migration patterns in the nineteenth century?

► How did conflicts between "modernizers" and "traditionalists" shape the development of Asian societies in the nineteenth century?

LOOKING BACK, LOOKING AHEAD

► How did Europeans' desire to gain access to the wealth of Asia shape world history from 1500 to 1900?

► What connections might one make between the events of the second half of the nineteenth century and role of Japan in regional and world affairs in the first half of the twentieth century?

> IN YOUR OWN WORDS

Imagine that you must give an oral report to the class answering the following question: **How did Asian leaders respond to the challenges posed by Western imperialism?** What would be the most important points and why?

27
THE AMERICAS IN THE AGE OF LIBERALISM
1810–1910

> **How did liberal political and economic ideas shape the development of the Americas in the nineteenth century?** Chapter 27 examines major trends in the nineteenth-century Americas. In the United States, Cuba, and Brazil slavery endured until the second half of the nineteenth century. In Spanish America land remained concentrated in the hands of colonial elites. By 1900 millions of immigrants from Europe, the Middle East, and Asia had settled in the Americas. New political systems and governing institutions emerged quickly in the United States, Canada, and Brazil, while in much of the rest of the continent political rivals struggled to share power. The United States managed to nurture internal markets and assume an influential place in both Atlantic and Pacific trade. Across Latin America, new nations with weak internal markets and often poorly consolidated political systems struggled to accumulate capital or industrialize.

Yaqui Woman Indians across the Americas found their world under assault during the nineteenth century as new nation-states completed the process of territorial consolidation begun in the colonial era. Yaqui people like the woman depicted here faced the dual pressures of the United States' westward expansion and Mexico's integration of northern borderlands. (Library of Congress LC-USZ62-104492)

✓ LearningCurve

After reading the chapter, use LearningCurve to retain what you've read.

> How and why did the process of nation-state consolidation vary across the Americas?

> Why did slavery last longer in the United States, Brazil, and Cuba than in the other republics of the Americas? How did patterns of resistance shape slavery and abolition?

> As Latin America became more integrated into the world economy, how did patterns of economic growth shape social relations and political culture?

> What factors shaped immigration patterns to the Americas? How did immigrants shape — and how were they shaped by — their new settings?

> In what ways did U.S. policies in the Caribbean and Central America resemble European imperialism? How did U.S. foreign policy depart from European imperialism?

How and why did the process of nation-state consolidation vary across the Americas?

Market Vendors in Mexico

Women sell fruits and vegetables at a market in San Luis Potosí, Mexico, around 1910 (© ullstein — Haeckel-Archiv/The Image Works)

A**T THE MOMENT OF THEIR INDEPENDENCE**, none of the nations of the Americas had consolidated what would become their national territory, and that process often took place violently. In countries such as Mexico and Argentina new governments failed to establish the trust needed for political stability. In the United States long-standing tensions and disagreements culminated in the Civil War, while in Cuba nationalists fought a long struggle for independence from Spain.

Liberalism and Caudillos in Spanish America

The nations that gained independence from the Spanish Empire in the Americas drew upon ideological currents that circulated in the Atlantic in the age of revolution in order to establish new frameworks of government and social organization (see Chapter 22). The dominant ideology of the era was **liberalism**. Liberals sought to create representative republics with strong central governments framed by constitutions that defined and protected individual rights, in particular the right to freely own and buy and sell private property. Beginning with the United States, colonies that became independent nations in the Americas all adopted liberal constitutions.

liberalism

▶ A philosophy whose principal ideas were equality and liberty; liberals demanded representative government and equality before the law as well as such individual freedoms as freedom of the press, freedom of speech, freedom of assembly, and freedom from arbitrary arrest.

CHAPTER LOCATOR | **How and why did the process of nation-state consolidation vary across the Americas?** | Why did slavery last longer in the U.S., Brazil, and Cuba than in other republics of the Americas?

814 CHAPTER 27 THE AMERICAS IN THE AGE OF LIBERALISM

1810–1825 Wars of independence in Latin America	**1879–1883** War of the Pacific
1845 First use of term *manifest destiny* in United States; Texas and Florida admitted into United States	**1886** Abolition of slavery in Cuba
1845–1847 Mexican-American War	**1888** Abolition of slavery in Brazil
1857–1861 Mexican Wars of Reform	**1889** Brazilian monarchy overthrown and republic established
1861–1865 U.S. Civil War	**1898** Spanish-American War
1865–1870 Paraguay War (War of Triple Alliance)	**1904** United States secures the rights to build and control the Panama Canal
1867 Dominion of Canada formed	**1910** Mexican Revolution
1868–1878 Cuban Ten Years' War	**1914** Panama Canal completed

The U.S. Constitution, in its earliest form, is an example of classic liberalism: it defined individual rights, but those individual rights were subordinated to property rights. Slaves were considered property rather than individuals with constitutional rights. Only property owners could vote, only men could own property, and the new government did not recognize the property of Indians. Thus, liberalism mainly served and protected oligarchs—the small number of individuals and families who had monopolized political power and economic resources since the colonial era. Liberalism preserved slavery, created tools that allowed the wealthy and powerful to continue to concentrate land ownership in the countryside, gave industrialists a free hand over their workers, and concentrated political power in the hands of those who held economic power.

By the end of the nineteenth century liberalism commingled with other ideologies such as Social Darwinism and scientific racism (see pages 736–737). This combination inspired the imperial ambitions of the United States toward Mexico and the Circum-Caribbean, the region that includes the Antilles as well as the lands that bound the Caribbean in Central America, southern North America, and northern South America.

Though liberalism provided the political and economic framework that replaced colonialism, nations of the Americas took different approaches. The United States deferred questions about centralized federal power over local state authority, as well as the legality of slavery, until its Civil War (1861–1865). After the North prevailed, economic growth under its liberal economic model accelerated. In Spanish America wars of independence left behind a weak consensus about government, which led to long cycles of civil war across many countries.

oligarchs
▶ The small number of individuals and families that monopolized political power and economic resources.

Circum-Caribbean
▶ The region encompassing the Antilles islands as well as the lands that bound the Caribbean Sea in Central America, southern North America, and northern South America.

| How did patterns of economic growth shape social and political culture in Latin America? | What factors shaped immigration patterns to the Americas? | How did U.S. policies in the Caribbean and Central America resemble European imperialism? | ☑ LearningCurve
Check what you know. |

The lack of a shared political culture among powerful groups in Spanish America created a crisis of confidence. Large landowners held great local power that they refused to yield to politicians in a distant capital. Political factions feared that if a rival faction won power, it would not abide by the rules and limits framed by the constitution, or that a rival would use its governing authority to crush its opponents. The power vacuum that resulted was often filled by caudillos, strong leaders who came to power and governed through their personal charisma and leadership abilities. This form of leadership is known as **caudillismo**. The rule of a caudillo, anchored in his charisma and the loyalty of his followers, often provided temporary stability amid the struggles between liberals and conservatives, but caudillos cultivated their own prestige at the expense of building stable political institutions.

caudillismo

▶ Government by charismatic figures who rule through personal power rather than the functioning of public institutions.

Mexico and the United States

The rumblings of independence first stirred Mexico in 1810. A century later, in 1910, the country was engulfed in the Mexican Revolution. In the century between these events, Mexico declined politically and economically from its status as the most prosperous and important colony of the Spanish Empire. It lost most of its national territory as Central American provinces broke away and as the United States expanded westward and captured, purchased, or otherwise wrangled away Mexico's northern lands.

Mexicans experienced political stabilization and economic growth again in the second half of the nineteenth century when liberal leaders, especially the dictator Porfirio Díaz (r. 1876–1910), imposed order and attracted foreign investment. But as Díaz himself is said to have remarked, "Poor Mexico, so far from God, so close to the United States."[1] The United States pursued territorial expansion under the doctrine of **manifest destiny**, by which the United States would absorb all the territory spanning from its original Atlantic states to the Pacific Ocean. In the process, the United States took over lands belonging to Indian nations and to Mexico (Map 27.1). And as the United States grew economically, investors from the United States drove railroad construction and land speculation in Mexico that stripped lands away from peasants, who rose up in the 1910 revolution.

manifest destiny

▶ The belief that God had foreordained the United States to cover the entire continent.

Mexico's woes after independence resulted mainly from the inability of its political leaders to establish a consensus about how to govern the new nation. The general who led the war against Spain, Agustín de Iturbide, proclaimed himself emperor in 1822. When he was deposed a year later, the country's southern provinces broke away, forming the new nations of Guatemala, Honduras, Nicaragua, El Salvador, and Costa Rica. For the next three decades, power in Mexico rested in the hands of regional caudillos and local bosses. The presidency changed hands frequently as rival factions competed against each other.

By contrast, the United States established a clearer vision of government, a vision embodied in the 1789 Constitution. Deep differences of opinion remained over questions such as the power of the federal government relative to state governments, which played out in debates about the future of slavery and of westward expansion. These differences created regional tensions that lasted throughout the early nineteenth century and culminated in the Civil War (1861–1865).

Economically, the United States remained integrated into the expanding and industrializing British Empire. But the United States faced deepening regional

CHAPTER LOCATOR | **How and why did the process of nation-state consolidation vary across the Americas?** | Why did slavery last longer in the U.S., Brazil, and Cuba than in other republics of the Americas?

816   CHAPTER 27   THE AMERICAS IN THE AGE OF LIBERALISM

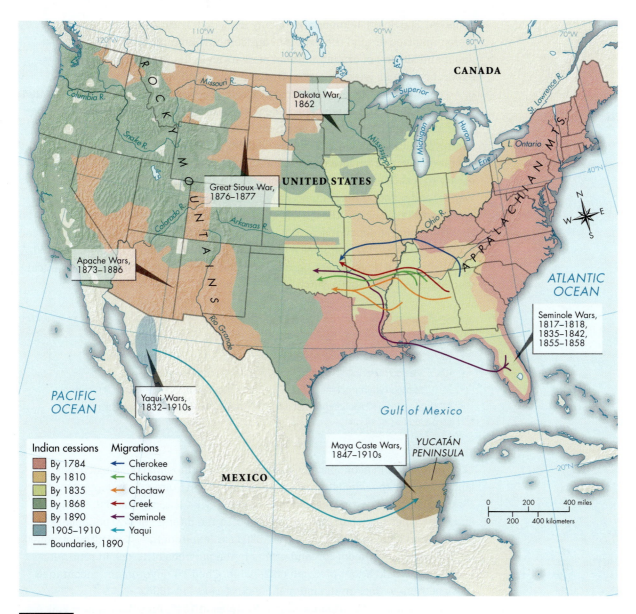

MAP 27.1 ■ Displacement of Indigenous Peoples, 1780s–1910s

The United States and Mexico waged repeated wars to claim the lands of Native American nations. This was the last stage of the process of conquest and dispossession that began with the arrival of Europeans in the Americas three centuries earlier. As national armies seized native lands, thousands of displaced native peoples were forcibly removed, leading to the deaths of thousands and the destruction of cultures.

differences: in the first half of the nineteenth century the North's economy and population grew faster than the South's, and the North became the center of immigration, banking, and industrialization. In the South slavery and tenant farming kept much of the population at the economic margins and weakened internal markets. Slavery also inhibited immigration, because immigrants avoided settling in areas where they had to compete for work with unfree labor.

The dichotomy between the economies of the U.S. North and South repeated itself in the difference between the economies of the United States and Latin

How did patterns of economic growth shape social and political culture in Latin America?

What factors shaped immigration patterns to the Americas?

How did U.S. policies in the Caribbean and Central America resemble European imperialism?

✓ LearningCurve
Check what you know.

America. The Spanish imperial economy imploded. Latin American economies were organized around the export of agricultural and mineral commodities like sugar and silver, not around internal markets as in the United States, and these export economies were disrupted by the independence process.

The fate of the major silver mine in Mexico illustrates the challenges presented by independence. La Valenciana in central Mexico was the most productive silver mine in the world. The machinery required to keep the mine functioning was destroyed during the wars of independence (1810–1821) and the mine ceased operation. Neither private investors nor the new government had the capital necessary to reactivate the mine after independence. Without the private profits, wages, and taxation that mining produced, Mexico's economy withered and its credit networks collapsed.

Thus, after independence, Mexico entered a vicious cycle: without capital and economic activity, tax revenues evaporated, public administration disintegrated, and the national government became unmanageable. In turn, the lack of political stability drove investors away.

> ### > Mexico Falls Behind the United States:

- 1800: Mexico produced half the goods and services that the United States did
- 1845: Mexico produced only 8 percent as much as the United States
- 1821: Mexico had a population of 6.2 million, while the United States had 3.9 million
- 1900: Mexico's population had risen to 13.6 million, while the U.S. population had increased to 76 million

Politically and economically weakened after independence, Mexico was vulnerable to expansionist pressure from the United States. At independence, Mexico's northern territories included much of what is today the U.S. Southwest and West. These northern territories attracted the interest of U.S. politicians, settlers, and land speculators. In the 1820s settlers from the U.S. South petitioned the Mexican government for land grants in the province of Texas, in return for which they would adopt Mexican citizenship. The U.S. government encouraged these settlers to declare the independence of Texas in 1836.

After Texas and Florida became U.S. states in 1845, President James Polk expanded its westward border, precipitating the Mexican-American War (1845–1847). In the **Treaty of Guadalupe Hidalgo** (1848), that followed Mexican defeat, Mexico ceded half its territory, including California, Nevada, Arizona, New Mexico, and parts of Colorado and Utah, to the United States.

Treaty of Guadalupe Hidalgo

▶ The 1848 treaty between the United States and Mexico in which Mexico ceded large tracts of land to the United States.

Liberal Reform in Mexico

In 1853 Mexican president Santa Anna unintentionally ushered in a new era of liberal political consolidation and economic reform by triggering a backlash against his sale of territory along the northern border to the United States. Many Mexicans saw his act as a betrayal of the nation and threw their support behind a new generation of liberal leaders. Beginning with the presidency of Ignacio Comonfort (pres. 1855–1858), these liberals carried out sweeping legal and economic changes called *La Reforma*, or "the reform."

CHAPTER LOCATOR | **How and why did the process of nation-state consolidation vary across the Americas?** | Why did slavery last longer in the U.S., Brazil, and Cuba than in other republics of the Americas?

Liberal reformers sought to make all individuals equal under the law and established property ownership as a basic right and national goal. The first major step in La Reforma was the Juarez Law (1855), which abolished legal privileges for military officers and members of the clergy. An even more consequential measure, the **Lerdo Law** (1856), banished another legacy of colonialism: "corporate lands," meaning lands owned by groups or institutions, such as the Catholic Church, rather than by individual property owners. Liberals wanted to redistribute church-owned lands among farmers who would own them as private parcels and who would profit from working them efficiently.

Lerdo Law
▶ An 1856 Mexican law that barred corporate landholdings.

These liberal reforms triggered a backlash from conservative landowners and the church. When liberals enshrined these laws and other reforms in a new constitution ratified in 1857, the Catholic Church threatened to excommunicate anyone who swore allegiance to it. Conservatives revolted, triggering a civil war called the Wars of Reform (1857–1861). Liberal forces led by Benito Juárez defeated the conservatives, who then conspired with French emperor Napoleon III to invite a French invasion of Mexico in 1862. French victory led to the installation of Napoleon III's Austrian cousin Maximilian of Habsburg as emperor of Mexico.

The deposed Juárez led a guerrilla war against the French troops backing Maximilian. Juárez's nationalists prevailed, restored Mexico's republic, and executed Maximilian. Conservatives had been completely discredited: they had conspired with another country to install a foreign leader through a military invasion.

Brazil: A New World Monarchy

Brazil gained independence in 1822 as a monarchy ruled by Emperor Pedro I, the son and heir of Portuguese emperor João IV. The creation of a Brazilian monarchy marked the culmination of a process that began in 1808, when Napoleon's armies crossed the Pyrenees from France to invade the Iberian Peninsula. Napoleon toppled the Spanish crown, but the Portuguese royal family, many of the government's bureaucrats, and most of the aristocracy fled aboard British warships to Portugal's colony, Brazil.

Before the seat of Portuguese power relocated to Brazil, colonial policies had restricted many activities in Brazil in order to keep the colony dependent and subordinate to Portugal. It was only with the arrival of the imperial court that Brazil gained its first printing press, library, and military and naval academies, as well as schools for engineering, medicine, law, and the arts.

With the flight of the emperor to Brazil in 1808 and the declaration of independence by his son in 1822, Brazil achieved something that had eluded Spanish-American nations: it retained the unifying symbol of the monarchy and continued to build upon the infrastructure of colonial administration. A liberal constitution adopted in 1824 lasted until a republican military coup in 1889. It established a two-chamber parliamentary system and a role for the emperor as a guide and intermediary in political affairs. Pedro I was not adept in this role and abdicated in 1831, leaving behind a regency governing in the name of his five-year-old son, Pedro II. In 1840 Pedro II declared himself an adult and assumed the throne. His rule, which lasted forty-nine years, provided the country with unusual political stability that helped keep Brazil from dividing into separate nations, as occurred in Spanish America, and avoided the internal strife that characterized the United States during that period.

How did patterns of economic growth shape social and political culture in Latin America?

What factors shaped immigration patterns to the Americas?

How did U.S. policies in the Caribbean and Central America resemble European imperialism?

☑ LearningCurve
Check what you know.

The nature of Brazil's independence nonetheless constrained its growth in the nineteenth century. Portugal had been economically and militarily dependent on Britain, and Britain transferred this dependency onto Brazil. Britain negotiated with Brazil a "Friendship Treaty" that allowed British industrial goods to enter the country with very low tariffs and granted British citizens in Brazil the right to be tried by British rather than Brazilian judges. The flood of cheap British imports inhibited Brazilian industrialization. British economic and political influence, as well as the special privileges enjoyed by British citizens in Brazil, were examples of **neocolonialism**, the influence that European powers and the United States exerted over politically and economically weaker countries after they gained their independence.

neocolonialism

▶ The re-establishment of political and economic influence over regions after they have ceased to be formal colonies.

> **QUICK REVIEW**

Why did Mexico struggle economically in the first half of the nineteenth century?

CHAPTER LOCATOR | How and why did the process of nation-state consolidation vary across the Americas? | **Why did slavery last longer in the U.S., Brazil, and Cuba than in other republics of the Americas?**

Slave Labor in Rio de Janeiro, Brazil

This lithograph by French traveler Jean-Baptiste Debret shows different facets of urban slavery in Rio de Janeiro. In the foreground slaves lay paving stones in a plaza, while behind them other slaves peddle food. A funeral procession passes in the background. (from *Voyage Pittoresque et Historique au Bresil*, 1824 color lithograph by Jean-Baptiste Debret [1768–1848] published in 1839/Bibliotheque Nationale, Paris, France/Archives Charmet/The Bridgeman Art Library)

Why did slavery last longer in the United States, Brazil, and Cuba than in other republics of the Americas? How did patterns of resistance shape slavery and abolition?

ACROSS THE FORMER COLONIES OF SPANISH AMERICA, the abolition of slavery quickly followed independence. Abolitionist pressure from Britain ended slavery in its Caribbean colonies in 1834, and the British navy suppressed the Atlantic slave trade. But slavery endured well into the nineteenth century in the United States, Cuba, and Brazil. In each of these countries the question of abolition became entwined with the disputes over the nature of government and authority.

Slave Societies in the Americas

Africans and their descendants were enslaved in every country of the Americas, from Canada to Chile. The experiences in slavery and freedom for Africans and African Americans, broadly defined here as the descendants of slaves brought from Africa to anywhere in the New World, varied considerably. Several factors

How did patterns of economic growth shape social and political culture in Latin America?

What factors shaped immigration patterns to the Americas?

How did U.S. policies in the Caribbean and Central America resemble European imperialism?

 **LearningCurve**
Check what you know.

Slaves Sold South from Richmond, 1853

This scene was painted by a British artist, based on scenes he witnessed in the U.S. South twenty years after slavery was abolished in the British Empire. Being "sold south," as this image depicts, was a terrifying fate. In addition to having their families ripped apart, those who were sold were sent to plantations where the labor regimes were famously harsh. Note the ways in which the artist depicts not only the slave families but also the white, mixed, and free black traders. (*After the Sale: Slaves Going South from Richmond*, 1853 [oil on canvas], by Eyre Crowe [1824–1910]/© Chicago History Museum, U.S.A./The Bridgeman Art Library)

> PICTURING THE PAST
ANALYZING THE IMAGE: How are images of families used in this depiction of slavery? How are whites and free blacks represented?
CONNECTIONS: Can you think of other examples of art with social or political messages? How would this painting compare in its effectiveness?

shaped their experiences: the nature of slave regimes in different economic regions, patterns of manumission (individual slaves gaining their freedom), the nature of abolition (the ending of the institution of slavery), and the proportion of the local population they represented.

The settlement of Africans as slaves was the most intense in areas that relied on plantation agriculture. Plantations were an unusual kind of farming: they were typically enormous tracts of land dedicated to cultivating a single crop on a scale so great that plantation regions usually supplied distant global markets. The massive scale of this kind of agriculture, along with the practice of importing African labor to sustain it, originated in the sugar region of northeastern Brazil under the Portuguese. African slaves played many other roles as well. From Buenos Aires to Boston, slavery was also widespread in port cities, fed by easy access to the slave trade and the demand for street laborers such as porters. And across the Americas, slaves—especially slave women—were forced into domestic service, a role that added sexual abuse to the miseries that slaves endured.

CHAPTER LOCATOR | How and why did the process of nation-state consolidation vary across the Americas? | Why did slavery last longer in the U.S., Brazil, and Cuba than in other republics of the Americas?

CHAPTER 27
822 THE AMERICAS IN THE AGE OF LIBERALISM

Independence and Abolition

Slavery and abolition became intertwined with the process of political independence. The different relationships between independence and abolition in the United States and Haiti shaped perceptions across the rest of the continent. In Haiti national independence was achieved amid a social revolution in which slaves turned against their oppressors. By contrast, the United States gained its independence in a war that created a liberal political regime that preserved the institution of slavery. When colonial elites elsewhere on the continent contemplated independence, they weighed whether the U.S. or the Haitian experience awaited them. As a result, in colonies where the unfree population was the largest, independence movements proceeded more gradually.

British efforts to keep their North American colonies, as well as a combination of moral and economic appeals for the abolition of slavery in British territories, hastened the end of the slave trade to the Americas. When British forces fought to prevent the independence of the United States, they offered freedom to slaves who joined them. Many slaves did so, and after the British defeat and withdrawal, they dispersed to Spanish Florida, the Caribbean, and West Africa.

In 1808 British abolitionists pressured their government to end the Atlantic slave trade to British colonies, and in 1834 Britain abolished slavery in Canada and its Caribbean colonies. In order to reduce economic competition with other countries still importing slaves and still using slave labor, the British government pressured other nations to follow suit. A British naval squadron patrolled the Atlantic to suppress the slave trade. The squadron captured slave ships, freed the slaves they carried, and resettled them in a colony the British government established in Sierra Leone in 1787 to settle former slaves who had sided with Britain in the American Revolution.

Unlike in the United States, in Spanish America independence forces enlisted the participation of slaves and offered freedom in return. As rebels triumphed, new national governments enacted gradual abolition. The first step toward abolition was typically taken through **free womb laws** that granted freedom to children born to slaves. These laws, passed across independent Spanish America between 1811 and 1825, created gradual abolition but did not impose an immediate financial loss on slaveholders. Similar laws hastened the abolition of slavery in the Northern states of the United States.

free womb laws
▶ A gradual form of abolition through which children born to slaves gain their freedom.

In Spanish America the conflicts that continued after independence accelerated the abolition process: within the cycle of violence and civil wars, rival factions competed to enlist the support of slaves and free blacks. In 1854 Peru became the last country in Spanish America to fully abolish slavery. The combination of free womb laws and manumission as a reward for military service meant that, unlike in the United States, by the time slavery was abolished in Latin American countries, most blacks had already gained their freedom (Map 27.2).

In the United States, even if independence occurred without abolition, the questions of nation building and slavery remained connected. The determination of Southern states to protect the slave regime was enshrined in the U.S. Constitution, which granted individual states considerable autonomy in such questions as slavery and freedom. As slavery was abolished in Northern states, westward expansion tested the political compromise between the North and South, culminating in the Civil War.

| How did patterns of economic growth shape social and political culture in Latin America? | What factors shaped immigration patterns to the Americas? | How did U.S. policies in the Caribbean and Central America resemble European imperialism? | ✓ LearningCurve Check what you know. |

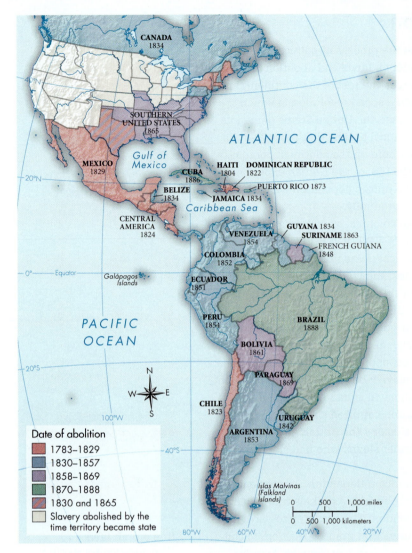

MAP 27.2 ■ Abolition in the Americas

The process of abolition in the Americas was gradual and varied across regions. In some areas, such as Mexico and parts of New England, slavery was abolished soon after independence, while in the U.S. South it lasted until the end of the Civil War. In Texas, slavery was abolished by the Mexican government, but when Texas became part of the United States, slavery was legally reinstated. In British territories, slavery was abolished in 1834. Across Latin America the abolition of slavery was hastened by civil wars that mobilized slaves as combatants. The last country to abolish slavery, Brazil, did so only in 1888.

> **MAPPING THE PAST**

ANALYZING THE MAP: How did the United States resemble Latin America in its patterns of abolition?
CONNECTIONS: Why did some countries abolish slavery earlier, and why did others do so much later?

Tensions between the North and the South reached a breaking point when Abraham Lincoln, committed to checking the spread of slavery, was elected president in 1860. Southern political leaders, fearing that Lincoln might abolish slavery, seceded and formed a new nation, the Confederate States of America. Lincoln declared the secession illegal and declared war on the seceding states to preserve the territorial integrity of the United States. The ensuing civil war resulted in the deaths of over 750,000 combatants and civilians.

The Emancipation Proclamation, which became effective January 1, 1863, abolished slavery in all states that remained opposed to the Union. It was intended as leverage to bring the rebel states back into the Union, not to abolish slavery altogether, because it freed slaves only in states that had seceded. Nevertheless, the proclamation hastened the demise of slavery. In 1865 Southern rebel states surrendered after Northern armies decimated their industrial, agricultural, and military capacity. Months later, the Thirteenth Amendment to the Constitution fully abolished slavery.

Two aspects made slavery in the United States different from slavery in Latin America: gradual abolition in the North made it a regional rather than a national institution, and the U.S. Civil War, followed by military occupation of the South (1865–1877), created a lasting regional backlash that codified racial segregation. This did not make the South entirely racist and the North entirely antiracist: segregation is a form of racism but hardly the only one. Instead race relations in the northern and western states of the United States resembled those of Latin America, where racial prejudice and the marginalization of African Americans were perpetuated through largely informal practices and values. Meanwhile,

CHAPTER LOCATOR | How and why did the process of nation-state consolidation vary across the Americas? | **Why did slavery last longer in the U.S., Brazil, and Cuba than in other republics of the Americas?**

CHAPTER 27
824 THE AMERICAS IN THE AGE OF LIBERALISM

the U.S. South erected a distinct legal edifice preserving white privilege that best resembled the oppressive white-minority regimes of South Africa and Rhodesia (see page 1007).

Abolition in Cuba and Brazil

Cuba and Brazil followed long and indirect paths to abolition. In Cuba nationalist rebels fought for independence from Spain in the Ten Years' War (1868–1878). Many slaves and free blacks joined the failed anticolonial struggle. Spanish authorities sought to defuse the tensions feeding that struggle by enacting the Moret Law in 1870, which granted freedom to slaves who fought on the Spanish side in the war, to the children of slaves born since 1868, and to slaves over age sixty. By 1878 Spanish forces had defeated the nationalists, but the conflict set in motion an irreversible process of abolition. In Brazil the 1871 Law of the Free Womb also granted freedom to children born to slaves, and an 1885 law granted freedom to slaves over age sixty. Slavery was finally abolished completely in Cuba in 1886 and in Brazil in 1888, making them the last regions of the Americas to end slavery.

Abolition did not come about solely through laws from the top down. Social pressure, often exerted by slaves themselves, contributed to abolition. For example, in Cuba many officers in the nationalist army, including its second-in-command, General Antonio Maceo, were free black abolitionists. In Brazil free blacks like engineer André Rebouças, journalist José do Patrocínio, and novelist Joaquim Machado de Assis were fervent abolitionists who shaped public opinion against slavery and found common cause with a republican movement that saw both slavery and monarchy as outdated.

Slave resistance, in its many forms, also intensified in the last years of the nineteenth century. Slaves ran off from plantations in growing numbers. In many cases, they settled in communities of runaway slaves, particularly in Brazil, where the vast interior offered opportunities to resettle out of the reach of former masters. In the years preceding abolition, in some regions of Brazil slave flight became so widespread that slaves might simply leave their plantation and hire themselves out to a nearby planter whose own slaves had also run away. In the end, the costs of slavery had become unsustainable.

QUICK REVIEW

What connection was there between independence struggles in Spanish America and the abolition of slavery in former Spanish colonies?

How did patterns of economic growth shape social and political culture in Latin America?

What factors shaped immigration patterns to the Americas?

How did U.S. policies in the Caribbean and Central America resemble European imperialism?

☑ LearningCurve
Check what you know.

As Latin America became more integrated into the world economy, how did patterns of economic growth shape social relations and political culture?

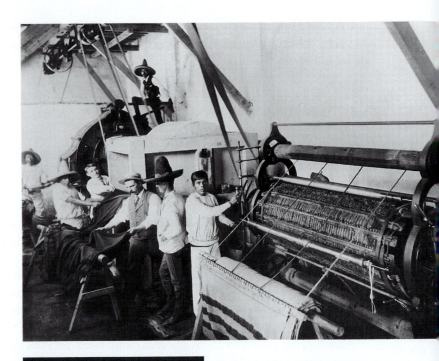

The Growth of Industry in Mexico

Workers at a textile mill in Mexico around 1900.
(© akg-images/The Image Works)

THE CONSOLIDATION OF A LIBERAL ORDER in the Americas through reforms that began in the 1850s and accelerated through conflicts like Mexico's Wars of Reform, the U.S. Civil War, and the Paraguay War in South America created stable conditions for a return of foreign investment that brought economic growth. But reforms intended to create a dynamic class of rural farmers served the opposite ends. In particular, liberalism created new economic pressures against rural workers and indigenous communities.

The Porfiriato and Liberal Stability in Mexico

When Porfirio Díaz became president of Mexico in 1876, he inherited a country in which much had been achieved: President Juárez had established national unity against the French invasion. He and his generation of liberal leaders and policymakers had also created a national legal and political framework based on the 1857 constitution. Conservatives had been defeated and discredited. But it was a country that faced enormous challenges: per capita income was less than it had been at independence in 1821. The country had barely four hundred miles

CHAPTER LOCATOR | How and why did the process of nation-state consolidation vary across the Americas? | Why did slavery last longer in the U.S., Brazil, and Cuba than in other republics of the Americas?

CHAPTER 27

826 THE AMERICAS IN THE AGE OF LIBERALISM

of railroad tracks. The Mexican government was bankrupt and in debt. Díaz's first challenge was to attract foreign investment.

Porfirio Díaz built a regime—the **Porfiriato**—with unprecedented stability and ruled, with a single term out of power, from 1876 to 1911. He ruled by the mantra *pan o palo*, "bread or the stick," rewarding supporters and ruthlessly punishing opponents. The political stability he created made Mexico a haven for foreign investment, particularly from the United States. Investment in industry increased from 25,000 to 30 million pesos, and the value of manufacturing doubled. Foreign trade increased tenfold, and the country became the third largest oil producer. Railroads rapidly expanded, facilitating the shipment of goods to the United States and connecting regions long isolated from each other and from national markets.

The Porfiriato was a modernizing regime, staffed with technocrats called *científicos*: engineers, agronomists, and other experts to whom Díaz granted great autonomy and lavish rewards. By contrast, the Porfiriato considered indigenous peoples racially inferior and suppressed them, often violently, using the mission of modernization and economic development to justify a range of abuses.

Economic progress enriched Díaz and his allies but proved perilous to rural communities. The rise in foreign investment and economic activity made land more valuable, which made small landholders vulnerable. The Lerdo Law, intended to encourage the growth of small farmers, now served the opposite goal as large landowners and speculative investors used it to challenge the legal rights to lands across the Mexican countryside. In addition, the 1883 Law of Barren Lands allowed real estate companies to identify land that was not being cultivated so it could be surveyed and auctioned off. The abuse of these laws by land speculators with ties to the regime, along with intimidation and violence, had devastating consequences: by 1910, 80 percent of rural peasants had no land. The increase in land values paradoxically reduced production: speculators from the United States bought large tracts of land not to farm but to hold as investments.

The Porfiriato and its liberal ideology favored the needs of foreign investors over its own citizens. Most of Mexico's 1910 population of 12 million remained tied to the land. The expansion of railroads into that land made it valuable, and liberal reforms provided the tools to transfer that value from peasants to capitalists. Given Mexico's proximity to the United States, that process was swifter and more intense than elsewhere in Latin America, and it led to the first great social upheaval of the twentieth century, the Mexican Revolution that erupted in 1910.

Porfiriato

▶ The regime of Porfirio Díaz, who presided in Mexico from 1876 to 1880 and again from 1884 to 1910.

Liberal Consolidation in South America

As in the United States and Mexico, the process of liberal nation-state consolidation in South America took place through military conflict. The War of the Triple Alliance, or Paraguay War (1865–1870), in which Paraguay fought Brazil, Argentina, and Uruguay, played a similar role to Mexico's Wars of Reform and the U.S. Civil War in consolidating liberalism in South America. In 1865 Paraguayan leader Francisco Solano López declared war against the three neighboring countries after political competition between Argentina and Brazil threatened Paraguay's use of Uruguay's Atlantic port in Montevideo. Landlocked Paraguay depended on Montevideo as a shipping point for its imports and exports. Paraguay fought a five-year war against much larger neighbors until it was defeated in 1870.

| How did patterns of economic growth shape social and political culture in Latin America? | What factors shaped immigration patterns to the Americas? | How did U.S. policies in the Caribbean and Central America resemble European imperialism? | ☑ LearningCurve Check what you know. |

The war was devastating for Paraguay, which lost more than half its national population, including most adult men. But victory, too, was traumatic for Argentina and Brazil. Argentines and Brazilians asked themselves why it had taken five years to defeat a much smaller neighbor. The war prompted debates about the need for economic modernization and the reform of national governments.

In Brazil, where Emperor Pedro II's calls for volunteers to enlist in the army fell on deaf ears, the army enlisted slaves who, if they served honorably and survived, would be granted freedom. What did it mean when the free citizens of a nation would not mobilize to defend it, and when a nation prevailed only through the sacrifices borne by its slaves? For many, especially military officers who were veterans of the conflict, the lesson was that being a monarchy that relied on slavery made Brazil a backward nation. Veteran officers and liberal opponents of the war formed a movement to create a liberal republic and abolish slavery. These republicans overthrew monarchy in 1889 and installed a liberal regime that lasted until 1930.

In Argentina, after the war with Paraguay, a succession of liberal leaders beginning with Domingo Sarmiento (pres. 1868–1874) also pressed modernizing reforms. Economic measures in Argentina were the most far-reaching and drew on the experience of the United States in settling its western frontier as a model. In a military campaign called the Conquest of the Desert (1878–1885), Argentine troops took control of the lands of Mapuche Indians in the southern region of Patagonia and opened new lands for sale to ranchers. The wars were accompanied by ambitious railroad construction that linked inland areas to the coast, the introduction of barbed wire fencing that intensified ranching capabilities, and the development of new strains of cattle and wheat that increased production. The Conquest of the Desert and the government's land distribution policies transformed Argentina's countryside into highly productive ranch lands and farmlands whose exports competed directly with the ranches of the North American West.

Latin America Re-enters the World Economy

The wars of independence in Spanish America interrupted the Atlantic and Pacific trade networks that had sustained the region's colonial economies. Amid the political instability that followed independence, investment dried up and trade networks collapsed. For rural peasants and indigenous communities, this was a benefit in disguise: the decline of trade made lands less valuable. The rents landowners could charge tenant farmers decreased, making it easier for peasants to gain access to land.

By the second half of the nineteenth century Latin American elites reached a compromise that combined liberal political ideas about the way national government should be structured with liberal economic policies that favored large landowners. Political stability and economic growth returned. Foreign investment intensified. By the turn of the twentieth century Latin American countries were firmly tied to the world economy. Indigenous and rural communities paid a high price for this return to economic growth: as the value of agricultural exports increased, so did the value of land. Governments, foreign investors, and large landowners seized lands through war, legal action, or coercion at a dizzying rate.

As Latin American governments stabilized, they consolidated control of national territory in part by eliminating, subjugating, or displacing indigenous

CHAPTER LOCATOR | How and why did the process of nation-state consolidation vary across the Americas? | Why did slavery last longer in the U.S., Brazil, and Cuba than in other republics of the Americas?

CHAPTER 27
828 THE AMERICAS IN THE AGE OF LIBERALISM

communities. Through this process, Latin American governments opened new lands for private ownership.

After the Conquest of the Desert in the 1870s and 1880s, the Argentine government sold off lands it took from indigenous communities. The land was inexpensive, but because it was sold in such large parcels, the few who could purchase it did so by mortgaging existing landholdings. Consequently, more than 20 million acres were sold to just 381 landowners, who created vast estates known as latifundios. In contrast, the Brazilian Land Law of 1850 restricted land ownership by prohibiting anyone from gaining title to land by settling it. The law was a response to pressure from Britain to end the slave trade: planters used the law to keep slaves or free workers on their plantations by preventing them from setting out to farm on their own.[2]

latifundios
▶ Large landed estates.

Liberal economic policies and the intensification of foreign trade concentrated land in the hands of wealthy exporters. Governments represented the interests of large landowners by promoting commodity exports and industrial imports. Brazil became the world's largest exporter of coffee and experienced a brief but intense boom in rubber production. Argentina's conquests on the frontier and economic modernization made it one of the most efficient and profitable exporters of grains and beef. Chile and Peru served the international market for fertilizers by exporting nitrates and bat guano.

These export booms depended on imported capital and technology. In the Circum-Caribbean this came mostly from investors in the United States, while in South America it came from Britain. (See "Individuals in Society: Henry Meiggs, Promoter and Speculator," page 830.) British capital and technology built Argentina's network of railroads and refrigerated meatpacking plants. By 1890 British companies controlled 90 percent of Chile's nitrate-mining industry.

The rise in the quantity and value of primary commodity exports concentrated wealth in the hands of oligarchs. Large landowners, such as Brazilian coffee planters, relied on cheap labor provided by slaves until 1888 and, increasingly, by tenant farmers and free laborers who worked for little pay. The exported coffee produced by these workers reaped profits so great that, although coffee planters were the main slaveholders, they could afford to give up slavery and pursue immigrant labor from Europe. In the late nineteenth century planters united to create colonization companies in southern European cities that promoted and subsidized immigration to Brazil. The planters combined economic liberalism with Social Darwinism: they believed that free workers were more efficient than slave laborers and that white workers were more productive than black ones.

QUICK REVIEW ‹

What groups benefitted most from economic growth in Latin America in the second half of the nineteenth century?

How did patterns of economic growth shape social and political culture in Latin America?

What factors shaped immigration patterns to the Americas?

How did U.S. policies in the Caribbean and Central America resemble European imperialism?

✓ LearningCurve
Check what you know.

Henry Meiggs, Promoter and Speculator

All throughout the Americas in the nineteenth century, opportunities beckoned. Henry Meiggs, born in upstate New York in 1811, responded to several of them, building and losing fortunes in Brooklyn, San Francisco, Chile, and Peru.

Meiggs, with only an elementary school education, began work at his father's shipyard. He soon started his own lumber business and did well until he lost everything in the financial panic of 1837. He rebuilt his business, and when gold was discovered in California in 1848, he filled a ship with lumber and sailed around Cape Horn to San Francisco, where he sold his cargo for $50,000, twenty times what he had paid for it. He then entered the lumber business, organizing crews of five hundred men to fell huge California redwoods and bring them to his steam sawmills. As his business flourished, he began speculating in real estate, which led to huge debts when the financial crisis of 1854 hit. In an attempt to save himself and his friends, Meiggs forged warrants for more than $900,000; when discovery of the fraud seemed imminent, he sailed with his wife and children for South America.

Although at one point Meiggs was so strapped for cash that he sold his watch, within three years of arriving in Chile, he had secured his first railway contract, and by 1867 he had built about 200 miles of rail lines in that country. In 1868 he went to Peru, which had less than 60 miles of track at the time. In the next nine years he would add 700 more.

Meiggs was not an engineer, but he was a good manager. He recruited experienced engineers from abroad and arranged purchase of foreign rolling stock, rails, and ties, acting as a promoter and developer. Much of the funding came from international investors in Peruvian bonds.

The most spectacular of the rail lines Meiggs built was Peru's Callao-Lima-Oroya line, which crosses the Andes at about seventeen thousand feet above sea level, making it the highest standard-gauge railway in the world. Because water was scarce in many areas along the construction site, it had to be transported up to workers, who were mostly local people. Dozens of bridges and tunnels had to be built, and casualties were high. Eight hundred people were invited to the banquet that marked the beginning of work on the Oroya Railway. Meiggs drummed up enthusiasm at the event by calling the locomotive the "irresistible battering ram of modern civilization."

In Peru Meiggs became known for his extravagance and generosity, and some charged that he bribed Peruvian officials on a large scale to get his projects approved. He was a good speaker and loved

The challenges in building the Callo-Lima-Oroya railroad across the Andes can be imagined from this picture of one of its many bridges. (From Elio Galessio, *Ferrocarriles del Perú: Un viaje a través de su Historia*. Reproduced with permission of the author.)

to entertain lavishly. In one example of his generosity, he distributed thousands of pesos and soles to the victims of the earthquake of 1868. He also contributed to the beautification of Lima by tearing down an old wall and putting a seven-mile-long park in its place.

Always the speculator, in 1877 Meiggs died poor, his debts exceeding his assets. He was beloved, however, and more than twenty thousand Peruvians, many of whom had labored on his projects, attended his funeral at a Catholic church in Lima.

QUESTIONS FOR ANALYSIS

1. What accounts for the changes in fortune that Meiggs experienced?
2. Were the Latin American governments that awarded contracts to Meiggs making reasonable decisions?
3. Should it matter whether Meiggs had to bribe officials to get the railroads built? Why or why not?

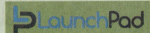

ONLINE DOCUMENT PROJECT

How did investors like Henry Meiggs fit into the larger context of Latin American nation building? Read descriptions of Latin America's past and visions of its future, and then complete a quiz and writing assignment based on the evidence and details from this chapter. *See inside the front cover to learn more.*

Immigrants in the Americas

Indian immigrants at a Jamaican banana plantation (top) and German immigrants in Brazil (bottom) at the turn of the twentieth century. Immigrants brought new cultures and worldviews to the Americas. (Jamaica: *Picturesque Jamaica*, by Adolphe Duperly & Son, England, circa 1905/Brazil: © The Print Collector/Heritage/The Image Works; © SZ Photo/Scherl/The Image Works)

DURING THE LATE NINETEENTH and early twentieth centuries unprecedented numbers of people from Europe, Asia, and the Middle East settled across North and South America. The largest wave of immigrants—some 28 million between 1860 and 1914—settled in the United States. Another 8 million had settled in Argentina and Brazil by 1930. This cycle of immigration was a product of liberal political and economic reforms that abolished slavery, established stable political systems, and created a framework for integrating immigrants as factory and farm laborers.

How did patterns of economic growth shape social and political culture in Latin America?

What factors shaped immigration patterns to the Americas?

How did U.S. policies in the Caribbean and Central America resemble European imperialism?

✔ LearningCurve
Check what you know.

Immigration to Latin America

In 1852 the Argentine political philosopher Juan Bautista Alberdi published *Bases and Points of Departure for Argentine Political Organization*, in which he argued that the development of his country depended on immigration. Indians and blacks, Alberdi maintained, lacked basic skills, and it would take too long to train them. Thus he pressed for massive immigration from northern Europe and the United States. Alberdi's ideas, guided by the aphorism "to govern is to populate," won immediate acceptance and were even incorporated into the Argentine constitution, which declared, "The Federal government will encourage European immigration." Other Latin American countries adopted similar policies promoting immigration to achieve similar goals.

Coffee barons in Brazil, *latifundiarios* (owners of vast estates) in Argentina, or investors in nitrate and copper mining in Chile made enormous profits that they reinvested in new factories. Latin America had been tied to the Industrial Revolution in Britain and northern Europe from the outset as a provider of raw materials and as a consumer of industrial goods. In the major exporting countries of Argentina, Brazil, and Mexico, domestic industrialization now began to take hold in the form of textile mills, food-processing plants, and mechanized transportation such as modern ports and railroads.

By the turn of the twentieth century, an industrial working-class had begun to emerge. In Brazil and Argentina these workers, who were mainly European immigrants, proved unexpectedly contentious: they brought with them radical ideologies that challenged liberalism, particularly anarchism and **anarcho-syndicalism**, a version of anarchism that advocated placing power in the hands of workers' unions. These workers clashed with bosses and political leaders who rejected the idea that workers had rights. The authorities suppressed worker organizations such as unions, and they resisted implementing labor laws such as a minimum wage, restrictions on child labor, the right to strike, or factory safety regulations.

Although Europe was a significant source of immigrants to Latin America, so were Asia and the Middle East. For example, in the late nineteenth and early twentieth centuries large numbers of Japanese arrived in Brazil, and by 1920 Brazil had the largest Japanese community in the world outside of Japan. From the Middle East, Lebanese, Turks, and Syrians also entered Brazil. Between 1850 and 1880, South Asian laborers went to Trinidad, Jamaica, St. Lucia, Grenada, and St. Vincent, mostly as indentured servants. When slavery was abolished in Cuba in 1886, some of the work in the sugarcane fields was done by Chinese indentured servants. Likewise, the abolition of slavery in Mexico led to the arrival of thousands of Chinese bonded servants.

Thanks to the influx of new arrivals, Buenos Aires, São Paulo, Mexico City, Montevideo, Santiago, and Havana experienced spectacular growth. By 1914 Buenos Aires in particular had emerged as one of the most cosmopolitan cities in the world, with a population of 3.6 million.

Immigrants brought wide-ranging skills that helped develop industry and commerce. In Argentina, Italian and Spanish settlers stimulated the expansion of the cattle industry and the development of the wheat and shoe industries. In Brazil, Swiss immigrants built the cheese business, Italians gained a leading role in the coffee industry, and Japanese farmers made the country self-sufficient in rice production. In Peru, Italians became influential in banking and the restaurant

anarcho-syndicalism

▶ A radical ideology that proposed the revolutionary reorganization of society into an egalitarian community ruled by workers' unions.

CHAPTER LOCATOR | How and why did the process of nation-state consolidation vary across the Americas? | Why did slavery last longer in the U.S., Brazil, and Cuba than in other republics of the Americas?

CHAPTER 27

832 THE AMERICAS IN THE AGE OF LIBERALISM

business, while the French dominated dressmaking as well as the jewelry and pharmaceutical businesses. Chinese laborers built Peruvian railroads, and in sections of large cities such as Lima, the Chinese dominated the ownership of shops and restaurants.

Immigration to the United States

After the Civil War ended in 1865, the United States underwent an industrial boom powered by exploitation of the country's natural resources. The federal government turned over vast amounts of land and mineral resources to private industrialists for development. In particular, railroad companies—the foundation of industrial expansion—received 130 million acres. By 1900 the U.S. railroad system, was 193,000 miles long, connected every part of the nation, and represented 40 percent of the railroad mileage in the world, and it was all built by immigrant labor.

Between 1860 and 1914, 28 million immigrants came to the United States. Though many became rural homesteaders, industrial America developed on the sweat and brawn of immigrants. As in South America, immigration fed the growth of cities.

Working conditions for new immigrants were often deplorable. Industrialization had created a vast class of workers who depended entirely on wage labor. Employers paid women and children much less than men. Because business owners resisted government efforts to install costly safety devices, working conditions in mines and mills were frightful. In 1913 alone, even after some safety measures had been instituted, twenty-five thousand people died in industrial accidents.

Immigrants in Hawaii

Fruit store owned and run by Chinese immigrants in Honolulu, Hawaii, around 1905.
(The Art Archive at Art Resource, NY)

How did patterns of economic growth shape social and political culture in Latin America?

What factors shaped immigration patterns to the Americas?

How did U.S. policies in the Caribbean and Central America resemble European imperialism?

✓ LearningCurve
Check what you know.

"The Chinese Must Go!"

Anti-immigrant sentiment intensified as immigration to the United States accelerated in the late nineteenth and early twentieth centuries. This 1880 campaign advertisement presented Chinese immigrants as a threat to native-born workers.

Workers responded to these conditions with strikes, violence, and, gradually, unionization.

Immigrants faced more than economic exploitation: they were also subjected to harsh ethnic stereotypes and faced pressure to assimilate culturally. An economic depression in the 1890s increased resentment toward immigrants. Powerful owners of mines, mills, and factories fought the organization of labor unions, fired thousands of workers, slashed wages, and ruthlessly exploited their workers. Workers in turn feared that immigrant labor would drive salaries lower. Some of this antagonism sprang from racism, some from old Protestant suspicions of Roman Catholicism, the faith of many of the new arrivals. Long-standing anti-Semitism against Jewish immigrants from eastern Europe intensified, while increasingly violent agitation against Asians led to race riots in California and finally culminated in the Chinese Exclusion Act of 1882, which denied Chinese laborers entrance to the country. Japanese immigration to the United States was restricted in 1907, so later Japanese immigrants settled in South America, especially Brazil.

Immigrants were received very differently in Latin America, where oligarchs encouraged immigration from Europe, the Middle East, and Japan because they believed these "whiter" workers were superior to native-born, often racially mixed workers. By contrast, in the United States the descendants of northern European Protestants developed prejudices and built social barriers out of their belief that Catholic Irish, southern and eastern European, or Jewish immigrants were not white enough.

CHAPTER LOCATOR | How and why did the process of nation-state consolidation vary across the Americas? | Why did slavery last longer in the U.S., Brazil, and Cuba than in other republics of the Americas?

834 CHAPTER 27 THE AMERICAS IN THE AGE OF LIBERALISM

Immigration to Canada

Canada was sparsely populated in the nineteenth century relative to other areas of the Americas. Provinces of the British colony gained governing autonomy after 1840 and organized a national government, the Dominion of Canada, in 1867 (Map 27.3). As in the United States and Latin America, the native peoples were pushed aside by Canada's development plans, and their population dropped by half or more during the century, many succumbing to the newcomers' diseases. French Canadians were the largest minority in the population, and they remained different in language, law, and religion.

Immigration to Canada increased in the 1890s. Between 1897 and 1912, 961,000 people entered Canada from the British Isles, 594,000 from Europe, and 784,000 from the United States. Some immigrants went to work in the urban factories of Hamilton, Toronto, and Montreal. However, most immigrants from continental Europe—Poles, Germans, Scandinavians, and Russians—flooded the midwestern plains and soon transformed the prairies into one of the world's greatest

---

MAP 27.3 ■ The Dominion of Canada, 1871

Shortly after the Dominion of Canada came into being as a self-governing nation within the British Empire in 1867, new provinces were added. Vast areas of Canada were too sparsely populated to achieve provincial status. Alberta and Saskatchewan did not become part of the Dominion until 1905; Newfoundland was added only in 1949.

How did patterns of economic growth shape social and political culture in Latin America?

What factors shaped immigration patterns to the Americas?

How did U.S. policies in the Caribbean and Central America resemble European imperialism?

✓ LearningCurve
Check what you know.

Russian Immigrant Women in Saskatchewan

These women were Doukhobors, members of a Christian religious sect who came to Canada from Russia seeking religious freedom from tsarist persecution. While most of the men took railroad jobs, the women planted the vast plains with rye, wheat, oats, and flax. Their farms and orchards flourished, and the Doukhobors played an important role in the development of western Canada. (Saskatchewan Archives Board, photo no. R-B 1964)

grain-growing regions. Mining also expanded, and British Columbia, Ontario, and Quebec produced large quantities of wood pulp, much of it sold to the United States. Canada's great rivers were harnessed to supply hydroelectric power for industrial and domestic use. But Canada remained a predominantly agricultural country, with less than 10 percent of its population engaged in manufacturing.

> **QUICK REVIEW**

How did racial attitudes shape immigration to the Americas in the second half of the nineteenth century?

CHAPTER LOCATOR | How and why did the process of nation-state consolidation vary across the Americas? | Why did slavery last longer in the U.S., Brazil, and Cuba than in other republics of the Americas?

In what ways did U.S. policies in the Caribbean and Central America resemble European imperialism? How did U.S. foreign policy depart from European imperialism?

BY 1890 THE UNITED STATES HAD CLAIMED the contiguous territories it acquired through purchase, war, and displacement. Its frontier was closed. The United States redirected its expansionist pressures outward, beginning with the remnants of the Spanish Empire: Cuba and Puerto Rico in the Caribbean, and the Philippine Islands and Guam in the Pacific.

U.S. Intervention in Latin America

Between 1898 and 1932 the U.S. government intervened militarily thirty-four times in ten nations in the Caribbean and Central America to extend and protect its economic interests. U.S. influence in the Circum-Caribbean was not new, however, and stretched back to the early nineteenth century. In 1823 President James Monroe proclaimed in the **Monroe Doctrine** that the United States would keep European influence out of Latin America. This bold assertion established Latin America as part of the U.S. sphere of influence. U.S. interventions in Latin America were also a byproduct of the manifest destiny ideal of consolidating national territory from the Atlantic to the Pacific. Often the easiest way to connect the two sides of the continent was through Latin America.

The California gold rush of the 1840s created pressure to move people and goods quickly and inexpensively between the eastern and western parts of the United States decades before its transcontinental railroad was completed in 1869. It was cheaper, faster, and safer to travel to the east or west coast of Mexico and Central America, traverse the continent where it was narrower, and continue the voyage by sea. The Panama Railway, the first railroad constructed in Central America, served exactly this purpose and was built with U.S. investment in 1855.

Monroe Doctrine

▶ Established a U.S. sphere of influence over the Americas by opposing European imperialism on the continent.

How did patterns of economic growth shape social and political culture in Latin America?

What factors shaped immigration patterns to the Americas?

How did U.S. policies in the Caribbean and Central America resemble European imperialism?

✓ LearningCurve
Check what you know.

837

Planters and politicians in the U.S. South, who faced pressure from northern abolitionists against the westward territorial expansion of the slave regime, responded by seeking opportunities to annex new lands in Latin America and the Caribbean. They eyed Cuba, the Dominican Republic, El Salvador, and Nicaragua. In Nicaragua, Tennessean William Walker employed a mercenary army to depose the government and install himself as president (1856–1857). One of his first acts was to reinstate slavery. He was overthrown by armies sent from Costa Rica, El Salvador, and Honduras.

By the end of the nineteenth century U.S. involvement in Latin America had intensified, first through private investment and then through military force. In 1893 a group of New York investors bought the foreign debt of the Dominican Republic and took control of its customs houses in order to repay investors and creditors. After the government propped up by the U.S. company fell, President Theodore Roosevelt intervened, introducing what would be known as the **Roosevelt Corollary** to the Monroe Doctrine, which stated that the United States, as a civilized nation, would correct the "chronic wrongdoing" of its neighbors, such as failure to protect U.S. investments.

To this end, in 1903 and 1904 Roosevelt deployed Marines to the Dominican Republic to protect the investments of U.S. firms. Marines occupied and governed the Dominican Republic again from 1916 to 1924. The violent and corrupt dictator Rafael Trujillo ruled from 1930 to 1961 with the support of the United States. When he eventually defied the United States, he was assassinated by rivals acting with the encouragement of the Central Intelligence Agency.

Versions of the Dominican Republic's experience played out across the Circum-Caribbean. These military occupations followed a similar pattern of using military force to protect private U.S. companies' investments. During repeated occupations, the U.S. military ruled like dictators and violently suppressed protest and resistance. And as U.S. forces departed, they left power in the hands of dictators who served U.S. interests. These dictators governed not through popular consent but through force, corruption, and the support of the United States.

Roosevelt Corollary

▶ A corollary to the Monroe Doctrine stating that the United States would "correct" what it saw as wrongdoing in neighboring countries.

The Spanish-American War

In Cuba a second war of independence erupted in 1895 after it had failed to gain freedom from Spain in the Ten Years' War (1868–1878). A brutal war of attrition ensued, and by 1898 the countryside was in ruins and Spanish colonial control was restricted to a handful of cities. Cuban nationalists were on the verge of defeating the Spanish forces and gaining independence. But before they could realize this goal, the United States intervened.

The U.S. intervention began with a provocative act: sailing the battleship *Maine* into Havana harbor. This was an aggressive act because the battleship was capable of bombarding the entire city. But soon after it laid anchor, the *Maine* exploded and sank, killing hundreds of sailors. The U.S. government accused Spain of sinking the warship, a charge Spain denied, and demanded that the Spanish government provide restitution. Regardless of the cause, the sinking of the *Maine* led to war between Spain and the United States over control of Cuba and the Philippines. From April to August 1898 the U.S. Navy and Marines fought and defeated Spanish forces in the Pacific and the Caribbean. With its victory, the

CHAPTER LOCATOR | How and why did the process of nation-state consolidation vary across the Americas? | Why did slavery last longer in the U.S., Brazil, and Cuba than in other republics of the Americas?

838 CHAPTER 27 THE AMERICAS IN THE AGE OF LIBERALISM

United States acquired Guam and Puerto Rico and launched a military occupation of Cuba and the Philippines.

Puerto Rico and Guam became colonies directly ruled by U.S. administrators, and residents of both island territories did not gain the right to elect their own leaders until after the Second World War. They remained commonwealths (territories that are not states) of the United States. The U.S. government also established direct rule in the Philippines, brushing aside the government established by Filipino nationalists who had fought for freedom from Spain. Nationalists then fought against the Unites States in an unsuccessful effort to establish an independent government in the Philippine-American War (1899–1902).

Cuba alone gained formal independence, but U.S. pressure limited that independence. The Platt Amendment, which the United States imposed as a condition of Cuban independence, gave the United States the power to cancel laws passed by the Cuban congress, withheld the Cuban government's right to establish foreign treaties, and granted the United States control over Guantanamo Bay, where it established a permanent naval base. Moreover, the United States militarily occupied Cuba in 1899–1902, 1906–1908, and 1912. Between 1917 and 1922 U.S. administrator Enoch Crowder governed the island.

The constraints that the U.S. government imposed on Cuban politics, along with its willingness to deploy troops and periodically establish military rule, created a safe and fertile environment for U.S. investment. By 1919 half of the island's sugar mills were owned by U.S. businesses. Small farms were consolidated into massive estates as twenty-two companies took hold of 20 percent of Cuba's national territory. U.S. companies like Coca-Cola and Hershey were among the new landowners that took control of their most important ingredient: sugar.

The United States imported its prevailing racial policies to its new Caribbean territories. In Cuba, U.S. authorities encouraged political parties to exclude black Cubans. Black war veterans established the Independent Party of Color in 1908 in order to press for political inclusion. The party was banned in 1910, and in 1912 its leaders organized a revolt that led to a violent backlash by the army and police, supported by U.S. Marines. The campaign against members of the party was followed by a wave of lynchings of black Cubans across the island.

In Puerto Rico the influence of U.S. racism was more direct. The United States carried out the involuntary sterilization of thousands of Puerto Rican women as part of a policy aimed at addressing what the government saw as overpopulation on the island. In addition, Puerto Rican men drafted into U.S. military service were organized into segregated units, as African Americans were.

The Panama Canal

U.S. imperialism in the Caribbean extended beyond Cuba and Puerto Rico to the prize the United States had pursued for decades: a canal to connect the Atlantic and Pacific Oceans. The canal would transport cargo between the east and west of the United States much less expensively than rail. In the mid-nineteenth century the U.S. railroad tycoon Cornelius Vanderbilt tried but failed to build a canal through Nicaragua. Later in the century, a consortium of French investors pursued the construction of a canal in the Columbian province of Panama. Engineers and laborers completed some excavation before the French company went bankrupt.

How did patterns of economic growth shape social and political culture in Latin America?

What factors shaped immigration patterns to the Americas?

How did U.S. policies in the Caribbean and Central America resemble European imperialism?

☑ LearningCurve
Check what you know.

839

After the Spanish-American War, U.S. authorities negotiated with the Colombian government for the right to continue the project started by the French company, but the Colombian congress balked at the U.S. government's demand that it should have territorial control of the canal. The U.S. government responded by encouraging an insurrection in Panama City and recognized the rebels as leaders of the new country of Panama. With the 1904 Isthmian Canal Convention, the new Panamanian government gave the United States permanent control over the canal and the land upon which it was built, which became known as the Canal Zone. The Canal Zone became an unincorporated U.S. territory.

Tens of thousands of migrant workers from around the Caribbean provided labor for construction of the canal, which opened in 1914. U.S. authorities instituted the same segregationist policies applied in their other Caribbean territories. Workers were divided into a "gold roll" of highly paid white U.S. workers and a "silver role" of mostly black workers, who came from Barbados, Panama, Nicaragua, Colombia and other parts of the Caribbean. They were paid lower wages, faced much higher rates of death and injury, and lived in less healthy conditions. The Canal Zone itself functioned as a segregated enclave: U.S. residents could move freely between it and Panamanian territory, but it was closed to Panamanians except those who entered through labor contracts.

> QUICK REVIEW

What motives were behind the United States' repeated military interventions in Latin America? How did the United States justify its actions?

CHAPTER SUMMARY

In the century after independence, political consolidation and economic integration varied across the Americas. The North of the United States became the continent's main engine of capital accumulation, immigration, and industrialization. In other regions political and economic conditions produced different results. In the U.S. South and Brazil reliance on slavery weakened internal markets, inhibited immigration, and slowed industrialization. In Spanish America the lack of a governing consensus until the second half of the nineteenth century led new countries to fall behind not only relative to other regions of the world but even relative to their past colonial experiences.

The cycle of war that began in the 1850s and continued for the next two decades reshaped the Americas politically and economically, consolidating a liberal order that placed great wealth in few hands while dealing misery and dislocation to many others. Liberalism had a modernizing influence on trade and industry, but it further concentrated wealth. Just as the United States waged wars against the Indians and pushed its frontier westward, so too did the countries of Latin America. Racial prejudice kept most African Americans at the social and economic margins.

CHAPTER LOCATOR | How and why did the process of nation-state consolidation vary across the Americas? | Why did slavery last longer in the U.S., Brazil, and Cuba than in other republics of the Americas?

By the beginning of the twentieth century, the economies of American nations were tightly integrated into the world economy, and powerful currents of immigration further deepened ties between countries. Industrialization that began in the northeast of the United States developed elsewhere in the continent, but the lead in industrialization held by the United States allowed it to increasingly impose its will over other nations. The economic and social dislocations produced by the liberal model of export-oriented economic growth also awoke growing social demands by the rural and urban poor. These boiled over the most dramatically in Mexico's 1910 revolution, but in cities to the south such as Buenos Aires, Argentina, and Santiago, Chile, workers' demands for the right to organize for better wages and for political representation were becoming too insistent to ignore.

 **CONNECTIONS** In the Americas the century or so between independence and World War I was a time of nation building. Colonial governments were overthrown, new constitutions were written, settlement was extended, slavery was ended, and immigrants from around the world settled across the continents. On the eve of World War I, there was reason to be optimistic about the future of all these countries.

World War I, the topic of the next chapter, affected these countries in a variety of ways. Canada followed Britain into the war in 1914 and sent six hundred thousand men to fight. The United States did not join the war until 1917, but quickly mobilized several million men and in 1918 began sending soldiers and materials in huge numbers. Even countries that maintained neutrality, as all the Latin American countries other than Brazil did, felt the economic impact of the war deeply, especially the increased demand for food and manufactured goods. For the working class the global demand for exported foods drove up the cost of living, but the profits that oligarchs accummulated fueled the process of industrialization.

How did patterns of economic growth shape social and political culture in Latin America?

What factors shaped immigration patterns to the Americas?

How did U.S. policies in the Caribbean and Central America resemble European imperialism?

☑ **LearningCurve**
Check what you know.

STEP 1 GET STARTED ONLINE

✓ **LearningCurve**

Now that you've read the chapter, make it stick by completing the LearningCurve activity.

STEP 2 EXPLAIN WHY IT MATTERS

Put your reading into practice. Identify each term below, and then explain why it matters in world history.

TERM	WHO OR WHAT & WHEN	WHY IT MATTERS
liberalism (p. 814)		
oligarchs (p. 815)		
Circum-Caribbean (p. 815)		
caudillismo (p. 816)		
manifest destiny (p. 816)		
Treaty of Guadalupe Hidalgo (p. 818)		
Lerdo Law (p. 819)		
neocolonialism (p. 820)		
free womb laws (p. 823)		
Porfiriato (p. 827)		
latifundios (p. 829)		
anarcho-syndicalism (p. 832)		
Monroe Doctrine (p. 837)		
Roosevelt Corollary (p. 838)		

STEP 3 MOVE BEYOND THE BASICS

To demonstrate a more advanced understanding of the development of the United States and the independent nations of Latin America in the nineteenth century, fill in the chart below with descriptions of the nature of government and degree of democratization, economic development, and the impact of race on society. How did race shape American societies in both South and North America?

	Government and Democracy	Economic Development	Race and Society
United States			
Latin America			

STEP 4

PUT IT ALL TOGETHER

Now, take a step back and try to explain the big picture. Remember to use specific examples from the chapter in your answers.

NEW NATIONS AND THE ABOLITION OF SLAVERY

▶ What role did political liberalism play in Latin American independence movements?

▶ How did the various new nations of the Americas deal with the issue of slavery? How would you explain the differences you note?

ECONOMIC AND DEMOGRAPHIC TRENDS

▶ Why did so many Latin American nations develop economies focused on the export of commodities? What were the advantages and disadvantages of such an approach to economic growth?

▶ What forces drew new immigrants to the Americas in the second half of the nineteenth century?

A NEW AMERICAN EMPIRE

▶ Why did so many Americans look to Latin America for new opportunities at the end of the nineteenth century?

▶ What policies and practices did the United States use to control the governments and economies of its Latin American neighbors?

LOOKING BACK, LOOKING AHEAD

▶ How did the process of nation building in the Americas differ from the nation building in Italy and Germany (see Chapter 24) that occurred in roughly the same time period?

▶ What new opportunities and challenges might the devastation of old nations of Europe in World War I have created for the new nations covered in this chapter?

> ## IN YOUR OWN WORDS

Imagine that you must give an oral report to the class answering the following question: **How did liberal political and economic ideas shape the development of the Americas in the nineteenth century?** What would be the most important points and why?

28
WORLD WAR AND REVOLUTION

1914–1929

> ### > In what ways did the First World War represent a fundamental turning point in world history?

Chapter 28 examines the First World War, the Russian Revolution, and the decade that followed these cataclysmic events. The First World War was long, global, indecisive, and tremendously destructive. All of the major combatant nations were traumatized and transformed by the war. In Russia, military defeat once again led to social and political unrest. This time, however, the tsarist regime did not survive and was replaced by history's first Communist state. When the war was finally over, the victorious Allies, led by Britain, France, and the United States, met in Paris to plan the peace to come. In the end, few left Paris satisfied with the results. The peace and prosperity the delegates sought lasted barely a decade.

 **LearningCurve**

After reading the chapter, use LearningCurve to retain what you've read.

Senegalese Soldier A *tirailleur* (literally, "skirmisher") from French West Africa who fought in Europe during the Great War. Across the bottom of this postcard image from the era, the soldier proclaimed his loyalty with the phrase "Glory to the Greater France," meaning France and its colonies. Note the two German *pickelhaube* (spike helmets) he wears on his head. (Private Collection/Archives Charmet/The Bridgeman Art Library)

> What were the long-term and immediate causes of World War I, and how did the conflict become a global war?

> How did total war affect the home fronts of the major combatants?

> What factors led to the Russian Revolution, and what was its outcome?

> What were the global consequences of the First World War?

> How did leaders deal with the political dimensions of uncertainty and try to re-establish peace and prosperity in the interwar years?

> In what ways were the anxieties of the postwar world expressed or heightened by revolutionary ideas in modern thought, art, and science and in new forms of communication?

What were the long-term and immediate causes of World War I, and how did the conflict become a global war?

Henri de Groux, *The Assault, Verdun*

An eerie portrayal by Belgian artist Henri de Groux (1867–1930) of French troops moving forward in a thick haze of smoke and perhaps clouds of diphosgene, a poisonous gas first used by the Germans at Verdun on June 22, 1916. (Musées des Deux Guerres Mondiales, Paris, France/The Bridgeman Art Library)

THE FIRST WORLD WAR CLEARLY MARKED a major break in the course of world history. The maps of Europe and southwest Asia were redrawn, nationalist movements took root and spread across Asia (see Chapter 29), America consolidated its position as a global power, and the world experienced, for the first time, industrialized, total war. Europe's Great Powers started the war and suffered the most. Imperialism also brought the conflict to the Middle East, Africa, and Asia, making this a global war of unprecedented scope.

Origins and Causes of the Great War

Any study of the Great War's origins must begin with nationalism (see Chapter 24), one of the major ideologies of the nineteenth century, and its armed companion, **militarism**, the glorification of the military as the supreme ideal of the state with all other interests subordinate to it. European concerns over national security, economies, welfare, identities, and overseas empires set nation against nation, alliance against alliance, and army against army until they all went to war at once.

militarism
▶ The glorification of the military as the supreme ideal of the state with all other interests subordinate to it.

CHAPTER LOCATOR | **What were the long-term and immediate causes of World War I, how did it become a global war?** | How did total war affect the home fronts of the major combatants?

1914
Assassination of Archduke Franz Ferdinand; Ottoman Empire joins Central Powers; German victories on the eastern front

1914–1918
World War I

1914
Japan joins the Triple Entente and seizes German holdings in China

1915
Italy joins the Triple Entente; German submarine sinks the *Lusitania*; Japan expands into southern Manchuria

1916
Battles of Verdun and the Somme; Irish Easter Rebellion; German Auxiliary Service Law requires seventeen- to sixty-year-old males to work for war effort; Rasputin murdered

1916–1918
Growth of antiwar sentiment throughout Europe

1917
United States declares war on Germany; Bolshevik Revolution in Russia

1917–1922
Civil war in Russia

1918
Treaty of Brest-Litovsk; revolution in Germany

1919
Treaty of Versailles; Freudian psychology gains popularity; Rutherford splits the atom; Bauhaus school founded

1920s
Existentialism, Dadaism, and surrealism gain prominence

1923
French and Belgian armies occupy the Ruhr

1924
Dawes Plan

1926
Germany joins League of Nations

1928
Kellogg-Briand Pact

Competition between nations intensified greatly when Germany became a unified nation-state and the most powerful country in Europe in 1871 (see page 726). A new era in international relations began, as Chancellor Bismarck declared Germany a "satisfied" power, having no territorial ambitions within Europe and desiring only peace.

But how to preserve the peace? Bismarck's first concern was to keep rival France diplomatically isolated and without military allies. His second concern was to prevent Germany from being dragged into a war between the two rival empires, Austria-Hungary and Russia, as they sought to fill the power vacuum created in the Balkans by the Ottoman Empire's decline (see pages 765–767). To these ends, Bismarck brokered a series of treaties and alliances, all meant to ensure the balance of power in Europe and to prevent the outbreak of war.

In 1890 Germany's new emperor, William II, forced Bismarck to resign and then abandoned many of Bismarck's efforts to ensure German security through promoting European peace and stability. William refused to renew a nonaggression pact Bismarck had signed with Russia, for example, which prompted France to court the tsar, offering loans and arms, and sign a Franco-Russian Alliance in 1892. With France and Russia now allied against Germany, Austria, and Italy, Great Britain's foreign policy became increasingly crucial. Many Germans and some Britons felt that the racially related Germanic and Anglo-Saxon peoples were natural allies. However, the good relations that had prevailed between Prussia and Great Britain since the mid-eighteenth century gave way after 1890 to a bitter Anglo-German rivalry.

There were several reasons for this development. Germany and Great Britain's commercial rivalry in world markets and Kaiser William's publicly expressed

What factors led to the Russian Revolution, and what was its outcome?

What were the global consequences of the First World War?

How did leaders deal with the political dimensions of uncertainty in the interwar years?

In what ways were the anxieties of the postwar world expressed in new forms of communication?

☑ LearningCurve
Check what you know.

847

intention to create a global German empire unsettled the British. Germany's decision in 1900 to add a fleet of big-gun battleships to its already-expanding navy also heightened tensions. British leaders considered the new battleships to be a military challenge to their long-standing naval supremacy. This decision coincided with the South African War (see page 756) between the British and the Afrikaners, which revealed widespread anti-British feeling around the world.

Thus British leaders set about shoring up their exposed position with their own alliances and agreements. Britain improved its relations with the United States, concluded an alliance with Japan in 1902, and in the Anglo-French Entente of 1904 settled all outstanding colonial disputes with France. Frustrated by Britain's closer relationship with France, Germany's leaders decided to test the entente's strength by demanding an international conference to challenge French control over Morocco. At the Algeciras (Spain) Conference in 1906, Germany's crude bullying only forced France and Britain closer together.

The Moroccan crisis was something of a diplomatic revolution. Britain, France, Russia, and even the United States began to view Germany as a potential threat. At the same time, German leaders began to suspect sinister plots to encircle Germany and block its development as a world power. In 1907 Russia and Britain settled their outstanding differences and signed the Anglo-Russian Agreement. This treaty, together with the earlier Franco-Russian Alliance of 1892 and Anglo-French Entente of 1904, served as a catalyst for the **Triple Entente**, the alliance of Great Britain, France, and Russia in the First World War (Map 28.1).

Triple Entente

▶ The alliance of Great Britain, France, and Russia in the First World War.

MAP 28.1 ■ European Alliances at the Outbreak of World War I, 1914

By the time war broke out, Europe was divided into two opposing alliances: the Triple Entente of Britain, France, and Russia and the Triple Alliance of Germany, Austria-Hungary, and Italy. Italy switched sides and joined the Entente in 1915.

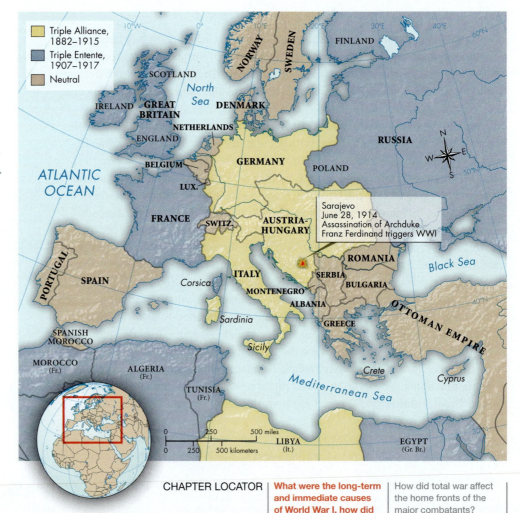

CHAPTER LOCATOR | **What were the long-term and immediate causes of World War I, how did it become a global war?** | How did total war affect the home fronts of the major combatants?

By 1909 Britain was psychologically, if not officially, in the Franco-Russian camp. Europe's leading nations were divided into two hostile blocs, both ill-prepared to deal with upheaval in the Balkans.

The Outbreak of War

By 1903 Balkan nationalism was asserting itself again. Serbia led the way, becoming openly hostile to both Austria-Hungary and the Ottoman Empire. The Slavic Serbs looked to Slavic Russia for support of their national aspirations. In 1908, to block Serbian expansion, Austria formally annexed Bosnia and Herzegovina. Serbia erupted in rage but could do nothing without Russia's support.

Then two nationalist wars, the first and second Balkan wars in 1912 and 1913, finally destroyed the centuries-long Ottoman presence in Europe (Map 28.2). This sudden but long-expected event elated Balkan nationalists but dismayed Austria-Hungary's leaders who feared that Austria-Hungary might next be broken apart.

Within this tense context, Serbian nationalist Gavrilo Princip assassinated Archduke Franz Ferdinand, heir to the Austro-Hungarian throne, and his wife, Sophie, on June 28, 1914, during a state visit to the Bosnian capital of Sarajevo.

MAP 28.2 ■ The Balkans, 1878–1914

The Ottoman Empire suffered large territorial losses after the Congress of Berlin in 1878 but remained a power in the Balkans. By 1914 ethnic boundaries that did not follow political boundaries had formed, and Serbian national aspirations threatened Austria-Hungary.

What factors led to the Russian Revolution, and what was its outcome?	What were the global consequences of the First World War?	How did leaders deal with the political dimensions of uncertainty in the interwar years?	In what ways were the anxieties of the postwar world expressed in new forms of communication?	✔ LearningCurve Check what you know.

Austria-Hungary's leaders held Serbia responsible and on July 23 presented Serbia with an unconditional ultimatum that included demands amounting to Austrian control of the Serbian state. When Serbia replied moderately but evasively, Austria declared war.

Of prime importance in Austria-Hungary's fateful decision was Germany's unconditional support. Kaiser William II and his chancellor, Theobald von Bethmann-Hollweg, realized that war between Austria and Russia was likely, for Russia could not stand by and watch the Serbs be crushed. Yet Bethmann-Hollweg hoped that while Russia (and its ally France) might go to war, Great Britain would remain neutral.

Anticipating a possible conflict, Europe's military leaders had been drawing up war plans and timetables for years, and now these, rather than diplomacy, began to dictate policy. Tsar Nicholas II ordered a partial mobilization against Austria-Hungary but almost immediately found this was impossible. Russia had assumed a war with both Austria and Germany, and it could not mobilize against one without mobilizing against the other. Therefore, Russia ordered full mobilization and in effect declared general war. The German general staff had also prepared for a two-front war. Its Schlieffen plan called for first knocking out France with a lightning attack through neutral Belgium to capture Paris before turning on a slower-to-mobilize Russia. On August 3 German armies invaded Belgium. Great Britain declared war on Germany the following day. In each country the great majority of the population rallied to defend its nation and enthusiastically embraced war in August 1914.

Stalemate and Slaughter

When the Germans invaded Belgium in August 1914, the Belgian army defended its homeland and then fell back to join a rapidly landed British army corps near the Franco-Belgian border. Instead of quickly capturing Paris in a vast encircling movement, German soldiers were advancing slowly along an enormous front. On September 6 the French attacked the German line at the Battle of the Marne. For three days France threw everything into the attack, forcing the Germans to fall back (Map 28.3).

The two stalled armies now dug in behind rows of trenches, mines, and barbed wire. A "no-man's land" of one hundred to three hundred yards lay between the two combatants. Eventually an unbroken line of trenches stretched over four hundred miles from the Belgian coast to the Swiss frontier. By November 1914 the slaughter on the western front had begun in earnest. For four years battles followed the same plan: after ceaseless heavy artillery shelling to "soften up" the enemy, young soldiers went "over the top" of the trenches in frontal attacks on the enemy's line.

The human cost of **trench warfare** was staggering, while territorial gains were minuscule. In the Battle of the Somme in summer 1916, the British and French gained an insignificant 125 square miles at a cost of 600,000 dead or wounded. The Germans lost 500,000 men. That same year the unsuccessful German campaign against Verdun cost 700,000 lives on both sides. The slaughter was made even greater by new weapons of war—including chemical gases, tanks, airplanes, flamethrowers, and the machine gun.

The Schlieffen Plan

- - - ▶ Planned German offensive
— ▶ Actual German offensive
▢ Neutral nations

GREAT BRITAIN
NETHERLANDS
BELGIUM
GERMANY
Brussels
Rhine R.
LUX.
Reims
Metz
Paris
Seine R.
Marne R.
FRANCE
SWITZ.

0   100   200 mi.
0   100   200 km

trench warfare
▶ Fighting behind rows of trenches, mines, and barbed wire; used in World War I with a staggering cost in lives and minimal gains in territory.

CHAPTER LOCATOR

What were the long-term and immediate causes of World War I, how did it become a global war?

How did total war affect the home fronts of the major combatants?

850 CHAPTER 28
WORLD WAR AND REVOLUTION

Legend (map)

- Triple Entente and allies
- Central Powers and allies
- Greatest extent of territory gained by Germany-Austria
- German submarine war zone
- Neutral nations
- Farthest advance by Central Powers on date marked
- Farthest advance by Entente Powers on date marked
- British naval blockade
- Major battle

Main map labels:

NORWAY, SWEDEN, FINLAND, Helsinki, Petrograd (St. Petersburg), DENMARK, Kiel, Jutland 1916, North Sea, Baltic Sea, ESTONIA, LATVIA, Riga, COURLAND, LITHUANIA, Vilnius, Moscow, RUSSIA, E. PRUSSIA, Masurian Lakes 1914, BELARUS, GREAT BRITAIN, Lusitania 1915, London, NETHERLANDS, GERMANY, Berlin, Tannenberg 1914, Warsaw, KINGDOM OF POLAND (Russia), Brest-Litovsk, Kiev, Farthest Russian advance, 1914, Armistice line, December 1917, March 1918, Treaty of Brest-Litovsk, March 1918, Dnieper R., BELGIUM, LUXEMBOURG, ALSACE-LORRAINE, Rhine R., Elbe R., Vistula R., Armistice line, November 1918, GALICIA, Farthest German military advance, See inset map, Paris, Seine R., Western front, SWITZERLAND, Bordeaux, FRANCE, Loire R., Garonne R., Rhône R., Aug. 1917, Caporetto 1917, Italian front, May 1915, AUSTRIA-HUNGARY, Vienna, Budapest, TRANSYLVANIA, ROMANIA, Bucharest, Danube R., Black Sea, Caspian Sea, March 1918, SPAIN, Ebro R., Corsica, Elba, ITALY, Rome, Sardinia, Balearic Is., Adriatic Sea, Po R., Sarajevo, SERBIA, MONTENEGRO, BULGARIA, ALBANIA, 1917–1918, 1916, 1915, GREECE, Balkan front, Dardanelles, Constantinople, OTTOMAN EMPIRE, Gallipoli 1915, Nov. 1917, Middle Eastern front, Mar. 1918, PERSIA, IRAQ, Al Kut 1915 1916 1917, Baghdad, Oct. 1918, Basra, ALGERIA (Fr.), Tunis, TUNISIA (Fr.), Sicily, Malta, Crete, Mediterranean Sea, Cyprus, SYRIA, Damascus, LIBYA (It.), EGYPT (Gr. Br.), Red Sea, Al Aqabah 1917

Scale: 200 / 400 miles; 200 / 400 kilometers

Compass: N W E S

The Western Front (inset)

Legend:
- Germany, 1914
- Greatest extent of territory gained by Germany, Sept. 1914
- Front at beginning of 1915
- German offensive, Summer 1918
- Major battle

Inset labels:

NETHERLANDS, Dover, Ostend, FLANDERS, Ghent, Antwerp, Louvain, Brussels, Liège, Ruhr R., Rhine R., Cologne, Schelde R., Calais, Ypres, English Channel, BELGIUM, Meuse R., Coblenz, Armistice line, November 1918, Arras, ARDENNES, LUX., GERMANY, Somme R., St. Quentin, Sedan, Amiens, Somme, Aisne R., ARGONNE FOREST, St. Mihiel, LORRAINE, Compiègne, Reims, Marne R., Verdun, Moselle R., Saar R., Belleau Wood, Marne I, Châlons-sur-Marne, Nancy, Paris, Seine R., Marne II, Chateau-Thierry, Strasbourg, ALSACE, FRANCE, Epinal, Mulhouse, Basel, SWITZ.

Scale: 0 / 25 / 50 miles; 0 / 25 / 50 kilometers

MAP 28.3 ■ The First World War in Europe

The trench war on the western front was concentrated in Belgium and northern France (inset), while the war in the east encompassed an enormous territory.

On the eastern front, the Russians moved into eastern Germany but suffered appalling losses against the Germans at the Battles of Tannenberg and the Masurian Lakes in August and September 1914 (see Map 28.3). German and Austrian forces then reversed the Russian advances of 1914 and forced the Russians to retreat deep into their own territory in the 1915 eastern campaign. A staggering 2.5 million Russians were killed, wounded, or taken prisoner.

These changing tides of victory and hopes of territorial gains brought neutral countries into the war. In May 1915 Italy joined the Triple Entente of Great Britain, France, and Russia in return for promises of Austrian territory. In September Bulgaria joined the Triple Alliance in order to settle old scores with Serbia.

The War Becomes Global

In October 1914 the Ottoman Empire joined with Austria and Germany, by then known as the Central Powers. A German alliance permitted the Turks to renounce the limitations on Ottoman sovereignty imposed by Europeans in the nineteenth century and also to settle old grievances with Russia, the Turks' historic enemy.

The entry of the Ottoman Turks pulled the entire Middle East into the war and made it truly a global conflict. While Russia attacked the Ottomans in the Caucasus, the British protected their rule in Egypt. In 1915, at the Battle of Gallipoli, British forces tried to take the Dardanelles and Constantinople from the Ottoman Turks but were badly defeated. Casualties were high on both sides and included thousands of Australians and New Zealanders.

The British had more success inciting Arabs to revolt against their Turkish overlords. The foremost Arab leader was Hussein ibn-Ali (1856–1931), who governed much of the Ottoman Empire's territory along the Red Sea (see Map 29.1, page 889). In 1915 Hussein won vague British commitments for an independent Arab kingdom. In return, he joined forces with the British under T. E. Lawrence, who in 1917 led Arab tribesmen and Indian soldiers in a successful guerrilla war against the Turks on the Arabian peninsula. In the Ottoman province of Iraq, Britain occupied Basra in 1914 and captured Baghdad in 1917. In 1918 British armies, aided by imperial forces from Egypt, India, Australia, and New Zealand, smashed the old Ottoman state. Thus war brought revolutionary change to the Middle East (see pages 888–895).

Japan, allied with the British since 1902, joined the Triple Entente on August 23, 1914, and began attacking German-controlled colonies and territories in the Pacific. Later that year Japan seized Germany's holdings on the Shandong (Shantung) Peninsula in China.

War also spread to colonies in Africa and East Asia. Colonized peoples provided critical supplies and fought in Europe, Africa, and the Ottoman Empire. More than a million Africans and Asians served in the various armies of the warring powers, with more than double that number serving as porters to carry equipment.

Many of these men joined up to get clothes (uniforms), food, and money for enlisting. Others did so because colonial recruiters promised them better lives when they returned home. Most were illiterate and had no idea of why they were going or what they would experience.

The war had a profound impact on these colonial troops. Fighting against and killing Europeans destroyed the impression that the Europeans were superhuman.

CHAPTER LOCATOR | **What were the long-term and immediate causes of World War I, how did it become a global war?** | How did total war affect the home fronts of the major combatants?

New concepts like nationalism and individual freedoms—ideals for which the Europeans were supposedly fighting—were carried home to become rallying cries for future liberation struggles.

A crucial turning point in the expanding conflict came in April 1917 when the United States declared war on Germany. American intervention grew out of the war at sea and sympathy for the Triple Entente. At the beginning of the war Britain and France established a naval blockade to strangle the Central Powers. In early 1915 Germany launched a counter-blockade using the new and deadly effective submarine. In May a German submarine sank the British passenger liner *Lusitania*. More than a thousand people died, including 139 U.S. citizens. President Woodrow Wilson protested vigorously. Germany was forced to restrict its submarine warfare for almost two years or face almost certain war with the United States.

Early in 1917 the German military command—confident that improved submarines could starve Britain into submission before the United States could come to its rescue—resumed unrestricted submarine warfare. This was a reckless gamble. The United States declared war on Germany and eventually tipped the balance in favor of the Triple Entente.

QUICK REVIEW

What role did nationalism play in the outbreak
of the First World War?

| What factors led to the Russian Revolution, and what was its outcome? | What were the global consequences of the First World War? | How did leaders deal with the political dimensions of uncertainty in the interwar years? | In what ways were the anxieties of the postwar world expressed in new forms of communication? | LearningCurve Check what you know. |

How did total war affect the home fronts of the major combatants?

> **PICTURING THE PAST**

ANALYZING THE IMAGE: How is neutral Belgium personified? What do you think the artist's purpose was?

CONNECTIONS: How did governments use propaganda and other means to unite people for the war effort?

THE WAR'S IMPACT ON CIVILIANS was no less massive than on the men crouched in trenches. Total war mobilized entire populations, led to increased state power, and promoted social equality. It also led to dissent and a growing antiwar movement.

Mobilizing for Total War

Within months of the outbreak of the First World War, national unity governments began to plan and control economic and social life in order to wage **total war**. Governments imposed rationing, price and wage controls, and even restrictions on workers' freedom of movement. These total-war economies blurred the old distinction between soldiers on battlefields and civilians at home. The ability of central governments to manage and control highly complicated economies increased and strengthened their powers, often along socialist lines.

Germany went furthest in developing a planned economy to wage total war. Soon after war began, the Jewish industrialist Walter Rathenau convinced the

total war

▶ Practiced by countries fighting in World War I, a war in which the government plans and controls all aspects of economic and social life in order to make the greatest possible military effort.

CHAPTER LOCATOR | What were the long-term and immediate causes of World War I, how did it become a global war? | **How did total war affect the home fronts of the major combatants?**

854   CHAPTER 28   WORLD WAR AND REVOLUTION

German government to set up the War Raw Materials Board to ration and distribute raw materials. Food was also rationed, and the board successfully produced substitutes, such as synthetic rubber and synthetic nitrates, for scarce war supplies. Following the terrible Battles of Verdun and the Somme in 1916, military leaders forced the Reichstag to accept the Auxiliary Service Law, which required all males between seventeen and sixty to work only at jobs considered critical to the war effort. Women also worked in war factories, mines, and steel mills.

France and Great Britain mobilized economically for total war less rapidly and less completely than Germany, as they could import materials from their colonies and from the United States. When it became apparent that the war was not going to end quickly, however, the Western Allies all passed laws giving their governments sweeping powers over all areas of the nation's daily life—including industrial and agricultural production, censorship, education, health and welfare, the curtailment of civil liberties, labor, and foreign aliens.

The Social Impact of War

The social impact of total war was no less profound than the economic impact, though again there were important national variations. The military's insatiable needs—nearly every belligerent power resorted to conscription to put soldiers in the field—created a tremendous demand for workers at home. This situation brought about momentous changes.

One such change was increased power and prestige for labor unions. Unions cooperated with war governments in return for real participation in important decisions. This entry of labor leaders into policymaking councils paralleled the entry of socialist leaders into the war governments.

Women's roles also changed dramatically. In every belligerent country, large numbers of women went to work in industry, transportation, and offices. Moreover, women became highly visible—not only as munitions workers but as bank tellers, mail carriers, and even police officers. Women also served as nurses and doctors at the front. (See "Individuals in Society: Vera Brittain," page 856.) In general, the war greatly expanded the range of women's activities and changed attitudes toward women. Although at war's end most women were quickly let go and their jobs were given back to the returning soldiers, their many-sided war effort caused Britain, Germany, and Austria to grant them the right to vote immediately after the war.

Recent scholarship has shown, however, that traditional views of gender— of male roles and female roles—remained remarkably resilient and that there was a significant conservative backlash in the postwar years. Even as the war progressed, many men, particularly soldiers, grew increasingly hostile toward women. Some were angry at mothers, wives, and girlfriends for urging them to enlist and fight in the horrible war. Soldiers with wives and girlfriends back home grew increasingly convinced that they were cheating on them. Others worried that factory or farm jobs had been taken by women and there would be no work when they returned home. Men were also concerned that if women received the vote at war's end, they would vote themselves into power.

War promoted social equality, blurring class distinctions and lessening the gap between rich and poor. Greater equality was reflected in full employment,

What factors led to the Russian Revolution, and what was its outcome? | What were the global consequences of the First World War? | How did leaders deal with the political dimensions of uncertainty in the interwar years? | In what ways were the anxieties of the postwar world expressed in new forms of communication? | ✓ LearningCurve Check what you know.

855

Although the Great War upended millions of lives, it struck Europe's young people with the greatest force. For Vera Brittain (1893–1970), as for so many in her generation, the war became life's defining experience, which she captured forever in her famous autobiography, *Testament of Youth* (1933).

Brittain grew up in a wealthy business family in northern England, bristling at small-town conventions and discrimination against women. Very close to her brother Edward, two years her junior, Brittain read voraciously and dreamed of being a successful writer. Finishing boarding school and beating down her father's objections, she prepared for Oxford's rigorous entry exams and won a scholarship to its women's college. Brittain also fell in love with Roland Leighton, an equally brilliant student from a literary family and her brother's best friend. All three, along with two more close friends, Victor Richardson and Geoffrey Thurlow, confidently prepared to enter Oxford in late 1914.

When war suddenly approached in July 1914, Brittain shared with millions of Europeans a thrilling surge of patriotic support for her government, a prowar enthusiasm she later played down in her published writings. She wrote in her diary that her "great fear" was that England would declare its neutrality and commit the "grossest treachery" toward France.* She seconded Roland's decision to enlist, agreeing with her sweetheart's glamorous view of war as "very ennobling and very beautiful." Later, exchanging anxious letters in 1915 with Roland in France, Vera began to see the conflict in personal, human terms. She wondered if any victory or defeat could be worth Roland's life.

Struggling to quell her doubts, Brittain redoubled her commitment to England's cause and volunteered

Vera Brittain was marked forever by her wartime experiences. (Hulton Archive/Getty Images)

as an army nurse. For the next three years she served with distinction in military hospitals in London, Malta, and northern France, repeatedly torn between the vision of noble sacrifice and the reality of human tragedy. She lost her sexual inhibitions caring for mangled male bodies, and she longed to consummate her love with Roland. Awaiting his return on leave on Christmas Day in 1915, she was greeted instead with a telegram: Roland had been killed two days before.

Roland's death was the first of the devastating blows that eventually overwhelmed Brittain's idealistic patriotism. In 1917 first Geoffrey and then Victor died from gruesome wounds. In early 1918, as the last great German offensive covered the floors of her war-zone hospital with maimed and dying German prisoners, the bone-weary Vera felt a common humanity and saw only more victims. A few weeks later brother Edward — her last hope — died in action. When the war ended, she was, she said, a "complete automaton," with "my deepest emotions paralyzed if not dead."

Returning to Oxford and finishing her studies, Brittain gradually recovered. She formed a deep, restorative friendship with another talented woman writer, Winifred Holtby, published novels and articles, and became a leader in the feminist campaign for gender equality. She also married and had children. But her wartime memories were always there. Finally, Brittain succeeded in coming to grips with them in *Testament of Youth*, her powerful antiwar autobiography. The unflinching narrative spoke to the experiences of an entire generation and became a runaway bestseller. Above all, perhaps, Brittain captured the ambivalent, contradictory character of the war, in which millions of young people found excitement, courage, and common purpose but succeeded only in destroying their lives with their superhuman efforts and futile sacrifices. Becoming ever more committed to pacifism, Brittain opposed England's entry into World War II.

*Quoted in the excellent study by P. Berry and M. Bostridge, *Vera Brittain: A Life* (London: Virago Press, 2001), p. 59; additional quotations are from pp. 80 and 136.

rationing according to physical needs, and a sharing of hardships. Society became more uniform and more egalitarian.

Growing Political Tensions

During the war's first two years, belief in a just cause and patriotic nationalism united soldiers and civilians behind their various national leaders. Each government employed censorship and propaganda to maintain popular support.

By spring 1916, however, cracks were appearing under the strain of total war. In April Irish nationalists in Dublin unsuccessfully rose up against British rule in the Easter Rebellion. Strikes and protest marches over inadequate food flared up on every home front. In April 1917 nearly half the French infantry divisions mutinied for two months after suffering enormous losses in the Second Battle of the Aisne. Later that year there was a massive mutiny of Russian soldiers supporting the revolution.

The Central Powers experienced the most strain. In October 1916 a young socialist assassinated Austria's chief minister. Conflicts among nationalities grew, and both Czech and Yugoslav leaders demanded autonomous democratic states for their peoples. By 1917 German political unity was also collapsing, and prewar social conflicts were re-emerging. A coalition of Socialists and Catholics in the Reichstag called for a compromise "peace without annexations or reparations." Thus Germany, like its ally Austria-Hungary and its enemy France, began to crack in 1917. But it was Russia that collapsed first and saved the Central Powers—for a time.

QUICK REVIEW

What steps did the major combatants take to harness the full power of their populations and economies?

Vladimir Lenin (center) with two other major figures of the Russian Revolution, Joseph Stalin (left) and Mikhail Kalinin (right). After Lenin's death in January 1924, Stalin moved to seize power and ruled the Soviet Union until his death in 1953. Kalinin was one of Lenin's earliest followers and then supported Stalin in the power struggle after Lenin's death. He was one of the few "old Bolsheviks" to survive Stalin's purges and received a large state funeral following his death from natural causes in 1946. (Photo by Keystone-France/Gamma-Keystone via Getty Images)

THE 1917 RUSSIAN REVOLUTION, directly related to the Great War, opened a new era with a radically new prototype of state and society that changed the course of the twentieth century.

The Fall of Imperial Russia

Imperial Russia in 1914 was still predominantly a rural and nonurbanized society. Russia came late to industrialization (see page 729), and, although rapidly expanding, industrialization was still in its early stages. Peasants made up perhaps 80 percent of the population. Besides the royal family and the nobility, the rest of Russian society consisted of the bourgeoisie (the elite, educated upper and middle classes, such as liberal politicians, propertied and professional classes, military officer corps, and landowners) and the proletariat (the popular masses, such as the urban working class, and rank-and-file soldiers and sailors). These two factions contended for power when the tsar abdicated in 1917.

Like their allies and their enemies, Russians embraced war with patriotic enthusiasm in 1914. For a moment Russia was united, but soon the war began to take its toll.

CHAPTER LOCATOR | What were the long-term and immediate causes of World War I, how did it become a global war? | How did total war affect the home fronts of the major combatants?

858
WORLD WAR AND REVOLUTION

CHAPTER 28

Russia quickly exhausted its supplies of shells and ammunition, and better-equipped German armies inflicted terrible losses—1.5 million casualties and nearly 1 million captured in 1915 alone. Russian soldiers were sent to the front without rifles. The Duma, Russia's lower house of parliament, and *zemstvos* (zemst-vohs), local governments, led the effort toward full mobilization on the home front. These efforts improved the military situation, but overall Russia mobilized less effectively for total war than did the other warring nations.

Although limited industrial capacity was a serious handicap in a war against highly industrialized Germany, Russia's real problem was leadership. A kindly, slightly dull-witted man, Tsar Nicholas II (r. 1894–1917) distrusted the moderate Duma and rejected popular involvement. As a result, the Duma, whose members came from the elite classes, and the popular masses became increasingly critical of the tsar's leadership and the appalling direction of the war. In response, Nicholas (who had no military background) traveled to the front in September 1915 to lead Russia's armies—and thereafter received all the blame for Russian losses.

His departure was a fatal turning point. His German-born wife, Tsarina Alexandra, took control of the government and the home front. She tried to rule absolutely in her husband's absence with an uneducated Siberian preacher, Rasputin, as her most trusted adviser. In a desperate attempt to right the situation, three members of the high aristocracy murdered Rasputin in December 1916. In this atmosphere of unreality, the government slid steadily toward revolution.

Large scale-strikes, demonstrations, and protest marches were now commonplace, as were bread shortages. On March 8, 1917, a women's bread march in Petrograd (formerly St. Petersburg) started riots, which spread throughout the city. While his ministers fled the city, the tsar ordered that peace be restored, but discipline broke down, and the soldiers and police joined the revolutionary crowd. The Duma declared a provisional government on March 12, 1917. Three days later, Nicholas abdicated.

"The Russian Ruling House"

This wartime cartoon captures the ominous, spellbinding power of Rasputin over Tsar Nicholas II and his wife, Alexandra. Rasputin's manipulations disgusted Russian public opinion and contributed to the monarchy's collapse. (© INTERFOTO/Alamy)

The Provisional Government

The **March Revolution** was joyfully accepted throughout the country. A new government formed in May 1917, with the understanding that an elected democratic government, ruling under a new constitution drafted by a future Constituent Assembly, would replace it when circumstances permitted. The provisional government established equality before the law; freedom of religion, speech, and assembly; the right of unions to organize and strike; and other classic liberal measures.

March Revolution

▶ The first phase of the Russian Revolution of 1917, in which unplanned uprisings led to the abdication of the tsar and the establishment of a transitional democratic government that was then overthrown in November by Lenin and the Bolsheviks.

What factors led to the Russian Revolution, and what was its outcome? | What were the global consequences of the First World War? | How did leaders deal with the political dimensions of uncertainty in the interwar years? | In what ways were the anxieties of the postwar world expressed in new forms of communication? | ✓ LearningCurve Check what you know.

859

The provisional government soon made two fatal decisions, however, that turned the people against the new government. First, it refused to confiscate large landholdings and give them to peasants, fearing that such drastic action in the countryside would only complete the disintegration of Russia's peasant army. Second, the government decided that the continuation of war was still the all-important national duty and that international alliances had to be honored. Neither decision was popular. The peasants believed that when the tsar's autocratic rule ended, so too did the nobles' title to the land, which was now theirs for the taking. The army believed that the March Revolution meant the end of the war.

Petrograd Soviet

▶ A counter-government that was a huge, fluctuating mass meeting of two to three thousand workers, soldiers, and socialist intellectuals.

From its first day, the provisional government had to share power (dual power) with a formidable rival that represented the popular masses—the **Petrograd Soviet** (or council) of Workers' and Soldiers' Deputies, an organization comprised of two to three thousand workers, soldiers, and socialist intellectuals. This counter-government, or half government, issued its own radical orders, further weakening the provisional government. Most famous of these was Army Order No. 1, issued in March 1917, which stripped officers of their authority and gave power to elected committees of common soldiers.

Order No. 1 led to a total collapse of army discipline. Soldiers began returning to their villages to get a share of the land that peasants were seizing from landowners, either through peasant soviets (councils) or by force, in a great agrarian upheaval. Through the summer of 1917, the provisional government, led from July by the socialist Alexander Kerensky, became increasingly more conservative and authoritarian as it tried to maintain law and order. The government was being threatened from one side by an advancing German army and from the other by proletarian forces, urban and rural alike, shouting "All power to the soviets!" and calling for an even more radical revolution.

Lenin and the Bolshevik Revolution

Among those leading the call for radical revolution was Vladimir Ilyich Lenin (1870–1924). Lenin became an enemy of imperial Russia when his older brother was executed for plotting to kill the tsar in 1887. As a law student Lenin studied Marxist doctrines with religious ferocity. Exiled to Siberia for three years because of socialist agitation, Lenin lived in western Europe after his release for seventeen years and developed his own revolutionary interpretations of Marxist thought (see page 716).

Three interrelated ideas were central for Lenin. First, he stressed that only violent revolution could destroy capitalism. Second, Lenin believed that a socialist revolution was possible even in an agrarian country like Russia. According to classical Marxist theory, a society must have reached the capitalist, industrial stage of development before its urban workers, the proletariat, can rise up and create a Communist society. Lenin thought that although Russia's industrial working class was small, the peasants, who made up the bulk of the army and navy, were also potential revolutionaries. Third, Lenin believed that at a given moment revolution was determined more by human leadership than by vast historical laws. He called for a highly disciplined workers' party, strictly controlled by a dedicated elite of intellectuals and full-time revolutionaries like him.

CHAPTER LOCATOR | What were the long-term and immediate causes of World War I, how did it become a global war? | How did total war affect the home fronts of the major combatants?

- The necessity of violent revolution
- The possibility of socialist revolution in Russia
- The importance of a disciplined workers' party led by committed revolutionaries

Lenin's ideas did not go unchallenged by other Russian Marxists. At a Social Democratic Labor Party congress in London in 1903, Lenin demanded a small, disciplined, elitist party; his opponents wanted a more democratic party with mass membership. The Russian Marxists split into two rival factions. Because his side won one crucial vote at the congress, Lenin's camp became known as **Bolsheviks**, or "majority group"; his opponents were Mensheviks, or "minority group."

In March 1917 Lenin and nearly all the other leading Bolsheviks were living in exile abroad or in Russia's remotest corners. After the March Revolution, the German government provided safe passage for Lenin across Germany and back into Russia, hoping he would undermine Russia's sagging war effort. They were not disappointed. Arriving in Petrograd on April 16, Lenin attacked at once, issuing his famous April Theses. To the Petrograd Bolsheviks' great astonishment, he rejected all cooperation with what he called the "bourgeois" provisional government, and instead called for exactly what the popular masses themselves were demanding: "All power to the soviets!" and "Peace, Land, Bread!" Bolshevik support increased through the summer, culminating in mass demonstrations in Petrograd on July 16–20 by soldiers, sailors, and workers. Lenin and the Bolshevik Central Committee had not planned these demonstrations and were completely unprepared to support them. Nonetheless, the provisional government labeled Lenin and other leading Bolsheviks traitors and ordered them arrested. Lenin had to flee to Finland.

Meanwhile, however, the provisional government itself was collapsing. The coalition between liberals and socialists was breaking apart as their respective power bases—bourgeoisie and proletariat—demanded they move further to the right or left. Prime Minister Kerensky's unwavering support for the war lost him all credit with the army, the only force that might have saved him and democratic government in Russia. In early September an attempted right-wing military coup failed as Petrograd workers organized themselves as Red Guards to defend the city and then convinced the coup's soldiers to join them. Although the workers' actions were organized by local unions and factories—the Bolshevik leaders had no hand in stopping the coup—the Bolsheviks gained more support nevertheless. Lenin, from his exile in Finland, now called for an armed Bolshevik insurrection before the Second All-Russian Congress of Soviets met in early November.

In October the Bolsheviks gained a fragile majority in the Petrograd Soviet. Lenin did not return to Russia until mid-October and even then remained in hiding. It was Lenin's supporter Leon Trotsky (1879–1940) who brilliantly executed the Bolshevik seizure of power. On November 6 militant Trotsky followers joined with trusted Bolshevik soldiers to seize government buildings and arrest provisional government members. That evening Lenin came out of hiding and took control of the revolution. The following day revolutionary forces seized the Winter Palace, and Kerensky capitulated. At the Congress of Soviets, a Bolshevik majority

Bolsheviks

▶ The majority group; this was Lenin's camp of the Russian party of Marxist socialism.

What factors led to the Russian Revolution, and what was its outcome? | What were the global consequences of the First World War? | How did leaders deal with the political dimensions of uncertainty in the interwar years? | In what ways were the anxieties of the postwar world expressed in new forms of communication? | ☑ LearningCurve
Check what you know.

861

declared that all power had passed to the soviets and named Lenin head of the new government.

The Bolsheviks came to power for three key reasons. First, by late 1917 democracy had given way to anarchy as the popular masses no longer supported the provisional government. Second, in Lenin and Trotsky the Bolsheviks had a truly superior leadership who were utterly determined to provoke a Marxist revolution. Third, the Bolsheviks appealed to soldiers, urban workers, and peasants who were exhausted by war and eager for socialism.

Dictatorship and Civil War

The Bolsheviks' true accomplishment was not taking power but keeping it and conquering the chaos they had helped create. Once again, Lenin was able to profit from developments over which he and the Bolsheviks had no control. Since summer 1917 an unstoppable peasant revolution had swept across Russia, as peasants divided among themselves the estates of the landlords and the church. Thus Lenin's first law, which supposedly gave land to the peasants, actually merely approved what peasants were already doing. Lenin then met urban workers' greatest demand with a decree giving local workers' committees direct control of individual factories.

The Bolsheviks proclaimed their regime a "provisional workers' and peasants' government," promising that a freely elected Constituent Assembly would draw up a new constitution. However, when Bolshevik delegates won fewer than one-fourth of the seats in free elections in November, the Constituent Assembly was permanently disbanded by Bolshevik soldiers acting under Lenin's orders.

Lenin then moved to make peace with Germany, at any price. That price was very high. Germany demanded the Soviet government surrender all its western territories in the Treaty of Brest-Litovsk (BREHST lih-TAWFSK), in March 1918. With Germany's defeat eight months later, the treaty was nullified, but it allowed Lenin time to escape the disaster of continued war and pursue his goal of absolute political power for the Bolsheviks—now renamed Communists—within Russia.

The war's end and the demise of the democratically elected Constituent Assembly revealed Bolshevik rule as a dictatorship. Officers of the old army organized so-called White opposition to the Bolsheviks in southern Russia, Ukraine, Siberia, and west of Petrograd and plunged the country into civil war from November 1917 to October 1922. The Whites came from many political factions and were united only by their hatred of the Bolsheviks—the Reds. In almost five years of fighting, 125,000 Reds and 175,000 Whites and Poles were killed before the Red Army under Trotsky's command claimed final victory.

The Bolsheviks' Red Army won for several reasons. Strategically, they controlled the center, while the disunited Whites attacked from the fringes. Moreover, the Whites' poorly defined political program failed to unite all of the Bolsheviks' foes under a progressive democratic banner. Most important, the Communists developed a better army, against which the divided Whites were no match.

The Bolsheviks also mobilized the home front. Establishing **War Communism**— the application of the total-war concept to a civil conflict—they seized grain from peasants, introduced rationing, nationalized all banks and industry, and required everyone to work. Although these measures contributed to a breakdown of nor-

The Russian Civil War, 1917–1922

- Ceded after Treaty of Brest-Litovsk, 1918
- Bolshevik territory, 1919
- Occupied by Allies, 1919
- → White Army forces
- — Boundary of U.S.S.R., 1921

War Communism

▶ The application of the total-war concept to a civil conflict; the Bolsheviks seized grain from peasants, introduced rationing, nationalized all banks and industry, and required everyone to work.

CHAPTER LOCATOR | What were the long-term and immediate causes of World War I, how did it become a global war? | How did total war affect the home fronts of the major combatants?

mal economic activity, they also served to maintain labor discipline and to keep the Red Army supplied.

Revolutionary terror also contributed to the Communist victory. The old tsarist secret police was re-established as the Cheka, which hunted down and executed thousands of real or supposed foes. During the so-called Red Terror of 1918–1920, the Cheka sowed fear, silenced opposition, and executed an estimated 250,000 "class enemies."

KEY EVENTS OF THE RUSSIAN REVOLUTION

1914	Russia enters World War I
1916–1917	Tsarist government in crisis
March 1917	March Revolution; Duma declares a provisional government; tsar abdicates; Petrograd Soviet issues Army Order No. 1
April 1917	Lenin returns from exile
October 1917	Bolsheviks gain a majority in the Petrograd Soviet
November 7, 1917	Bolsheviks seize power; Lenin named head of new Communist government
March 1918	Treaty of Brest-Litovsk; Trotsky becomes head of the Red Army
1917–1922	Civil war
1922	Civil war ends; Lenin and the Bolshevik Communists take control of Russia

Finally, foreign military intervention in the civil war ended up helping the Communists. The Allies sent troops to prevent war materiel that they had sent to the provisional government from being captured by the Germans. After the Soviet government nationalized all foreign-owned factories without compensation and refused to pay foreign debts, Western governments began to support White armies. While these efforts did little to help the Whites' cause, they did permit the Communists to appeal to the ethnic Russians' patriotic nationalism.

QUICK REVIEW

How were the Bolsheviks able to defeat their rivals and take control of Russia?

| **What factors led to the Russian Revolution, and what was its outcome?** | What were the global consequences of the First World War? | How did leaders deal with the political dimensions of uncertainty in the interwar years? | In what ways were the anxieties of the postwar world expressed in new forms of communication? | ✓ **LearningCurve** Check what you know. |

> What were the global consequences of the First World War?

IN SPRING 1918 THE GERMANS LAUNCHED their last major attack against France. It failed, and Germany was defeated. The armistice came in November, and in January 1919, as civil war spread in Russia and chaos engulfed much of eastern Europe, the victorious Western Allies came together in Paris hoping to establish a lasting peace. The eventual peace settlement, however, failed to establish a lasting peace or to resolve the issues that had brought the world to war.

The End of the War

Peace and an end to the war did not come easily. Victory over revolutionary Russia had temporarily boosted sagging German morale, and in spring 1918 the German army attacked France once more. The German offensive was turned back in July at the Second Battle of the Marne, where 140,000 fresh American soldiers saw action. Adding 2 million men in arms to the war effort by August, the late but massive American intervention decisively tipped the scales in favor of Allied victory.

By September British, French, and American armies were advancing steadily on all fronts. On October 4 the German emperor formed a new, more liberal German government to sue for peace. As negotiations over an armistice dragged on, the frustrated German people rose up. On November 3 sailors in Kiel (keel) mutinied, and throughout northern Germany soldiers and workers established revolutionary councils on the Russian soviet model. Austria-Hungary surrendered to the Allies the same day. With army discipline collapsing, Kaiser William abdicated and fled to Holland. Socialist leaders in Berlin proclaimed a German republic on November 9 and agreed to tough Allied terms of surrender. The armistice went into effect on November 11, 1918.

The Paris Peace Treaties

Seventy delegates from twenty-seven nations attended the opening of the Paris Peace Conference at the Versailles Palace on January 18, 1919. The delegates met with great expectations. A young British diplomat later wrote that the victors

CHAPTER LOCATOR | What were the long-term and immediate causes of World War I, how did it become a global war? | How did total war affect the home fronts of the major combatants?

CHAPTER 28
864 WORLD WAR AND REVOLUTION

"were journeying to Paris . . . to found a new order in Europe. We were preparing not Peace only, but Eternal Peace."[1]

This idealism was strengthened by President Wilson's January 1918 peace proposal, the Fourteen Points. Wilson stressed national self-determination and the rights of small countries and called for the creation of a **League of Nations**, a permanent international organization designed to protect member states from aggression and avert future wars.

The real powers at the conference were the United States, Great Britain, and France. Germany and Russia were excluded, and Italy's role was limited. Almost immediately the three Allies began to quarrel. President Wilson insisted that the first order of business be the League of Nations. Wilson had his way, although Prime Ministers Lloyd George of Great Britain and, especially, Georges Clemenceau of France were unenthusiastic. They were primarily concerned with punishing Germany.

The "Big Three" were soon in a stalemate over Germany's fate. Although personally inclined to make a somewhat moderate peace with Germany, Lloyd George felt pressured for a victory worthy of the sacrifices of total war. Clemenceau also wanted revenge and lasting security for France, which, he believed, required the creation of a buffer state between France and Germany, Germany's permanent demilitarization, and vast German reparations. Wilson, supported by Lloyd George, would hear none of this.

In the end, Clemenceau agreed to a compromise. He gave up the French demand for a Rhineland buffer state in return for a formal defensive alliance with the United States and Great Britain. Both Wilson and Lloyd George also promised their countries would come to France's aid if it was attacked.

The **Treaty of Versailles** was the first step toward re-establishing international order, though it was an order that favored the victorious Allies. Germany's colonies were given to France, Britain, and Japan as League of Nations mandates. Germany's territorial losses within Europe were minor: Alsace-Lorraine was returned to France, and parts of Germany were ceded to the new Polish state (see Map 28.4). The treaty limited Germany's army to one hundred thousand men and allowed no new military fortifications in the Rhineland.

More harshly, the Allies declared that Germany (with Austria) was responsible for the war and therefore had to pay reparations equal to all civilian damages caused by the war. The actual reparations figure was not set, however, leaving open the possibility that it might be set at a reasonable level in the future when tempers had cooled.

Other agreements reached in Paris also had far-reaching consequences for the course of the twentieth century. In eastern Europe, Poland regained its independence (see Map 19.1, page 570), and the independent states of Austria, Hungary, Czechoslovakia, and a larger Romania were created out of the Austro-Hungarian Empire (see Map 28.4). A greatly expanded Serbian monarchy united Slavs in the western Balkans and took the name Yugoslavia.

Promises of independence made to Arab leaders were largely brushed aside, and Britain and France extended their power in the Middle East, taking advantage of the breakup of the Ottoman Empire. As League of Nations mandates, the French received Lebanon and Syria, and Britain took Iraq and Palestine. Palestine was to include a Jewish national homeland first promised by Britain in 1917 in the Balfour Declaration (see page 891). These Allied acquisitions, although officially

League of Nations

▶ A permanent international organization established during the 1919 Paris Peace Conference to protect member states from aggression and avert future wars.

Treaty of Versailles

▶ The 1919 peace settlement that ended World War I; it declared Germany responsible for the war, limited Germany's army to one hundred thousand men, and forced Germany to pay huge reparations.

What factors led to the Russian Revolution, and what was its outcome? | **What were the global consequences of the First World War?** | How did leaders deal with the political dimensions of uncertainty in the interwar years? | In what ways were the anxieties of the postwar world expressed in new forms of communication? | ✓ LearningCurve Check what you know.

865

MAP 28.4 ■ Territorial Changes in Europe After World War I

The Great War brought tremendous changes to eastern Europe. Empires were shattered, new nations were established, and a dangerous power vacuum was created by the relatively weak states established between Germany and Soviet Russia.

> MAPPING THE PAST

ANALYZING THE MAP: What territory did Germany lose, and to whom? What new independent states were formed from the old Russian empire?

CONNECTIONS: How were the principles of national self-determination applied to the redrawing of Europe after the war? Did this theory work out?

League of Nations mandates, were one of the most imperialistic elements of the peace settlement. Another was mandating Germany's holdings in China to Japan (see page 901). Germany's African colonies were mandated to Great Britain, France, South Africa, and Belgium. The mandates system left colonial peoples in the Middle East, Asia (see Chapter 29), and Africa bitterly disappointed and demonstrated that the age of Western and Eastern imperialism lived on.

CHAPTER LOCATOR | What were the long-term and immediate causes of World War I, how did it become a global war? | How did total war affect the home fronts of the major combatants?

American Rejection of the Versailles Treaty

The 1919 peace settlement was not perfect, but for war-shattered Europe it was an acceptable beginning. The remaining problems could be worked out in the future. Such hopes were dashed, however, when the United States quickly reverted to its prewar preferences for isolationism and the U.S. Senate, led by Republican Henry Cabot Lodge, rejected the Versailles treaty. Wilson rejected all attempts at compromise on the treaty, ensuring that it would never be ratified in any form and that the United States would never join the League of Nations. Moreover, the Senate refused to ratify Wilson's defensive alliance with France and Great Britain. Using U.S. action as an excuse, Great Britain also refused to ratify its defensive alliance with France. Betrayed by its allies, France stood alone, and the great hopes of early 1919 had turned to ashes by year's end.

QUICK REVIEW

How did the American, British, and French visions of the postwar peace differ?

| What factors led to the Russian Revolution, and what was its outcome? | **What were the global consequences of the First World War?** | How did leaders deal with the political dimensions of uncertainty in the interwar years? | In what ways were the anxieties of the postwar world expressed in new forms of communication? | ☑ LearningCurve Check what you know. |

867

How did leaders deal with the political dimensions of uncertainty and try to re-establish peace and prosperity in the interwar years?

THE PURSUIT OF REAL AND LASTING PEACE in the first half of the interwar years proved difficult for many reasons. Germany hated the Treaty of Versailles. France was fearful and isolated. Britain was undependable, and the United States had turned its back on Europe's problems. Eastern Europe was in ferment, and no one could predict Communist Russia's future. Moreover, the international economic situation was poor and was greatly complicated by war debts and disrupted patterns of trade. Yet for a time, from 1925 to late 1929, it appeared that peace and stability were within reach.

Germany and the Western Powers

Nearly all Germans and many other observers immediately and for decades after believed the Versailles treaty represented a harsh dictated peace and should be revised or repudiated as soon as possible. Many right-wing Germans believed there had been no defeat; instead they believed German soldiers had been betrayed by liberals, Marxists, Jews, and other "November criminals" who had surrendered in order to seize power.

Historians have recently begun to reassess the treaty's terms, however, and many scholars currently view them as relatively reasonable. They argue that much of the German anger toward the Allies was based more on perception than reality. With the collapse of Austria-Hungary, the dissolution of the Ottoman Empire, and the revolution in Russia, Germany emerged from the war an even stronger power in eastern Europe than before, and economically stronger and more populated than France or Great Britain. Moreover, when contrasted with

CHAPTER LOCATOR | What were the long-term and immediate causes of World War I, how did it become a global war? | How did total war affect the home fronts of the major combatants?

the extremely harsh Treaty of Brest-Litovsk that Germany had forced on Lenin's Russia, and the peace terms Germany intended to impose on the Allies if they won the war, the Versailles treaty was far from being a vindictive and crippling peace. Had it been, Germany could hardly have become the economic and military juggernaut that it was only twenty years later.

This is not to say, however, that France did not seek some degree of revenge on Germany for both the Franco-Prussian War (see page 726) and the Great War. Most of the war on the western front had been fought on French soil. The expected reconstruction costs and the amount of war debts owed to the United States were staggering. Thus the French believed that heavy German reparations were an economic necessity that could hold Germany down indefinitely and would enable France to realize its goal of security.

The British soon felt differently. Prewar Germany had been Great Britain's second-best market, and after the war a healthy, prosperous Germany appeared to be essential to the British economy. In addition, the British were suspicious of France's army—the largest in Europe—and the British and French were at odds over their League of Nations mandates in the Middle East.

While France and Britain drifted in different directions, the Allied reparations commission completed its work, and in 1921 the young German republic—known as the Weimar Republic—made its first reparations payment. Then in 1922, wracked by rapid inflation and political assassinations and motivated by hostility and arrogance as well, the Weimar Republic announced its inability to pay more and proposed a reparations moratorium for three years.

The British were willing to accept a moratorium, but the French were not. Led by their prime minister, Raymond Poincaré (1860–1934), they decided they had to either call Germany's bluff or see the entire peace settlement dissolve to France's great disadvantage. So in January 1923 French and Belgian armies occupied the Ruhr district, industrial Germany's heartland, creating the most serious international crisis of the 1920s.

Strengthened by a wave of patriotism, the German government ordered the people of the Ruhr to stop working and to resist French occupation nonviolently. The French responded by sealing off not only the Ruhr but also the entire Rhineland from the rest of Germany, letting in only enough food to prevent starvation.

By summer 1923 France and Germany were engaged in a great test of wills. French armies could not collect reparations from striking workers at gunpoint. But French occupation was paralyzing Germany and its economy, and the German government was soon forced to print money to pay its bills. Prices soared, and German money rapidly lost all value. Many retired and middle-class people saw their savings wiped out. Many Germans felt betrayed. They hated and blamed the Western governments, their own government, big business, the Jews, the workers, and the Communists for their misfortune.

In August 1923, as the mark's value fell and political unrest grew throughout Germany, Gustav Stresemann (1878–1929) became German chancellor. Stresemann adopted a compromising attitude. He called off the peaceful resistance campaign in the Ruhr and in October agreed in principle to pay reparations but asked for a re-examination of Germany's ability to pay. Poincaré accepted. Thus, after five years of hostility and tension, Germany and France, with British and American help, decided to try compromise and cooperation.

French Occupation of the Ruhr, 1923–1925

What factors led to the Russian Revolution, and what was its outcome?

What were the global consequences of the First World War?

How did leaders deal with the political dimensions of uncertainty in the interwar years?

In what ways were the anxieties of the postwar world expressed in new forms of communication?

✓ LearningCurve
Check what you know.

869

Hope in Foreign Affairs

In 1924 an international committee of financial experts headed by American banker Charles G. Dawes met to re-examine reparations. Under the terms of the resulting **Dawes Plan** (1924), Germany's yearly reparations were reduced and linked to the level of German economic prosperity. Germany would also receive large loans from the United States to promote German recovery, as well as to pay reparations to France and Britain, thus enabling those countries to repay the large sums they owed the United States. This circular flow of international payments was complicated and risky, but it worked for a while, facilitating a worldwide economic recovery in the late 1920s.

This economic settlement was matched by a political settlement. In 1925 European leaders met in Locarno, Switzerland. Germany and France solemnly pledged to accept their common border, and both Britain and Italy agreed to fight either France or Germany if one invaded the other. Stresemann also agreed to settle boundary disputes with Poland and Czechoslovakia by peaceful means, and France promised those countries military aid if Germany attacked them.

Other developments also strengthened hopes for international peace. In 1926 Germany joined the League of Nations, and in 1928 fifteen countries signed the Kellogg-Briand Pact. The signing nations "condemned and renounced war as an instrument of national policy."

Hope in Democratic Government

European domestic politics also offered reason for hope. During the Ruhr occupation and the great inflation, Germany's republican government appeared ready to collapse. In 1923 Communists momentarily entered provincial governments. In November an obscure politician named Adolf Hitler proclaimed a "national socialist revolution" in a Munich beer hall. Hitler's plot to seize government control was poorly organized and easily crushed. Hitler was sentenced to prison, where he outlined his theories and program in his book *Mein Kampf* (*My Struggle*, 1925).

The moderate businessmen who tended to dominate the various German coalition governments believed that economic prosperity demanded good relations with the Western powers, and they supported parliamentary government at home. Elections were held regularly, and as the economy boomed in the aftermath of the Dawes Plan, republican democracy appeared to have growing support among a majority of Germans. There were, however, sharp political divisions in the country. Many unrepentant nationalists and monarchists populated the right and the army. Members of Germany's Communist Party received directions from Moscow, and they accused the Social Democrats of betraying the revolution.

France's situation was similar to Germany's. Communists and socialists battled for the workers' support. After 1924 the democratically elected government rested mainly in the hands of moderate coalitions, and business interests were well represented. France's great accomplishment was rapid rebuilding of its war-torn northern region, and good times prevailed until 1930.

Britain, too, faced challenges after 1920. The great problem was unemployment, which hovered around 12 percent throughout the 1920s. The state provided unemployment benefits and a range of additional social services. These and other

Dawes Plan

▶ The product of the reparations commission, accepted by Germany, France, and Britain, that reduced Germany's yearly reparations, made payment dependent on German economic prosperity, and granted Germany large loans from the United States to promote recovery.

Mein Kampf

▶ Adolf Hitler's autobiography, published in 1925, which also contains Hitler's political ideology.

CHAPTER LOCATOR | What were the long-term and immediate causes of World War I, how did it become a global war? | How did total war affect the home fronts of the major combatants?

870 CHAPTER 28
WORLD WAR AND REVOLUTION

measures kept living standards from seriously declining, defused class tensions, and pointed the way to the welfare state Britain established after World War II.

The wartime trend toward greater social equality continued, however, helping maintain social harmony. Relative social harmony was accompanied by the rise of the Labour Party. Committed to moderate, "revisionist" socialism (see page 743), the Labour Party under Ramsay MacDonald (1866–1937) governed the country in 1924 and 1929–1935.

The British Conservatives under Stanley Baldwin (1867–1947) showed the same compromising spirit on social issues, and Britain experienced only limited social unrest in the 1920s and 1930s. In 1922 Britain granted southern, Catholic Ireland full autonomy after a bitter guerrilla war. Thus developments in both international relations and domestic politics gave the leading democracies cause for cautious optimism in the late 1920s.

QUICK REVIEW

What developments in the 1920s gave some observers
hope that lasting peace and stability were possible?

| What factors led to the Russian Revolution, and what was its outcome? | What were the global consequences of the First World War? | **How did leaders deal with the political dimensions of uncertainty in the interwar years?** | In what ways were the anxieties of the postwar world expressed in new forms of communication? | ✓ LearningCurve Check what you know. |

871

In what ways were the anxieties of the postwar world expressed or heightened by revolutionary ideas in modern thought, art, and science and in new forms of communication?

Unlocking the Power of the Atom

Many of the fanciful visions of science fiction came true in the twentieth century, although not exactly as first imagined. This 1927 cartoon satirizes a professor who has split the atom and has unwittingly destroyed his building and neighborhood in the process. In the Second World War scientists harnessed the atom in bombs and decimated faraway cities and their inhabitants. (© Mary Evans Picture Library/The Image Works)

M**ANY PEOPLE HOPED THAT HAPPIER TIMES** would return after the war, along with the familiar prewar ideals of peace, prosperity, and progress. These hopes were in vain. Great numbers of men and women felt themselves increasingly adrift in an age of anxiety and continual crisis.

Uncertainty in Philosophy and Religion

Before 1914 most people in the West still believed in Enlightenment philosophies of progress, reason, and individual rights. As the century began, progress was a daily reality, apparent in the rising living standard, the taming of the city, the

CHAPTER LOCATOR

What were the long-term and immediate causes of World War I, how did it become a global war?

How did total war affect the home fronts of the major combatants?

CHAPTER 28
872   WORLD WAR AND REVOLUTION

spread of political rights to women and workers, and the growth of state-supported social programs.

Even before the war, however, the German philosopher Friedrich Nietzsche (NEE-chuh) (1844–1900) called such faith in reason into question. In the first of his *Untimely Meditations* (1873), he argued that Western civilization overemphasized rationality and stifled the passions and animal instincts that drive human activity and true creativity. Nietzsche believed that reason, democracy, progress, and respectability were outworn social and psychological constructs that suffocated self-realization and excellence. Rejecting religion, Nietzsche claimed that Christianity embodied a "slave morality" that glorified weakness, envy, and mediocrity. Little read during his lifetime, Nietzsche attracted growing attention in the early twentieth century.

The First World War accelerated the revolt against established philosophical certainties. Logical positivism, often associated with Austrian philosopher Ludwig Wittgenstein (VIHT-guhn-shtighn) (1889–1951), rejected most concerns of traditional philosophy as nonsense and argued that life must be based on facts and observation. Others looked to **existentialism** for answers. Highly diverse and even contradictory, existential thinkers were loosely united in a search for moral values in an anxious and uncertain world. Often inspired by Nietzsche, they did not believe that a supreme being had established humanity's fundamental nature and given life its meaning. In the words of the French existentialist Jean-Paul Sartre (ZHAWN-pawl SAHR-truh) (1905–1980), "Man's existence precedes his essence. . . . To begin with he is nothing. He will not be anything until later, and then he will be what he makes of himself."[2]

In contrast, the loss of faith in human reason and in continual progress led to a renewed interest in Christianity. After World War I several thinkers and theologians began to revitalize Christian fundamentals, and intellectuals increasingly turned to religion between about 1920 and 1950. Sometimes described as Christian existentialists because they shared the loneliness and despair of atheistic existentialists, these believers felt that religion was one meaningful answer to terror and anxiety.

existentialism
▶ The name given to a highly diverse and even contradictory philosophy that stresses the meaninglessness of existence and the search for moral values in a world of terror and uncertainty.

The New Physics

Starting at the turn of the century, a series of discoveries challenged the established certainties of Newtonian physics. An important first step toward the new physics was the British physicist J. J. Thomson's 1897 discovery of subatomic particles, which proved that atoms were not stable and unbreakable. The following year Polish-born physicist Marie Curie (1867–1934) and her French husband, Pierre (1859–1906), discovered radium and demonstrated that it constantly emits subatomic particles and thus does not have a constant atomic weight. Building on this, German physicist Max Planck (1858–1947) showed in 1900 that subatomic energy is emitted in uneven little spurts, which Planck called "quanta," and not in a steady stream, as previously believed.

In 1905 the German-Jewish genius Albert Einstein (1879–1955) further undermined Newtonian physics. His theory of special relativity postulated that time and space are relative to the observer's viewpoint and that only the speed of light is constant for all frames of reference in the universe. In addition, Einstein's theory

What factors led to the Russian Revolution, and what was its outcome?

What were the global consequences of the First World War?

How did leaders deal with the political dimensions of uncertainty in the interwar years?

In what ways were the anxieties of the postwar world expressed in new forms of communication?

✔ LearningCurve
Check what you know.

873

stated that matter and energy are interchangeable and that even a particle of matter contains enormous levels of potential energy.

In the 1920s breakthrough followed breakthrough, with some discoveries raising new doubts about reality. The implications of the new theories and discoveries were disturbing to millions of people in the 1920s and 1930s. The new universe was strange and troubling, and, moreover, science appeared distant from human experience and human problems.

Freudian Psychology

With physics presenting an uncertain universe so unrelated to ordinary human experience, questions about the power and potential of the human mind assumed special significance. The findings and speculations of psychologist Sigmund Freud (1856–1939) were particularly disturbing.

Before Freud, most psychologists assumed that human behavior resulted from rational thinking by the conscious mind. By analyzing dreams and hysteria, Freud developed a very different view of the human psyche. Freud concluded that human behavior was governed by three parts of the self: the **id**, **ego**, and **superego**. The irrational unconscious, which he called the id, was driven by sexual, aggressive, and pleasure-seeking desires and was locked in constant battle with the mind's two other parts: the rationalizing conscious—the ego—which mediates what a person can do, and ingrained moral values—the superego—which specify what a person should do. Thus for Freud human behavior was a product of a fragile compromise between instinctual drives and the controls of rational thinking and moral values.

id, ego, superego
▶ Freudian terms for the primitive, irrational unconscious (id), the rationalizing conscious that mediates what a person can do (ego), and the ingrained moral values that specify what a person should do (superego).

Twentieth-Century Literature

Western literature was also influenced by the general intellectual climate of pessimism, relativism, and alienation. Some novelists used the stream-of-consciousness technique with its reliance on internal monologues to explore the psyche. The most famous stream-of-consciousness novel is *Ulysses*, published by Irish novelist James Joyce (1882–1941) in 1922. Abandoning conventional grammar and blending foreign words, puns, bits of knowledge, and scraps of memory together in bewildering confusion, the language of *Ulysses* was intended to mirror modern life itself.

Creative writers rejected the idea of progress; some even described "anti-utopias," nightmare visions of things to come. In 1918 Oswald Spengler (1880–1936) published *The Decline of the West*, in which he argued that Western civilization was in its old age and would soon be conquered by East Asia. Likewise, T. S. Eliot (1888–1965) depicted a world of growing desolation in his famous poem *The Waste Land* (1922). Franz Kafka's (1883–1924) novels portrayed helpless individuals crushed by inexplicably hostile forces.

Modern Architecture, Art, and Music

modernism
▶ A variety of cultural movements at the end of the nineteenth century and beginning of the twentieth that rebelled against traditional forms and conventions of the past.

Like scientists and intellectuals, creative artists rejected old forms and old values after the war. **Modernism** in architecture, art, and music meant constant experimentation and a search for new kinds of expression.

CHAPTER LOCATOR | What were the long-term and immediate causes of World War I, how did it become a global war? | How did total war affect the home fronts of the major combatants?

CHAPTER 28
874 WORLD WAR AND REVOLUTION

The United States pioneered in the new architecture. In the 1890s the Chicago School of architects, led by Louis H. Sullivan (1856–1924), used cheap steel, reinforced concrete, and electric elevators to build skyscrapers and office buildings lacking almost any exterior ornamentation. The buildings of Frank Lloyd Wright (1867–1959) were renowned for their sometimes-radical design, their creative use of wide varieties of materials, and their appearance of being part of the landscape.

In Europe architectural leadership centered in German-speaking countries. In 1919 Walter Gropius (1883–1969) merged the schools of fine and applied arts at Weimar into a single interdisciplinary school, the Bauhaus. Throughout the 1920s the Bauhaus, with its stress on **functionalism** and good design for everyday life, attracted enthusiastic students from all over the world.

functionalism

▶ The principle that buildings, like industrial products, should serve the purpose for which they were made as well as possible.

Eiffel Tower, 1926

The works of the French artist Robert Delaunay (1885–1941) represent most of the major art styles of the early twentieth century, including modernism, abstraction, futurism, fauvism, cubism, and Orphism. His early renderings of the Eiffel Tower (1909–1912), the iconic symbol of urbanization, the machine age, and, as a radio tower, limitless communication, possess features drawn from several of these styles. His later paintings of the Eiffel Tower, such as the one shown here, draw on a much wider palette of brilliant colors, reflecting aspects of a style known as Orphism, with which he is most closely identified. (*Eiffel Tower*, 1926, oil on canvas by Robert Delaunay [1885–1941]/Private Collection/Photo © Christie's Images/The Bridgeman Art Library)

What factors led to the Russian Revolution, and what was its outcome?

What were the global consequences of the First World War?

How did leaders deal with the political dimensions of uncertainty in the interwar years?

In what ways were the anxieties of the postwar world expressed in new forms of communication?

✓ LearningCurve Check what you know.

875

Art increasingly took on a nonrepresentational, abstract character. New artistic styles grew out of a revolt against French impressionism, which was characterized by an overall feeling, or impression, of light falling on a real-life scene before the artist's eyes, rather than an exact copy of objects. Though individualistic in their styles, "postimpressionists" and "expressionists" were united in their desire to depict unseen inner worlds of emotion and imagination.

In 1907 in Paris the famous Spanish painter Pablo Picasso (1881–1973), along with Georges Braque, Marcel Duchamp, and other artists, established cubism—an artistic approach concentrated on a complex geometry of zigzagging lines and sharply angled overlapping planes. Since the Renaissance, artists had represented objects from a single viewpoint and had created unified human forms. Cubism represented a radical new view of reality.

The ultimate stage in the development of abstract, nonrepresentational art occurred around 1910. Artists such as the Russian-born Wassily Kandinsky (1866–1944) turned away from nature completely.

Radicalization accelerated after World War I. The most notable new developments were New Objectivity, Dadaism, and surrealism. Paintings inspired by the New Objectivity were provocative, emotionally disturbing, and harshly satirical. Dadaism attacked all accepted standards of art and behavior, delighting in outrageous conduct. Surrealists painted fantastic worlds of wild dreams and complex symbols.

Developments in modern music were strikingly parallel to those in painting. Attracted by the emotional intensity of expressionism, composers depicted unseen inner worlds of emotion and imagination. Likewise, modernism in opera and ballet flourished. Led by Viennese composer Arnold Schönberg (SHUHN-buhrg) (1874–1951), some composers turned their backs on long-established musical conventions. As abstract painters arranged lines and color but did not draw identifiable objects, so modern composers arranged sounds without creating recognizable harmonies.

Movies and Radio

In the decades following the First World War, motion pictures became the main entertainment of the masses worldwide. Motion pictures offered ordinary people a temporary escape from the hard realities of international tensions, uncertainty, unemployment, and personal frustrations. Motion pictures also became powerful tools of indoctrination, especially in countries with dictatorial regimes.

Radio also dominated popular culture after the war. In 1920 the first major public broadcasts were made in Great Britain and the United States. Every major country quickly established national broadcasting networks. In the United States these were privately owned and financed by advertising. In Europe, China, Japan, India, and elsewhere the typical pattern was direct government control. By the late 1930s more than three-fourths of the households in both democratic Great Britain and dictatorial Germany had at least one radio. Radio was well suited for promoting patriotism and spreading political propaganda. Radios were revolutionary in that they were capable of reaching all of a nation's citizens at once, offering them a single perspective on current events, and teaching them a single national language and pronunciation.

CHAPTER LOCATOR | What were the long-term and immediate causes of World War I, how did it become a global war? | How did total war affect the home fronts of the major combatants?

876 CHAPTER 28
WORLD WAR AND REVOLUTION

The International Appeal of Cinema

A movie house in Havana, Cuba, in 1933 showing two American films made in 1932: *El Rey de la Plata* (*Silver Dollar*) starring Edward G. Robinson and *6 horas de Vida* (*Six Hours to Live*) featuring Warner Baxter. The partially visible poster in the upper right is advertising *El último varon sobre la Tierra* (*The Last Man on Earth*), an American-produced Spanish-language movie staring Raul Roulien, first released in Spain in January 1933. (Walker Evans [1903–1975]/© Copyright 1933. Cinema, 1933, printed ca. 1970. Gelatin silver print. Gift of Arnold H. Crane, 1971 [1971.646.12]) © Walker Evans Archive, Metropolitan Museum of Art, New York, NY, USA/Image copyright © The Metropolitan Museum of Art/Image source: Art Resource, NY)

QUICK REVIEW

How did the new physics challenge Enlightenment certainties?

What factors led to the Russian Revolution, and what was its outcome?

What were the global consequences of the First World War?

How did leaders deal with the political dimensions of uncertainty in the interwar years?

In what ways were the anxieties of the postwar world expressed in new forms of communication?

 LearningCurve
Check what you know.

CHAPTER SUMMARY

Nationalism, militarism, imperialism, and the alliance system increased political tensions across Europe at the end of the nineteenth century. Franz Ferdinand's assassination in 1914 sparked a regional war that soon became global. Four years of stalemate and slaughter followed. Entire societies mobilized for total war, and government powers greatly increased. Women earned greater social equality, and labor unions grew. Many European countries adopted socialism as a realistic economic blueprint.

Horrible losses on the eastern front led to Russian tsar Nicholas II's abdication in March 1917. A provisional government controlled by moderate social democrats replaced him but refused to withdraw Russia from the war. A second Russian revolution followed in November 1917, led by Lenin and his Communist Bolshevik Party. The Bolsheviks established a radical regime, smashed existing capitalist institutions, and posed an ongoing challenge to Europe and its colonial empires.

The "war to end war" brought only a fragile truce. The Versailles treaty took away Germany's colonies, limited its military, and demanded admittance of war guilt and exorbitant war reparations. Separate treaties redrew the maps of Europe and the Middle East. Allied wartime solidarity faded, and Germany remained unrepentant, setting the stage for World War II. Globally, the European powers refused to extend self-determination to their colonies, instead creating a mandate system that sowed further discontent among colonized peoples.

In the 1920s moderate political leaders sought to create an enduring peace and rebuild prewar prosperity though compromise. By decade's end they seemed to have succeeded: Germany experienced an economic recovery, France rebuilt its war-torn regions, and Britain's Labour Party expanded social services. Ultimately, however, these measures were short-lived.

The war's horrors, particularly the industrialization of war that slaughtered millions, shattered Enlightenment ideals and caused widespread anxiety. In the interwar years philosophers, artists, and writers portrayed these anxieties in their work. Movies and the radio initially offered escape but soon became powerful tools of indoctrination and propaganda.

CHAPTER LOCATOR | What were the long-term and immediate causes of World War I, how did it become a global war? | How did total war affect the home fronts of the major combatants?

CHAPTER 28
878   WORLD WAR AND REVOLUTION

 **CONNECTIONS** The Great War continues to influence global politics and societies. To understand the origins of many modern world conflicts, one must study first the intrigues and treaties and the revolutions and upheavals that were associated with this first truly world war.

In Chapter 30 we will see how the conflict contributed to a worldwide depression, the rise of totalitarian dictatorships, and a Second World War more global and destructive than the first. In the Middle East the Ottoman Empire came to an end, allowing France and England to carve out mandated territories—including modern Iraq, Palestine/Israel, and Lebanon—that remain flash points for violence and political instability in the twenty-first century. Nationalism, the nineteenth-century European ideology of change, took root in Asia, partly driven by Wilson's promise of self-determination. In Chapter 29 the efforts of various nationalist leaders—Atatürk in Turkey, Gandhi in India, Mao Zedong in China, Ho Chi Minh in Vietnam, and others—to throw off colonial domination will be examined, as well as the rise of ultranationalism in Japan, which led it into World War II and to ultimate defeat.

America's entry into the Great War placed it on the world stage, a place it has not relinquished as a superpower in the twentieth and twenty-first centuries. Russia, too, eventually became a superpower, but this outcome was not so clear in 1919 as its leaders fought for survival in a vicious civil war. By the outbreak of World War II Joseph Stalin had solidified Communist power, and the Soviet Union and the United Sates would play leading roles in defeating totalitarianism in Germany and Japan. But at war's end, as explained in Chapter 31, the two superpowers found themselves opponents in a Cold War that lasted for much of the rest of the twentieth century.

ONLINE DOCUMENT PROJECT

Calling Young Women to War

What words and images did governments use to recruit women to serve in World War I?

Examine several recruitment posters aimed at women, and then complete a quiz and writing assignment based on the evidence and details from this chapter. *See inside the front cover to learn more.*

What factors led to the Russian Revolution, and what was its outcome? | What were the global consequences of the First World War? | How did leaders deal with the political dimensions of uncertainty in the interwar years? | In what ways were the anxieties of the postwar world expressed in new forms of communication? | ✓ **LearningCurve** Check what you know.

879

GET STARTED ONLINE

LearningCurve

Now that you've read the chapter, make it stick by completing the LearningCurve activity.

STEP 1

STEP 2

EXPLAIN WHY IT MATTERS

Put your reading into practice. Identify each term below, and then explain why it matters in world history.

TERM	WHO OR WHAT & WHEN	WHY IT MATTERS
militarism (p. 846)		
Triple Entente (p. 848)		
trench warfare (p. 850)		
total war (p. 854)		
March Revolution (p. 859)		
Petrograd Soviet (p. 860)		
Bolsheviks (p. 861)		
War Communism (p. 862)		
League of Nations (p. 865)		
Treaty of Versailles (p. 865)		
Dawes Plan (p. 870)		
Mein Kampf (p. 870)		
existentialism (p. 873)		
id, ego, superego (p. 874)		
modernism (p. 874)		
functionalism (p. 875)		

STEP 3

MOVE BEYOND THE BASICS

To demonstrate a more advanced understanding of the nature and consequences of "total war," fill in the chart below with descriptions of the military, political, social, and economic impact of total war. In what ways was total war a conflict between nations as opposed to armies?

	Military	Political	Social	Economic
Impact of Total War				

STEP 4 PUT IT ALL TOGETHER

Now, take a step back and try to explain the big picture. Remember to use specific examples from the chapter in your answers.

WORLD WAR I

▶ What factors contributed to the division of Europe into two hostile blocs? Why did European leaders fail to resolve the tensions and conflicts that led to this situation?

▶ How did political leaders channel their nation's resources into the war effort? How did their policies affect European society and government?

THE RUSSIAN REVOLUTION

▶ How did the war undermine the tsarist regime in Russia? How did the tsar himself contribute to the collapse of his government?

▶ To what extent did Lenin dictate the course of events during the Russian Revolution? To what extent did he merely take advantage of opportunities as they presented themselves?

THE POSTWAR WORLD

▶ What steps did Western leaders take to repair the political and economic damage of World War I? Why were the new political and economic systems they created so fragile?

▶ How did the experience of World War I shape Western thought and culture in the 1920s?

LOOKING BACK, LOOKING AHEAD

▶ Compare and contrast the peace settlements that followed the Napoleonic wars and World War I. Which was more successful? Why?

▶ Argue for or against the following statement: "The roots of the economic crisis and global conflicts of the 1930s and 1940s can be found in the failures of the 1920s." What evidence can you present to support your position?

> ## IN YOUR OWN WORDS

Imagine that you must give an oral report to the class answering the following question: **In what ways did the First World War represent a fundamental turning point in world history?** What would be the most important points and why?

29
NATIONALISM IN ASIA

1914–1939

> **How did nationalism shape developments across Asia in the decades following the First World War?** Chapter 29 examines nationalist movements in Asia in the decades following the First World War. The First World War sped the development of modern Asian nationalism. Before 1914 the nationalist gospel of anti-imperialist political freedom and racial equality had already won converts among Asia's westernized, educated elites. In the 1920s and 1930s it increasingly won the allegiance of the masses. Between the outbreaks of the First and Second World Wars, each Asian country developed a distinctive national movement rooted in its own unique culture and history. And as in Europe, nationalist movements gave rise in Asia to conflict both within large, multiethnic states and between independent states.

LearningCurve

After reading the chapter, use LearningCurve to retain what you've read.

Kasturba Gandhi Wife of Indian political leader Mohandas Gandhi, Kasturba was barely fourteen years old and he thirteen when the marriage took place. Kasturba (1869–1944) supported Gandhi through decades of struggle for Indian independence. Here she spins cotton on a charkha, or spinning wheel, part of Gandhi's campaign for Indians to become self-sufficient by making their own cloth and freeing themselves from imported British goods. (© Dinodia Photo Library/The Image Works)

> Why did modern nationalism develop in Asia between the First and Second World Wars, and what was its appeal?

> How did the Ottoman Empire's collapse in World War I shape nationalist movements in the Middle East?

> What role did Gandhi and his campaign of militant nonviolence play in leading India to independence from the British?

> How did nationalism shape political developments in East and Southeast Asia?

> Why did modern nationalism develop in Asia between the First and Second World Wars, and what was its appeal?

IN THE LATE NINETEENTH and early twentieth centuries the peoples of Asia adapted the European ideology of nationalism to their own situations. The First World War profoundly affected Asian nationalist aspirations by altering relations between Asia and Europe. For four years Asians watched Europeans vilifying and destroying each other. Japan's defeat of imperial Russia in 1905 (see page 729) had shown that an Asian power could beat a European Great Power; now for the first time Asians saw the entire West as divided and vulnerable.

Asian Reaction to the War in Europe

The Great War was a global conflict, but some peoples were affected more significantly than others. The Japanese and Ottoman Turks were directly involved, fighting with the Allies and Central Powers, respectively. The Chinese, who overthrew their emperor in 1911, were more concerned with internal events and the threat from Japan than they were with war in Europe. In British India and French Indochina the war's impact was unavoidably greater. Total war required the British and the French to draft their colonial subjects into the conflict.

An Indian or Vietnamese soldier who fought in France and came in contact there with democratic and republican ideas, however, was less likely to accept foreign rule when he returned home. The British and the French therefore had to make rash promises to gain the support of these colonial peoples and other allies during the war, suggesting in many cases that colonial peoples would move toward self-rule once victory was achieved. After the war the nationalist genie the colonial powers had called on refused to slip meekly back into the bottle.

U.S. President Wilson's war aims also raised the hopes of peoples under imperial rule. In January 1918 Wilson proposed his Fourteen Points (see page 884), whose key idea was national self-determination for the peoples of Europe and the Ottoman Empire. Wilson recommended in Point 5 that in all colonial questions

CHAPTER LOCATOR |

Why did modern nationalism develop in Asia between the First and Second World Wars, and what was its appeal?

How did the Ottoman Empire's collapse in World War I shape nationalist movements in the Middle East?

884 CHAPTER 29 NATIONALISM IN ASIA

1904–1905
Russo-Japanese War ends in Russia's defeat

1916
Sykes-Picot Agreement divides Ottoman Empire; Lucknow Pact forms alliance between Hindus and Muslims in India; New Culture Movement in China begins

1917
Balfour Declaration establishes Jewish homeland in Palestine

1919
Amritsar Massacre in India; May Fourth Movement in China; Treaty of Versailles; Afghanistan achieves independence

1920
King of Syria deposed by French; Gandhi launches campaign of nonviolent resistance against British rule in India

1920s–1930s
Large numbers of European Jews immigrate to Palestine; Hebrew becomes common language

1923
Sun Yatsen allies Nationalist Party with Chinese Communists; Treaty of Lausanne ends war in Turkey; Mustafa Kemal begins to modernize and secularize Turkey

1925
Reza Shah Pahlavi proclaims himself shah of Persia and begins modernization campaign

1927
Jiang Jieshi, leader of Chinese Nationalist Party, purges his Communist allies

1930
Gandhi leads Indians on march to the sea to protest the British salt tax

1931
Japan occupies Manchuria

1932
Iraq gains independence in return for military alliance with Great Britain

1934
Mao Zedong leads Chinese Communists on Long March; Philippines gains self-governing commonwealth status from United States

1937
Japanese militarists launch attack on China; Rape of Nanjing

"the interests of native populations be given equal weight with the desires of European governments," and he seemed to call for national self-rule. This message had enormous appeal for educated Asians, fueling their hopes of freedom.

The Mandates System

After winning the war, the Allies tried to re-establish or increase their political and economic domination of their Asian and African colonies. Although fatally weakened, Western imperialism remained very much alive in 1918, partly because President Wilson was no revolutionary. At the Paris Peace Conference Wilson compromised on colonial questions in order to achieve some of his European goals and create the League of Nations.

The compromise at the Paris Peace Conference between Wilson's vague, moralistic idealism and the European determination to maintain control over colonial empires was a system of League of Nations mandates over Germany's former colonies and the old Ottoman Empire. Article 22 of the League of Nations Covenant, which was part of the Treaty of Versailles, assigned territories "inhabited by peoples incapable of governing themselves" to various "developed nations." "The well-being and development of such peoples" was declared "a sacred trust of civilization." The **Permanent Mandates Commission**, whose members came from European countries with colonies, was created to oversee the developed nations' fulfillment of their international responsibility. Thus the League elaborated a new

Permanent Mandates Commission

▶ A commission created by the League of Nations to oversee the developed nations' fulfillment of their international responsibility toward their mandates.

What role did Gandhi and his campaign of militant nonviolence play in leading India to independence from the British?

How did nationalism shape political developments in East and Southeast Asia?

☑ LearningCurve
Check what you know.

principle—development toward the eventual goal of self-government—but left its implementation to the colonial powers themselves.

The mandates system demonstrated that Europe was determined to maintain its imperial power and influence. Bitterly disappointed patriots throughout Asia saw the system as an expansion of the imperial order. Yet Asian patriots did not give up. They preached national self-determination and struggled to build mass movements capable of achieving freedom and independence.

In this struggle Asian nationalists were encouraged by Soviet communism. After seizing power in 1917, Lenin declared that the Asian inhabitants of the new Soviet Union were complete equals of the Russians with a right to their own development. The Communists also denounced European and American imperialism and pledged to support revolutionary movements in colonial countries. The example, ideology, and support of Soviet communism exerted a powerful influence in the 1920s and 1930s, particularly in China and French Indochina (see page 901).

Nationalism's Appeal

There were at least three reasons for the upsurge of nationalism in Asia. First and foremost, nationalism provided the most effective means of organizing anti-imperialist resistance both to direct foreign rule and to indirect Western domination. Second, nationalism called for fundamental changes and challenged old political and social practices and beliefs. As in Russia after the Crimean War, in Turkey after the Ottoman Empire's collapse, and in Japan after the Meiji Restoration, the nationalist creed after World War I went hand in hand with acceptance of modernization by the educated elites. Third, nationalism offered a vision of a free and prosperous future, and provided an ideology to ennoble the sacrifices the struggle would require.

Nationalism also had a dark side. As in Europe (see page 715), Asian nationalists developed a strong sense of "we" and "they." "They" were often the enemy. European imperialists were just such a "they," and nationalist feeling generated the will to challenge European domination. But, as in Europe, Asian nationalism also stimulated bitter conflicts and wars between peoples, in three different ways.

First, as when the ideology of nationalism first developed in Europe in the early 1800s (see pages 715–716), Asian (and African) elites were often forced to create a national identity in colonies that Europeans had artificially created, or in multiethnic countries held together by authoritarian leaders but without national identities based on shared ethnicities or histories. Second, nationalism stimulated conflicts between relatively homogeneous peoples in large states, rallying, for example, Chinese against Japanese and vice versa. Third, nationalism often heightened tensions between ethnic or religious groups within states. In nearly all countries there were ancient ethnic and religious differences and rivalries. Imperial rulers of colonial powers and local authoritarian rulers exploited these ethnic and religious differences to "divide and conquer" the peoples in their empires. When the rigid imperial rule ended, the different national, religious, or even ideological factions turned against each other, each seeking to either seize control of or divide the existing state, and to dominate the enemy "they" within its borders.

CHAPTER LOCATOR | **Why did modern nationalism develop in Asia between the First and Second World Wars, and what was its appeal?** | How did the Ottoman Empire's collapse in World War I shape nationalist movements in the Middle East?

CHAPTER 29
886 NATIONALISM IN ASIA

Nationalism's appeal in Asia was not confined to territories under direct European rule. Europe and the United States had forced even the most solid Asian states, China and Japan, to accept unequal treaties (see page 795) and humiliating limitations on their sovereignty. Thus the nationalist promise of genuine economic independence and true political equality with the West appealed as powerfully in old but weak states like China as in colonial territories like British India.

QUICK REVIEW

What was the mandates system, and how did it contribute to the intensification of Asian nationalism?

What role did Gandhi and his campaign of militant nonviolence play in leading India to independence from the British?

How did nationalism shape political developments in East and Southeast Asia?

✓ LearningCurve
Check what you know.

How did the Ottoman Empire's collapse in World War I shape nationalist movements in the Middle East?

Mustafa Kemal

Surnamed Atatürk, meaning "father of the Turks," Mustafa Kemal and his supporters imposed revolutionary changes aimed at modernizing and westernizing Turkish society and the new Turkish government. Dancing here with his adopted daughter at her high-society wedding, Atatürk often appeared in public in elegant European dress — a vivid symbol for the Turkish people of his radical break with traditional Islamic teaching and custom. (Hulton Archive/Getty Images)

THE MOST FLAGRANT ATTEMPT TO EXPAND Western imperialism occurred in southwest Asia (Map 29.1). There the British and the French successfully encouraged an Arab revolt in 1916 and destroyed the Ottoman Empire. Europeans then sought to replace Turks as principal rulers throughout the region. Turkish, Arab, and Persian nationalists, as well as Jewish nationalists arriving from Europe, reacted violently. They struggled to win nationhood, and as the Europeans were forced to make concessions, they sometimes came into sharp conflict with each other, most notably in Palestine.

CHAPTER LOCATOR | Why did modern nationalism develop in Asia between the First and Second World Wars, and what was its appeal? | **How did the Ottoman Empire's collapse in World War I shape nationalist movements in the Middle East?**

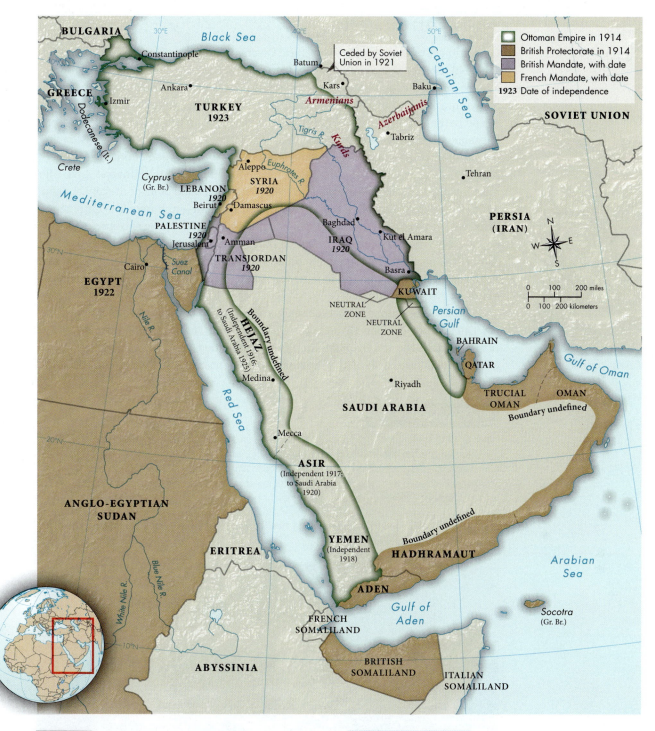

MAP 29.1 ■ The Partition of the Ottoman Empire, 1914–1923

By 1914 the Ottoman Turks had been pushed out of the Balkans, and their Arab provinces were on the edge of revolt. That revolt erupted in the First World War and contributed greatly to the Ottomans' defeat. When the Allies then attempted to implement their plans, including independence for the Armenian people, Mustafa Kemal arose to forge in battle the modern Turkish state.

> **MAPPING THE PAST**

ANALYZING THE MAP: What new countries were established as a result of the partition of the Ottoman Empire? Where were mandates established? What might you conclude about European views of the Middle East based on how Europe divided up the region?

CONNECTIONS: How might the collapse of the Ottoman Empire in World War I have contributed to the current situation in the Middle East?

What role did Gandhi and his campaign of militant nonviolence play in leading India to independence from the British?	How did nationalism shape political developments in East and Southeast Asia?	✓ LearningCurve Check what you know.

The Arab Revolt

Long subject to European pressure, the Ottoman Empire failed to reform and modernize in the late nineteenth century (see pages 765–767). Declining international stature and domestic tyranny led to revolutionary activity among idealistic exiles and young army officers who wanted to seize power and save the Ottoman state. These patriots, the so-called Young Turks, succeeded in the 1908 revolution, and subsequently they were determined to hold together the remnants of the vast multiethnic empire. Defeated in the Balkan war of 1912 and stripped of practically all territory in Europe, the Young Turks redoubled their efforts in southwest Asia. The most important of their possessions were Syria—consisting of modern-day Lebanon, Syria, Israel, the West Bank, the Gaza Strip, and Jordan—and Iraq. The Ottoman Turks also claimed the Arabian peninsula but exercised only loose control there.

For centuries the largely Arab populations of Syria and Iraq had been tied to their Ottoman rulers by their common faith in Islam (though there were Christian Arabs as well). Yet beneath the surface, ethnic and linguistic tensions simmered between Turks and Arabs.

Young Turk actions after 1908 made the embryonic "Arab movement" a reality. The majority of Young Turks promoted a narrow Turkish nationalism. They further centralized the Ottoman Empire and extended the sway of Turkish language and culture. In 1909 the Turkish government brutally slaughtered thou-

The Armenian Atrocities

When in 1915 some Armenians welcomed Russian armies as liberators after years of persecution, the Ottoman government ordered a genocidal mass deportation of its Armenian citizens from their homeland in the empire's eastern provinces. American ambassador to Constantinople Henry Morgenthau included this photo in his 1918 autobiography, *Ambassador Morganthau's Story*, with this caption: "Scenes like this were common all over the Armenian provinces in the spring and summer months of 1915. Death in its several forms — massacres, starvation, exhaustion — destroyed the larger part of the refugees. The Turkish policy was that of extermination under the guise of deportation." (© Bettmann/Corbis)

CHAPTER LOCATOR | Why did modern nationalism develop in Asia between the First and Second World Wars, and what was its appeal? | **How did the Ottoman Empire's collapse in World War I shape nationalist movements in the Middle East?**

890 CHAPTER 29 NATIONALISM IN ASIA

sands of Armenian Christians, a prelude to the wholesale massacre of more than a million Armenians during the First World War. Meanwhile, Arab discontent grew.

During World War I the Turks aligned themselves with Germany and Austria-Hungary (see page 852). As a result, the Young Turks drew all of the Middle East into what had been up to that point a European war. Arabs opposed to Ottoman rule found themselves allied with the British, who encouraged the alliance with vague promises of an independent Arab kingdom. After British victories on the Arab peninsula in 1917 and 1918, many Arab patriots expected a large, unified Arab state to rise from the dust of the Ottoman collapse. Within two years, however, Arab nationalists felt bitterly betrayed by Great Britain and its allies.

Arab bitterness was partly directed at secret wartime treaties between Britain and France to divide and rule the old Ottoman Empire. In the 1916 **Sykes-Picot Agreement**, Britain and France secretly agreed that France would receive modern-day Lebanon, Syria, and much of southern Turkey, and Britain would receive Palestine, Jordan, and Iraq. The Sykes-Picot Agreement contradicted British promises concerning Arab independence after the war and left Arab nationalists feeling cheated and betrayed.

A related source of Arab frustration was Britain's wartime commitment to a Jewish homeland in Palestine. The **Balfour Declaration** of November 1917, made by the British foreign secretary Arthur Balfour, offered British support for the idea of a Jewish homeland in Palestine. Some British Cabinet members believed the Balfour Declaration would appeal to German, Austrian, and American Jews and thus help the British war effort. Others sincerely supported the Zionist vision of a Jewish homeland (see page 894), but also believed that Jews living in this homeland would be grateful to Britain and thus help maintain British control of the Suez Canal.

In 1914 Jews made up about 11 percent of the predominantly Arab population in the Ottoman territory that became, under British control, Palestine. The "national home for the Jewish People" mentioned in the Balfour Declaration implied to the Arabs—and to the Zionist Jews as well—some kind of Jewish state that would be incompatible with majority rule.

After failed efforts at the Paris Peace Conference to secure Arab independence, Arab nationalists met in Damascus at the General Syrian Congress in 1919 and unsuccessfully called again for political independence. Ignoring Arab opposition, the British mandate in Palestine formally incorporated the Balfour Declaration and its commitment to a Jewish national home. In March 1920 the Syrian National Congress proclaimed Syria independent, with Faisal bin Hussein as king. A similar congress declared Iraq an independent kingdom.

Western reaction to events in Syria and Iraq was swift and decisive. A French army stationed in Lebanon attacked Syria, taking Damascus in July 1920. Faisal fled, and the French took over. Meanwhile, the British put down an uprising in Iraq and established effective control there. Western imperialism appeared to have replaced Turkish rule in the Middle East (see Map 29.1).

The Turkish Revolution

Days after the end of the First World War, French and then British troops entered Constantinople to begin a five-year occupation of the Ottoman capital. A treaty forced on the helpless sultan dismembered Turkey and reduced it to a puppet

Sykes-Picot Agreement
▶ The 1916 secret agreement between Britain and France that divided up the Arab lands of Lebanon, Syria, southern Turkey, Palestine, Jordan, and Iraq.

Balfour Declaration
▶ A 1917 statement by British foreign secretary Arthur Balfour that supported the idea of a Jewish homeland in Palestine.

What role did Gandhi and his campaign of militant nonviolence play in leading India to independence from the British?

How did nationalism shape political developments in East and Southeast Asia?

✓ LearningCurve
Check what you know.

state. Great Britain and France occupied parts of Turkey, and Italy and Greece claimed shares as well. In 1919 Greek armies carried by British ships landed on the Turkish coast at Smyrna and advanced into the interior. Turkey seemed finished.

But Turkey produced a great leader and revived to become an inspiration to the entire Middle East. Mustafa Kemal (1881–1938), considered the father of modern Turkey, was a military man sympathetic to the Young Turk movement. After the armistice, he watched with anguish the Allies' aggression and the sultan's cowardice. In early 1919 he began working to unify Turkish resistance.

The sultan, bowing to Allied pressure, initially denounced Kemal, but the cause of national liberation proved more powerful. The catalyst was the Greek invasion and attempted annexation of much of western Turkey.

Refusing to acknowledge the Allied dismemberment of their country, the Turks battled on through 1920 despite staggering defeats. The next year the Greeks advanced almost to Ankara, the nationalist stronghold in central Turkey. There Mustafa Kemal's forces took the offensive and won a great victory. The Greeks and their British allies sued for peace. The resulting **Treaty of Lausanne** (1923) recognized a truly independent Turkey (see Map 29.1).

Mustafa Kemal believed Turkey should modernize and secularize along Western lines. His first moves, beginning in 1923, were political. Kemal called on the National Assembly to depose the sultan and establish a republic and had himself elected president. Kemal savagely crushed the demands for independence of ethnic minorities within Turkey like the Armenians and the Kurds, but he realistically abandoned all thought of winning back lost Arab territories. He then created a one-party system in order to work his will.

Kemal's most radical changes pertained to religion and culture. Profoundly influenced by the example of western Europe, Mustafa Kemal set out to limit religious influence in daily affairs. Kemal decreed a revolutionary separation of church and state. Secular law codes inspired by European models replaced religious courts. State schools replaced religious schools and taught such secular subjects as science, mathematics, and social sciences.

Mustafa Kemal also struck down many entrenched patterns of behavior. Women, traditionally secluded and inferior to males in Islamic society, received the right to vote. Civil law on a European model, rather than the Islamic code, now governed marriage. Women could seek divorces, and no man could have more than one wife at a time. Men were forbidden to wear the tall red fez of the Ottoman era. The old Arabic script was replaced with a new Turkish alphabet based on Roman letters, which facilitated massive government efforts to spread literacy after 1928. Finally, in 1935, surnames on the European model were introduced. The National Assembly granted Mustafa Kemal the surname Atatürk, which means "father of the Turks."

By his death in 1938, Atatürk and his supporters had consolidated their revolution. Government-sponsored industrialization was fostering urban growth and new attitudes, encouraging Turks to embrace business and science. Poverty persisted in rural areas, as did some religious discontent among devout Muslims. But like the Japanese after the Meiji Restoration, the Turkish people had rallied around the nationalist banner to repulse European imperialism and were building a modern secular nation-state.

Treaty of Lausanne
▶ The 1923 treaty that ended the Turkish war and recognized the territorial integrity of a truly independent Turkey.

CHAPTER LOCATOR | Why did modern nationalism develop in Asia between the First and Second World Wars, and what was its appeal? | **How did the Ottoman Empire's collapse in World War I shape nationalist movements in the Middle East?**

892 NATIONALISM IN ASIA

CHAPTER 29

Modernization Efforts in Persia and Afghanistan

In Persia (renamed Iran in 1935) strong-arm efforts to build a unified modern nation ultimately proved less successful than in Turkey. In the late nineteenth century Persia had also been subject to extreme foreign pressure, which stimulated efforts to reform the government as a means of reviving Islamic civilization. In 1906 a nationalistic coalition of merchants, religious leaders, and intellectuals revolted. The despotic shah was forced to grant a constitution and establish a national assembly, the **Majlis**.

Yet the 1906 Persian revolution was doomed to failure, largely because of European imperialism. In 1907 Britain and Russia divided the country into spheres of influence. Britain's sphere ran along the Persian Gulf; the Russian sphere encompassed the whole northern half of Persia (see Map 29.1). Thereafter Russia intervened constantly. It blocked reforms, occupied cities, and completely dominated the country by 1912. When Russian power collapsed in the Bolshevik Revolution, British armies rushed into the power vacuum. By bribing corrupt Persians, Great Britain in 1919 negotiated a treaty allowing the installation of British "advisers" in every government department.

The Majlis refused to ratify the treaty, and the blatant attempt to make Persia a British satellite aroused the national spirit. In 1921 reaction against the British brought to power a military dictator, Reza Shah Pahlavi (1877–1944), who proclaimed himself shah in 1925 and ruled until 1941.

Inspired by Turkey's Mustafa Kemal, Reza Shah had three basic goals: to build a modern nation, to free Persia from foreign domination, and to rule with an iron fist. The challenge was enormous. Persia was a vast, undeveloped country. The rural population was mostly poor and illiterate, and among the Persian majority were sizable ethnic minorities with their own aspirations. Furthermore, Iran's powerful religious leaders hated Western (Christian) domination but were equally opposed to a more secular, less Islamic society.

To realize his vision of a strong Persia, the shah created a modern army, built railroads, and encouraged commerce. He won control over ethnic minorities such as the Kurds in the north and Arab tribesmen on the Iraqi border. He reduced the privileges granted to foreigners and raised taxes on the powerful Anglo-Persian Oil Company. Yet Reza Shah was less successful than Atatürk.

Because the European-educated elite in Persia was smaller than the comparable group in Turkey, the idea of re-creating Persian greatness on the basis of a secularized society attracted relatively few determined supporters. Many powerful religious leaders turned against Reza Shah, and he became increasingly brutal, greedy, and tyrannical.

Afghanistan, meanwhile, was nominally independent in the nineteenth century, but the British imposed political restrictions and constantly meddled in the country's affairs. In 1919 emir Amanullah Khan (1892–1960) declared war on the British government in India and won complete independence for the first time. Amanullah then decreed revolutionary modernizing reforms designed to hurl his primitive country into the twentieth century. Amanullah pushed too hard and too fast, however, and the result was tribal and religious revolt, civil war, and retreat from reform. Islam remained both religion and law. A powerful but

Majlis

▶ The national assembly established by the despotic shah of Iran in 1906.

Afghanistan Under Amanullah Khan

What role did Gandhi and his campaign of militant nonviolence play in leading India to independence from the British?

How did nationalism shape political developments in East and Southeast Asia?

✔ LearningCurve
Check what you know.

primitive patriotism enabled Afghanistan to win political independence from the West, but not to build a modern society.

Gradual Independence in the Arab States

French and British mandates forced Arab nationalists to seek independence by gradual means after 1920. Arab nationalists were indirectly aided by Western taxpayers who wanted cheap—that is, peaceful—empires. As a result, Arabs won considerable control over local affairs in the mandated states, except Palestine, though the mandates remained European satellites in international and economic affairs.

In Iraq the British chose Faisal bin Hussein, whom the French had deposed in Syria, as king. Faisal obligingly gave British advisers broad behind-the-scenes control. The king also accepted British ownership of Iraq's oil fields. Given the severe limitations imposed on him, Faisal (r. 1921–1933) proved to be an able ruler, gaining his peoples' support and encouraging moderate reforms. In 1932 he secured Iraqi independence at the price of a restrictive long-term military alliance with Great Britain.

Egypt had been occupied by Great Britain since 1882 (see page 767) and had been a British protectorate since 1914. Following intense nationalist agitation after the Great War, Great Britain in 1922 proclaimed Egypt formally independent but continued to occupy the country militarily and control its politics. In 1936 the British agreed to restrict their troops to their bases in the Suez Canal Zone.

The French compromised less in their handling of their mandated Middle East territories. Following the Ottoman Empire's collapse after World War I, the French designated Lebanon as one of several ethnic enclaves within a larger area that became part of the French mandate of Syria. They practiced a policy of divide and rule and generally played off ethnic and religious minorities against each other. In 1926 Lebanon became a separate republic but remained under the control of the French mandate. Arab nationalists in Syria finally won promises of Syrian independence in 1936 in return for a friendship treaty with France.

In short, the Arab states gradually freed themselves from Western political mandates but not from Western military threats or from pervasive Western influence. Since large Arab landowners and urban merchants increased their wealth and political power after 1918, they often supported the Western hegemony. Radical nationalists, on the other hand, recognized that Western control of the newly discovered Arab oil fields was proof that economic independence and genuine freedom had not yet been achieved.

Arab-Jewish Tensions in Palestine

Relations between the Arabs and the West were complicated by the tense situation in the British mandate of Palestine, and that situation deteriorated in the interwar years. Both Arabs and Jews denounced the British, who tried unsuccessfully to compromise with both sides. Arab nationalist anger, however, was aimed primarily at Jewish settlers. The key issue was Jewish migration from Europe to Palestine.

Jewish nationalism, known as Zionism, took shape in Europe in the late nineteenth century. The Zionist movement encouraged some of the world's Jews to

CHAPTER LOCATOR | Why did modern nationalism develop in Asia between the First and Second World Wars, and what was its appeal? | **How did the Ottoman Empire's collapse in World War I shape nationalist movements in the Middle East?**

894 CHAPTER 29 NATIONALISM IN ASIA

settle in Palestine, but until 1921 the great majority of Jewish emigrants preferred the United States.

After 1921 the situation changed radically. An isolationist United States drastically limited immigration from eastern Europe, where war and revolution had kindled anti-Semitism. Moreover, the British began honoring the Balfour Declaration despite Arab protests. Thus Jewish immigration to Palestine from turbulent Europe in the interwar years grew rapidly, particularly after Adolf Hitler became German chancellor in 1933. By 1939 Palestine's Jewish population had increased almost fivefold since 1914 and accounted for about 30 percent of all inhabitants.

Jewish settlers in Palestine faced formidable difficulties. Although much of the land purchased by the Jewish National Fund was productive, the sellers of such land were often wealthy absentee Arab landowners who cared little for their Arab tenants' welfare. When the Jewish settlers replaced those long-time Arab tenants, Arab farmers and intellectuals burned with a sense of injustice. Moreover, most Jewish immigrants came from urban backgrounds and preferred to establish new cities like Tel Aviv or to live in existing towns, where they competed with the Arabs. The land issue combined with economic and cultural friction to harden Arab protest into hatred.

The British gradually responded to Arab pressure and tried to slow Jewish immigration. This effort satisfied neither Jews nor Arabs, and by 1938 the two communities were engaged in an undeclared civil war.

On the eve of the Second World War, the frustrated British proposed an independent Palestine with the number of Jews permanently limited to only about one-third of the total population. Zionists felt themselves in grave danger of losing their dream of an independent Jewish state.

Nevertheless, in the face of adversity Jewish settlers gradually succeeded in forging a cohesive community in Palestine. Hebrew, for centuries used only in religious worship, was revived as a living language in the 1920s–1930s to bind the Jews in Palestine together. Despite its slow beginnings, rural development achieved often remarkable results. The key unit of agricultural organization was the **kibbutz** (kih-BOOTS), a collective farm on which each member shared equally in the work, rewards, and defense. An egalitarian socialist ideology also characterized industry, which grew rapidly. By 1939 a new but old nation was emerging in the Middle East.

kibbutz
▶ A Jewish collective farm on which each member shared equally in the work, rewards, and defense.

QUICK REVIEW

What kind of state did Mustafa Kemal build in Turkey? How did his accomplishments serve as a model for other nationalist leaders in the Middle East?

What role did Gandhi and his campaign of militant nonviolence play in leading India to independence from the British?

How did nationalism shape political developments in East and Southeast Asia?

✓ LearningCurve
Check what you know.

What role did Gandhi and his campaign of militant nonviolence play in leading India to independence from the British?

Gandhi on the Salt March, June 1930

A small, frail man, Gandhi possessed enormous courage and determination. His campaign of nonviolent resistance to British rule inspired the Indian masses and mobilized a nation. Here he is shown walking on his famous march to the sea to protest the English-Indian government's monopoly on salt production. (akg-images)

THE NATIONALIST MOVEMENT IN BRITISH INDIA grew out of two interconnected cultures, Hindu and Muslim. While the two joined together to challenge British rule, they also came to see themselves as fundamentally different. Nowhere has modern nationalism's power both to unify and to divide been more strikingly demonstrated than in India.

British Promises and Repression

When the First World War began, the British feared an Indian revolt. Instead Indians supported the war effort. About 1.2 million Indian soldiers and laborers voluntarily served in Europe, Africa, and the Middle East. The British government in India and the native Indian princes sent large supplies of food, money, and ammunition. In return, the British opened more good government jobs to Indians and made other minor concessions.

CHAPTER LOCATOR | Why did modern nationalism develop in Asia between the First and Second World Wars, and what was its appeal? | How did the Ottoman Empire's collapse in World War I shape nationalist movements in the Middle East?

As the war in distant Europe ground on, however, inflation, high taxes, food shortages, and a terrible influenza epidemic created widespread suffering and discontent. The prewar nationalist movement revived stronger than ever, and moderates and radicals in the Indian National Congress Party (see page 784) joined forces. Moreover, in 1916 Hindu leaders in the Congress Party hammered out an alliance—the **Lucknow Pact**—with India's Muslim League. The Lucknow Pact forged a powerful united front of Hindus and Muslims and called for putting India on equal footing with self-governing British dominions like Canada, Australia, and New Zealand.

The British response to the Lucknow Pact was mixed. In August 1917 the British called for the development of self-governing institutions in India, but the proposed self-government was much more limited than that granted the British dominions. In late 1919 the British established a dual administration: part Indian and elected, part British and authoritarian. Sensitive matters like taxes, police, and the courts remained solely in British hands.

Old-fashioned authoritarian rule also seriously undermined whatever positive impact this reform might have had. The 1919 Rowlatt Acts indefinitely extended wartime "emergency measures" designed to curb unrest and root out "conspiracy." The result was a wave of rioting across India.

Under these tense conditions a crowd of some ten thousand gathered to celebrate a Sikh religious festival in an enclosed square in the Sikh holy city of Amritsar in the northern Punjab province. Unknown to the crowd, the local English

Lucknow Pact
▶ A 1916 alliance between the Hindus leading the Indian National Congress and the Muslim League.

British Man Fishing in India

British colonial officials, such as this gentleman reposing in a wicker chair while fishing in India around 1925, enjoyed lifestyles that were often much more comfortable than would have been the case back in England. Gardeners, chauffeurs, maids, cooks, and other personal servants, like the three men helping the fisher, were commonly hired to wait on the colonists hand and foot. Some justified the lifestyle as demonstrating the refinements of civilization — part of the white man's burden. (Photograph by Ralph Ponsonby Watts/© Mary Evans Picture Library/The Images Works)

What role did Gandhi and his campaign of militant nonviolence play in leading India to independence from the British?

How did nationalism shape political developments in East and Southeast Asia?

✓ LearningCurve
Check what you know.

commander, General Reginald Dyer, had banned all public meetings that very day. Dyer marched his troops into the square and, without warning, ordered them to fire into the crowd until the ammunition ran out. Official British records of the Amritsar Massacre list 379 killed and 1,137 wounded, but these figures remain hotly contested as being too low. Tensions flared, and India stood on the verge of more violence and repression. That India took a different path to national liberation was due largely to Mohandas K. Gandhi (1869–1948), the most influential Indian leader of modern times.

The Roots of Militant Nonviolence

Gandhi grew up in a well-to-do family, and after his father's death, he went to study law in England, where he passed the English bar. Upon returning to India, he decided in 1893 to try a case for some wealthy Indian merchants in the British colony of Natal (part of modern South Africa).

In Natal Gandhi took up the plight of the expatriate Indian community. White plantation owners had been importing thousands of poor Indians as indentured laborers since the 1860s. Some of these Indians, after completing their period of indenture, remained in Natal as free persons and economic competitors. In response, the Afrikaner (of Dutch descent) and British settlers passed brutally discriminatory laws. Poor Indians had to work on plantations or return to India. Rich Indians, who had previously had the vote in Natal, lost that right in 1896. Gandhi undertook his countrymen's legal defense.

Meanwhile, Gandhi was searching for a spiritual theory of social action. He studied Hindu and Christian teachings and gradually developed a weapon for the poor and oppressed that he called **satyagraha** (suh-TYAH-gruh-huh). Gandhi conceived of satyagraha, loosely translated as "soul force," as a means of striving for truth and social justice through love and a willingness to suffer the oppressor's blows, while trying to convert him or her to one's views of what is true and just. Its tactic was active nonviolent resistance.

When South Africa's white government severely restricted Asian immigration and internal freedom of movement, Gandhi put his philosophy into action and organized a nonviolent mass resistance campaign. Thousands of Indian men and women marched in peaceful protest and withstood beatings, arrest, and imprisonment.

In 1914 South Africa's exasperated whites agreed to many of the Indians' demands. They passed a law abolishing discriminatory taxes on Indian traders, recognized the legality of non-Christian marriages, and permitted the continued immigration of free Indians.

Gandhi's Resistance Campaign in India

In 1915 Gandhi returned to India a hero. The masses hailed him as a mahatma, or "great soul"—a Hindu title of veneration for a man of great knowledge and humanity. In 1920 Gandhi launched a national campaign of nonviolent resistance to British rule. He urged his countrymen to boycott British goods, jobs, and honors and told peasants not to pay taxes.

The nationalist movement had previously touched only the tiny, prosperous, Western-educated elite. Now both the illiterate masses of village India and the

satyagraha

▶ Loosely translated as "soul force," which Gandhi believed was the means of striving for truth and social justice through love, suffering, and conversion of the oppressor.

CHAPTER LOCATOR | Why did modern nationalism develop in Asia between the First and Second World Wars, and what was its appeal? | How did the Ottoman Empire's collapse in World War I shape nationalist movements in the Middle East?

898 CHAPTER 29 NATIONALISM IN ASIA

educated classes heard Gandhi's call for militant nonviolent resistance. It particularly appealed to the masses of Hindus who were not members of the warrior caste or the so-called military races and who were traditionally passive and nonviolent. The British had regarded ordinary Hindus as cowards. Gandhi told them that they could be courageous and even morally superior. Under Gandhi's leadership, the Indian National Congress became a mass political party, welcoming members from every ethnic group and cooperating closely with the Muslim minority.

In 1922 some Indian resisters turned to violence, murdering twenty-two policemen. Savage riots broke out, and Gandhi abruptly called off his campaign. Arrested for fomenting rebellion, Gandhi served two years in prison. Upon his release Gandhi set up a commune, established a national newspaper, and set out to reform Indian society and improve the lot of the poor. For Gandhi moral improvement, social progress, and the national movement went hand in hand. Above all, Gandhi nurtured national identity and self-respect.

During Gandhi's time in prison the Indian National Congress had splintered into various factions, and Gandhi spent the years after his release quietly trying to reunite the organization. In 1929 the radical nationalists, led by Jawaharlal Nehru (1889–1964), pushed through the National Congress a resolution calling for virtual independence within a year. The British stiffened in their resolve against Indian independence, and Indian radicals talked of a bloody showdown.

Into this tense situation Gandhi masterfully reasserted his leadership, taking a hard line toward the British but insisting on nonviolent methods. He organized a massive resistance campaign against the tax on salt. From March 12 to April 6, 1930, Gandhi led fifty thousand people in a spectacular march to the sea, where he made salt in defiance of the law. A later demonstration at the British-run Dharasana salt works resulted in many of the 2,500 nonviolent marchers being beaten senseless by policemen in a brutal and well-publicized encounter. Over the next months the British

India, ca. 1930

arrested Gandhi and sixty thousand other protesters for making and distributing salt. But the protests continued, and in 1931 the frustrated and unnerved British released Gandhi from jail and sat down to negotiate with him over Indian self-rule. Negotiations resulted in a new constitution, the Government of India Act, in 1935, which greatly strengthened India's parliamentary representative institutions and gave Indians some voice in the administration of British India.

Despite his best efforts, Gandhi failed to heal a widening split between Hindus and Muslims. Indian nationalism, based largely on Hindu symbols and customs, increasingly disturbed the Muslim minority. Tempers mounted, and both sides committed atrocities. By the late 1930s Muslim League leaders were calling for the creation of a Muslim nation in British India, a "Pakistan," or "land of the pure." As in Palestine, the rise of conflicting nationalisms in India based on religion would lead to tragedy (see pages 962–963).

QUICK REVIEW <

Why did the British find it so difficult to suppress the Indian independence movement?

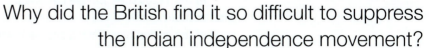

What role did Gandhi and his campaign of militant nonviolence play in leading India to independence from the British?

How did nationalism shape political developments in East and Southeast Asia?

✓ LearningCurve
Check what you know.

How did nationalism shape political developments in East and Southeast Asia?

The Fate of a Chinese Patriot

On May 30, 1925, Shanghai police opened fire on a group of Chinese demonstrators who were protesting unfair labor practices and wages and the foreign imperialist presence in their country. The police killed nine people and wounded many others, touching off nationwide and international protests and attacks on foreign offices and businesses. This political cartoon shows the fate of the Chinese patriots at the hands of warlords and foreign imperialists. (© Library of Congress, LC-USZ62-99451)

> PICTURING THE PAST

ANALYZING THE IMAGE: Which figures represent Chinese warlords, foreign imperialists, and Chinese patriots? What does the cartoon suggest about the fate of the Chinese demonstrators? What emotions are these images trying to evoke in the person viewing the cartoon?

CONNECTIONS: Why might foreign imperialists and Chinese warlords work together to put down the demonstrations?

BECAUSE OF THE EFFORTS OF THE MEIJI REFORMERS, nationalism and modernization were well developed in Japan by 1914 (see pages 796–797). Initially China lagged behind, but after 1912 the pace of nationalist development began to quicken.

In the 1920s the Chinese nationalist movement managed to reduce the power and influence both of the warlords who controlled large territories in the interior and of the imperialist West. These achievements were soon undermined, how-

CHAPTER LOCATOR | Why did modern nationalism develop in Asia between the First and Second World Wars, and what was its appeal? | How did the Ottoman Empire's collapse in World War I shape nationalist movements in the Middle East?

ever, by an internal civil war followed by war with an expanding Japan. Nationalism also flourished elsewhere in Asia, scoring a major victory in the Philippines.

The Rise of Nationalist China

The 1911 Revolution led by Sun Yatsen (1866–1925) overthrew the Qing Dynasty, ending imperial rule in China. Sun Yatsen proclaimed China a republic and thereby opened an era of unprecedented change for Chinese society. In 1912 Sun Yatsen turned over leadership of the republican government to the other central figure in the revolution, Yuan Shigai (Yüan Shih-k'ai). Called out of retirement to save the dynasty, Yuan (1859–1916) betrayed the Qing Dynasty's Manchu leaders and convinced the revolutionaries that he could unite the country peacefully and prevent foreign intervention. Once elected president of the republic, however, Yuan concentrated on building his own power. In 1913 he used military force to dissolve China's parliament and ruled as a dictator. China's first modern revolution had failed.

The extent of the failure became apparent only after Yuan's death in 1916, when the central government in Beijing almost disintegrated. For more than a decade thereafter, power resided in a multitude of local military leaders, the so-called warlords. Their wars, taxes, and corruption created terrible suffering.

Foreign imperialism intensified the agony of warlordism. Japan's expansion into Shandong and southern Manchuria during World War I (see page 852) angered China's growing middle class and enraged China's young patriots (see Map 29.2, page 907). On May 4, 1919, five thousand students in Beijing exploded against the decision of the Paris Peace Conference to leave the Shandong Peninsula in Japanese hands. This famous incident launched the **May Fourth Movement**, which opposed both foreign domination and warlord government.

The May Fourth Movement, which was both strongly pro-Marxist and passionately anti-imperialist, looked to the October 1917 Bolshevik Revolution in Russia as a model for its own nationalist revolution. In 1923 Sun Yatsen decided to ally his Nationalist Party, or Guomindang, with Lenin's Communist Third International and the newly formed Chinese Communist Party. The result was the first of many so-called national liberation fronts.

Sun, however, was no Communist. In his *Three Principles of the People*, elaborating on the official Nationalist Party ideology — nationalism, democracy, and people's livelihood — nationalism remained of prime importance. Democracy, in contrast, had a less exalted meaning. Sun equated it with firm rule by the Nationalists, who would improve people's lives through land reform and welfare measures.

Sun planned to use the Nationalist Party's revolutionary army to crush the warlords and reunite China under a strong central government. When Sun unexpectedly died in 1925, Jiang Jieshi (traditionally called Chiang Kai-shek) (1887–1975) took his place. In 1926 and 1927 Jiang led Nationalist armies in a successful attack on warlord governments in central and northern China. In 1928 the Nationalists established a new capital at Nanjing.

In fact, national unification was only skin-deep. China remained a vast agricultural country plagued by foreign concessions, regional differences, and a lack of modern communications. Moreover, the uneasy alliance between the Nationalist Party and the Chinese Communist Party had turned into a bitter, deadly rivalry.

May Fourth Movement
▶ A Chinese nationalist movement against foreign imperialists; it began as a student protest against the decision of the Paris Peace Conference to leave the Shandong Peninsula in the hands of Japan.

What role did Gandhi and his campaign of militant nonviolence play in leading India to independence from the British?

How did nationalism shape political developments in East and Southeast Asia?

☑ LearningCurve
Check what you know.

Fearful of Communist subversion of the Nationalist government, Jiang decided in April 1927 to liquidate his left-wing "allies" in a bloody purge. Chinese Communists went into hiding and vowed revenge.

China's Intellectual Revolution

Nationalism was the most powerful idea in China between 1911 and 1929, but it was only one aspect of a complex intellectual revolution, generally known as the **New Culture Movement**. The New Culture Movement was founded around 1916 by young Western-oriented intellectuals in Beijing. These intellectuals attacked Confucian ethics, which subordinated subjects to rulers, sons to fathers, and wives to husbands. As modernists, they advocated new and anti-Confucian virtues: individualism, democratic equality, and the critical scientific method. They also promoted the use of simple, understandable written language as a means to clear thinking and mass education. China, they said, needed a whole new culture, a radically different worldview.

New Culture Movement
▶ An intellectual revolution, sometimes called the Chinese Renaissance, that attacked traditional Chinese, particularly Confucian, culture and promoted Western ideas of science, democracy, and individualism, from around 1916 to 1923.

Many intellectuals thought the radical worldview China needed was Marxist socialism. Though undeniably Western, Marxism provided a means of criticizing Western dominance, thereby salving Chinese pride. Chinese Communists could blame China's pitiful weakness on rapacious foreign capitalistic imperialism. Thus Marxism, as modified by Lenin and applied by the Bolsheviks in the Soviet Union, appeared as a means of catching up with the hated but envied West. For Chinese believers, it promised salvation soon.

Chinese Communists could and did interpret Marxism-Leninism to appeal to the masses—the peasants. Mao Zedong (Mao Tse-tung) in particular quickly recognized the impoverished Chinese peasantry's enormous revolutionary potential. Mao's (1893–1976) first experiment in peasant revolt—the Autumn Harvest Uprising of September 1927—was not successful, but Mao learned quickly. He advocated equal distribution of land and broke up his forces into small guerrilla groups. After 1928 he and his supporters built up a self-governing Communist soviet, centered at Ruijin (Juichin) in southeastern China, and dug in against Nationalist attacks.

China's intellectual revolution also stimulated profound changes in popular culture and family life. After the 1911 Revolution Chinese women enjoyed increasingly greater freedom and equality and gradually gained unprecedented educational and economic opportunities. Thus rising nationalism and the intellectual revolution interacted with monumental changes in Chinese family life. (See "Individuals in Society: Ning Lao, a Chinese Working Woman," page 904.)

From Liberalism to Ultranationalism in Japan

The Meiji reformers' spectacular success deeply impressed Japan's fellow Asians. The Japanese, alone among Asia's peoples, had mastered modern industrial technology by 1910 and had fought victorious wars against both China and Russia. The First World War brought more triumphs. In 1915 Japan seized Germany's Asian holdings and retained most of them as League of Nations mandates. The Japanese economy expanded enormously. Profits soared as Japan won new markets that wartime Europe could no longer supply.

CHAPTER LOCATOR | Why did modern nationalism develop in Asia between the First and Second World Wars, and what was its appeal? | How did the Ottoman Empire's collapse in World War I shape nationalist movements in the Middle East?

902 CHAPTER 29 NATIONALISM IN ASIA

Japanese Suffragists

In the 1920s Japanese women pressed for political emancipation in demonstrations like this one, but they did not receive the right to vote until 1946. Like these suffragists, some young Japanese women adopted Western fashions. Most workers in modern Japanese textile factories were women. (Time Life Pictures/Getty Images)

In the early 1920s Japan made further progress on all fronts. In 1922 Japan signed a naval arms limitation treaty with the Western powers and returned some of its control over the Shandong Peninsula to China. These conciliatory moves reduced tensions in East Asia. At home Japan seemed headed toward genuine democracy. The electorate expanded twelvefold between 1918 and 1925 as all males over twenty-five won the vote. Two-party competition was intense. Japanese living standards were the highest in Asia. Literacy was universal.

Japan's remarkable rise was accompanied by serious problems. Japan had a rapidly growing population but scarce natural resources. As early as the 1920s Japan was exporting manufactured goods in order to pay for imports of food and essential raw materials. Deeply enmeshed in world trade, Japan was vulnerable to every boom and bust. These economic realities broadened support for Japan's colonial empire. Before World War I Japanese leaders saw colonial expansion primarily in terms of international prestige and national defense. Now, in the 1920s, Japan's colonies also seemed essential for markets, raw materials, and economic growth.

Japan's rapid industrial development also created an imbalanced "dualistic" economy. The modern sector consisted of a handful of giant conglomerate firms, the **zaibatsu**, or "financial combines." Zaibatsu firms wielded enormous economic power and dominated the other sector of the economy, an unorganized multitude of peasant farmers and craftsmen. The result was financial oligarchy, corruption of government officials, and a weak middle class.

zaibatsu
▶ Giant conglomerate firms in Japan.

Behind the façade of party politics, Japanese elites jockeyed savagely for power. Cohesive leadership, which had played such an important role in Japan's modernization by the Meiji reformers, had ceased to exist. By far the most serious challenge to peaceful progress was fanatical nationalism. As in Europe, ultranationalism first emerged in Japan in the late nineteenth century but did not flower fully until the First World War and the 1930s.

Though their views were often vague, Japan's ultranationalists shared several fundamental beliefs. They were violently anti-Western. They rejected

What role did Gandhi and his campaign of militant nonviolence play in leading India to independence from the British?

How did nationalism shape political developments in East and Southeast Asia?

☑ LearningCurve
Check what you know.

903

Ning Lao, a Chinese Working Woman

The voice of the poor and uneducated is often muffled in history. Thus *A Daughter of Han*, a rare autobiography of an illiterate working woman as told to an American friend, Ida Pruitt, offers unforgettable insights into the evolution of ordinary Chinese life and family relations.

Ning Lao was born in 1867 to poor parents in the northern city of Penglai on the Shandong Peninsula. Her foot binding was delayed to age nine, since she "loved so much to run and play." She described the pain when the bandages were finally drawn tight: "My feet hurt so much that for two years I had to crawl on my knees."* Her arranged marriage at age fourteen was a disaster. She found that her husband was a drug addict ("in those days everyone took opium to some extent") who sold everything to pay for his habit. Yet "there was no freedom then for women," and "it was no light thing for a woman to leave her house" and husband. Thus Ning Lao endured her situation until her husband sold their four-year-old daughter to buy opium. Taking her remaining baby daughter, she fled.

Taking off her foot bandages, Ning Lao became a beggar. Her feet began to spread, quite improperly, but she walked without pain. And the beggar's life was "not the hardest one," she thought, for a beggar woman could go where she pleased. To better care for her child, Ning Lao became a servant and a cook in prosperous households. Some of her mistresses were concubines (secondary wives taken by rich men in middle age), and she concluded that concubinage resulted in nothing but quarrels and heartache. Hot tempered and quick to take offense and leave an employer, the hard-working woman always found a new job quickly. In time she became a peddler of luxury goods to wealthy women confined to their homes.

The two unshakable values that buoyed Ning Lao were a tough, fatalistic acceptance of life — "Only fortune that comes of itself will come. There is no use to seek for it" — and devotion to her family. She eventually returned to her husband, who had mellowed, seldom took opium, and was "good" in those years. She reflected, "But I did not miss him when he died. I had my newborn son and I was happy. My house was established. . . . Truly all my life I spent thinking of my family." Her lifelong devotion was reciprocated by her son and granddaughter, who cared for her well in her old age.

Ning Lao's remarkable life story encompasses both old and new Chinese attitudes toward family life. Her son moved to the capital city of Beijing, worked in an office, and had only one wife. Her granddaughter, Su Teh, studied in missionary schools and became a college teacher and a determined foe of arranged marriages. She personified the trend toward greater freedom for Chinese women.

Generational differences also highlighted changing political attitudes. When the Japanese invaded China and occupied Beijing in 1937, Ning Lao thought that "perhaps the Mandate of Heaven had passed to the Japanese . . . and we should listen to them as our new masters." Her nationalistic granddaughter disagreed. She urged resistance and the creation of a new China, where the people governed themselves. Leaving to join the guerrillas in 1938, Su Teh gave her savings to her family and promised to continue to help them. One must be good to one's family, she said, but one must also work for the country.

The tough and resilient Ning Lao (right) with Ida Pruitt.
(Reproduced with permission of Eileen Hsu-Balzer)

*Ida Pruitt, *A Daughter of Han: The Autobiography of a Chinese Working Woman* (New Haven, Conn.: Yale University Press, 1945), p. 22. Other quotations are from pages 83, 62, 71, 182, 166, 235, and 246.

QUESTIONS FOR ANALYSIS

1. Compare the lives of Ning Lao and her granddaughter. In what ways were they different and similar?
2. In a broader historical perspective, what do you find most significant about Ning Lao's account of her life? Why?

ONLINE DOCUMENT PROJECT

How did China's conflicts with the Western powers and Japan affect its people? Read the excerpts from Ning Lao's autobiography, and then complete a quiz and writing assignment based on the evidence and details from this chapter. *See inside the front cover to learn more.*

democracy, big business, and Marxist socialism. Reviving old myths, they stressed the emperor's godlike qualities and the samurai warrior's code of honor, obedience, and responsibility. Despising party politics, they assassinated moderate leaders and plotted armed uprisings to achieve their goals. Above all else, the ultranationalists preached foreign expansion.

The ultranationalists were noisy and violent in the 1920s, but it took the Great Depression of the 1930s to tip the scales decisively in their favor. The worldwide depression hit Japan like a tidal wave in 1930. Exports and wages collapsed; unemployment and raw suffering soared. The ultranationalists blamed the system, and people listened.

Japan Against China

Among those who listened with particular care were young Japanese army officers in Manchuria, the underpopulated, resource-rich province of northeastern China controlled by the Japanese army since its victory over Russia in 1905. The rise of Chinese nationalism embodied in the Guomindang unification of China challenged Japanese control over Manchuria. In response, junior Japanese officers in Manchuria, in cooperation with top generals in Tokyo, secretly manufactured an excuse for aggression in late 1931. They blew up some Japanese-owned railroad tracks near the city of Shenyang (Mukden) and then, with reinforcements rushed in from Korea, quickly occupied all of Manchuria in "self-defense."

When the League of Nations condemned Japanese aggression in Manchuria, Japan resigned in protest. Japanese aggression in Manchuria proved that the army, though reporting directly to the Japanese emperor, was an independent force subject to no outside control.

For China the Japanese conquest of Manchuria was disastrous. Japanese aggression in Manchuria drew attention away from modernizing efforts. The Nationalist government promoted a massive boycott of Japanese goods but lost interest in social reform. Above all, the Nationalist government after 1931 completely neglected land reform and the Chinese peasants' grinding poverty.

Having abandoned land reform, partly because they themselves were often landowners, the Nationalists under Jiang Jieshi devoted their energies between 1930 and 1934 to great campaigns of encirclement and extermination of the Communists' rural power base in southeastern China. In 1934 they closed in for the kill, but, in one of the most incredible sagas of modern times, the main Communist army broke out, beat off attacks, and retreated 6,000 miles in twelve months to a remote region on the northwestern border (Map 29.2). Of the estimated 100,000 men and women who began the **Long March**, only 8,000 to 10,000 reached the final destination in Yan'an. There Mao built up his forces once again, established a new territorial base, and won local peasant support by taking aggressive action to improve peasant life.

Long March

► The 6,000-mile retreat of the Chinese Communist army to a remote region on the northwestern border of China, during which tens of thousands lost their lives.

> **> Mao's Unprecedented Pro-Peasant Policies:**

- Communist forces did not pillage and rape as imperialist and warlord armies had always done
- The Communists set up schools to teach illiterate peasants to read and write
- The Communists established health clinics to provide the peasants with basic medical care
- Communist armies helped the peasants plant and harvest their crops
- Communist courts tried the warlords and landlords for crimes against the peasants

In Japan politics became increasingly chaotic. In 1937 the Japanese military and the ultranationalists were in command. Unable to force China to cede more territory in northern China, they used a minor incident near Beijing as a pretext for a general attack. This marked the beginning of what became World War II in Asia. The Nationalist government, which had just formed a united front with the

Japanese Atrocities in China

In this August 1938 photograph, Japanese soldiers taunt their young Chinese prisoners before executing them. (Hulton Archive/Getty Images)

CHAPTER LOCATOR | Why did modern nationalism develop in Asia between the First and Second World Wars, and what was its appeal? | How did the Ottoman Empire's collapse in World War I shape nationalist movements in the Middle East?

MAP 29.2 ■ **The Chinese Communist Movement and the War with Japan, 1927–1938**

After urban uprisings ordered by Stalin failed in 1927, Mao Zedong succeeded in forming a self-governing Communist soviet in mountainous southern China. Relentless Nationalist attacks between 1930 and 1934 finally forced the Long March to Yan'an, where the Communists were well positioned for guerrilla war against the Japanese.

Communists, fought hard, but Japanese troops quickly took Beijing and northern China. After taking the port of Shanghai, the Japanese launched an immediate attack up the Yangzi River.

Foretelling the horrors of World War II, the Japanese air force bombed Chinese cities and civilian populations with unrelenting fury. Nanjing, the capital, fell in December 1937. Entering the city, Japanese soldiers went berserk and committed dreadful atrocities over seven weeks. The "Rape of Nanjing" combined with other Japanese atrocities to outrage world opinion. The Western powers denounced Japanese aggression but, with tensions rising in Europe, took no action.

What role did Gandhi and his campaign of militant nonviolence play in leading India to independence from the British?

How did nationalism shape political developments in East and Southeast Asia?

✓ LearningCurve
Check what you know.

By late 1938 Japanese armies occupied sizable portions of coastal China (see Map 29.2). But the Nationalists and the Communists had retreated to the interior, and both refused to accept defeat. In 1939, as Europe edged toward another great war, China and Japan were bogged down in a savage stalemate, providing a spectacular example of conflicting nationalisms.

Striving for Independence in Southeast Asia

The tide of nationalism was also rising in Southeast Asia. Nationalists in French Indochina, the Dutch East Indies, and the Philippines urgently wanted genuine political independence and freedom from foreign rule. In both French Indochina and the Dutch East Indies they ran up against an imperialist stone wall. The obstacle to Filipino independence came from America and Japan.

The French in Indochina, as in all their colonies, resisted all efforts to move toward self-government. This uncompromising attitude stimulated the growth of an equally stubborn Communist opposition under Ho Chi Minh (1890–1969), which despite ruthless repression emerged as the dominant anti-French force in Indochina.

Uncle Sam as Schoolmaster

In this cartoon that first appeared on the cover of *Harper's Weekly* in August 1898, unruly students identified as a "Cuban Ex-patriot" and a "Guerilla" are being disciplined with a switch by a stern Uncle Sam as he tries to teach them self-government. The gentleman to the left reading a book is José Miguel Gómez, one of Cuba's revolutionary heroes, while the Filipino insurrectionist Emilio Aguinaldo is made to wear a dunce cap and stand in the corner. The two well-behaved girls to the right represent Hawaii and Puerto Rico.

| Why did modern nationalism develop in Asia between the First and Second World Wars, and what was its appeal? | How did the Ottoman Empire's collapse in World War I shape nationalist movements in the Middle East?

In the East Indies—modern Indonesia—the Dutch made some concessions after the First World War, establishing a people's council with very limited law-making power. But in the 1930s the Dutch cracked down hard, jailing all the important nationalist leaders. Like the French, the Dutch were determined to hold on.

In the Philippines, however, a well-established nationalist movement achieved greater success. By the late nineteenth century the Filipino population was 80 percent Catholic. Filipinos shared a common cultural heritage and a common racial origin. Education, especially for girls, was advanced for Southeast Asia. Economic development helped to create a westernized elite, which turned first to reform and then to revolution in the 1890s. As in Egypt and Turkey, long-standing intimate contact with Western civilization created a strong nationalist movement at an early date.

Filipino nationalists were bitterly disillusioned when the United States, having taken the Philippines from Spain in the Spanish-American War of 1898, ruthlessly beat down a patriotic revolt and denied the universal Filipino desire for independence. As the imperialist power in the Philippines, the United States encouraged education and promoted capitalistic economic development. And as in British India, an elected legislature was given some real powers.

As in India and French Indochina, demands for independence grew. One important contributing factor was American racial attitudes. Americans treated Filipinos as inferiors and introduced segregationist practices borrowed from the American South. American racism made passionate nationalists of many Filipinos. However, it was the Great Depression that had the most radical impact on the Philippines.

As the United States collapsed economically in the 1930s, the Philippines suddenly appeared to be a liability rather than an asset. American farm groups lobbied for protection from cheap Filipino sugar. To protect American jobs, labor unions demanded an end to Filipino immigration. Responding to public pressure, in 1934 Congress made the Philippines a self-governing commonwealth and scheduled independence for 1944. Sugar imports were reduced, and immigration was limited to only fifty Filipinos per year.

The Spanish-American War in the Philippines, 1898

QUICK REVIEW

How did ideological conflicts shape the struggle to create a unified, genuinely independent nation in China?

What role did Gandhi and his campaign of militant nonviolence play in leading India to independence from the British?

How did nationalism shape political developments in East and Southeast Asia?

☑ LearningCurve
Check what you know.

CHAPTER SUMMARY

The Ottoman Empire's collapse in World War I left a power vacuum that both Western imperialists and Asian nationalists sought to fill. Strong leaders, such as Turkey's Mustafa Kemal led successful nationalist movements in Turkey, Persia, and Afghanistan. British and French influence over the League of Nations–mandated Arab states declined in the 1920s and 1930s as Arab nationalists pushed for complete independence. The situation in Palestine, where the British had promised both Palestinians and Jewish Zionists independent homelands, deteriorated in the interwar years as increasingly larger numbers of European Jews migrated there.

Gandhi's active, nonviolent resistance campaign, which he called satyagraha, convinced the British that colonial rule in India was over, and India won independence in 1947. Regrettably, following independence, extreme Muslim and Hindu religious nationalism threatened to tear India apart.

China's 1911 Revolution successfully ended the ancient dynastic system before the Great War, while the 1919 May Fourth Movement renewed nationalist hopes after it. Jiang Jieshi's Nationalist Party and Mao Zedong's Communists, however, would violently contest who would rule over a unified China. Japan, unlike China, industrialized early and by the 1920s seemed headed toward genuine democracy, but militarists and ultranationalists then launched an aggressive campaign of foreign expansion which contributed to the buildup to World War II. As the Great Depression took hold, Filipino nationalists achieved independence from the United States.

 **CONNECTIONS** Just as nationalism drove politics and state-building in Europe in the nineteenth century, so it took root across Asia in the late nineteenth and early twentieth centuries. While nationalism in Europe developed out of a desire to turn cultural unity into political reality, in Asia nationalist sentiments drew their greatest energy from opposition to European imperialism and domination. Asian modernizers also pressed the nationalist cause by demanding an end to outdated conservative traditions that they argued only held back the development of modern, independent nations capable of throwing off Western domination and existing as equals with the West.

The nationalist cause in Asia took many forms and produced some of the twentieth century's most remarkable leaders. In Chapter 32 we will discuss how nationalist leaders across Asia shaped the freedom struggle and the resulting independence according to their own ideological and personal visions. China's Mao Zedong is the giant among the nationalist leaders who emerged in Asia, but he replaced imperialist rule with one-party Communist rule. Gandhi's dream of a unified India collapsed with the partition of British India into Hindu India and Muslim Pakistan and Bangladesh. India and Pakistan remain bitter, and nuclear-armed, enemies today, as we will see in Chapter 33. Egypt assumed a prominent position in the Arab world after World War II under Gamal Nasser's leadership and, after a series of wars with Israel, began to play a significant role in efforts to find a peaceful resolution to the Israeli-Palestinian conflict. That conflict, however,

CHAPTER LOCATOR | Why did modern nationalism develop in Asia between the First and Second World Wars, and what was its appeal? | How did the Ottoman Empire's collapse in World War I shape nationalist movements in the Middle East?

910 CHAPTER 29 NATIONALISM IN ASIA

continues unabated as nationalist and religious sentiments inflame feelings on both sides. Ho Chi Minh eventually forced the French colonizers out of Vietnam, only to face another Western power, the United States, in a long and deadly war. As described in Chapter 32, a unified Vietnam finally gained its independence in 1975, but, like China, the country was under one-party Communist control.

Japan remained an exception to much of what happened in the rest of Asia. After a long period of isolation, the Japanese implemented an unprecedented program of modernization and westernization in the late 1800s. Japan continued to model itself after the West when it took control of former German colonies as mandated territories after the Great War and occupied territory in China, Korea, Vietnam, Taiwan, and elsewhere. In the next chapter we will see how ultranationalism drove national policy in the 1930s, ultimately leading to Japan's defeat in World War II.

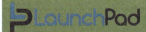

ONLINE DOCUMENT PROJECT

Foreign Intervention in China

How did China's conflicts with the Western powers and Japan affect its people?

Read the excerpts from Ning Lao's autobiography, and then complete a quiz and writing assignment based on the evidence and details from this chapter. *See inside the front cover to learn more.*

What role did Gandhi and his campaign of militant nonviolence play in leading India to independence from the British?

How did nationalism shape political developments in East and Southeast Asia?

✔ LearningCurve
Check what you know.

CHAPTER 29 STUDY GUIDE

 STEP 1

GET STARTED ONLINE

 **LearningCurve**

Now that you've read the chapter, make it stick by completing the LearningCurve activity.

 **STEP 2**

EXPLAIN WHY IT MATTERS

Put your reading into practice. Identify each term below, and then explain why it matters in world history.

TERM	WHO OR WHAT & WHEN	WHY IT MATTERS
Permanent Mandates Commission (p. 885)		
Sykes-Picot Agreement (p. 891)		
Balfour Declaration (p. 891)		
Treaty of Lausanne (p. 892)		
Majlis (p. 893)		
kibbutz (p. 895)		
Lucknow Pact (p. 897)		
satyagraha (p. 898)		
May Fourth Movement (p. 901)		
New Culture Movement (p. 902)		
zaibatsu (p. 903)		
Long March (p. 906)		

 **STEP 3**

MOVE BEYOND THE BASICS

To demonstrate a more advanced understanding of nationalist movements in Turkey, India, China, and Japan, fill in the table below with descriptions of four key factors that shaped the development of nationalist movements in each country: political and social context, ideology, movement goals, and internal divisions. How did Western imperialism shape each movement?

	Political and Social Context	Ideology	Movement Goals	Internal Divisions
Turkey				
India				
China				
Japan				

STEP 4 **PUT IT ALL TOGETHER** Now, take a step back and try to explain the big picture. Remember to use specific examples from the chapter in your answers.

NATIONALISM IN THE MIDDLE EAST

▶ What role did Western powers play in the Middle East after World War I? How did the Western presence shape Middle Eastern nationalist movements?

▶ What was the relationship between Islam and nationalism in the postwar Middle East?

NATIONALISM IN INDIA

▶ What was Gandhi's contribution to the Indian nationalist movement? In what ways did he transform the movement?

▶ Why did it prove so difficult for Hindus and Muslims to maintain a united front against the British?

NATIONALISM IN EAST AND SOUTHEAST ASIA

▶ Why did competing nationalist movements emerge in China? What common origins and beliefs did the movements share?

▶ How did nationalism contribute to Japan's rise to regional dominance? How did it undermine Japan's domestic political stability?

LOOKING BACK, LOOKING AHEAD

▶ How did Asian nationalism in the twentieth century differ from European nationalism in the nineteenth century? What explains the differences you note?

▶ World War I played a crucial role in stimulating Asian nationalism. Looking ahead, what role might you anticipate World War II playing in shaping the ongoing development of Asian nationalist movements?

> **IN YOUR OWN WORDS**

Imagine that you must give an oral report to the class answering the following question: **How did nationalism shape developments across Asia in the decades following the First World War?** What would be the most important points and why?

30

THE GREAT DEPRESSION AND WORLD WAR II

1929–1945

> **How did the economic suffering created by the Great Depression contribute to the outbreak of World War II?** Chapter 30 examines the Great Depression and World War II. In 1929 the interconnected global economy collapsed. In the wake of the Great Depression, people everywhere looked to new leaders for relief, some democratically elected, many not. A global trend toward dictatorship produced a particularly ruthless brand of totalitarianism that reached its fullest realization in the Soviet Union, Nazi Germany, and Japan in the 1930s. Germany's and Japan's aggressive expansion sparked World War II. By war's end, millions had died on the battlefields and in the bombed-out cities. Millions more died in the Holocaust, in Stalin's Soviet Union from purges and forced imposition of communism, and during Japan's quest to create an "Asia for Asians."

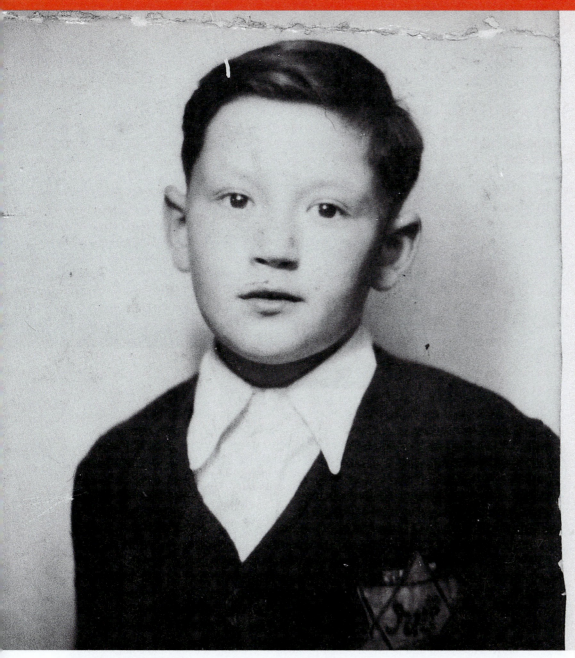

Jewish Boy in Nazi-Controlled France Israel Lichtenstein, wearing a Jewish star, was born in Paris in 1932. His father was one of an estimated 1 million Jews who died in the Auschwitz concentration camp. Israel and his mother were also sent to a concentration camp, but they escaped and survived the Holocaust by going into hiding until the end of the war. Israel later immigrated to the nation of Israel. (United States Holocaust Memorial Museum, courtesy of Israel Lichtenstein)

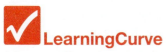

LearningCurve

After reading the chapter, use LearningCurve to retain what you've read.

> What caused the Great Depression, and what were its consequences?

> What was the nature of the new totalitarian dictatorships, and how did they differ from conservative authoritarian states and from each other?

> How did Stalin and the Communist Party build a totalitarian order in the Soviet Union?

> How did Italian fascism develop?

> Why were Hitler and his Nazi regime initially so popular, and how did their actions lead to World War II?

> How did Germany and Japan build empires in Europe and Asia, and how did the Allies defeat them?

What caused the Great Depression, and what were its consequences?

Louisville Flood Victims, 1937

During the Great Depression, Louisville, Kentucky, was hit by the worst flood in its history. The famous documentary photographer Margaret Bourke-White captured this image of African American flood victims lining up for food. Not only does the billboard message mock the Depression-era conditions, but the smiling white family appears to be driving its car through the line of people, drawing attention to America's race and class differences. (Margaret Bourke-White/Time-Life Pictures/Getty Images)

LIKE THE GREAT WAR, the Great Depression must be spelled with capital letters. Beginning in 1929 an exceptionally long and severe economic depression struck the entire world with ever-greater intensity, and recovery was uneven and slow. The social and political consequences of prolonged economic collapse were enormous and were felt worldwide.

The Economic Crisis

Though economic activity was already declining moderately in many countries by early 1929, the U.S. stock market crash in October of that year really started the Great Depression. The American stock market boom was built on borrowed money. Two factors explain why. First, the wealth gap (or income inequality) between America's rich and poor reached its greatest extent in the twentieth century in 1928–1929. One percent of Americans then held 70 percent of all America's wealth. Eventually, with not enough money to go around, the 99 percent had to

CHAPTER LOCATOR | **What caused the Great Depression, and what were its consequences?** | What was the nature of the new totalitarian dictatorships?

1921
New Economic Policy in Soviet Union

1922
Mussolini seizes power in Italy

1924–1929
Buildup of Nazi Party in Germany

1925
Hitler, *Mein Kampf*

1927
Stalin comes to power in Soviet Union

1928
Stalin's first five-year plan

1929
Start of collectivization in Soviet Union; Lateran Agreement

1929–1939
Great Depression

1931
Japan invades Manchuria

1932–1933
Famine in Ukraine

1933
Hitler appointed chancellor in Germany; Nazis begin control of state and society

1935
Mussolini invades Ethiopia; creation of U.S. Works Progress Administration as part of New Deal

1936
Start of great purges under Stalin; Spanish Civil War begins

1936–1937
Popular Front government in France

1939
Germany occupies Czech lands and invades Poland; Britain and France declare war on Germany, starting World War II

1940
Japan signs formal alliance with Germany and Italy; Germany defeats France; Battle of Britain

1941
Germany invades Soviet Union; Japan attacks Pearl Harbor; United States enters war

1941–1945
The Holocaust

1944
Allied invasion at Normandy

1945
Atomic bombs dropped on Japan; World War II ends

borrow to make even basic purchases—as a result, the cost of farm credit, installment loans, and home mortgages skyrocketed. Then a point was reached where the 99 percent could borrow no more, so they stopped buying.

Second, wealthy investors and speculators took increasingly greater investment risks. One such popular risk was to buy stocks by paying only a small fraction of the total purchase price and borrowing the remainder from their stockbrokers or from banks. Such buying "on margin" was extremely dangerous. When prices started falling, the hard-pressed margin buyers started selling to pay their debts. The result was a financial panic. Countless investors and speculators were wiped out in a matter of days or weeks, and the New York stock market's crash started a domino effect that hit most of the world's major stock exchanges

The financial panic in the United States triggered a worldwide financial crisis. Throughout the 1920s American bankers and investors had lent large sums to many countries, and as panic spread, New York bankers began recalling their short-term loans. Frightened citizens around the world began to withdraw their bank savings, leading to general financial chaos. The recall of American loans also accelerated the collapse in world prices, as business people dumped goods in a frantic attempt to get cash to pay what they owed.

How did Stalin and the Communist Party build a totalitarian order in the Soviet Union?	How did Italian fascism develop?	Why were Hitler and his Nazi regime initially so popular, how did their actions lead to WWII?	How did Germany and Japan build empires in Europe and Asia, how did the Allies defeat them?	✔ LearningCurve Check what you know.

The financial chaos led to a drastic decline in production in country after country. Countries now turned inward and tried to go it alone. Many followed the American example, in which protective tariffs were raised to their highest levels ever in 1930 to seal off shrinking national markets for American producers only.

Although historians' opinions differ, two factors probably best explain the relentless slide to the bottom from 1929 to early 1933. First, the international economy lacked leadership able to maintain stability when the crisis came. Neither the seriously weakened British nor the United States—the world's economic leaders—stabilized the international economic system in 1929. Instead Britain and the United States cut back international lending and erected high tariffs.

Second, in almost every country, governments cut their budgets and reduced spending instead of running large deficits to try to stimulate their economies. That is, governments needed to put large sums of money into the economy to stimulate job growth and spending. After World War II such a "counter-cyclical policy," advocated by the British economist John Maynard Keynes (1883–1946), became a well-established weapon against depression. But in the 1930s orthodox economists generally regarded Keynes's prescription with horror.

Mass Unemployment

The need for large-scale government spending was tied to mass unemployment. The 99 percent's halt in buying contributed to the financial crisis, which led to production cuts, which in turn caused workers to lose their jobs and have even less money to buy goods. This led to still more production cuts, and unemployment soared.

> **> Mass Unemployment at Its Peak:**
>
> - Britain: 18 percent
> - Germany: 25 percent
> - Australia: 32 percent
> - The United States: 33 percent

Mass unemployment created great social problems. Poverty increased dramatically, although in most industrialized countries unemployed workers generally received some meager unemployment benefits or public aid that prevented starvation. Millions of unemployed people lost their spirit, and homes and ways of life were disrupted in countless personal tragedies. Only strong government action could deal with the social powder keg preparing to explode.

The New Deal in the United States

The Great Depression and the response to it marked a major turning point in American history. Herbert Hoover (U.S. pres. 1929–1933) and his administration initially reacted with limited action. When the financial crisis struck Europe with full force in summer 1931 and boomeranged back to the United States, banks failed and unemployment soared. In 1932 industrial production fell to about 50 percent of its 1929 level.

New Deal

▶ Franklin Delano Roosevelt's plan to reform capitalism through forceful government intervention in the economy.

In these desperate circumstances Franklin Delano Roosevelt (U.S. pres. 1933–1945) won a landslide presidential victory in 1932 with promises of a "**New Deal** for the forgotten man." Roosevelt's basic goal was to preserve capitalism by reforming it. Rejecting socialism and government ownership of industry, Roosevelt advocated forceful federal government intervention in the economy. His commitment to national relief programs marked a profound shift from the traditional stress on family support and local community responsibility.

CHAPTER LOCATOR | **What caused the Great Depression, and what were its consequences?** | What was the nature of the new totalitarian dictatorships?

CHAPTER 30
918 THE GREAT DEPRESSION AND WORLD WAR II

As in Asia, Africa, and Latin America, American farmers were hard hit by the Great Depression, and agricultural recovery became a top priority. Innovative programs, such as the 1933 Agricultural Adjustment Act, aimed to raise prices and farm income by limiting production.

Roosevelt then attacked mass unemployment. New federal agencies launched a vast range of public works projects so the federal government could directly employ as many people as financially possible. The Works Progress Administration (WPA), set up in 1935, employed one-fifth of the entire U.S. labor force at some point in the 1930s, and these workers constructed public buildings, bridges, and highways.

Following the path blazed by Germany's Bismarck in the 1880s (see page 740), the U.S. government in 1935 established a national social security system with old-age pensions and unemployment benefits. The 1935 National Labor Relations Act declared collective bargaining to be U.S. policy, and union membership more than doubled. In general, between 1935 and 1938 government rulings and social reforms chipped away at the privileges of the wealthy and tried to help ordinary people.

Despite undeniable accomplishments in social reform, the New Deal was only partly successful as a response to the Great Depression. Some economic progress was made, but the New Deal never did pull the United States out of the depression; only the Second World War did that.

The European Response to the Depression

The American stock market's collapse in October 1929 set off a chain of economic downturns that hit Europe, particularly Germany and Great Britain, the hardest. Postwar Europe had emerged from the Great War deeply in debt and in desperate need of investment capital to rebuild. The United States became the primary creditor and financier. Germany borrowed, for example, to pay Britain war reparations, and then Britain took that money and repaid its war debts and investment loans to America. When the American economy crashed, the whole circular system crashed with it.

Of all the Western democracies, the Scandinavian countries under socialist leadership responded most successfully to the challenge of the Great Depression. When the economic crisis struck in 1929, Sweden's socialist government pioneered the use of large-scale deficits to finance public works projects and thereby maintain production and employment. Scandinavian governments also increased social welfare benefits. All this spending required a large bureaucracy and high taxes. Yet both private and cooperative enterprise thrived, as did democracy. Some observers considered Scandinavia's welfare socialism an appealing middle way between what they considered to be sick capitalism and cruel communism or fascism.

In Britain, Ramsay MacDonald's Labour government (1929–1931) and, after 1931, the Conservative-dominated coalition government followed orthodox economic theory. The budget was balanced, but unemployed workers received barely enough welfare support to live. Nevertheless, the economy recovered considerably after 1932, reflecting the gradual reorientation of the British economy. Britain concentrated increasingly on the national, rather than the international, market. Old export industries, such as textiles and coal, continued to decline, but new

How did Stalin and the Communist Party build a totalitarian order in the Soviet Union?　　How did Italian fascism develop?　　Why were Hitler and his Nazi regime initially so popular, how did their actions lead to WWII?　　How did Germany and Japan build empires in Europe and Asia, how did the Allies defeat them?　　✓ LearningCurve Check what you know.

919

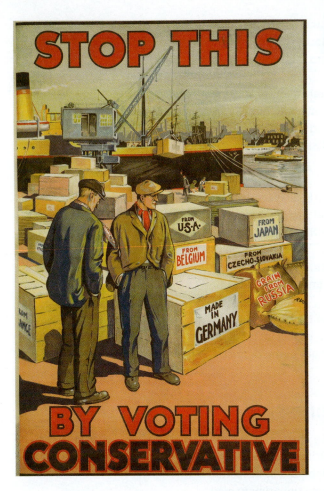

> PICTURING THE PAST

ANALYZING THE IMAGE: Where are the goods on the dock from? What do the Conservatives want stopped? **CONNECTIONS:** Was this attitude toward foreign goods unique to England? What other countries held similar views? What effect did such attitudes have on the world-wide depression?

industries, such as automobiles and electrical appliances, grew. These developments encouraged British isolationism and often had devastating economic consequences for Britain's far-flung colonies and dominions, which depended heavily upon reciprocal trade with Great Britain and the United States.

The Great Depression came late to France as it was relatively less industrialized and more isolated from the world economy. But once the depression hit, it stayed. Economic stagnation both reflected and heightened an ongoing political crisis, as liberals, democratic socialists, and Communists fought for control of the French government with conservatives and the far right. The latter groups agitated against parliamentary democracy and turned to Mussolini's Italy and Hitler's Germany for inspiration. At the same time, the Communist Party and many workers looked to Stalin's Russia for guidance.

Frightened by the growing popularity of Hitler- and Mussolini-style right-wing dictatorships at home and abroad, the Communist, Socialist, and Radical Parties in France formed an alliance—the **Popular Front**—for the May 1936 national elections. Following its clear victory, the Popular Front government launched a far-reaching program of social and economic reform. Popular with workers and the lower middle class, these measures were quickly sabotaged by rapid inflation, rising wages, a decline in overseas exports, and cries of socialist revolution from frightened conservatives. Politically, the Popular Front lost many left-wing supporters when it failed to back the republican cause in the Spanish Civil War, while Hitler and Mussolini openly armed and supported Franco's nationalists (see page 936). In June 1937, with the country hopelessly divided, the Popular Front collapsed.

Popular Front

▶ A New Deal–inspired party in France that encouraged unions and launched a far-reaching program of social reform.

Worldwide Effects

The Great Depression's magnitude was unprecedented, and its effect rippled well beyond Europe and the United States. Because many countries and colonies in Africa, Asia, and Latin America were nearly totally dependent on one or two commodities for income, the implementation of protectionist trade policies by the leading industrial nations had devastating effects.

CHAPTER LOCATOR | **What caused the Great Depression, and what were its consequences?** | What was the nature of the new totalitarian dictatorships?

The Great Depression hit the vulnerable commodity economies of Latin America especially hard. With foreign sales plummeting, Latin American countries could not buy the industrial goods they needed from abroad. The global depression provoked a profound shift toward economic nationalism after 1930, as popularly based governments worked to reduce foreign influence and gain control of their own economies and natural resources. These efforts were fairly successful. By the late 1940s factories in Argentina, Brazil, and Chile could generally satisfy domestic consumer demand for the products of light industry. But as in Hitler's Germany, the deteriorating economic conditions in Latin America also gave rise to dictatorships, some of them modeled along European Fascist lines (pages 976–980).

The Great Depression marked a decisive turning point in the development of African nationalism. For the first time, educated Africans faced widespread unemployment. African peasants and small business people who had been drawn into world trade, and who sometimes profited from booms, also felt the economic pain, as did urban workers. In some areas the result was unprecedented mass protest.

While Asians were somewhat affected by the Great Depression, the consequences varied greatly by country or colony and were not as serious generally as they were elsewhere. That being said, where the depression did hit, it was often severe. The price of rice fell by two-thirds between 1929 and 1932. Also crippling to the region's economies was Asia's heavy dependence on raw material exports. With debts to local moneylenders fixed in value and taxes to colonial governments hardly ever reduced, many Asian peasants in the 1930s struggled under crushing debt and suffered terribly.

When the Great Depression reached China in the early 1930s, it hit the rural economy the hardest. China's economy depended heavily on cash-crop exports and these declined dramatically, while cheap foreign agricultural goods—such as rice and wheat—were dumped in China. Agricultural prices in 1932 were only 41 percent of 1921 prices, and rural incomes fell by over 50 percent between 1931 and 1934. While Chinese industrial production dropped off after 1931, it quickly recovered. Much of this growth was in the military sector, as China tried to catch up with the West and also prepare for war with Japan.

In Japan the terrible suffering caused by the Great Depression caused ultranationalists and militarists to call for less dependence on global markets and the expansion of a self-sufficient empire. Such expansion began in 1931 when Japan invaded Chinese Manchuria, which became a major source of the raw materials needed to feed Japanese industrial growth (see Chapter 29). Japan recovered more quickly from the Great Depression than any other major industrial power because of prompt action by the civilian democratic government, but the government and large corporations continued to be blamed for the economic downturn. By the mid-1930s this lack of confidence, combined with the collapsing international economic order, Europe's and America's increasingly isolationist and protectionist policies, and a growing admiration for Nazi Germany and its authoritarian, militaristic model of government, had led the Japanese military to topple the civilian authorities and dictate Japan's future.

QUICK REVIEW <

How did the world's governments respond to challenges posed by the Great Depression?

| How did Stalin and the Communist Party build a totalitarian order in the Soviet Union? | How did Italian fascism develop? | Why were Hitler and his Nazi regime initially so popular, how did their actions lead to WWII? | How did Germany and Japan build empires in Europe and Asia, how did the Allies defeat them? | ✔ LearningCurve Check what you know. |

What was the nature of the new totalitarian dictatorships, and how did they differ from conservative authoritarian states and from each other?

The Spread of Fascism

In the 1920s and 1930s most European countries had Fascist sympathizers. The British Union of Fascists, led by Sir Oswald Mosley, modeled itself on Mussolini's nationalist Fascist Party. Its members were highly visible in their black uniforms, but they never numbered more than a few thousand and never elected a member to Parliament. Here Mosley and his Black Shirts prepare to march through London's Jewish East End in October 1936. Antifascist demonstrators attacked Mosley's followers and stopped the march. (Central Press/Getty Images)

BOTH CONSERVATIVE AND RADICAL totalitarian dictatorships arose in Europe in the 1920s and the 1930s. Although they sometimes overlapped in character and practice, they were profoundly different in essence.

Conservative Authoritarianism

The traditional form of antidemocratic government in world history was conservative authoritarianism. Like Russia's tsars and China's emperors, the leaders of such governments relied on obedient bureaucracies, vigilant police departments, and trustworthy armies to control society. They forbade or limited popular participation in government and often jailed or exiled political opponents. Yet they had neither the ability nor the desire to control many aspects of their subjects' lives. As long as the people did not try to change the system, they often enjoyed considerable personal independence.

CHAPTER LOCATOR | What caused the Great Depression, and what were its consequences? | **What was the nature of the new totalitarian dictatorships?**

922 CHAPTER 30 THE GREAT DEPRESSION AND WORLD WAR II

After the First World War, conservative authoritarianism revived, especially in Latin America. Conservative dictators also seized power in Spain and Portugal, and in the less-developed eastern part of Europe. There were several reasons for this development. These lands lacked strong traditions of self-government, and many new states, such as Yugoslavia, were torn by ethnic conflicts. Dictatorship appealed to nationalists and military leaders as a way to repress such tensions and preserve national unity. Large landowners and the church were still powerful forces in these predominantly agrarian areas and often looked to dictators to protect them from progressive land reform or Communist agrarian upheaval. Conservative dictatorships were concerned more with maintaining the status quo than with mobilizing the masses or forcing society into rapid change or war.

Radical Totalitarian Dictatorships

By the mid-1930s a new kind of radical dictatorship—termed totalitarian—had emerged in the Soviet Union, Germany, and, to a lesser extent, Italy. It can be argued that totalitarianism began with the total war effort of 1914–1918 (see Chapter 28), as governments acquired total control over all areas of society in order to achieve one supreme objective: victory. This provided a model for future totalitarian states.

In 1956 American historians Carl Friedrich and Zbigniew Brzezinski identified at least six key features of modern totalitarian states.[1] The six features are (1) an official ideology that demanded adherence from everyone, that touched every aspect of a citizen's existence, and that promised to lead to a "perfect final stage of mankind"; (2) a single ruling party, whose "passionate and unquestionably-dedicated-to-the-ideology" members were drawn from a small percentage of the total population (following Lenin's "vanguard of the proletariat" model; see page 860), hierarchically organized, and led by one charismatic leader, the "dictator"; (3) complete control of "all weapons of armed combat"; (4) complete monopoly of all means of mass communication; (5) a system of terror, physical and psychic, enforced by the party and the secret police; and (6) central control and direction of the entire economy.

While all these features were present in Stalin's Communist Soviet Union and Hitler's Nazi Germany, there were some major differences. Most notably, Soviet communism seized private property for the state and sought to level society by crushing the middle classes. Nazi Germany also criticized big landowners and industrialists but, unlike the Communists, did not try to nationalize private property, so the middle classes survived. This difference in property and class relations led some scholars to speak of "totalitarianism of the left"—Stalinist Russia—and "totalitarianism of the right"—Nazi Germany.

Moreover, Soviet Communists ultimately had international aims: they sought to unite the workers of the world. Mussolini and Hitler claimed they were interested in changing state and society on a national level only. Both Mussolini and Hitler used the term fascism to describe their movements' supposedly "total" and revolutionary character. Orthodox Marxist Communists argued that the Fascists were powerful capitalists seeking to destroy the revolutionary working class and thus protect their enormous profits. So while Communists and Fascists both sought the overthrow of existing society, their ideologies clashed, and they were enemies.

totalitarianism
▶ A radical dictatorship that exercises complete political power and control over all aspects of society and seeks to mobilize the masses for action.

fascism
▶ A movement characterized by extreme, often expansionist nationalism, anti-socialism, a dynamic and violent leader, and glorification of war and the military.

How did Stalin and the Communist Party build a totalitarian order in the Soviet Union?

How did Italian fascism develop?

Why were Hitler and his Nazi regime initially so popular, how did their actions lead to WWII?

How did Germany and Japan build empires in Europe and Asia, how did the Allies defeat them?

✓ LearningCurve
Check what you know.

923

European Fascist movements shared many characteristics, including extreme nationalism; an anti-socialism aimed at destroying working-class movements; a crushing of human individualism; alliances with powerful capitalists and landowners; and glorification of war and the military. Fascists, especially in Germany, also embraced racial homogeneity. Indeed, while class was the driving force in communist ideology, race and racial purity were profoundly important to Nazi ideology.

Although 1930s Japan has sometimes been called a Fascist society, most recent scholars disagree with this label. Some European Fascist ideas did appear attractive to Japanese political philosophers, such as nationalism, militarism, the corporatist economic model, and a single, all-powerful political party. However, there were also various ideologically unique forces at work in Japan, including ultranationalism, militarism (building on the historic role of samurai warriors in Japanese society), reverence for traditional ways, emperor worship, and the profound changes to Japanese society beginning with the Meiji Restoration in 1867 (see page 796). These also contributed to the rise of a totalitarian, but not Fascist, state before the Second World War.

> **QUICK REVIEW**

What were the most important differences between the totalitarian states established in Germany, the Soviet Union, and Japan?

CHAPTER LOCATOR | What caused the Great Depression, and what were its consequences? | What was the nature of the new totalitarian dictatorships?

CHAPTER 30
924   THE GREAT DEPRESSION AND WORLD WAR II

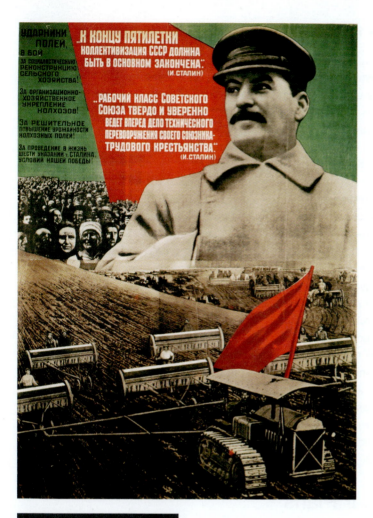

Soviet Collectivization Poster

Soviet leader Joseph Stalin ordered a nationwide forced collectivization campaign from 1929 to 1933. Following communist theory, the government created large-scale collective farms by seizing land and forcing peasants to work on it. In this idealized 1932 poster, farmers are encouraged to complete the five-year plan of collectivization, while Stalin looks on approvingly. The outcome instead was a disaster. Millions of people died in the resulting human-created famine. (Deutsches Plakat Museum, Essen, Germany/Archives Charmet/ The Bridgeman Art Library)

How did Stalin and the Communist Party build a totalitarian order in the Soviet Union?

JOSEPH STALIN (1879–1953) cautiously consolidated his power and eliminated his enemies in the mid-1920s. Then in 1928 he launched the first **five-year plan**— a "revolution from above,"[2] as he so aptly termed it, to transform Soviet society along socialist lines. Stalin and the Communist Party used constant propaganda, enormous sacrifice, and unlimited violence and state control to establish a dynamic, modern totalitarian state in the 1930s.

five-year plan

▶ Launched by Stalin in 1928 and termed the "revolution from above," its goal was to modernize the Soviet Union and generate a Communist society with new attitudes, new loyalties, and a new socialist humanity.

| How did Stalin and the Communist Party build a totalitarian order in the Soviet Union? | How did Italian fascism develop? | Why were Hitler and his Nazi regime initially so popular, how did their actions lead to WWII? | How did Germany and Japan build empires in Europe and Asia, how did the Allies defeat them? | ☑ LearningCurve Check what you know. |

From Lenin to Stalin

By spring 1921 Lenin and the Bolsheviks had won the civil war, but they ruled a shattered and devastated land. Facing economic disintegration, the worst famine in generations, riots by peasants and workers, and an open rebellion by previously pro-Bolshevik sailors at Kronstadt, Lenin changed course. In March 1921 he announced the **New Economic Policy (NEP)**, which re-established limited economic freedom in an attempt to rebuild agriculture and industry. Peasant producers could sell their surpluses in free markets, as could private traders and small handicraft manufacturers. Heavy industry, railroads, and banks, however, remained wholly nationalized.

The NEP was successful both politically and economically. Politically, it was a necessary but temporary compromise with the Soviet Union's overwhelming peasant majority. Economically, the NEP brought rapid recovery. In 1926 industrial output surpassed prewar levels, and peasants were producing almost as much grain as before the war.

As the economy recovered, an intense power struggle began in the Communist Party's inner circles, for Lenin left no chosen successor when he died in 1924. The principal contenders were Stalin and Leon Trotsky. While Trotsky appeared to be the stronger of the two, in the end Stalin won because he gained the party's support, the only genuine source of power in the one-party state.

Stalin gradually achieved absolute power between 1922 and 1927. He used the moderates to crush Trotsky and then turned against the moderates and destroyed them as well. Stalin's final triumph came at the party congress of December 1927, which condemned all deviation from the general party line as formulated by Stalin.

The Five-Year Plans

The 1927 party congress marked the end of the NEP and the beginning of socialist five-year plans. The first five-year plan had staggering economic objectives. In just five years, total industrial output was to increase by 250 percent and agricultural production by 150 percent. By 1930 economic and social change was sweeping the country in a frenzied effort to modernize, much like the Industrial Revolution in Europe in the 1800s (see Chapter 23), and dramatically changing the lives of ordinary people, sometimes at great personal cost.

Stalin unleashed his "second revolution" because, like Lenin, Stalin and his militant supporters were deeply committed to socialism as they understood it. Stalin was also driven to catch up with the advanced and presumably hostile Western capitalist nations. Domestically, there was the peasant problem. For centuries peasants had wanted to own the land, and finally they had it. Sooner or later, the Communists reasoned, the peasants would become conservative capitalists and threaten the regime. Stalin therefore launched a preventive war against the peasantry to bring it under the state's absolute control.

That war was **collectivization**—the forcible consolidation of individual peasant farms into large, state-controlled enterprises. Beginning in 1929 peasants were ordered to give up their land and animals and become members of collective farms. As for the kulaks, the better-off peasants, Stalin instructed party workers to "break their resistance, to eliminate them as a class."[3] Stripped of land and

New Economic Policy (NEP)

▶ Lenin's 1921 policy re-establishing limited economic freedom in an attempt to rebuild agriculture and industry in the face of economic disintegration.

collectivization

▶ Stalin's forcible consolidation of individual peasant farms into large, state-controlled enterprises.

CHAPTER LOCATOR | What caused the Great Depression, and what were its consequences? | What was the nature of the new totalitarian dictatorships?

926 CHAPTER 30 THE GREAT DEPRESSION AND WORLD WAR II

livestock, many starved or were deported to forced-labor camps for "re-education." Because almost all peasants were poor, the term *kulak* soon meant any peasant who opposed the new system.

Forced collectivization led to disaster. Many peasants slaughtered their animals and burned their crops in protest. Nor were the state-controlled collective farms more productive. Grain output barely increased, and collectivized agriculture made no substantial financial contribution to Soviet industrial development during the first five-year plan.

In Ukraine Stalin instituted a policy of all-out collectivization with two goals: to destroy all expressions of Ukrainian nationalism, and to break the Ukrainian peasants' will so they would accept collectivization and Soviet rule. Stalin began by purging Ukraine of its intellectuals and political elite. He then set impossibly high grain quotas for the collectivized farms. This grain quota had to be turned over to the government before any peasant could receive a share. The result was a terrible man-made famine, called in Ukrainian the *Holodomor* (Hunger-extermination), in Ukraine in 1932 and 1933, which probably claimed 3 to 5 million lives. Many scholars and dozens of governments and international organizations have declared Stalin's and the Soviet government's policies a deliberate act of genocide.

Collectivization was a cruel but real victory for Communist ideologues who were looking to institute their brand of communism and to crush opposition as much as improve production. By 1938, 93 percent of peasant families had been herded onto collective farms at a horrendous cost in both human lives and resources. Regimented as state employees and dependent on the state-owned tractor stations, the collectivized peasants were no longer a political threat.

The industrial side of the five-year plans was more successful. Soviet industry produced about four times as much in 1937 as in 1928. No other major country had ever achieved such rapid industrial growth. Heavy industry led the way, and urban development accelerated: more than 25 million people migrated to cities to become industrial workers during the 1930s.

The sudden creation of dozens of new factories demanded tremendous resources. Funds for industrial expansion were collected from the people through heavy hidden sales taxes. Firm labor discipline also contributed to rapid industrialization. Trade unions lost most of their power, and individuals could not move without police permission. When factory managers needed more hands, they were sent "unneeded" peasants from collective farms.

Foreign engineers were hired to plan and construct many of the new factories. Highly skilled American engineers, hungry for work in the depression years, were particularly important until newly trained Soviet experts began to replace them after 1932. Thus Stalin's planners harnessed the skill and technology of capitalist countries to promote the surge of socialist industry.

Life and Culture in Soviet Society

Daily life was hard in Stalin's Soviet Union. There were constant shortages, and scarcity of housing was a particularly serious problem. A relatively lucky family received one room for all its members and shared both a kitchen and a toilet with others on the floor. Less fortunate people built scrap-lumber shacks in shantytowns. Despite these hardships, many Communists saw themselves as heroically

How did Stalin and the Communist Party build a totalitarian order in the Soviet Union? | How did Italian fascism develop? | Why were Hitler and his Nazi regime initially so popular, how did their actions lead to WWII? | How did Germany and Japan build empires in Europe and Asia, how did the Allies defeat them? | ☑ LearningCurve Check what you know.

927

building the world's first socialist society while capitalism crumbled and fascism rose in the West.

Offsetting the hardships were the important social benefits Soviet workers received, such as old-age pensions, free medical services and education, and day-care centers for children. Unemployment was almost unknown. Moreover, there was the possibility of personal advancement. Rapid industrialization required massive numbers of trained experts. Thus the Stalinist state broke with the egalitarian policies of the 1920s and provided tremendous incentives to those who acquired specialized skills. A growing technical and managerial elite joined the political and artistic elites in a new upper class, whose members were rich and powerful.

Soviet society's radical transformation profoundly affected women's lives. The Russian Bolshevik Revolution immediately proclaimed complete equality of rights for women. In the 1920s divorce and abortion were made easily available, and women were urged to work outside the home. After Stalin came to power, however, he encouraged a return to traditional family values.

The most lasting changes for women involved work and education. Peasant women continued to work on farms, and millions of women now toiled in factories and heavy construction. The more determined women entered the ranks of the better-paid specialists in industry and science. By 1950, 75 percent of all doctors in the Soviet Union were women.

Culture was thoroughly politicized through constant propaganda and indoctrination. Party activists lectured workers in factories and peasants on collective farms, while newspapers, films, and radio broadcasts recounted socialist achievements and warned of capitalist plots.

Stalinist Terror and the Great Purges

In the mid-1930s the push to build socialism and a new society culminated in ruthless police terror and a massive purging of the Communist Party. In late 1934 Stalin's number-two man, Sergei Kirov, was mysteriously murdered. Although Stalin himself probably ordered Kirov's murder, he used the incident to launch a reign of terror.

In August 1936 sixteen prominent "Old Bolsheviks"—party members before the 1917 revolution—confessed to all manner of plots against Stalin in spectacular public show trials in Moscow. Then in 1937 the secret police arrested a mass of lesser party officials and newer members, torturing them and extracting confessions for more show trials. In addition to the party faithful, union officials, managers, intellectuals, army officers, and countless ordinary citizens were struck down. In all, at least 8 million people were arrested, and millions of these were executed. Those not immediately executed were sent to gulags—labor camps from which few escaped. Many were simply worked to death as they provided convict labor for Stalin's industrialization drive in areas of low population.

Stalin's mass purges remain baffling, for most historians believe those purged posed no threat and confessed to crimes they had not committed. Some historians have challenged the long-standing interpretation that blames the great purges on Stalin's cruelty or madness. They argue that Stalin's fears were exaggerated but genuine and were shared by many in the party and in the general population.[4]

CHAPTER LOCATOR | What caused the Great Depression, and what were its consequences? | What was the nature of the new totalitarian dictatorships?

CHAPTER 30
928 THE GREAT DEPRESSION AND WORLD WAR II

Women and Children Prisoners

Millions of Soviet citizens were sent to forced-labor prison camps from 1929 to 1953, and over 1.5 million died. Ten to 20 percent of these prisoners were women, many of them found guilty of nothing more than being married to men considered enemies of the state. This photo, taken around 1932, shows a woman and possibly her two children performing hard manual labor in one of these camps. (© akg-images/The Image Works)

Historians who have accessed recently opened Soviet archives, however, continue to hold that Stalin was intimately involved and personally directed the purges, abetted by amenable informers, judges, and executioners. In short, a ruthless and paranoid Stalin found large numbers of willing collaborators for crime as well as for achievement.

QUICK REVIEW ‹

What were the economic and ideological goals of the Soviet five-year plans? To what extent were those goals achieved?

How did Stalin and the Communist Party build a totalitarian order in the Soviet Union? | How did Italian fascism develop? | Why were Hitler and his Nazi regime initially so popular, how did their actions lead to WWII? | How did Germany and Japan build empires in Europe and Asia, how did the Allies defeat them? | ✓ LearningCurve Check what you know.

929

How did Italian fascism develop?

Mussolini Leading a Parade in Rome

Benito Mussolini was a master showman who drew on Rome's ancient heritage to promote Italian fascism. He wanted a grand avenue to stage triumphal marches with thousands of troops, so he had the Way of the Imperial Forums built through the old city. Here Mussolini rides at the head of a grand parade in 1932 to inaugurate the new road, passing the Roman Coliseum, one of the focal points along the route. (© Stefano Bianchetti/Corbis)

MUSSOLINI'S FASCIST MOVEMENT and his seizure of power in 1922 were important steps in the rise of dictatorships between the two world wars. Mussolini and his supporters were the first to call themselves "Fascists." His dictatorship was brutal and theatrical, and it contained elements of both conservative authoritarianism and modern totalitarianism.

The Seizure of Power

In the early twentieth century Italy was a liberal state with civil rights and a constitutional monarchy. On the eve of the First World War, the parliamentary regime granted universal male suffrage. But there were serious problems. Poverty was widespread, and many peasants were more attached to their villages and local interests than to the national state. Church-state relations were often tense. Class differences were also extreme, and by 1912 the Socialist Party's radical wing led the powerful revolutionary socialist movement.[5]

CHAPTER LOCATOR | What caused the Great Depression, and what were its consequences? | What was the nature of the new totalitarian dictatorships?

World War I worsened the political situation. Having fought on the Allied side almost exclusively for purposes of territorial expansion, the parliamentary government disappointed Italian nationalists with Italy's modest gains at the Paris Peace Conference. Workers and peasants also felt cheated: to win their support during the war, the government had promised social and land reform, which it failed to deliver after the war.

The Russian Revolution inspired and energized Italy's revolutionary socialist movement, and radical workers and peasants began occupying factories and seizing land in 1920. These actions scared and mobilized the property-owning classes. Thus by 1921 revolutionary socialists, antiliberal conservatives, and frightened property owners were all opposed—though for different reasons—to the liberal parliamentary government.

Into these crosscurrents of unrest and fear stepped Benito Mussolini (1883–1945). Mussolini began his political career as a Socialist Party leader and radical newspaper editor before World War I. Expelled from the Italian Socialist Party for supporting the war, and wounded on the Italian front in 1917, Mussolini returned home and began organizing bitter war veterans into a band of Fascists—from the Italian word for "a union of forces."

At first Mussolini's program was a radical combination of nationalist and socialist demands. As such, it competed directly with the well-organized Socialist Party and failed to attract followers. When Mussolini realized his violent verbal assaults on rival Socialists won him growing support from conservatives and the frightened middle classes, he began to shift gears and to exalt nation over class.

Mussolini and his private army of **Black Shirts** also turned to physical violence. Few people were killed, but Socialist newspapers, union halls, and local Socialist Party headquarters were destroyed. A skillful politician, Mussolini convinced his followers they were opposing the "Reds" while also making a real revolution of the little people against the established interests.

With the government breaking down in 1922, partly because of the chaos created by his Black Shirt bands, Mussolini stepped forward as the savior of order and property. In October 1922 thirty thousand Fascists marched on Rome, threatening the king and demanding he appoint Mussolini prime minister. Victor Emmanuel III (r. 1900–1946) forced to choose between Fascists or Socialists, asked Mussolini to form a new cabinet. Thus, after widespread violence and a threat of armed uprising, Mussolini seized power "legally."

Black Shirts

▶ A private army under Mussolini that destroyed Socialist newspapers, union halls, and local Socialist Party headquarters, eventually pushing Socialists out of the city governments of northern Italy.

The Regime in Action

In 1924 Mussolini declared his desire to "make the nation Fascist"[6] and imposed a series of repressive measures. Press freedom was abolished, elections were fixed, and the government ruled by decree. Mussolini arrested his political opponents, disbanded all independent labor unions, and put dedicated Fascists in control of Italy's schools. He created a Fascist youth movement, Fascist labor unions, and many other Fascist organizations. By year's end Italy was a one-party dictatorship under Mussolini's unquestioned leadership.

Mussolini was only primarily interested, however, in personal power. Rather than destroy the old power structure, he remained content to compromise with the conservative classes that controlled the army, the economy, and the state.

| How did Stalin and the Communist Party build a totalitarian order in the Soviet Union? | How did Italian fascism develop? | Why were Hitler and his Nazi regime initially so popular, how did their actions lead to WWII? | How did Germany and Japan build empires in Europe and Asia, how did the Allies defeat them? | ✔ LearningCurve Check what you know. |

931

He controlled labor but left big business to regulate itself, profitably and securely. There was no land reform.

Mussolini also drew increasing support from the Catholic Church. In the **Lateran Agreement** of 1929, he recognized the Vatican as a tiny independent state and agreed to give the church heavy financial support. The pope in return urged Italians to support Mussolini's government.

Like Stalin and Hitler, Mussolini favored a return of traditional roles for women. He abolished divorce and told women to stay at home and produce children. In 1938 women were limited by law to a maximum of 10 percent of the better-paying jobs in industry and government.

Mussolini's government passed no racial laws until 1938 and did not persecute Jews savagely until late in the Second World War, when Italy was under Nazi control. Nor did Mussolini establish a truly ruthless police state. Only twenty-three political prisoners were condemned to death between 1926 and 1944. Mussolini's Fascist Italy, though repressive and undemocratic, was never really totalitarian.

Lateran Agreement

▶ A 1929 agreement that recognized the Vatican as an independent state, with Mussolini agreeing to give the church heavy financial support in return for the pope's public support.

> **QUICK REVIEW**

Why is it inaccurate to describe Mussolini's Fascist Italy as a totalitarian state?

CHAPTER LOCATOR | What caused the Great Depression, and what were its consequences? | What was the nature of the new totalitarian dictatorships?

CHAPTER 30
932 THE GREAT DEPRESSION AND WORLD WAR II

Why were Hitler and his Nazi regime initially so popular, and how did their actions lead to World War II?

Young People in Hitler's Germany

This photo from 1930 shows Hitler admiring a young boy dressed in the uniform of Hitler's storm troopers, a paramilitary organization of the Nazi Party that supported Hitler's rise to power in the 1920s and early 1930s. Only a year after the founding of the storm troopers in 1921, Hitler began to organize Germany's young people into similar paramilitary groups in an effort to militarize all of German society. The young paramilitaries became the Hitler Youth, who eventually numbered in the millions. (Popperfoto/Getty Images)

THE MOST FRIGHTENING DICTATORSHIP developed in Nazi Germany. Nazism asserted an unlimited claim over German society and proclaimed the ultimate power of its aggressive leader, Adolf Hitler. Nazism's aspirations were truly totalitarian.

The Roots of Nazism

Nazism grew out of many complex concepts, of which the most influential were extreme nationalism and racism. These ideas captured the mind of the young Adolf Hitler (1889–1945) and evolved into Nazism.

The son of an Austrian customs official, Hitler did poorly in high school and dropped out at age sixteen. He then headed to Vienna, where he was exposed to extreme Austro-German nationalists who believed Germans to be a superior

Nazism

▶ A movement born of extreme nationalism and racism and dominated by Adolf Hitler from 1933 until the end of World War II in 1945.

How did Stalin and the Communist Party build a totalitarian order in the Soviet Union?

How did Italian fascism develop?

Why were Hitler and his Nazi regime initially so popular, how did their actions lead to WWII?

How did Germany and Japan build empires in Europe and Asia, how did the Allies defeat them?

✓ **LearningCurve**
Check what you know.

933

people and central Europe's natural rulers. They advocated union with Germany and violent expulsion of "inferior" peoples from the Austro-Hungarian Empire.

From these extremists Hitler eagerly absorbed virulent anti-Semitism, racism, and hatred of Slavs. He developed an unshakable belief in the crudest distortions of Social Darwinism (see page 736), the superiority of Germanic races, and the inevitability of racial conflict. Anti-Semitism and racism became Hitler's most passionate convictions.

Hitler greeted the Great War's outbreak as a salvation. The struggle and discipline of serving as a soldier in the war gave his life meaning, and when Germany suddenly surrendered in 1918, Hitler's world was shattered. Convinced that Jews and Marxists had "stabbed Germany in the back," he vowed to fight on.

In late 1919 Hitler joined a tiny extremist group in Munich called the German Workers' Party. By 1921 Hitler had gained absolute control of this small but growing party, now renamed the National Socialist German Worker's Party, or Nazi Party. A master of mass propaganda and political showmanship, Hitler worked his audiences into a frenzy with wild attacks on the Versailles treaty, the Jews, war profiteers, and Germany's Weimar Republic.

In late 1923 Germany under the Weimar Republic was experiencing unparalleled hyperinflation and seemed on the verge of collapse (see page 868). Hitler, inspired by Mussolini's recent victory, attempted an armed uprising in Munich. Despite the failure of the poorly organized plot and Hitler's arrest, Nazism had been born.

Hitler's Road to Power

At his trial Hitler violently denounced the Weimar Republic and attracted enormous publicity. From the unsuccessful revolt, Hitler concluded he had to gain power legally through electoral competition. During his brief prison term he dictated *Mein Kampf* (*My Struggle*), in which he expounded on his basic ideas on race and anti-Semitism, the notion of territorial expansion based on "living space" for Germans, and the role of the leader-dictator, called the *Führer* (FYOUR-uhr).

The Nazis remained a small splinter group until the 1929 Great Depression shattered economic prosperity. By the end of 1932 an incredible 43 percent of the labor force was unemployed. Industrial production fell by one-half between 1929 and 1932. No factor contributed more to Hitler's success than this economic crisis.

Hitler rejected free-market capitalism and advocated government programs to promote recovery. He pitched his speeches to middle- and lower-middle-class groups and to skilled workers. As the economy collapsed, great numbers of these people "voted their pocketbooks"[7] and deserted the conservative and moderate parties for the Nazis. In the 1930 election the Nazis won 6.5 million votes and 107 seats, and in July 1932 they gained 14.5 million votes—38 percent of the total— and became the largest party in the Reichstag.

Hitler and the Nazis appealed strongly to German youth. In 1931 almost 40 percent of Nazi Party members were under thirty, compared with 20 percent of Social Democrats. National recovery, exciting and rapid change, and personal advancement made Nazism appealing to millions of German youths.

Hitler also came to power because of the breakdown of democratic government. Germany's economic collapse in the Great Depression convinced many voters that the country's republican leaders were stupid and corrupt. Disunity on the left was another nail in the republic's coffin. The Communists refused to

CHAPTER LOCATOR | What caused the Great Depression, and what were its consequences? | What was the nature of the new totalitarian dictatorships?

934 CHAPTER 30
THE GREAT DEPRESSION AND WORLD WAR II

cooperate with the Social Democrats, even though the two parties together out-numbered the Nazis in the Reichstag.

Finally, Hitler excelled in backroom politics. In 1932 he succeeded in gaining support from key people in the army and big business who thought they could use him to their own advantage. Many conservative and nationalistic politicians thought similarly. Thus in January 1933 President Paul von Hindenburg (1847–1934) legally appointed Hitler, leader of Germany's largest party, as German chancellor.

The Nazi State and Society

Hitler quickly established an unshakable dictatorship. When the Reichstag build-ing was partly destroyed by fire in February 1933, Hitler blamed the Communist Party. He convinced President von Hindenburg to sign dictatorial emergency acts that abolished freedom of speech and assembly and most personal liberties. He also called for new elections in an effort to solidify his political power.

When the Nazis won only 44 percent of the votes, Hitler outlawed the Com-munist Party and arrested its parliamentary representatives. Then on March 23, 1933, the Nazis forced through the Reichstag the so-called **Enabling Act**, which gave Hitler absolute dictatorial power for four years.

Hitler and the Nazis took over the government bureaucracy, installing many Nazis in top positions. Hitler next outlawed strikes and abolished independent labor unions, which were replaced by the Nazi Labor Front. Professional people—doctors and lawyers, teachers and engineers—also saw their independent organi-zations swallowed up in Nazi associations. Publishing houses and universities were put under Nazi control, and students and professors publicly burned forbid-den books. Modern art and architecture were ruthlessly prohibited. Life became violently anti-intellectual. By 1934 a brutal dictatorship characterized by frighten-ing dynamism and total obedience to Hitler was already largely in place.

In June 1934 Hitler ordered his elite personal guard—the SS—to arrest and shoot without trial roughly a thousand long-time Nazi storm troopers. Shortly thereafter army leaders swore a binding oath of "unquestioning obedience" to Adolf Hitler. The SS grew rapidly. Under Heinrich Himmler (1900–1945), the SS took over the political police (the Gestapo) and expanded its network of concen-tration camps.

From the beginning, German Jews were a special object of Nazi persecution. By late 1934 most Jewish lawyers, doctors, professors, civil servants, and musi-cians had been banned from their professions. In 1935 the infamous Nuremberg Laws classified as Jewish anyone having three or more Jewish grandparents and deprived Jews of all rights of citizenship. By 1938 roughly one-quarter of Germa-ny's half million Jews had emigrated, sacrificing almost all their property in order to leave Germany.

In late 1938 the attack on the Jews accelerated and grew more violent. On November 9 and 10, 1938, the Nazis initiated a series of well-organized attacks against Jews throughout Nazi Germany and some parts of Austria. This infamous event is known as Kristallnacht, or Night of Broken Glass, after the broken glass that littered the streets following the frenzied destruction of Jewish homes, shops, synagogues, and neighborhoods by German civilians and uniformed storm troop-ers. Many historians consider this night the beginning of Hitler's Final Solution against the Jews (see page 942), and after this event it became very difficult for Jews to leave Germany.

Enabling Act
▶ An act pushed through the Reichstag by the Nazis that gave Hitler absolute dictatorial power for four years.

How did Stalin and the Communist Party build a totalitarian order in the Soviet Union?

How did Italian fascism develop?

Why were Hitler and his Nazi regime initially so popular, how did their actions lead to WWII?

How did Germany and Japan build empires in Europe and Asia, how did the Allies defeat them?

☑ LearningCurve
Check what you know.

Some Germans privately opposed these outrages, but most went along or looked the other way. Although this lack of response reflected the individual's helplessness in a totalitarian state, it also reflected the strong popular support Hitler's government enjoyed.

Hitler's Popularity

Hitler had promised the masses economic recovery— "work and bread"—and he delivered. The Nazi Party launched a large public works program to pull Germany out of the depression. In 1935 Germany turned decisively toward rearmament. Unemployment dropped steadily, and by 1938 the Nazis boasted of nearly full employment. For millions of Germans economic recovery was tangible evidence that Nazi promises were more than show and propaganda.

For ordinary German citizens, in contrast to those deemed "undesirable," Hitler's government offered greater equality and more opportunities. In 1933 class barriers in Germany were generally high. Hitler's rule introduced changes that lowered these barriers. The new Nazi elite included many young and poorly edu-cated dropouts, rootless lower-middle-class people like Hitler who rose to the top with breathtaking speed. More generally, however, the Nazis tolerated privilege and wealth only as long as they served party needs. The well-educated classes held on to most of their advantages, and only a modest social leveling occurred in the Nazi years

Not all Germans supported Hitler, and a number of German groups actively resisted him after 1933. Tens of thousands of political enemies were imprisoned, and thousands were executed. In the first years of Hitler's rule, the principal resist-ers were trade-union Communists and Socialists. Catholic and Protestant churches produced a second group of opponents. Their efforts were directed primarily at preserving genuine religious life, however, not at overthrowing Hitler. Finally, in 1938 and again during the war, some high-ranking army officers, who feared the consequences of Hitler's reckless aggression, plotted, unsuccessfully, against him.

Aggression and Appeasement, 1933–1939

After Germany's economic recovery and Hitler's success in establishing Nazi con-trol of society, he turned to the next item on his agenda: aggressive territorial expansion. Germany's withdrawal from the League of Nations in October 1933 indicated its determination to rearm. When in March 1935 Hitler established a general military draft and declared the "unequal" Versailles treaty disarmament clauses null and void, leaders in Britain, France, and Italy issued a rather tepid joint protest and warned him against future aggressive actions.

But the emerging united front against Hitler quickly collapsed. Britain adopted a policy of appeasement, granting Hitler everything he could reasonably want (and more) in order to avoid war. British appeasement, which practically dictated French policy, had the support of many powerful British conservatives who, as in Germany, underestimated Hitler. The British people, still horrified by the memory, the costs, and the losses of the First World War, generally supported pacifism rather than war.

In March 1936 Hitler suddenly marched his armies into the demilitarized Rhineland, violating the Treaties of Versailles and Locarno. France would not move without British support, and Britain refused to act. As Britain and France opted for appeasement and the Soviet Union watched all developments suspiciously,

Italy's Ethiopian Campaign, 1935–1936

CHAPTER LOCATOR | What caused the Great Depression, and what were its consequences? | What was the nature of the new totalitarian dictatorships?

CHAPTER 30
936 THE GREAT DEPRESSION AND WORLD WAR II

Hitler found powerful allies. In October 1936 Italy and Germany established the so-called Rome-Berlin Axis. Japan, which wanted support for its occupation of Manchuria, also joined the Axis alliance (see page 905).

At the same time, Germany and Italy intervened in the Spanish Civil War (1936–1939), where their support helped General Francisco Franco's Fascist movement defeat republican Spain. Republican Spain's only official aid in the fight against Franco came from the Soviet Union.

In late 1937 Hitler moved forward with his plans to crush Austria and Czechoslovakia as the first step in his long-contemplated drive to the east for living space. By threatening Austria with invasion, Hitler forced the Austrian chancellor in March 1938 to put local Nazis in control of the government. The next day German armies moved in unopposed, and Austria became two provinces of Greater Germany (Map 30.1).

MAP 30.1 ■ The Growth of Nazi Germany, 1933–1939

Until March 1939 Hitler brought ethnic Germans into the Nazi state; then he turned on the Slavic peoples, whom he had always hated. He stripped Czechoslovakia of its independence and prepared for an attack on Poland in September 1939.

How did Stalin and the Communist Party build a totalitarian order in the Soviet Union?

How did Italian fascism develop?

Why were Hitler and his Nazi regime initially so popular, how did their actions lead to WWII?

How did Germany and Japan build empires in Europe and Asia, how did the Allies defeat them?

✔ LearningCurve
Check what you know.

937

Simultaneously, Hitler demanded that the pro-Nazi, German-speaking territory of western Czechoslovakia—the Sudetenland—be turned over to Germany. Democratic Czechoslovakia was prepared to defend itself, but appeasement triumphed again. In September 1938 British prime minister Arthur Neville Chamberlain (1869–1940) flew to Germany three times in fourteen days. In these negotiations Chamberlain and the French agreed with Hitler that the Sudetenland should be ceded to Germany immediately. Sold out by the Western powers, Czechoslovakia gave in.

Hitler's armies occupied the remainder of Czechoslovakia in March 1939. This time, there was no possible rationale of self-determination for Nazi aggression. When Hitler used the question of German minorities in Danzig as a pretext to confront Poland, Chamberlain declared that Britain and France would fight if Hitler attacked his eastern neighbor. Hitler did not take these warnings seriously and pressed on.

Then, in an about-face that stunned the world, sworn enemies Hitler and Stalin signed a nonaggression pact in August 1939. Each dictator promised to remain neutral if the other became involved in war. An attached secret protocol divided eastern Europe into German and Soviet zones "in the event of a political and territorial reorganization."[8] Stalin agreed to the pact for three reasons: he distrusted Western intentions, he needed more time to build up Soviet industry and military reserves, and Hitler offered territorial gain.

For Hitler, everything was now set. On September 1, 1939, the Germans attacked Poland from three sides. Two days later, Britain and France, finally true to their word, declared war on Germany. The Second World War had begun.

> ## QUICK REVIEW

What role did economic factors play both in Hitler's rise to power and his popularity once in power?

CHAPTER LOCATOR | What caused the Great Depression, and what were its consequences? | What was the nature of the new totalitarian dictatorships?

CHAPTER 30
938 THE GREAT DEPRESSION AND WORLD WAR II

How did Germany and Japan build empires in Europe and Asia, and how did the Allies defeat them?

NAZI SOLDIERS SCORED ENORMOUS SUCCESSES in Europe until late 1942, establishing a vast empire of death and destruction. Japan attacked the United States in December 1941 and then moved to expand their empire throughout Asia and the Pacific Ocean. Eventually, the mighty coalition of Britain, the United States, and the Soviet Union overwhelmed the aggressors in manpower and military strength.

Hitler's Empire in Europe, 1939–1942

Using planes, tanks, and trucks in the first example of a blitzkrieg, or "lightning war," Hitler's armies crushed Poland in four weeks. The Soviet Union quickly took its share agreed to in the secret protocol—the eastern half of Poland and the Baltic states of Lithuania, Estonia, and Latvia. In the west French and British armies dug in; they expected another war of attrition and economic blockade. But in spring 1940 the Nazi lightning war struck again. After occupying Denmark, Norway, and Holland, German motorized columns broke through southern Belgium and into France.

blitzkrieg
▶ "Lightning war" using planes, tanks, and trucks, first used by Hitler to crush Poland in four weeks.

| How did Stalin and the Communist Party build a totalitarian order in the Soviet Union? | How did Italian fascism develop? | Why were Hitler and his Nazi regime initially so popular, how did their actions lead to WWII? | **How did Germany and Japan build empires in Europe and Asia, how did the Allies defeat them?** | ✓ LearningCurve Check what you know. |

939

Vichy France, 1940

Occupied by Germany

Annexed by Germany

As Hitler's armies poured into France, aging marshal Henri-Philippe Pétain formed a new French government—the so-called Vichy (VIH-shee) government—and accepted defeat. By July 1940 Hitler ruled practically all of western continental Europe; Italy was an ally, the Soviet Union a friendly neutral (Map 30.2). Only Britain, led by Winston Churchill (1874–1965), remained unconquered.

To prepare for an invasion of Britain, Germany first needed to gain control of the air. In the Battle of Britain, which began in July 1940, German planes attacked British airfields and key factories. In September Hitler began indiscriminately bombing British cities to break British morale. British aircraft factories increased production, and Londoners defiantly dug in. By September Britain was winning the air war, and Hitler abandoned his plans for an immediate German invasion of Britain.

Hitler now allowed his lifetime obsession of creating a vast eastern European empire for the "master race" to dictate policy. In June 1941 Germany broke the Nazi-Soviet nonaggression pact and attacked the Soviet Union. By October Leningrad was practically surrounded, Moscow was besieged, and most of Ukraine had

EVENTS LEADING TO WORLD WAR II

1919	Treaty of Versailles is signed
1921	Hitler heads National Socialist German Worker's Party (Nazis)
1922	Mussolini seizes power in Italy
1927	Stalin takes control of the Soviet Union
1929–1939	Great Depression
1931	Japan invades Manchuria
January 1933	Hitler is appointed chancellor of Germany
March 1933	Reichstag passes the Enabling Act, granting Hitler absolute dictatorial power
October 1933	Germany withdraws from the League of Nations
1935	Nuremberg Laws deprive Jews of all rights of citizenship
March 1935	Hitler announces German rearmament
October 1935	Mussolini invades Ethiopia and receives Hitler's support
March 1936	German armies move unopposed into the demilitarized Rhineland
October 1936	Rome-Berlin Axis created
1936–1939	Spanish Civil War
1937	Japan invades China
March 1938	Germany annexes Austria
September 1938	Munich Conference: Britain and France agree to German seizure of the Sudetenland from Czechoslovakia
March 1939	Germany occupies the rest of Czechoslovakia; appeasement ends in Britain
August 1939	Nazi-Soviet nonaggression pact is signed
September 1, 1939	Germany invades Poland
September 3, 1939	Britain and France declare war on Germany

CHAPTER LOCATOR | What caused the Great Depression, and what were its consequences? | What was the nature of the new totalitarian dictatorships?

CHAPTER 30

940 THE GREAT DEPRESSION AND WORLD WAR II

Legend:
- Axis powers and their allies
- Occupied by Germany and its allies
- Allied powers and their allies
- Neutral nations
- Boundary of Greater Germany
- Major battle

Siege of Leningrad, Sept. 1941–Jan. 1944

Germans repulsed, Dec. 1941

Moscow Oct. 1941–Jan. 1942

Siege of Stalingrad, Aug. 21, 1942–Jan. 31, 1943

Germany surrenders, May 8, 1945

Siege, Sept. 1939 Uprising, Aug.–Sept. 1944

Kursk July–Aug. 1943

Dnieper Aug.–Dec. 1943

Battle of Britain, fall 1940

Invasion of Normandy June 6, 1944

Battle of the Bulge Dec. 1944

Axis troops occupy Vichy France, Nov. 10 and 11, 1942

Allies invade Sicily and Italy, July–Sept. 1943

Rome (Liberated June 1944)

Monte Cassino May 1944

Salerno Sept. 1943

Casablanca Nov. 1942

Axis troops evacuated, May 1943

Joined Allies, Nov. 1942

Sicily July 1943

Battle for Crete, May 20–June 1, 1941

El Alamein autumn 1942

MAP 30.2 ■ World War II in Europe and Africa, 1939–1945

The map shows the extent of Hitler's empire at its height, before the Battle of Stalingrad in late 1942 and the subsequent advances of the Allies until Germany surrendered on May 7, 1945.

been conquered. But the Soviets did not collapse, and when a severe winter struck German armies outfitted in summer uniforms, the invaders were stopped.

Although stalled in Russia, Hitler ruled an enormous European empire. He now began building a **New Order** based on the guiding principle of Nazi totalitarianism: racial imperialism. Hitler envisioned a vast eastern colonial empire where enslaved Poles, Ukrainians, and Russians would die or be killed off while Germanic peasants would resettle the abandoned lands. Himmler and the elite

New Order

▶ Hitler's program, based on the guiding principle of racial imperialism, which gave preferential treatment to the Nordic peoples above "inferior" Latin peoples and, at the bottom, "subhuman" Slavs and Jews.

How did Stalin and the Communist Party build a totalitarian order in the Soviet Union?

How did Italian fascism develop?

Why were Hitler and his Nazi regime initially so popular, how did their actions lead to WWII?

How did Germany and Japan build empires in Europe and Asia, how did the Allies defeat them?

☑ LearningCurve Check what you know.

SS corps, supported by military commanders and German policemen, implemented a program of destruction in the occupied territories to create a "mass settlement space" for Germans.

The Holocaust

Finally, the Nazi state condemned all European Jews to extermination in the Holocaust. After Warsaw fell in 1939, the Nazis forced Jews in the occupied territories to move to urban ghettos, while German Jews were sent to occupied Poland. After Germany attacked Russia in June 1941, forced expulsion spiraled into extermination. In late 1941 Hitler and the Nazi leadership, in some still-debated combination, ordered the SS to speed up planning for "the final solution of the Jewish question."[9] Throughout the Nazi empire Jews were systematically arrested, packed like cattle onto freight trains, and dispatched to extermination camps.

Arriving at their destination, small numbers of Jews were sent to nearby slave labor camps, where they were starved and systematically worked to death. (See "Individuals in Society: Primo Levi," page 944.) Most victims were taken to "shower rooms," which were actually gas chambers. By 1945 about 6 million Jews had been murdered.

Who was responsible for this terrible crime? After the war historians laid the guilt on Hitler and the Nazi leadership. Beginning in the 1990s studies appeared revealing a much broader participation of German people in the Holocaust and popular indifference (or worse) to the Jews' fate.[10] In most occupied countries local non-German officials also cooperated in the arrest and deportation of Jews.

Japan's Asian Empire

By late 1938, 1.5 million Japanese troops were bogged down in China, holding a great swath of territory but unable to defeat the Nationalists and the Communists (see pages 905–908). In 1939, as war broke out in Europe, the Japanese redoubled their ruthless efforts. Implementing a savage policy of "kill all, burn all, destroy all," Japanese troops committed shocking atrocities, including the so-called Rape of Nanjing. During Japan's war in China—the second Sino-Japanese War (1937–1945)—the Japanese are estimated to have killed 4 million Chinese people.

In August 1940 the Japanese announced the formation of a self-sufficient Asian economic zone. Although they spoke of liberating Asia from Western imperialism and of "Asia for the Asians," their true intentions were to eventually rule over a vast Japanese empire. Ultranationalists moved to convince Japan's youth that Japan had a sacred liberating mission in Asia.

For the moment, however, Japan needed allies. In September 1940 Japan signed a formal alliance (the Axis alliance) with Germany and Italy, and Vichy France granted the Japanese domination over northern French Indochina. The United States, upset with Japan's occupation of Indochina and fearing embattled Britain would collapse if it lost its Asian colonies, froze scrap iron sales to Japan and applied further economic sanctions in October.

As 1941 opened, Japan's leaders faced a critical decision. In 1941 the United States was the world's largest oil producer and supplied over 90 percent of

Holocaust

▶ The attempted systematic extermination of all European Jews and other "undesirables" by the Nazi state during World War II.

Axis powers and their allies
Occupied by Germany and its allies
■ Extermination camp
● Major concentration camp
◆ Site of mass killing
★ Ghetto

The Holocaust, 1941–1945

CHAPTER LOCATOR | What caused the Great Depression, and what were its consequences? | What was the nature of the new totalitarian dictatorships?

CHAPTER 30
942 THE GREAT DEPRESSION AND WORLD WAR II

Japan's oil needs. Japan had only a year and a half's worth of military and economic oil reserves, which the war in China and the Japanese military and merchant navies were quickly drawing down. On July 26, 1941, President Roosevelt embargoed all oil exports to Japan and froze its assets in the United States. Japan now had to either recall its forces from China or go to war before running out of oil. It chose war.

On December 7, 1941, Japan launched a surprise attack on the U.S. fleet in Pearl Harbor in the Hawaiian Islands. Japan hoped to cripple its Pacific rival, gain time to build a defensible Asian empire, and eventually win an ill-defined compromise peace.

The Japanese attack was a limited success. The Japanese sank or crippled every American battleship, but by chance all the American aircraft carriers were at sea and escaped unharmed. Hours later the Japanese destroyed half of the American Far East Air Force stationed at Clark Air Base in the Philippines. Americans were humiliated by these unexpected defeats, which soon overwhelmed American isolationism and brought the United States into the war.

Hitler immediately declared war on the United States. Simultaneously, Japanese armies successfully attacked European and American colonies in Southeast Asia. After American forces surrendered the Philippines in May 1942, Japan held a vast empire in Southeast Asia and the western Pacific (Map 30.3).

The Japanese claimed they were freeing Asians from Western imperialism, and they called their empire the Greater East Asian Co-Prosperity Sphere. Most local populations were glad to see the Western powers go, but Asian faith in "co-prosperity" and support for Japan steadily declined as the war progressed. Although the Japanese set up anticolonial governments and promised genuine independence, real power always rested with Japanese military commanders and their superiors in Tokyo. Moreover, the Japanese never treated local populations as equals, and the occupiers exploited local peoples for Japan's wartime needs.

The Japanese often exhibited great cruelty toward prisoners of war and civilians. For example, Dutch, Indonesian, and perhaps as many as two hundred thousand Korean women were forced to provide sex for Japanese soldiers as "comfort women." Recurring cruel behavior aroused local populations against the invaders.

The Grand Alliance

While the Nazis and the Japanese built their empires, Great Britain, the United States, and the Soviet Union joined together in an unlikely military pact called the Grand Alliance. Grand Alliance leaders agreed to a **Europe first policy**. Only after defeating Hitler would the Allies mount an all-out attack on Japan. To encourage mutual trust, the Allies adopted the principle of the unconditional surrender of Germany and Japan, and no unilateral treaties. This policy cemented the Grand Alliance because it denied Germany and Japan any hope of dividing their foes.

The Grand Alliance's military resources were awesome. The United States possessed a unique capacity to wage global war with its large population and mighty industry. The British economy was totally and effectively mobilized, and the country became an important staging area for the war in Europe. As for the Soviet Union, so great was its economic strength that it might well have defeated Germany without Western help.

Europe first policy

▶ The military strategy, set forth by Churchill and adopted by Roosevelt, that called for the defeat of Hitler in Europe before the United States launched an all-out strike against Japan in the Pacific.

How did Stalin and the Communist Party build a totalitarian order in the Soviet Union?

How did Italian fascism develop?

Why were Hitler and his Nazi regime initially so popular, how did their actions lead to WWII?

How did Germany and Japan build empires in Europe and Asia, how did the Allies defeat them?

✔ LearningCurve
Check what you know.

943

Most Jews deported to Auschwitz were murdered as soon as they arrived, but the Nazis made some prisoners into slave laborers, and a few of these survived. Primo Levi (1919–1987), an Italian Jew, became one of the most influential witnesses to the Holocaust and its death camps.

Like many in Italy's small Jewish community, Levi's family belonged to the urban professional classes. The young Primo Levi graduated in 1941 from the University of Turin with highest honors in chemistry. Since 1938, when Italy introduced racial laws, he had faced growing discrimination, and two years after graduation he joined the antifascist resistance movement. Quickly captured, he was deported to Auschwitz with 650 Italian Jews in February 1944. Stone-faced SS men picked only ninety-six men and twenty-nine women to work in their respective labor camps. Levi was one of them.

Nothing had prepared Levi for what he encountered. The Jewish prisoners were kicked, punched, stripped, branded with tattoos, crammed into huts, and worked unmercifully. Hoping for some sign of prisoner solidarity in this terrible environment, Levi found only a desperate struggle of each against all and enormous status differences among prisoners. Many stunned and bewildered newcomers, beaten and demoralized by their bosses — the most privileged prisoners — collapsed and died. Others struggled to secure their own privileges, however small, because food rations and working conditions were so abominable that ordinary Jewish prisoners perished in two to three months.

Sensitive and noncombative, Levi found himself sinking into oblivion. But instead of joining the mass of the "drowned," he became one of the "saved" — a complicated surprise with moral implications that he would ponder all his life. As Levi explained in *Survival in Auschwitz* (1947), the usual road to salvation in the camps was some kind of collaboration with German power.[*] Savage German criminals were released from prison to become brutal camp guards; non-Jewish political prisoners competed for jobs entitling them to better conditions; and, especially troubling for Levi, a small number of Jewish men plotted and struggled for the power of life and death over other Jewish prisoners. Though not one of these Jewish bosses, Levi believed that he himself, like almost all survivors, had entered the "gray zone" of moral compromise. Only a very few superior individuals, "the stuff of saints and martyrs," survived the death camps without shifting their moral stance.

For Levi, compromise and salvation came from his profession. Interviewed by a German technocrat for the camp's synthetic rubber program, Levi performed brilliantly in scientific German and savored his triumph as a Jew over Nazi racism. Work in the warm camp laboratory offered Levi opportunities to pilfer equipment that could then be traded to other prisoners for food and necessities. Levi also gained critical support from three saintly prisoners who refused to do wicked and hateful acts. And he counted "luck" as essential for his survival: in the camp infirmary with scarlet fever in February 1945 as advancing Russian armies prepared to liberate the camp, Levi was not evacuated by the Nazis and shot to death like most Jewish prisoners.

After the war Primo Levi was forever haunted by the nightmare that the Holocaust would be ignored or forgotten. Always ashamed that so many people whom he considered better than himself had perished, he wrote and lectured tirelessly to preserve the

Primo Levi, who never stopped thinking, writing, and speaking about the Holocaust. (© Gianni Giansanti/Sygma/Corbis)

[*]Primo Levi, *Survival in Auschwitz: The Nazi Assault on Humanity*, rev. ed. 1958 (London: Collier Books, 1961), pp. 79–84, and *The Drowned and the Saved* (New York: Summit Books, 1988). These powerful testimonies are highly recommended.

memory of Jewish victims and guilty Nazis. Wanting the world to understand the Jewish genocide in all its complexity so that never again would people tolerate such atrocities, he grappled tirelessly with his vision of individual choice and moral compromise in a hell designed to make the victims collaborate and persecute each other.

QUESTIONS FOR ANALYSIS

1. Describe Levi's experience at Auschwitz. How did camp prisoners treat each other? Why?
2. What does Levi mean by the "gray zone"? How is this concept central to his thinking?
3. Will a vivid historical memory of the Holocaust help prevent future genocide? Why or why not?

ONLINE DOCUMENT PROJECT

What choices did Holocaust survivors face? Listen to testimonies from Holocaust survivors, and then complete a quiz and writing assignment based on the evidence and details from this chapter. *See inside the front cover to learn more.*

The War in Europe, 1942–1945

Halted at the gates of Moscow and Leningrad in 1941, the Germans renewed their offensive against the Soviet Union in 1942 and attacked Stalingrad in July. The Soviet armies counterattacked, quickly surrounding the entire German Sixth Army of 300,000 men. By late January 1943 only 123,000 soldiers were left to surrender. In summer 1943 the larger, better-equipped Soviet armies took the offensive and began to push the Germans back (see Map 30.2).

Not yet prepared to attack Germany directly through France, the Western Allies engaged in heavy fighting in North Africa (see Map 30.2). In autumn 1942 British forces defeated German and Italian armies at the Battle of El Alamein (el a-luh-MAYN) in Egypt. Shortly thereafter an Anglo-American force took control of the Vichy French colonies of Morocco and Algeria.

Having driven the Axis powers from North Africa by spring 1943, Allied forces invaded Italy. War-weary Italians deposed Mussolini, and the new Italian government accepted unconditional surrender in September 1943. But German commandos rescued Mussolini and made him head of a puppet government. German armies seized Rome and all of northern Italy. After almost two years of fighting, the German armies in Italy finally surrendered on April 29, 1945. Two days earlier Mussolini had been captured by partisan forces, and he was executed the next day.

On June 6, 1944, American and British forces under General Dwight Eisenhower landed on the beaches of Normandy, France. From there, they pushed inland and broke through the German lines. In March 1945 American troops crossed the Rhine and entered Germany.

The Soviets had been advancing steadily since July 1943, and on April 26, 1945, the Red Army met American forces on the Elbe River in Germany. As Soviet forces fought their way into Berlin, Hitler committed suicide in his bunker on April 30. On May 7 the remaining German commanders capitulated.

The War in the Pacific, 1942–1945

In April 1942 the Japanese devised a plan to take Port Moresby in New Guinea and also destroy U.S. aircraft carriers in an attack on Midway Island (see Map 30.3). Having broken the secret Japanese code, the Americans skillfully won a series of decisive naval victories. First, in the Battle of the Coral Sea in May 1942, an American carrier force halted the Japanese advance on Port Moresby. Then, in the Battle of Midway in June 1942, American pilots sank all four of the attacking Japanese aircraft carriers and established overall naval equality with Japan in the Pacific.

The United States gradually won control of the sea and air as it geared up its war industry. In July 1943 the Americans and their Australian allies opened an "island-hopping" campaign toward Japan. By 1944 hundreds of American submarines were hunting in "wolf packs," decimating shipping and destroying economic links in Japan's far-flung, overextended empire.

The Pacific war was brutal and atrocities were committed on both sides. Aware of Japanese atrocities in China and the Philippines, the U.S. forces seldom took Japanese prisoners after the Battle of Guadalcanal in August 1942, killing even those rare Japanese soldiers who offered to surrender. American forces moving across the central and western Pacific in 1943 and 1944 faced unyielding resistance, and this resistance hardened soldiers as American casualties kept rising. A product of spiraling violence, mutual hatred, and dehumanizing racial stereotypes, the war's brutality intensified as it moved toward Japan.

In June 1944 U.S. bombers began a relentless bombing campaign of the Japanese home islands. In October 1944 American forces under General Douglas MacArthur landed on Leyte Island in the Philippines. In the ensuing Battle of Leyte Gulf, the Japanese lost 13 large warships, including 4 aircraft carriers, while the Americans lost only 3 small ships. The Japanese navy was practically finished.

In spite of massive defeats, Japanese troops continued to fight on. Indeed, the bloodiest battles of the Pacific war took place on Iwo Jima in February 1945 and on Okinawa in June 1945. American commanders believed that an invasion of Japan might cost 1 million American casualties and possibly 10 to 20 million Japanese lives. In fact, Japan was almost helpless,

A Hiroshima Survivor Remembers

Yasuko Yamagata was seventeen when she saw the brilliant blue-white "lightning flash" that became a fiery orange ball consuming everything that would burn. Thirty years later Yamagata painted this scene, her most unforgettable memory of the atomic attack. An incinerated woman, poised as if running with her baby clutched to her breast, lies near a water tank piled high with charred corpses. (GE15-05 drawn by Yasuko Yamagata, Hiroshima Peace Memorial Museum)

CHAPTER LOCATOR | What caused the Great Depression, and what were its consequences? | What was the nature of the new totalitarian dictatorships?

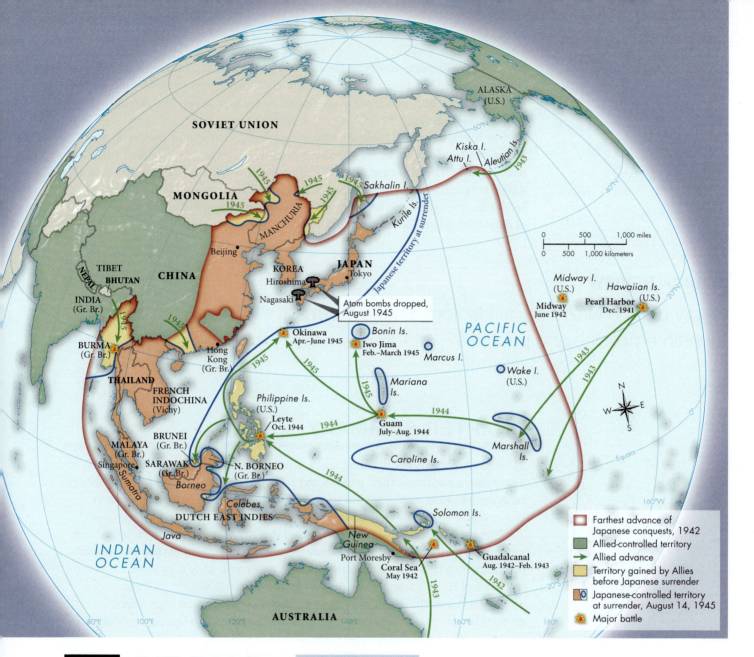

MAP 30.3 ■ World War II in the Pacific

Japanese forces overran an enormous amount of territory in 1942, which the Allies slowly recaptured in a long, bitter struggle.

> MAPPING THE PAST

ANALYZING THE MAP: Locate the extent of the Japanese empire in 1942, and compare it to the Japanese-controlled territory at surrender in 1945. Where was the fighting in the Pacific concentrated?

CONNECTIONS: How was the course of the war's end in Europe different from that of Asia, and what does this suggest about the difficulties that the Allies faced in fighting the Japanese?

its industry and cities largely destroyed by intense American bombing. As the war in Europe ended in April 1945, Japanese leaders were divided. Hardliners argued that surrender was unthinkable. A peace faction argued that Japan should seek a negotiated end to the war.

On July 26 Truman, Churchill, and Stalin issued the Potsdam Declaration, which demanded unconditional surrender. The declaration left unclear whether

How did Stalin and the Communist Party build a totalitarian order in the Soviet Union?

How did Italian fascism develop?

Why were Hitler and his Nazi regime initially so popular, how did their actions lead to WWII?

How did Germany and Japan build empires in Europe and Asia, how did the Allies defeat them?

✔ LearningCurve
Check what you know.

the Japanese emperor would be treated as a war criminal. The Japanese, who considered Emperor Hirohito a god, sought clarification and amnesty for him. The Allies remained adamant that the surrender be unconditional. The Japanese felt compelled to fight on.

On August 6 and 9, 1945, the United States dropped atomic bombs on Hiroshima and Nagasaki in Japan. Also on August 9, Soviet troops launched an invasion of the Japanese puppet state of Manchukuo (Manchuria, China). To avoid a Soviet invasion and further atomic bombing, the Japanese announced their surrender on August 14, 1945. The Second World War, which had claimed the lives of more than 50 million soldiers and civilians, was over.

> QUICK REVIEW

How did the Nazi's racial ideology shape German wartime policies and priorities?

CHAPTER SUMMARY

The 1929 American stock market crash triggered a Great Depression. Western democracies expanded their powers and responded with relief programs. Authoritarian and Fascist regimes arose to replace some capitalist democracies. Only World War II ended the depression.

The radical totalitarian dictatorships of the 1920s and 1930s were repressive, profoundly antiliberal, and exceedingly violent. Mussolini set up the first Fascist government, a one-party dictatorship, but it was never truly a totalitarian state on the order of Hitler's Germany or Stalin's Soviet Union.

In the Soviet Union Stalin launched a socialist "revolution from above" to modernize and industrialize the U.S.S.R. Mass purges of the Communist Party in the 1930s led to the imprisonment and deaths of millions.

Hitler and the Nazi elite rallied support with a totalitarian ideology that combined racism and extreme nationalism. The Great Depression caused German voters to turn to Adolph Hitler and the Nazis for relief. After Hitler declared the Versailles treaty disarmament clause null and void, British and French leaders tried appeasement. On September 1, 1939, his unprovoked attack on Poland forced the Allies to declare war, starting World War II.

Nazi armies first seized Poland and Germany's western neighbors and then turned east. Here Hitler planned to build a New Order based on racial imperialism. In the Holocaust that followed, millions of Jews and other "undesirables" were systematically exterminated. In Asia the Japanese created the Greater East Asian Co-Prosperity Sphere as a vehicle of Japanese domination and control. After Japan attacked Pearl Harbor, the United States entered the war. In 1945 the Grand Alliance of the United States, Britain, and the Soviet Union defeated Germany and Japan.

CHAPTER LOCATOR | What caused the Great Depression, and what were its consequences? | What was the nature of the new totalitarian dictatorships?

948 CHAPTER 30
THE GREAT DEPRESSION AND WORLD WAR II

CONNECTIONS If anyone still doubted the interconnectedness of all the world's inhabitants following the Great War, those doubts faded as events on a truly global scale touched everyone as never before. First a Great Depression shook the financial foundations of the wealthiest capitalist economies and the poorest producers of raw materials and minerals. Another world war followed, bringing global death and destruction. At war's end, as we shall see in Chapter 31, the world's leaders revived Woodrow Wilson's idea of a League of Nations and formed the United Nations in 1946 to prevent such tragedies from ever reoccurring.

Although the United Nations was an attempt to bring nations together, the postwar world became more divided than ever. Chapter 31 will describe how two new superpowers—the United States and the Soviet Union—emerged from World War II to engage one another in the Cold War for nearly the rest of the century. Then in Chapters 32 and 33 we will see how less developed nations in Asia, Africa, and Latin America emerged after the war. Many of them did so by turning the nineteenth-century European ideology of nationalism against its creators, breaking the bonds of colonialism.

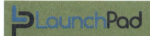

ONLINE DOCUMENT PROJECT
Remembering the Holocaust
What choices did Holocaust survivors face?

Listen to testimonies from Holocaust survivors, and then complete a quiz and writing assignment based on the evidence and details from this chapter. *See inside the front cover to learn more.*

How did Stalin and the Communist Party build a totalitarian order in the Soviet Union?

How did Italian fascism develop?

Why were Hitler and his Nazi regime initially so popular, how did their actions lead to WWII?

How did Germany and Japan build empires in Europe and Asia, how did the Allies defeat them?

☑ **LearningCurve**
Check what you know.

CHAPTER 30 STUDY GUIDE

STEP 1 GET STARTED ONLINE

 **LearningCurve**

Now that you've read the chapter, make it stick by completing the LearningCurve activity.

STEP 2 EXPLAIN WHY IT MATTERS

Put your reading into practice. Identify each term below, and then explain why it matters in world history.

TERM	WHO OR WHAT & WHEN	WHY IT MATTERS
New Deal (p. 918)		
Popular Front (p. 920)		
totalitarianism (p. 923)		
fascism (p. 923)		
five-year plan (p. 925)		
New Economic Policy (NEP) (p. 926)		
collectivization (p. 926)		
Black Shirts (p. 931)		
Lateran Agreement (p. 932)		
Nazism (p. 933)		
Enabling Act (p. 935)		
blitzkrieg (p. 939)		
New Order (p. 941)		
Holocaust (p. 942)		
Europe first policy (p. 943)		

STEP 3 MOVE BEYOND THE BASICS

To demonstrate a more advanced understanding of the totalitarian regimes of the 1920s and 1930s, fill in the chart below with descriptions of the ideologies and policies of the governments of the Soviet Union, Italy, and Germany. How did ideology shape the policies of each government?

	Ideology	Social Policy	Economic Policy	Foreign Policy
The Soviet Union				
Italy				
Germany				

PUT IT ALL TOGETHER

Now, take a step back and try to explain the big picture. Remember to use specific examples from the chapter in your answers.

THE GREAT DEPRESSION

▶ Compare and contrast the response to the Great Depression in the United States, France, Britain, Germany, and the Scandinavian countries. How would you explain the similarities and differences you note?

▶ What light does the Great Depression shed on the nature of global economic connections in the 1920s and 1930s? How did an economic crisis that began in the United States and Europe spread to Asia, Africa, and Latin America?

THE AGE OF DICTATORS

▶ In your opinion, was Italy under Mussolini a totalitarian state? Why or why not?

▶ Compare and contrast Stalinism and Nazism. What were the most important differences between the two ideologies? How did both systems use the persecution of "outsiders" to promote loyalty and obedience to the regime?

THE SECOND WORLD WAR

▶ What role did race play in the German and Japanese drive for territorial expansion? Is it fair to describe World War II, in Europe and in the Pacific, as a racial war?

▶ In your opinion, why did the Allies win the war? What role did industrial production play in the Allied victory? What other factors were important?

LOOKING BACK, LOOKING AHEAD

▶ Argue for or against the following proposition: "World War II was the inevitable consequence of the destruction of World War I and the fatally flawed peace treaties produced at its conclusion." What evidence can you present to support your position?

▶ What similarities and differences do you see between the Great Depression of the 1930s and the global economic crisis of the early twenty-first century? Could the contemporary crisis lead to another "Age of Dictators"? Why or why not?

> ## IN YOUR OWN WORDS

Imagine that you must give an oral report to the class answering the following question: **How did the economic suffering created by the Great Depression contribute to the outbreak of World War II?** What would be the most important points and why?

31

DECOLONIZATION, REVOLUTION, AND THE COLD WAR

1945–1968

> **How did decolonization and the Cold War shape global developments in the decades following World War II?** Chapter 31 examines political and economic developments in the decades following World War II. In the aftermath of World War II, the immediate challenge was to repair the enormous damage done by the fighting. This challenge was complicated by rivalry between the United States and the Soviet Union that developed into a tense but nonviolent conflict known as the Cold War. Devastated by war, the nations of Europe could no longer hold onto their overseas empires, and nearly every colonial territory gained formal independence between 1945 and the early 1960s. A revolution in China consolidated Communist rule. At the same time, remarkable growth and economic prosperity occurred in the postwar era. There were, however, limits to postwar prosperity, and these decades of economic growth did not resolve underlying tensions and conflicts.

New Leadership in Africa Kwame Nkrumah, nationalist leader and first prime minister of Ghana after its independence in 1957. (Photo by Underwood Archives/Getty Images)

LearningCurve
After reading the chapter, use LearningCurve to retain what you've read.

> How did the Cold War and decolonization shape the postwar world?

> How did religion and the legacies of colonialism affect the formation of new nations in South Asia and the Middle East after World War II?

> How did the Cold War shape reconstruction, revolution, and decolonization in East and Southeast Asia?

> What factors influenced decolonization in Africa after World War II?

> Why did populism emerge as such a powerful political force in Latin America?

> Why did the world face growing social unrest in the 1960s?

> How did the Cold War and decolonization shape the postwar world?

United Nations Programs at Work, 1951

As part of a UN assistance program, the United Nations Children's Fund (UNICEF) provided milk to children in Greece in the aftermath of civil war in that country.

(© Amerika Haus/SZ Photo/The Image Works)

Cold War

▶ The postwar conflict between the United States and the Soviet Union.

THE BITTER RIVALRY BETWEEN the United States and the Soviet Union divided postwar Europe and became a **Cold War**—not an outright military confrontation between nations, but a long, tense standoff. As the Cold War took shape, activists and observers around the world debated the meaning of freedom and independence in a postcolonial world.

The Cold War and the Division of Europe

The Cold War originated in disputes over the political outcome of the war. During talks among the three major powers—the United States, Britain, and the Soviet Union—held toward the end of the war, Soviet leader Joseph Stalin insisted that control of eastern Europe was the best way to guarantee military security from Germany. When Harry Truman demanded free elections throughout eastern Europe, Stalin refused.

Truman's tough stance was bolstered by the fact that the United States was the only country that possessed atomic weapons at the end of the war. Just as the

CHAPTER LOCATOR | **How did the Cold War and decolonization shape the postwar world?** | How did religion and the legacies of colonialism affect the new nations in South Asia and the Middle East?

954 **CHAPTER 31** DECOLONIZATION, REVOLUTION, AND THE COLD WAR

1945 United Nations established	**1957** Formation of Common Market
1946–1955 Populist Juan Perón leads Argentina	**1957–1964** Decolonization in sub-Saharan Africa
1947 Independence of India	**1957–1975** War between North and South Vientam
1948 Marshall Plan aid in Europe; independence of Israel	**1959** Cuban Revolution
1949 Chinese Revolution; formation of NATO	**1960** Brazil's new capital, Brasília, inaugurated
1949–present Harsh restrictions against religion and speech in China	**1961** Building of Berlin Wall
1950–1953 Korean War	**1962** Cuban missile crisis
1953–1964 Khrushchev implements policy of de-Stalinization in the Soviet Union	**1964–1965** Civil Rights Act and Voting Rights Act passed in United States
1956 Nasser nationalizes Suez Canal Company; Soviet invasion of Hungary	**1965** Great Proletarian Cultural Revolution in China
	1967 Six-Day War in Israel

U.S. sense of security came from having a monopoly on the atomic bomb, Stalin pursued security for the Soviet Union by militarily occupying eastern Europe and imposing obedient governments that would provide a buffer against the threat of western European aggression.

President Harry Truman misread these occupations as a campaign for world domination. Communist movements beyond Stalin's occupation zone in Greece and China fed these fears. In October 1945 Truman issued the **Truman Doctrine**, aimed at "containing" communism to areas already occupied by the Soviet army by providing military and economic support to governments threatened by Communist control.

Truman asked Congress for military aid for Greece and Turkey to prevent the spread of communism. Soon after, Secretary of State George C. Marshall proposed a broader package of economic and food aid—the **Marshall Plan**—to help Europe rebuild. Stalin refused Marshall Plan assistance for all of eastern Europe, where he had established Soviet-style Communist dictatorships. The Soviet Union's aid and support for the overthrow of the democratically elected Czechoslovakian government in February 1948 shocked the U.S. Congress into action, and on April 2, 1948, it voted for the Marshall Plan.

On July 24, 1948, Stalin blocked all road traffic through the Soviet zone of Germany to Berlin. The Western allies responded with an airlift of provisions to the West Berliners. After 324 days the Soviets backed down. In 1949 the United States

Truman Doctrine
▶ American policy of preventing the spread of Communist rule.

Marshall Plan
▶ American plan for providing economic aid to Europe to help it rebuild.

How did the Cold War shape revolution and decolonization in East and Southeast Asia?	What factors influenced decolonization in Africa after World War II?	Why did populism emerge as such a powerful political force in Latin America?	Why did the world face growing social unrest in the 1960s?	☑ LearningCurve Check what you know.

NATO

▶ The North Atlantic Treaty Organization, an anti-Soviet military alliance of Western nations.

superpowers

▶ Countries whose military (or economic) might dwarfed that of other countries.

formed an anti-Soviet military alliance of Western governments: the North Atlantic Treaty Organization (**NATO**). Stalin countered by tightening his hold on his satellites, later united in the Warsaw Pact. Europe was divided into two hostile blocs. British prime minister Winston Churchill warned that an "iron curtain has descended across the Continent."[1]

The Soviet Union, with its massive army arrayed across eastern Europe, and the United States, with its industrial strength and atomic weapons, emerged from the war as **superpowers** whose might dwarfed that of other countries. Superpower status reached an awkward balance after the Soviet Union developed its own atomic weapons in 1949. Both nations pitched themselves into a military and geopolitical confrontation that stopped short of outright war: the Cold War (Map 31.1).

A deep ideological divide defined the rivalry between the United States and the Soviet Union. The United States saw itself as the defender of a "free world" governed by liberal principles such as free markets, private property, and individ-

MAP 31.1 ■ Cold War Europe in the 1950s

Europe was divided by an "iron curtain" during the Cold War. None of the Communist countries of eastern Europe were participants in the Marshall Plan.

CHAPTER LOCATOR | How did the Cold War and decolonization shape the postwar world? | How did religion and the legacies of colonialism affect the new nations in South Asia and the Middle East?

956 CHAPTER 31 DECOLONIZATION, REVOLUTION, AND THE COLD WAR

ual rights protected by democratic constitutions. The Soviet Union defined itself as the defender of the rights of workers and peasants against their exploiters, the rights of colonial peoples against their colonizers, and economic development based on rational production and equitable distribution. The Cold War sharpened the distinctions between these models, creating opposing paths that the superpowers pressured other countries to follow.

The United Nations

In 1945 representatives of fifty nations met in San Francisco to draft a charter for a new intergovernmental organization called the United Nations. Like that of its predecessor, the League of Nations (see Chapter 28), the immediate goal of the United Nations was to mediate international conflicts in order to preserve peace. But in 1945 the founders of the United Nations foresaw a more ambitious role for the new body than the League of Nations had played: beyond conflict resolution, the UN would support the decolonization of territories under foreign rule; promote economic development; and expand access to health care, protection for workers, environmental conservation, and gender equity.

The United Nations was divided into two bodies: a General Assembly that met annually and included all nations that signed the UN Charter; and a Security Council made up of the five main regional powers (the United States, the Soviet Union, the United Kingdom, China, and France), each of which held veto power over the council's decisions, making it a body that in effect only functioned through unanimous consent.

The UN gave critical support to decolonization efforts. Its charter defended the right of self-determination, and it served as a forum for liberation movements to advocate for their claims, negotiate the terms of independence, or define new national boundaries. In addition, UN member nations volunteered military forces to serve around the world as peacekeepers.

The Politics of Liberation

The term *Third World* emerged in the 1950s when many observers viewed Africa, Asia, and Latin America as a single entity, different from both the capitalist, industrialized "First World" and the Communist, industrialized "Second World." The Cold War rivalry between the United States and the Soviet Union reinforced this "three-bloc" perspective, which staked out separate camps for the superpowers, and created a third general category for everyone else. Despite differences in history and culture, most so-called Third World countries in Africa, Asia, and Latin America were poor and economically underdeveloped. They also shared many characteristics that encouraged the development of a common consciousness about their marginalization and ideologies for defining their future.

The roots of many liberation movements in these countries went back well before the Second World War and often as far back as the nineteenth century. After the Second World War weakened the colonial powers, nationalist movements in the colonies became more insistent. As nations fought against colonial rule, their quest for liberation took many forms. Economically, they pursued national industrialization and development to end dependence on industrialized

How did the Cold War shape revolution and decolonization in East and Southeast Asia?

What factors influenced decolonization in Africa after World War II?

Why did populism emerge as such a powerful political force in Latin America?

Why did the world face growing social unrest in the 1960s?

☑ LearningCurve
Check what you know.

957

nations. Politically, they sought alliances within the industrializing world to avoid the neocolonial influences of more powerful nations. Intellectually, they reacted against Western assumptions of white supremacy.

The former colonies faced intense pressure to align themselves ideologically and economically with either the United States or the Soviet Union, and few could resist the pressure or the incentives those powers brought to bear. Nonetheless, to varying degrees, they tried to operate independently from the two superpowers in a number of ways. In 1955 leaders of twenty-nine recently independent nations in Asia and Africa met in Bandung, Indonesia, to create a framework for political and economic cooperation to help them emerge from colonialism without having to resubordinate their nations either to their former colonizers or to pressures from the Cold War superpowers. The participants outlined principles for rejecting pressure from the superpowers and supporting decolonization. In 1961 nations participating in the Bandung Conference met in Yugoslavia to form a Non-Aligned Nations Movement.

Dependency and Development Theories

In 1948 the United Nations established the Economic Commission for Latin America (ECLA) in Santiago, Chile, to study economic development. Under the direction of Argentine economist Raúl Prebisch, ECLA produced one of Latin America's most influential intellectual contributions of the twentieth century: a diagnosis of reasons why Latin America, like other less industrialized regions of the world, remained economically and technologically dependent on Europe and the United States, along with prescriptions for remedying that dependency. These ideas formed what became known as **dependency theory**.

According to dependency theory, countries in Latin America, Africa, and Asia were trapped in the position of borrowers of capital and technology, and producers of primary commodities such as agricultural and mineral goods. Since western Europe and the United States industrialized in the nineteenth century, they secured a lasting economic advantage magnified by colonialism and neocolonialism, which reorganized production and consumption around the world for their benefit.

According to this analysis, the prosperity of Europe and the United States was built on the impoverishment of other regions of the world because the products that industrialized countries made were worth more than the agricultural or mineral exports of other nations. This inequality in the market value of goods increased over time as the relative value of commodities such as coffee or copper decreased relative to the value of manufactured goods like automobiles or technologically advanced goods like computer software.

How could this pattern be broken? One approach was **modernization theory**, championed by U.S. economist Walt Whitman Rostow. He suggested that societies passed through phases of development from primitive to modern, and that adopting the political, economic, or cultural practices of places like the United States was the best remedy for poverty. Modernization theory shaped foreign aid programs: the U.S. government deployed armies of experts around the world to advise governments and communities on how to modernize. These technicians

dependency theory
▶ The belief that development in some areas of the world locks other nations into underdevelopment.

modernization theory
▶ The belief that all countries evolved in a linear progression from traditional to mature.

CHAPTER LOCATOR | **How did the Cold War and decolonization shape the postwar world?** | How did religion and the legacies of colonialism affect the new nations in South Asia and the Middle East?

CHAPTER 31
958 DECOLONIZATION, REVOLUTION, AND THE COLD WAR

often did not understand local conditions, believing that the American way was the only way, and these projects were often riddled with unintended negative consequences. As a result, many people began to mistrust these experts.

To peoples emerging from colonialism, dependency theory offered a more appealing path. Dependency theorists rejected liberalism because they believed free-market capitalism reinforced social and economic problems by inhibiting the accumulation of wealth in dependent regions. Instead they favored state intervention to remake national economies so that resources would be distributed more equitably. Prebisch advocated a practice that became common in much of the world: **import substitution industrialization (ISI)**. Under ISI policies, countries imposed trade barriers to keep certain foreign products out and provided subsidies to develop domestic industries that could make the same goods. Some dependency theorists suggested that even ISI was not enough, and that deeper social reforms were needed, such as the redistribution of farmlands from large landowners to rural workers, as well as state control of major industries and banks.

The governments that attempted land redistribution or the nationalization of foreign firms often faced a fierce backlash by landowners, foreign corporations, and political conservatives. In many cases, reformist governments were deposed in military coups supported by the United States. The U.S. reaction against reformers in countries like Guatemala, where the elected government was overthrown in a coup organized by the United States in 1954, pushed reformers in other countries into more radical and defiant approaches. In Cuba a revolutionary movement led by Fidel Castro took power in 1959. Castro's regime executed a deep social and economic transformation of Cuba, including the redistribution of land and urban properties. This pressure from the United States pushed revolutionary Cuba into an alliance with the Soviet Union. The Argentine military strategist who worked closely with Castro, Che Guevara, became an icon of radical revolutionary liberation. He built his ideas for social change into a revolutionary theory, Guevarism, which suggested that private property and wage labor were forms of exploitation that could be overthrown by free workers volunteering their labor to help liberate others.

One of the most influential areas where the idea of liberation crystallized was a movement within the Catholic Church called **liberation theology**. The movement emerged in Latin America amid reforms of church doctrine carried out by Pope John XXIII (pontificate 1958–1963), who called on clergy to engage more directly with the contemporary world. In 1968 the Latin American Council of Bishops gathered in Medellín, Colombia, and invoked dependency theory as it called on clergy to exercise a "preferential option for the poor," by working toward "social justice," including land redistribution, the recognition of peasants' and labor unions, and denouncing economic dependency and neocolonialism.

Drawing on dependency theory and sometimes verging on revolutionary Marxism, priests attracted to liberation theology often challenged governments and fought against landowners and business owners they saw as oppressors. After the 1970s, Popes John Paul II (pontificate 1978–2005) and Benedict XVI (pontificate 2005–2013) suppressed liberation theology and silenced its most outspoken thinkers. Advocates of liberation theology greeted the naming of a pope from Latin America, Francis, in 2013 as a return to the focus on fighting poverty and social exclusion within the Catholic Church.

import substitution industrialization (ISI)
▶ The use of trade barriers to keep certain products out of one's country so that domestic industry can emerge and produce the same goods.

liberation theology
▶ A movement within the Catholic Church to support the poor in situations of exploitation that emerged with particular force in Latin America in the 1960s.

How did the Cold War shape revolution and decolonization in East and Southeast Asia?

What factors influenced decolonization in Africa after World War II?

Why did populism emerge as such a powerful political force in Latin America?

Why did the world face growing social unrest in the 1960s?

✓ LearningCurve
Check what you know.

Interpreting the Postcolonial Experience

Many intellectuals who came of age during and after the struggle for political emancipation embraced a vision of solidarity among peoples oppressed by colonialism and racism. Some argued that genuine freedom required a total rejection of Western values in addition to an economic and political break with the former colonial powers. Frantz Fanon (1925–1961), a French-trained black psychiatrist from the Caribbean island of Martinique, argued that decolonization is always a violent and totally consuming process whereby one "species" of men, the colonizers, is completely replaced by an absolutely different species—the colonized. Fanon believed that throughout Africa and Asia the former imperialists and their local collaborators—the "white men with black faces"—remained the enemy.

As countries gained independence, some writers looked beyond wholesale rejection of the industrialized powers. They, too, were anti-imperialist, but they were often also activists and cultural nationalists who celebrated the rich histories and cultures of their peoples. Many did not hesitate to criticize their own leaders or fight oppression and corruption.

The Nigerian writer Chinua Achebe (1930–2013) rendered these themes with sharp insight. Achebe sought to restore his people's self-confidence by reinterpreting the past. For Achebe, the "writer in a new nation" had first to embrace the "fundamental theme" that Africans had their own culture before the Europeans came and that it was the duty of writers to help Africans reclaim their past. Achebe took up this task in his 1958 novel *Things Fall Apart*, which brings to life the men and women of an Ibo village at the beginning of the twentieth century, with all their virtues and frailties. In later novels Achebe portrayed the post-independence disillusionment of many writers and intellectuals, which reflected trends in many developing nations in the 1960s and 1970s: the rulers seemed increasingly corrupted by Western luxury and estranged from the rural masses. From the 1970s onward, Achebe was active in the struggle for democratic government in Nigeria.

Novelist V. S. Naipaul, born in Trinidad in 1932 of Indian parents, also castigated governments in the developing countries for corruption, ineptitude, and self-deception. Another of Naipaul's recurring themes is the poignant loneliness and homelessness of people uprooted by colonialism and Western expansion.

> ## QUICK REVIEW

What was dependency theory, and how did activists and reformers apply it to countries in Latin America, Africa, and Asia?

CHAPTER LOCATOR | How did the Cold War and decolonization shape the postwar world?

How did religion and the legacies of colonialism affect the new nations in South Asia and the Middle East?

960 CHAPTER 31 DECOLONIZATION, REVOLUTION, AND THE COLD WAR

How did religion and the legacies of colonialism affect the formation of new nations in South Asia and the Middle East after World War II?

The Non-Aligned Movement

Indira Gandhi, daughter of Jawaharlal Nehru, became prime minister of India in 1966. She is shown here at a 1966 meeting of the Non-Aligned Nations Movement, seated between Yugoslav president Josip Tito (left) and Egyptian president Gamal Abdel Nasser (right). (© Sueddeutsche Zeitung Photo/The Image Works)

AS EUROPE MOVED TOWARD GREATER economic unity in the postwar era, nationalist independence movements in former colonies dramatically reversed centuries of overseas imperial expansion. The three South Asian countries created through independence from Britain and subsequent partition, India, Pakistan, and Bangladesh, reflected the dominant themes of national renaissance and modernization that characterized the end of colonialism, but ethnic and religious rivalries greatly complicated their renewal and development.

The nationalists who guided the formation of modern states in the Arab world struggled to balance Cold War pressures from the United States and the Soviet Union, as well as the tension between secular modernization and Islam. In many cases, these pressures resulted in the formation of one-party dictatorships that became corrupt and failed to alleviate poverty. At the heart of this world, Jewish nationalists founded the state of Israel following the Second World War. The Zionist claim to a homeland came into sharp, and often violent, conflict with the rights and claims of the Palestinian people displaced by the creation of Israel.

| How did the Cold War shape revolution and decolonization in East and Southeast Asia? | What factors influenced decolonization in Africa after World War II? | Why did populism emerge as such a powerful political force in Latin America? | Why did the world face growing social unrest in the 1960s? | ✓ **LearningCurve** Check what you know. |

Independence in India, Pakistan, and Bangladesh

World War II accelerated the drive toward Indian independence begun by Mohandas Gandhi (see page 898). In 1942 Gandhi called on the British to "quit India" and threatened another civil disobedience campaign. He and the other Indian National Congress Party leaders were soon after arrested and were jailed for much of the war. Meanwhile, the Congress Party's prime rival skillfully seized the opportunity to increase its influence.

Muslim League

▶ Political party in colonial India that advocated for a separate Muslim homeland after independence.

The Congress Party's rival was the **Muslim League**, led by the English-educated lawyer Muhammad Ali Jinnah (1876–1948). Jinnah feared Hindu domination of an independent Indian state led by the Congress Party. Asserting the right of Muslim areas to separate from the Hindu majority, Jinnah called on the British government in March 1940 to grant the Muslim and Hindu peoples separate national states, in recognition of what he saw as their essentially separate national identities. Gandhi regarded Jinnah's two-nation theory as untrue and as promising the victory of hate over love.

Britain agreed to speedy independence for India after 1945, but conflicts between Hindu and Muslim nationalists led to murderous clashes in 1946. When it became clear that Jinnah and the Muslim League would accept nothing less than an independent state of Pakistan, the British mediated a partition that created a predominantly Hindu nation and a predominantly Muslim nation. On August 14, 1947, India and Pakistan gained political independence from Britain as two separate nations (Map 31.2).

Massacres and mass expulsions followed independence. Perhaps a hundred thousand Hindus and Muslims were slaughtered, and an estimated 5 million became refugees. Gandhi labored to ease tensions between Hindus and Muslims, but in the aftermath of riots in January 1948, he was killed by a Hindu gunman who resented what he saw as Gandhi's appeasement of Muslims.

Jawaharlal Nehru (1889–1964) and the Indian National Congress Party ruled India for a generation and introduced major social reforms. Hindu women gained legal equality, including the right to vote, to seek divorce, and to marry outside their castes. The constitution abolished the untouchable caste. In practice, less discriminatory atti-

MAP 31.2 ■ The Partition of British India, 1947

Violence and fighting were most intense where there were large Hindu and Muslim minorities — in Kashmir, the Punjab, and Bengal. The tragic result of partition, which occurred repeatedly throughout the world in the twentieth century, was a forced exchange of populations and greater homogeneity on both sides of the border.

CHAPTER LOCATOR | How did the Cold War and decolonization shape the postwar world?

How did religion and the legacies of colonialism affect the new nations in South Asia and the Middle East?

962 CHAPTER 31
DECOLONIZATION, REVOLUTION, AND THE COLD WAR

tudes toward women and untouchables evolved slowly—especially in rural villages, where 85 percent of the people lived.

The Congress Party leadership pursued nationalist, state-driven economic development, but population growth of about 2.4 percent per year consumed much of the increased output of economic expansion. The relocation of millions during the partition of Indian and Pakistan exacerbated poverty. The Congress Party maintained neutrality in the Cold War, distancing itself from both the United States and the Soviet Union. Instead India became one of the most avid advocates of a "third force" of nonaligned nations.

At independence, Pakistan was divided between eastern and western provinces separated by more than a thousand miles of Indian territory, as well as by language, ethnic background, and social custom. The Bengalis of East Pakistan were neglected by the central government, which remained in the hands of West Pakistan's elite after Jinnah's death. In 1971 the Bengalis revolted and won their independence as the new nation of Bangladesh after a violent civil war. Bangladesh, a secular parliamentary democracy, struggled to find political and economic stability amid famines and flooding.

Arab Socialism in the Middle East

In the postwar period, new Arab states in the Middle East emerged from long legacies of colonial rule. These new nations embraced **Arab socialism**, a modernizing, secular, and nationalist project of nation building aimed at economic development, a strong military and Pan-Arab unity that would deter imperial impulses from Europe or the superpowers. Arab socialism focused on modernization and state formation rather than ideological Marxism.

Arab socialism held particular significance for women in Middle Eastern societies. It cast aside religious restrictions on women's dress, education, occupations, and public activities. In countries like Egypt and Iraq, Western dress, the openness of education, and access to professions enjoyed by urban, typically affluent women symbolized an embrace of modernity.

In 1952 army officers overthrew Egypt's monarchy and expelled the British military force that the king had allowed to occupy the country. The movement's leader, Gamal Abdel Nasser (1918–1970), built a nationalist regime aimed at eradicating the vestiges of European colonialism, as well as creating an economic transformation through land redistribution and state support for industrialization. Applying the principles of Arab socialism, Nasser pursued the secularization of Egyptian society and equal opportunity for women and men, and created an extensive social welfare network.

Nasser's National Charter called for the nationalization of railroads, mines, ports, airports, dams, banks, utilities, insurance companies, and heavy industries. In the countryside the size of landholdings were limited and large estates broken up.

In 1956 Nasser took a symbolic and strategic step toward nationalizing Egypt's economy when he ordered the army to take control of the Suez Canal, still held by Britain and France. A coalition of British, French, and Israeli forces invaded to retake the canal. The Soviet Union offered support to Egypt. To prevent Soviet intervention and a Soviet-Egyptian alliance, the United States negotiated a cease-fire that granted Egypt control of the Suez Canal against the wishes

Arab socialism
▶ A modernizing, secular, and nationalist project of nation building aimed at economic development and the development of a strong military.

How did the Cold War shape revolution and decolonization in East and Southeast Asia?

What factors influenced decolonization in Africa after World War II?

Why did populism emerge as such a powerful political force in Latin America?

Why did the world face growing social unrest in the 1960s?

☑ LearningCurve
Check what you know.

963

of the British and French governments. Alongside control of the canal, Nasser's other main economic goal was the construction of a massive hydroelectric dam—the Aswan Dam—on the Nile River, which would provide electricity and control flooding to intensify agriculture. Nasser negotiated the funding and technical expertise for building the damn with both the United States and the Soviet Union, eventually settling on Soviet aid. The Suez crisis and the construction of the Aswan Dam were examples of a nationalist leader like Nasser successfully playing the superpowers against each other.

Nationalist military officers in other Arab countries emulated Nasser's public political profile and socialist developmental projects. In countries like Syria and Iraq, these nationalists formed the Pan-Arab socialist Ba'ath Party. Syria briefly merged with Egypt from 1958 until 1961, forming the United Arab Republic. Ba'athist military officers who resented Nasser's control of Syria revolted against Egypt and established a new national Syrian government dominated by the Ba'ath Party. In Iraq the Ba'ath Party formed part of the military movement that in 1958 overthrew the British-backed monarchy, leading to a long reign by Ba'athist leaders that ended when a U.S. military invasion toppled Saddam Hussein in 2003.

The Arab-Israeli Conflict

Palestinian Arabs, as well as Arabs in new states, strenuously opposed Jewish settlement in Palestine (see pages 894–895). The British announced in early 1947 their intention to withdraw from Palestine in 1948. The difficult problem of a Jewish homeland was dumped in the lap of the United Nations. In November 1947 the UN General Assembly passed a plan to partition Palestine into two separate states—one Arab and one Jewish (Map 31.3). The Jews accepted, and the Arabs rejected, the partition of Palestine.

By early 1948 an undeclared civil war raged in Palestine. When the British mandate ended on May 14, 1948, the Jews proclaimed the state of Israel. Arab countries immediately attacked, but Israeli forces drove off the invaders and conquered more territory. Roughly nine hundred thousand Palestinian refugees fled or were expelled from old Palestine. The war left an enormous legacy of Arab bitterness toward Israel and its political allies, Great Britain and the United States. In 1964 a loose union of Palestinian refugee groups opposed to Israel joined together, under the leadership of Yasir Arafat (1929–2004), to form the **Palestine Liberation Organization (PLO)**.

Palestine Liberation Organization (PLO)

▶ Created in 1964, a loose union of Palestinian refugee groups opposed to Israel and united in the goal of gaining Palestinian home rule.

Nationalist leaders in neighboring Syria and Egypt cultivated political support at home through fierce opposition to Israel and threats to crush it militarily. This tension repeatedly erupted into war. On June 1, 1967, when Syrian and Egyptian armies massed on Israel's borders, the Israeli government launched surprise air strikes that destroyed most of the Egyptian, Syrian, and Jordanian air forces. Over the next five days Israeli armies took control of the Sinai Peninsula and the Gaza Strip from Egypt, the West Bank and East Jerusalem from Jordan, and the Golan Heights from Syria. In the Six-Day War (also known as the 1967 Arab-Israeli War), Israel proved itself to be the pre-eminent military force in the region, and it expanded the territory under its control threefold.

After the war Israel began to build large Jewish settlements in the Gaza Strip and the West Bank, home to millions of Palestinians. On November 22, 1967, the UN Security Council adopted Resolution 242, which contained a "land for peace"

CHAPTER LOCATOR | How did the Cold War and decolonization shape the postwar world?

How did religion and the legacies of colonialism affect the new nations in South Asia and the Middle East?

964 CHAPTER 31 DECOLONIZATION, REVOLUTION, AND THE COLD WAR

MAP 31.3 ■ **The Middle East After 1947**

The partition of Palestine by the United Nations resulted in the creation of Israel in 1948, which faced repeated conflicts with rival Arab states.

Legend:
- Jewish state after UN partition of Palestine, 1947
- Area added by Israel after War of 1948–1949
- Area controlled by Israel after Six-Day War, 1967
- Israeli-occupied area after Yom Kippur War, 1973
- Area united as United Arab Republic, 1958–1961

formula by which Israel was called upon to withdraw from the occupied territories, and in return the Arab states were to withdraw all claims to Israeli territory, cease all hostilities, and recognize the sovereignty of the Israeli state. The tension between rival territorial claims persisted.

QUICK REVIEW <

How did religious divisions complicate India's transition from colony to independent nation?

How did the Cold War shape revolution and decolonization in East and Southeast Asia?

What factors influenced decolonization in Africa after World War II?

Why did populism emerge as such a powerful political force in Latin America?

Why did the world face growing social unrest in the 1960s?

 LearningCurve
Check what you know.

> How did the Cold War shape reconstruction, revolution, and decolonization in East and Southeast Asia?

Communist China Poster Art

One of the most popular art forms in Communist China was poster art, millions of copies of which were printed to adorn the walls of homes, offices, factories, and businesses. This uniquely Chinese form contained neither abstract, modern, or bourgeois elements nor classical Chinese art styles. Such posters glorified the state, its leaders, and the heroes of the revolution. The two young women in this poster wear uniforms and caps bearing the Communist red star, the five points of which represent the five components of Communist society: the youth, the army, the peasants, the workers, and the intellectuals. (Courtesy, Chinese Poster Collection, University of Westminster, London)

> PICTURING THE PAST

ANALYZING THE IMAGE: Who is depicted, and what are they doing? What message do you think the artist seeks to convey with this image?

CONNECTIONS: What social function or application might posters such as this one have? Is this sort of expression unique to Communist societies, or can you think of examples of other types of art that promote public messages?

IN ASIA JAPAN'S DEFEAT ended the Second World War, but other conflicts continued: nationalists in territories colonized by European nations intensified their struggle for independence, and in China Nationalist and Communist armies confronted each other in a renewed civil war. In 1949 Communist forces under Mao Zedong triumphed and established the People's Republic of China. The Communist victory in China shaped the nature of Japan's reconstruction, as its U.S. occupiers determined that an industrially and economically strong Japan would serve as a counterweight to Mao. U.S. fear of the spread of communism drew the country into conflicts in Korea and Vietnam, intensifying the stakes in the decolonization struggle across East and Southeast Asia.

CHAPTER LOCATOR | How did the Cold War and decolonization shape the postwar world? | How did religion and the legacies of colonialism affect the new nations in South Asia and the Middle East?

966 CHAPTER 31
DECOLONIZATION, REVOLUTION, AND THE COLD WAR

The Communist Victory in China

When Japan surrendered to the Allies in August 1945, Communists and Nationalists both rushed to seize evacuated territory. Communists and Nationalists had fought each other before the Second World War, but had put aside their struggle to resist Japanese invasion. With the war over, the Nationalists and Communists resumed their conflict. By 1948 the Nationalist forces disintegrated before the better-led, more determined Communists. The following year Nationalist leader Jiang Jieshi and 2 million mainland Chinese fled to Taiwan, and in October 1949 Mao Zedong proclaimed the People's Republic of China (Map 31.4).

Communism triumphed in China for many reasons. Mao Zedong and the Communists had avoided pitched battles and concentrated on winning peasant support and forming a broad anti-Japanese coalition. By reducing rents, promising land redistribution, enticing intellectuals, and spreading propaganda, they emerged in peasant eyes as the true patriots, the genuine nationalists.

Between 1949 and 1954 the Communists consolidated their rule. They seized the vast landholdings of a minority of landlords and rich peasants and distributed the land to 300 million poor peasants. Meanwhile, as Mao admitted in 1957, mass arrests led to eight hundred thousand "class enemies" being summarily executed; the true figure is probably much higher. Millions more were deported to forced-labor camps.

Mao and the party looked to the Soviet Union for inspiration in the early 1950s. China adopted collective agriculture and Soviet-style five-year plans to promote rapid industrialization. Russian specialists built many Chinese factories, and the Soviets provided considerable economic aid. In the cultural and intellectual realms, too, the Chinese followed the Soviet example. Basic civil and political rights were abolished. Temples and churches were closed. They enthusiastically promoted Soviet Marxist ideas concerning women and the family. Full equality, work outside the home, and state-supported child care became primary goals.

In 1958 China broke from the Marxist-Leninist course of development and began to go its own way. Mao proclaimed a **Great Leap Forward** in which industrial growth would be based on small-scale backyard workshops and steel mills run by peasants living in gigantic self-contained communes. The intended great leap produced an economic disaster, as land in the countryside went untilled when peasants turned to industrial production. As many as 30 million people died in famines that swept the country in 1960–1961. When Soviet premier Nikita Khrushchev criticized Chinese policy in 1960, Mao condemned him and his

MAP 31.4 ■ Decolonization in Asia

After the Second World War, countries colonized by Britain, France, the Netherlands, and the United States gained their independence. In cases such as Vietnam and Indonesia, independence came through armed struggles against colonizers who were reluctant to leave.

Great Leap Forward

▶ Mao Zedong's acceleration of Chinese development in which industrial growth was to be based on small-scale backyard workshops run by peasants living in gigantic self-contained communes.

How did the Cold War shape revolution and decolonization in East and Southeast Asia?

What factors influenced decolonization in Africa after World War II?

Why did populism emerge as such a powerful political force in Latin America?

Why did the world face growing social unrest in the 1960s?

✔ LearningCurve
Check what you know.

Great Proletarian Cultural Revolution

▶ A movement launched by Mao Zedong that attempted to purge the Chinese Communist Party of long-serving bureaucrats and recapture the revolutionary fervor of his guerrilla struggle.

Red Guards

▶ Radical cadres formed of Chinese youth who would attack anyone identified as an enemy of either the Chinese Communist Party or Chairman Mao.

Russian colleagues as detestable "modern revisionists." The Russians cut off economic and military aid, splitting the Communist world apart.

Mao lost influence in the party after the Great Leap Forward fiasco and the Sino-Soviet split, but in 1965 he staged a dramatic comeback, launching the **Great Proletarian Cultural Revolution**. He sought to purge the party and to recapture the revolutionary fervor of the guerrilla struggle (see page 902). The army and the nation's young people responded enthusiastically, organizing themselves into radical cadres called **Red Guards**. Students denounced their teachers and practiced rebellion in the name of revolution. Mao's thoughts, through his speeches and writings, were collected in the *Little Red Book*, which became scripture to the Red Guards.

The Red Guards sought to erase all traces of "feudal" and "bourgeois" culture and thought. Ancient monuments and countless works of art, antiques, and books were destroyed. Party officials, professors, and intellectuals were exiled to remote villages to purify themselves with heavy labor. Universities were shut down for years. Thousands of people died, many of them executed, and millions more were sent to rural forced-labor camps.

Conflict in Korea

As tensions rose in Europe, the Cold War spread to Asia. In 1945 Korea was divided into Soviet and American zones of occupation, which in 1948 became Communist North Korea and anticommunist South Korea. When the Russian-backed Communist forces of North Korea invaded South Korea in spring 1950, President Truman sent U.S. troops to lead a UN coalition force to stop what he interpreted as a coordinated Communist effort to dominate Asia.

The Korean War (1950–1953) was bitterly fought, but ended in a stalemate. The well-equipped North Koreans conquered most of the peninsula, but the South Korean, American, and UN troops rallied and drove their foes north to the Chinese border. At that point China intervened and pushed the South Koreans and Americans back south. In 1953 a fragile truce was negotiated, and the fighting stopped. Thus the United States extended its policy of containing communism to Asia, but drew back from invading Communist China and possibly provoking nuclear war.

Japan's American Reconstruction

Japan, like Germany, was formally occupied by all the Allies, but real power resided in American hands. U.S. general Douglas MacArthur exercised almost absolute authority. MacArthur and the Americans had a revolutionary plan for defeated Japan, introducing reforms designed to make Japan a free, democratic society along American lines.

Japan's sweeping American revolution began with demilitarization and a systematic purge of convicted war criminals and wartime collaborators. The American-dictated constitution of 1946 allowed the emperor to remain the "symbol of the State." Real power resided in the Japanese Diet, whose members were popularly elected. A bill of rights granted basic civil liberties and freed all political prisoners. Article 9 of the new constitution abolished the Japanese armed forces and renounced war. The American occupation left Japan's powerful bureaucracy

The Korean War

SOVIET UNION

CHINA

Chosin Reservoir

Farthest UN advance Nov. 1950

Yalu R.

NORTH KOREA

Pyongyang

Sea of Japan

Demilitarized zone 1953

38th Parallel

Seoul

SOUTH KOREA

Inchon landing Sept. 15, 1950

UN defensive line Sept. 1950

Yellow Sea

Pusan

JAPAN

→ North Korean invasion, June–Sept. 1950

→ UN offensive, Sept.–Nov. 1950

→ Communist Chinese offensive, Nov. 1950–Jan. 1951

CHAPTER LOCATOR | How did the Cold War and decolonization shape the postwar world? | How did religion and the legacies of colonialism affect the new nations in South Asia and the Middle East?

CHAPTER 31

968 DECOLONIZATION, REVOLUTION, AND THE COLD WAR

largely intact and used it to implement fundamental social and economic reforms. The occupation promoted the Japanese labor movement, introduced antitrust laws, and granted Japanese women equality before the law. The occupation also imposed revolutionary land reform that strengthened the small independent farmers who became staunch defenders of postwar democracy.

America's efforts to remake Japan in its own image were powerful but short-lived. As Mao's forces prevailed in China, however, American leaders began to see Japan as a potential ally, not as an object of social reform. The American command began purging leftists and rehabilitating prewar nationalists. When the occupation ended in 1952, Japan regained independence, and the United States retained its vast military complex in Japan. Japan became the chief Asian ally of the United States in its efforts to contain the spread of communism in East Asia.

The Vietnam War

French Indochina experienced the bitterest struggle for independence in Southeast Asia. With financial backing from the United States, France tried to reimpose imperial rule there after the Communist and nationalist guerrilla leader Ho Chi Minh (1890–1969) declared an independent republic in 1945. French forces were decisively defeated in the 1954 Battle of Dien Bien Phu. At the subsequent international peace conference, French Indochina gained independence. Laos and Cambodia became separate states, and Vietnam was temporarily divided into separately governed northern and southern regions pending elections to select a single unified government within two years. The South Vietnamese government refused to hold the elections, and civil war between it and the Communist Democratic Republic of Vietnam, or North Vietnam, broke out.

Cold War fears and U.S. commitment to the ideology of containment drove the United States to get involved in Vietnam. President Dwight D. Eisenhower (elected in 1952) refused to sign the Geneva Accords that temporarily divided the country, and provided military aid to help the south resist North Vietnam. Eisenhower's successor, John F. Kennedy, increased the number of American "military advisers." In 1964 President Lyndon Johnson greatly expanded America's role in the Vietnam conflict.

The American strategy was to "escalate" the war sufficiently to break the will of the North Vietnamese and their southern allies without resorting to "overkill," which might risk war with the entire Communist bloc. South Vietnam received massive military aid. Large numbers of American forces joined in

Baseball in Japan

Though baseball arrived in Japan in the late nineteenth century, it increased in popularity during U.S. occupation. This photo from 1950 shows children in their baseball uniforms, with a U.S. Jeep in the background. (Courtesy: CSU Archives/The Everett Collection)

How did the Cold War shape revolution and decolonization in East and Southeast Asia?

What factors influenced decolonization in Africa after World War II?

Why did populism emerge as such a powerful political force in Latin America?

Why did the world face growing social unrest in the 1960s?

✓ LearningCurve
Check what you know.

The Vietnam War

CHINA

NORTH VIETNAM

Hanoi
U.S. air raids
late 1960s, 1972

Dien Bien Phu

Gulf of Tonkin

LAOS

Gulf of Tonkin incident
Aug. 1964

Vientiane

17th parallel
demarcation line
(Geneva Accords,
1954)

Demilitarized
zone (DMZ)

THAILAND

Da Nang

Invasion of Laos
Feb. 6–March 1971

Ho Chi Minh Trail

Mekong R.

CAMBODIA

Invasion of
Cambodia
April 29–
June 29, 1970

SOUTH VIETNAM

Phnom
Penh

Gulf of
Thailand

Saigon
Surrender of
South Vietnam
1975

combat. The United States bombed North Vietnam with ever-greater intensity. But there was no invasion of North Vietnam or naval blockade of its ports.

Most Americans initially saw the war as part of a legitimate defense against communism, but the combined effect of watching the results of the violent conflict on the nightly television news and experiencing the widening dragnet of a military draft spurred a growing antiwar movement. By 1967 a growing number of critics had denounced the American presence in Vietnam as an intrusion into a complex and distant civil war. The north's Tet Offensive in January 1968, a major attack on South Vietnamese cities, failed militarily but shook Americans' confidence in their government's ability to manage the conflict. Within months President Johnson announced he would not stand for re-election, and he called for negotiations with North Vietnam.

Elected in 1968, President Richard Nixon sought to disengage America gradually from Vietnam. He intensified the continuous bombardment of the enemy while simultaneously pursuing peace talks with the North Vietnamese. He also began a slow process of transferring the burden of the war to the South Vietnamese army, cutting American forces there from 550,000 to 24,000 in four years. Nixon finally reached a peace agreement with North Vietnam in 1973 that allowed the remaining American forces to complete their withdrawal in 1975.

The Vietnamese Communists unified their country in 1975 and began the process of nation building. Millions of Vietnamese civilians faced reprisals for aligning with the United States, including Hmong and Degar peoples (such as the Mnong) and other ethnic minorities. They first fled to refugee camps elsewhere in Southeast Asia and later settled as refugees in the United States. (See "Individuals in Society: Sieng, a Mnong Refugee in an American High School," page 1038.)

> **QUICK REVIEW**

How did the Communist victory in China shape U.S. policy toward Japan and Vietnam?

CHAPTER LOCATOR | How did the Cold War and decolonization shape the postwar world? | How did religion and the legacies of colonialism affect the new nations in South Asia and the Middle East?

970 CHAPTER 31 DECOLONIZATION, REVOLUTION, AND THE COLD WAR

What factors influenced decolonization in Africa after World War II?

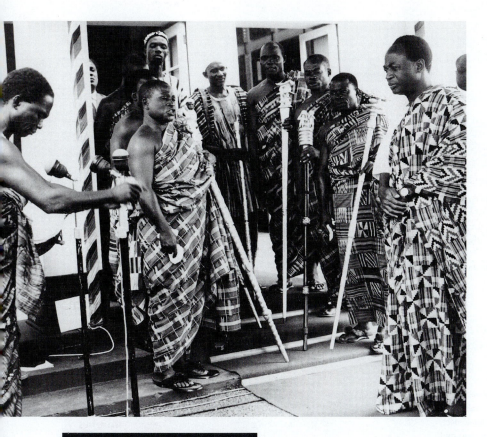

The Opening of Parliament in Ghana

As part of an ancient ritual, two medicine men pour out sacred oil and call on the gods to bless the work of the Second Parliament and President Kwame Nkrumah, standing on the right. The combination of time-honored customs and modern political institutions was characteristic of African states after they secured independence. (AP Photo)

BY 1964 MOST OF AFRICA had gained independence (Map 31.5). Only Portugal's colonies and white-dominated southern Africa remained beyond the reach of African nationalists. The rise of independent states in sub-Saharan Africa came about as a reaction against Western imperialism and through the growth of African nationalism.

The Growth of African Nationalism

African nationalism resembled similar movements in Asia and the Middle East in its reaction against European colonialism, but there were two important differences. First, because the imperial system and Western education did not solidify in Africa until after 1900 (see pages 758–759), national movements came of age in the 1920s and reached maturity after 1945. Second, Africa's multiplicity of ethnic groups, coupled with colonial boundaries that often bore no resemblance to

How did the Cold War shape revolution and decolonization in East and Southeast Asia?	**What factors influenced decolonization in Africa after World War II?**	Why did populism emerge as such a powerful political force in Latin America?	Why did the world face growing social unrest in the 1960s?	☑ LearningCurve Check what you know.

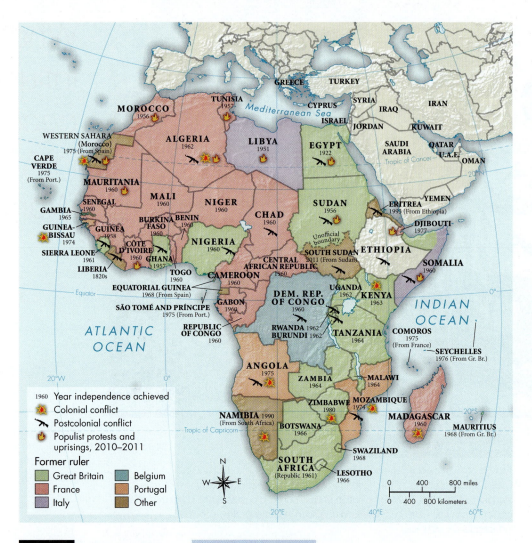

MAP 31.5 ■ Decolonization in Africa, 1947 to the Present

Most African territories achieved statehood by the mid-1960s, as European empires passed away, unlamented.

Map legend:
- 1960 Year independence achieved
- Colonial conflict
- Postcolonial conflict
- Populist protests and uprisings, 2010–2011

Former ruler
- Great Britain
- France
- Italy
- Belgium
- Portugal
- Other

> MAPPING THE PAST

ANALYZING THE MAP: How many African states achieved independence after 1945? How many experienced some sort of postcolonial conflict?

CONNECTIONS: How did the imperialist legacy serve to complicate the transition to stable, independent nations in Africa and Latin America?

existing ethnic geography, greatly complicated the development of political—as distinct from cultural—nationalism. Was a modern national state based on ethnic or clan loyalties? Was it to be a continent-wide union of all African peoples? Would the multiethnic territories carved out by European empires become the new African nations? Such questions were not fully addressed until after 1945.

The first nationalist impetus came from the United States and the Caribbean. The most renowned participant in this "black nationalism" was W. E. B. Du Bois (1868–1963). The cofounder of the National Association for the Advancement of Colored People (NAACP) in the United States, Du Bois organized Pan-African congresses in Paris during the Paris Peace Conference in 1919 and in Brussels

CHAPTER LOCATOR | How did the Cold War and decolonization shape the postwar world? | How did religion and the legacies of colonialism affect the new nations in South Asia and the Middle East?

972 CHAPTER 31
DECOLONIZATION, REVOLUTION, AND THE COLD WAR

in 1921. **Pan-Africanists** sought black solidarity and, eventually, a vast self-governing union of all African peoples. Jamaican-born Marcus Garvey (1887–1940) was the most influential Pan-Africanist, rallying young, educated Africans to his call of "Africa for the Africans."

In the 1920s a surge of anticolonial nationalism swept educated Africans in French and British colonies. African intellectuals in Europe formulated and articulated *négritude*, or blackness: racial pride, self-confidence, and joy in black creativity and the black spirit. This westernized African elite pressed for better access to government jobs, modest steps toward self-government, and an end to humiliating discrimination.

The mass protests that accompanied the deprivations of the Great Depression, in particular the **cocoa holdups** of 1930–1931 and 1937–1938, fueled the new nationalism. Cocoa dominated the British colonial economy in the Gold Coast (which became Ghana). As prices plummeted after 1929, cocoa farmers refused to sell their beans to the British firms that fixed prices and monopolized exports. Now farmers organized cooperatives to cut back production and sell their crops directly to European and American chocolate manufacturers. The cocoa holdups mobilized the population against the foreign companies and demonstrated the power of mass organization and protest.

The repercussions of the Second World War in Africa greatly accelerated the changes begun in the 1930s. Many African soldiers who served in India had been powerfully impressed by Indian nationalism. As African mines and plantations strained to meet wartime demands, towns mushroomed into cities, which became centers of discontent and hardship.

Western imperialism also changed. The principle of self-government was written into the United Nations charter and was supported by Great Britain's postwar Labour government. Thus the key issue for Great Britain's various African colonies was their rate of progress toward self-government. The British and the French were in no rush, but an emerging group of African nationalist leaders was less patient. These postwar African leaders formed an elite by virtue of their advanced Western education, and they were profoundly influenced by Western thought. But compared with the interwar generation of educated Africans, they were more radical and had humbler social origins.

Postwar African nationalists pragmatically accepted prevailing colonial boundaries to avoid border disputes and achieve freedom as soon as possible. Sensing a loss of power, traditional rulers sometimes became the new leaders' worst political enemies. Skillfully, the new leaders channeled postwar hope and discontent into support for mass political organizations that offset this traditional authority. These organizations staged gigantic protests and became political parties.

Ghana Shows the Way

The most charismatic of this generation of African leaders was Kwame Nkrumah (KWA-may ihn-CROO-mah) (1909–1972). Nkrumah spent ten years studying in the United States, where he was influenced by European socialists and Marcus Garvey. Under his leadership the Gold Coast — which he renamed "Ghana" — became the first sub-Saharan state to emerge from colonialism.

Nkrumah came to power by building a radical party that appealed particularly to modern groups — veterans, merchant women, union members, urban toughs,

Pan-Africanists
▶ People who sought black solidarity and envisioned a vast self-governing union of all African peoples.

cocoa holdups
▶ Mass protests in the 1930s by Gold Coast producers of cocoa who refused to sell their beans to British firms and instead sold them directly to European and American chocolate manufacturers.

How did the Cold War shape revolution and decolonization in East and Southeast Asia?

What factors influenced decolonization in Africa after World War II?

Why did populism emerge as such a powerful political force in Latin America?

Why did the world face growing social unrest in the 1960s?

✓ LearningCurve
Check what you know.

973

and cocoa farmers. Rejecting halfway measures, Nkrumah and his Convention People's Party staged strikes and riots.

After he was arrested in 1950, Nkrumah campaigned from jail and saw his party win a smashing victory in the 1951 national elections. Called from prison to head the transitional government, Nkrumah and his nationalist party defeated westernized moderates and more traditional political rivals in free elections. In 1957 Ghana became independent. After Ghana's breakthrough, independence for other African colonies followed rapidly. The main problem in some colonies was the permanent white settlers, not the colonial officials. Wherever white settlers were numerous, as in Kenya, Algeria, and Rhodesia, they fought to preserve their privileged position.

French-Speaking Regions

Decolonization took a different course in French-speaking Africa. The events in the French North African colony of Algeria in the 1950s and early 1960s help clarify France's attitude toward its sub-Saharan African colonies.

Algeria's large, and mostly Catholic, European population—known as the **pieds-noirs** (black feet) because its members wore black shoes instead of sandals—was determined to keep Algeria part of France. In November 1954 Algeria's anticolonial movement, the **National Liberation Front** (FLN), began a bitter war for independence. After the FLN won and created an independent Algerian state in 1962, an estimated 900,000 of the 1.25 million Europeans and indigenous Jews fled.

The long and violent anticolonial war in Algeria, following Indochina's military victory, sharply divided France and undermined its political stability. As a result, it was difficult for France to respond to nationalists in its other African colonies until Charles de Gaulle returned to power in 1958. Seeking to maximize France's influence over the future independent nations, de Gaulle devised a divide-and-rule strategy. He divided the French West Africa and French Equatorial Africa federations into thirteen separate governments. Plebiscites were called in each territory to ratify the new arrangement. An affirmative vote meant continued ties with France; a negative vote signified immediate independence and a complete break with France.

De Gaulle's gamble was shrewd. The educated black elite identified with France and dreaded an abrupt separation. They also wanted French aid to continue. France had given the vote to its educated colonial elite after the Second World War, and about forty Africans held French parliamentary seats after 1946. For these reasons, French Africa's leaders tended to be moderate in their pursuit of independence.

In Guinea, however, a young nationalist named Sékou Touré (1922–1984) led his people to overwhelmingly reject the new constitution in 1958. Inspired by Ghana's Nkrumah, Touré laid it out to de Gaulle face-to-face: "We have one prime and essential need: our dignity. But there is no dignity without freedom. . . . We prefer freedom in poverty to opulence in slavery."[2]

Though peoples that had been colonized by France and Britain often found paths for independence, those of other regions of Africa struggled with the colonial policies of other European nations less prepared to acknowledge the wave of decolonization. Portugal's dictatorship hoped to keep its colonies in perpetuity.

pieds-noirs
▶ The predominantly Catholic French population in the French colony of Algeria, called "black feet" because they wore black shoes instead of sandals.

National Liberation Front
▶ The victorious anticolonial movement in Algeria.

To ensure this, the Portuguese regime intensified white settlement and repression of nationalist groups in its colonies of Angola and Mozambique.

Belgium, a long-time practitioner of colonial paternalism coupled with harsh, selfish rule in its enormous Congo colony (see page 754), had always discouraged the development of an educated elite. When Belgium abruptly decided to grant independence in 1959 after intense riots, the fabric of Congo's government and society broke down. The mineral-rich nation stabilized under the U.S.-backed dictatorship of Mobutu Sese Seko, who renamed the country Zaire. Mobutu's corruption deepened poverty as the tremendous wealth generated from mining went into the hands of foreign companies and Mobutu's family and cronies.

QUICK REVIEW

Why was the process of decolonization more difficult and tumultuous in some African colonies than in others?

| How did the Cold War shape revolution and decolonization in East and Southeast Asia? | **What factors influenced decolonization in Africa after World War II?** | Why did populism emerge as such a powerful political force in Latin America? | Why did the world face growing social unrest in the 1960s? | ✓ LearningCurve Check what you know. |

975

Why did populism emerge as such a powerful political force in Latin America?

Revolutionaries in Cuba

Che Guevara (left) and Fidel Castro (right), whose successful revolution in Cuba inspired armed movements across Latin America. (© United Archives/Topfoto/The Image Works)

IN THE DECADES AFTER THE SECOND WORLD WAR, Latin American nations struggled to find a political balance that integrated long-excluded groups such as women, workers, and peasants in the face of growing anxiety and resistance by liberal oligarchs. Populist politicians rose to power by building a base of support among the urban and rural poor. They often combined charisma with promises of social change, particularly through national economic development that would create more and better job opportunities. Revolutionary leader Fidel Castro carved an alternative path in Cuba. Castro went beyond the reforms advocated by populists and sought an outright revolutionary transformation of Cuban society.

Economic Nationalism in Mexico

Although Spain's Central and South American colonies and Portuguese Brazil won political independence in the early nineteenth century, the new nations struggled to achieve genuine economic independence. Latin American countries

CHAPTER LOCATOR | How did the Cold War and decolonization shape the postwar world? | How did religion and the legacies of colonialism affect the new nations in South Asia and the Middle East?

had developed as producers of foodstuffs and raw materials exported to Europe and the United States in return for manufactured goods and capital investment. This exchange brought considerable economic development but exacted a heavy price: neocolonialism (see page 819). The Great Depression further hampered development and provoked a shift toward **economic nationalism**, a systematic effort by nationalists to end neocolonialism and to free their national economies from U.S. and western European influences.

Economic nationalism and industrialization were especially successful in the largest countries in Latin America: Mexico, Brazil, and Argentina. In Mexico, Lázaro Cárdenas, elected president in 1934, carried out sweeping economic reforms. Millions of acres of large estates were divided among small farmers or were returned undivided to Indian communities. State-supported Mexican businessmen built many small factories to meet domestic needs. In 1938 Cárdenas nationalized the petroleum industry. The 1930s also saw the flowering of a distinctive Mexican culture that proudly celebrated cultural mixture and intermarriage between Indians, Africans, and Europeans.

The presidents who followed Cárdenas used the state's power to promote industrialization, and the Mexican economy grew consistently through the 1970s. While the country's economic health improved, social inequities remained. The upper and middle classes reaped the lion's share of the benefits of this economic growth.

economic nationalism

▶ A systematic effort by Latin American nationalists to end neocolonialism and to free their national economies from American and western European influences.

The Plaza of the Three Cultures in Tlatelolco, Mexico City

Modern apartment buildings rise behind Aztec ruins and a Spanish church built in 1536. Mexican authorities massacred student protesters at this plaza to suppress unrest before the 1968 Summer Olympics in the city. (© Macduff Everton/The Image Works)

How did the Cold War shape revolution and decolonization in East and Southeast Asia?	What factors influenced decolonization in Africa after World War II?	**Why did populism emerge as such a powerful political force in Latin America?**	Why did the world face growing social unrest in the 1960s?	✔ LearningCurve Check what you know.

Populism in Argentina and Brazil

populists

▶ Politicians who appealed to the working class and poor with appeals to nationalism and to social justice.

Argentina and Brazil's postwar economic development was shaped by a rising cadre of **populist** politicians. Earlier liberal politicians had dismissed the electoral potential of the working class and denied it the right to vote. But as pressure for universal voting rights intensified, first for men and then for women, large numbers of Latin Americans who had never been given a political voice gained it, beginning with universal male suffrage in Argentina in 1912 and Mexico in 1917. Women gained the right to vote across Latin America in the decades that followed. To appeal to new voters, populist candidates promised schools and hospitals, higher wages, and nationalist projects that would create more industrial jobs.

At the turn of the century Argentina's economy prospered through its liberal export boom (see Chapter 27), but industrialization followed only haltingly and the economy faltered. Populist Juan Perón, an army colonel, was elected president in 1946 with support of Argentina's unions. Juan Perón's charismatic wife Eva, known by her nickname Evita, played a vital role in promoting Perón. Once in power, Perón embarked on an ambitious scheme to transform Argentina's economy: the government would purchase all of the country's agricultural exports in order to negotiate their sale abroad at a higher price. He would reinvest the profits in industry and raise worker wages to stimulate demand.

Perón's scheme worked in the immediate postwar period, when European agricultural production had not yet recovered and the international price of Argentina's exports was high. But when commodity prices declined, Perón reduced government payments to farmers, who ceased to bring their harvests to market. In the coming decades Argentina never returned to the high rates of economic growth it enjoyed at the beginning of the century. Despite these economic setbacks, Perón initially remained highly popular, buoyed by the popular appeals made by Evita. (See "Individuals in Society: Eva Perón," page 979.)

After Evita died of cancer in 1952, much of the magic slipped away. Amid the stagnating economy even Perón's union supporters faltered, and he responded harshly to press criticism. In 1955 the armed forces deposed Perón, and he fled to exile in Spain. The military ruled Argentina for the next three years. Nonetheless, Perón remained the most popular politician in the country. Presidential candidates could not win without discreetly winning the exiled Perón's endorsement, and this veiled support for Perón by civilian leaders prompted repeated military interventions. The 1955–1958 military government was the first of several, including a dictatorship that ruled from 1966 to 1973.

In Brazil, reacting against the economic and political liberalism through which coffee planters dominated the country, the armed forces installed a state governor, Getúlio Vargas, as president in 1930. Vargas initiated democratic reforms, but veered into a nationalist dictatorship known as the "New State" (1937–1945), inspired by European fascism. Despite his harsh treatment of opponents, he was popular with the masses and was elected to a new term as president in 1950, now reinvented as a populist who promised nationalist economic reforms that would favor industrial workers. The armed forces and conservatives mistrusted Vargas's appeals to workers and organized to depose him in 1954. Before they could act, Vargas killed himself.

Juscelino Kubitschek, elected in 1955, continued to build upon Vargas's populism and nationalism. Between 1956 and 1960 Kubitschek's government borrowed

CHAPTER LOCATOR | How did the Cold War and decolonization shape the postwar world? | How did religion and the legacies of colonialism affect the new nations in South Asia and the Middle East?

CHAPTER 31

978 DECOLONIZATION, REVOLUTION, AND THE COLD WAR

INDIVIDUALS IN SOCIETY
Eva Perón

When Eva Perón died of cancer at age thirty-three on July 26, 1952, the state radio broadcaster sadly announced that "today at 20:25 Eva Perón, Spiritual Leader of the Nation, entered immortality." Argentina went into official mourning; although Perón had never held an official political office, she was accorded a state funeral. Immediately after her death her corpse was embalmed, with the intention of putting it on public display forever in a planned memorial larger than the Statue of Liberty.

Often called Evita (the Spanish diminutive of Eva), she was one of five illegitimate children born near Buenos Aires to Juan Duarte and Juana Ibarguren. Duarte returned to his legitimate wife and children when Eva was a year old, leaving Juana and her children destitute and dependent on Juana's sewing for their existence. As they grew older all the children had to work, but Eva apparently also dreamed of becoming an actress.

At fifteen Eva Duarte moved to the cosmopolitan city of Buenos Aires. Although she had little formal education and no connections, she possessed beauty and charisma, and soon she joined a professional theater group with which she toured nationally. She also modeled, appeared in a few movies, and then obtained regular employment as a character on a radio series. By 1943, although only twenty-three years old, she was one of the highest-paid actresses in the country.

In 1943 Eva met widowed Colonel Juan Perón, then secretary of labor and social welfare in the military government that had seized power that year. Juan Perón had grand ambitions, intending to run for president. Eva Duarte became his partner and confidante, and she won him support among the Argentine masses. In 1945 Juan Perón and Eva Duarte married.

A year later Perón won the presidency. Eva had gone out on the campaign trail and organized support for her husband from *los descamisados* (the shirtless ones), her name for Argentina's poor. When Perón assumed the presidency, Eva, though not officially appointed, became the secretary of labor. Having come from a childhood of poverty herself, she now worked tirelessly for the poor, for the working classes, and with organized labor. She instituted a number of social welfare measures and promoted a new Ministry of Health, which resulted in the creation of new hospitals and disease-treatment programs. In 1948 she established the Eva Perón Welfare Foundation, which grew into an immense semiofficial welfare agency, helping the poor throughout Argentina and even contributing to victims of natural disasters in other countries.

Eva Perón waves to supporters from the balcony of the presidential palace, Casa Rosada, in Buenos Aires, on October 17, 1951. (Archivo Clarin/AP Photo)

From early on, Eva Perón had supported women's suffrage, and in September 1947 Argentine women won the right to vote. Eva then formed the Female Perónist Party, which by 1951 had five hundred thousand members. Thousands of Argentine women have credited Eva's example as a reason for their involvement in politics. In 1951 she seemed ready to run for vice president beside her husband. The huge base of women, the poor, and workers assured them victory. Her declining health, however, forced her to turn down the nomination. Juan Perón won the election by over 30 percent, but when Eva died the following year, his authoritarian rule and bad economic policies lost him support, and a military junta forced him into exile.

Eva Perón's life story is an amazing one, but what happened following her death is just as extraordinary. Before the massive monument intended to hold her embalmed body could be built, the military seized power, and her body disappeared. Seventeen years later the generals finally revealed that it was in a tomb in Milan, Italy. Juan Perón, living in Spain with his third wife, had the body exhumed and brought to Spain, where he kept it in his house. Perón returned to Argentina in 1973 and won the presidential election, but died the following year. His wife, Isabelita Perón, succeeded him as president. Juan and Eva's bodies were briefly displayed together at his funeral and then, finally, buried.

Source: Nicholas Fraser and Marysa Navarro, *Evita: The Real Life of Eva Perón* (New York: Norton, 1976).

QUESTIONS FOR ANALYSIS

1. Why do you think Eva Perón was adored by the Argentine people when she died?
2. What were some of the welfare and government programs that Eva Perón promoted?

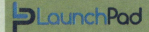

ONLINE DOCUMENT PROJECT

What were the political implications of Eva Perón's public presentation of herself? Examine photos of Eva Perón, and then complete a quiz and writing assignment based on the evidence and details from this chapter. *See inside the front cover to learn more.*

heavily from abroad to promote industry and build the futuristic new capital of Brasília in the midst of a wilderness.

In 1961 leftist populist João Goulart became Brazil's president. Goulart sought social and economic reforms, including the redistribution of land and limits on the profits multinational corporations could take out of the country. In 1964 a military coup backed by the United States deposed Goulart. The armed forces held power for the next twenty-one years.

Communist Revolution in Cuba

Cuba remained practically an American colony until the 1930s, when a series of rulers with socialist and Communist leanings seized and lost power. Cuba's political institutions were weak and its politicians corrupt. In March 1952 Fulgencio Batista (1901–1973) staged a coup with American support and instituted a repressive authoritarian regime that favored wealthy Cubans and multinational corporations.

The Cuban Revolution led by Fidel Castro (b. 1927) began in 1953 and finally overthrew the Cuban government on New Year's Day 1959. Castro had not come to power as a Communist: his main aim had been to regain control of Cuba's economy and politics from the United States. But U.S. efforts to overthrow him and to starve the Cuban economy drove him to form an alliance with the Soviet Union, which agreed to place nuclear missiles in Cuba to protect against another U.S. invasion. When President John F. Kennedy demanded the missiles be removed, the military and diplomatic brinksmanship of the 1962 Cuban missile crisis ensued. In 1963 the United States placed a complete commercial and diplomatic embargo on Cuba that has remained in place ever since.

Castro now declared himself a Marxist-Leninist and relied on Soviet military and economic support. Under Castro, medical attention and education became free and widely accessible. But such reforms were achieved at great cost and through the suppression of political dissent. Political opponents were jailed or exiled. Meanwhile, economic reforms were improvised with ideological objectives rather than economic logic, which often resulted in productive inefficiency and scarcity of foodstuffs and other goods.

Cuba

> **QUICK REVIEW**

What groups in Latin American society found the populist message appealing? What groups were most actively opposed to the implementation of the populist agenda?

CHAPTER LOCATOR | How did the Cold War and decolonization shape the postwar world? | How did religion and the legacies of colonialism affect the new nations in South Asia and the Middle East?

CHAPTER 31
980   DECOLONIZATION, REVOLUTION, AND THE COLD WAR

Registering to Vote

African American residents of Hattiesburg, Mississippi, register to vote in 1964. The sign on the wall indicates that their names will be published in the newspaper for two consecutive weeks, making African Americans vulnerable to violent reprisals for registering to vote. (© 1976 Matt Herron/ Take Stock/The Image Works)

Why did the world face growing social unrest in the 1960s?

IN THE 1950S AND 1960S the United States and the Soviet Union, as well as both western and eastern Europe, rebounded economically from the combined strains of the Great Depression and the Second World War. But these decades of economic growth did not resolve underlying tensions and conflicts.

The Soviet Union Struggles to Move Beyond Stalin

Though the "Great Patriotic War of the Fatherland" had fostered Russian nationalism and a relaxation of totalitarian terror, Stalin's new rivalry with the United States provided him with an excuse to re-establish a harsh dictatorship. Stalin reasserted control of the government and society through the reintroduction of five-year plans. Once again, Soviet central planners favored heavy and military industry over consumer goods, housing, and collectivized agriculture. Stalin exported this system to eastern Europe. Rigid ideological indoctrination, attacks

How did the Cold War shape revolution and decolonization in East and Southeast Asia?

What factors influenced decolonization in Africa after World War II?

Why did populism emerge as such a powerful political force in Latin America?

Why did the world face growing social unrest in the 1960s?

✓ LearningCurve
Check what you know.

981

on religion, and a lack of civil liberties were soon facts of life in the region's one-party states. Only Yugoslavia's Josip Tito (1892–1980) could resist Soviet domination successfully because there was no Russian army in Yugoslavia.

In 1953 the aging Stalin died. Even as his heirs struggled for power, they realized that reforms were necessary because of the widespread fear and hatred of Stalin's political terrorism. They curbed secret police powers and gradually closed many forced-labor camps. Change was also necessary for economic reasons. Agriculture was in bad shape, and shortages of consumer goods discouraged hard work. Moreover, Stalin's foreign policy had led directly to a strong Western alliance, isolating the Soviet Union.

The Communist Party leadership was badly split on just how much change to permit. Reformers, led by Nikita Khrushchev (1894–1971), argued for major innovations and won. Khrushchev spoke out in a "secret speech" against Stalin and his crimes and initiated a series of reforms known as **de-Stalinization** in the West. Khrushchev eased foreign policy, declaring that "peaceful coexistence" with capitalism was possible. The government relaxed controls over heavy industry and the military and shifted some resources from these areas to consumer goods, improving standards of living substantially throughout the 1960s.

De-Stalinization stimulated rebelliousness in the eastern European satellites. Poland won greater autonomy in 1956 after extensive protests forced the Soviets to allow a new Communist government. The people of Budapest, Hungary, installed a liberal Communist reformer as their new chief in October 1956. The rebellion was short-lived. After the new government promised free elections and renounced Hungary's military alliance with Moscow, the Soviet Army invaded and crushed the revolution, killing around 2,700 protesters. When the United States did not come to their aid, Hungarians and most eastern Europeans concluded that their only hope was to strive for small domestic gains while obediently following Russia in foreign affairs.

In August 1961, amid concerns about growing defections to the West, the East German government began construction of a wall between East and West Berlin. It also built a ninety-mile-long barrier between the three allied sectors of West Berlin and East Germany, thereby completely cutting off West Berlin.

By late 1962 party opposition to Khrushchev's policies had gained momentum. De-Stalinization was seen as a dangerous threat to party authority. Moreover, Khrushchev's policy toward the West was erratic and ultimately unsuccessful. In 1962 Khrushchev ordered the installation of nuclear missiles in Cuba, triggering the military standoff known as the Cuban missile crisis. After a tense diplomatic crisis Khrushchev backed down and removed the missiles. Two years later, Communist Party leaders removed Khrushchev in a bloodless coup. After Leonid Brezhnev (1906–1982) and his supporters took over in 1964, they talked quietly of Stalin's "good points," stopped further liberalization, and launched a massive arms buildup.

de-Stalinization

▶ The liberalization of the post-Stalin Soviet Union, led by reformer Nikita Khrushchev during his years as the head of the Soviet Union (1953–1964).

Western Europe's Postwar Challenge

In 1945 much of western Europe was devastated by the war, and prospects for a swift recovery looked bleak. Nonetheless, in the decades that followed, demo-

CHAPTER LOCATOR | How did the Cold War and decolonization shape the postwar world? | How did religion and the legacies of colonialism affect the new nations in South Asia and the Middle East?

982 CHAPTER 31 DECOLONIZATION, REVOLUTION, AND THE COLD WAR

cratic governments took root throughout western Europe and thrived in an atmosphere of civil liberties and individual freedom. Progressive Catholics and their Christian Democratic political parties were particularly influential. In Italy and Germany Christian Democrats took power, rejecting fascism and putting their faith in democracy. Socialists and Communists active in the resistance against Hitler returned with renewed prestige, especially in France and Italy. In the immediate postwar years welfare measures such as family allowances, health insurance, and increased public housing were enacted throughout much of Europe.

The Cold War prevented the allies occupying Germany from finding a political settlement, resulting in a partition between a Soviet-controlled German Democratic Republic (East Germany) and a Federal Republic of Germany (West Germany). Under its first postwar chancellor, Konrad Adenauer, West Germany recovered from near total devastation in World War II and became the leading economic power in Europe. A fierce opponent of communism, Adenauer forged close ties with the United States and fully supported efforts at European unity. He also initiated dialogues with leaders of Europe's Jewish community and with Israel to encourage a reconciliation of the Jewish and German peoples following the Holocaust.

European nations followed different paths to postwar recovery. West Germany balanced a free-market economy with an extensive social welfare network, while France resorted to central planning. But amid the destruction and uncertainty brought by two world wars caused by Europeans and fought in Europe, many Europeans believed that only unity could forestall future European conflicts.

The experience of close cooperation among European states for Marshall Plan aid led European leaders to pursue economic unity. France, West Germany, Italy, Belgium, the Netherlands, and Luxembourg joined together in 1952 to control and integrate their steel and coal production. In 1957 the six nations of the Coal and Steel Community signed the Treaty of Rome, creating the European Economic Community, popularly known as the **Common Market**. The treaty's primary goal was a gradual reduction of all tariffs among the six in order to create a single market.

Common Market
▶ The European Economic Community created in 1957.

The Common Market was a great success, encouraging hopes of rapid progress toward political as well as economic union. In the 1960s, however, a resurgence of more traditional nationalism in France led by Charles de Gaulle, French president from 1958 to 1969, frustrated these hopes. Viewing the United States as the main threat to genuine French independence, he withdrew all French military forces from NATO and developed France's own nuclear weapons. De Gaulle also thwarted initial efforts of Denmark, Ireland, Norway, and the United Kingdom to join the Common Market.

Migrant laborers, mainly from southern Italy, North Africa, Turkey, Greece, and Yugoslavia, also shaped western European societies and drove their economic recovery. Tens of millions of migrant workers made it possible for western European economies to continue to grow beyond their postwar labor capacity. Governments at first labeled the migrants as "guest workers" to signal their temporary status, though in practice many chose to remain in their new homes. As their communities became more settled, migrants faced a backlash from majority populations.

How did the Cold War shape revolution and decolonization in East and Southeast Asia?

What factors influenced decolonization in Africa after World War II?

Why did populism emerge as such a powerful political force in Latin America?

Why did the world face growing social unrest in the 1960s?

✔ LearningCurve
Check what you know.

983

America's Economic Boom and Civil Rights Revolution

The Second World War ended the Great Depression in the United States, bringing about a great economic boom. By the end of the war, the United States had the strongest economy and held several advantages over its past commercial rivals: its industry and infrastructure had not been damaged by war. In the first decades following the war, U.S. manufactured goods saturated markets around the world.

Postwar America experienced a genuine social revolution as well: after a long struggle African Americans began to experience major victories against the deeply entrenched system of segregation and discrimination. In 1954 the NAACP won a landmark decision in the Supreme Court, which ruled in *Brown v. Board of Education* that "separate educational facilities are inherently unequal." Civil rights leader Martin Luther King, Jr. (1929–1968) challenged inequality by using Gandhian methods of nonviolent peaceful resistance.

With African American support in key Northern states, Democrat Lyndon Johnson won the 1964 presidential election. Johnson secured enactment of the 1964 **Civil Rights Act**, which prohibited discrimination in public services and on the job, and the 1965 Voting Rights Act, which prohibited discrimination in voting. In the mid-1960s President Johnson began an "unconditional war on poverty" that promised the kind of fundamental social reform that had succeeded in western Europe after the Second World War.

Civil Rights Act

▶ The 1964 U.S. act that prohibited discrimination in public services and on the job.

The World in 1968

In 1968 pressures for social change boiled over into protests worldwide. Students across Latin America and western Europe, Czechoslovaks weary of the harshness of Soviet domination, activists for civil rights and women's rights in the United States along with opponents of the U.S. war in Vietnam all took loudly to the streets. The world seemed to be at a tipping point between the goals of conservative defenders of the existing social and political order and those of a young generation energized by the possibility of radical and swift change.

In Czechoslovakia the "Prague Spring"—a brief period of liberal reform and loosening of political controls—unfolded as reformers in the Czechoslovakian Communist Party gained a majority and replaced a long-time Stalinist leader with Alexander Dubček (DOOB-chehk), whose new government launched dramatic reforms. Dubček and his allies called for "socialism with a human face." Communist leaders in the Soviet Union and other eastern European states feared that they would face similar demands for reform from their own citizens. Protests against the excesses of Communist rule erupted in Poland and Yugoslavia.

In France, students went on strike over poor university conditions. When government forces punished those protesters harshly, a much larger and more radical wave of student protests erupted. The students were soon joined by a general strike carried out by France's labor unions. Similar student movements erupted across western Europe.

In Latin America students rose in protest as well. In Argentina students in the industrial city of Córdoba went on strike against the military dictatorship that had been in place since 1966. Joined by factory workers, the protesters took control of the city in an event known as the Cordobazo. In Brazil a national student

CHAPTER LOCATOR | How did the Cold War and decolonization shape the postwar world? | How did religion and the legacies of colonialism affect the new nations in South Asia and the Middle East?

984 CHAPTER 31 DECOLONIZATION, REVOLUTION, AND THE COLD WAR

strike challenged the military dictatorship that had been in power since 1964. In Mexico City, where the Olympic games were scheduled to be held, students used the international visibility of the event to protest the heavy-handed government. In each case the students challenged the authoritarian excesses of their regimes, but they were also animated by the example offered by revolutionary Cuba, which suggested that directly confronting the political regime could bring revolutionaries to power, and that once in power, they could quickly transform their societies.

In the United States protests against the Vietnam War and against the military draft erupted on college campuses nationwide. These protests marked an increase in popular mobilization in a country where civil rights marches in the South now extended to protests against discrimination and police violence in cities like Boston and Chicago. Protesters around the world were aware of each other, and their sense that they participated in a worldwide movement against the abuses of the established order empowered them.

Protesters and reformers faced violent reactions from the powerful political and economic groups they challenged. If 1968 seemed to be the peak of young radicals' aspirations for social transformation, this was because it also marked the intensification of the reaction against their efforts. Conservatives reacted against more than the protests of 1968: they sought to slow or sometimes reverse the dramatic changes that had taken place in the postwar era.

In October 1968 Soviet troops and tanks flooded into Czechoslovakia, crushing the Prague Spring and unseating Dubček. Supporters of the Prague Spring faced harsh persecution. In Cuba, where revolutionary dreams of liberation were increasingly subsidized by the Soviet Union, Castro was obligated to support the Soviet crackdown.

Around the world, protests were followed by violent crackdowns. The Mexican government massacred protesters, many of them students in Tlatelolco. The Argentine army and paramilitary groups launched a violent campaign to retake the city of Córdoba from protesters. In Brazil, the military regime reacted to protests by imposing a harsh new national security law that made criticizing the government an offense punishable by imprisonment. Around the world, revolutionary violence met with increasingly violent repression.

The Soviet Invasion of Prague, 1968

Czech demonstrators throw torches and wave flags in an attempt to stop a tank as the Soviet army crushes the protests of the Prague Spring in 1968. (© Libor Hajsky/epa/Corbis)

QUICK REVIEW <

What tensions and conflicts fueled the protest movements of the late 1960s?

| How did the Cold War shape revolution and decolonization in East and Southeast Asia? | What factors influenced decolonization in Africa after World War II? | Why did populism emerge as such a powerful political force in Latin America? | **Why did the world face growing social unrest in the 1960s?** | ✓ LearningCurve Check what you know. |

CHAPTER SUMMARY

The decades after the Second World War were an era of rebuilding after the destruction caused by years of war. In Germany and Japan in particular, rebuilding also meant charting a new political and economic path.

For the United States and the Soviet Union rebuilding had other meanings. For both countries, it meant building a military and ideological complex with which to confront each other in the Cold War. This involved building rival networks of military and economic alliances. In each country individually, rebuilding took other forms: in the Soviet Union it meant seeking the means to reform the system of political terror and coercion through which Stalin had ruled; in the United States it meant struggling to overcome the structures of white supremacism and other forms of racial discrimination that divided society and oppressed millions of citizens.

In Asia, Africa, and the Middle East rebuilding meant dismantling European colonialism to reconstitute independent states or to build new independent states. Here the idea of rebuilding took on its deepest meaning: learning how to replace not just colonial institutions but colonial mentalities, patterns of production, forms of education, and ways of relating to each other with new versions that were not dictated by colonizers.

In Latin America rebuilding meant finding the means to overcome patterns of social exclusion—especially of rural workers—that were legacies of its colonial experience, as well as finding a political formula that could integrate long-excluded groups. It also meant finding the means to build industry and develop economically, overcoming patterns of dependency. In the end, the decades after 1945 showed how much was possible through mass movements, advancing industrialization, and political self-determination. But the balance of these years also showed how much more work remained to overcome poverty, underdevelopment, and neocolonialism.

 **CONNECTIONS** The great transformations experienced by peoples around the world following the Second World War can best be compared to the age of revolution in the late eighteenth and early nineteenth centuries (see Chapter 22). In both eras peoples rose up to undertake the political, economic, social, and cultural transformation of their societies, and in both eras history seemed to accelerate as a quick succession of events had impacts across the globe.

Liberation movements spanning the globe sought not only to end imperial domination and remove social boundaries imposed by white racism, but also to make deeper changes in how peoples perceived themselves and their societies. As radical and new as these ideas were, they nonetheless owed much to the Enlightenment ideals about liberal individual rights.

Though the social revolutions in countries like China and Cuba and the independence movements across Africa, Asia, and the Middle East brought unprecedented

CHAPTER LOCATOR | How did the Cold War and decolonization shape the postwar world? | How did religion and the legacies of colonialism affect the new nations in South Asia and the Middle East?

986 CHAPTER 31 DECOLONIZATION, REVOLUTION, AND THE COLD WAR

deep and fast changes, they were only the first steps in remaking societies that had been created by centuries of colonialism. Uprooting the legacies of colonialism—in the form of poverty, continued domination of economies by foreign powers, limited industrialization, and weak states—remained a daunting challenge that societies continued to face in the future.

ONLINE DOCUMENT PROJECT

Gender Roles and Populism in Argentina

What were the political implications of Eva Perón's public presentation of herself?

Examine photos of Eva Perón, and then complete a quiz and writing assignment based on the evidence and details from this chapter. *See inside the front cover to learn more.*

| How did the Cold War shape revolution and decolonization in East and Southeast Asia? | What factors influenced decolonization in Africa after World War II? | Why did populism emerge as such a powerful political force in Latin America? | Why did the world face growing social unrest in the 1960s? | ✔ LearningCurve Check what you know. |

CHAPTER 31 STUDY GUIDE

STEP **1** **GET STARTED ONLINE**

LearningCurve

Now that you've read the chapter, make it stick by completing the LearningCurve activity.

STEP **2** **EXPLAIN WHY IT MATTERS**

Put your reading into practice. Identify each term below, and then explain why it matters in world history.

TERM	WHO OR WHAT & WHEN	WHY IT MATTERS
Cold War (p. 954)		
Truman Doctrine (p. 955)		
Marshall Plan (p. 955)		
NATO (p. 956)		
superpowers (p. 956)		
dependency theory (p. 958)		
modernization theory (p. 958)		
import substitution industrialization (ISI) (p. 959)		
liberation theology (p. 959)		
Muslim League (p. 962)		
Arab socialism (p. 963)		
Palestine Liberation Organization (PLO) (p. 964)		
Great Leap Forward (p. 967)		
Great Proletarian Cultural Revolution (p. 968)		
Red Guards (p. 968)		
Pan-Africanists (p. 973)		
cocoa holdups (p. 973)		
pieds-noirs (p. 974)		
National Liberation Front (p. 974)		
economic nationalism (p. 977)		
populists (p. 978)		
de-Stalinization (p. 978)		
Common Market (p. 982)		
Civil Rights Act (p. 982)		

> IN YOUR OWN WORDS

Imagine that you must give an oral report to the class answering the following question: **How did decolonization and the Cold War shape global developments in the decades following World War II?** What would be the most important points and why?

STEP 3 — MOVE BEYOND THE BASICS

To demonstrate a more advanced understanding of postwar decolonization, fill in the chart below with descriptions of the decolonization process and its aftermath in the Middle East, Africa, and South Asia. What are the most important differences in the decolonization experience in each region? How would you explain the differences you note?

	Decolonization Process	Post-Independence Developments
The Middle East		
Africa		
South Asia		

STEP 4 — PUT IT ALL TOGETHER

Now, take a step back and try to explain the big picture. Remember to use specific examples from the chapter in your answers.

ASIA AND THE MIDDLE EAST

▶ How did Asian and Middle Eastern nationalists drawn on Western ideas and models during the struggle for independence?

▶ What explains the dominant role the Israeli/Palestinian issue has played in Middle Eastern politics since 1945?

AFRICA AND LATIN AMERICA

▶ How did the circumstances under which Latin American and sub-Saharan African nations gained independence shape their subsequent development?

▶ Why was the Cuban Revolution such an important turning point in Latin American history?

THE LIMITS OF POSTWAR PROSPERITY

▶ To what extent were the protest movements of the 1960s a product of postwar affluence? What other factors contributed to their emergence?

▶ What were the most important forces for change in the postwar era? What important continuities were there between the pre- and postwar periods?

LOOKING BACK, LOOKING AHEAD

▶ Argue for or against the following proposition: "The European wars of the first half of the twentieth century made decolonization possible. Without them, the Western imperial system might still be in existence." What evidence can you present to support your position?

▶ In your opinion, in the next several decades will South and East Asia overtake Europe and North America as the dominant regions in the global economy? Why or why not?

32

LIBERALIZATION

1968–2000S

> Why did liberalization emerge as a such a powerful force in the second half of the twentieth century, and what were the consequences of this development? Chapter 32 examines the impact of liberalization in the late twentieth century. In the 1970s two currents ran against each other in much of the world. The radicalism of liberation in decolonization, revolutions, and mass social movements continued. But alongside this current ran a different one whose influence was undeniable by the 1990s: liberalization. After the Second World War, the United States had championed liberal economic policies, but this objective ran against the desires of other countries to protect and promote their own industrialization and economic development. But in the last decades of the century, the U.S. drive for global liberalization of trade experienced greater success, while reform movements in the Eastern bloc and in Latin America pursued human rights and political liberalization.

Sandinista Soldier in Nicaragua Street art in Jinotega, Nicaragua, shows an armed female soldier of the Sandinista National Liberation Front picking coffee beans in her military camouflage. The Sandinistas overthrew the U.S.-backed dictator Anastasio Somoza in 1979. After their victory, the Socialist Sandinistas ruled Nicaragua until 1990 and then returned to power in 2006. (© Thalia Watmough/aliki image library/Alamy)

> What were the short-term and long-term consequences of the OPEC oil embargo?

> How did war and revolution reshape the Middle East?

> What effect did the Cold War and debt crisis have on Latin America?

> How did white-minority rule end in southern Africa?

> How have East and South Asian nations pursued economic development, and how have political regimes shaped those efforts?

> How did decolonization and the end of the Cold War change Europe?

✓ **LearningCurve**
After reading the chapter, use LearningCurve to retain what you've read.

> What were the short-term and long-term consequences of the OPEC oil embargo?

Oil in Nigeria

A Nigerian woman ferries fuel drums across Warri Harbor, near an abandoned oil tanker. Nigeria's oil has brought great profits to some, but boom-and-bust cycles and corruption keep wealth out of the hands of most Nigerians. (© George Steinmetz/Corbis)

IN 1973 WAR ERUPTED AGAIN between Israel and its neighbors Egypt and Syria. The conflict became known as the Yom Kippur War. Armed with advanced weapons from the Soviet Union, Egyptian and Syrian armies came close to defeating Israel before the U.S. government airlifted sophisticated arms to Israel. Israel counterattacked, reaching the outskirts of both Cairo and Damascus before the fighting ended. Arab oil-exporting countries retaliated against U.S. support for Israel by imposing an embargo on oil sales to countries that had supported Israel during the war.

Amid the oil embargo, the war in Vietnam, and political conflict within the United States, U.S. political and economic influence as a global superpower seemed to decline.

The OPEC Oil Embargo

In 1960 oil-exporting countries formed a cartel called OPEC (the Organization of the Petroleum Exporting Countries) in order to coordinate production and raise prices. In 1973 OPEC countries agreed to an embargo, withholding oil sales to

CHAPTER LOCATOR | **What were the short-term and long-term consequences of the OPEC oil embargo?** | How did war and revolution reshape the Middle East?

992 CHAPTER 32 LIBERALIZATION

1973 Yom Kippur War; OPEC oil embargo	**1990–1991** Persian Gulf War
1979 Islamic revolution in Iran; second oil shock	**1991** Congress Party in India embraces Western capitalist reforms
1980 Rhodesian white minority rulers surrender power and the nation is renamed Zimbabwe	**1991–2001** Civil war in Yugoslavia
1980–1988 Iran-Iraq War	**1993** Formation of European Union
1982 Falklands (or Malvinas) War leads to the collapse of the Argentine junta	**1994** North American Free Trade Agreement goes into effect between Canada, Mexico, and the United States
1985 Glasnost leads to greater freedom of speech and expression in the Soviet Union	**1994** Nelson Mandela elected president of South Africa
1987 Palestinian intifada	**2003–2011** Second Persian Gulf War
1989 Collapse of Berlin Wall; "NO" campaign in Chile; Tiananmen Square protests suppressed in China	**2007** Hamas seizes control of Gaza Strip from Palestinian Authority
1989–1991 Fall of communism in Soviet Union and eastern Europe	**2009–2014** Popular uprisings and protests across the Middle East

the United States and western Europe in response to U.S. support for Israel in the Yom Kippur War. As a result of the embargo, the price of oil increased almost overnight from $3 to $12 per barrel, quadrupling energy costs.

OPEC's ability to disrupt the world economy, and the U.S. government's powerlessness to reverse the disruption, suggested a new world order. Brazil's military leaders, for example, distanced themselves from their traditional alliance with the United States and built relations with OPEC countries.

Oil prices remained high and peaked again in the second oil shock of 1979 as a result of the Iranian revolution, which ousted the secular government and brought religious leaders to power. In the United States soaring energy costs sapped economic growth and also triggered inflation, making prices rise at a time when earning power was diminished, a combination dubbed stagflation. Europe and Japan, heavily dependent on oil imports, resorted to bicycle and mass transit use to reduce their energy needs, as well as intense development of nuclear power generation.

In the decade after the first oil shock, OPEC countries such as Saudi Arabia deposited their huge profits in large international banks. This money, which began as oil profits and circulated the world as bank loans, was known as **petrodollars**. In this economic cycle, the higher prices that consumers around the world paid for fuel generated profits for oil exporters that they invested in large banks. In turn,

petrodollars
▶ The global recirculation by international banks of profits from the higher price of oil.

What effect did the Cold War and debt crisis have on Latin America?	How did white-minority rule end in southern Africa?	How have East and South Asian nations pursued economic development?	How did decolonization and the end of the Cold War change Europe?	✔ LearningCurve Check what you know.

these banks loaned this capital out to foreign governments. Many industrializing countries faced both high energy costs and heavy debts amassed through petro-dollar loans.

In the United States, as stagflation and the 1979 second oil shock drove rising inflation, the Federal Reserve Bank raised interest rates. Increased interest rates in the United States made it more expensive to borrow money, which slowed economic activity and led to an economic recession. The United States was not the only country to experience this recession: countries that exported goods to the United States faced reduced demand for their goods, and countries that borrowed from U.S. banks found that the interest on their debts increased as well. In industrializing nations the rapid increase in interest on their heavy debts became a crippling burden, triggering a global crisis. Debtor nations became dependent on U.S. assistance to restructure unsustainable loans; the U.S. government was able to impose neoliberal free-market reforms for the first time.

Beginning in the 1980s neoliberal policies increasingly shaped the world economy. **Neoliberalism** promoted free-market policies and the free circulation of capital across national borders. Debtor countries needed to continue to borrow in order to pay the interest on the debts they held, and their ability to secure loans now depended on their adherence to a set of liberal principles known as the **Washington Consensus**: policies that restricted public spending, lowered import barriers, privatized state enterprises, and deregulated markets.

The forces unleashed by the Yom Kippur War and the OPEC oil embargo of 1973 at first tipped the scale in favor of less industrialized nations, but by the 1980s the scale had swung back as debt and liberalization shifted power back to the most economically powerful countries, in particular the United States. The experiences of Mexico and Nigeria reflect the effects of the boom-and-bust cycle ignited by the oil embargo.

Mexico Under the PRI

By the 1960s Mexico was a democracy that functioned like a dictatorship. The Institutional Revolutionary Party (PRI) held nearly every public office. The PRI controlled both labor unions and federations of businessmen. More than a party, it was a vast system of patronage. Even at the landfills where the most desperately poor scavenged through trash, a PRI official collected a cut of their meager earnings. Mexico's road from the nationalist economic project that emerged from the 1910 revolution to the liberal reforms of the 1960s and 1970s is also the story of the PRI.

The PRI claimed the reform legacy of the Mexican Revolution. But these claims were undermined when PRI politicians ordered the deadly crackdown on student protesters in 1968 (see page 984). The party that had defined itself as the agent of progress and change became the reactionary party preserving a corrupt order.

In 1970 the PRI chose and elected as president populist Luis Echeverría, who sought to reclaim the mantle of reform by nationalizing utilities and increasing social spending. Echeverría and his successor, José López Portillo, embarked on massive development projects financed through projected future earnings of the state oil monopoly PEMEX. Amid inflation, corruption, and the decline of oil prices

neoliberalism
► A return to policies intended to promote free markets and the free circulation of capital across national borders.

Washington Consensus
► Policies restricting public spending, lowering import barriers, privatizing state enterprises, and deregulating markets.

CHAPTER LOCATOR | What were the short-term and long-term consequences of the OPEC oil embargo? | How did war and revolution reshape the Middle East?

994 CHAPTER 32 LIBERALIZATION

and demand during the global recession of the 1980s, the Mexican government fell into the debt crisis, and was compelled to embrace the Washington Consensus, which meant restricted spending, opening trade borders, and privatization.

The PRI was further undermined by its inept and corrupt response to a devastating earthquake that struck Mexico City in 1986. Two years later the PRI faced its first real presidential election challenge. Cuauhtémoc Cárdenas, who was the son of populist Lázaro Cárdenas, ran against PRI candidate Carlos Salinas de Gortari. On election night, as the vote counting favored Cárdenas, the government declared that the computers tabulating the votes had crashed and declared Gortari the winner. The PRI-controlled congress ordered the ballots burned afterward. The PRI now governed through simple fraud. In its last years holding power, the PRI pursued liberalization of the economy, negotiating a free-trade agreement with the United States and Canada, the North American Free Trade Agreement (NAFTA), which went into effect in 1994.

The debt crisis forced the PRI government to abandon the nationalist development project created in the decades after the 1910 revolution and to embrace economic liberalism, but the experience with neoliberalism proved equally corrupt. Mexico continued to face economic crises such as a 1994 financial panic. As the PRI's power slipped and as Mexico's trade with the United States intensified, violent drug cartels proliferated, especially in Mexico's northern border states, and competed for the lucrative drug trade into the United States.

Nigeria, Africa's Giant

After Nigeria gained independence from Britain in 1960, its key constitutional question was the relationship between the central government and its ethnically distinct regions (see Map 31.5, page 972). Under the federal system created after independence, each region had a dominant ethnic group and a corresponding political party. After independence Nigeria's ethnic rivalries intensified, and in 1967 they erupted in the Biafran war in which the Igbo ethnic group in southeastern Nigeria fought unsuccessfully to form a separate nation. The war lasted three years and resulted in famine that left millions dead.

The wealth generated by oil exports in the 1970s had contradictory effects on Nigerian society. On one hand, a succession of military leaders who held power after a 1966 coup grew increasingly corrupt throughout the 1970s. On the other hand, oil wealth allowed the country to rebuild after the Biafran war. By the mid-1970s Nigeria had the largest middle and professional classes on the continent outside of South Africa. Nigeria's oil boom in the 1970s resembled Mexico's experience: the expectation of future riches led to growing indebtedness, and when global demand and oil prices collapsed amid the global recession of the early 1980s, Nigeria faced a corrosive debt crisis.

Oil wealth allowed Nigeria to develop one innovative solution to its ethnic divisions: the construction of a modernist new capital, Abuja, modeled on Brazil's project in Brasília (see page 978). Located in the center of the country at the confluence of major regional and ethnic boundaries, Abuja symbolized equal representation in government. Residential areas in the new city were divided by ethnicity, but shopping and services were located between them to encourage commingling.

What effect did the Cold War and debt crisis have on Latin America?

How did white-minority rule end in southern Africa?

How have East and South Asian nations pursued economic development?

How did decolonization and the end of the Cold War change Europe?

✓ LearningCurve
Check what you know.

995

Except for an early period of civilian rule, Muslim army officers ruled Nigeria until 1998, when the brutal military dictator General Sani Abacha suddenly died. Nigerians adopted a new constitution in 1999, and that same year they voted in free elections and re-established civilian rule. Elections in 2003 ended thirty-three years of military rule. Nonetheless, ethnic tensions remained. Since 2000 ethnic riots have left thousands dead in the predominantly Muslim northern Nigerian states.

> **QUICK REVIEW**

How did the oil shocks of the 1970s contribute to the growing influence of neoliberal economic policies on the global economy in subsequent decades?

CHAPTER LOCATOR | What were the short-term and long-term consequences of the OPEC oil embargo? | **How did war and revolution reshape the Middle East?**

996 CHAPTER 32
LIBERALIZATION

Protest messages along with images of Che Guevara and peace doves adorn the wall separating the Palestinian West Bank from Jerusalem, in the background. (SIPA/Sipa USA)

How did war and revolution reshape the Middle East?

THE 1973 YOM KIPPUR WAR had a lasting effect across the Middle East. Egypt and Syria had again been defeated, but Israelis also felt more vulnerable after the war. The oil embargo empowered oil-exporting nations like Saudi Arabia, Libya, and Iraq. The Middle East faced deepening divisions, which added to the conflict between Israel and its neighbors. Rising Islamic militancy led to revolution in Iran, as well as a spreading religious challenge to the rule of secular, modernizing dictatorships in countries like Egypt.

The Palestinian-Israeli Conflict

After the 1973 war, the United States recognized the need to become more actively involved in the Middle East. Peacemaking efforts by U.S. president Jimmy Carter led to the Camp David Accords in 1979, which normalized relations between Israel and its neighbors Egypt and Jordan. With the prospect of border wars between Israel and its neighbors diminished, political attention turned to the conflict between Israel and Palestinian nationalist organizations. Tensions between

| What effect did the Cold War and debt crisis have on Latin America? | How did white-minority rule end in southern Africa? | How have East and South Asian nations pursued economic development? | How did decolonization and the end of the Cold War change Europe? | ✓ LearningCurve Check what you know. |

Syria and Israel shifted from their border into Lebanon, where Syria backed the militia Hezbollah. Hezbollah condemned the 1978 and 1982 Israeli invasions of Lebanon aimed at eradicating the Palestine Liberation Organization's control of southern Lebanon, and had as one of its stated objectives the complete destruction of the state of Israel.

In 1987 young Palestinians in the occupied territories of the Gaza Strip and the West Bank began the **intifada**, a prolonged campaign of civil disobedience against Israeli soldiers. Inspired increasingly by Islamic fundamentalists, the Palestinian uprising eventually posed a serious challenge not only to Israel but also to the secular Palestine Liberation Organization (PLO), long led from abroad by Yasir Arafat. The result was an unexpected and mutually beneficial agreement in 1993 between Israel and the PLO. Israel agreed to recognize Arafat's organization and start a peace process that granted Palestinian self-rule in Gaza and called for self-rule throughout the West Bank in five years. In return, Arafat renounced violence and abandoned the demand that Israel must withdraw from all land occupied in the 1967 war.

The peace process increasingly divided Israel. In 1995 a right-wing Jewish extremist assassinated Prime Minister Yitzhak Rabin. In 1996 a coalition of opposition parties won a slender majority, charging the Palestinian leadership with condoning anti-Jewish terrorism. The new Israeli government limited Palestinian self-rule where it existed and expanded Jewish settlements in the West Bank. On the Palestinian side, dissatisfaction with the peace process grew.

Failed negotiations between Arafat and Israel in 2000 unleashed an explosion of violence between Israelis and Palestinians known as the Second Intifada. In 2003 the Israeli government began to build a barrier around the West Bank, which met with opposition from Israelis and Palestinians alike.

The death of Yasir Arafat, the PLO's long-time leader, in November 2004 marked a turning point in the Israeli-Palestinian conflict. Mahmoud Abbas, Arafat's pragmatic successor, found little room for negotiation. In January 2006 Hamas, a Sunni Muslim political party, won a majority in the Palestinian legislature. Considered by Israel to be a terrorist organization, Hamas had gained widespread support from many Palestinians for the welfare programs it established in the West Bank and Gaza Strip.

Immediately after the Hamas victory, Israel, the United States, and the European Union suspended aid to the Palestinian Authority, the governing body of the West Bank and Gaza Strip established by the 1994 peace agreement. Since then, economic and humanitarian conditions for Palestinians living in the Gaza Strip have deteriorated.

Egypt: Arab World Leader

In 1977 Egypt's president, Anwar Sadat (1918–1981), negotiated a peace settlement with Israel known as the Camp David Accords. Each country gained: Egypt got back the Sinai Peninsula, which Israel had taken in the 1967 Six-Day War (see Map 31.3, page 965), and Israel obtained peace and normal relations with Egypt. Israel also kept the Gaza Strip. Some Arab leaders denounced Sadat's initiative as treason.

After Sadat was assassinated by Islamic radicals in 1981, Egyptian relations with Israel deteriorated, but Egypt and Israel maintained their fragile peace as

intifada

▶ A prolonged campaign of civil disobedience by Palestinian youth against Israeli soldiers; the Arabic word *intifada* means "shaking off."

CHAPTER LOCATOR | What were the short-term and long-term consequences of the OPEC oil embargo? | **How did war and revolution reshape the Middle East?**

998 CHAPTER 32 LIBERALIZATION

Sadat's successor, Hosni Mubarak, took office. In return for helping to stabilize the region, the United States gave Egypt billions of dollars in development, humanitarian, and military aid. This aid failed to yield economic development, and Mubarak ruled with an increasingly dictatorial hand, silencing all opposition and punishing, torturing, and killing anyone perceived as a threat to his rule.

In December 2010 demonstrations broke out in Tunisia against the twenty-three-year authoritarian rule of President Zine Ben Ali, leading to his downfall on January 14, 2011. This populist revolt soon spread across North Africa and the Middle East, including Egypt. After three weeks of increasingly large demonstrations, coordinated through social media, Mubarak stepped down as president in 2011 and was arrested soon after. Libya, located between Tunisia and Egypt, also witnessed an uprising against its dictatorial leader of forty-two years, Muammar Gaddafi. Gaddafi struggled violently to remain in power, but was deposed and killed amid European and U.S. air strikes. That same year, a lengthy and intense civil war erupted in Syria.

The "Arab Spring" uprisings that swept the Middle East shook a political order that had rested in the hands of the armed forces and pursued secular, nationalist objectives. The reaction against these regimes was often religious and culturally conservative. The political transitions resulting from this upheaval tended to pit secular and religious factions against each other amid debates over the nature of government and social reform.

Revolution and War in Iran and Iraq

In oil-rich Iran foreign powers competed for political influence in the decades after the Second World War, and the influence of the United States in particular helped trigger a revolutionary backlash. In 1953 Iran's prime minister, Muhammad Mossadegh (1882–1967), tried to nationalize the British-owned Anglo-Iranian Oil Company, forcing the pro-Western shah Muhammad Reza Pahlavi (r. 1941–1979) to flee to Europe. However, loyal army officers, with the help of the American CIA, quickly restored the shah to his throne.

Pahlavi set out to build a powerful modern nation to ensure his rule. The shah undermined the power bases of the traditional politicians—large landowners and religious leaders—by means of land reform, secular education, and increased power for the central government. Modernization surged forward, accompanied by widespread corruption and harsh dictatorship. The result was a violent reaction against modernization and secular values. Led by the Islamic cleric Ayatollah Ruholla Khomeini, the fundamentalists deposed the shah in 1979 and tried to build their vision of a true Islamic state.

Iran's Islamic republic frightened its neighbors. Iraq, especially, feared that Iran—a nation of Shi'ite Muslims—would succeed in getting Iraq's Shi'ite majority to revolt against its Sunni leaders (Map 32.1). In September 1980 Iraq's ruler, Saddam Hussein (1937–2006), launched a surprise attack against Iran. The Iran-Iraq War last eight years and resulted in the death of hundreds of thousands of soldiers on both sides before ending in a modest victory for Iran in 1988.

Saddled with the costs of war, Hussein eyed Kuwait's great oil wealth. In August 1990 he ordered his forces to overrun his tiny southern neighbor and proclaimed its annexation to Iraq. To Saddam's surprise, his troops were driven out of Kuwait by an American-led, United Nations–sanctioned military coalition.

| What effect did the Cold War and debt crisis have on Latin America? | How did white-minority rule end in southern Africa? | How have East and South Asian nations pursued economic development? | How did decolonization and the end of the Cold War change Europe? | ☑ LearningCurve Check what you know. |

999

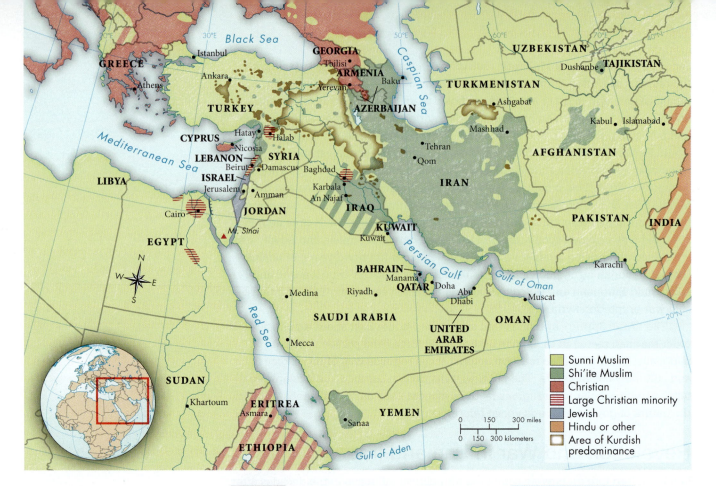

MAP 32.1 ■ Abrahamic Religions in the Middle East and Surrounding Regions

Islam, Judaism, and Christianity, which all trace their origins back to the patriarch Abraham, have significant populations in the Middle East. Since the 1979 Iranian revolution, Shi'ites throughout the region have become more vocal in their demands for equality and power. One of the largest stateless ethnic groups, the Kurds, who follow various religions, has become a major player in the politics of the region, especially in Iraq and Turkey, where the group seeks Kurdish independence.

> **MAPPING THE PAST**

ANALYZING THE MAP: Which religion dominates? Where are the largest concentrations of Jews and Christians in the Middle East located?
CONNECTIONS: How have divisions between Shi'ite and Sunni Muslims contributed to war in the region?

The United Nations Security Council imposed economic sanctions on Iraq as soon as it invaded Kuwait, and these sanctions continued after the Persian Gulf War to force Iraq to destroy its stockpiles of chemical and biological weapons. Sparked by allegations that Iraq still had such weapons, an American-led invasion of Iraq in 2003 began the Second Persian Gulf War and overthrew Saddam Hussein's regime. The invasion led to a lengthy U.S. occupation and a violent insurgency against U.S. military forces, which remained in Iraq until 2011.

As secular Iraq staggered, the Iran revolutionary regime seemed to moderate. Executive power in Iran was divided between a Supreme Leader and twelve-member Guardian Council selected by high Islamic clerics, and a popularly elected president and parliament. A reform movement pressed for relaxation of strict Islamic decrees and elected a moderate, Muhammad Khatami (b. 1943), as presi-

CHAPTER LOCATOR | What were the short-term and long-term consequences of the OPEC oil embargo? | **How did war and revolution reshape the Middle East?**

CHAPTER 32
1000 LIBERALIZATION

dent in 1997 and again in 2001. The Supreme Leader, controlling the army and the courts, vetoed Khatami's reforms and jailed some of the religious leadership's most vocal opponents.

In 2005 dubious election returns gave the presidency to conservative populist Mahmoud Ahmadinejad (b. 1956). Ahmadinejad won re-election in 2009 after a bitterly contested challenge from moderates. The government suppressed a "green revolution" of protests that broke out after news of the election results. In 2013 opposition groups came together to support the election of Hassan Rouhani, a centrist cleric who promised civil rights reforms and has made overtures to the West in the hopes of relieving economic sanctions in return for negotiating an end to Iran's nuclear weapons program.

QUICK REVIEW

What role has the United States played in Middle Eastern politics since the 1973 Yom Kippur War? What impact have U.S. policies and interventions had on the region?

| What effect did the Cold War and debt crisis have on Latin America? | How did white-minority rule end in southern Africa? | How have East and South Asian nations pursued economic development? | How did decolonization and the end of the Cold War change Europe? | ☑ LearningCurve Check what you know. |

What effect did the Cold War and debt crisis have on Latin America?

The Mothers of the Plaza de Mayo

Mothers and grandmothers demand information about their children and grandchildren who were "disappeared" by the Argentine military junta in a protest in Buenos Aires. (Eduardo Di Baia/AP Photo)

AFTER THE CUBAN REVOLUTION IN 1959, the United States financed and armed military dictatorships to suppress any dissent that might lead to communism and to secure U.S. influence in the region. Many elected governments were toppled in military coups that brought right-wing military dictatorships to power with U.S. military and financial support.

Civil Wars in Central America

Central America experienced the greatest violence in Latin America during the Cold War. In the second half of the twentieth century nationalists in Central America sought economic development that was less dependent on the United States and U.S. corporations, and groups of peasants and urban workers began to press for political rights and improved living standards. Through the lens of the Cold War, Central American conservatives and the United States government saw these groups as Communists who should be suppressed. In turn, many workers and peasants radicalized and formed Marxist revolutionary movements. The

CHAPTER LOCATOR | What were the short-term and long-term consequences of the OPEC oil embargo? | How did war and revolution reshape the Middle East?

CHAPTER 32
1002 LIBERALIZATION

result of this conflict, and of U.S. support for right-wing governments and forces was hundreds of thousands of deaths.

In Guatemala reformist president Jacobo Arbenz was deposed in a military coup organized by the CIA in 1954. Subsequent Guatemalan leaders backed by the U.S. government violently suppressed peasant movements, resulting in the likely death of over two hundred thousand mostly indigenous people.

El Salvador and Nicaragua, too, faced civil wars. In 1979 the Sandinista movement overthrew dictator Anastasio Somoza Debayle. The Sandinistas, who conducted a revolutionary transformation of Nicaragua inspired by Communist rule in Cuba, were undermined by war with a U.S.-trained and U.S.-financed insurgent army called the Contras. In El Salvador a right-wing death squad killed Archbishop Oscar Romero in 1980 for speaking out against their violence.

U.S. policies that encouraged one faction to fight against the other deepened political instability and repression and intensified these civil wars. Acting against U.S. wishes, in 1986 Costa Rican president Oscar Arias mediated peace talks among the warring factions in Nicaragua, El Salvador, and Guatemala, which ended the wars and initiated open elections in each country, with former armed rivals competing instead at the ballot box.

Boom and Bust in Chile

In the 1960s Chilean voters pushed for greater social reforms, culminating in the election of the Marxist candidate Salvador Allende as president in 1970. Allende redistributed land and nationalized foreign businesses including copper mines, drawing fiery opposition from conservative Chileans, foreign businesses, and the U.S. government. U.S. president Richard Nixon created a clandestine task force to organize an "invisible blockade" to disrupt the Chilean economy by withholding economic aid and quietly instructing U.S. companies not to trade with or invest in Chile.

In 1973 Chile's armed forces deposed Allende, who killed himself rather than surrender as the military stormed the palace. A **junta**, or council of commanders of the branches of the armed forces, took power. Its leader, General Augusto Pinochet (1915–2006), instituted radical economic reforms, giving neoliberal economists a free hand to remake Chile into a showcase of free-market economics. Schools, health care, pensions, and public services were turned over to private companies. Regulatory protections for industry were slashed, and land was concentrated into the hands of large agricultural corporations. Pinochet's economic program was supported by lavish U.S. economic aid.

The reforms created a boom-and-bust cycle in which Chile became especially vulnerable to global economic changes. At its peak, Chile's economy grew at 8 percent per year. The costs of the reforms were just as intense. Income inequality soared: a handful of Chileans tied to big business conglomerates and banks made

A Contra Rebel

A member of the Contra paramilitary force, which was armed and trained by the United States to fight against the socialist Sandinista government in Nicaragua. (© Bill Gentile/ZUMAPRESS.com)

junta

▶ A government headed by a council of commanders of the branches of the armed forces.

What effect did the Cold War and debt crisis have on Latin America? | How did white-minority rule end in southern Africa? | How have East and South Asian nations pursued economic development? | How did decolonization and the end of the Cold War change Europe? | ✔ LearningCurve Check what you know.

1003

fortunes, while workers faced job loss and an increasing cost of living. In 1975 the implementation of reforms that cut social programs and caused mass unemployment left half of the country's children malnourished. The 1982 recession in Chile put one-third of Chileans out of work.

Pinochet dealt violently with his critics. Thousands disappeared, and tens of thousands were tortured. These human rights abuses brought international condemnation and resistance within Chile. Groups of women who had lost children or spouses banded together with the protection of the Catholic Church and embroidered quilts known as *arpilleras*, rendering images of their missing relatives or other experiences with repression. Catholic leaders investigated human rights abuses, uncovering mass graves that served as proof of the dictatorship's violence.

Amid the excesses of Pinochet's dictatorship, opponents and even many allies looked for ways to curb his power and find the path for redemocratization. After the 1982 economic crisis, businessmen began to join with opposition groups to press for liberalization. Opposition groups proposed a return to democracy that maintained the major elements of free-market reforms. These groups banded together and called for Chileans to vote "NO" in the 1989 referendum on whether Pinochet would remain in power. The "NO" prevailed, and Chile held its first democratic elections in two decades.

The opposition alliance in Chile resembled many other alliances around the world that sought transitions from authoritarian rule: political opponents who advocated for human rights joined forces with business groups that sought markets in order to produce a postdictatorship democracy founded on free-market principles and support for human rights.

The Dirty War in Argentina

The Argentine military either held power or set the political rules for decades after it deposed populist Juan Perón in 1955 (see page 978). By 1973 the armed forces conceded that their efforts to "de-Perónize" the country had failed. They allowed Perón to return, and he was again elected president, with his third wife, María Estela, known as Isabelita, as vice president. Soon after the election, Juan Perón died and Isabelita Perón become president, She faced daunting circumstances: Marxist groups waged a guerrilla war against the regime, while the armed forces and death squads waged war on them.

In March 1976 a military junta took power and announced a Process of National Reorganization. The generals waged a "dirty war," seeking to kill and "disappear" people whom they considered a destructive "cancer" on the nation. Argentine military forces killed between fourteen thousand and thirty thousand of their fellow citizens during the dirty war.

A handful of mothers whose children had disappeared began appearing in the Plaza de Mayo in front of the presidential palace holding pictures of their missing children and carrying signs reading "Where are they?" A growing organization of the Mothers of the Plaza de Mayo was soon joined by the Grandmothers, who demanded the whereabouts of children born to women who were detained and disappeared while pregnant. These mothers were only kept alive until they gave birth. Their children were placed with adoptive families tied to the police or armed forces. Unlike in Chile and Brazil, in Argentina senior Catholic clergy did

CHAPTER LOCATOR | What were the short-term and long-term consequences of the OPEC oil embargo? | How did war and revolution reshape the Middle East?

CHAPTER 32
1004 LIBERALIZATION

not advocate for human rights or the protection of dissidents. Instead Argentine bishops praised the coup and defended the military regime until it ended in 1983.

In 1982, emboldened by its success in eradicating its opposition, the Argentine junta occupied a set of islands off of its southern coast that were claimed by Britain. Known in Britain as the Falklands and in Argentina as the Malvinas, the islands were home to a small British settlement. Britain resisted the invasion and the Falklands/Malvinas War resulted in a humiliating defeat for the Argentine junta. After the war the junta abruptly called for elections, and a civilian president took office in 1983.

The new president, Raúl Alfonsín, faced a debt crisis similar to Mexico's. He also had to figure out how to mete out justice for the crimes committed by the junta, whose members were tried and convicted. Their convictions created a backlash in the armed forces, which forced the government to halt prosecutions. Alfonsín was succeeded by Carlos Menem, who tried a different approach. Menem pardoned the junta members and embarked on free-market reforms, privatizing businesses and utilities and reducing trade barriers. Investment flooded in, and Argentina seemingly put the past to rest.

As the capacity to attract foreign investment through privatization ran out by the end of the century, Argentina faced economic crisis again. In 2001, amid a run on banks and a collapse of the Argentine peso, the country had five different presidents in a single month. Eventually, the economy stabilized during the presidency of Néstor Kirchner, succeeded by his wife, Cristina Fernández de Kirchner. Cristina Fernández de Kirchner resumed the prosecution of those responsible for violence during the dirty war.

Development and Dictatorship in Brazil

Brazil's military dictatorship, in power since 1964, pursued a different economic model than Chile's and Argentina's. Though Brazil's generals began with liberal reforms, they moved to a nationalist project of increased state control of industry, restrictions on imports, and heavy investments in energy and transportation infrastructure. They initially experienced great success, with annual growth rates averaging 11 percent between 1968 and 1973. This growth depended on cheap imported oil and harsh political repression. When the oil embargo threatened to cripple the country's accelerating industrialization, the generals borrowed heavily from abroad to subsidize fuel costs and conduct costly alternative energy projects.

The Brazilian cycle of borrowing petrodollars to subsidize oil imports and development projects was ruinous for the country. By the end of the 1970s Brazil had the largest foreign debt in the developing world. When the second oil shock hit in 1979, and as the U.S. government raised interest rates, making Brazil's debt more expensive to manage, the country entered what became known as a "lost decade" of recession and inflation. In the 1980s the economic crisis set the tone for a transition to democracy: as the generals made painful cuts to public services and as Brazilians faced crippling inflation and recession, people overwhelmingly turned against military rule and supported redemocratization.

As in Chile, Brazil's transition to democracy was shaped by liberalization. Business groups, which had grown uneasy with the dictatorship's borrowing and central planning, joined forces with human rights advocates to return the "rule of law," rather than arbitrary rule by generals. Unlike in Chile, the debt left behind

| What effect did the Cold War and debt crisis have on Latin America? | How did white-minority rule end in southern Africa? | How have East and South Asian nations pursued economic development? | How did decolonization and the end of the Cold War change Europe? | ✓ LearningCurve Check what you know. |

1005

by Brazil's military leaders drove liberal economic reforms. In order to sustain its debt payments, the Brazilian government accepted the Washington Consensus, reducing public spending and opening the economy to imports and foreign investment. Within this changed climate, in 1994 Brazilians elected Fernando Henrique Cardoso. Cardoso carried out the deepest and most sustained liberal reforms Brazil had seen since the 1930s.

> **QUICK REVIEW**

What explains the rise of authoritarian governments throughout Latin America during this period?

CHAPTER LOCATOR | What were the short-term and long-term consequences of the OPEC oil embargo? | How did war and revolution reshape the Middle East?

1006 CHAPTER 32 LIBERALIZATION

How did white-minority rule end in southern Africa?

Student Demonstrations Against Apartheid

Police fire tear gas at anti-apartheid protesters in 1989 at Witwatersrand University in Johannesburg. (Ulli Michel/Reuters/Landov)

THE RACIALLY SEGREGATED SYSTEM OF APARTHEID in South Africa was part of a larger system of white-minority rule that included Portuguese Angola and Mozambique, the government of Ian Smith in Rhodesia, and South African control of the former German colony of Namibia. In the 1970s the buffer of neighboring white-minority governments around South Africa crumbled. Domestic and foreign pressure brought a political transition to majority rule in Namibia and South Africa in the 1990s.

Portuguese Decolonization and Rhodesia

At the end of World War II Portugal was the poorest country in western Europe and was ruled by a dictatorship, but it still claimed an immense overseas empire that included Angola, Mozambique, Guinea-Bissau, and Cape Verde. Unlike other European colonial leaders, the Portuguese dictator António Salazar (1889–1970) refused to consider ending colonial rule. Without government support for independence, nationalists in Portugal's colonies resorted to armed insurrections. By the

What effect did the Cold War and debt crisis have on Latin America?

How did white-minority rule end in southern Africa?

How have East and South Asian nations pursued economic development?

How did decolonization and the end of the Cold War change Europe?

✓ LearningCurve Check what you know.

1007

early 1970s independence movements in Angola, Cape Verde, Guinea-Bissau, and Mozambique all fought guerrilla wars against the Portuguese army and colonial militias. The human toll was immense, and Portuguese officers returning from the colonies deposed the dictator in 1974. Guinea-Bissau and Cape Verde became independent that same year; Angola and Mozambique gained independence a year later. The nationalist movements that took power were all Marxist. Their radicalism was a product of their long struggle against oppression, inequality, and lack of access to their countries' resources.

The end of colonialism in Angola and Mozambique shifted the political landscape of southern Africa. Mozambique helped rebels fighting white-minority rule in Rhodesia, while the South African government saw independent Angola as a threat to apartheid and to its control over Namibia. The block of white-minority rule had been shattered, but neither Angola nor Mozambique would soon find peace.

The new government of Mozambique faced a guerrilla movement financed by Rhodesia. As Angola became independent, it faced immediate invasions from Zaire (encouraged by the United States) and South Africa. The new president of Angola, Agostinho Neto (1922–1978), requested military aid from Cuba. Until the late 1980s tens of thousands of Cuban troops faced off with the South African Defense Forces and mercenary armies to defend the government of Angola.

In the British colony of Rhodesia white settlers were a small minority of the population who declared independence on their own in order to avoid sharing power with the black majority. In 1965 they established a white-minority government under Ian Smith. The new Rhodesian state faced international condemnation for its treatment of black citizens, including the first economic sanctions imposed by the United Nations.

The Zimbabwe African People's Union (ZAPU) fought a guerrilla war against Rhodesia's white regime. Rebuffed by the United States and Britain, ZAPU turned to China and the Soviet Union for support. When Mozambique gained independence in 1974, its government allowed ZAPU and other guerrilla groups to use neighboring Mozambican territory as a staging ground to launch attacks on Rhodesia, making it impossible for the Ian Smith government to endure. Negotiations led to an open election in 1980 that ZAPU leader Robert Mugabe won easily. The new Mugabe government renamed the country Zimbabwe after an ancient city-state that predated colonial rule.

South Africa Under Apartheid

apartheid
▶ The system of racial segregation and discrimination that was supported by the Afrikaner government in South Africa.

African National Congress (ANC)
▶ The main black nationalist organization in South Africa, led by Nelson Mandela.

In 1948 the ruling South African National Party created a racist and segregationist system of discrimination known as **apartheid**, meaning "apartness" or "separation." The population was divided into four legally unequal racial groups: whites, blacks, Asians, and racially mixed "coloureds." South Africa was the most highly industrialized country in Africa at this time. Good jobs in the cities were reserved for whites. Blacks were restricted to outlying townships plagued by poverty, crime, and mistreatment from white policemen.

By the 1950s black South Africans and their allies mounted peaceful protests. A turning point came in 1960, when police in the township of Sharpeville fired at demonstrators and killed sixty-nine black demonstrators. The main black nationalist organization—the **African National Congress (ANC)**—was outlawed but sent

CHAPTER LOCATOR | What were the short-term and long-term consequences of the OPEC oil embargo? | How did war and revolution reshape the Middle East?

CHAPTER 32
1008 LIBERALIZATION

some of its leaders abroad. Other ANC members, led by a young lawyer, Nelson Mandela (1918–2013), stayed in South Africa to mount armed resistance. In 1962 Mandela was captured and sentenced to life imprisonment.

In the 1970s the South African government fell into the hands of "securocrats," military and intelligence officers who directed the state's resources into policing apartheid and dominating South Africa's neighbors by force. They adopted a policy known as the "total strategy," which intensified repression of black activists at home and launched military strikes against ANC and South West Africa People's Organization (SWAPO) camps operating in neighboring countries. At the United Nations, African leaders denounced the South African government, and activists in countries around the world pressured their governments to impose economic sanctions against the South African regime. South Africa's white leaders responded with a program of cosmetic reforms in 1984 to improve their international standing.

The reforms provoked a backlash. In the segregated townships young black militants took to the streets, clashing with heavily armed white security forces. Across the border with Angola, South African troops engaged in escalating conflicts with Angolan, ANC, SWAPO, and Cuban forces. Mounting casualties and defeat in major battles shook white South Africans' confidence.

Isolated politically, besieged by economic sanctions, and defeated on the battlefield, South African president Frederik W. de Klerk opened a dialogue with ANC leaders in 1989. He lifted the state of emergency imposed in 1985, legalized the ANC, and freed Mandela in February 1990. Mandela suspended the ANC's armed struggle and negotiated an agreement with de Klerk calling for universal suffrage, which meant black-majority rule.

In May 1994 Mandela was elected president of South Africa. Heading the new "government of national unity," which included de Klerk as vice president, Mandela and the South African people set about building a multiracial democracy. Seeking to sustain the economy built through South Africa's industrialization and to avoid white flight, Mandela repudiated his Marxist beliefs and reassured domestic and foreign investors of his commitment to liberalization.

Political Change in Africa Since 1990

Democracy's rise in South Africa was part of a trend toward elected civilian rule that swept through sub-Saharan Africa after 1990. The end of the Cold War that followed the breakup of the Soviet Union in 1990 transformed Africa's relations with Russia and the United States. Communism's collapse in Europe brought an abrupt end to Communist aid to Russia's African clients. U.S. support for pro-Western dictators, no matter how corrupt or repressive, declined as well. But the decrease in support for dictators left a power vacuum in which ethnic conflicts intensified, with often-disastrous results.

For instance, in the early 1990s the United States cut off decades of support for the anticommunist General Mobutu Sese Seko (1930–1997), who seized power in 1965 in Zaire (the former Belgian Congo, renamed the Democratic Republic of the Congo in 1997) and looted the country. Opposition groups toppled the tyrant in 1997, and a civil war ensued that left an estimated 5.4 million dead by 2007.

The agreement by national independence leaders across the continent to respect colonial borders prevented one kind of violence, but resulted in another.

| What effect did the Cold War and debt crisis have on Latin America? | **How did white-minority rule end in southern Africa?** | How have East and South Asian nations pursued economic development? | How did decolonization and the end of the Cold War change Europe? | ✓ LearningCurve Check what you know. |

1009

Greenpoint Stadium, Cape Town, South Africa

This modern stadium, complete with a retractable roof, was built especially for the 2010 soccer World Cup and seats sixty-eight thousand people. The 2010 matches marked the first time the World Cup was held in Africa. South Africa's successful handling of this global event became a matter of great pride for the country and the continent. To the left of the stadium is Cape Town, with the famous Table Mountain in the distance. (© AfriPics.com/Alamy)

In countries whose national boundaries had been created by colonial powers irrespective of historic divisions, ethnic strife sometimes boiled over into deep violence, such as the genocides of ethnic Hutus by Tutsis in Burundi in 1972 and by Tutsis of Hutus in 1993 and 1994 in Rwanda, which left hundreds of thousands dead. A test of the alternative to preserving national boundaries came amid efforts to ease tensions that had created famine and hardship in Sudan. In 2011, 98 percent of the electorate in southern Sudan voted to break away and form a new country, South Sudan. The early promise of peace after separation has been challenged by increased ethnic and political violence in South Sudan.

Amid these conflicts, political and economic reform has occurred in other African nations where years of mismanagement and repression had delegitimized one-party rule. Above all, the strength of the democratic opposition rested on a growing class of educated urban Africans. Postindependence governments enthusiastically expanded opportunities in education, especially higher education. The result was a growing middle class of educated professionals who chafed at the ostentatious privilege of tiny closed elites and pressed for political reforms that would democratize social and economic opportunities. Thus after 1990 sub-Saharan Africa accompanied the global trend toward liberalization and human rights.

> **QUICK REVIEW**

Why did South Africa's white-minority government agree to end apartheid?

CHAPTER LOCATOR | What were the short-term and long-term consequences of the OPEC oil embargo? | How did war and revolution reshape the Middle East?

The Election of Benazir Bhutto

Pakistan's Benazir Bhutto became the first female prime minister of a Muslim nation in 1988. (SIPA/Spa USA)

How have East and South Asian nations pursued economic development, and how have political regimes shaped those efforts?

CHINA, JAPAN, AND THE COUNTRIES that became known as the "Asian Tigers" (South Korea, Hong Kong, Singapore, and Taiwan) experienced fantastic economic growth in the last decades of the twentieth century. The Chinese Communist Party maintained tight political control amid liberalization and economic growth. Japan's economy stagnated in the 1990s and struggled to recover amid growing competition from its neighbors. In South Asia tensions between India and Pakistan remained.

China's Economic Resurgence

Mao's Cultural Revolution of 1965–1969 created chaos and a general crisis of confidence, especially in the cities (see page 967). Intellectuals, technicians, and purged party officials launched a counterattack on the radicals and regained much of their influence by 1969. This shift opened the door to a limited but lasting reconciliation between China and the United States in 1972.

After Mao's death in 1976, Chinese leader Deng Xiaoping (1904–1997) and his supporters initiated the "Four Modernizations": agriculture, industry, science and

What effect did the Cold War and debt crisis have on Latin America?

How did white-minority rule end in southern Africa?

How have East and South Asian nations pursued economic development?

How did decolonization and the end of the Cold War change Europe?

☑ LearningCurve
Check what you know.

1011

technology, and national defense. China's 800 million peasants were allowed to farm in small family units rather than in large collectives and to "dare to be rich" by producing crops of their choice. Peasants responded enthusiastically, increasing food production by more than 50 percent by 1984.

The successful use of free markets in agriculture encouraged further experimentation. Foreign capitalists were allowed to open factories in southern China and to export their products around the world. Private enterprise was permitted in cities. China's Communist Party also drew on the business talent of "overseas" Chinese in Hong Kong and Taiwan who understood world markets and sought cheap labor. The Chinese economy grew rapidly between 1978 and 1987, and per capita income doubled in these years.

Most large-scale industry remained state owned, however, and the Communist Party zealously preserved its monopoly on political power. When the worldwide movement for political liberalization took root in China in the 1980s, the government banned demonstrations and slowed economic liberalization. Inflation soared to more than 30 percent a year. The economic reversal, the continued lack of political freedom, and the conviction that Chinese society was becoming more corrupt led idealistic university students to spearhead demonstrations in 1989.

More than a million people streamed into Beijing's central **Tiananmen Square** in support of the students' demands. The government declared martial law and ordered the army to clear the students. Masses of courageous citizens blocked the

Tiananmen Square

▶ The site of a Chinese student revolt in 1989 at which Communists imposed martial law and arrested, injured, or killed hundreds of students.

Tiananmen Square, 1989

Protesters in Tiananmen Square surround a towering figure of the Goddess of Democracy built by Chinese art students. The statue was eventually destroyed by Chinese soldiers.
(© Peter Turnley/Corbis)

> PICTURING THE PAST

ANALYZING THE IMAGE: What do you think this statue symbolized for demonstrators in Tiananmen Square?

CONNECTIONS: Why has the Goddess of Democracy become a lasting symbol of the 1989 student movement?

CHAPTER LOCATOR | What were the short-term and long-term consequences of the OPEC oil embargo? | How did war and revolution reshape the Middle East?

CHAPTER 32
1012 LIBERALIZATION

soldiers' entry into the city for two weeks, but in the early hours of June 4, 1989, tanks rolled into Tiananmen Square. At least seven hundred students died as a wave of repression, arrests, and executions descended on China.

As communism fell in eastern Europe and the Soviet Union broke apart, China's rulers felt vindicated. They believed their action had preserved Communist power, prevented chaos, and demonstrated the limits of reform. China became politically Communist and economically capitalist. In 2001 China joined the World Trade Organization, completing its immersion in the liberal global economy.

> ### > The Chinese Economy (1978–2012)

- Nine percent average annual rate of growth and 16 percent average annual growth of foreign trade
- Average per capita income in China doubled every ten years
- March 2011 China replaced Japan as the world's second-largest economy

"Japan, Inc." and the "Asian Tigers"

Japan's postwar economic recovery, like Germany's, proceeded slowly at first. But during the Korean War, the Japanese economy took off and grew with spectacular speed. Between 1950 and 1970 Japan's economic growth averaged a breathtaking 10 percent a year.

Japan's emergence as an economic superpower fascinated outsiders. Many Asians and Africans looked to Japan for the secrets of successful modernization, but some of Japan's Asian neighbors again feared Japanese exploitation. In the 1970s and 1980s some Americans and Europeans accused **"Japan, Inc."** of an unfair alliance between government and business and urged their own governments to retaliate.

In Japan's system of managed capitalism, the government protected its industry from foreign competition, decided which industries were important, and then made loans and encouraged mergers to create powerful firms in those industries. The government rewarded large corporations and encouraged them to develop extensive industrial and financial activities. But the 1990s saw Japan's economy stagnate amid the bursting of a speculative bubble that crippled banks and led to record postwar unemployment as the country faced competition from industrializing neighbors in Asia.

The "Asian Tigers," named for their economic development, replicated the rapid industrialization that characterized Japan. Both South Korea and Taiwan were underdeveloped countries in the early postwar years—poor, small, agricultural, densely populated, and lacking natural resources.

They each pursued development through a similar series of reforms. First, land reform allowed small farmers to become competitive producers as well as consumers. Second, governments stimulated business through lending, import barriers, and control of labor. Third, nationalist leaders (Park Chung Hee in South Korea and Jiang Jieshi in Taiwan) maintained stability at the expense of democracy. When Park was assassinated in 1979, South Korea faced an even more authoritarian regime until democracy was established at the end of the 1980s. By the late 1990s South Korea had one of the largest economies in the world.

"Japan, Inc."

▶ A nickname from the 1980s used to describe the intricate relationship of Japan's business world and government.

Asian "Economic Tigers"

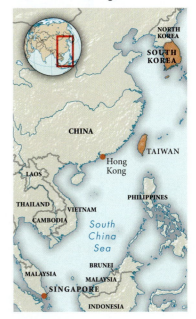

What effect did the Cold War and debt crisis have on Latin America?

How did white-minority rule end in southern Africa?

How have East and South Asian nations pursued economic development?

How did decolonization and the end of the Cold War change Europe?

☑ LearningCurve
Check what you know.

In 1949, after Jiang Jieshi had fled to Taiwan with his Nationalist troops and around 2 million refugees, he re-established the Republic of China (ROC) in exile. Over the next fifty years Taiwan created one of the world's most industrialized economies, becoming a leader in electronic manufacturing and design. Mainland China continued to claim Taiwan, considering it part of "One China."

Development Versus Democracy in India and Pakistan

Jawaharlal Nehru's daughter, Indira Gandhi (no relation to Mohandas Gandhi) (1917–1984), became prime minister of India in 1966. She dominated Indian political life for a generation. In 1975 she subverted parliamentary democracy and proclaimed a state of emergency. Gandhi applied her emergency powers across a broad range of areas, including combating corruption, quelling labor unrest, and jailing political opponents. She also initiated a campaign of mass sterilization to reduce population growth. More than 7 million men were forcibly sterilized in 1976. Many believed that Gandhi's emergency measures marked the end of liberal democracy, but in 1977 Gandhi called for free elections in which she suffered a spectacular electoral defeat. Her successors fell to fighting among themselves, and in 1980 she returned to power in an equally stunning electoral victory.

Separatist ethnic nationalism plagued Indira Gandhi's last years in office. India remained a patchwork of religions, languages, and peoples, always threatening to further divide the country along ethnic or religious lines. Most notable were the 15 million Sikhs of the Punjab in northern India (see Map 31.2, page 962), with their own religion, distinctive culture, and aspirations for greater autonomy for the Punjab. By 1984 some Sikh radicals were fighting for independence. Gandhi cracked down hard and was assassinated by Sikhs in retaliation. Violence followed as Hindu mobs slaughtered over a thousand Sikhs throughout India.

One of Indira Gandhi's sons, Rajiv Gandhi, was elected prime minister in 1984 by a landslide sympathy vote. Rajiv Gandhi departed from the Congress Party's socialism and prepared the way for Finance Minister Manmohan Singh to introduce market reforms, capitalist development, and Western technology and investment from 1991 onward. These reforms were successful, and since the 1990s India's economy has experienced explosive growth.

Though the Congress Party held power in India almost continuously after 1947, in the 1990s Hindu nationalists increasingly challenged the party's grip on power. These nationalists argued that India was based, above all, on Hindu culture and religion. The Hindu nationalist party, known as the BJP, finally gained power in 1998. The new government immediately tested nuclear devices, asserting its vision of a militant Hindu nationalism. In 2004 the United Progressive Alliance (UPA), a center-left coalition dominated by the Congress Party, regained control of the government and elected Manmohan Singh as prime minister. Under Narendra Modi, credited with the rapid economic growth of Gujarat state, the BJP returned to power after a sweeping electoral victory in 2014.

After Pakistan announced that it had developed nuclear weapons in 1998, relations between Pakistan and India worsened. In 2001 the two nuclear powers seemed poised for conflict until intense diplomatic pressure from the United States and other nations brought them back from the abyss of nuclear war. Tensions

CHAPTER LOCATOR | What were the short-term and long-term consequences of the OPEC oil embargo? | How did war and revolution reshape the Middle East?

CHAPTER 32
1014 LIBERALIZATION

again increased in 2008 when a Pakistan-based terrorist organization carried out a terrorist attack in Mumbai, India's largest city, killing 164 and wounding over 300.

In the decades following the separation of Bangladesh, Pakistan alternated between civilian and military rule. General Muhammad Zia-ul-Haq, who ruled from 1977 to 1988, drew Pakistan into a close alliance with the United States, but relations with the United States chilled as Pakistan pursued its nuclear weapons program. In 1996 a fundamentalist Muslim group, the Taliban, seized power in Afghanistan, Pakistan's neighbor to the west. The Taliban's leadership allowed al-Qaeda to use Afghanistan as a base for launching acts of terrorism like the attack on the U.S. World Trade Center and the Pentagon in 2001. Following that attack, the United States invaded Afghanistan, driving the Taliban from power.

When the United States invaded Afghanistan in 2001, Pakistani dictator General Pervez Musharraf (b. 1943) renewed the alliance with the United States, and Pakistan received billions of dollars in U.S. military aid. But U.S. combat against radical terrorist groups drove militants into regions of northwest Pakistan, where they undermined the government's already-tenuous control. Cooperation between Pakistan and the United States in the war was often strained.

In 2007 Musharraf attempted to reshape the country's Supreme Court by replacing the chief justice with one of his close allies, bringing about calls for his impeachment. Former prime minister Benazir Bhutto (1953–2007) returned from exile to challenge Musharraf's increasingly repressive military rule. She was assassinated while campaigning. After being defeated at the polls in 2008, Musharraf resigned and went into exile in London. Asif Ali Zardari (b. 1955), Benazir Bhutto's husband, won the presidency by a landslide in the elections that followed.

QUICK REVIEW <

What challenges do China and India face as they attempt to sustain the spectacular economic growth of recent decades?

| What effect did the Cold War and debt crisis have on Latin America? | How did white-minority rule end in southern Africa? | How have East and South Asian nations pursued economic development? | How did decolonization and the end of the Cold War change Europe? | ✓ LearningCurve Check what you know. |

1015

How did decolonization and the end of the Cold War change Europe?

Fall of the Berlin Wall

A man stands atop the partially destroyed Berlin Wall flashing the *V* for victory sign as he and thousands of other Berliners celebrate the opening of the Berlin Wall in November 1989. Within a year the wall was torn down, communism collapsed, and the Cold War ended. (Lionel Cironneau/AP Photo)

détente

▶ The progressive relaxation of Cold War tensions.

IN THE LATE 1960S AND EARLY 1970S the United States and the Soviet Union pursued a relaxation of Cold War tensions that became known as **détente** (day-TAHNT). Détente stalled when Brezhnev's Soviet Union invaded Afghanistan to save an unpopular Marxist regime. President Jimmy Carter reacted with alarm at the spread of Soviet influence.

Carter's successor, Ronald Reagan (U.S. pres. 1981–1989), further re-ignited the Cold War by calling the Soviet Union the "evil empire" and deploying nuclear arms in western Europe. Reagan found conservative allies in British prime minister Margaret Thatcher and German chancellor Helmut Kohl. But as Reagan, Thatcher, and Kohl rekindled the Cold War, the Soviet Union underwent a cycle of reform that culminated in the release of Soviet control over eastern Europe and the dismantling of the Soviet Union.

CHAPTER LOCATOR | What were the short-term and long-term consequences of the OPEC oil embargo? | How did war and revolution reshape the Middle East?

The Limits of Reform in the Soviet Union and Eastern Europe

After their 1968 military intervention in Czechoslovakia, Soviet leaders worked to restore order and stability. Free expression and open protest disappeared throughout their satellite nations. Dissidents were blacklisted or imprisoned in jails or mental institutions. A rising standard of living helped ensure stability as well. The privileges enjoyed by the Communist Party elite also served as incentives for such elites to do as the state wished. Beneath this appearance of stability, however, the Soviet Union underwent a social revolution. The urban population expanded rapidly, as did the number of highly trained scientists, managers, and specialists. These educated people read, discussed, and formed definite ideas about social questions ranging from pollution to urban transportation, fostering the growth of Soviet public opinion.

When Mikhail Gorbachev (b. 1931) became premier in 1985, he set out to reform the Soviet system with policies he called democratic socialism. The first set of reforms was intended to transform and restructure the economy. This limited economic restructuring, **perestroika**, permitted freer prices, more autonomy for state enterprises, and the establishment of some profit-seeking private cooperatives. Gorbachev also launched a campaign of openness, or **glasnost**, introduced in 1985. Where censorship and uniformity had long characterized public discourse, the new frankness approached free speech and marked a significant shift.

Democratization under Gorbachev led to the first free elections in the Soviet Union since 1917. Gorbachev and the party remained in control, but an independent minority was elected in 1989 to a revitalized Congress of People's Deputies. Democratization encouraged demands for greater autonomy from non-Russian minorities, especially in the Baltic region and in the Caucasus.

Finally, Gorbachev brought "new political thinking" to foreign affairs. He withdrew Soviet troops from Afghanistan in 1989 and sought to reduce Cold War tensions. Gorbachev pledged to respect the political choices of eastern Europe's peoples. Soon after, a wave of peaceful revolutions swept across eastern Europe, overturning Communist regimes.

Poland led the way. In August 1980 strikes grew into a working-class revolt. Led by Lech Wałęsa (lehk vah-LEHN-suh) (b. 1943), workers organized the independent trade union **Solidarity**. Communist leaders responded by imposing martial law in December 1981 and arresting Solidarity's leaders. Though outlawed, Solidarity maintained its organization and strong popular support. By 1988 labor unrest and inflation had brought Poland to the brink of economic collapse. Solidarity pressured Poland's Communist Party leaders into legalizing Solidarity and allowing free elections in 1989 for some seats in the Polish parliament. Solidarity won every contested seat. A month later Solidarity member Tadeusz Mazowiecki (1927–2013) was sworn in as prime minister.

Czechoslovakia's Velvet Revolution followed the dramatic changes in Poland and led to the peaceful ouster of Communist leaders. The Czech movement for democracy grew out of massive street protests led by students and intellectuals and resulted in the election of Václav Havel (VAH-slahf HAH-vuhl) as president in 1989. (See "Individuals in Society: Václav Havel," page 1018.)

Only in Romania was revolution violent. Communist dictator Nicolae Ceauşescu (chow-SHEHS-koo) (1918–1989) unleashed his security forces on

perestroika
▶ Economic restructuring and reform implemented by Soviet premier Mikhail Gorbachev that permitted an easing of government price controls on some goods, more independence for state enterprises, and the establishment of profit-seeking private cooperatives to provide personal services for consumers.

glasnost
▶ Soviet premier Mikhail Gorbachev's popular campaign for openness in the government and the media.

Solidarity
▶ Led by Lech Wałęsa, a free and democratic Polish trade union that worked for the rights of workers and political reform.

| What effect did the Cold War and debt crisis have on Latin America? | How did white-minority rule end in southern Africa? | How have East and South Asian nations pursued economic development? | **How did decolonization and the end of the Cold War change Europe?** | ✓ LearningCurve Check what you know. |

1017

INDIVIDUALS IN SOCIETY
Václav Havel

On the night of November 24, 1989, the revolution in Czechoslovakia reached its climax. Three hundred thousand people had poured into Prague's historic Wenceslas Square to continue the massive protests that had erupted a week earlier after the police savagely beat student demonstrators. Now all eyes were focused on a high balcony. There an elderly man with a gentle smile and a middle-aged intellectual wearing jeans and a sports jacket stood arm in arm and acknowledged the cheers of the crowd. "Dubček-Havel," the people roared. "Dubček-Havel!" Alexander Dubček, who represented the failed promise of reform communism in the 1960s (see page 984), was symbolically passing the torch to Václav Havel, who embodied the uncompromising opposition to communism that was sweeping the country. That very evening, the hard-line Communist government resigned, and soon Havel was the unanimous choice to head a new democratic Czechoslovakia. Who was this man to whom the nation turned in 1989?

Václav Havel, playwright, dissident leader, and the first postcommunist president of the Czech Republic. (Chris Niedenthal/Black Star)

Born in 1936 into a prosperous, cultured, upper-middle-class family, the young Havel was denied admission to the university because of his class origins. Loving literature and philosophy, he gravitated to the theater, became a stagehand, and emerged in the 1960s as a leading playwright. His plays were set in vague settings, developed existential themes, and poked fun at the absurdities of life and the pretensions of communism. In his private life, Havel thrived on good talk, Prague's lively bar scene, and officially forbidden rock 'n' roll.

In 1968 the Soviets rolled into Czechoslovakia, and Havel watched in horror as a tank commander opened fire on a crowd of peaceful protesters in a small town. "That week," he recorded, "was an experience I shall never forget."[*] The free-spirited artist threw himself into the intellectual opposition to communism and became its leading figure for the next twenty years. The costs of defiance were enormous. Purged and blacklisted, Havel lifted barrels in a brewery and wrote bitter satires that could not be staged. In 1977 he and a few other dissidents publicly protested Czechoslovakian violations of the Helsinki Accords on human rights, and in 1989 this Charter '77 group became the inspiration for Civic Forum, the democratic coalition that toppled communism. Havel spent five years in prison and was constantly harassed by the police.

Havel's thoughts and actions focused on truth, decency, and moral regeneration. In 1975, in a famous open letter to Czechoslovakia's Communist boss, Havel wrote that the people were indeed quiet, but

only because they were "driven by fear. . . . Everyone has something to lose and so everyone has reason to be afraid." Havel saw lies, hypocrisy, and apathy undermining and poisoning all human relations in his country: "Order has been established — at the price of a paralysis of the spirit, a deadening of the heart, and a spiritual and moral crisis in society."[†]

Yet Havel saw a way out of the Communist quagmire. He argued that a profound but peaceful revolution in human values was possible. Such a revolution could lead to the moral reconstruction of Czech and Slovak society, where, in his words, "values like trust, openness, responsibility, solidarity and love" might again flourish and nurture the human spirit. Havel was a voice of hope and humanity who inspired his compatriots with a lofty vision of a moral postcommunist society. As president of his country from 1989 to 2003, Havel continued to speak eloquently on the great questions of our time.

QUESTIONS FOR ANALYSIS

1. Why did Havel oppose Communist rule? How did his goals differ from those of Dubček and other advocates of reform communism?
2. Havel has been called a "moralist in politics." Is this a good description of him? Why or why not?

[†]Quoted ibid., p. 110.

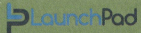

ONLINE DOCUMENT PROJECT

How did people in Czechoslovakia overturn the existing social and political order? Explore the efforts of dissidents to produce a peaceful revolution, and then complete a quiz and writing assignment based on the evidence and details from this chapter. *See inside the front cover to learn more.*

[*]Quoted in M. Simmons, *The Reluctant President: A Political Life of Václav Havel* (London: Methuen, 1991), p. 91.

protesters, sparking an armed uprising. After Ceauşescu's forces were defeated, he and his wife were captured and executed.

Amid growing resistance, the Hungarian Communist Party scheduled free elections for early 1990. Hungarians tore down the barbed wire that separated Hungary and Austria (see Map 31.1, page 956) and opened their border to refugees from East Germany. As thousands of East Germans passed through Czechoslovakia and Hungary on their way to West Germany, a protest movement arose in East Germany. East Germany's leaders relented and opened the Berlin Wall in November 1989, before being swept aside. An "Alliance for Germany" won general elections and negotiated an economic union with West Germany.

Two factors contributed to the rapid reunification of East and West Germany. First, in the first week after the Berlin Wall opened, almost 9 million East Germans poured across the border into West Germany. Almost all returned home, but their experiences in the West aroused long-dormant hopes of unity and change. Second, West German chancellor Helmut Kohl was successful in convincing American, Soviet, and European leaders that they need not fear a reunified Germany. In 1991 East and West Germany merged into a single nation under West Germany's constitution and laws.

The great postcommunist tragedy was Yugoslavia, whose federation of republics and regions had been held together under Josip Tito's Communist rule. After Tito's death in 1980, power passed increasingly to the republics. Rising territorial and ethnic tensions were intensified by economic decline and charges of ethnically inspired massacres during World War II. The revolutions of 1989 accelerated the breakup of Yugoslavia. Serbian president Slobodan Milošević (SLOH-buh-dayn muh-LOH-suh-vihch) (1941–2006) attempted to grab land from other republics and unite all Serbs in a "greater Serbia." His ambitions led to civil wars that between 1991 and 2001 engulfed Kosovo, Slovenia, Croatia, and Bosnia-Herzegovina (Map 32.2). In 1999 Serbian aggression prompted NATO air strikes, led by the United States, against the Serbian capital of Belgrade as well as against Serbian military forces until Milošević relented. Milošević was voted out of office in 2000. The new Serbian government extradited him to a United Nations war crimes tribunal in the Netherlands to stand trial for crimes against humanity.

Recasting Russia Without Communism

Amid anticommunist upheavals in eastern Europe, the Soviet Union itself transitioned away from Communist Party rule. In February 1990 the Soviet Communist Party was defeated in local elections throughout the country. Gorbachev responded by asking Soviet citizens to ratify a new constitution that abolished the Communist Party's monopoly on political power and expanded the power of the Congress of People's Deputies. Gorbachev's eroding power and unwillingness to risk a popular election for the presidency strengthened his rival, Boris Yeltsin (1931–2007), the former mayor of Moscow. In May 1990, as leader of the Russian parliament, Yeltsin announced that Russia would declare its independence from the Soviet Union. In June 1991 Yeltsin was elected president of the Russian Federation within the Soviet Union, placing him in direct confrontation with Gorbachev, who wanted to keep the Soviet Union together amid carefully managed reforms.

In August 1991 Gorbachev survived an attempted coup by Communist Party hardliners and their allies in the armed forces. Not only did their coup attempt fail,

| What effect did the Cold War and debt crisis have on Latin America? | How did white-minority rule end in southern Africa? | How have East and South Asian nations pursued economic development? | **How did decolonization and the end of the Cold War change Europe?** | ✓ LearningCurve Check what you know. |

1019

MAP 32.2 ■ **The Breakup of Yugoslavia**

Yugoslavia had the most ethnically diverse population in eastern Europe. The Republic of Croatia had substantial Serbian and Muslim minorities, and Bosnia-Herzegovina had large Muslim, Serbian, and Croatian populations, none of which had a majority. In June 1991 Serbia's brutal effort to seize territory and unite all Serbs in a single state brought a tragic civil war to the region.

but it also hastened the end of the Soviet Union. Yeltsin emerged as a popular hero for his dramatic resistance to the coup attempt.

In the aftermath of the attempted military takeover, an anticommunist revolution swept the Russian Federation as the Communist Party was outlawed and its property confiscated. Yeltsin and his liberal allies declared Russia independent and withdrew from the Soviet Union. All the other Soviet republics followed suit. Gorbachev agreed to their independence, and the Soviet Union ceased to exist on December 25, 1991 (Map 32.3).

As Boris Yeltsin presided over newly independent Russia, he sought to create economic conditions that would prevent a return to communism. Yeltsin opted for breakneck liberalization. This shock therapy, which followed methods similar to radical free-market policies in Chile and other parts of Latin America, freed prices on 90 percent of all Russian goods. The government also launched a rapid privatization of industry and turned thousands of factories and mines over to new private companies. However, instead of producing the hoped for prosperity, prices soared and production collapsed.

CHAPTER LOCATOR | What were the short-term and long-term consequences of the OPEC oil embargo? | How did war and revolution reshape the Middle East?

MAP 32.3 ■ Russia and the Successor States

After the attempt in August 1991 to depose Gorbachev failed, an anticommunist revolution swept the Soviet Union. Led by Russia and Boris Yeltsin, the republics that formed the Soviet Union declared their sovereignty and independence. Eleven of the fifteen republics then formed a loose confederation called the Commonwealth of Independent States, but the integrated economy of the Soviet Union dissolved into separate national economies, each with its own goals and policies.

Rapid economic liberalization had harsh consequences for Russia. Powerful state industrial monopolies became powerful private monopolies that cut production and raised prices in order to maximize profits. The managerial elite worked with organized crime to prevent the formation of would-be competitors. A new capitalist elite acquired great wealth and power, while the vast majority of people fell into poverty. As the quality of public services and health care declined, life expectancies fell. In 2003 Russia's per capita income was lower than at any time since 1978, essentially erasing the economic progress gained over the past twenty-five years.

The election of Yeltsin's handpicked successor, President Vladimir Putin (b. 1952), in 2000 ushered in a new era of "managed democracy." Putin's stress on public order and economic reform was popular, even as he became progressively

What effect did the Cold War and debt crisis have on Latin America?

How did white-minority rule end in southern Africa?

How have East and South Asian nations pursued economic development?

How did decolonization and the end of the Cold War change Europe?

☑ LearningCurve
Check what you know.

more authoritarian. Putin consolidated the power and authority of the state around himself and his closest advisers, closing off the development of democratic pluralism and an independent legal system in Russia.

Putin carried out a brutal military campaign against the primarily Muslim republic Chechnya (CHEHCH-nyuh) (see Map 32.3, inset) that in 1991 declared its independence. Up to two hundred thousand Chechen civilians are estimated to have been killed between 1994 and 2011. Many more became refugees. Chechen resistance to Russian domination continued, often in the form of attacks such as a suicide bombing at Moscow's airport in 2011.

Unable to run for re-election in 2008, Putin handpicked a successor, Dmitry Medvedev, to be president, and took the position of Russian prime minister for himself. He remained the main power broker and returned to the presidency in 2012. Liberal reforms doomed much of Russia's industry, and its economy depended increasingly on oil and natural gas exports.

Political and ethnic divisions threatened peace and stability among the post-Soviet republics. Rival claims between the Republic of Georgia and the Russian Federation over the territory of South Ossetia led to war in 2008 in which Russian forces quickly defeated their Georgian rivals and established the pro-Russian autonomy of the region. In Ukraine, in 2014 pro-Western protesters toppled a president who refused to sign agreements with the European Union. In the aftermath of the uprising, Russian forces occupied Ukrainian province of Crimea along the Black Sea and backed secessionist movements in ethnically Russian regions of the Ukraine.

Integration and Reform in Europe

Building on integration efforts in the 1940s and 1950s established through NATO and the Common Market (see page 982), at the end of the twentieth century European nations moved toward greater unity. France and Germany took the lead in pushing for a monetary union among Common Market members. The **European Union (EU)**, established in 1993, allowed for the free movement of people and goods among its original twelve member countries; created a common currency, the euro (2002); and formed a European Parliament.

The loss by western European countries of their colonies in Africa and Asia was a major incentive to unify within Europe because it dramatically shifted their access to markets and resources. For five centuries overseas empires not only provided the engine for economic development at home but also shaped international relations. As the cycle of colonialism ended, nations that had related to each other with the crutch of overseas empires now needed to forge new relationships directly with one another—the first time they had ever done so since the cycle of colonialism accompanied the process of nation-state formation. The result was an unprecedentedly close degree of economic and political integration.

European leaders embraced, or at least accepted, a neoliberal, free-market vision of capitalism. The most radical economic changes had been implemented in the 1980s by Margaret Thatcher (1925–2013) in Britain, who drew inspiration from Pinochet's Chile. Other governments also introduced austerity measures to slow the growth of public spending and the welfare state. Many individuals suffered under the impact of these reductions in public spending and social welfare, and the threat of unemployment shaped the outlook of a whole generation. Harder

European Union (EU)
▶ An economic and political alliance of twelve European nations formed in 1993 that has since grown to include twenty-seven European nations.

CHAPTER LOCATOR | What were the short-term and long-term consequences of the OPEC oil embargo? | How did war and revolution reshape the Middle East?

CHAPTER 32
1022 LIBERALIZATION

times meant that more women entered or remained in the workforce after they married.

In the 1990s Germany and France continued to lead the push for integration. French president François Mitterrand (1916–1996) and German chancellor Helmut Kohl (b. 1930) pursued a monetary union of European Community members, and the Maastricht Treaty of 1992 created a single EU currency, the euro. In 1993 the European Community rechristened itself the European Union (EU).

The success of the euro encouraged the EU to accelerate plans for an ambitious enlargement to the east. On May 1, 2004, the EU started admitting eastern European countries. By 2007 the EU had twenty-seven member states. Future candidates for membership include Croatia, Macedonia, former parts of the Soviet Union, and Turkey (Map 32.4).

MAP 32.4 ■ The European Union, 2014

No longer divided by ideological competition and the Cold War, much of today's Europe has banded together in a European Union.

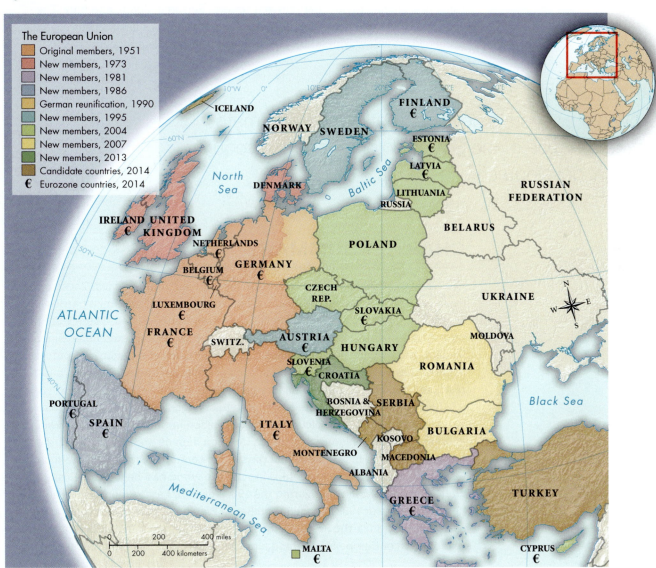

| What effect did the Cold War and debt crisis have on Latin America? | How did white-minority rule end in southern Africa? | How have East and South Asian nations pursued economic development? | **How did decolonization and the end of the Cold War change Europe?** | ✓ LearningCurve Check what you know. |

A proposed EU constitution binding EU member states even closer together was scheduled to go into effect in 2007. First, however, it needed to be approved by voters in all member countries. In 2005 voters in France and Holland voted overwhelmingly against the constitution and threw the entire process into confusion. The rejected constitution was replaced with the Treaty of Lisbon in 2007. The new treaty kept most of the reforms contained in the original European constitution, but it revised the political structure of the EU bureaucracy. By November 2009 all members had approved it, and the Lisbon treaty came into force on December 1, 2009.

The economic crisis that began in 2008 tested the European Union and the euro. Countries that had adopted the euro currency had to meet stringent fiscal standards and imposed budget cuts and financial austerity. The resulting reductions in health care and social benefits hit ordinary citizens hard. A global economic recession magnified these difficulties. National governments could no longer manage their own currencies to promote recovery, and governments were forced to slash budgets to meet debt obligations. Economic austerity brought ruinous economic cycles that crippled Greece, Portugal, Spain, and Italy. The consequences of liberalization in Europe resembled the consequences elsewhere: economic growth was greater, but economic hardships were deeper.

> **QUICK REVIEW**

How did economic developments in the aftermath of the collapse of the Soviet Union shape subsequent political developments in Russia?

CHAPTER SUMMARY

In 1976 most of the world was governed by undemocratic regimes. These regimes came in many different types: some were controlled by Communist parties and others by right-wing military officers loyal to the United States. There were dictatorships ruled by nationalist leaders, strongmen who unseated independence leaders, and by members of families that owned much of a nation's resources. Some of these dictators created an illusion of governing democratically, but they restricted opposition or required one-party rule.

Some dictatorships created the space to engage in utopian projects to remake nations. Even when such dictatorships succeeded in their goals, they did so at enormous costs measured in debt and inflation, famine and malnutrition, the tattering of public institutions, and the reliance on repression to maintain order.

By the mid-1980s dictatorships around the world had begun to fall, and democratic transitions followed. During the 1980s most of Latin America returned to democracy, and in 1989 the fall of the Berlin Wall began a wave of political and economic change in the Soviet Union and eastern Europe. The end of the Cold War division of Europe accelerated a process of integration and unification that

CHAPTER LOCATOR | What were the short-
term and long-term
consequences of the
OPEC oil embargo?

How did war and
revolution reshape the
Middle East?

CHAPTER 32
1024 LIBERALIZATION

had its roots in reconstruction after the Second World War and the process of decolonization that dismantled European empires. Alongside political transitions, a wave of economic liberalization, often promoted by the United States, swept the world. Trade and economic activity increased as a result of liberalization, but it also created growing gaps between rich and poor.

 **CONNECTIONS** The experiences of people living under authoritarian regimes varied greatly. Many supported the regimes from which they drew privileges or found a reassuring sense of order. Others avoided political questions and stayed out of trouble.

Many, however, resisted the regimes. For some, a closed political system meant the only tools available were armed resistance. Guerrilla movements against authoritarian regimes were common, though the imbalance in their resources meant they mostly met with violent ends at the hands of security forces. Another form of resistance proved more effective: nonviolent, and ostensibly nonpolitical, resistance was harder for regimes to repress. Mothers asking for the whereabouts of missing children or quilting the scenes of their grief in Argentina and Chile, or workers organizing an independent union in Poland, found ways to challenge their regimes.

The most successful resistance was often opposition that was not explicitly ideological, such as the defense of human rights, or the establishment of the rule of law that would restrict a regime's arbitrary power. These pressures had a similar effect when applied to right-wing or socialist dictatorships alike: they were liberalizing. As dictatorships in Latin America, East Asia, and eastern Europe moved toward multiparty democracy, and as the Soviet bloc disintegrated, those countries shared a historical moment in which liberal economic and political reforms swept the world.

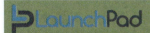

ONLINE DOCUMENT PROJECT
Václav Havel: Planning a Nonviolent Revolution

How did people in Czechoslovakia overturn the existing social and political order?

Explore the efforts of dissidents to produce a peaceful revolution, and then complete a quiz and writing assignment based on the evidence and details from this chapter. *See inside the front cover to learn more.*

What effect did the Cold War and debt crisis have on Latin America?

How did white-minority rule end in southern Africa?

How have East and South Asian nations pursued economic development?

How did decolonization and the end of the Cold War change Europe?

LearningCurve Check what you know.

STEP 1 **GET STARTED ONLINE**

✓ **LearningCurve**

Now that you've read the chapter, make it stick by completing the LearningCurve activity.

STEP 2 **EXPLAIN WHY IT MATTERS**

Put your reading into practice. Identify each term below, and then explain why it matters in world history.

TERM	WHO OR WHAT & WHEN	WHY IT MATTERS
petrodollars (p. 993)		
neoliberalism (p. 994)		
Washington Consensus (p. 994)		
intifada (p. 998)		
junta (p. 1003)		
apartheid (p. 1008)		
African National Congress (ANC) (p. 1008)		
Tiananmen Square (p. 1012)		
"Japan, Inc." (p. 1013)		
détente (p. 1016)		
perestroika (p. 1017)		
glasnost (p. 1017)		
Solidarity (p. 1017)		
European Union (EU) (p. 1022)		

STEP 3 **MOVE BEYOND THE BASICS**

To demonstrate a more advanced understanding of the impact of economic developments and policies on recent world history, fill in the chart below with descriptions of key economic events and their consequences. In your opinion, has liberalization had an overall positive impact on global economic development in the last fifty years? Why or why not?

	Description	Consequences
OPEC Oil Embargo		
Economic Liberalization in Latin America		
Economic Liberalization in China		
Economic Liberalization in the Aftermath of the Collapse of the Soviet Union		
The 2008 Financial Crisis		

STEP 4 — PUT IT ALL TOGETHER

Now, take a step back and try to explain the big picture. Remember to use specific examples from the chapter in your answers.

THE MIDDLE EAST AND ASIA

▶ What are the most important *internal* divisions within the Islamic societies of the Middle East?

▶ In your opinion, how stable is China's combination of economic liberalism and political authoritarianism? What does China's history since 1945 tell us about the likelihood of political liberalization in China in coming decades?

LATIN AMERICA AND AFRICA

▶ What policies and practices did Latin American authoritarian leaders employ to maintain their hold on power? Why did so many dictatorships give way to democracy in the late twentieth century?

▶ What light do the recent histories of Nigeria and South Africa shed on the challenges facing sub-Saharan Africa as the region enters the twenty-first century?

THE END OF THE COLD WAR

▶ How would you explain the pattern of post–Cold War development in Eastern Europe? Why were some states more successful than others?

▶ What forces were behind the push toward greater European unity in the late twentieth century? What might explain the increasing reluctance of ordinary Europeans to support further steps toward unification?

LOOKING BACK, LOOKING AHEAD

▶ Compare and contrast the economic relationship between the West and the rest of the world in 1900 and in 2000. What changed? What stayed the same?

▶ In your opinion, will liberal economic policies continue to dominate global economic activity in the next several decades? Why or why not?

> IN YOUR OWN WORDS

Imagine that you must give an oral report to the class answering the following question: **Why did liberalization emerge as a such a powerful force in the second half of the twentieth century, and what were the consequences of this development?** What would be the most important points and why?

33

THE CONTEMPORARY WORLD IN HISTORICAL PERSPECTIVE

> **How is our understanding of the present shaped by our understanding of the past?**

Chapter 33 examines the contemporary world in historical perspective. Since the end of the Cold War, many nations around the world have undergone transitions from dictatorship to democracy, and a growing number of nations have pursued free trade. These new experiences have been shaped by past struggles, and they have intensified global connections, aided by revolutions in communications and information technology. Amid these changes, stubborn regional and political conflicts remain in many parts of the world, and the experiences of poverty and marginalization continue to be widespread. But this is also a world in which, as in the past, humans have had the ability to shape, adapt, and transform the problems they confront.

> Does the contemporary world reflect the "end of history"?

> How have migration and the circulation of capital and technology continued to shape the world?

> What challenges did social reformers address at the turn of the twenty-first century?

> How have science and technology kept pace with population change?

The Digital Revolution People throughout the world have embraced the ease and convenience of mobile phone technology, which has increased dramatically since the introduction of the first cellular phone in 1985. (Masterfile/Royalty-Free)

LearningCurve
After reading the chapter, use LearningCurve to retain what you've read.

> Does the contemporary world reflect the "end of history"?

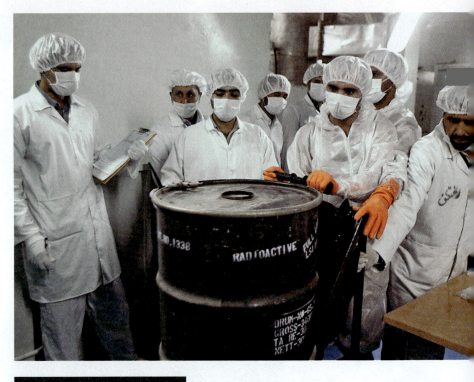

Iranian Nuclear Energy Program

Despite threats of sanctions from the United States, France, Germany, Great Britain, and Russia, Iran continues to develop its nuclear energy program. Here Iranian scientists move a container of radioactive uranium. (Behrouz Mehri/AFP/Getty Images)

IN 1989, AS THE BERLIN WALL FELL and the Soviet system disintegrated, a historian wrote a provocative article called "The End of History?" in which he argued that the collapse of the Soviet system meant the triumph of liberalism as a political and economic philosophy. The argument, and the essay's title, begged an interesting question. Was liberalism the ultimate stage of human political and economic development?

Around the world at the turn of the twenty-first century, liberalism certainly emerged as the dominant political and economic philosophy. But there have been limits to liberalism's reach and its effectiveness as a solution to political and economic problems. For instance, economic liberalism has tended to increase social inequality and the disparity of wealth between nations and regions in ways that are not sustainable. As a result, the rise of liberalism has been met by a growing range of social activism aimed at reducing social inequality; gender, ethnic, and racial marginalization; and the environmental costs of economic development.

The tension between liberalism and activism is one example of the kinds of contradictory and competing pressures that shape the contemporary world. For instance, the earth's growing population has increased demands for food produc-

1950s Beginning of green revolution	**1997** Chemical Weapons Convention goes into effect, banning the production of chemical weapons; Kyoto Protocol on global warming
1969–1979 Strategic Arms Limitation Talks (SALT) between the Soviet Union and United States	**2000–2010** Warmest decade in recorded history
1970 Treaty on the Non-Proliferation of Nuclear Weapons	**2001** Al-Qaeda attacks on World Trade Center and U.S. Pentagon
1981 UN World Health Organization International Code of Marketing of Breast-Milk Substitutes	**2001** U.S. invasion and occupation of Afghanistan
1989 United Nations Convention on the Rights of the Child	**2003** U.S.-led coalition invades Iraq; Human Genome Project completes sequencing of human genome
1994 Zapatista Army for National Liberation insurrection in Chiapas, Mexico	

tion, prompting a revolution in agricultural sciences. Although new technologies have helped meet the world's demand for food, the diversion of water resources and the expansion of farming at the expense of forests remind us that new technologies often bring unintended costs. Similarly, the end of the Cold War has been met not with peace but with regional conflicts around the world. And with the intensification of communications, increase in travel, and the spread of technology, capital and liberal ideology have been met with conservative, often religious reactions in different regions of the world. Increasingly, those reactions have had a global impact as militants pursue their causes in the United States and Europe.

Complexity and Violence in a Multipolar World

When the Cold War ended, the existing global political alignment yielded to new regional relationships in which many middle powers exerted increased influence. Increasingly assertive **middle powers**, countries with significant economic influence either in relation to their neighbors or in broader trade networks, jockeyed for regional leadership.

middle powers
▶ Countries with significant economic influence that became increasingly assertive regional leaders after the Cold War.

> **Middle Powers:**

- South America: Brazil
- The Spanish-speaking Americas: Mexico
- Europe: France and Germany
- Sub-Saharan Africa: Nigeria and South Africa
- The Middle East: Turkey, Egypt, Iran, and Israel
- Asia: China, India, and Japan

What challenges did social reformers address at the turn of the twenty-first century?	How have science and technology kept pace with population change?	✓ LearningCurve Check what you know.

While the end of the Cold War reduced superpower pressures that intensified regional conflicts, other factors continued to feed conflicts around the world. In the 1990s civil wars in Bosnia, Kosovo, Rwanda, and Afghanistan killed over a million people and created hundreds of thousands of refugees. Since 2000 new and continuing wars have caused millions more deaths and new refugees. Rivalries between ethnic groups often lay at the heart of these wars.

An Expanding Atomic Age

After the bombing of Hiroshima and Nagasaki in 1945 (see page 946), the United States briefly held a monopoly on atomic weapons. Since then, a growing number of nations have developed nuclear arms.

The Cold War arms race resulted in intense competition for the development of increasingly powerful atomic weapons, and it also meant massive spending in the United States, the Soviet Union, and Europe on the development of other military technology. While the superpowers and their closest allies sought to restrict access to nuclear weapons, they sold huge numbers of conventional arms to other nations.

Amid the Cold War arms race, atomic tests brought fear that radiation would enter the food chain. Concerned scientists called for a ban on atomic bomb testing. In 1963 the United States, Great Britain, and the Soviet Union reached an agreement, eventually joined by more than 150 countries, to ban nuclear tests in the atmosphere. In 1970 more than sixty countries signed the Treaty on the Non-Proliferation of Nuclear Weapons, designed to halt the spread of nuclear weapons to states that did not yet have them and to reduce stockpiles of existing bombs held by the nuclear powers. It seemed that the nuclear arms race might yet be reversed.

This outcome did not come to pass. French and Chinese leaders disregarded the test ban and by 1968 had developed their own nuclear weapons, although they later signed the nonproliferation treaty. India also developed nuclear weapons and in 1974 exploded an atomic device. Meanwhile, the nuclear arms race between the Soviet Union and the United States was so intense that after the 1960s both sides sought ways of slowing it and negotiated shared limits to their nuclear arsenals. A series of treaties between 1969 and 2010 have brought substantial reductions in nuclear weapons stockpiles.

India's nuclear test in 1974 in turn frightened Pakistan, which pursued its own nuclear weapons. In 1998 both India and Pakistan tested nuclear devices within weeks of each other. Other nations discreetly pursued nuclear arms without publicly stating that they possessed them.

In the 1950s Israel began developing nuclear weapons, and it is generally believed to have had an arsenal of nuclear weapons since the 1970s. Israel's apparent nuclear superiority was threatening to Arab states that for decades had tried to vanquish Israel. When Iraq attempted, with help from France, to develop nuclear capability in the 1980s, Israel responded by attacking and destroying the Iraqi nuclear reactor in June 1981.

The risks associated with the proliferation of nuclear weapons helped mobilize the international community and contributed to positive developments through the 1980s and 1990s. Between 1983 and 2003 Argentina, Romania, Brazil, South Africa, and Libya all agreed to abandon their nuclear weapons programs. Several

CHAPTER LOCATOR | **Does the contemporary world reflect the "end of history"?** | How have migration and the circulation of capital and technology shaped the world?

CHAPTER 33
1032 THE CONTEMPORARY WORLD IN HISTORICAL PERSPECTIVE

of the former Soviet republics that possessed nuclear arsenals returned their nuclear weapons to Russia. International agencies monitored exports of nuclear material, technology, and missiles that could carry atomic bombs. These measures encouraged confidence in global cooperation and in the nonproliferation treaty, which was extended indefinitely in 1995.

Despite these efforts, nuclear proliferation has continued. In 2003 the United States accused Iran of seeking to build nuclear weapons, and ongoing diplomatic efforts, sanctions, and other punitive measures have failed to induce Iran to limit its nuclear program. There is also the threat that enriched nuclear materials will fall into the hands of terrorist organizations or that countries possessing nuclear weapons technology would share it with other nations.

In the new century, long-standing tensions between North Korea and the United States, which had never signed a peace treaty to end the 1950–1953 Korean War, intensified over North Korea's pursuit of nuclear weapons and ballistic missile technology. As each side accused the other of failing to live up to its agreements, North Korea tested its first nuclear device in 2006. A year later, North Korea agreed to shut down its major nuclear facility at Yŏngbyŏn in exchange for thousands of tons of fuel oil from the West and the release of $25 million in frozen North Korean funds. In 2009, however, North Korea ended all diplomatic talks, expelled all nuclear inspectors, and conducted a nuclear test. In the years that followed, North Korean authorities have engaged in nuclear brinksmanship.

Al-Qaeda and Afghanistan

In the Middle East and Central Asia, conflicts that had involved the superpowers continued beyond the Cold War. The 1979 Soviet invasion of Afghanistan, as well as the Iranian revolution, which was followed by the Iran-Iraq War, led to enduring political upheaval that continued to draw the United States into violent conflicts in the twenty-first century.

In Afghanistan rebel groups supported by the United States fought the Soviet armed forces occupying the country, and forced a Soviet withdrawal in 1989. In 1996, after years of civil war, a puritanical Islamic movement called the Taliban filled the military and political vacuum left by the Soviet Union. The Taliban pursued a radical religious transformation of Afghan society, in particular by imposing harsh restrictions on women. The Taliban government provided safe haven in Afghanistan for a terrorist organization called al-Qaeda. In the 1990s, led by Osama bin Laden (1957–2011), al-Qaeda attacked U.S. diplomatic and military targets in Africa and the Middle East.

On September 11, 2001, al-Qaeda militants hijacked four passenger planes in the United States. They flew two of them into the World Trade Center buildings in New York City and a third into the Pentagon in Washington, D.C. A fourth, believed to be targeting the White House or the U.S. Capitol, crashed into a field in rural Pennsylvania. These terrorist attacks killed almost three thousand people. In response, the U.S. government demanded that the Taliban government in Afghanistan surrender the al-Qaeda leadership it hosted. When the Taliban refused, the United States formed a military coalition including NATO members as well as Russia, Pakistan, and rebel groups in Afghanistan. The coalition mounted an invasion, deposed the Taliban, and pursued al-Qaeda.

What challenges did social reformers address at the turn of the twenty-first century?

How have science and technology kept pace with population change?

☑ LearningCurve
Check what you know.

Pedestrians race for safety as the World Trade Center towers collapse after being hit by jet airliners. (Amy Sanetta/AP Photo)

After the U.S.-led coalition deposed the Taliban in 2001 and installed a new government in Afghanistan, it faced a protracted guerrilla war against Taliban forces that controlled rural areas. The conflict in Afghanistan spread to Pakistan, where some members of al-Qaeda found refuge, and acts of terrorism increased around the world in the years following the invasion of Afghanistan.

Through years of war, the United States and allied governments devastated al-Qaeda's leadership and reduced its reach, but local groups acting in conflicts in the Middle East and Africa continued to act under al-Qaeda's name. Militants with loose ties to al-Qaeda set off multiple bombs in a Madrid train station on March 11, 2004, killing 191 and wounding over 1,800. In London on July 7, 2005, terrorist bombs killed 56 people and injured more than 700. At least three of the bombers were British citizens of Pakistani descent with unclear links to al-Qaeda. A suicide bomber who may have had links to al-Qaeda has also been blamed for the 2007 assassination of Pakistani presidential candidate Benazir Bhutto. In 2011 U.S. intelligence services identified bin Laden's hideout in Pakistan in a compound located near the country's main military academy in Abbottabad. In a night raid, U.S. forces killed bin Laden.

U.S. military action against al-Qaeda and the Taliban spilled over into another conflict in the Middle East when the U.S. government invaded Iraq in 2003. In the decade following the conclusion of the Persian Gulf War (1990–1991), Iraq faced international economic sanctions along with constant political and military pressure from the United States to surrender its chemical and biological weapons stockpiles. After 2001, amid the U.S. invasion of Afghanistan, U.S. president George W. Bush accused Iraq of rebuilding its nuclear, chemical, and biological weapons programs. To build domestic support for an invasion, the U.S. government also falsely implied that there were connections between Iraq and al-Qaeda. In 2002 UN inspectors found no weapons of mass destruction. France, Russia, China, Germany, and a majority of the smaller states argued for continued weapons monitoring, and France threatened to veto any resolution authorizing an invasion of Iraq. Rather than risk this veto, the United States and Britain claimed that earlier Security Council resolutions provided sufficient authorization and invaded Iraq in 2003.

CHAPTER LOCATOR | **Does the contemporary world reflect the "end of history"?** | How have migration and the circulation of capital and technology shaped the world?

1034 CHAPTER 33 THE CONTEMPORARY WORLD IN HISTORICAL PERSPECTIVE

A coalition of U.S.-led forces quickly defeated the Iraqi military, and in the power vacuum that ensued, armed groups representing all three main factions in Iraq—Sunni Muslims, Shi'ite Muslims, and Kurds—carried out daily attacks on Iraqi military and police, government officials, religious leaders, and civilians. Estimates of Iraqi deaths since the beginning of the war in 2003 and the U.S. withdrawal in 2011 ranged from 100,000 to over 1 million. Though the U.S. military occupation ended in 2011, the violence continued. Paradoxically, though the connection between al-Qaeda and the government of Saddam Hussein implied by President Bush did not exist, postwar Iraq became a place where militant groups that identified with al-Qaeda proliferated.

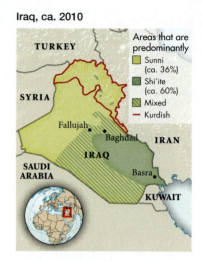

Iraq, ca. 2010

Areas that are predominantly
- Sunni (ca. 36%)
- Shi'ite (ca. 60%)
- Mixed
- Kurdish

TURKEY
SYRIA
Fallujah
Baghdad
IRAN
IRAQ
SAUDI ARABIA
Basra
KUWAIT

QUICK REVIEW

What contemporary trends and developments demonstrate some of the limits of liberalism?

What challenges did social reformers address at the turn of the twenty-first century?

How have science and technology kept pace with population change?

✔ LearningCurve
Check what you know.

How have migration and the circulation of capital and technology continued to shape the world?

The Bazaar Economy

These merchant women selling vegetables in Pisac, Peru, form part of an informal economy. (© Juergen Ritterbach/vario Images RM/age fotostock)

MUCH OF THE HISTORY IN THIS TEXTBOOK is driven by the circulation of peoples over great distances. Migration continues to be one of the great engines of history, though its experience exposes one of the major contradictions in the way liberalization has been conducted: governments have pressed for the free circulation of goods and capital, but have sought to limit the movement of people across borders.

Migration

National immigration policies vary considerably. In Europe the process of integration has meant that European Union member countries permit the free movement of citizens from other EU nations. But in many other cases, restrictions on migration have increased even as barriers to trade and investment have fallen.

The border between the United States and Mexico reflects many of the challenges of contemporary migrations. As the United States conquered land that had belonged to Mexico in the nineteenth century (see Chapter 27), it restricted the movement of migrants northward across the border. At the beginning of the twenty-first century the U.S. government began building a wall at its border with

CHAPTER LOCATOR | Does the contemporary world reflect the "end of history"? | How have migration and the circulation of capital and technology shaped the world?

1036 CHAPTER 33
THE CONTEMPORARY WORLD IN HISTORICAL PERSPECTIVE

Mexico, further restricting the circulation of people even as the United States and Mexico negotiated a free-trade agreement that made it easier for goods and capital to cross the border.

Similar trade agreements, coupled with similar restrictions on migration, exist between the United States and many Central American and Caribbean nations. The United States is by far the leading source of foreign investment in those countries. And the United States has participated in military conflicts in all of those countries over the past century. Still, within the United States, the most intense public discussions about Latin America surround the restriction of migration.

In many cases, restrictions on immigration have increased in countries where national economic growth has slowed. For instance, as Japanese industry boomed in the 1980s, the country welcomed descendants of Japanese emigrants who had settled in South America in the first half of the century to come to Japan as guest workers. As manufacturing and economic growth stagnated in the 1990s, this circuit of migration to Japan dwindled. During the same period millions of people, first from South Korea and then Vietnam, Cambodia, and Laos, whose countries had experienced great upheavals in conflicts involving the United States, found legal refuge in the United States. (See "Individuals in Society: Sieng, a Mnong Refugee in an American High School," page 1038.)

Though pursuit of economic opportunity and flight from persecution are the major factors that drive international migration, other factors shape the creation of migratory circuits. A migratory circuit is a deep connection created between two regions through an initial experience of migration that results in a greater circulation of people. These migratory circuits have often followed experiences of violence. For instance, circuits of migration to the United States have often followed U.S. military actions, such as wars in Southeast Asia and Korea or military interventions in Latin America.

Migrants usually become ethnic, religious, or linguistic minorities in the countries where they settle, and they commonly face discrimination. Sometimes this discrimination is expressed in violence and oppression. In turn, discrimination and social pressures have also triggered violent reactions from ethnic minorities, such as riots in the Paris suburbs in 2007 and Stockholm in 2013 to protest discrimination experienced by Middle Eastern and North African migrants. When migrants lack legal standing, as is the case for millions in the United States, they can fall prey to criminal organizations or be exploited by employers.

Urbanization

Cities in Africa, Asia, and Latin America expanded at an astonishing pace after 1945. Many doubled or even tripled in size in a single decade (Table 33.1). In 1950 there were only eight **megacities** (5 million or more inhabitants), and only two were in developing countries. Of the fifty-nine megacities anticipated to exist by 2015, forty-eight will be outside North America and Europe.

megacities
▶ Cities with populations of 5 million people or more.

What caused this urban explosion? First, the overall population growth in the developing nations was critical. Urban residents gained substantially from a medical revolution that provided improved health care but only gradually began to reduce the size of their families. Second, more than half of all urban growth comes from rural migration. Manufacturing jobs in the developing nations were concentrated in cities.

What challenges did social reformers address at the turn of the twenty-first century?

How have science and technology kept pace with population change?

✓ LearningCurve
Check what you know.

INDIVIDUALS IN SOCIETY

Sieng, a Mnong Refugee in an American High School

In 2008, at a large urban high school in the U.S. South, Sieng, a seventeen-year-old Mnong refugee, recited the Pledge of Allegiance in his JROTC class. His aspiration to join the U.S. Marine Corps was an act of belonging that bridged both his life in the United States and his sense of his family and its history.

The Mnong are among a diverse group of ethnic minorities, known broadly as Montagnards, whose communities stretch across the central highlands of Vietnam. They are also a religious minority in Vietnam — many had converted to Christianity. During the Vietnam War, many Mnong provided military service alongside the United States, particularly with the U.S. Army Special Forces. After the war ended in 1975, the Mnong faced persecution and over time many fled the country, joining the current of refugees who resettled in camps in Thailand, Malaysia, the Philippines, and later Cambodia. Sieng's family left Vietnam when he was a child in the late 1990s. He recalled his journey:

> We had a hard time in Vietnam, so we had to leave. We didn't have no choice because we had no food, and no land. And [the Vietnamese government] wanted my dad and took my grandpa. So we left in the night and went through the jungle. We walked and walked and got lost. So me and my dad tried to find the way and we found a house. Some people let us sleep there and also gave us food. Then we got to a [refugee] camp in Cambodia and stayed there for a year. I didn't have school in Vietnam, and I didn't have school at the camp. Then we came here.

Arriving in the United States at the age of sixteen, Sieng was not literate in Mnong, Vietnamese, or English, the language of his new school. Sieng aspired to become a Marine so he could help other refugees and his family. He explained, "A man needs to take care of the family too, and that's what I want to do. The Marines will help me take care of my family."

For Sieng, being a refugee instilled a sense of pride, a sense of what he and his family had overcome in coming to the United States, and a sense of what he desired for the future. As the oldest male child, Sieng was, in his words, "second in command" in the home while his father worked the third shift at a shipping facility. In the United States Sieng was an ethnic minority and a refugee with limited English skills. He was misunderstood. A classmate in a world history class asked him where he was from in Mexico, and the question made him indignant:

Hmong students and their teaching assistant at a high school in Wisconsin recite the Pledge of Allegiance. (Morry Gash/AP Photo)

> I am a *refugee*, not an immigrant! I am *Mnong*, not Vietnamese! But people call me Spanish. Some kids once asked me to say something in Spanish. . . . And Mexican students think I'm Chinese. They say, *"Hey Chino! Hey Chino!"* I get mad when they do this because I am more like American. My grandpa worked with Americans [in the war].

In a diverse school, amid other immigrants and ethnic minorities, Sieng found comfort in his identity as a refugee, reflecting on his family's past, its connection to the United States, and his role facilitating its journey, as he confronted a new environment, struggling to be understood.

Source: Liv T. Dávila, "Performing Allegiance: An Adolescent Refugee's Construction of Patriotism in JROTC," *Educational Studies* 39.5 (2014), in press. Reprinted by permission of Taylor & Francis LLC (http://www.tandfonline.com).

QUESTIONS FOR ANALYSIS

1. What aspects of Sieng's experience reflect broader patterns of migration?
2. How does Sieng's experience as a refugee shape his identity?
3. What role does JROTC play in Sieng's sense of belonging?

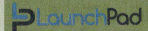

ONLINE DOCUMENT PROJECT

What are the key issues surrounding immigration reform? Examine documents related to the debate over U.S. immigration reform, and then complete a quiz and writing assignment based on the evidence and details from this chapter. *See inside the front cover to learn more.*

TABLE 33.1 ■ Urban Population as a Percentage of Total Population in the World and in Eight Major Areas, 1925–2025

Area	1925	1950	1975	2000	2025 (est.)
World Total	21%	28%	39%	50%	63%
North America	54	64	77	86	93
Europe	48	55	67	79	88
Soviet Union	18	39	61	76	87
East Asia	10	15	30	46	63
Latin America	25	41	60	74	85
Africa	8	13	24	37	54

Note: Little more than one-fifth of the world's population was urban in 1925. In 2000 the total urban proportion in the world was about 50 percent. According to United Nations experts, the proportion should reach two-thirds by about 2025. The most rapid urban growth will occur in Africa and Asia, where the move to cities is still in its early stages.

Newcomers have streamed to the cities even when industrial jobs have been scarce, seeking any type of employment. Many migrants were pushed into cities. As large landowners found it more profitable to produce export crops, their increasingly mechanized operations reduced the need for agricultural laborers. Ethnic or political unrest in the countryside can also push migrants into cities. These push factors have been particularly strong in Latin America, with its neocolonial pattern of large landowners and foreign companies that exported food and raw materials.

Most of the exploding numbers of urban poor earned precarious livings in a **bazaar economy** comprised of petty traders and unskilled labor. In the bazaar economy, which echoed early preindustrial markets, regular salaried jobs were rare and highly prized, and a complex world of tiny, unregulated businesses and service occupations predominated. Peddlers and pushcart operators hawked their wares, and sweatshops and home-based workers manufactured cheap goods for popular consumption. This bazaar economy grew prodigiously as migrants streamed to the cities.

After 1945 large-scale urban migration profoundly affected traditional family patterns in developing countries, just as it had during the Industrial Revolution. Particularly in Africa and Asia, the great majority of migrants to cities were young men. There were several reasons for this pattern. Much of the movement to cities was temporary or seasonal. Moreover, the cities were expensive, and prospects there were uncertain. Only after a man secured a genuine foothold did he marry or send for his wife and children.

For rural women, the consequences of male out-migration to cities were mixed. Asian and African women found themselves heads of households, faced with managing the farm, feeding the children, and running their own lives. African and Asian village women had to become unprecedentedly self-reliant and independent. As a result, rural women in Africa and Asia began to gain some rights and opportunities, but they faced limitations as well.

Migration patterns in Latin America differed from this model. Whole families generally migrated, often to squatter settlements, much more commonly than in Asia and Africa. These families frequently belonged to the class of landless

bazaar economy

▶ An economy with few salaried jobs and an abundance of tiny, unregulated businesses such as peddlers and pushcart operators.

What challenges did social reformers address at the turn of the twenty-first century?

How have science and technology kept pace with population change?

✓ LearningCurve
Check what you know.

laborers, which was generally larger in Latin America than in Africa and Asia. Migration was also more likely to be permanent. Another difference was that single women were as likely as single men to move to the cities, in part because women were in high demand as domestic servants. Even so, in Latin America urban migration seems to have had less of an impact on family patterns and on women's attitudes than it did in Asia and Africa.

In cities the concentration of wealth in few hands has resulted in unequal consumption, education, health care, and employment. The gap between rich and poor around the world can be measured both between the city and the country-side, and within cities (Map 33.1). Wealthy city dwellers in developing countries

---

MAP 33.1 ■ The Global Distribution of Wealth, ca. 2010

This size-comparison map, arranged according to global wealth distribution, vividly illustrates the gap in wealth between the Northern and Southern Hemispheres. The two small island nations of Japan and the United Kingdom have more wealth than all the nations of the Southern Hemisphere combined, although wealth creation in India and Brazil has advanced significantly. The wealthiest countries are also the most highly urbanized. As market capitalism expands in China, Vietnam, and other Asian countries and in Latin America and Africa, the relative-size ratios on the map will continue to change and evolve. Tiny Iceland, whose GDP is less than $20 billion, nevertheless has one of the highest per capita GDPs in the world.

> MAPPING THE PAST

ANALYZING THE MAP: Which three countries are the wealthiest? Where are the poorest countries concentrated?

CONNECTIONS: How were the two small nations of Japan and the United Kingdom able to acquire such enormous wealth?

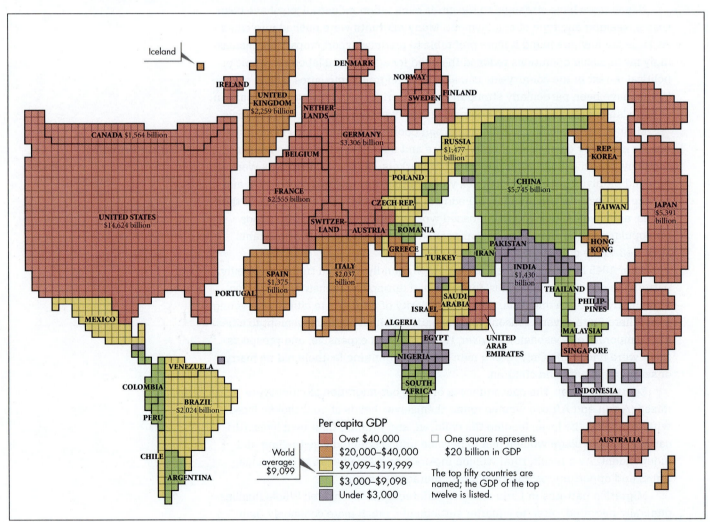

Per capita GDP

- Over $40,000
- $20,000–$40,000
- $9,099–$19,999 — World average: $9,099
- $3,000–$9,098
- Under $3,000

☐ One square represents $20 billion in GDP

The top fifty countries are named; the GDP of the top twelve is listed.

CHAPTER LOCATOR | Does the contemporary world reflect the "end of history"? | **How have migration and the circulation of capital and technology shaped the world?**

often had more in common with each other than with their poorer urban and rural people in their own country. As a result, the elites have often favored globalization that connects them with wealthier nations.

Multinational Corporations

A striking feature of global interdependence beginning in the early 1950s was the rapid emergence of **multinational corporations**, or multinationals, which are business firms that operate in a number of different countries and tend to adopt a global rather than a national perspective. Their rise was partly due to the revival of capitalism after the Second World War, increasingly free international economic relations, and the worldwide drive for rapid industrialization. Multinationals treated the world as one big market, coordinating complex activities across political boundaries and escaping political controls and national policies.

The impact of multinational corporations, especially on less industrialized countries, has been mixed. The presence of multinationals helped spread the products and values of consumer society to elites in the developing world. Critics considered this part of the process of neocolonialism, whereby local elites abandoned their nation's interests and contributed to continued foreign domination.

Multinational corporations are among the main beneficiaries of economic liberalism: growing openness of national markets and growing economic integration allow corporations to move goods, capital, and technology more fluidly and more intensely. But the growing interconnectedness of world markets comes with

multinational corporations
▶ Business firms that operate in a number of different countries and tend to adopt a global rather than a national perspective.

Multinational Companies in China

A Gap clothing store is reflected in the windows of an Apple store in Shanghai, China.
(© Jeffrey Greenberg/The Image Works)

What challenges did social reformers address at the turn of the twenty-first century?	How have science and technology kept pace with population change?	✓ LearningCurve Check what you know.

costs. In particular, it has meant increased economic volatility such as the banking crisis that swept the United States and Europe in 2008 and plunged countries into deep and long recessions.

The recession created particular hardship in Greece, Italy, Spain, and Portugal. Monetary policy for the euro was set for the currency zone as a whole and was strongly influenced by its most powerful economies, Germany and France, which resisted expanding the monetary supply to relieve the most afflicted economies in the Eurozone. The tension between the economic policymaking of Germany and France and the deep economic crisis in southern Europe threatened European economic unity.

> **QUICK REVIEW**

What are the most important factors driving contemporary migration patterns? What steps have states taken to shape or limit the movement of people across borders?

CHAPTER LOCATOR | Does the contemporary world reflect the "end of history"? | How have migration and the circulation of capital and technology shaped the world?

CHAPTER 33

1042 THE CONTEMPORARY WORLD IN HISTORICAL PERSPECTIVE

Equal Marriage in Argentina

Latin America's first same-sex marriage occurred in Tierra del Fuego, Argentina, in 2009. (Tierra del Fuego Government/Reuters/Landov)

What challenges did social reformers address at the turn of the twenty-first century?

AS MOVEMENTS FOR HUMAN RIGHTS and social reform gained ground in the 1960s and 1970s, activists increasingly looked beyond national borders to form alliances. Movements for women's rights, nuclear disarmament, environmental protection, and addressing climate change all became both local and global efforts. For example, the global anti-apartheid movement kept pressure on nations to apply economic and political sanctions on the white minority regime in South Africa. But at the same time, the anti-apartheid movement served as a means to address local problems. For instance, in Brazil anti-apartheid activism helped draw attention to the country's own racial inequalities.

The 1977 Nestlé boycott exemplified the kinds of success such movements could achieve as well as their limitations. Critics charged that the Swiss company's intense marketing of powdered baby formula in poor countries or regions with little access to clean water posed a risk to children. Activists called on consumers around the world to boycott Nestlé products.

At first, Nestlé dismissed the boycott and sought to discredit the movement. However, widespread condemnation of Nestlé continued to mount, and in 1981 the UN World Health Organization responded to the campaign by developing a

What challenges did social reformers address at the turn of the twenty-first century?

How have science and technology kept pace with population change?

 LearningCurve
Check what you know.

1043

set of voluntary standards regulating the marketing of infant formula in poorer countries where access to clean water was precarious. In 1984 Nestlé agreed to follow the standards. The movement succeeded, but its success raised questions: multinational corporations operate beyond the reach of single governments and often operate in regions with weak regulatory or investigatory structures or in countries where repressive political systems shield them from scrutiny. As a result, it is hard to hold them accountable when their conduct is unethical. At the same time, social movements and nongovernmental organizations also acted outside the realm of public accountability.

Environmentalism

The modern environmental movement began with concerns about chemical waste, rapid consumption of energy and food supplies, global deforestation, and threats to wildlife. By the 1970s citizens had begun joining together in nongovernmental organizations to pursue preservation or restoration of the natural environment.

The environmental movement is actually several different movements, each with its own agenda. American biologist and writer Rachel Carson was an early proponent of the environmental health movement. In *Silent Spring* (1962), she warned of the dangers of pesticides and pollution. Environmentalists like Carson acted out of concern that all living things were connected and that damage to one part of an ecological system could have consequences across that ecosystem.

The conservation movement, represented in the United States by the Sierra Club and the Audubon Society, seeks to protect the biodiversity of the planet and emphasizes the spiritual and aesthetic qualities of nature. The ecology movement consists of different groups with somewhat similar agendas, ranging from politically active green parties to the nongovernmental organization Greenpeace. These organizations are concerned about a wide range of environmental issues, and they often highlight the connections between the environment, on the one hand, and social, economic, and political developments, on the other.

global warming

▶ The belief of the majority of the world's scientists that hydrocarbons produced through the burning of fossil fuels have caused a greenhouse effect that has increased global temperatures over time.

Environmentalists today are especially concerned about **global warming**, the increase of global temperatures over time caused by the buildup of carbon in the atmosphere that captures heat. As a result of global warming, average temperatures have increased worldwide in recent decades, a trend that most scientists expect will intensify without curbs on carbon emissions. Scientists believe that man-made climate change began with the Industrial Revolution in the eighteenth century. The subsequent release of hydrocarbons produced through the burning of fossil fuels—coal, oil, natural gas—have caused a greenhouse effect that traps these gases and heats up earth's atmosphere. Paradoxically, industrialization and increased consumption in the developing world meant diminished global inequalities but intensified global carbon emissions.

International concerns over the potentially catastrophic consequences of global warming resulted in a 1997 agreement, the Kyoto Protocol, which amended the United Nations Framework Convention on Climate Change. Countries that ratify the Kyoto Protocol agree to reduce their emissions of carbon dioxide and five other greenhouse gases. As of April 2014, 191 countries had ratified it. The most

CHAPTER LOCATOR | Does the contemporary world reflect the "end of history"? | How have migration and the circulation of capital and technology shaped the world?

CHAPTER 33
1044 THE CONTEMPORARY WORLD IN HISTORICAL PERSPECTIVE

notable exception was the United States. The United Nations and environmental activists have continued to pursue an international environmental accord that can bring all nations into a shared effort to combat climate change.

Lesbian, Gay, and Transgender Rights

By the early 1970s a global gay rights movement championed the human rights of lesbian, gay, and transgendered people. The movement intensified in the 1980s as it became clear that governments neglected medical research and treatment for people sick with AIDS, which they dismissed as a "gay disease." The organization Act Up's advocacy campaign for AIDS research created a powerful symbol using the words "Silence = Death" inside a pink triangle to represent the AIDS crisis.

By the 1990s gay rights activists had broadened their efforts to challenge discrimination in employment, education, and public life. In 1995 Canada became the first country to allow same-sex marriage. In the ensuing years many European countries followed suit. But the legalization of same-sex marriage was not only a Western achievement: by 2013 Argentina, South Africa, Ecuador, and Uruguay had legalized same-sex marriage, while many other nations provided legal protections for families that stopped shy of marriage. Argentina led the way in legal support for transgendered people and made sexual reassignment surgery a legal right in 2012.

Women's Right to Equality

The 1995 United Nations Fourth World Conference on Women, held in Beijing, China, called on the world community to take action in twelve areas of critical concern to women: poverty, access to education and training, access to health

What challenges did social reformers address at the turn of the twenty-first century?

How have science and technology kept pace with population change?

☑ LearningCurve
Check what you know.

care, violence against women, women and war, economic inequality with men, political inequality with men, creation of institutions for women's advancement, lack of respect for women's rights, stereotyping of women, gender inequalities and the environment, and violation of girl children's rights.[1] These are concerns that all women share, although degrees of inequality vary greatly from one country to another.

feminization of poverty
► The issue that those living in extreme poverty are disproportionately women.

The **feminization of poverty**, the disproportionate number of women living in extreme poverty, applies to even the wealthiest countries, where two out of every three poor adults are women. There are many causes for this phenomenon. Because women are primarily responsible for child care in many cultures, they have less time and opportunity for work. Male labor migration increases the number of households headed by women and thus the number of families living in poverty. Job restrictions, discrimination, and limited access to education reduce women's employment options. Birthrates are higher among poor women, particularly among adolescents. The poorest women usually suffer most from government policies, usually legislated by men, which restrict their access to reproductive health care and family planning.

Women have made gains in the workplace, making up 38 percent of the nonfarm-sector global workforce in the early 2000s, as compared to 35 percent in 1990. But segregated labor markets remain the rule, with higher-paying jobs reserved for men. In the farm sector, women produce more than half of all the food and up to 80 percent of subsistence crops grown in Africa. Because this is informal labor and often unpaid, these women laborers are denied access to loans, and many cannot own the land they farm.

Social class continues to be a major divider of women's opportunities. Over the course of the twentieth century women from more affluent backgrounds experienced far greater gains in access to education, employment, and political representation than women in poverty did.

Children: The Right to Childhood

In 1989 the United Nations General Assembly adopted the Convention on the Rights of the Child, which spelled out a number of rights that are due every child. These include civil and human rights and economic, social, and cultural rights. It is not difficult to see why such a document was necessary. Globally, a billion children live in poverty—one in every two children in the world. The convention also addresses other concerns, including the fact that children make up half the world's refugees, and the problems of child labor and exploitation, sexual violence and sex trafficking, police abuse of street children, HIV/AIDS orphans, lack of access to education, and lack of access to adequate health care. The United States and Somalia remain the only two United Nations member nations that have not ratified the treaty.

As the twenty-first century began, nearly a billion people—mostly women denied equitable access to education—were illiterate. Increasing economic globalization has put pressure on all governments to improve literacy rates and educational opportunities; the result has been reduced gender inequalities in education. The greatest gains in literacy have occurred in South Asia and the Middle East.

CHAPTER LOCATOR | Does the contemporary world reflect the "end of history"? | How have migration and the circulation of capital and technology shaped the world?

CHAPTER 33
1046 THE CONTEMPORARY WORLD IN HISTORICAL PERSPECTIVE

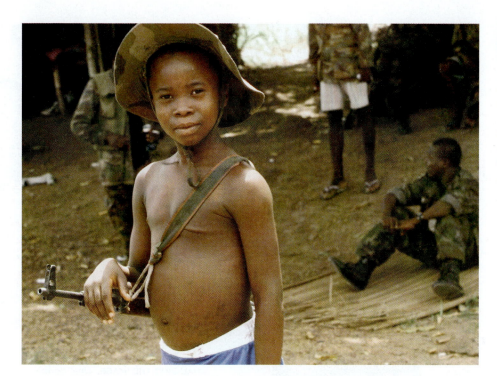

Mexico pioneered a new approach to combating poverty that has been implemented in a growing number of countries. Conditional cash transfer, or CCT, provides a stipend to families who meet certain goals, such as keeping their children in school. This approach addresses poverty directly, while enlisting families to work toward its long-term solution by increasing education levels, which will broaden opportunities for new generations. Versions of the program have been introduced across Latin America, Asia, and the Middle East.

QUICK REVIEW <

What global trends have led to the feminization of poverty?

What challenges did social reformers address at the turn of the twenty-first century?

How have science and technology kept pace with population change?

☑ LearningCurve
Check what you know.

> How have science and technology kept pace with population change?

Protest Against Genetically Modified Foods

Chilean demonstrators oppose the introduction of genetically modified crops. The banner reads, "I do not want transgenic crops in Chile: Movement for Food Sovereignty." (Eliseo Fernandez/Reuters/Landov)

> PICTURING THE PAST

ANALYZING THE IMAGE: What do the costumes suggest about the protesters' views about the effects of genetically modified foods?
CONNECTIONS: What are some of the advantages and disadvantages of the scientific engineering of food crops?

SINCE 1950 THE WORLD'S POPULATION has increased from 2.5 billion people to over 7 billion. This population growth has been matched by increasing demand for food and has placed growing strains on natural resources. Advances in agriculture and medicine have helped offset this challenge, while technological innovations in areas such as transportation and communications have increased the complexity of interactions among the world's growing number of people.

Intensified Agriculture and the Green Revolution

As the world's population grew in the second half of the twentieth century, food production strained to keep pace, prompting a greater emphasis on rural development and agricultural sciences. Before 1939 the countries of Asia, Africa, and Latin America had collectively produced more grain than they consumed. After 1945, as their populations soared, they began importing food from countries like

CHAPTER LOCATOR | Does the contemporary world reflect the "end of history"? | How have migration and the circulation of capital and technology shaped the world?

the United States. Although crops might fail in poor countries, starvation seemed a thing of the past.

Then, in 1966 and 1967, India was hit with a devastating famine. That close brush with mass starvation created widespread alarm that population growth was outpacing food production. The American scientist Paul Ehrlich envisioned a grim future in his 1968 bestseller *The Population Bomb*, which warned of a population crisis. Ehrlich was not the first scientist to make such dire predictions, and like Thomas Malthus before him (see page 689), he failed to understand the adaptability of farmers and agricultural technology to keep pace with population growth.

Technological improvements countered such nightmarish visions and offered hope. Plant scientists set out to develop new genetically engineered seeds. The first breakthrough came in Mexico in the 1950s when an American-led team developed new strains of high-yield wheat. These varieties enabled farmers to double their yields, though the plants demanded greater amounts of fertilizer and water for irrigation. Mexican wheat production soared. Thus began the transformation of agriculture in some poor countries—the so-called **green revolution**.

In the 1960s American-backed scientists in the Philippines developed a new hybrid "miracle rice" that required more fertilizer and water but yielded more and grew much faster than ordinary rice. Asian scientists developed similar hybrid strains of rice to meet local conditions.

As they applied green revolution technologies, many Asian countries experienced rapid increases in grain production. Farmers in India increased production more than 60 percent in fifteen years. China followed with its own highly successful version of the green revolution.

The green revolution offered new hope to industrializing nations, though its benefits often flowed to large landowners and export farms that could afford the necessary investments in irrigation and fertilizer. Experiences in China and other Asian countries showed, however, that even peasant families with tiny farms could gain substantially. Indeed, the green revolution's greatest successes occurred in Asian countries with broad-based peasant ownership of land. Conversely, the green revolution spread most slowly in regions with low rates of peasant landownership.

As the practice of planting genetically engineered crops to increase production grew in the late twentieth and early twenty-first centuries, many feared that such foods would have still-unknown harmful effects on the human body. The loss of biodiversity was also of growing concern. When one or two genetically engineered seeds replaced all the naturally occurring local seeds in an area, food security was threatened. With a shrinking diversity of plants and animals, farmers find it more difficult to find alternatives if the dominant hybrid seed in use becomes susceptible to a particular disease or pest or if a significant climate change occurs.

green revolution
▶ The increase in food production stemming from the introduction of high-yielding wheat, hybrid seeds, and other advancements.

Slowing Population Growth

By the 1970s and 1980s population growth in the industrialized countries had begun to fall significantly. By the 1990s some European leaders were expressing concern that low birthrates threatened national economies by reducing the labor force, the tax base, and the number of consumers. Between 1970 and 1975 China registered the fastest five-year birthrate decline in recorded history. Other

What challenges did social reformers address at the turn of the twenty-first century?

How have science and technology kept pace with population change?

✓ LearningCurve
Check what you know.

countries, especially in Latin America and East Asia, experienced declines in fertility. Fertility in most of the developing world could fall below the replacement level (2.1 children per woman) before 2100.

There were several reasons for this decline in fertility among women in the developing world. As fewer babies died of disease or malnutrition, families needed fewer births to guarantee the survival of the number of children they wanted. Better living conditions, urbanization, and more education encouraged women to have fewer children.

In the early 1960s the introduction of the birth control pill allowed women to take control of their own fertility. Family planning was now truly possible. In the early twenty-first century, more than half of the world's couples practiced some form of birth control, up from one in eight just forty years earlier.

The Medical Revolution

The medical revolution began in the late 1800s with the development of the germ theory of disease (see page 731) and continued rapidly after World War II. Scientists discovered vaccines for many of the most deadly diseases. According to the United Nations World Health Organization, medical advances reduced deaths from smallpox, cholera, and plague by more than 95 percent worldwide between 1951 and 1966.

Medical advances significantly lowered death rates and lengthened life expectancies worldwide. Children became increasingly likely to survive their early years, although infant and juvenile mortality remained far higher in poor countries than in rich ones. By 1980 the average inhabitant of the developing countries could expect to live about fifty-four years, although life expectancy at birth varied from forty to sixty-four years depending on the country. In industrialized countries, life expectancy at birth averaged seventy-one years.

The medical benefits of scientific advances have been limited by unequal access to health care, which is more readily available to the wealthy than the poor. Between 1980 and 2000 the number of children under the age of five dying annually of diarrhea dropped by 60 percent through the global distribution of a cheap sugar-salt solution mixed in water. Still, over 1.5 million children worldwide continue to die each year from diarrhea, primarily in poorer nations. Deaths worldwide from HIV/AIDS, malaria, and tuberculosis were concentrated in the world's poorest regions, while tuberculosis remained the leading killer of women worldwide.

In 2007 the United Nations calculated that 36 million persons globally were infected with HIV, the virus that causes AIDS, and that AIDS was the world's fourth-leading cause of death. About 90 percent of all persons who die from AIDS and 86 percent of those currently infected with HIV live in sub-Saharan Africa (Map 33.2). In Africa HIV/AIDS is most commonly spread through heterosexual sex. Widespread disease and poverty are also significant factors in that Africans already suffering from other illnesses such as malaria or tuberculosis are less resistant to HIV and have less access to health care for treatment.

Another critical factor contributing to the spread of AIDS in Africa is the continued political instability of many countries—particularly those in the corridor running from Uganda to South Africa. This region was the scene of brutal civil and liberation wars that resulted in massive numbers of refugees, a breakdown

CHAPTER LOCATOR | Does the contemporary world reflect the "end of history"? | How have migration and the circulation of capital and technology shaped the world?

CHAPTER 33
1050 THE CONTEMPORARY WORLD IN HISTORICAL PERSPECTIVE

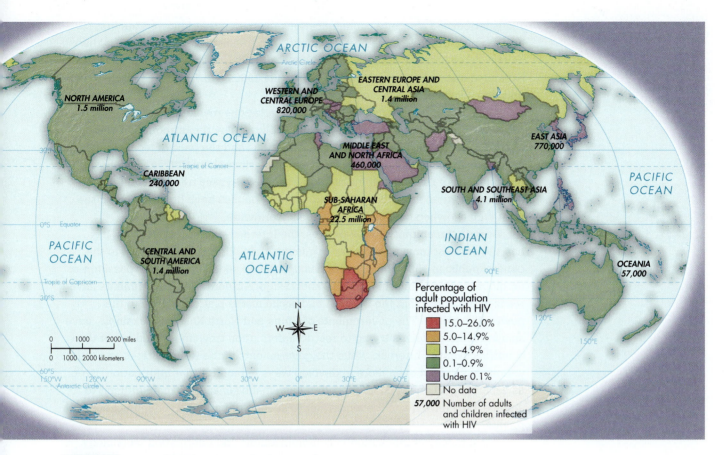

MAP 33.2 ■ People Living with HIV/AIDS Worldwide, ca. 2010

As this map illustrates, Africa has been hit the hardest by the HIV/AIDS epidemic. It currently has fifteen to twenty times more identified cases than any other region of the world. AIDS researchers expect that in the coming decade, however, Russia and South and East Asia will overtake and then far surpass Africa in the number of infected people. (Source: Data from World Health Organization, www.whosea.org)

in basic health-care services, and the destruction of family and cultural networks. The people living in this area in the countries of Uganda, Rwanda, Burundi, Zaire/Congo, Angola, Zimbabwe, Mozambique, and South Africa have been decimated by HIV/AIDS. Since 2001 relatively inexpensive AIDS drugs that are widely available in the West have been dispensed freely to many of those infected in Africa and Asia, but the availability of these drugs has generally failed to keep up with the need.

A Digital Revolution

The invention of moving pictures, the telephone, and other communications technologies between 1875 and 1900 prepared the way for a twentieth-century era of mass communications. In parallel, new information-processing technologies began with development of adding and calculating machines and culminated in the development of the first computers during the Second World War. As computing and communications technologies converged, they created the "information age." The global availability and affordability of radios and television sets in the

What challenges did social reformers address at the turn of the twenty-first century?

How have science and technology kept pace with population change?

✓ LearningCurve
Check what you know.

1950s introduced a second communications revolution that followed the first revolution brought by telegraph and telephone. The transistor radio penetrated the most isolated hamlets of the world. Though initially less common, television use expanded into nearly every country during the 1960s and 1970s, even if there was only one television in a village.

The third, and perhaps greatest, communications revolution occurred with the first Apple personal computers in 1976, followed by the introduction of cell phones in 1985. The use of mass communications and the pace of technological development in communications have exploded since then. Cell phones allowed individuals and nations in the developing world to bypass traditional telephone lines, installation, and other obstacles, and cell phones have become among the most widely owned communications tools worldwide.

Despite the ubiquity of cell phones, the Internet, or World Wide Web, has had the greatest impact on human communication. First made available to the general public in 1994, the Internet has opened up seemingly infinite possibilities for global access to information and knowledge. Authoritarian governments have realized the threat that the Internet and social media platforms pose to their power and control. The governments of China and North Korea, for example, have spent millions of dollars trying to restrict information traveling in and out of their countries over the Internet, while the governments of the United States and other nations have spent even more to develop ways to monitor that information. Even as expanding means of communication have made censorship more difficult to enforce, they have made it even harder to keep information or communications private.

The intensity of innovation in communications and information technology created new business giants. Apple, Microsoft, Google, and IBM are entities that stand at the forefront of the contemporary world, and they absorb and distribute enormous amounts of capital. The success of these technology companies and the proliferation of computer, cellular telephone and Internet use are remarkable changes, but they also deepen a stubborn continuity: deep socioeconomic inequalities between countries and within countries. The unevenness of both the production and consumption of computer technology has resulted in a **digital divide**, meaning the gap in access to Internet and computer and telecommunications resources. This gap is the greatest between nations like the United States, western European countries, and Japan and nations in Africa and South or Southeast Asia. The digital divide also exists between the wealthy and poor, as well as between urban and rural areas within countries.

digital divide

▶ The gap between levels of access to computing, Internet, and telecommunications between rich and poor regions and populations.

> ## QUICK REVIEW

What challenges and opportunities have been created by the third communications revolution?

CHAPTER LOCATOR | Does the contemporary world reflect the "end of history"? | How have migration and the circulation of capital and technology shaped the world?

CHAPTER SUMMARY

The end of the Cold War confrontation between superpowers has resulted in a world in which regional tensions endure and sometimes become international conflicts. Consequently, in a way similar to its actions in the Cold War era, the United States after 1990 continued to be involved in military conflicts far from home in regions ranging from the Balkans to Libya, Iraq, and Afghanistan. These conflicts have also spurred arms races that have led to the emergence of new nuclear powers in South Asia and East Asia.

The transitions to economic and political liberalism in the former Soviet bloc and in Latin America were particularly dramatic expressions of the rise of liberalism worldwide, which included the economic and political integration of Europe and the emergence of China as an economic superpower. Growing interconnectedness of world markets has meant increased economic volatility, such as the global financial market crisis of 2008. Cycles of economic growth and crisis, as well as contradictory experiences of integration and regional conflict, are tensions of the modern world rooted in historical experiences.

 **CONNECTIONS** The present shapes the ways we ask questions about the past. Understanding of the past also shapes our questions about the present and the future. Our history of world societies shows that the forces that shape the world we live in have deep roots: Globalization reaches back for centuries. Current armed conflicts are based on historic tensions often rooted in ethnic differences or legacies of colonialism. The gaps between rich and poor countries, and between the rich and poor within countries, have sometimes been diminished by advances in science and technology or by reforms in social policy. But science, technology, and public policy also deepen those inequalities, as uneven industrialization and the digital divide reflect.

We find these competing tensions throughout history, and we find them often recurring over time and place: our relationship with the past is one of continuity and change. The study of history allows us to frame questions about complex, competing, and often-contradictory experiences. Asking these questions sharpens our focus on not only the past but also the present. We are shaped by history. But we also make it.

ONLINE DOCUMENT PROJECT

The Immigration Debate

What are the key issues surrounding immigration reform?

Examine documents related to the debate over U.S. immigration reform, and then complete a quiz and writing assignment based on the evidence and details from this chapter. *See inside the front cover to learn more.*

What challenges did social reformers address at the turn of the twenty-first century?

How have science and technology kept pace with population change?

✔ **LearningCurve**
Check what you know.

CHAPTER 33 STUDY GUIDE

STEP 1   GET STARTED ONLINE

 **LearningCurve**

Now that you've read the chapter, make it stick by completing the LearningCurve activity.

STEP 2   EXPLAIN WHY IT MATTERS

Put your reading into practice. Identify each term below, and then explain why it matters in world history.

TERM	WHO OR WHAT & WHEN	WHY IT MATTERS
middle powers (p. 1031)		
megacities (p. 1037)		
bazaar economy (p. 1039)		
multinational corporations (p. 1041)		
global warming (p. 1044)		
feminization of poverty (p. 1046)		
green revolution (p. 1049)		
digital divide (p. 1052)		

STEP 3   MOVE BEYOND THE BASICS

To demonstrate a more advanced understanding of the impact of global trends on Asia, Africa, and Latin America, fill in the chart below with descriptions of the impact in the following key areas: urbanization, population growth, and technology and science. In what ways has the social and economic history of these three regions converged in recent decades? In what ways has it diverged?

	Urbanization	Population Growth	Technological and Scientific Developments
Asia			
Africa			
Latin America			

STEP 4 **PUT IT ALL TOGETHER** Now, take a step back and try to explain the big picture. Remember to use specific examples from the chapter in your answers.

LIBERALISM AND GLOBALIZATION

▶ What particular challenges do multinational corporations pose to developing nations?

▶ How would you explain the tendency of governments around the world to remove barriers to the circulation of goods and capital and at the same time that they erect new barriers to cross-border migration?

SOCIAL MOVEMENTS

▶ What are the most important obstacles to the formulation and implementation of a coordinated global response to climate change?

▶ Why do women and children remain the most vulnerable populations on the planet?

SCIENCE AND TECHNOLOGY

▶ In your opinion, will recent advances in communication technology lead to more or less political and individual freedom? Why?

▶ What challenges and opportunities have been created by recent advances in science and technology?

LOOKING BACK, LOOKING AHEAD

▶ In what ways does the current era of globalization differ from earlier period of accelerating global contacts?

▶ A hundred years from now, will the nation-state still be the basic unit of social and political organization? Why or why not?

> **IN YOUR OWN WORDS**

Imagine that you must give an oral report to the class answering the following question: **Why did liberalization emerge as a such a powerful force in the second half of the twentieth century, and what were the consequences of this development?** What would be the most important points and why?

ENDNOTES

Chapter 16

1. Thomas Benjamin, *The Atlantic World: Europeans, Africans, Indians and Their Shared History, 1400–1900* (Cambridge: Cambridge University Press, 2009), p. 141.
2. Herbert S. Klein, "Profits and the Causes of Mortality," in *The Atlantic Slave Trade*, ed. David Northrup (Lexington, Mass.: D. C. Heath, 1994), p. 116.

Chapter 19

1. Quoted in G. L. Mosse et al., eds., *Europe in Review* (Chicago: Rand McNally, 1964), p. 156.
2. Orlando Patterson, *Slavery and Social Death* (Cambridge, Mass.: Harvard University Press, 1982), p. 255.

Chapter 20

1. P. D. Curtin, *Economic Change in Precolonial Africa: Senegambia in the Era of the Slave Trade* (Madison: University of Wisconsin Press, 1975), pp. 34–35; J. A. Rawley, *The Transatlantic Slave Trade: A History* (Lincoln: University of Nebraska Press, 2005).
2. Quoted in R. Hallett, *Africa to 1875* (Ann Arbor: University of Michigan Press, 1970), p. 151.
3. Ibid., pp. 35–38.
4. P. E. Lovejoy, *Transformations in Slavery: A History of Slavery in Africa* (Cambridge: Cambridge University Press, 1992), p. 25, Table 2.1, "Trans-Saharan Slave Trade, 650–1600."
5. J. Iliffe, *Africans: The History of a Continent* (Cambridge: Cambridge University Press, 1995), p. 77.
6. R. Shell, *Children of Bondage: A Social History of the Slave Society at the Cape of Good Hope, 1652–1838* (Hanover, N.H.: University Press of New England, 1994), pp. 285–289.
7. R. Blackburn, *The Making of New World Slavery: From the Baroque to the Modern, 1492–1800* (New York: Verso, 1998), pp. 79–80.
8. *Equiano's Travels: The Interesting Narrative of the Life of Olaudah Equiano*, ed. P. Edwards (Portsmouth, N.H.: Heinemann, 1996), p. 23–26.
9. Rawley, *The Transatlantic Slave Trade*, pp. 45–47.
10. Robert W. July, *A History of the African People* (Prospect Heights, Ill.: Waveland Press, 1998), p. 171.
11. Robert W. July, *Precolonial Africa: An Economic and Social History* (New York: Scribner's, 1975), pp. 269–270.
12. A. G. Hopkins, *An Economic History of West Africa* (New York: Columbia University Press, 1973), p. 119.
13. P. Manning, *Slavery and African Life: Occidental, Oriental, and African Slave Trades* (New York: Cambridge University Press, 1990), pp. 22–23 and chap. 3, pp. 38–59.

Chapter 23

1. N. F. R. Crafts, *British Economic Growth During the Industrial Revolution* (Oxford: Oxford University Press, 1985), p. 32.
2. See especially J. Brenner and M. Rama, "Rethinking Women's Oppression," *New Left Review* 144 (March–April 1984): 33–71, and sources cited there.
3. Joel Mokyr, *The Enlightened Economy: An Economic History of Britain, 1700–1850* (New Haven, Conn.: Yale University Press, 2009), pp. 460–461.
4. Ibid., p. 455.
5. Quoted in D. Geary, ed., *Labour and Socialist Movements in Europe Before 1914* (Oxford: Berg, 1989), p. 29.

Chapter 24

1. Jonathan Sperber, *The European Revolutions, 1848–1851*, 2d ed. (Cambridge: Cambridge University Press, 2005), pp. 40–47.
2. J. McKay, *Tramways and Trolleys: The Rise of Urban Mass Transport in Europe* (Princeton, N.J.: Princeton University Press, 1976), p. 81.

Chapter 25

1. Iliffe, *Africans*, p. 169.
2. Lovejoy, *Transformations in Slavery*, p. 15.
3. R. Oliver, *The African Experience* (New York: Icon Editions, 1991), pp. 164–166.

Chapter 27

1. Jürgen Buchenau, *Mexican Mosaic: A Brief History of Mexico* (Wheeling, Ill.: Harlan-Davidson, 2008), p. 2
2. David Rock, *Argentina, 1516–1987: From Spanish Colonization to Alfonsín* (Berkeley: University of California Press, 1987), p. 154; Emilia Viotti da Costa, *The Brazilian Empire: Myths and Histories* (Chapel Hill: University of North Carolina Press, 2000), p. 78.

Chapter 28

1. Quoted in H. Nicolson, *Peacemaking 1919* (New York: Grosset & Dunlap Universal Library, 1965), pp. 8, 31–32.
2. Quoted in John Macquarrie, *Existentialism* (New York: Penguin Books, 1972), p. 15.

Chapter 30

1. Carl J. Friedrich and Zbigniew K. Brzezinski, *Totalitarian Dictatorship and Autocracy*, 2d ed. (Cambridge, Mass.: Harvard University Press, 1965), pp. 21–23.
2. See Robert C. Tucker, *Stalin in Power: The Revolution from Above, 1928–1941* (New York: W. W. Norton, 1992).
3. Robert Service, *Stalin: A Biography* (Cambridge, Mass.: Harvard University Press, 2005), p. 266.
4. M. Malia, *The Soviet Tragedy: A History of Socialism in Russia, 1917–1991* (New York: Free Press, 1995), pp. 227–270; see also the controversial work by historian John Archibald Getty, *Origins of the Great Purges: The Soviet Communist Party Reconsidered, 1933–1938* (New York: Cambridge University Press, 1985).
5. R. Vivarelli, "Interpretations on the Origins of Fascism," *Journal of Modern History* 63 (March 1991): 41.
6. Christopher Seton-Watson, *Italy from Liberalism to Fascism, 1870–1925* (London: Methuen, 1967), p. 661.
7. W. Brustein, *The Logic of Evil: The Social Origins of the Nazi Party, 1925–1933* (New Haven, Conn.: Yale University Press, 1996), pp. 52, 182.
8. Izidors Vizulis, *The Molotov-Ribbentrop Pact of 1939: The Baltic Case* (New York: Praeger, 1990), p. 16.
9. Jeremy Noakes and Geoffrey Pridham, eds., "Message from Hermann Göring to Reinhard Heydrich, 31 July, 1941," in *Documents on Nazism, 1919–1945* (New York: Viking Press, 1974), p. 486.
10. See, for example, Christopher Browning, *Ordinary Men: Reserve Police Battalion 101 and the Final Solution in Poland* (New York: HarperCollins, 1992); Robert Gellately, *Backing Hitler: Consent and Coercion in Nazi Germany* (Oxford: Oxford University Press, 2001); Ian Kershaw, *Hitler, the Germans, and the Final Solution* (New Haven, Conn.: Yale University Press, 2008).

Chapter 31

1. Winston Churchill, "Sinews of Peace" (the Iron Curtain Speech), delivered at Westminster College in Fulton, Missouri, March 5, 1946, in Robert Rhodes James, ed., *Winston S. Churchill: His Complete Speeches, 1897–1963*. Vol. 7: *1943–1949* (New York: Chelsea House, 1974), p. 7509.
2. Quoted in R. Hallett, *Africa Since 1875: A Modern History* (Ann Arbor: University of Michigan Press, 1974), pp. 378–379.

Chapter 33

1. United Nations, "Critical Areas of Concern," *Report of the Fourth World Conference on Women* (New York: United Nations Department for Policy Coordination and Sustainable Development, 1995), ch. 1, annex II, ch. 3, pp. 41–44, http://www.un.org/esa/gopher-data /conf/fwcw/off/a--20.en. See also Population Reference Bureau, *Women of Our World 2005* (Washington, D.C.: Population Reference Bureau, 2005) for the latest data and ten-year follow-up to the Beijing meeting.

INDEX

A note about the index: Key terms and the pages where they are defined appear in boldface. Names of individuals appear in boldface. Letters in parentheses following pages refer to: *(i)* illustrations, including photographs and artifacts as well as information in captions; *(f)* figures, including charts and graphs; *(m)* maps; *(t)* tables

Abbottabad, 1034
Abolition of slavery, 815*(t)*, 821, 823, 825
Abraham (prophet), 1000*(i)*
Absenteeism, of clergy, 514–515
Absolutism
    Austria, 515*(t)*
    described, ***523***–528
    divine right of kings, 525
    enlightened absolutism, ***568***–569, 577, 581
    France, 524–525
    Prussia, 515*(t)*
    Russia, 539–543
    Spain, 523–524
Adal, 585*(t)*, 592, 593, 593*(m)*
Adolphus, Gustavus, 521
Afghanistan
    independence, 885*(t)*
    modernization efforts, 885*(t)*, 893–894
Africa
    Afrikaners, 755*(m)*, ***756***–758, 848, 898, 1008
    Algeria
        anticolonial war, 974
        National Liberation Front, ***974***, 991*(i)*
        pieds-noirs, ***974***
    apartheid
        described, 758, 1007, ***1008***–1009
        global anti-apartheid movements, 1043
        student demonstrations, 1007*(i)*
    bananas, from Asia (900–1100 C.E.), 589
    decolonization in, 971–975, 972*(m)*
    early modern states and societies (1400–1800), 582–609
        big picture, 609*(i)*
        chronology, 585*(t)*
        CONNECTIONS, 606–607
        overview, 582–583
        summary, 606
    East Africa
        Portuguese in, 595
        Swahili city-state, ***594***–595, 606
    Ethiopia
        Coptic Christianity, ***593***, 593*(m)*, 594, 609
        Muslim and European incursions (1500–1630), 585*(t)*, 593–594
        Mussolini's campaigns, 917*(t)*, 936*(m)*, 940*(t)*
        Prester John (mythical Christian monarch), 593, 606

    ethnic groups, 971
    French-speaking, decolonization, 974–975
    Great Depression and, 921
    HIV/AIDS, 1050
    Mansa Musa (king), 460*(i)*
    Mogadishu
        commercial prosperity, 595
        trade with Middle East, 459
    Pan-Africanists, ***973***
    plantains, from Asia (900–1100 C.E.), 589
    Portuguese in (European expansion), 463–464
    protectorates in, 754, 755*(m)*, 758
    South Africa
        Afrikaners, 755*(m)*, ***756***–758, 848, 898, 1008
        diamond mining, 757, 757*(i)*
        middle power, ***1031***, 1031*(t)*
        nineteenth century, 756–758
        South African War (1899–1902), 751*(t)*, 758, 762, 848
    sub-Saharan Africa
        decolonization, 955*(t)*
        HIV/AIDS, 1050
    Sudan
        famine (2011), 1010
        Hausaland, 584, 586*(m)*, 588
        Kanem-Bornu, 585*(t)*, 586*(m)*, 588
        Songhai kingdom, 585*(t)*, 586*(m)*, 587–588
    Timbuktu
        described, 587–588
        Leo Africanus in, 587
        map, 465*(i)*
        Portuguese in (1480s), 464, 583
        trade, 590, 590*(m)*
    Tuareg, ***590***
    urban population (1925–2025), 1039*(t)*
    West Africa, 584–586, 606, 609
        Benin forest kingdom, 586–587
        daily life, 588–590
        early modern period (1400–1800), 583–591, 586*(m)*
        famine (1738–1756), 585*(t)*
        industry, 590–591
        Senegambian states, 584–586
        stateless societies, 584–586, 606, 609
        trade, 590*(m)*, 590–591
African National Congress (ANC), ***1008***
Afrikaners, 755*(m)*, ***756***–758, 848, 898, 1008
Afroeurasian trade world
    described, 456–460, 480
    Indian Ocean, 456–459
    map (fifteenth century), 458*(m)*
    Middle East, 459
    peoples and cultures, 458–459
Age-grade systems, ***585***
Agricultural Adjustment Act (1933), 919
Agriculture
    collectivization, Soviet Union, 917*(t)*, 925*(i)*, ***926***–927, 981

    contemporary world in historical perspective, 1048–1049
    enclosure movement, ***573***, 683, 719
    kibbutz, ***895***
Ahmed Arabi, 751*(t)*
Aisne, Battle of, 857
Akbar, 487*(t)*, 493, 495–496, 499*(i)*, 500, 508
Alberdi, Juan Bautista, 832
Alchemy, Scientific Revolution, 555
Alcohol use
    Hong Xiuquan, 792
    Ming China, alcoholic drink from fermented rice, 618
    pre-Reformation Catholic clergy, 498*(t)*, 514
    realist movement and, 738
Alexander II of Russia, 724*(i)*, 729, 730
Alexander I of Russia, 662–663, 712*(i)*
Alexander VI (pope), 466
Alexandria
    anti-European riots (1882), 770
    Ptolemy's *Geography*, ***462***, 465–466, 552–553
Algeria
    anticolonial war, 974
    French conquest (1830), 751*(t)*, 767
    National Liberation Front, ***974***, 991*(i)*
    pieds-noirs, ***974***
Ali (Muhammad's cousin and son-in-law), 492
Ali, Muhammad
    described, 766, 767–769
    modernization of Egypt (1805–1849), 751*(t)*, 776
    picture, 769*(i)*
Alooma, Idris, 585*(t)*, 588
Alternate residence system, ***627***, 629
American reconstruction, of Japan, 968–969
American Revolution (1775–1783)
    framing Constitution, 651–652
    independence from Britain, 650–651
    key events, 651*(t)*
    origins of, 649–650
    Treaty of Paris, 487*(t)*, 505, 645*(t)*, ***647***, 651, 651*(t)*, 652
Americas
    Creoles, 473, 523, 576, 577–578, ***672***–673
    immigration patterns to, 835–836
    nineteenth-century liberalism (1810–1910), 812–843
        big picture, 843*(i)*
        chronology, 812*(t)*
        CONNECTIONS, 841
        overview, 812–813
        summary, 840–841
    reconquista, 462, 465, 471, 472
    Spain's voyages (fifteenth century), 464–466
    viceroyalties, 472
Amritsar Massacre, 885*(t)*, 898
Anarcho-syndicalism, ***832***

Anatolia, 487

Andean civilizations
  Callao-Lima-Oroya rail line, 830, 830(i)
  Inca Empire
    Atahualpa, 469, 471
    described, *469*
    Spanish conquest, 468–471
  khipus, 469

Angels, French illustration (1848), 721(i)

Animals
  Columbian exchange, *474*–475, 483
  dragons, 594(i)

Animism, 753

Antifederalists, 652

Antilles islands, Circum-Caribbean, *815*, 829, 838

Anti-Semitism
  Dreyfus affair, 739(i), **741**
  Mein Kampf (Hitler), *870*, 917(t), 934
  nineteenth-century Europe, 742–743

Antiwar sentiment (1916–1918), 847(t)

Apartheid
  described, 758, 1007, ***1008*–1009**
  global anti-apartheid movements, 1043
  student demonstrations, 1007(i)

Appeasement, 936–937, 940(t), 948

Apple personal computers, communications revolution, 1052

Apple store, Shanghai, 1041(i)

Aqueducts, Paris (after 1870), 732

Arab-Israeli conflict, 955(t), 964–965, 965(m), 998

Arabs
  Arab Revolt (1916–1918), 890–891
  emirs, 893
  Jewish-Arab tensions, Palestine, 894–895

Arab socialism, *963*–964

Arab Spring, 999

Aragon, Ferdinand of, 462, 466, 499

Architecture
  Coliseum in Rome, 930(i)
  modernism, **874**–875, 876
  Taj Mahal, 487(t), 496

Argentina
  Great Depression, 921
  Perón, Eva, 978–979
  Perón, Juan, 955(t), 978–979, 1004
  populism, 978–980

Arguin, 457(t), 464

Aristotle
  Aristotelian universe (imagination, sixteenth century), 550(i)
  Bacon and, 556
  Galen and, 558
  Galileo and, 559
  Scientific Revolution and, 552–553, 578
  slavery and, 480
  universities, High Middle Ages, 550(i)

Arkwright, Richard, 683(t), 689

Armenians
  Armenian Genocide, 890(i), 891
  brass bowl, 504(i)
  Safavid dynasty, 500, 503–504

Arts
  Mughal Empire, 494–495
  Ottoman Empire, 494–495
  rococo style, 551(t), 575
  romanticism, **717**, 858, 860, 861, 923
  Safavid Empire, 494–495

Ashikaga Shogunate, 624

Asia
  bananas, in Africa (900–1100 C.E.), 589
  decolonization, 697(m)
  Great Depression and, 921

imperialism (1800–1914), 780–811
  big picture, 810(i)
  British rule in India, 782–785
  China's decline, 791–796
  chronology, 783(t)
  CONNECTIONS, 809
  Dutch East Indies, 787–788
  map (1914), 786(m)
  migrations in Pacific region, 800–805
  opening of Japan, 795–796
  overview, 780–781
  similarities and differences, Asian countries, 806–807
  summary, 808–809
Japan's Asian Empire, 942–943
nationalism (1914–1939), 882–913
  appeal of, 886–887
  Arab Revolt (1916–1918), 890–891
  Asia reaction to World War I, 884–885
  big picture, 913(i)
  chronology, 885(t)
  CONNECTIONS, 910–911
  development, 884–887
  nationalism's appeal, 886–887
  Ottoman Empire's collapse, 888, 889(m)
  overview, 882
  Southeast Asia, independence, 908–909
  summary, 910
  Turkish Revolution, 891–892
plantains, in Africa (900–1100 C.E.), 589
Portuguese in Asia (European expansion), 463–464
rebuilding era (after World War II), 986

Astrolabe, 462–463, 463(i)

Astrology, Scientific Revolution and, 555, 579

Astronomy
  heliocentrism, 559
  Scientific Revolution, 553
  telescopic observations, Galileo, 554(i)

Atahualpa, 469, 471

Atatürk, 879, 885(m), 888(i), 889(m), 892, 893, 910

Atlantic Enlightenment, 577–578

Atomic bombs
  ban on testing (1963), 1032
  Hiroshima and Nagasaki, 917(t), 946(i), 947(m), 948, 1032

Atomist philosophers, 557

Atoms
  Boyle and, 558
  humans and atoms, realist perspective, 738
  splitting of, 847(t), 872(i)
  subatomic particles (J. J. Thomson's discovery, 1897), 738

Augsburg, Peace of, 517(m), 518, 520, 521

Aurangzeb, 487(t), 493, 500, 507

Auschwitz concentration camp, 915(i), 944, 945

Austerlitz, Battle of, 662

Australia
  gold discovery, 803
  map (nineteenth century), 801(m)
  mass unemployment, Great Depression, 918

Austria
  absolutism, 515(t)
  Congress of Vienna, *712*, 713(t), 714(m), 724, 729
  Hitler's takeover (1938), 937
  Joseph II, 551(t), 569
  per capita levels of industrialization (1750–1913), 692(t)
  Quadruple Alliance, 664, 712, 713

Austrian Habsburgs, 515(t), 527(m), 527–528

Austro-Hungarian Empire, 741–742, 744, 849, 865, 866(m), 934

Austro-Prussian War of 1866, 728, 728(m)

Authoritarianism, conservative, 922–923

Aztecs **(Mexica)**
  described, *469*
  Nahuatl language, 470
  Spanish conquest, 468–471
  Tenochtitlán, invasion of, 469, 469(m)

Ba'ath Party, 964

Bacon, Francis, 556–557, 557(t), 558, 560

Bacterial revolution, 732

Balfour Declaration, 865, 885(t), **891**

Bananas, Africa (900–1100 C.E.), 589

Bangladesh, famine, 963

Banking
  Bank of France (1800), 661
  crisis (2008), 1042

Bankruptcy
  Belgian banks and, 695
  Egypt (1876), 770, 776
  Estates General, *654*, 658(t), 676
  Louis XVI, 654
  Ottoman state, 751(t), 767
  Porfiriato and, 827
  Spain, 524

Banners, 621

Baseball, in Japan, 969(i)

Bastille, storming of, 654–655, 658(t)

Batista, Fulgencio, 980

Bayle, Pierre, 562, 564(t)

Bazaar economy, 1036(i), **1039**

Beccaria, Cesare, 568

Beethoven, Ludwig van, 737

Belgium
  Belgian banks and bankruptcy, 695
  industrialization (1830s), 683(t), 694
  Leopold II, 750(i), 754, 756
  per capita levels of industrialization (1750–1913), 692(t)
  "rape of Belgium," 854(i)

Below Stairs (Rowlandson), 597(i)

Benin forest kingdom, 586–587

Berbers, Tuareg, 590

Berlin
  Borsig ironworks, 691(i)
  Rome-Berlin Axis, 937, 940(t)
  street fighting (1848), 718(i)

Berlin Conference, 751(t), **754**

Berlin Wall, 955(t), 956(m), 993(t), 1016(i), 1019, 1024, 1030

Bhakti movement, 497

Biafran war, 995

Bile, bodily humors, 558

Bill of Rights (1689), **531**

Bill of Rights (1791), 651–652, 651(t)

Birth control pill, 1050

Bismarck, Otto von, 919
  Berlin Conference, 751(t), **754**
  German unification (1866–1871), 713(t), 726, 728(m), 728–729

Black bile, bodily humor, 558

Black Code (1685), 666

Black Death, disappearance (after 1720), 573

Black Legend, 479

Black Shirts, 922(i), **931**

Blitzkrieg, 939

Blood, bodily humor, 558

Bloody Sunday (1905), 730

Bodily humors, 558

Bolshevik Revolution, 847(t), 860–862, 928

Bolsheviks, *861*
Bombings
    Hiroshima and Nagasaki, 917*(t)*, 946*(i)*,
        947*(m)*, 948, 1032
    Madrid train bombings, 1034
    suicide bombings, 1022, 1034
Book of the Sea (Piri Reis), 487*(t)*, 497
Books
    China (ca. 1500–1600), 613*(t)*, 618
    French book trade, 572*(i)*
    publishing (ca. 1700–1789), 551*(t)*, 575
Borodino, Battle of, 663
Borsig ironworks, 691*(i)*
Bourgeoisie, 645, **717**, 744, 858, 861
Bourke-White, Margaret, 916*(i)*
Bows, Mongols, 623
Boxers, 696, 783*(t)*, **794**
Boyle, Robert, 557*(t)*, 558
Brahe, Tycho, 553, 557, 557*(t)*
Brasilia, 955*(t)*, 980, 995
Brass bowl, Armenian, 504*(i)*
Brazil
    Brasilia, 955*(t)*, 980, 995
    Great Depression, 921
    independence, 819–820
    Kubitschek, 978, 980
    middle power, **1031**, 1031*(t)*
    populism, 978, 980
    Portuguese in, 471, 472
    Rio de Janeiro
        growth (1900s), 832
        Napoleon's troop, 675
        Peddlers in Rio de Janeiro (sketch),
            602*(i)*
        Slave Labor in Rio de Janeiro
            (lithograph), 821*(i)*
    slavery abolished, 815*(t)*, 825
Brest-Litovsk, Treaty of, 847*(t)*, 863*(t)*
Brezhnev, Leonid, 982, 1016
Bride wealth, *459*, 589
Bridges
    Nguyen Dynasty, 788
    Peru's Callao-Lima-Oroya rail line, 830,
        830*(i)*
    Works Progress Administration and, 919
Britain
    Battle of Britain, 917*(t)*, 940
    Crimean War, 729, 729*(m)*, 886
    early labor movement, 704–705
    Industrial Revolution, 682–690
    mass unemployment, Great Depression,
        918
British Empire in India, 505
Brittain, Vera, 856–857
Brzezinski, Zbigniew, 923
Buddhism
    canon law, 622
    Maitreya Buddha, 613
    Zen
        Hideyoshi and, 638
        Muromachi culture, 624–625
Burke, Edmund, 645*(t)*

Cabot, John, 467
caesars, title, 540
Calicut, Port of, 456*(i)*, 464
California, gold discovery, 803
Caliphate, Sokoto, 751*(t)*, **753**
Callao-Lima-Oroya rail line, 830, 830*(i)*
Calvin, John, 516
Calvinism
    Edict of Nantes, 515*(t)*, 524, 525
    predestination, 516
Camel caravans, salt, 591*(i)*

Canada
    Cartier in, 467
    Dominion of Canada (1867), 815*(t)*, 835,
        835*(m)*
    gold discovery, 803
    immigration certificate (1885), 804*(i)*
    immigration to (nineteenth century),
        835–836, 836*(m)*
    New France, 527, 537
    Treaty of Paris, 647
Canals
    Grand Canal, 614
    Panama Canal, 773, 815*(t)*, 839–840
    Suez Canal, 751*(t)*, 768, 768*(m)*, 783*(t)*,
        891, 963
Canon law, Buddhist texts, 622
Canon of Problems, 617
Canon of the Pulse, 617
Cape Colony, 585*(t)*, 597, 597*(m)*
Capitalism
    EU formation and, 1022
    global distribution of wealth, 1040*(m)*
    Hitler's view, 934
    "Japan, Inc.," **1013**–1014
    Khrushchev's view, 982
    Lenin's view, 860
    multinational corporations, 1040*(m)*
    New Deal, 917*(t)*, **918**–919, 920*(i)*
    Swahili civilization, 595
Capital punishment
    On Crimes and Punishments (Beccaria),
        568
    Second Republic of France, 721
Captaincies, *472*
Caravan routes, salt transportation, 591*(i)*
Caravel, *462*, 480, 604*(i)*
Carbon emissions, 1044–1045
Caribbean islands
    Circum-Caribbean, *815*, 829, 838
    colonization (1612–1697), 515*(t)*, 535, 537
Carlos III, 577
Carlos IV, 577
Carpet weaving, 487*(t)*, 494, 495*(i)*
Cartesian dualism, 557*(t)*, 562
Cartier, Jacques, 467
Caste system
    reform of, Rammohun Roy, 785
    untouchables, 962, 963
    varnas, 649
Castiglione, Guiseppe, 620*(i)*
Castles, Tokugawa shoguns and, 628
Castro, Fidel, 959, 976, 976*(i)*, 980, 985
Catalan Atlas (1375), 460*(i)*
Catherine the Great of Russia, 543, 551*(t)*,
    568–569, 651
Catholic Church (Roman Catholic Church,
    Western Christian Church)
    criticism, Protestant Reformation,
        514–516
    excommunication, 564*(t)*, 819
    Galileo, 559
    Inquisition, 516, 559
    liberation theology, *959*
    religious orders
        Dominicans, 479, 637, 790
        Franciscans, 479, 637
        Jesuits, 514*(i)*, **517**–518
Catholic Enlightenment, 566
Catholic League, 521
Catholic Reformation
    Council of Trent, 517

Counter-Reformation, 516
    described, 516–518
caudillismo, **816**
Cavour, Camillo Benso di, 725–726
Celibacy, neglect of (Roman Catholic
    Church, early sixteenth century), 514
Cell phones, 1052
Chamberlain, Arthur Neville, 938
Chancellor of Germany, Hitler, 917*(t)*, 935,
    940*(t)*
Chang'an, 614
Charles III of Spain, 645
Charles II of England, 515*(t)*, 526, 531, 537
Charles II of Spain, 526
Charles I of England, 515*(t)*, 529, 530, 531
Charles V (Holy Roman Emperor)
    abdication, 518
    Augsburg agreement, 517*(m)*, 518, 520, 521
    Luther and, 515–516
    New Laws, 472–473
    Safavid Persia, 489
    transatlantic slave trade, 472
    Valladolid debate, **479**
Chattel, *585*, 596, 606
Chechnya, Russian invasions, 1022
Chemistry, Scientific Revolution, 558
Children
    factory work and, 698–699
    filial piety, 616
    in military, 1047*(i)*
    Mines Act of 1842, 683*(t)*, **700**
    right to childhood, 1046–1047
Chile
    Great Depression, 921
    1982 economic crisis, 1004
China
    books availability (ca. 1500–1600), 613*(t)*,
        618
    Boxers, 696, 783*(t)*, **794**
    civil service examinations (merit-based
        examination system)
        defined, **616**
        Ming China, 616, 617
    Classical Age (to 221 B.C.E.)
        Hubei province, 619
        yin and yang, 617
    decline (nineteenth century), 791–796
    famine (1960–1961), 967
    foot binding, 793, 904
    Forbidden City, 614*(i)*
    Great Depression (1930s), 921
    Japan's aggression (1914–1939), 905–908
    Japan's Asian empire, 942–943
    Jesuits in, 514*(i)*
    Macao, 476, 613*(t)*, 636
    May Fourth Movement, 885*(t)*, **901**, 910
    middle power, **1031**, 1031*(t)*
    Ming Dynasty, *612*–619
        civil service examinations, 616, 617
        daily life, 618–619
        decline, 619
        founding, 612–614
        map, 613*(m)*
        Mongols and Great Wall, 615–616
        overview, 610
        Zhu Yuanzhang, 612–613
    multinational corporations, 1041*(i)*
    Nanjing
        capital, 614, 614*(i)*, 901, 907
        Chengzu and, 614
        Matteo Ricci (missionary) in, 636
        Rape of Nanjing, 885*(t)*, 907, 942
        tree planting, Ming government, 619
        Zhu's conquest (1356), 613

China (continued)
  nationalism, 901–902
  Nationalist Party, 885(t), 901, 910
  New Culture Movement, 885(t), *902*
  Nina Lao, 904–905
  1911 Revolution, *794*, 901, 902, 910
  Opium War, 783(t), 791–*792*
  People's Republic of China, 966, 967, 967(m)
  per capita levels of industrialization (1750–1913), 692(t)
  Qing Dynasty
    banners, *621*
    emperors, 622–623
    imperial expansion, 623
    Manchus, 506, 620–623
    map, 621(m)
    overview, 610
  railroads (1876), 793(i)
  Revolution of 1911, *794*, 901, 902, 910
  scholar-official class
    portrait of Jiang Shunfu, 612(i)
    Qing Dynasty, 622
    Taiping rebels (1853), 793
  self-strengthening movement, 793–794
  Shanghai
    Apple store, 1041(i)
    first railroad in China, 793(i)
    Japanese attack (1937), 907
    multinational companies, 1041(i)
    protest incident (May 30, 1925), 900(i)
  Sino-Japanese War, 783(t), 793, 794, 799, 942
  Taiping Rebellion, 783(t), 792–793
  Tiananmen Square, 993(t), 1012(i), *1012*–1013
  Yangzi River
    Grand Canal, 614
    Japanese attack (1937), 907
  Yellow River
    Grand Canal, 614
    Ming Dynasty decline, 619
  yin and yang, 617
  Zhou Dynasty, Mandate of Heaven, 904
Chinese Communism
  Mao Zedong
    Great Leap Forward, *967*–968
    Great Proletarian Cultural Revolution, 955(t), *968*
    Long March, 885(t), *906*, 907(m)
    pro-peasant policies, 906(t)
    Red Guards, *968*
  Nationalist Party, 885(t), 901, 910
Chinese Rebellions (1851–1911), 793(m)
Chinese Renaissance, 885(t), *902*
Chinese Revolution, 955(t)
Chintz, 501(i)
Chocolate
  cocoa holdups, 973
  Enlightenment (Age of Enlightenment), 575
Cholera, 732, 784, 1050
Christianity
  Coptic Christianity, *593*, 593(m), 594, 609
  division of Christendom, Protestant Reformation, 562(t)
  reconquista (750–1492), Americas, 462, 465, 471, 472
Chronology
  African states and societies (1400–1800), 585(t)
  Asia and the Pacific (imperialism,1800–1914), 783(t)

contemporary world in historical perspective, 1031(t)
East Asia (1400 c.e.–1800 c.e.), 613(t)
Europe (nineteenth century), 713(t)
European expansion (1450–1600), 457(t)
European expansion (1500–1750), 515(t)
Great Depression, 917(t)
imperialism (1800–1914), 751(t)
Industrial Revolution, 683(t)
Islamic world powers (1300–1800), 487(t)
liberalization (1968–2000s), 993(t)
Nationalism in Asia (1914–1939), 885(t)
Revolutionary era (1775–1825), 645(t)
World War I, 847(t)
World War II, 917(t)
Churchill, Winston, 940, 943, 947, 956
Circum-Caribbean, *815*, 829, 838
Cities
  megacities, *1037*, 1039
  Mughal Empire, 495–496
  Ottoman Empire, 495–496
  Safavid Empire, 495–496
Citizenship of Jews, Nuremberg Laws, 935, 940(t)
City-states
  Kilwa, 585(t), 595
  Swahili city-state, *594*–595, 606
Civil Constitution of the Clergy, 655, 658(t)
Civilizing mission, 752, 762, 776
Civil Rights Act, 955(t), *984*
Civil service examinations (merit-based examination system)
  defined, *616*
  Ming China, 616, 617
  scholar-official class
    portrait of Jiang Shunfu, 612(i)
    Qing Dynasty, 622
    Taiping rebels (1853), 793
Civil wars
  English Civil War (1642–1649), 515(t), 530, 530(m)
  Japan (1467–1600), 613(t), 625
  Netherlands (1568–1578), 518
  Russian Civil War, 847(t), 862, 862(m), 863(t)
  Spanish Civil War, 917(t), 920, 937, 940(t)
  Syria, 999
  U.S. Civil War, 815, 815(t), 816
Class-consciousness, *704*, 705, 709, 717
Classes (social classes)
  nineteenth-century Europe, 733–734
  scholar-official class
    portrait of Jiang Shunfu, 612(i)
    Qing Dynasty, 622
    Taiping rebels (1853), 793
Classic of Filial Piety, 616
Clergy
  absenteeism, 514–515
  alcohol use, pre-Reformation Catholic clergy, 498(t), 514
Climate change
  global warming, 1031(t), *1044*–1045, 1045(i)
  United Nations Framework Convention on Climate Change, 1044–1045
Cocoa holdups, *973*
Coercive Acts, 650, 651(t)
Coffeehouses (mid-fifteenth century, Islamic world), 498, 498(i)
Coins
  Nobunaga and, 625–626
  Tokugawa Shogunate, 629
Colbert, Jean-Baptiste, 515(t), 527, 536–537

Cold War
  Cuban missile crisis, 955(t), 980, 982
  defined, *954*
  described, 954–957
  détente, 1016
  map of Europe (1950s), 956(m)
  NATO, 955(t), *956*, 956(m), 983
Coleridge, Samuel Taylor, 737
Coliseum in Rome, 930(i)
Collectivization, 917(t), 925(i), *926*–927, 981
Colonialism
  Africa, impact after 1900, 758–759
  England, 535–537
  France, 535–537
  neocolonialism, *820*
    economic nationalism, *977*
    multinational corporations, 1041
  Spanish and Portuguese, 471–473
Colonization, Caribbean islands (1612–1697), 515(t), 535, 537
Columbian exchange, *474*–475, 483
Columbus, Christopher
  Afroeurasian trade world (before Columbus), 456–460, 480
  voyages, 457(t), 462, 464–466, 466(m)
Combination Acts, 683(t), *705*
"Comfort women," 943
Common Market, 955(t), *983*, 1022
Common Sense (Paine), 645(t), 650
Communes, 967
Communications revolution
  Australia, 801(m)
  digital divide, *1052*, 1053
  digital revolution, 1029(i), 1051–1052, 1053
Communism. *See also* Chinese Communism
  collectivization of agriculture, Stalin, 917(t), 925(i), *926*–927, 981
  Poster art, Communist China, 966(i)
  Stalin's great purges, 858(i), 914, 917(t), 928–929, 948
  War Communism, *862*
Communist Manifesto, 713(t), 717
Compass, 462, 551
Compulsory education, 741
Concentration camps, 758, 915(i), 935, 939(i), 942(m)
Concordat of 1801, 661
Concubines
  defined, *490*
  Edo period, 629, 632
  Hürrem, 487(t), 491, 491(i)
  Ning Lao's opinion, 904
  Ottoman Empire, 490
  Plum in the Golden Vase (novel, Ming China), 618(t)
  Shah Jahan, 496
  transatlantic slave trade, 752
The Condition of the Working Class in England (Engels), 683(t), 703
Confucianism, Neo-, 634
Congress of Vienna, *712*, 713(t), 714(m), 724, 729
CONNECTIONS
  African states and societies (1400–1800), 606–607
  Asia and the Pacific (imperialism,1800–1914), 809
  contemporary world in historical perspective, 1053
  East Asia (1400 c.e.–1800 c.e.), 639
  European expansion (1450–1600), 481
  European expansion (1500–1750), 544
  Great Depression, 949
  imperialism (1800–1914), 777

Islamic world powers (1300–1800), 509
liberalization (1968–2000s), 1025
Nationalism in Asia (1914–1939), 910–911
Revolutionary era (1775–1825), 677
World War II, 949
Conquistadors
Cortés, 457(t), 468–471
Pizarro, 457(t), 468, 469, 469(m), 471
Conrad, Joseph, 751(t), 763
Conservatism, *712*–715
Conservative authoritarianism, 922–923
Constantinople, Ottoman Empire, 487–489
Constitution, U.S.
framing, 651–652
limitations of liberty and equality, 652
Constitutionalism, *529*–532
Consumerism, 581
Consumer revolution, 572, 575, 576(i)
Contemporary world in historical
perspective, 1028–1055, 1031–1032
big picture, 1055(i)
children: right to childhood, 1046–1047
chronology, 1031(t)
CONNECTIONS, 1053
digital revolution, 1029(i), 1051–1052, 1053
"The End of History?" article, 1030
environmentalism, 1044–1045
expanding atomic age, 1032–1033
feminization of poverty, *1046*
global warming, 1031(t), *1044*–1045,
1045(i)
green revolution, 1001, 1031(t), *1049*
HIV/AIDS
ACT UP organization, 1045
deaths from, 1050
orphans, 1046
sub-Saharan Africa, 1050
worldwide (ca. 2010), 1051(m)
intensified agriculture, 1048–1049
lesbian, gay, and transgendered people,
1045
medical revolution, 1050–1051
middle powers, *1031*, 1031(t)
migration, 1036–1038
multinational corporations
accountability, 1044
Batista and, 980
in China, 1041(i)
described, *1041*–1042
developing nations and, 1055
Goulart and, 980
Nestlé boycott, 1043–1044
overview, 1043
population growth, slowing down,
1049–1050
al-Qaeda
Afghanistan and, 1033–1035
September 11 terrorist attacks, 1031(t),
1033, 1034(i)
Sieng (Mnong refugee in American high
school), 1038
summary, 1053
urbanization
bazaar economy, 1036(i), *1039*
contemporary world, 1037, 1039–1041,
1039(t)
global wealth distribution (ca. 2010),
1040(m), 1040–1041
megacities, *1037*, 1039
population, eight major areas (1925–
2025), 1039(t)
violence and complexity in multipolar
world, 1031–1032
women's right to equality, 1045–1046

Continental System, *662*
Contra rebel, 1003(i)
Conversations on the Plurality of Worlds
(Fontenelle), 559(i)
Conversions, indigenous peoples, 479
Copernicus, Nicolaus
Copernican hypothesis, *553*, 557(t)
*On the Revolutions of the Heavenly
Spheres*, 553, 557(t)
Coptic Christianity, *593*, 593(m), 594, 609
Coques, Gonzales, 532(i)
Coral Sea, Battle of the, 946
Cornwallis, Charles, 505
Cort, Henry, 686
Cortés, Hernán, 457(t), 468–471
Cossacks, 515(t), 538, *540*, 541
Cottage industry, *573*, 684(m), 684–685
Council of Trent, 517
Cow milking, Inca women, 471(i)
Cowrie shells, 459, *591*
Craft guilds, 705
Creoles, 473, 523, 576, 577–578, *672*–673
Crimean War, 729, 729(m), 886
Cromwell, Oliver, 515(t), 530–531, 537, 684
Crystal Palace, 683(t), *689*
Cuba
Castro, Fidel, 959, 976, 976(i), 980, 985
map, 980(m)
slavery abolished, 815(t), 825
Ten Years' War, 815(t), 825, 838
Cuban missile crisis, 955(t), 980, 982
Cuban Revolution (1959), 955(t), 980, 989,
1002
Cults
Maitreya Buddha cult, 613
Tonghak movement, 799
Curie, Marie, 873
Customs Union, *Zollverein*, 683(t), 694, 726
Cyprus
Great Britain (1787) and, 767
Ottoman Empire, 487(t), 489
Czechoslovakia, German occupation (1939),
917(t), 938, 940(t)

Dadaism, 847(t), 876
da Gama, Vasco, 456(i), 464, 585(t), 593(m),
595
Daily life (home life)
Ming Dynasty, 618–619
Soviet Union, under Stalin's reign,
927–928
Tokugawa Shogunate, 629–632
West Africa (1400–1800), 588–590
daimyo, *625*, 627(i)
Dalai Lamas, Gelug-pa sect and, 616
d'Alembert, Jean le Rond, 564, 564(t)
Dancing
geishas, 630
kabuki theater, 611(i), *630*, 630(i)
Darwin, Charles
evolution theory, *736*–737
*On the Origin of Species by the Means of
Natural Selection*, 713(t), 736
Social Darwinism, *737*, 761, 815, 829, 934
Dawes Plan, 847(t), *870*
Deaths
HIV/AIDS, 1050
infanticide, 792, 808
malaria (1980–2000), 1050
smallpox (1951–1966), 1050
Debates
European debates about indigenous
peoples, 479
Valladolid debate, *479*

De Beers Mining Company, 757
Declaration of Independence, 649(i), *650*,
651(t), 676
Declaration of Pillnitz, 656, 658(t)
Decolonization
in Africa, 971–975, 972(m)
in Asia, 967(m)
French-speaking Africa, 974–975
sub-Saharan Africa, 955(t)
United Nations, 957
Deism, *564*
Delacroix, Eugène, 737
Delaunay, Robert, 875(i)
Demographic changes, Enlightenment,
572–573
Dengel, Lebna, 593
Dependency theory, *958*
Descartes, René, 557, 557(t), 558, 567
Dessalines, Jean Jacques, 668(t), 669, 670
de-Stalinization, 955(t), *982*
Détente, *1016*
Determinism, 562, 564(t), 738
Development theories
dependency theory, *958*
modernization theory, *958*–959, 961
Devshirme, *490*
*Dialogue on the Two Chief Systems of the
World* (Galileo), 559
Diamond mining, South Africa, 757, 757(i)
Diasporas, 802, 808
Diaz, Bartholomew, 464
Díaz, Porfirio, 816, 827
Díaz del Castillo, Bernal, 464
Diderot, Denis, 564(t), 565, 566
Dien Bien Phu, Battle of, 969
Digital divide, *1052*, 1053
Digital revolution, 1029(i), 1051–1052, 1053
Dioceses, Council of Trent's impact, 517
The Directory, 658(t), 659, 661, 676
Diseases
cholera, 732, 784, 1050
Columbian exchange, *474*–475, 483
germ theory, 713(t), *732*, 1050
HIV/AIDS
ACT UP organization, 1045
deaths from, 1050
orphans, 1046
sub-Saharan Africa, 1050
worldwide (ca. 2010), 1051(m)
malaria
deaths (1980–2000), 1050
Ming Dynasty, 618
quinine, 760(i), 761
transatlantic slave trade, 598
West Africa, 589
yellow fever, 732, 790
Divine animals, dragons, 594(i)
Divine right of kings, *525*
Division of labor, sexual, 699–700, 699(t)
Divorce
Bolshevik Revolution, 928
Edo period, 632
under Mussolini's government, 932
National Assembly, 655, 892
National Congress Party and, 962
Southeast Asian peoples, 459
Dominicans, 479, 637, 790
Dominion of Canada (1867), 815(t), 835,
835(m)
Doña Marina (Malintzin), 470, 470(i)
Dragons, 594(i)
Drama, Nō theater, *625*, 638
Dreyfus affair, 739(i), *741*
Droughts, Ming decline, 619

Dualism, Cartesian, 557(t), 562
Dutch Cape Colony, 585(t), 597, 597(m)
Dutch East India Company, 457(t), 476–477, 502, 535, 585(t), 597, 606
Dutch East Indies, 787–788
Dutch Republic
    republicanism, 531–532
    trade (seventeenth century), 535, 536(m)
    transatlantic slave trade, 535

Early modern period (Europe, 1500–1750), 512–547
    big picture, 547(i)
    Catholic Reformation
        Council of Trent, 517
        described, 516–518
    chronology, 515(t)
    CONNECTIONS, 544
    Enlightenment (1690–1789), 561–578
        Atlantic Enlightenment, 577–578
        Catholic Enlightenment, 566
        in chronology, 551(t)
        contributing factors, 562(t)
        defined, **561**
        deism, **564**
        demographic changes, 572–573
        early period, 561–563
        economic change, 572–573
        enlightened absolutism, **568**–569, 577, 581
        globalization and, 562(t)
        International Enlightenment, 566–568
        Jewish Enlightenment (Haskalah), **569**, 569(m), 571
        major figures in, 564(t)
        overview, 548–549
        philosophes, 551(t), **563**–565, 568, 569, 575
        Protestant Reformation and, 562(t)
        public sphere, 568, 572, **575**, 578
        race concept, 565–566
        Scientific Revolution and, 562(t)
        Scottish Enlightenment, 564(t), 567, 568, 577
        summary, 578–579
        transatlantic slave trade, 573–575, 574(m)
        urban life, 575
    mercantilism
        colonial wars and, 537–538
        defined, **527**
        Navigation Acts, 515(t), **537**, 684
    overview, 512–513
    Peace of Utrecht, 526, 526(m), 538
    Protestant Reformation, 514–516
    Scientific Revolution (1500–1700), 548–560
        alchemy, 555
        Aristotle and, 552–553, 578
        astrology and, 555, 579
        astronomy, 553
        chemistry, 558
        in chronology, 551(t)
        contributors, 557(t)
        Copernican hypothesis, 553, 557(t)
        magic, 555
        methods of science, 556–558
        natural history and empire, 554–555
        Newton's synthesis, 553–554
        overview, 548–549
        physics, 553
        religion and science, 559
        society and science, 559–560
        thought to 1550, 552–553

        sovereignty, **521**
        state-building, 520
        summary, 544
        trade, 534–538
Earthquakes
    Mexico City (1986), 995
    Peru (1868), 830
East Africa
    Mogadishu
        commercial prosperity, 595
        trade with Middle East, 459
    Portuguese in, 595
    Swahili city-state, **594**–595, 606
East Asia
    Chang'an, 614
    1400 C.E.–1800 C.E., 610–641
        big picture, 641(i)
        chronology, 613(t)
        CONNECTIONS, 639
        map (ca. 1600), 635(m)
        overview, 610–611
        summary, 638–639
    Korea, Three Kingdoms Period, 618(t)
    urban population (1925–2025), 1039(t)
Easter Island society, 801
Eastern Europe, anti-Semitism (1873), 713(t), 742–743
East Germany, Berlin Wall, 955(t), 956(m), 993(t), 1016(i), 1019, 1024, 1030
Economic crisis, Chile (1982), 1004
Economic liberalism
    activism and, 1030–1031
    defined, **568**
    laissez faire, **715**, 716, 720, 761
    multinational corporations, 1041
    Smith, Adam, 564(t), 568
Economic nationalism, 976–**977**
Edict of Nantes, 515(t), 524, 525
Ego, **874**
Egypt
    Alexandria
        anti-European riots (1882), 770
        Ptolemy's *Geography*, **462**, 465–466, 552–553
    Ali, Muhammad
        life, 766, 767–769
        modernization of Egypt, 751(t), 776
        picture, 769(i)
    imperialism in, 767–768, 770
    middle power, **1031**, 1031(t)
    modernization
        1805, 683(t), 696
        1805–1849, 751(t), 776
    Nasser, Gamal Abdel, 910, 955(t), 961(i), 963–964
    Suez Canal, 751(t), 768, 768(m), 783(t), 891, 963
Eiffel Tower, 875(i)
Einstein, Albert, 873–874
Eisenhower, Dwight D., 945, 969
El Alamein, Battle of, 945
Eliot, T. S., 874
Elizabeth I, 502, 516, 529
Emancipation Proclamation, 824
emirs, 893
Empiricism, **557**–558
Enabling Act, **935**, 940(t)
Enclosure movement, **573**, 683, 719
Encomienda system, **472**–473, 479, 789
Encyclopedia: The Rational Dictionary of the Sciences, the Arts, and the Crafts, 551(t), 564, 564(t)
"The End of History?" article, 1030
Engels, Friedrich, 683(t), 703, 717

England
    colonialism, 535–537
    Factory Acts, 683(t), **698**
    Glorious Revolution, 515(t), 531
    Mines Act of 1842, 683(t), **700**
English Civil War (1642–1649), 515(t), 530, 530(m)
Enlightened absolutism, 568–569, 577, 581
Enlightenment (1690–1789), 561–578
    Atlantic Enlightenment, 577–578
    Catholic Enlightenment, 566
    in chronology, 551(t)
    contributing factors, 562(t)
    defined, **561**
    deism, **564**
    demographic changes, 572–573
    early period, 561–563
    economic change, 572–573
    enlightened absolutism, **568**–569, 577, 581
    globalization and, 562(t)
    International Enlightenment, 566–568
    Jewish Enlightenment (Haskalah), **569**, 569(m), 571
    major figures in, 564(t)
    overview, 548–549
    philosophes, 551(t), **563**–565, 568, 569, 575
    Protestant Reformation and, 562(t)
    public sphere, 568, 572, **575**, 578
    race concept, 565–566
    Scientific Revolution and, 562(t)
    Scottish Enlightenment, 564(t), 567, 568, 577
    summary, 578–579
    transatlantic slave trade, 573–575, 574(m)
    urban life, 575
Entertainment
    coffeehouses (mid-fifteenth century, Islamic world), 498, 498(i)
    kabuki theater, 611(i), **630**, 630(i)
Entrepôts
    Mogadishu, 595
    port of Malacca, 456
    Senegambian states, 584
Environmentalism, 1044–1045
Epidemics
    influenza epidemic (1918), 897
    Muhammad's view, 497
    smallpox
        Ming Dynasty, 619
        Native Americans (sixteenth century), 469, 473, 598
        reduced deaths (1951–1966), 1050
        vaccination, 700
        variolation, 637
Equiano, Olaudah, 566, 585(t), 599–601, 600(i)
Estates General, **654**, 658(t), 676
Estonian serfs, 519, 519(i)
Ethiopia
    Coptic Christianity, **593**, 593(m), 594, 609
    Muslim and European incursions (1500–1630), 585(t), 593–594
    Mussolini's campaigns, 917(t), 936(m), 940(t)
    Prester John (mythical Christian monarch), 593, 606
Ethnic groups
    Africa, 971
    nationalism and, 715–716, 722
    Nigeria, 995
    Ottomans, 488(m)
    race and, 480

Euclid, 636
Eunuchs
    Aurangzeb and, 500
    Kanem-Bornu kingdom, 588
    Ming Dynasty, 615
    Zheng He, 457, 458(m), 613(t), 633–634,
        641
Europe
    Hitler's empire (1939–1942), 939–942
    revolutions of 1848 (central Europe),
        722–723
    urban population (1925–2025), 1039(t)
    World War II
        Nazi occupation (1939–1942), 939–942
        war in Europe (1942–1945), 942–943
European Economic Community (Common
    Market), 955(t), **983**, 1022
European expansion (1450–1600), 454–483
    big picture, 483(i)
    causes of, 461–462
    chronology, 457(t)
    Columbian exchange, **474**–475, 483
    CONNECTIONS, 481
    exploration
        northern European powers, 467
        rise of, 462–463
    France, 467
    Geography, Ptolemy's, **462**, 465–466,
        552–553
    Indian Ocean, Afroeurasian trade world,
        456–459
    indigenous peoples
        conversions, 479
        European debates, 479
        population loss and economic
            exploitation, 472–473
    Magellan, 466, 481
    map, 465(m)
    Marco Polo, 457, 457(t)
    overview, 454–455
    Portuguese in Africa and Asia, 463–464
    race concept, 479–480
    Spain
        Americas, 464–466
        Aztec and Inca empires, 468–471
        encomienda system, **472**–473, 479, 789
        Pacific, 466–467
    summary, 480–481
    technology, 462–463
    Treaty of Tordesillas, 457(t), **466**, 471
European Union (EU), 993(t), 998, **1022**–
    1024, 1023(m)
Europe's first policy, **943**
Evolution, **736**–737
Excommunication, 564(t), 819
Executions
    Charles I of England, 515(t), 530
    Coliseum in Rome, 930(i)
    death penalty
        On Crimes and Punishments
            (Beccaria), 568
        Second Republic of France, 721
    guillotine, 657(i), 659, 659(i)
    purges of Stalin, 858(i), 914, 917(t),
        928–929, 948
    Reign of Terror, **657**–659, 658(t), 676
    Robespierre, 659(i)
    Suleiman's son, Mustafa, 491
    Tiananmen Square, 1013
    witch-hunts, 518
Existentialism, 847(t), **873**, 1018
Extermination
    Armenian Genocide, 890(i), 891
    Holocaust, 942, 942(m)

hunger-extermination, Ukraine, 917(t),
    925(i), 926, 927
Extraterritoriality, **792**

Factories
    families and children, 698–699
    Industrial Revolution, 684–685, 697–701
    new class of factory owners, 703
    work in, 697–698
Factory Acts, 683(t), **698**
Factory-forts, **502**, 602
Faisal bin Hussein (king), 891, 894
Families
    factory work and, 698–699
    filial piety, 616
    nineteenth-century Europe, 734–736
    nuclear, 589
Famines
    Bangladesh, 963
    Biafran war, 995
    China (1960–1961), 967
    collectivization campaign, Stalin, 917(t),
        925(i), **926**–927, 981
    Edo Period, 631
    Europe (seventeenth century), 520
    Great Famine in Ireland (1845–1851), 698,
        713(t), 720, 741
    India (1966–1967), 1049
    Malthus and, 690
    Senegambian coast to Upper Nile (1680s),
        585(t), 590
    Sudan (2011), 1010
    Ukraine (1932–1933), 917(t), 925(i), 926,
        927
    West Africa (1738–1756), 585(t)
Fascism
    Black Shirts, 922(i), **931**
    defined, **925**
    described, 930–932
    Japan (1930s) and, 924
    Mussolini
        Black Shirts, 922(i), **931**
        Ethiopian campaigns, 917(t), 936(m),
            940(t)
        fascism, **925**, 930–932
        Lateran Agreement, 917(t), **932**
        in parade, 930(i)
        regime in action, 931–932
        seizes power in Italy, 917(t), 930–931
    spread, 922(i)
Fatehpur Sikri, 495–496, 499(i)
Feminism
    Brittain's efforts, 856
    separate spheres, 735–736
    woman, in French illustration (Triumph of
        Democratic Republics, 1848), 721(i)
Feminization of poverty, **1046**
Ferdinand, Franz, 847(t), 849, 878
Ferdinand I, 722
Ferdinand II, 527
Ferdinand III, 527
Ferdinand of Aragon, 462, 466, 499
Ferdinand VII, 662, 673
Filial piety, 616
Final Solution, 935, 942
Fire
    Aristotelian universe (imagination,
        sixteenth century), 550(i)
    Aristotle, 552
    sati practice, 500
First policy, Europe, **943**
"First principles," Descartes, 558
Five-year plans, 917(t), **925**, 925(i), 926–
    927, 967, 981

Florida, admitted to U.S. (1845), 815(t)
Fontenelle, 559(i)
Foot binding, 793, 904
Foraging, hunter-gatherers, 468
Forbidden City, 614(i)
Fourier, Charles, 716(t)
France
    absolutism, 524–525
    Algeria conquest, 751(t), 767
    book trade, 572(i)
    colonialism, 535–537
    Congress of Vienna, **712**, 713(t), 714(m),
        724, 729
    Crimean War, 729, 729(m), 886
    European expansion, 467
    Great Depression, 920
    mercantilism, 515(t), 527, 536
    middle power, **1031**, 1031(t)
    Paris
        Notre Dame Cathedral, 737–738
        salons, 551(t), 560, 565, 567(i), **575**, 577
        sans-culottes, **656**, 657(i), 658(t), 667
        Treaty of Paris, 487(t), 505, 645(t), **647**,
            651, 651(t), 652
    per capita levels of industrialization
        (1750–1913), 692(t)
    Popular Front, 917(t), **920**
    Republican France (nineteenth century),
        740–741
    revolutions (1848), 720–722
    Saint Bartholomew's Day massacre, 518
    Sykes-Picot Agreement, 885(t), **891**
    Thirty Years' War
        described, **520**–521
        map of Europe (after 1648), 522(m)
        Peace of Westphalia, 521, 524
Franciscans, 479, 637
Francis II of Austria, 656
Francis I of France, 489
Franco, Francisco, 920, 937
Franco-Prussian War, 728(m), 729, 740, 797
Frederick the Great, 551(t), 568–569, 570(m)
Frederick William IV, 718(i), 723
Free people of color, 549(i), 577, 665–666, 670
Free will, 516, 562
Free womb laws, **823**, 825
French Revolution (1789–1799)
    breakdown of old order, 653–654
    constitutional monarchy, 655
    The Directory, 658(t), 659, 661, 676
    key events, 658(t)
    National Assembly, 654–655
    National Convention, 655–659
    Reflections on the Revolution in France
        (Burke), 645(t)
    Reign of Terror, **657**–659, 658(t), 676
Fresco, Persian princess (Safavid Dynasty),
    485(i)
Freud, Sigmund, 874
Freudian psychology, 847(t), 874
Friedrich, Carl, 923
Frobisher, Martin, 467
Functionalism, **875**
Fur trade, 534(i)

Galileo, 553–554, 554(i), 557, 557(t), 559
Gallipoli, Battle of, 852
Gambling, pre-Reformation Catholic clergy,
    498(t), 514
Gandhi, Kasturba, 883(i)
Gandhi, Mohandas
    King, Martin Luther, Jr., 984
    resistance campaign in India, 898–899
    satyagraha, 885(t), **898**–899, 910

Gardens
    Mughal Empire, 496–497
    Ottoman Empire, 496–497
    Safavid Empire, 496–497
Garibaldi, Giuseppe, 725(m), 726, 727, 727(i)
Gas chambers, 939(i), 942
Gay rights, 1045
Geishas, 630
Gelug-pa sect, 616
Gender roles, separate spheres, *699*–700, 735–736, 744
General will, 565
Geneva
    Geneva Accords, 969
    Protestant Reformation, 516
Genius
    Colbert's financial genius, 527
    Einstein, 873–874
    Shakespeare, 785
Genoa
    Afroeurasian trade world, 460
    John Cabot, 467
Genocide
    Armenian Genocide, 890(i), 891
    Rwanda, 1010, 1032
Geography, Ptolemy's, *462,* 465–466, 552–553
George, Saint, 594(i)
German Auxiliary Service Law, 847(t)
German Confederation of the Rhine, 662, 662(m)
German Empire
    Reichstag, 740, 743, 855, 857, 934, 935, 940(t)
    up to Great War, 740
Germany
    Franco-Prussian War, 728(m), 729, 740, 797
    Great Depression, 918, 934
    middle power, *1031,* 1031(t)
    per capita levels of industrialization (1750–1913), 692(t)
    rebuilding era (after World War II), 986
    social security laws (1883), 713(t), 740, 919
    unification (1866–1871), 713(t), 726, 728(m), 728–729
    Zollverein, 683(t), 694, 726
Germ theory, 713(t), ***732***, 1050
Gestapo, 935
Girondists, 656
Glasnost, 993(t), ***1017***
Global economy
    global wealth distribution (ca. 2010), 1040(m), 1040–1041
    Latin America (nineteenth century), 828–829
    trade (sixteenth and seventeenth centuries), 477(m)
Globalization
    beginnings (sixteenth century), 454, 483
    Enlightenment and, 562(t)
    state-building efforts (European powers, seventeenth century), 547
    throughout history, 1053, 1055
Global warming, 1031(t), ***1044***–1045, 1045(i)
Glorious Revolution, 515(t), 531
Glückel of Hameln, 533, 533(i)
Gold, discovery, 803
Goulart, João, 980
Government of India Act (1935), 899
Granada, Spain conquers (1492), 462

Grand Alliance, 943, 948
Grand Canal, 614
Grand Empire, 662–664, 663(m)
Gravitation, universal law of, 554, 557(t)
Gray zone of moral compromise, 944
Great Britain
    in 1707, 537
    Congress of Vienna, *712,* 713(t), 714(m), 724, 729
    Cyprus and (1878), 767
    development (up to Great War), 741–742
    per capita levels of industrialization (1750–1913), 692(t)
    Quadruple Alliance, 664, 712, 713
    Reform Bill (1832), 713(t), 719
    social reform (1906–1914), 713(t), 719–720, 741
    Sykes-Picot Agreement, 885(t), *891*
Great Depression (1929–1939), 916–921
    big picture, 951(i)
    chronology, 917(t)
    cocoa holdups, *973*
    CONNECTIONS, 949
    economic crisis, 916–918
    European response, 919–920
    Louisville flood victims, 916(i)
    mass unemployment, 918
    New Deal, 917(t), 918–919, *918*–919, 920(i)
    overview, 914
    summary, 948
    worldwide effects, 920–921
Great Exhibition (1851), 683(t), 689
Great Famine in Ireland (1845–1851), 698, 713(t), 720, 741
Great Fear, 655, 658(t)
Great Leap Forward, 967–968
Great migration, 774–775
Great Mutiny / Great Revolt, 783
Great Northern War (1700–1721), 541
Great Patriotic War of the Fatherland, 981
Great Proletarian Cultural Revolution, 955(t), ***968***
Great purges, 858(i), 914, 917(t), 928–929, 948
Great Revolt, 783, 783(m), 783(t)
Great sword hunt of Hideyoshi, 626
Great Wall, Mongols, 615–616
Great white walls, 775
Greenhouse effect, 1044
Green revolution, 1001, 1031(t), ***1049***
Gropius, Walter, 875
Guadalcanal, Battle of, 946
Guadalupe Hidalgo, Treaty of, 818
Guevara, Che, 959, 976(i), 997(i)
Guillotine, 657(i), 659, 659(i)
Gunboat diplomacy, 796

Habsburg monarchy
    Austrian Habsburgs, 527(m), 527–528
    War of the Spanish Succession, 515(t), 525–526, 526(m), 528, 537–538, 671
Haitian Revolution (1791–1804)
    key events, 668(t)
    L'Ouverture, Toussaint, 645(t), 668–670
    map, 667(m)
    Saint-Domingue slave revolt, 665(i), 665–668
Hardy, Thomas, 738
Hargreaves, James, 682(i), 683(t)
Harvey, William, 557(t), 558
Haseki mosque complex, 491
Haskalah (Jewish Enlightenment), ***569***, 569(m), 571

Hastings, Warren, 505
Hausaland, 584, 586(m), 588
Havel, Václav, 1017–1018
Hawaii, Pearl Harbor attacks, 917(t), 943, 948
Heart of Darkness (Conrad), 751(t), 763
Heaven
    Christianized version of Aristotle, 552
    Mandate of Heaven, 904
    On the Revolutions of the Heavenly Spheres, 553, 557(t)
    sati practice, 500
Heavenly Kingdom of Great Peace (Taiping), 793
Hebrew people
    Abraham, 1000(i)
    Isaiah, 600
Heliocentrism, 559
Henry (prince), 463–464
Henry II of France, 489
Henry IV of France, 515(t), 524
Henry of Navarre, 518
Henry VIII, 516
Heresy
    Galileo, 559
    Inquisition, 516, 559
Herzl, Theodor, 743
Hideyoshi, Toyotomi, 610, 624(i), 626(m), 626–627, 634, 638
High Middle Ages, 550(i), 551
Himmler, Heinrich, 935, 941–942
Hindenburg, Paul von, 935
Hinduism
    Marathas (Hindu militant group), 503(m), 507, 508
    Ottoman Empire and Hindus, 500
    Upanishads, 785
Hiroshima and Nagasaki, atomic bombs, 917(t), 946(i), 947(m), 948, 1032
Historical and Critical Dictionary (Bayle), 562, 564(t)
Hitler, Adolf
    appeasement, 936–937, 940(t), 948
    as chancellor of Germany, 917(t), 935, 940(t)
    empire in Europe, 939–942
    Enabling Act, *935*, 940(t)
    Final Solution, 935, 942
    Mein Kampf, *870*, 917(t), 934
    Nazism and, 933–934
    New Order program, *941*, 948
    popularity, 936
    road to power, 934–935
    SS corps, 935, 941–942, 944
HIV/AIDS
    ACT UP organization, 1045
    deaths from, 1050
    orphans, 1046
    sub-Saharan Africa, 1050
    worldwide (ca. 2010), 1051(m)
Hobson, J. A., 751(t), 762–763
Holocaust
    Auschwitz, 915(i), 944, 945
    in chronology, 917(t)
    concentration camps, 758, 915(i), 935, 939(i), 942(m)
    defined, *942*
    Final Solution, 935, 942
    gas chambers, 939(i), 942
    gray zone of moral compromise, 944
    map, 942(m)
Holodomor, 927
Holy Alliance, 713–714
Holy Office, 516, 559

Holy Roman Empire
  Charles V
    abdication, 518
    Augsburg agreement, 517(m), 518,
      520, 521
    Luther and, 515–516
    New Laws, 472–473
    Safavid Persia, 489
    transatlantic slave trade, 472
    Valladolid debate, **479**
Homosexuality
  lesbian, gay, and transgendered people,
    1045
  marriage
    legalization in countries, 1045
    Tierra del Fuego (2009), 1043(i)
  samurai, 630
Hong Xiuquan, 792
Hoover, Herbert, 918
Hubei province, 619
Hugo, Victor, 737–738
Human rights
  Bill of Rights (1689), **531**
  Bill of Rights (1791), 651–652, 651(t)
  children: right to childhood, 1046–1047
  Declaration of Independence, 649(i),
    651(t), 676
  women's right to equality, 1045–1046
Humayun, 493
Hume, Marcel, 564(t), 567–568
Humors, bodily, 558
Hunchback of Notre Dame (Hugo), 737–738
Hungary
  Austro-Hungarian Empire, 741–742, 744,
    849, 865, 866(m), 934
  per capita levels of industrialization
    (1750–1913), 692(t)
  Soviet invasion, 955(t)
Hunger-extermination, Ukraine, 917(t),
    925(i), 926, 927
Hunter-gatherers, 468
Hürrem, 487(t), 491, 491(i)
Hussein, Saddam, 964, 999, 1000, 1035

Ice age, little, 508, 520, 619
Id (Freudian term), **874**
imams, 492
Immigration
  to Canada (nineteenth century), 835–836,
    836(m)
  of Jews to Palestine (1920s–1930s),
    885(m)
  to Latin America (late nineteenth
    century), 832–833
  to U.S. (nineteenth century), 833–834
Immortality
  "On the Immortality of the Soul"
    (Mendelssohn, M.), 571
  philosophes and, 564
Imperialism (1800–1914), 748–811
  before 1880, 751–754
  Africa, 750–753
  in Asia, 760–761
  Asia and the Pacific, 780–811
    big picture, 810(i)
    British rule in India, 782–785
    China's decline, 791–796
    chronology, 783(t)
    CONNECTIONS, 809
    Dutch East Indies, 787–788
    map (1914), 786(m)
    migrations in Pacific region, 800–805
    opening of Japan, 795–796
    overview, 780–781

similarities and differences, Asian
  countries, 806–807
summary, 808–809
Berlin Conference, 751(t), **754**
big picture, 779(i)
causes of, 761–762
chronology, 751(t)
civilizing mission, 752, 762, 776
colonialism's impact on Africa, 758–759
CONNECTIONS, 777
critics of, 762–763
in Egypt, 767–768, 770
new imperialism (1880–1914), 751(t),
  761–764
New Order, **941**, 948
overview, 748
responses, 763–764
Rhodes, 757, 758
scramble for Africa, 754–756, 755(m)
Social Darwinism, **737**, 761, 815, 829, 934
South Africa, 756–758
summary, 776
trade and social change, Africa, 750–753
"White Man's Burden" (Kipling), 751(t),
  762, 763
Import substitution industrialization (ISI),
  798, **959**
Impressionism, 876
Inca Empire
  Atahualpa, 469, 471
  described, **469**
  Spanish conquest, 468–471
Indentured laborers, **803**–804 535, 808,
  832, 898
India
  British rule, 782–785
  caste system, reform, 785
  famine (1966–1967), 1049
  Gandhi, Mohandas
    King, Martin Luther, Jr., 984
    resistance campaign in India, 898–899
    satyagraha, 885(t), **898**–899, 910
  independence, 955(t), 962, 962(m)
  map (1707–1805), 503(m)
  middle power, **1031**, 1031(t)
  Mughal Empire (1526–1827)
    Akbar, 487(t), 493, 495–496, 499(i), 500,
      508
    Aurangzeb, 487(t), 493, 500, 507
    city building, 495–496
    coffeehouses, 498, 498(i)
    cultural advances, 494–498
    decline of power, 506–508, 507(m)
    defined, 493
    described, 493
    Indian Ocean trade, 502
    intellectual advances, 497
    map, 493(m)
    merchant networks, 502–504
    non-Muslims, 499–500
    overview, 484
    religious trends, 497
    summary, 508–509
    trade routes' impact, 501–505
  Muslim League, 897, 899, **962**
  per capita levels of industrialization
    (1750–1913), 692(t)
India Act of 1784, 505
Indian Civil Service, **785**
Indian National Congress, 783(t), **785**, 808,
  897, 899, 962
Indian Ocean
  Afroeurasian trade world, 456–459
  Mughal, Ottoman, Safavid empires, 502

Indigenous peoples
  conversions, 479
  displacement (1780s–1910s), 817(m)
  European debates, 479
  population loss and economic
    exploitation, 472–473
Individualism
  New Culture Movement, 885(t), **902**
  socialism *versus*, 716
Individuals in Society
  Ali, Muhammad, 769, 769(i)
  Brittain, Vera, 856–857
  Doña Marina (Malintzin), 470, 470(i)
  Equiano, Olaudah, 566, 585(t), 599–601,
    600(i)
  Garibaldi, Giuseppe, 725(m), 726, 727,
    727(i)
  Glückel of Hameln, 533, 533(i)
  Havel, Václav, 1017–1018
  Hürrem, 487(t), 491, 491(i)
  Levi, Primo, 944–945
  L'Ouverture, Toussaint, 645(t), 668–670
  Meiggs, 830
  Mendelssohn, Moses, 569, 571
  Ning Lao, 904–905
  Perón, Eva, 978–979
  Rizal, José, 790
  Sieng (Mnong refugee in American high
    school), 1038
  Tan Yunxian, 617
  Wedgwood, Josiah, 687
Inductive reasoning, 557
Industrialization
  global consequences (1800–1914), 771–773
  import substitution industrialization, 798,
    959
  Japan (nineteenth century), 798
  Russia(1890–1900), 713(t), 730
Industrial Revolution (1780–1850)
  Britain, 682–690
  chronology, 683(t)
  continental industrialization (ca. 1850),
    694(m)
  defined, **684**
  factories, 684–685
  global picture, 695–696
  iron law of wages, **690**
  national and international variations,
    691–693
  responses to, 703–704
  slavery and, 706
  technological innovations, 684–685
Industrious revolution, Japan, 629
Industry
  cottage industry, **573**, 684(m), 684–685
  putting-out system, 503, 684, 693, 698
  West Africa (1400–1800), 590–591
Inertia, law of, **553**, 557(t)
Infanticide, 792, 808
Influenza epidemic (1918), 897
Information age, 1051–1052
Inquisition, 516, 559
Intellectual life
  Mughal Empire, 497
  Ottoman Empire, 497
  Safavid Empire, 497
International Enlightenment, 566–568
Internet, digital divide, **1052**, 1053
Interwar years, 868–871
intifada, 993(t), **998**
Iran
  Majlis, 893
  middle power, **1031**, 1031(t)
  nuclear energy program, 1030(i)

Iraq
  Hussein, Saddam, 964, 999, 1000, 1035
  OPEC oil embargo and, 997
Ireland, Great Famine (1845–1851), 698,
  713(t), 720, 741
Iron curtain, 956, 956(m)
Iron law of wages, **690**
Isabella of Castile, 462, 466, 499
Isaiah (prophet), 600
Islam
  imams, 492
  Mecca
    coffeehouses, 498
    Mansa Musa at, 460(i)
    Zheng He in, 634
  Muhammad
    Ali (Muhammad's cousin and son-in-
      law), 492
    Sunna, 492
  Sufism
    described, 497, 498
    Qizilbash, **490**, 492, 497
Islamic civilization
  Mughal Empire (1526–1827)
    Akbar, 487(t), 493, 495–496, 499(i), 500,
      508
    Aurangzeb, 487(t), 493, 500, 507
    city building, 495–496
    coffeehouses, 498, 498(i)
    cultural advances, 494–498
    decline of power, 506–508, 507(m)
    defined, 493
    described, 493
    Indian Ocean trade, 502
    intellectual advances, 497
    map, 493(m)
    merchant networks, 502–504
    non-Muslims, 499–500
    overview, 484
    religious trends, 497
    summary, 508–509
    trade routes' impact, 501–505
  Ottoman Empire (1299–1922)
    Armenian Genocide, 890(i), 891
    in chronology, 487(t)
    city building, 495–496
    coffeehouses, 498, 498(i)
    Constantinople, 487–489
    cultural advances, 494–498
    decline of power, 506–508, 507(m),
      765–767
    defined, **487**
    expansion, 487–490
    height of, 487(t), 488(m)
    Hürrem, 487(t), 491, 491(i)
    Indian Ocean trade, 502
    intellectual advances, 497
    janissaries, **490**, 491, 766
    map, 488(m)
    merchant networks, 502–504
    non-Muslims, 499–500
    Osman (ruler), 487, 487(t)
    overview, 484
    partition (1914–1923), 889(m)
    reform, 765–767
    religious trends, 497
    slavery, 490
    summary, 508–509
    Tanzimat, 751(t), **766**
    trade routes' impact, 501–505
  Safavid Empire (1501–1722)
    city building, 495–496
    coffeehouses, 498, 498(i)
    cultural advances, 494–498

decline of power, 506–508, 507(m)
  defined, **490**
  described, 490–492
  Indian Ocean trade, 502
  intellectual advances, 497
  map, 492(m)
  merchant networks, 502–504
  non-Muslims, 499–500
  overview, 484
  religious trends, 497
  Shah Abbas, 485(i), 487(t), 492, 492(m),
    494, 495, 496(i), 504
  summary, 508–509
  trade routes' impact, 501–505
Seljuk Turks, 488
Sufism
  described, 497, 498
  Qizilbash, **490**, 492, 497
Suleiman the Magnificent
  building program, 496(i)
  Hürrem, 487(t), 491, 491(i)
  intellectual advances, 497
  reign of, 487(t), 488(m), 489, 508
  1300–1800, 484–511
    big picture, 511(i)
    chronology, 487(t)
    CONNECTIONS, 509
    merchant networks, 502–504
    overview, 484–485
    summary, 508–509
Isma'il, 487(t), **490**, 492
Israel
  independence, 955(t), 964, 965(m)
  middle power, **1031**, 1031(t)
  Six-Day War, 955(t), 964–965, 965(m), 998
  Zionism, **743**, 891, 894–895, 910, 961
Italy
  Mussolini
    Black Shirts, 922(i), **931**
    Ethiopian campaigns, 917(t), 936(m),
      940(t)
    fascism, **925**, 930–932
    Lateran Agreement, 917(t), **932**
    in parade, 930(i)
    regime in action, 931–932
    seizes power in Italy, 917(t), 930–931
  per capita levels of industrialization
    (1750–1913), 692(t)
  unification of (1859–1870), 713(t),
    725–726
Ivan III, 539–540
Ivan IV, 540
Ivan the Terrible, 515(i), 540, 541, 544

Jacobin Club, **656**, 657, 676
Jahangir, 493, 495, 499(i), 500, 502
James I, 529–530
Janissaries, **490**, 491, 766
Japan
  American reconstruction, 968–969
  Asian Empire, 942–943
  baseball in, 969(i)
  China-Japan relations (1914–1939),
    905–908
  civil wars (1467–1600), 613(t), 625
  Fascism (1930s) and, 924
  Great Depression (1930s), 921
  Hiroshima and Nagasaki, atomic bombs,
    917(t), 946(i), 947(m), 948, 1032
  industrialization (nineteenth century),
    798
  industrious revolution, 629
  Meiji Restoration, 783(t), **796**–799, 900–
    902, 903

Middle Ages (1400–1800), 624–638
middle power, **1031**, 1031(t)
Muromachi culture, 624–625
Nō theater, **625**, 638
opening of, 795–796
Pearl Harbor attacks, 917(t), 943, 948
rebuilding era (after World War II), 986
Russo-Japanese War (1904–1905), 713(t),
  718(t), **799**, 885(t)
Sino-Japanese War, 783(t), 793, 794, 799,
  942
Tokugawa Shogunate (Edo period)
  alternate residence system, **627**, 629
  chronology, 613(t)
  commercialization and growth of
    towns, 629
  daily life, 629–632
  government, 627–628
  kabuki theater, 611(i), **630**, 630(i)
  map, 628(m)
  Matsumoto Yonesaburo, 611(i)
  overview, 610
World War II, 942–943
"Japan, Inc.," **1013**–1014
Jasperware, 687(i)
Java War, **788**
Jerusalem
  Hürrem in, 491
  Suleiman's reconstruction, 495
Jesuits, 514(i), **517**–518
Jewish Enlightenment (Haskalah), **569**,
  569(m), 571
Jews
  anti-Semitism
    Dreyfus affair, 739(i), **741**
    eastern Europe (1873), 713(t), 742–743
    Mein Kampf (Hitler), **870**, 917(t), 934
  Arab-Jewish tensions, Palestine, 894–895
  Balfour Declaration, 865, 885(t), **891**
  expulsion
    from Russia, 742, 742(i)
    from Spain (1492), 499
  Glückel of Hameln, 533, 533(i)
  immigration to Palestine (1920s–1930s),
    885(m)
  kibbutz, **895**
  Mendelssohn, Moses, 569, 571
  Ottoman Empire, 499–500
  Pale of Settlement, 551(t), 569, 569(m)
  Zionism, **743**, 891, 894–895, 910, 961
Jiang Jieshi (Chiang Kai-shek), 885(t), 901,
  905–906, 910, 967, 1013, 1014
jihads, **753**
jizya, **500**
John Paul II, 959
Johnson, Lyndon, 969, 970, 984
Joliet, Louis, 537
Joseph II of Austria, 551(t), 569
The Journey to the West (novel, Ming
  China), 618(t)
Joyce, James, 874
Juárez, Benito, 819, 826
junta, 979, 993(t), 1002(i), **1003**–1005

Kabuki theater, 611(i), **630**, 630(i)
Kafka, Franz, 874
Kamakura Shogunate, 624
Kanem-Bornu kingdom, 585(t), 586(m), 588
Kangxi emperor, 525, 622, 623, 637
Kant, Immanuel, 564(t), 568
Karlsbad Decrees, 714
Kashmir, partition of British India (1947),
  962(m)
Kellogg-Briand Pact, 847(t), 870

Kemal, Mustafa, 879, 885(m), 888(i), 889(m), 892, 893, 910
Kennedy, John F., 969, 980
Kepler, Johannes, 553, 554, 555, 557(t), 559
Keynes, John Maynard, 918
Khanates, 540
Khipus, 469
Khrushchev, Nikita, 955(t), 967–968, 982
Kibbutz, 895
Kilwa city-state, 585(t), 595
King, Martin Luther, Jr., 984
Kinship relations
  Kurds, 1000(m)
  West Africa, 584–586, 606, 609
Kipling, Rudyard, 751(t), 762, 763
Kirov, Sergei, 928
Korea
  division of, 968
  Three Kingdoms Period, 618(t)
Korean War, 955(t), 968, 968(m), 1013, 1033
Kristallnacht, 935
Kubitschek, Juscelino, 978, 980
Kunduchi pillar tomb, 592(i)
Kyoto Protocol, 1031(t), 1044–1045

Laissez faire, 715, 716, 720, 761
La Salle, René-Robert Cavelier, 537
Las Casas, Bartolomé de, 479
Lateran Agreement of 1929, 917(t), 932
Latifundios, 829, 832
Latin America
  conservative authoritarianism in, 923
  Great Depression, 920–921
  immigration to (late nineteenth century), 832–833
  populism, 976–980
  rebuilding era (after World War II), 986
  re-entry into world economy (nineteenth century), 828–829
  revolutions, 671–676
    key events, 675(t)
    map (ca. 1780 and 1830), 674(m)
    origins of, 671–673
    resistance, rebellion, independence, 673–675, 674(m)
  urban population (1925–2025), 1039(t)
  U.S. intervention, 837–838
  Wars of Independence (1810–1825), 815(t), 818, 828
Laud, William, 530
Lausanne, Treaty of, 885(t), 892
Law of inertia, 553, 557(t)
Law of universal gravitation, 554, 557(t)
Lawrence, T. E. (Lawrence of Arabia), 852
Laws
  Buddhist texts, 622
  Combination Acts, 683(t), 705
  great white walls, 775
  Mines Act of 1842, 683(t), 700
  Navigation Acts, 515(t), 537, 684
League of Nations
  defined, 865
  Germany in, 847(t)
  Mandates system, 885–886
Leclerc, Charles-Victor-Emmanuel, 667(m), 668(t)
Legislative Assembly, 656, 658(t)
Leibniz, Gottfried Wilhelm von, 562, 564(t)
Lenin, Vladimir Ilyich
  New Economic Policy, 917(t), 926
  photo, 858(i)
Leopold II (Habsburg Empire), 569
Leopold II of Belgium, 750(i), 754, 756

Lepanto, Ottoman Empire, 487(t), 489, 506
Lerdo Law, 819
Lesbian, gay, and transgendered people, 1045
Levi, Primo, 944–945
Leyte Gulf, Battle of, 946
Liberalism
  defined, 715, 814
  in Spanish America, 814–816
Liberalization (1968–2000s), 990–1027
  apartheid
    described, 758, 1007, 1008–1009
    global anti-apartheid movements, 1043
    student demonstrations, 1007(i)
  big picture, 1027(i)
  chronology, 993(t)
  CONNECTIONS, 1025
  European Union, 993(t), 998, 1022–1024, 1023(m)
  glasnost, 993(t), 1017
  "Japan, Inc.," 1013–1014
  junta, 979, 993(t), 1002(i), 1003–1005
  neoliberalism, 994–995, 1003, 1022
  overview, 990
  perestroika, 1017
  Solidarity, 1017
  summary, 1024–1025
  Tiananmen Square, 993(t), 1012(i), 1012–1013
  Washington Consensus, 994–995, 1006
Liberation movements, 677, 957–958, 986
Liberation theology, 959
Libya, OPEC oil embargo and, 997
Lichtenstein, Israel, 915(i)
Life energy (qi), 617
Lincoln, Abraham, 824
Literature, 717, 858, 860, 861, 923
  The Journey to the West (novel, Ming China), 618(t)
  khipus, 469
  Ming Dynasty, 618, 638
  realism, 713(t), 738, 744
  romanticism, 717, 858, 860, 861, 923
  Upanishads, 785
"Little ice age," 508, 520, 619
Locke, John, 531, 559(i), 562–563, 564(t), 567, 646
Locomotive, *Rocket*, 683(t), 688
Logical positivism, 873
Long March, 885(t), 906, 907(m)
Louisville Flood Victims, Great Depression, 916(i)
Louis XIV
  absolutism, 525
  expansion of France, 525–526
  painting, 513(i)
  reign, 515(t)
  at Versailles, 515(t), 528
  War of the Spanish Succession, 515(t), 525–526, 526(m), 528, 537–538, 671
Louis XV, 645(t), 653
Louis XV chairs, 576(i)
Louis XVI, 645(t), 654, 656, 658(t), 664
Louis XVIII, 664, 720
L'Ouverture, Toussaint, 645(t), 668–670
Loyola, Ignatius, 517
Lucknow Pact, 885(t), 897
Luddites, 703
Lusitania (British passenger liner), 847(t), 853
Lutheranism
  Augsburg agreement, 517(m), 518, 520, 521
  map (1555), 517(m)

Macao, 476, 613(t), 636
Macartney, George, 613(t), 638
Magellan, Ferdinand, 457(t), 466–467, 481
Magic, Scientific Revolution and, 555
Mahmud II, 751(t), 766, 768
Maitreya Buddha, 613
Maize (corn)
  Europe, late seventeenth century, 475
  West Africa (sixteenth century), 589
Majlis, 893
Malaria
  deaths (1980–2000), 1050
  Ming Dynasty, 618
  quinine, 760(i), 761
  transatlantic slave trade, 598
  West Africa, 589
Males, yin and yang principle, 617
Mali (ca. 1200–1450)
  Mansa Musa (king), 460(i)
  Timbuktu
    described, 587–588
    Leo Africanus in, 587
    map, 465(i)
    Portuguese in (1480s), 464, 583
    trade, 590, 590(m)
Malintzin (Doña Marina), 470, 470(i)
Malthus, Thomas, 690, 703, 1049
Manchester, Strike of, 683(t)
Manchuria
  Japanese in
    expansion, 847(t)
    invasion, 917(t)
Manchus, 506, 620–623
Mandate of Heaven, 904
Mandates system, 885–886
Manichaeism, 613
Manifest destiny, 815(t), 816, 837
Manila
  Port of Manila, 457(t), 476
  Rizal in, 790
Mansa Musa (king), 460(i)
Manumission, 597, 600, 822, 823
Maori people, 773, 802
Mao Zedong
  Great Leap Forward, 967–968
  Great Proletarian Cultural Revolution, 955(t), 968
  Long March, 885(t), 906, 907(m)
  pro-peasant policies, 906(t)
  Red Guards, 968
Marathas (Hindu militant group), 503(m), 507, 508
March Revolution, 859–860, 861, 863(t)
Marco Polo, 457, 457(t)
Market vendors, Mexico (1910), 814(i)
Marne, Battle of the, 850, 864
Marquette, Jacques, 537
Marriage, bride wealth, 459, 589
Marshall Plan, 955
Martyrs
  gray zone of moral compromise, 944
Massachusetts Bay Colony (1630), 536
Mass unemployment, Great Depression, 918
"Master race," 940
Mathematics, *Principia Mathematica*, 554, 563
Matsumoto Yonesaburo, 611(i)
May 30, 1925 (protest incident in Shanghai), 900(i)
May Fourth Movement, 885(t), 901, 910
Mazarin, Jules, 524

Mecca
  coffeehouses, 498
  Mansa Musa at, 460(i)
  Zheng He in, 634
Medici, Catherine de', 491
Medicine
  humors (blood, phlegm, black bile,
    yellow bile), 558
  revolution, contemporary world in
    historical perspective, 1050–1051
  Scientific Revolution, 558
  Tan Yunxian, 617
Medvedev, Dimitri, 1022
Megacities, *1037*, 1039
Mehmed V, 767
Mehmet, Takiyuddin, 497
Mehmet II, 486(i), 487–488
Meiggs, Henry, 830
Meiji Oligarchs, 796
Meiji Restoration, 783(t), *796*–799, 900–902,
  903
Mein Kampf, *870*, 917(t), 934
Mendelssohn, Felix, 571
Mendelssohn, Moses, 569, 571
Mercantilism
  colonial wars and, 537–538
  defined, *527*
  Navigation Acts, 515(t), *537*, 684
Merchants
  networks, Islamic empires, 502–504
  putting-out system, 503, 684, 693, 698
Mesoamerica
  Aztecs (Mexica)
    described, *469*
    Nahuatl language, 470
    Spanish conquest, 468–471
  Tenochtitlán (Aztec city)
    invasion of, 469, 469(m)
Mestizos, 470, 473, 646, 672, 673
Metternich, Klemens von, 712(i), 713–715
Mexican-American War (1845–1847), 815(t),
  818
Mexico
  economic nationalism, 976–**977**
  liberal reform (nineteenth century),
    818–819
  liberal stability, 826–827
  market ventors (1910), 814(i)
  middle power, *1031*, 1031(t)
  Porfiriato, 827
  Wars of Reform (1857–1861), 815(t), 819,
    826, 827
Mexico City
  earthquake (1986), 977(i)
  mining school (1792), 551(t)
  Plaza of the Three Cultures, 977(i)
  Tlatelolco, 977(i), 985
Middle class, 715
Middle East
  Afroeurasian trade world, 459
  map (after 1947), 965(m)
  rebuilding era (after World War II), 986
Middle Passage, *599*–601, 603
Middle powers, *1031*, 1031(t)
Midway, Battle of, 946
Migration chain, *775*
Migrations
  contemporary world in historical
    perspective, 1036–1038
  great migration, *774*–775
  Pacific region (nineteenth century),
    800–805
Militarism, *846*
Military, children in, 1047(i)

Milking of cow, Inca women, 471(i)
Mines Act of 1842, 683(t), *700*
Ming Dynasty, *612*–619
  civil service examinations, 616, 617
  daily life, 618–619
  decline, 619
  founding, 612–614
  map, 613(m)
  Mongols and Great Wall, 615–616
  overview, 610
  Zhu Yuanzhang, 612–613
Mining school, Mexico City, 551(t)
Miracle rice, 1049
Mitterrand, François, 1023
Mnong people, 970, 1038
Mobile phones, 1052
Moctezuma II, 469, 471
Modernism, *874*–875, 875(i), 876, 902
Modernization
  Afghanistan, 885(t), 893–894
  defined, *724*
  Egypt
    1805, 683(t), 696
    1805–1849, 751(t), 776
  Germany unification (1866–1871), 713(t),
    726, 728(m), 728–729
  Italy unification (1859–1870), 713(t),
    725–726
  Persia, 885(t), 893
  Russia, 729–730
Modernization theory, *958*–959, 961
Mogadishu
  commercial prosperity, 595
  trade with Middle East, 459
Monet, Claude, 688
Mongols
  Great Wall and, 615–616
  khanates, 540
  in Moscow, 539–540
  in Russia, 539–540
Monroe Doctrine, *837*
Montesquieu, 563, 564(t), 565, 566, 646
Moral compromise, gray zone, 944
Moral economy, *520*
Moscow
  Communist Party, 870
  Hitler attacks, 940
  Mongols, 539–540
  Napoleon in, 663, 663(m)
  suicide bombing (2011), 940
Mosley, Oswald, 922(i)
Mosques
  Haseki mosque complex, 491
  in Isfahan, 495
  Shehzade Mosque, 495
  of Suleiman, 491, 495
  Suleimaniye Mosque, 495
Mountain, *656*
Movies (nineteenth century), 876, 877(i)
Mughal Empire (1526–1827)
  Akbar, 487(t), 493, 495–496, 499(i), 500, 508
  Aurangzeb, 487(t), 493, 500, 507
  city building, 495–496
  coffeehouses, 498, 498(i)
  cultural advances, 494–498
  decline of power, 506–508, 507(m)
  defined, 493
  described, 493
  Indian Ocean trade, 502
  intellectual advances, 497
  map, 493(m)
  merchant networks, 502–504
  non-Muslims, 499–500
  overview, 484

  religious trends, 497
  summary, 508–509
  trade routes' impact, 501–505
Muhammad (prophet)
  Ali (Muhammad's cousin and son-in-law),
    492
  Sunna, 492
Mulattos, 604, 672
Multinational corporations
  accountability, 1044
  Batista and, 980
  in China, 1041(i)
  described, *1041*–1042
  developing nations and, 1055
  Goulart and, 980
  Nestlé boycott, 1043–1044
Muromachi culture, 624–625
Music, *717*, 858, 860, 861, 923
  Mendelssohn, Felix, 571
  modernism, *874*–875, 876
  Nō theater, *625*, 638
  romanticism, *717*, 858, 860, 861, 923
  troubadours, 497
Musikiysky, Grigory, 542(i)
Muslim League, 897, 899, *962*
Muslims, in Ethiopia (1500–1630), 585(t),
  593–594
Mussolini, Benito
  Black Shirts, 922(i), *931*
  Ethiopian campaigns, 917(t), 936(m), 940(t)
  fascism, *925*, 930–932
  Lateran Agreement, 917(t), *932*
  in parade, 930(i)
  regime in action, 931–932
  seizes power in Italy, 917(t), 930–931
Myths, Prester John (mythical Christian
  monarch), 593, 606

Nadir Shah, 508
Nagasaki and Hiroshima, atomic bombs,
  917(t), 946(i), 947(m), 948, 1032
Nahuatl language, 470
Nanjing
  capital
    fall (December 1937), 907
    moved to Beijing, 614, 614(i)
    Nationalist Party (1928), 901
  Chengzu and, 614
  Matteo Ricci (missionary) in, 636
  Rape of Nanjing, 885(t), 907, 942
  tree planting, Ming government, 619
  Zhu's conquest (1356), 613
Nantes, Edict of, 515(t), 524, 525
Naples, independence from Habsburg rule
  (1734), 568
Napoleon Bonaparte (Napoleon I)
  coronation of, 660(i)
  expansion in Europe, 661–662
  Grand Empire, *662*–664, 663(m)
  rule of France, 645(t), 660–661
Napoleonic Code, *661*
Narva, Battle of, 541
Nasser, Gamal Abdel, 910, 955(t), 961(i),
  963–964
National Assembly, *654*
National Congress, Indian, 783(t), *785*, 808,
  897, 899, 962
National Convention, 655–659
Nationalism
  Asia (1914–1939), 882–913
    appeal of, 886–887
    Arab Revolt (1916–1918), 890–891
    Asia reaction to World War I, 884–885
    big picture, 913(i)

chronology, 885(t)
CONNECTIONS, 910–911
development, 884–887
nationalism's appeal, 886–887
Ottoman Empire's collapse, 888, 889(m)
overview, 882
Southeast Asia, independence, 908–909
summary, 910
Turkish Revolution, 891–892
defined, **715**–716
Nazism and, 933
nineteenth-century Europe, 715–716,
739–744
Zionism, **743**, 891, 894–895, 910, 961
Nationalist Party, Chinese, 885(t), 901, 910
National Labor Relations Act, 919
***National Liberation Front, 974**, 991(i)
National self-determination, 865, 866(m),
884, 886
**NATO (North Atlantic Treaty
Organization)**
air strikes, Serbian aggression, 1019
Cold War, 955(t), **956**, 956(m), 983
de Gaulle and, 983
EU and, 1022
formation, 955(t)
Taliban and al-Qaeda, 1033
Natural history, Scientific Revolution,
554–555
***Navigation Acts**, 515(t), **537**, 684
Nazi Germany
Enabling Act, **935**, 940(t)
growth, 936–938, 937(m)
New Order, **941**, 948
state and society, 935–936
Nazi Party
buildup (1924–1929), 917(t)
storm troopers, 933(i), 935
***Nazism**
defined, **933**
extreme nationalism, 933
Hitler and, 933–934
racism and, 933
roots of, 933–934
***Neocolonialism, 820**
economic nationalism, **977**
multinational corporations, 1041
***Neo-Confucianism**, 634
***Neoliberalism, 994**–995, 1003, 1022
Nestlé boycott, 1043–1044
Netherlands, civil wars (1568–1578), 518
***New Culture Movement**, 885(t), **902**
***New Deal**, 917(t), **918**–919, 920(i)
***New Economic Policy (NEP)**, 917(t), **926**
New France, 527, 537
New Guinea, invasion by Japanese (1942),
946
***New imperialism** (1880–1914), 751(t),
761–764
New Laws, 472–473
New Objectivity, 876
***New Order, 941**, 948
New physics, 873–874
Newton, Isaac
alchemy, 555
law of universal gravitation, **554**, 557(t)
Principia Mathematica, 554, 563
synthesis, 553–554
Newtonian physics, new physics
challenges, 873–874
New Zealand
Maori people, 773, 802
World War I, 852
Nezahualpi, 455(i)

***Nguyen Dynasty**, 787(i), **788**
Nietzsche, Friedrich, 873
Nigeria
middle power, **1031**, 1031(t)
Yoruba people, 587
Night of Broken Glass, 935
***1911 Revolution, 794**, 901, 902, 910
1982 economic crisis, Chili, 1004
Nineteenth-century Europe, 710–747
anti-Semitism, 742–743
big picture, 747(i), 951(i)
chronology, 713(t), 917(t)
class and social inequality, 733–734
cocoa holdups, **973**
CONNECTIONS, 745, 949
conservatism (after 1815), 712–713
economic crisis, 916–918
European response, 919–920
families, 734–736
Great Britain, social reform, 713(t),
719–720, 741
great migration, **774**–775
Hitler's success and, 934
liberalism and middle class, 715
Louisville flood victims, 916(i)
map (1815), 714(m)
mass unemployment, 918
modernization, 724–730
defined, **724**
Germany unification (1866–1871),
713(t), 726, 728(m), 728–729
Italy unification (1859–1870), 713(t),
725–726
Russia, 729–730
nationalism, 715–716, 739–744
New Deal, 917(t), **918**–919, 920(i)
overview, 710–711, 914
political and social situation (after 1815),
712–713
Revolutions of 1848, 713(t), 718–723
science for masses, 736–737
socialism, 715–716, 743–744
stock market crash of 1929, 916–917, 919,
948
suffrage trends, 739–740
summary, 744, 948
unemployment, 916(i), 918–919, 921
urban development, 731–733
worldwide effects, 920–921
Ning Lao, 904–905
Nkrumah, Kwame, 953(i), 971(i), 973–974
Nobunaga, Oda, 625–626
***Nomads**
Turks
Qizilbash, **490**, 492, 497
Seljuk Turks, 488
Timur (Turkish leader), 486, 487,
487(m), 490
victory at Mohács, 489
Nongovernmental organizations, 1044
Non-violent resistance, satyagraha, 885(t),
898–899, 910
Normandy, Allied invasion, 917(t)
North Africa
Algeria
anticolonial war, 974
National Liberation Front, **974**, 991(i)
pieds-noirs, **974**
Arguin, 457(t), 464
North America, urban population (1925–
2025), 1039(t)
North Korea
division of Korea, 968
Korean War, 955(t), 968, 968(m), 1013, 1033

***Nō theater, 625**, 638
Notre Dame Cathedral, 737–738
Nuclear energy program, Iran, 1030(i)
Nuclear families, 589
Nuremberg Laws, 935, 940(t)

***oba**, 584(i), **587**
***October Manifesto, 730**
Ogé, Vincent, 666, 668(t)
Old Testament, Copernican system and,
559
***Oligarchs, 815**
Latin America, 829, 834, 841
liberalism and, 815
Meiji Oligarchs, 796
zaibatsu, 798, **903**
Oligarchy
Bank of France (1800), 661
Dutch Republic, 531
Olympic games (Mexico City, 1964), 977(i),
985
Omdurman, Battle of, 760(i)
On Crimes and Punishments (Beccaria),
568
"On the Immortality of the Soul"
(Mendelssohn, M.), 571
*On the Origin of Species by the Means of
Natural Selection* (Darwin), 713(t),
736
On the Revolutions of the Heavenly Spheres
(Copernicus), 553, 557(t)
On the Structure of the Human Body
(Vesalius), 556(i), 557(t)
OPEC oil embargo, 992–994, 993(t), 997,
1005
***Opium War**, 783(t), 791–**792**
Orphans, HIV/AIDS, 1046
Orphism, 875(i)
Osaka, Battle of, 613(t), 636
***Osman**, 487, 487(t)
Ottoman Empire (1299–1922)
Armenian Genocide, 890(i), 891
Austrian Habsburgs, 515(t), 527(m),
527–528
in chronology, 487(t)
city building, 495–496
coffeehouses, 498, 498(i)
Constantinople, 487–489
cultural advances, 494–498
decline of power, 506–508, 507(m),
765–767
defeat, at Lepanto, 487(t), 489, 506
defined, **487**
expansion, 487–490
height of, 487(t), 488(m)
Hürrem, 487(t), 491, 491(i)
Indian Ocean trade, 502
intellectual advances, 497
janissaries, **490**, 491, 766
Mahmud II, 751(t), 766, 768
map, 488(m)
merchant networks, 502–504
non-Muslims, 499–500
Osman (ruler), 487, 487(t)
overview, 484
partition (1914–1923), 889(m)
reform, 765–767
religious trends, 497
slavery, 490
Suleiman the Magnificent
building program, 496(i)
Hürrem, 487(t), 491, 491(i)
intellectual advances, 497
reign of, 487(t), 488(m), 489, 508

Ottoman Empire *(continued)*
summary, 508–509
Tanzimat, 751*(t)*, **766**
trade routes' impact, 501–505
Owen, Robert, 705

Pacific region
Easter Island society, 801
migrations (nineteenth century), 800–805
World War II in, 946–948, 947*(m)*
Paine, Thomas, 645*(t)*, 650
Paintings
modernism, **874**–875, 875*(i)*, 876
Saint George, 594*(i)*
The Young Scholar and His Wife
(Coques), 532*(i)*
Palaces
Crystal Palace, 683*(t)*, 689
Mughal Empire, 495–496
Ottoman Empire, 495–496
Safavid Empire, 495–496
Suleiman, 495–496
Pale of Settlement, 551*(t)*, 569, 569*(m)*
Palestine
Arab-Jewish tensions, 894–895
Balfour Declaration, 865, 885*(t)*, **891**
immigration of Jews (1920s–1930s),
885*(m)*
intifada, 993*(t)*, **998**
Palestine Liberation Organization (PLO),
964, 998
Palm oil, **750**
Pan-Africanists, **973**
Panama Canal, 773, 815*(t)*, 839–840
Pankhurst, Christabel, 711*(i)*
Paracelsus, 557, 558
Paraguay War, 815*(t)*, 826, 827
Paris
Notre Dame Cathedral, 737–738
salons, 551*(t)*, 560, 565, 567*(i)*, **575**, 577
sans-culottes, **656**, 657*(i)*, 658*(t)*, 667
Treaty of Paris, 487*(t)*, 505, 645*(t)*, **647**,
651, 651*(t)*, 652
Partitions
Africa, European imperialism, 755*(m)*
British India (1947), 962*(m)*
Ottoman Empire (1914–1923), 889*(m)*
Poland (1772–1795), 570*(m)*
Paşa, Lütfi, 489
Pasteur, Louis, 713*(t)*, 732
Patriarchy
Abraham (prophet), 1000*(i)*
European societies (seventeenth
century), 520
Paul III (pope), 516–517
Peace of Augsburg, 517*(m)*, 518, 520, 521
Peace of Utrecht, 526, 526*(m)*, 538
Peace of Westphalia, 521, 524
Pearl Harbor attacks, 917*(t)*, 943, 948
Pears' soap advertisement, 752*(i)*
Peasants
collectivization of agriculture, Stalin,
917*(t)*, 925*(i)*, **926**–927, 981
early modern period (Europe), 519–520
Estonian serfs, 519, 519*(i)*
Mao's pro-peasant policies, 906*(t)*
Peddlers in Rio de Janeiro (sketch), 602*(i)*
Pedro I, 819
Peninsulares, **672**
Pennsylvania, quaker colony, 536
People's Republic of China, 966, 967, 967*(m)*
Pepper harvest, 461*(i)*
Per capita levels of industrialization (1750–
1913), 692*(t)*

perestroika, **1017**
Permanent Mandates Commission,
885–886
Perón, Eva, 978–979
Perón, Isabelita, 1004
Perón, Juan, 955*(t)*, 978–979, 1004
Perry, Mathew, 783*(t)*, 795–796
Persian Empire
carpet weaving, 487*(t)*, 494, 495*(i)*
modernization efforts, 885*(t)*, 893
Peru, Callao-Lima-Oroya rail line, 830,
830*(i)*
Peter the Great, 515*(t)*, 519*(i)*, 541–543,
544, 569, 627
Petrodollars, **993**–994, 1005
Petrograd Soviet, **860**
Philip II of Spain, 518, 554
Philosophes, 551*(t)*, **563**–565, 568, 569, 575
*Philosophicae Naturalis Principia
Mathematica* (Newton), 554, 563
Philosophy
Aristotle
Aristotelian universe (imagination,
sixteenth century), 550*(i)*
Bacon and, 556
Galen and, 558
Galileo and, 559
Scientific Revolution and, 552–553, 578
slavery and, 480
universities, High Middle Ages, 550*(i)*
atomist, 557
Descartes, 557, 557*(t)*, 558, 567
determinism, 562, 564*(t)*, 738
empiricism, **557**–558
existentialism, 847*(t)*, **873**, 1018
free will, 516, 562
Locke, 531, 559*(i)*, 562–563, 564*(t)*, 567,
646
logical positivism, 873
Mendelssohn, Moses, 569, 571
Neo-Confucianism, 634
Nietzsche, 873
Rousseau, 564–565, 564*(t)*, 566
sensationalism, **563**
Sufism
described, 497, 498
Qizilbash, **490**, 492, 497
Voltaire, 561*(i)*, 563–564, 564*(t)*, 565,
567*(i)*, 637
Wittgenstein, 873
Phlegm, bodily humor, 558
Physics
Scientific Revolution, 553
special relativity theory, 873–874
Picasso, Pablo, 876
pieds-noirs, **974**
Pilgrims, at Plymouth (1620), 536
Pillar tomb, Kunduchi, 592*(i)*
Piri Reis, 487*(t)*, 497
Pius IX, 725
Pius V, 489
Pius VII, 660*(i)*, 661
Pizarro, Francisco, 457*(t)*, 468, 469, 469*(m)*,
471
Planck, Max, 873
Plantains, Africa (900–1100 c.e.), 589
Plants, Columbian exchange, **474**–475,
483
Plays, kabuki theater, 611*(i)*, **630**, 630*(i)*
Plaza of the Three Cultures, 977*(i)*
Plebiscites, 661, 722, 974
Plum in the Golden Vase (novel, Ming
China), 618*(t)*
Plymouth (1620), 536

Poetry
troubadours, 497
"White Man's Burden" (Kipling), 751*(t)*,
762, 763
Poincaré, Raymond, 869
Poland
blitzkrieg, **939**
German invasion (1939), 917*(t)*, 938,
940*(t)*
partition of (1772–1795), 570*(m)*
Solidarity movement, 1017
Pompeii, Wedgwood's imitation Greek
vases, 687
Popular Front, 917*(t)*, **920**
Population growth
contemporary world in historical
perspective, 1049–1050
eight major areas (1925–2025), 1039*(t)*
indigenous peoples, loss and economic
exploitation, 472–473
iron law of wages, **690**
Malthus, 690, 703, 1049
Populism
Argentina, 978–980
Brazil, 978, 980
Perón, Juan, 955*(t)*, 978–979, 1004
Porfiriato, **827**
Port Moresby, invasion by Japanese (1942),
946
Port of Calicut, 456*(i)*, 464
Port of Manila, 457*(t)*, 476
Portugal
caravel, **462**, 480, 604*(i)*
da Gama, 456*(i)*, 464, 585*(t)*, 593*(m)*,
595
expansion
in Africa and Asia (1450–1600),
463–464
in Brazil, 471, 472
colonial administration, 471–473
East Africa, 595
Sapi-Portuguese Saltcellar, 604*(i)*
Treaty of Tordesillas, 457*(t)*, **466**, 471
Poster art, Communist China, 966*(i)*
Potato famine in Ireland (1845–1851), 698,
713*(t)*, 720, 741
Potosi silver mines, 523
Potsdam Declaration, 947–948
Poverty
feminization of poverty, **1046**
sans-culottes, **656**, 657*(i)*, 658*(t)*, 667
Prague Spring, 984, 985, 985*(i)*
Predestination, 516
Premarital sex, Southeast Asian peoples,
459
Prester John (mythical Christian monarch),
593, 606
Principia Mathematica (Newton), 554,
563
Proletariat, **717**, 858, 860, 861, 923
Prophets
Abraham, 1000*(i)*
Isaiah, 600
Prostitution
coffeehouses (mid-fifteenth century,
Islamic world), 498, 498*(i)*
Edo period, 629, 630
Europe (late nineteenth century), 735
Ming China, 618
Taiping Rebellion and, 793
Protectorates
in Africa, 754, 755*(m)*, 758
defined, **754**
England (1653–1658), 515*(t)*, 530–531

Protestant Reformation
Catholic Reformation
Council of Trent, 517
Counter-Reformation, 516
described, 516–518
Council of Trent and, 517
criticism of Catholic Church, 514–516
defined, **514**
early modern period (Europe), 514–516
Enlightenment and, 562(t)
Protestants
Calvinism
Edict of Nantes, 515(t), 524, 525
predestination, 516
Lutheranism
Augsburg agreement, 517(m), 518,
520, 521
map (1555), 517(m)
Protestant Union (1608), 521
Puritans, 529(i), **530**–531
Protest movements (1960s), 984–985, 989
Proudhon, Pierre-Joseph, 716(t)
Prussia
absolutism, 515(t)
Austro-Prussian War of 1866, 728, 728(m)
Congress of Vienna, **712**, 713(t), 714(m),
724, 729
Franco-Prussian War, 728(m), 729, 740, 797
Frederick the Great, 551(t), 568–569,
570(m)
Holly Alliance, 713–714
Quadruple Alliance, 664, 712, 713
Psychology, Freudian, 847(t), 874
Ptolemy's Geography, **462**, 465–466,
552–553
Public sphere, 568, 572, **575**, 578
Purges, great, 858(i), 914, 917(t), 928–929,
948
Puritans, 529(i), **530**–531
Put It All Together (big picture)
African states and societies (1400–1800),
609(i)
Asia and the Pacific
(imperialism,1800–1914), 810(i)
contemporary world in historical
perspective, 1055(i)
East Asia (1400 C.E.–1800 C.E.), 641(i)
Europe (nineteenth-century), 747(i)
European expansion (1450–1600), 483(i)
European expansion (1500–1750), 547(i)
Great Depression, 951(i)
imperialism (1800–1914), 779(i)
Islamic world powers (1300–1800), 511(i)
liberalization (1968–2000s), 1027(i)
Nationalism in Asia (1914–1939), 913(i)
Revolutionary era (1775–1825), 679(i)
World War I, 881(i)
World War II, 951(i)
Putting-out system, 503, 684, 693, 698

al-Qaeda
Afghanistan and, 1033–1035
September 11 terrorist attacks, 1031(t),
1033, 1034(i)
qi (vital energy), 617
Qianlong emperor, 620(i), 623, 638
Qing Dynasty
banners, **621**
emperors, 622–623
imperial expansion, 623
Manchus, 506, 620–623
map, 621(m)
overview, 610
Qizilbash, **490**, 492, 497

Quadruple Alliance, 664, 712, 713
Quaker colony, Pennsylvania, 536
Queen Mother, 589(i)
Quinine, **761**

Race concept
Enlightenment and, 565–566
European expansion, 479–480
master race, 940
scientific definition, 480
Racism
anti-Semitism
Dreyfus affair, 739(i), **741**
eastern Europe (1873), 713(t), 742–743
Mein Kampf (Hitler), **870**, 917(t), 934
apartheid
described, 758, 1007, **1008**–1009
global anti-apartheid movements, 1043
student demonstrations, 1007(i)
Nazism and, 933
New Order, **941**, 948
Radio (nineteenth century), 876
Railroads
China (1876), 793(i)
steam locomotive, Rocket, 683(t), **688**
Rape
"rape of Belgium," 854(i)
Rape of Nanjing, 885(t), 907, 942
Rasputin, 847(t), 859, 859(i)
Razin, Stenka, 515(t), 541
Realism, 713(t), 738, 744
Rebuilding era (after World War II), 986
Reconquista (750–1492), Americas, 462,
465, 471, 472
Red Guards, **968**
Reflections on the Revolution in France
(Burke), 645(t)
Reform Bill in Great Britain (1832), 713(t),
719
Refugees
Palestine Liberation Organization, **964**,
998
Sieng (Mnong refugee in American high
school), 1038
Reichstag, 740, 743, 855, 857, 934, 935,
940(t)
Reign of Terror, **657**–659, 658(t), 676
Reincarnation
Buddhism, 616
third Dalai Lama, 616
Religions
animism, 753
Manichaeism, 613
Mughal Empire, 497
Ottoman Empire, 497
Safavid Empire, 497
Scientific Revolution, 559
Zoroastrianism, 500
Religious orders
Dominicans, 479, 637, 790
Franciscans, 479, 637
Jesuits, 514(i), **517**–518
Rembrandt, 533(i)
Renaissance, Chinese, 885(t), **902**
Representative assemblies, 527, 654
Republican France (nineteenth century),
740–741
Republicanism, **531**–532
Revisionism, **743**
Revolutionary era (1775–1825), 642–679
American Revolution (1775–1783)
framing Constitution, 651–652
independence from Britain, 650–651
key events, 651(t)

origins of, 649–650
Treaty of Paris, 487(t), 505, 645(t), **647**,
651, 651(t), 652
big picture, 679(i)
chronology, 645(t)
CONNECTIONS, 677
French Revolution (1789–1799)
breakdown of old order, 653–654
constitutional monarchy, 655
The Directory, 658(t), 659, 661, 676
key events, 658(t)
National Assembly, 654–655
National Convention, 655–659
Reflections on the Revolution in France
(Burke), 645(t)
Reign of Terror, **657**–659, 658(t), 676
Haitian Revolution (1791–1804)
key events, 668(t)
L'Ouverture, Toussaint, 645(t), 668–670
map, 667(m)
Saint-Domingue slave revolt, 665(i),
665–668
Latin American revolutions, 671–676
key events, 675(t)
map (ca. 1780 and 1830), 674(m)
origins of, 671–673
resistance, rebellion, independence,
673–675, 674(m)
overview, 642–643
Seven Years' War, 505, 575, 600, 645(t),
647, 648(m), 676
summary, 676
Revolutions
communications revolution
Australia, 801(m)
digital divide, **1052**, 1053
digital revolution, 1029(i), 1051–1052,
1053
consumer revolution, 572, 575, 576(i)
Cuban Revolution (1959), 955(t), 980, 989,
1002
Glorious Revolution, 515(t), 531
green revolution, 1001, 1031(t), **1049**
medicine, contemporary world in
historical perspective, 1050–1051
1911 Revolution, China, **794**, 901, 902, 910
Russian Revolution (1905), 713(t), 730(m)
Russian Revolution (1917), 858–863
Bolshevik Revolution, 847(t), 860–862,
928
fall of Imperial Russia, 858–859
key events, 863(t)
March Revolution, **859**–860, 861, 863(t)
provisional government, 859–860
Turkish Revolution, 891–892
Revolutions of 1848, 713(t), 718–723
Rhodes, Cecil, 757, 758
Rhodesia, 993(t), 1007, 1008
Ricardo, David, 690, 703
Ricci, Mateo, 636
Rice
alcoholic drink, Ming China, 618
miracle rice, 1049
Richelieu, Cardinal, 521, 524
Rio de Janeiro
growth (1900s), 832
Napoleon's troop, 675
Peddlers in Rio de Janeiro (sketch), 602(i)
Slave Labor in Rio de Janeiro (lithograph),
821(i)
Rizal, José, 790
Robespierre, Maximilien, 656, 657, 658(t),
659(i), 676
Rocket (steam locomotive), 683(t), **688**

Rococo art style, 551(t), 575
The Romance of the Three Kingdoms (novel, Ming China), 618(t)
Romanov, Michael, 540
Romanticism, 713(t), **737**–738, 744
Rome-Berlin Axis, 937, 940(t)
Roosevelt, Franklin Delano, 918–919, 943
Roosevelt, Theodore, 771(i), 838
Roosevelt Corollary, **838**
Rousseau, Jean-Jacques, 564–565, 564(t), 566
Rowlandson, Thomas, 597(i)
Rudolphine Tables, 557(t)
Ruhr, occupation of, 847(t), 869, 869(m), 870
Russia
    absolutism, 539–543
    Bolshevik Revolution, 847(t), 860–862, 928
    Catherine the Great, 543, 551(t), 568–569, 651
    Congress of Vienna, **712**, 713(t), 714(m), 724, 729
    Cossacks, 515(t), 538, **540**, 541
    Crimean War, 729, 729(m), 886
    expansion of empire, 540–541, 543(m)
    expansion (1462–1689), 543(m)
    expulsion of Jews, 742, 742(i)
    Holy Alliance, 713–714
    industrialization surge (1890–1900), 713(t), 730
    Ivan III, 539–540
    Ivan IV, 540
    Ivan the Terrible, 515(i), 540, 541, 544
    modernization, 729–730
    Mongols in, 539–540
    Moscow
        Communist Party, 870
        Hitler attacks, 940
        Mongols, 539–540
        Napoleon in, 663, 663(m)
        suicide bombing (2011), 940
    Pale of Settlement, 551(t), 569, 569(m)
    per capita levels of industrialization (1750–1913), 692(t)
    Peter the Great, 515(t), 519(i), 541–543, 544, 569, 627
    Quadruple Alliance, 664, 712, 713
    Russo-Japanese War (1904–1905), 713(t), 718(t), **799**, 885(t)
    Tartars, 491, 538, 569
    Time of Troubles (1598–1613), 515(t), 540
Russian Civil War, 847(t), 862, 862(m), 863(t)
Russian Revolution (1905), 713(t), 730(m)
Russian Revolution (1917), 858–863
    Bolshevik Revolution, 847(t), 860–862, 928
    fall of Imperial Russia, 858–859
    key events, 863(t)
    March Revolution, *859*–860, 861, 863(t)
    provisional government, 859–860
Russo-Japanese War (1904–1905), 713(t), 718(t), **799**, 885(t)
Rwanda genocide, 1010, 1032

Safavid Empire (1501–1722)
    city building, 495–496
    coffeehouses, 498, 498(i)
    cultural advances, 494–498
    decline of power, 506–508, 507(m)
    defined, **490**
    described, 490–492
    Indian Ocean trade, 502
    intellectual advances, 497
    Isma'il, 487(t), 490, 492

map, 492(m)
merchant networks, 502–504
non-Muslims, 499–500
overview, 484
religious trends, 497
Shah Abbas, 485(i), 487(t), 492, 492(m), 494, 495, 496(i), 504
summary, 508–509
trade routes' impact, 501–505
Saint Bartholomew's Day massacre, 518
Saint-Domingue slave revolt, 665(i), 665–668
Saint-Simon, Henri de, 716(t)
Salons, 551(t), 560, 565, 567(i), **575**, 577
Salt
    Sapi-Portuguese Saltcellar, 604(i)
    transportation, camel caravans, 591(i)
Salvation, predestination, 516
Samarkand, 486
Sans-culottes, **656**, 657(i), 658(t), 667
Sanskrit, *Upanishads*, 785
Sapi-Portuguese Saltcellar, 604(i)
Sardinia, Crimean War, 729, 729(m), 886
Sartre, Jean-Paul, 873
sati practice, 500
Satyagraha, 885(t), **898**–899, 910
Saudi Arabia
    OPEC oil embargo and, 997
    petrodollars, 993
Sayings of a Female Doctor (Tan Yunxian), 617
Scholar-official class
    portrait of Jiang Shunfu, 612(i)
    Qing Dynasty, 622
    Taiping rebels (1853), 793
Schönberg, Arnold, 876
Sciences, nineteenth-century Europe, 736–737
Scientific Revolution (1500–1700), 548–560
    alchemy, 555
    Aristotle and, 552–553, 578
    astrology and, 555, 579
    astronomy, 553
    chemistry, 558
    in chronology, 551(t)
    contributors, 557(t)
    Copernican hypothesis, 553, 557(t)
    Enlightenment and, 562(t)
    magic, 555
    methods of science, 556–558
    natural history and empire, 554–555
    Newton's synthesis, 553–554
    overview, 548–549
    physics, 553
    religion and science, 559
    society and science, 559–560
    thought to 1550, 552–553
Scottish Enlightenment, 564(t), 567, 568, 577
Second Coalition, 658(t), 660, 661
Second Socialist International, 713(t)
Segregation
    apartheid
        described, 758, 1007, **1008**–1009
        global anti-apartheid movements, 1043
        student demonstrations, 1007(i)
Self-immolation, 500
Self-strengthening movement, China, 793–794
Seljuk Turks, 488
Senegambian states, 584–586
Sensationalism, **563**
Separate spheres, **699**–700, 735–736, 744
Sepoys, **505**, 783

September 11 terrorist attacks, 1031(t), 1033, 1034(i)
Sepúlveda, Juan Ginés de, 479
Serfs, Estonian, 519, 519(i)
Seven Years' War, 505, 575, 600, 645(t), 647, 648(m), 676
Sexual division of labor, 699–700, 699(t)
Shah Abbas, 485(i), 487(t), 492, 492(m), 494, 495, 496(i), 504
Shah Jahan, 487, 493, 496
Shahs, **490**
Shakespeare, William, 785
Shanghai
    Apple store, 1041(i)
    first railroad in China, 793(i)
    Japanese attack (1937), 907
    multinational companies, 1041(i)
    protest incident (May 30, 1925), 900(i)
Shehzade Mosque, 495
Shogunate
    Ashikaga Shogunate, 624
    Kamakura Shogunate, 624
    Tokugawa Shogunate (Edo period)
        alternate residence system, **627**, 629
        chronology, 613(t)
        commercialization and growth of towns, 629
        daily life, 629–632
        government, 627–628
        kabuki theater, 611(i), **630**, 630(i)
        map, 628(m)
        Matsumoto Yonesaburo, 611(i)
        overview, 610
Shore trading, **602**
Sieng (Mnong refugee in American high school), 1038
Sigismund I, 491
Silent Spring (Carson), 1044
Silesia, 647
Silver, Potosi silver mines, 523
Silver Pavilion, 625
Sin, *sati* practice, 500
Sinking, of *Lusitania* (British passenger liner), 847(t), 853
Sino-Japanese War, 783(t), 793, 794, 799, 942
Six-Day War, 955(t), 964–965, 965(m), 998
Slave Labor in Rio de Janeiro (lithograph), 821(i)
Slavery
    abolition, 815(t), 821, 823, 825
    apartheid in South Africa
        described, 758, 1007, **1008**–1009
        global anti-apartheid movements, 1043
        student demonstrations, 1007(i)
    Aristotle and, 480
    chattel, **585**, 596, 606
    encomienda system, **472**–473, 479, 789
    free people of color, 549(i), 577, 665–666, 670
    Industrial Revolution and, 706
    manumission, 597, 600, 822, 823
    Ottoman Empire, 490
    Spanish America (nineteenth century), 821–825
Smallpox
    Ming Dynasty, 619
    Native Americans (sixteenth century), 469, 473, 598
    reduced deaths (1951–1966), 1050
    vaccination, 700
    variolation, 637
Smith, Adam, 564(t), 568
Social Darwinism, **737**, 761, 815, 829, 934

Social hierarchies
 caste system, reform, 785
 early modern period (Europe), 519–520
Socialism
 Arab socialism, *963*–964
 described, *716*–717
 nineteenth-century Europe, 715–716,
  743–744
Social security
 Germany (1883), 713(*t*), 740, 919
 United States (1935), 919
Society of Jesus, 517–518
Sokoto caliphate, 751(*t*), *753*
Solidarity, *1017*
Somme, Battle of the, 850
Songhai kingdom, 585(*t*), 586(*m*), 587–588
Sorting, 602
South Africa
 Afrikaners, 755(*m*), *756*–758, 848, 898,
  1008
 apartheid
  described, 758, 1007, *1008*–1009
  global anti-apartheid movements, 1043
  student demonstrations, 1007(*i*)
 diamond mining, 757, 757(*i*)
 middle power, *1031*, 1031(*t*)
 nineteenth century, 756–758
 South African War (1899–1902), 751(*t*),
  758, 762, 848
South America, liberal consolidation
 (nineteenth century), 827–828
Southeast Asia
 Afroeurasian trade world, Indian Ocean,
  456–459
 independence in, 908–909
 premarital sex, 459
South Korea
 division of Korea, 968
 Korean War, 955(*t*), 968, 968(*m*), 1013, 1033
Sovereignty, 521
Soviet Union
 collectivization of agriculture, 917(*t*),
  925(*i*), *926*–927, 981
 five-year plans, Stalin, 917(*t*), *925*, 925(*i*),
  926–927, 967, 981
 German invasion (1941), 917(*t*), 940(*t*)
 invasion of Hungary (1956), 955(*t*)
 life and culture, under Stalin's reign, 732
 New Economic Policy, 917(*t*), *926*
 rebuilding era (after World War II), 986
 urban population (1925–2025), 1039(*t*)
Spain
 absolutism, 523–524
 colonial administration, 471–473
 European expansion
  Americas, 464–466
  Aztec and Inca empires, 468–471
  encomienda system, *472*–473, 479, 789
  Pacific, 466–467
 Granada conquered (1492), 462
 reconquista (750–1492), Americas, 462,
  465, 471, 472
 Thirty Years' War
  described, *520*–521
  map of Europe (after 1648), 522(*m*)
  Peace of Westphalia, 521, 524
 Treaty of Tordesillas, 457(*t*), *466*, 471
 voyages to Americas (fifteenth century),
  464–466
 War of the Spanish Succession, 515(*t*),
  525–526, 526(*m*), 528, 537–538, 671
Spanish America
 liberalism in, 814–816
 slavery (nineteenth century), 821–825

Spanish-American War (1898), 762, 790,
  815(*t*), 838–839, 909, 909(*m*)
Spanish Civil War, 917(*t*), 920, 937, 940(*t*)
Special relativity theory, 873–874
Spengler, Oswald, 874
Spinning jenny, 682(*i*), 683(*t*), *685*
Spinoza, Baruch, 562, 564(*t*), 565
Spirits, animism, 753
Splitting the atom, 847(*t*), 872(*i*)
Sports
 baseball in Japan, 969(*i*)
 Coliseum in Rome, 930(*i*)
 Cromwell's state, 530
 Summer Olympics (Mexico City, 1964),
  977(*i*), 985
Spring
 Arab Spring, 999
 Prague Spring, 984, 985, 985(*i*)
 Silent Spring (Carson), 1044
Sri Lanka, Dutch East India Company and,
  502, 535
SS corps, 935, 941–942, 944
Stadholder, 532
Stagflation, 993, 994
Stalin, Joseph
 collectivization of agriculture, 917(*t*),
  925(*i*), *926*–927, 981
 comes to power in Soviet Union, 917(*t*)
 de-Stalinization, 955(*t*), *982*
 five-year plans, 917(*t*), *925*, 925(*i*), 926–
  927, 967, 981
 great purges, 858(*i*), 914, 917(*t*), 928–929,
  948
 life and culture under, 927–928
 Potsdam Declaration, 947–948
Stalingrad, Battle of, 941(*m*)
Stamp Act, 649, 650, 651(*t*)
Starvation
 Armenian Genocide, 890(*i*), 891
 India (1966–1967), 1049
 Magellan expedition, 467
 by Nazis, 942
 potato famine in Ireland (1845–1851),
  698, 713(*t*), 720, 741
Stateless societies
 Kurds, 1000(*m*)
 West Africa, 584–586, 606, 609
Steam engines, 683(*t*), *685–686*
Steam locomotive, *Rocket*, 683(*t*), *688*
Stephenson, George, 683(*t*), 688
Stereotypes
 United States immigrants, 834
 War in Pacific, 946
 of women, 1046
Stock market crash
 of 1873, 713(*t*), 742
 of 1929, 916–917, 919, 948
Storm troopers, 933(*i*), 935
Street fighting in Berlin (1948), 718(*i*)
Strikes
 October Manifesto, *730*
 Strike of Manchester (1810), 683(*t*)
Submarine warfare, 847(*t*), 851(*m*), 853,
  946
Sub-Saharan Africa
 decolonization, 955(*t*)
 HIV/AIDS, 1050
Sudan
 famine (2011), 1010
 Hausaland, 584, 586(*m*), 588
 Kanem-Bornu, 585(*t*), 586(*m*), 588
 Songhai kingdom, 585(*t*), 586(*m*), 587–588
Suez Canal, 751(*t*), 768, 768(*m*), 783(*t*), 891,
  963

Suez Canal Company, 955(*t*)
Suez crisis, 964
Suffrage
 Japanese suffragists (1920s), 903(*i*)
 nineteenth-century Europe, 739–740
Sufism
 described, 497, 498
 Qizilbash, *490*, 492, 497
Sugar, transatlantic slave trade, 475–
  476
Suicide
 Hitler, 945
 Nobunaga, 626
 self-immolation, 500
 suicide bombings, 1022, 1034
 widow suicide, 500, 808
Suleimaniye Mosque, 495
Suleiman the Magnificent
 building program, 496(*i*)
 Hürrem, 487(*t*), 491, 491(*i*)
 intellectual advances, 497
 reign of, 487(*t*), 488(*m*), 489, 508
Sullivan, Louis H., 875
Sultans, 488
Summer Olympics (Mexico City, 1964),
  977(*i*), 985
Sunna, 492
Sun Yatsen, 794, 805, 885(*t*), 901
Superego, 874
Superpowers, 956
Surat, factory-forts, 502
Surrealism, 847(*t*), 876
Survival in Auschwitz (Levi), 944
Swahili city-state, *594*–595, 606
Sweated industries, 734
Swords
 great sword hunt of Hideyoshi, 626
 The Traitor: Degradation of Alfred
  Dreyfus (illustration), 739(*i*)
Sykes-Picot Agreement, 885(*t*), *891*
Syria
 civil war (2011), 894
 Faisal bin Hussein (king), 891, 894

Taghza, *587*, 590, 590(*m*)
Taino people, 466
Taiping Rebellion, 783(*t*), *792*–793
Taizu, Zhu Yuanzhang, 613–615, 619
Taj Mahal, 487(*t*), 496
Taliban, 1015, 1033–1034
Tan Yunxian, 617
Tanzania, Kunduchi pillar tomb, 592(*i*)
Tanzimat, 751(*t*), *766*
Tariff protection, *694*, 706
Tartars, 491, 538, 569
Tea Act, 650, 651(*t*)
Technology
 communications revolution
  Australia, 801(*m*)
  digital divide, *1052*, 1053
  digital revolution, 1029(*i*), 1051–1052,
   1053
 European expansion (1450–1600),
  462–463
Telescopic observations of moon, 554(*i*)
Tellier, François le, 525
Tennis Court Oath, 653(*i*), 654, 658(*t*)
Tenochtitlán (Aztec city), invasion of, 469,
  469(*m*)
Ten Years' War, Cuba, 815(*t*), 825, 838
Terror
 Reign of Terror, *657*–659, 658(*t*), 676
 Stalin's great purges, 858(*i*), 914, 917(*t*),
  928–929, 948

Terrorism
   Madrid train bombings, 1034
   al-Qaeda
      Afghanistan and, 1033–1035
      September 11 terrorist attacks, 1031(t), 1033, 1034(i)
   suicide bombings, 1022, 1034
Testament of Youth (Brittain), 856
Texas, admitted to U.S. (1945), 815(t)
Texcoco, Nezahualpi (ruler), 455(i)
Thatcher, Margaret, 1016, 1022
Theory of special relativity, 873–874
Thermidorian reaction, 658(t), **659**
Thermodynamics, 736
Third World countries, 957
Thirty Years' War
   described, **520**–521
   map of Europe (after 1648), 522(m)
   Peace of Westphalia, 521, 524
Three Kingdoms Period, in Korea, 618(t)
Tiananmen Square, 993(t), 1012(i), **1012**–1013
Timbuktu
   described, 587–588
   Leo Africanus in, 587
   map, 465(i)
   Portuguese in (1480s), 464, 583
   trade, 590, 590(m)
Time of Troubles (1598–1613), 515(t), 540
Timur (Turkish leader), 486, 487, 487(m), 490
Tlatelolco, 977(i), 985
Tobacco
   Ming China, 618
   Virginia colony, 535
Todar Mal, 493
Tokugawa Shogunate (Edo period)
   alternate residence system, **627**, 629
   chronology, 613(t)
   commercialization and growth of towns, 629
   daily life, 629–632
   government, 627–628
   kabuki theater, 611(i), **630**, 630(i)
   map, 628(m)
   Matsumoto Yonesaburo, 611(i)
   overview, 610
Toltecs, Nahuatl language, 470
Tombs, Kunduchi pillar tomb, 592(i)
Tonghak movement, 799
Tordesillas, Treaty of, 457(t), **466**, 471
Torture
   On Crimes and Punishments, 568
   Galileo and, 559
   great purges, 858(i), 914, 917(t), 928–929, 948
   Mubarak and, 999
   Pinochet's dictatorship, 1004
   Prussia and, 569
   witch-hunts, 518
Totalitarianism (totalitarian dictatorships), **923**–924
   conservative authoritarianism, 920–921
   fascism
      Black Shirts, 922(i), **931**
      defined, **925**
      described, 930–932
      Japan (1930s) and, 924
      spread, 922(i)
Total war
   Reign of Terror, **657**–659, 658(t), 676
   World War I, 854–855
Toure, Muhammad, 585(t), 587–588
Touré, Sékou, 974

Towns, Edo period, 629
Trade
   African trading states, nineteenth century, 750–753
   Afroeurasian trade world, 456–460, 480
      Indian Ocean, 456–459
      map (fifteenth century), 458(m)
      Middle East, 459
      peoples and cultures, 458–459
   coins
      Nobunaga and, 625–626
      Tokugawa Shogunate, 629
   Columbian exchange, **474**–475, 483
   early modern period (Europe), 534–538
   entrepôts
      Mogadishu, 595
      port of Malacca, 456
      Senegambian states, 584
   factory-forts, **502**, 602
   French book trade, 572(i)
   furs, 534(i)
   global trade (sixteenth and seventeenth centuries), 477(m)
   import substitution industrialization, 798, **959**
   Indian Ocean
      Afroeurasian trade world, 456–459
      Mughal, Ottoman, Safavid empires, 502
   shore trading, **602**
   triangle trade, 573, 602–603, 603(t)
   West Africa (1400–1800), 590(m), 590–591
   World Trade Organization, 1013
Trafalgar, Battle of, 662
The Traitor: Degradation of Alfred Dreyfus (illustration), 739(i)
Transatlantic slave trade (ca. 1500–1900), 598–605
   African societies, impact, 603–605
   antislavery movement (1860s), 754
   Asians and, 775
   beginnings, 457(t), 475–476, 596–598
   British abolitionists (1808), 821, 823
   decline (1860s), 750–752, 751(t), 776
   Dutch trading empire, 535
   economy after 1700 c.e., 574(m), 574–575
   Enlightenment period, 573–575, 574(m)
   Equiano, Olaudah, 566, 585(t), 599–601, 600(i)
   Genoa and Venice, 460
   map, 476(m)
   Middle Passage, **599**–601, 603
   race concept, 479–480
   Senegambian peoples, 585
   slave volumes (1501–1866), 605(f)
   sugar and, 475–476
Transgendered people, 1045
Transportation, mass public (nineteenth-century Europe), 732
Travels of Sir John Mandeville, 462
Trench warfare, **850**, 851(m)
Trent, Council of, 517
Triangle trade, 573, 602–603, 603(t)
Triple Alliance (1882–1915), 848(m), 852
Triple Entente, **848**, 851(m), 852, 853
Triumph of Democratic Republics (French illustration, 1848), 721(i)
Trotsky, Leon, 861, 862, 863(t), 926
Troubadours, 497
Truman, Harry, 947–948, 954–955, 968
Truman Doctrine, **955**
Truth
   "first principles," Descartes, 558
   satyagraha and, 885(t), **898**–899, 910
   science and, 736

Tuareg, **590**
Turkey
   middle power, **1031**, 1031(t)
   Turkish Revolution, 891–892
Turks
   Qizilbash, **490**, 492, 497
   Seljuk Turks, 488
   Tartars, 491, 538, 569
   Timur (Turkish leader), 486, 487, 487(m), 490
   victory at Mohács, 489
   Young Turks, 751(t), **767**, 890, 891, 892
Turner, Joseph M. W., 688
Tyranny, 531, 646

Ukraine
   collectivization of agriculture, Stalin, 917(t), 925(i), **926**–927, 981
   famine (1932–1933), 917(t), 925(i), 926, 927
   German attack (1941), 940–941
ulama, **492**, 500
Unemployment
   Chile, 1004
   Great Depression, 916(i), 918–919, 921
   Hitler's Germany and, 934, 936
   "little ice age," 508, 520, 619
   postwar, in Japan, 1004
United Nations (UN)
   formation, 955(t), 957
   United Nations Framework Convention on Climate Change, 1044–1045
United States (U.S.)
   Civil War (1861–1865), 815, 815(t), 816
   enters World War II, 917(t)
   immigration to (nineteenth century), 833–834
   Latin America, intervention in, 837–838
   manifest destiny, 815(t), **816**, 837
   mass unemployment, Great Depression, 918
   Mexican-American War (1845–1847), 815(t), 818
   per capita levels of industrialization (1750–1913), 692(t)
   rebuilding era (after World War II), 986
   September 11 terrorist attacks, 1031(t), 1033, 1034(i)
   social security system (1935), 919
   Spanish-American War (1898), 762, 790, 815(t), 838–839, 909, 909(m)
   Vietnam War, 955(t), 969–970, 970(m)
Universal gravitation, law of, **554**, 557(t)
Untouchables, 962, 963
Upanishads, 785
Urban areas
   Enlightenment period, 575
   nineteenth-century Europe, 731–733
Urbanization
   bazaar economy, 1036(i), **1039**
   contemporary world, 1037, 1039–1041, 1039(t)
   global wealth distribution (ca. 2010), 1040(m), 1040–1041
   megacities, **1037**, 1039
   population, eight major areas (1925–2025), 1039(t)
Urban VIII (pope), 559
Uthman dan Fodio, 751(t), 753
Utrecht, Peace of, 526, 526(m), 538

Vaccination
   germ theory, 732
   smallpox, 700

Valladolid debate, **479**
Variolation, 637
Varnas, 649
Vatican, Lateran Agreement of 1929, 917(t), **932**
Venice, Afroeurasian trade world, 460
Verdun, Battle of, 846(i), 847(t), 850, 855
Vernacular literature, Ming Dynasty, 618, 638
Versailles
    Louis XIV at, 515(t), 528
    Treaty of Versailles, 865, 867
Vesalius, Andreas, 556(i), 557(t), 558
Vespucci, Amerigo, 456
Vespucci, Juan, 468(i)
Viceroyalties, **472**
Vietnam
    Mnong people, 970, 1038
    Nguyen Dynasty, 787(i), **788**
Vietnam War, 955(t), 969–970, 970(m)
Virtue
    filial piety, 616
Vital energy (qi), 617
Viziers, **489**, 490, 491, 506
Volcanic eruptions
    Mount Asama (1783), 631
Voltaire, 561(i), 563–564, 564(t), 565, 567(i), 637
Voting Rights Act, 955(t), 984

Wałęsa, Lech, 1017
Walker, William, 838
War Communism, **862**
War of the Pacific (1879–1883), 815(t)
War of the Spanish Succession, 515(t), 525–526, 526(m), 528, 537–538, 671
War of Triple Alliance, 815(t), 826, 827
Warriors, Qizilbash, **490**, 492, 497
Warsaw Ghetto, 939(i)
Wars of Independence in Latin America (1810–1825), 815(t), 818, 828
Wars of Reform, Mexican (1857–1861), 815(t), 819, 826, 827
Washington Consensus, **994**–995, 1006
Water frame, **685**
Water Margin (novel, Ming China), 618(t)
Watt, James, 683(t), 686
Wayna Daga, Battle of, 593
Wealth
    bride wealth, **459**, 589
    global distribution (ca. 2010), 1040(m), 1040–1041
    Mansa Musa, 460(i)
    mercantilism
        colonial wars and, 537–538
        defined, **527**
        Navigation Acts, 515(t), **537**, 684
    oligarchs, **815**
        Latin America, 829, 834, 841
        liberalism and, 815
        Meiji Oligarchs, 796
        zaibatsu, 798, **903**
    oligarchy
        Bank of France (1800), 661
        Dutch Republic, 531
    wealth gap, Great Depression, 916
Wedgwood, Josiah, 687
Wellesley, Richard, 505
West Africa
    Benin forest kingdom, 586–587
    daily life, 588–590

    early modern period (1400–1800), 583–591, 586(m)
    famine (1738–1756), 585(t)
    industry, 590–591
    Senegambian states, 584–586
    stateless societies, 584–586, 606, 609
    trade, 590(m), 590–591
Western Europe, post war challenge, 982–983
Western front (World War I)
    Battle of the Somme, 850
    Battle of Verdun, 846(i), 847(t), 850, 855
    trench warfare, **850**, 851(m)
West Germany, Berlin Wall, 955(t), 956(m), 993(t), 1016(i), 1019, 1024, 1030
Westphalia, Peace of, 521, 524
White man's burden, **762**
"White Man's Burden" (Kipling), 751(t), 762, 763
Widow suicide, 500, 808
Will
    free will, 516, 562
    general will, **565**
Witch-hunts, 518
Wittgenstein, Ludwig, 873
Women
    "comfort women," 943
    feminism
        Brittain's efforts, 856
        separate spheres, 735–736
        woman, in French illustration (Triumph of Democratic Republics, 1848), 721(i)
    feminization of poverty, **1046**
    foot binding, 793, 904
    French salons, 551(t), 560, 565, 567(i), **575**, 577
    rape
        "rape of Belgium," 854(i)
        Rape of Nanjing, 885(t), 907, 942
    right to equality, 1045–1046
    sati practice, 500
    widow suicide, 500, 808
    witch-hunts, 518
    yin and yang, 617
Wordsworth, William, 703, 737
Working classes
    The Condition of the Working Class in England (Engels), 683(t), 703
    factories, Industrial Revolution, 684–685, 697–701
    proletariat, **717**, 858, 860, 861, 923
    sweated industries, 734
Works Progress Administration, 917(t), 919
World Trade Organization, 1013
World War I, 844–881
    Armenian Genocide, 890(i), 891
    Battle of the Marne, 850, 864
    Battle of the Somme, 850
    Battle of Verdun, 846(i), 847(t), 850, 855
    big picture, 881(i)
    Brittain and, 856–857
    chronology, 847(t)
    CONNECTIONS, 879
    end of war, 864
    in Europe, 851(m)
    global consequences, 864–867
    global effort, 852–853
    growing political tensions, 857
    interwar years, 868–871
    Lusitania (British passenger liner) sinks, 847(t), 853

    origins and causes, 846–849
    outbreak of war, 849–850
    overveiw, 844
    Paris peace treaties, 864–865
    social impact, 855, 857
    stalemate and slaughter, 850, 852
    summary, 878
    territorial changes after war, 866(m)
    total war, 854–855
    Treaty of Versailles, 865, 867
    Triple Entente, **848**, 851(m), 852, 853
World War II, 933–948
    big picture, 951(i)
    chronology, 917(t)
    CONNECTIONS, 949
    end (1945), 917(t), 948
    Europe
        Nazi occupation (1939–1942), 939–942
        war in Europe (1942–1945), 942–943
    events leading to, chronology, 940(t)
    Grand Alliance, 943, 948
    Great Patriotic War of the Fatherland, 981
    Hiroshima and Nagasaki, atomic bombs, 917(t), 946(i), 947(m), 948, 1032
    interwar years, 868–871
    Japanese Empire, 942–943
    map of Europe and Africa, 941(m)
    Nazism's roots, **933**–934
    overview, 914
    in Pacific, 946–948, 947(m)
    Pearl Harbor attacks, 917(t), 943, 948
    start (1939), 917(t), 938
    summary, 948
Wright, Frank Lloyd, 875
Wu (Empress Wu), 491

yang and yin, 617
Yangzi River
    Grand Canal, 614
    Japanese attack (1937), 907
Yaqui people, 813(i), 817(m)
Yasuko Yamagata, 946(i)
Yellow bile, bodily humor, 558
Yellow fever, 732, 790
Yellow River
    Grand Canal, 614
    Ming Dynasty decline, 619
yin and yang, 617
Yom Kippur War, **965**(m), 992, 993, 993(t), 994, 997
Yoruba people, 587
The Young Scholar and His Wife (Coques), 532(i)
Young Turks, 751(t), **767**, 890, 891, 892
Yuan Grand Canal, 614

zaibatsu, 798, **903**
Zen
    Hideyoshi and, 638
    Muromachi culture, 624–625
Zheng He, 457, 458(m), 613(t), 633–634, 641
Zhou Dynasty, Mandate of Heaven, 904
Zhu Yuanzhang, 612–613
Zimbabwe
    Rhodesia, 993(t), 1007, 1008
    Zimbabwe African People's Union, 1008
Zionism, **743**, 891, 894–895, 910, 961
Zola, Émile, 738
Zollverein, 683(t), 694, 726
Zoroastrianism, 500

About the Authors

John P. McKay (Ph.D., University of California, Berkeley) is professor emeritus at the University of Illinois. He has written or edited numerous works, including the Herbert Baxter Adams Prize-winning book *Pioneers for Profit: Foreign Entrepreneurship and Russian Industrialization, 1885–1913*.

Patricia Buckley Ebrey (Ph.D., Columbia University), professor of history at the University of Washington in Seattle, specializes in China. She has published numerous journal articles and *The Cambridge Illustrated History of China*, as well as several monographs. In 2010 she won the Shimada Prize for outstanding work of East Asian Art History for *Accumulating Culture: The Collections of Emperor Huizong*.

Roger B. Beck (Ph.D., Indiana University) is Distinguished Professor of African and twentieth-century world history at Eastern Illinois University. His publications include *The History of South Africa*, a translation of P. J. van der Merwe's *The Migrant Farmer in the History of the Cape Colony, 1657–1842*, and more than a hundred articles, book chapters, and reviews. He is a former treasurer and Executive Council member of the World History Association.

Clare Haru Crowston (Ph.D., Cornell University) teaches at the University of Illinois, where she is currently associate professor of history. She is the author of *Fabricating Women: The Seamstresses of Old Regime France, 1675–1791*, which won the Berkshire and Hagley Prizes. She edited two special issues of the *Journal of Women's History*, has published numerous journal articles and reviews, and is a past president of the Society for French Historical Studies.

Merry E. Wiesner-Hanks (Ph.D., University of Wisconsin-Madison) taught first at Augustana College in Illinois, and since 1985 at the University of Wisconsin-Milwaukee, where she is currently UWM Distinguished Professor in the department of history. She is the coeditor of the *Sixteenth Century Journal* and the author or editor of more than twenty books, most recently *The Marvelous Hairy Girls: The Gonzales Sisters and Their Worlds* and *Gender in History*. She is the former Chief Reader for Advanced Placement World History.

Jerry Dávila (Ph.D., Brown University) is Jorge Paulo Lemann Professor of Brazilian History at the University of Illinois. He is the author of *Dictatorship in South America*; *Hotel Trópico: Brazil and the Challenge of African Decolonization*, winner of the Latin Studies Association Brazil Section Book prize; and *Diploma of Whiteness: Race and Social Policy in Brazil, 1917–1945*. He has served as president of the Conference on Latin American History.